£41.50

?/86

LEARNING AND MEMORY
A Biological View

LEARNING AND MEMORY
A Biological View

Edited by

Joe L. Martinez, Jr.
Department of Psychology
University of California
Berkeley, California

Raymond P. Kesner
Department of Psychology
University of Utah
Salt Lake City, Utah

1986

ACADEMIC PRESS, INC.
Harcourt Brace Jovanovich, Publishers
Orlando   San Diego   New York   Austin
Boston   London   Sydney   Tokyo   Toronto

ACADEMIC PRESS, INC.
Orlando, Florida 32887

United Kingdom Edition published by
ACADEMIC PRESS INC. (LONDON) LTD.
24-28 Oval Road, London NW1 7DX

LIBRARY OF CONGRESS CATALOGING-IN-PUBLICATION DATA

Main entry under title:

Learning and memory.

Includes index.
1. Memory—Physiological aspects.   2. Learning—
Physiological aspects.   I. Martinez, Joe L.
II. Kesner, Raymond P.
QP406.L43   1986   591.1'88   85-18648
ISBN 0-12-474990-9 (alk. paper)
ISBN 0-12-474991-7 (paperback)

PRINTED IN THE UNITED STATES OF AMERICA

86 87 88 89   9 8 7 6 5 4 3 2 1

This volume is dedicated to our wives Janice Martinez and Laya Kesner. Our creative endeavors are sustained by their patience, support, and understanding.

CONTENTS

3 ANATOMICAL CORRELATES OF NEURONAL PLASTICITY
Keith A. Crutcher

III
PHARMACOLOGY AND BIOCHEMISTRY

4 MEMORY: DRUGS AND HORMONES
Joe L. Martinez, Jr.

5 BIOCHEMICAL CORRELATES OF LEARNING AND MEMORY
Adrian J. Dunn

6 APPLIED ASPECTS OF MEMORY RESEARCH: AGING

Steven F. Zornetzer

IV
MODEL SYSTEMS

7 MEMORY: ELECTROPHYSIOLOGICAL ANALOGS

Timothy J. Teyler

8 MEMORY: INVERTEBRATE MODEL SYSTEMS

W. Jackson Davis

V

LESIONS

12 NEUROBIOLOGICAL VIEWS OF MEMORY
Raymond P. Kesner

CONTRIBUTORS

Numbers in parentheses indicate the pages on which the authors' contributions begin.

ROBERT F. BERMAN (341), Department of Psychology, Wayne State University, Detroit, Michigan 48202

JAMES E. BLACK (55), Department of Psychology, University of Illinois, Champaign, Illinois 61820

KEITH A. CRUTCHER (83), Department of Anatomy, University of Utah School of Medicine, Salt Lake City, Utah 84132

W. JACKSON DAVIS (267), Thimann Laboratories, University of California, Santa Cruz, California 95064

NELSON H. DONEGAN (3), Department of Psychology, Stanford University, Stanford, California 94305

ADRIAN J. DUNN (165), Department of Neuroscience, University of Florida College of Medicine, Gainesville, Florida 32610

WILLIAM T. GREENOUGH (55), Departments of Psychology and Anatomical Sciences and Neural and Behavioral Biology Program, University of Illinois at Urbana-Champaign, Champaign, Illinois 61820

BRUCE S. KAPP (299), Department of Psychology, University of Vermont, Burlington, Vermont 05405

RAYMOND P. KESNER (399), Department of Psychology, University of Utah, Salt Lake City, Utah 84112

JOE L. MARTINEZ, JR. (127), Department of Psychology, University of California, Berkeley, California 94720

DAVID S. OLTON (379), Department of Psychology, The Johns Hopkins University, Baltimore, Maryland 21218

JEFFREY P. PASCOE (299), Department of Psychology, University of Vermont, Burlington, Vermont 05405

TIMOTHY J. TEYLER (237), Neurobiology Department, Northeastern Ohio Universities College of Medicine, Rootstown, Ohio 44272

RICHARD F. THOMPSON (3), Department of Psychology, Stanford University, Stanford, California 94305

STEVEN F. ZORNETZER (203), Office of Naval Research, Arlington, Virginia 22217

PREFACE

One of the great scientific questions of our day is: How is information acquired and stored in the brain? Animals and humans are capable of modifying their behavior as a result of experience. Since each one of us is unique, it follows that learning is the property of the individual organism. And, if behavior depends on the coordinated action of nerves, muscles, and glands, then it follows that permanently learned responses have to depend on physical changes in these tissues. This is the focus of this book. What physical changes are induced in the organism by learning and what changes must occur for there to be learning? We call this area of study the neurobiology of learning and memory.

Today there is an increasing interest in the teaching of an undergraduate course in the neurobiology of learning and memory. Unfortunately, there is no comprehensive up-to-date textbook available. Teachers usually rely on a series of articles in journals or books which cover specific research topics. The only book that could be easily used as a text was *Brain and Learning*, edited by Tim Teyler and published in 1978. This book is no longer in print. With Teyler's book in mind as a model we embarked on a formulation of a comprehensive textbook about the neurobiology of learning and memory. We believe that an edited book provides a greater variety of views and is more representative of the ongoing research in the field.

Each author was asked to present a historical introduction and to present an overview of the critical studies and ideas in their area of expertise. The topics were selected to examine different historical perspectives, levels of analysis, methods of approach, subject populations, and theoretical views. In addition to a brief historical introduction to each specific topic, the first chapter, written by Richard Thompson, deals exclusively with a review of historical traditions that influenced current research on the biological basis of learning and memory. In addition Thompson's chapter details some of the exciting recent findings from his laboratory which indicate that the engram for a simple classically conditioned skeletal response may be in the cerebellum.

Within the context of brain–behavior relations, the mechanisms and processes associated with the acquisition and storage of information are studied at many levels. For example, James Black and William Greenough in Chapter 2 and Keith Crutcher in Chapter 3 emphasize the importance of anatomical mechanisms that could mediate learning, plasticity, and memory storage in young and adult animals. Interestingly, research indicates that learning in mammalian brain may involve the formation of new connections between neurons. Joe Martinez in Chapter 4 reviews data showing that peripheral hormones and particularly opioid peptides may influence complex behavior such as learning and memory. Adrian Dunn in Chapter 5 addresses the question of the contribution of individual neurotransmitter systems to learning and Steven Zornetzer in Chapter 6 examines the psychopathology of aging. There is current intense interest in memory decline associated with aging and Alzheimer's disease, which primarily affects aged populations.

Timothy Teyler in Chapter 7 explores an electrophysiological phenomenon called long-term potentiation which may be a model of the way the central nervous system stores information. Jackson Davis in Chapter 8 reviews studies of learning and memory conducted in invertebrate systems. Many think that a fundamental understanding of the neural basis of learning will only emerge from studying simple creatures such as invertebrates, and recent rapid progress supports this view. On the other hand, Bruce Kapp and Jeffrey Pascoe in Chapter 9 present what is known about learning in complex vertebrate systems. Others think that invertebrates are too simple to reveal the mystery of how the mammalian brain stores information. Interestingly, rapid progress in our understanding of the mechanisms of learning in vertebrates supports this view as well. Robert Berman in Chapter 10 discusses the consequences to learning and memory of manipulating active brain processes by direct stimulation of various brain nuclei.

David Olton in Chapter 11 discusses the use of the lesion technique in learning and memory research. Pavlov once noted by way of analogy that you do not study how a radio works by breaking the tubes. Yet, many of the recent and most exciting advances in understanding memory processes from both a behavioral and neurobiological level have come from lesion studies. Finally, Ray Kesner in Chapter 12 presents a new neurobehavioral analysis of the structure of memory formation which utilizes lesion analysis to a great degree and explores human memory pathology. Thus, this book touches upon most of the empirical and theoretical aspects of the neurobiology of learning and memory.

The book is intended for advanced undergraduate students that have had an introductory physiological psychology course, graduate students, and research workers in the field of memory. Nevertheless, the nonspecialist who is seeking to understand the biological basis of memory research, current theory, and the frontier of knowledge in this area will also benefit from this book.

Joe L. Martinez, Jr.
Raymond P. Kesner

I

HISTORICAL INTRODUCTION

1

THE SEARCH FOR THE ENGRAM*

Richard F. Thompson and Nelson H. Donegan

INTRODUCTION

When the mind wills to recall something, nerve impulses are inclined toward different parts of the brain until they come upon that part where the traces are left of the thing which it wishes to remember, for these traces are nothing else than the circumstances that the synapses of the brain through which the nerve impulses have already taken their course on presentation of the object, have thereby acquired a greater facility than the rest to be opened again the same way by the nerve impulses which come to them; so that these nerve impulses coming upon the synapses enter therein more readily than into the others.

This quotation from Descartes (1650) was given by Lashley (1950), who suggested the substitution of just a few words to make Descartes' view quite modern. The original quotation went:

"When the mind wills to recall something, this volition causes the little gland, by inclining successively to different sides, to impel the animal spirits toward different parts of the brain, until they come upon that part where the traces are left of the thing which it wishes to remember," and so on. Descartes was of course a dualist, and for him the mind acted through the pineal gland on the brain. But leaving out that part, he gives a thoroughly modern "use" theory of brain substrates of learning and memory.

* Supported in part by ONR Grant #N00014-83-K-0238, NSF Grant #BNS 8117115, and by grants from the Sloan Foundation and the McKnight Foundation.

3

A BRIEF HISTORY

The development of views of brain function, learning, and memory constitutes much of the history of psychology. Experimental psychology traces its origins to Wilhelm Wundt who founded the first psychology laboratory in Leipzig in 1879. Wundt developed the method of introspection—analyzing one's experience and sensations into their essential elements—a method that was also used in early studies of animal behavior, casually by Rommanes (1881), systematically and analytically by Morgan (1894). Wundt's approach was particularly successful in the analysis of sensations. In fact, he and his students told us what types of skin receptors ought to exist almost 100 years ago.

Americans flocked to Wundt's laboratory, among them William James, who established the young field of psychology in the U.S. with his classic text, *Principles of Psychology,* in 1890. James's approach was empirical and pragmatic, and his thinking was strongly influenced by the British associationists (e.g., Locke and Hume). The basic notion that we learn associations by contiguity—associative learning—stems from this tradition. James illustrated how the brain might build on reflexes to learn by association. He developed a more realistic analysis of mental phenomena than Wundt's school and was the first to define *selective* attention—when you attend, you not only concentrate, but you concentrate on one thing to the exclusion of others.

Wundt's approach was very productive in early days, analyzing elements of sensations, but after that there was really nowhere to go and the various followers of Wundt developed endless arguments about the more subtle aspects of sensory experience, for example, does a given color induce excitement or calm? Some of these debates resembled the medieval scholastic debates. The approach was self-limiting and gradually died out. Wundt felt that his method could not be applied to higher mental processes like memory and thought, but others attempted to do so.

During this period, the intellectual climate was very much influenced by Darwin's theory of evolution. Of importance to psychology was Darwin's proposal that the mental and behavioral traits of a species are shaped by the same process as the species' morphology—natural selection. Thus, a trait exhibited by one species should be represented to some degree in related species. This idea gave rise to the dicipline of comparative psychology, with the initial task being to trace the evolution of the human mind by comparing human intellectual abilities with the intellectual abilities of various animal species as revealed by natural observation (with the observer developing an explanation of behavior by placing him or herself in the place of the animal and introspecting on how the animal felt and thought about the situation [Rommanes, 1881; Morgan, 1894]) and later by systematic experimentation (Thorndike, 1898).

The notion that animals had minds caused few problems for most people when various primates, or even rats, were considered; but the paramecium was another matter. Endless debates grew up over where mind began in evolution. The uncertainty over where mind began in evolution and the uncritical use of introspection and anecdotes about clever animals led to a rather unsatisfactory understanding of animal behavior.

Edward Thorndike, an undergraduate at Wesleyan in the early 1890s, read James' text, became enthralled, and entered graduate school at Harvard and studied with James. He was fascinated by animal intelligence and began training chicks in his room (his landlady threw him out, and James took Thorndike and his chicks into his own basement). To survive, Thorndike later had to accept a fellowship at Columbia, where he did his classic work on cats in puzzle boxes (1898). He concluded that his subjects learned to solve the problems he set for them (e.g., how to release a door to escape from a box and gain access to food) by trail and error rather than insight. From his experimental results he formulated his law of effect: The probability of a given behavior increases if it is associated with reward and decreases if it is associated with punishment. Thorndike was the first to use an experimental approach to the study of animal learning, an approach that emphasized objectivity in observation and replicability and quantification of results—demands quite different from selective, casually introspective accounts given by Rommanes. Thorndike's approach revolutionized the study of animal learning.

Meanwhile, parallel developments were occurring in Russia. The eminent physiologist Sechenov published a paper in about 1870 on "Who must investigate the problems of psychology?" Answer: physiologists. How? By studying reflexes. His view and his books were condemned by the Czarist censor committee, and a court action was started against him but was later dropped. His writings (Sechenov, 1863) exerted a profound influence on two young physiologists, Pavlov and Bechterev. Pavlov acknowledges two major intellectual debts—to Sechenov and to Edward Thorndike, whose objective measurements of animal behavior impressed him greatly.

When Pavlov discovered the conditioned salivary response, he believed that this "psychic reflex" provided a method for studying the physiology and functions of the cerebral cortex in animals. His impact on the West was gradual and was exerted much more in terms of the vast body of data his laboratory collected on conditioned reflexes and in terms of his basic approach to investigating learning, using conditioned reflexes, than in terms of his theory of brain function. At first Pavlov did not take the neuron doctrine seriously and attempted to explain the learning phenomena he observed in terms of waves of excitation and inhibition spreading across the cortex, and their effects on cortical representations of stimulus events. An early study in Pavlov's laboratory by Zeliony, in 1911, seemed to show that the neocortex was essential for conditioned responses, and this became the accepted dogma, held more dogmatically by some of his students than by Pavlov himself (see Pavlov, 1927).

Bechterev also investigated conditioned reflexes and used such tasks as leg flexion and other skeletal muscle responses. Initially, his work had a greater impact on the West than did Pavlov's, but the influence of both was like that of Thorndike's work. All three demonstrated the value of objective methods to measure learning in animals and their use in the study of brain function.

Meanwhile, in the West, students of animal behavior were still required to interpret results in terms of the conscious experience of the animal during training. At the University of Chicago, John B. Watson completed his PhD under Angell, a psychologist, and Donaldson, a neurologist, in 1903, and stayed on to complete a paper in 1907 investigating the sensations and experiences the rat used to solve the problem of the maze. In 1908, he accepted a professorship at Johns Hopkins and increasingly rebelled against interpretations of behavior in terms of consciousness. In 1913, he published a paper entitled "Psychology as a Behaviorist Views It" that founded behaviorism and led ultimately to the disappearance of the introspectionist school.

Watson emphasized that to understand behavior, all that was necessary was to measure the stimuli that went in and the responses that came out. Consciousness or awareness was an unnecessary construct. For Watson, much of behavior could be explained in terms of learning. His view of learning was that of Bechterev, Pavlov, and Thorndike: The elements out of which all learned behavior is built are conditioned reflexes and trial-and-error learning shaped by rewards and punishments. However, unlike Pavlov and Bechterev, Watson largely ignored neurophysiology and placed all emphasis on a switchboard association notion of learning not too different from James' view and Descartes' much earlier view.

Watson established behaviorism at about the same time that logical positivism came to the fore in the philosophy of science: All science is measurements, and theories are simply ways of relating sets of measurements. Psychology had to begin with the establishment of relations between stimuli and responses and the laws stating how these relationships change as a function of experience.

At least four major theories of learning developed from Thorndike's, and to a lesser extent Watson's, influence: the systematic and mechanistic system of Clark Hull (1943) emphasizing reinforcement through drive reduction as the mechanism for learning; Guthrie's (1935) notion of elemental stimulus–response (S–R) associations established through contiguity; Skinner's (1938) focus on the law of effect, and his demonstrations of the effects of a wide range of schedules of reward and punishment on operant behaviors; and Tolman's development of a form of behaviorism that emphasized the cognitive nature of animal behavior. The approaches of Hull, Guthrie, and Tolman explained learning in terms of abstract associative principles arrived at through behavioral analysis, as opposed to physiological mechanisms, although Hull initially tried to cast his postulates in physiological terms.

In the 1940s and 1950s, these were the dominant theories of learning. The majority of workers did not really follow any one theory, but were more empirical in approach. But as a result of these theories and the research they stimulated, much was learned about learning in animals—a very large data base was developed. The influence of these theoretical approaches is still with us today: Hull–Spence by, for example, Wagner and Rescorla; Guthrie by stimulus sampling theory (e.g., Estes, 1959); Skinner by the large fields of behavioral engineering and psychopharmacology; and Tolman's impact is still being felt, as in Menzel's work on "cognitive mapping in chimpanzees" (Menzel, 1978) and in work on spatial memory in rats (O'Keefe & Nadel, 1978, "The hippocampus as a cognitive map.") Indeed, the modern field of cognitive psychology owes Tolman a debt—if rats can have purposes, goals, and plans, why can't humans?

The modern approach to understanding learning and memory in terms of their biological substrates was begun in the US by Karl Lashley, then a graduate student working with John Watson:

> In 1914, I think, Watson called attention of his seminar to the French edition of Bechterev, and that winter the seminar was devoted to translation and discussion of the book. In the spring I served as a sort of unpaid assistant and we constructed apparatus and planned experiments together. We simply attempted to repeat Bechterev's experiments. We worked with withdrawal reflexes, knee jerk, pupil. Watson took the initiative in all this, but he was also trying to photograph the vocal cord, so I did much of the actual experimental work. I devised drainage tubes for the parotid and submaxiallary ducts and planned the salivary work which I published. As we worked with the method, I think our

enthusiasm for it was somewhat dampened. Watson tried to establish conditioned auditory reflexes in the rat and failed. Our whole program was then disrupted by the move to the lab in Meyer's clinic. There were no adequate animal quarters there. Watson started work with the infants as the next best material available. I tagged along for awhile, but disliked the babies and found me a rat lab in another building. We accumulated a considerable amount of experimental material on the conditioned reflex which has never been published. Watson saw it as a basis for a systematic psychology and was not greatly concerned with the nature of the reaction itself. I got interested in the physiology of the reaction and the attempt to trace conditioned reflex paths through the nervous system started my program of cerebral work. (Letter of May 14, 1935, K. S. Lashley to E. R. Hilgard, reproduced with the kind permission of E. R. Hilgard).

One has the feeling that then and throughout his life, Lashley wanted to believe in localization of the memory trace, but his own results kept confounding his belief (see Lashley, 1950).

Karl Lashley began his search for the engram at Johns Hopkins University in a collaborative study with Sheppard Franz, who worked at St. Elizabeth's Hospital in Washington, DC. Franz had studied with Wundt in Leipzig (1896) and took his degree with Cattell in 1898. He developed an extensive research program concerned with recovery of function after brain damage in humans and animals and became skeptical of precise localization of intellectual functions in the cerebral cortex.

Lashley and Franz (1917) gave a very balanced and modern treatment of the issues of localization. They considered at length the experimental problems of distinguishing between effects of cortical lesions on memories, per se, or on sensory or motor capabilities. In their experiments, they focused on the frontal cortex of the rat and used a simple maze, which they termed a kinesthetic-motor habit, and an inclined plane box. In the latter, the animal had to learn to climb on top of the box, depress the elevated end of an inclined plane, then climb down and go to the food in the now opened box below the inclined plane. (Today, this would be viewed as a rather "cognitive" behavior for a rat.) Even very large frontal lesions did not impair learning or memory for the simple maze. However, the largest bilateral frontal lesions caused loss of the inclined-plane box habit. Interestingly, some of these lesions included much of the hippocampus as well. Smaller lesions had no effect. In their discussion, the notions of mass-action and equipotentiality were raised although these terms, per se, were not used until later (Lashley, 1929). Lashley and Franz were greatly struck by the resistance of well-learned habits to cortical insult: "The destruction of cortical tissue has not been extensive enough to prove that learning may take place wholly at the level of the subcortical centers but the evidence at hand is sufficient to justify more extensive experiments upon this point" (Lashley & Franz, 1917, p. 133).

Lashley continued to pursue localization of the memory trace in the cerebral cortex, culminating in his classic 1929 monograph. There he stated the extreme cortical localization view, the switchboard theory, and proceeded to demolish it experimentally. He concluded that memory traces were stored in the cerebral cortex but were not localized. He did not consider in any detail the alternative possibility he and Franz had raised earlier that memory traces for certain forms of learning might in fact be localized subcortically. Nevertheless, Lashley continued in search of the cortical engram and in 1950 drew his oft-quoted conclusion:

> This series of experiments has yielded a good bit of information about what and where the memory trace is not. It has discovered nothing directly of the real nature of the engram. I sometimes feel, in reviewing the evidence on the localization of the memory trace, that the necessary conclusion is that learning just is not possible. It is difficult to conceive of a mechanism which can satisfy the conditions set for it. Nevertheless, in spite of such evidence against it, learning does sometimes occur (Lashley, 1950, pp. 477–478).

The lesion approach to localization of the memory trace poses many problems of interpretation, as noted by Pavlov, Lashley, and many others:

> Notwithstanding the best surgical technic employed by some of these investigators, certain objections are particularly inherent in the method of extirpation. First, the gross mutilation of so fine and complex an organ as the brain is likely to have effects more widespread than simply the absence of the removed part. It is in the words of Pavlov, as if one struck a delicate machine with a sledge hammer and then studied the results. Furthermore, a three-legged stool falls when any one leg is removed, although that leg is now wholly responsible for holding up the stool—an analogy often used by Adolf Meyer (Brogden & Gantt, 1942a, p. 437).

Lashley moved from the University of Chicago to Harvard in 1937 and became director of the Yerkes Laboratory in Orange Park Florida in 1942. He disliked Cambridge and travelled there only once a year to give two weeks of seminars in order to keep his chair. At Orange Park, as at Chicago earlier, he had many of the people with him who became leaders in the fields of brain and behavior: Beach, Hebb, Schneirla, Leeper, Krechevsky–Krech, Griffin, Chow, Nissen, Riesen, Sperry, Pribram, Evarts, and many others. A major goal at Orange Park was to define the functions of primate association cortex. Much of our initial understanding of the behavioral roles of association cortex came from this work. Learning tasks were the primary method used to define the various behavioral functions of association areas—as in complex discriminations. However, Lashley remained pessimistic about ever understanding brain substrates of learning and memory as such.

In spite of Lashley's misgivings, this approach has continued to be productive. Particularly elegant contemporary examples that focus on memory include Mishkin's analysis of the brain substrates of pattern vision in the monkey (Mishkin, 1978), which interestingly can serve as an animal model of certain forms of human aphasia (primary visual cortex → visual association areas → cross hemispheres via corpus callosum → temporal association areas) and Goldman–Rakic's studies (Goldman–Rakic, 1984) of the essential circuitry in delayed response or short-term memory (parietal association areas → prefrontal cortex of sulcus principalis → interhemispheric communication).

Lashley's 1929 monograph brought the developing field at that time almost to a halt. The switchboard theory seemed to be wrong, but what were the alternatives? One direction was field theory. Gestalt psychologists Wertheimer, Koffka, and Köhler, developed notions of perceptions and memories existing as electric fields in the brain and Köhler did a number of animal studies recording dc potential from the cortex, with inconclusive results. Lashley and Sperry followed up these notions by implating conducting and insulating sheets in the cortex, with negative results. Field theory of brain substrates of memory today is represented by such workers as Roy John (1967), and perhaps to some degree by Karl Pribram in his holographic analogy (1971).

In 1949 Lashley's former student, Donald Hebb, published a theory of brain function and learning that he hoped would rescue the field. It had an extraordinary impact and indeed revitalized the field. Basically, it was a modified switchboard theory. A given memory was represented by a set of neurons that had developed increased functional connections. However, the neurons were not localized to one place but thought to be distributed: A given memory was represented by a network—the cell assembly—in the cortex, and the same neuron could participate in more than one memory. Hebb was deliberately vague about this, but quite specific about the synaptic mechanism, which has come to be termed the Hebb synapse—a special case of use-strengthening connections. Hebb's specific theory was perhaps less important then the fact that he developed a connectionistic view that could work.

Electrical stimulation of the brain as a tool for the localization of neural circuits constituting a memory trace was first used systematically in a now classic series of studies in the laboratory of W. Horsley Gantt at Johns Hopkins. Gantt, Loucks, Brogden, and others working in Gantt's laboratory attempted to define the "relation of conditioned reflex function to anatomic pathways" using electrical stimulation to elicit the behavioral response to be conditioned, that is, as an unconditioned stimulus (US). Loucks (1936) showed that a leg flexion elicited by stimulation of the motor area of the cerebral cortex could not be conditioned to a conditioned stimulus (CS). However, Brodgen and Gantt, in an extremely important series of experiments, demonstrated that electrical stimulation of the cerebellum could serve as an effective unconditioned stimulus (US) (1942). In brief, they found that a variety of movements elicited by cerebellar stimulation could be conditioned to tone or light CSs. Responses as diverse as forelimb flexion and discrete closure of the ipsilateral eyelid conditioned easily, although diffuse body movements due to contractions of the axial musculature did not. The movements that conditioned well were discrete, adaptive responses that would have avoided noxious stimuli of the sort that would normally have elicited the unconditioned responses.

The fundamental limitation of electrical stimulation of the brain as a tool for localization of the memory trace is, of course, that the effective action could be remote from the site of stimulation. Indeed, electrical stimulation of many sites in the brain can serve as a CS. (But the more modern approach of using microstimulation with a stimulating microelectrode can at least localize the site of stimulation and appears to have much promise [see Davis et al., 1982; Mauk & Thompson, 1984, and below]). However, the same is not true when the electrical stimulus serves as a US. Only a limited number of sites can elicit behavioral responses, and some of these are ineffective for conditioning (e.g., motor cortex). To our knowledge, the cerebellar stimulation as a US effect of Brogden and Gantt is the most impressive in the early literature.

MODERN APPROACHES TO THE PROBLEM OF LOCALIZATION

The problem of localizing "memory traces" has been the greatest barrier to progress in analyzing neurobiological substrates of learning and memory in the mammalian brain, as previously noted. In considering the issue of localization, it seems useful to distinguish between the neural circuitry essential for the development and expression of a particular form of learning—the memory trace circuit—and the subset of neural elements that exhibit the training-induced plasticity necessary for the development of such behavior. We will term the latter subset of elements the "memory trace." Assuming that in many learned behaviors the sites of plasticity are more central than the principal sensory systems or the motor neurons, we will use the term "sensory-motor circuit" to designate the part of the memory trace circuit that does not include the memory trace.

The premise that memory traces are localized does not necessarily imply that a particular trace has a single anatomical location. Rather, the memory trace circuit might involve a number of loci, parallel circuits, and feedback loops. We would argue that for a given form of learning, there is a discrete set of loci whose neuronal elements exhibit the essential neuronal plasticity defining the memory trace. Recent evidence strongly supports his view, at least for classically conditioned skeletal muscle responses (e.g., McCormick & Thompson, 1984a,b, see below and Chapter 9, this volume).

For simpler forms of learning, it seems evident that at least some components of the sensory-motor circuit and the memory trace must be localized. An animal trained to a particular conditioned stimulus will not respond to a very different conditioned stimulus and must be given additional training to do so. This fact, the existence of stimulus specificity, argues strongly that sensory-specific information is to some degree preserved in the elements of the memory trace. In addition, a well-trained animal usually exhibits a precise, stereotyped learned response. The fact that activation of motor neurons can be highly selective implies that the motor portion of the memory trace circuit must itself show specificity. Both the sensory-specific and motor-specific aspects of learning imply localization of the memory trace circuit.

To date, the most widely used methods for localizing the memory trace circuit have been lesions (see Chapter 11, this volume), including reversible lesions as with disruptive electrical stimulation and electrophysiological recording. Pharmacological, biochemical, and anatomical methods have been used only recently to address the issue of localization (see Chapters 3, 4, 5, & 6, this volume).

In a typical lesion experiment, animals are trained on some task, a candidate brain structure is destroyed, and the animal is allowed to recover. Subjects are then tested on the previously learned task and their postlesion performance is compared to their prelesion performance. Outcomes range from abolition of the learned behavior with no recovery over time to varying degrees of deficits with or without recovery, to no effect on performance. The problem, as with all other localization techniques, is how to interpret the results. If the lesion abolishes the learned behavior and the effect is selective (e.g., the animal is still capable of generating the behavior used to index learning) and nonspecific factors such as generalized depression of activity or motivational deficits can be ruled out, then two interpretations are indicated. The first is that the lesioned structure is part of the circuitry involved in generating the learned response—the memory trace circuit. This does not mean, however, that the lesioned structure contains the neural elements exhibiting the plasticity necessary for the development of the learned behavior. The second possibility is that the lesioned structure exerts a modulatory influence on the learned response circuit. If, on the other hand, the lesion has no effect on performance of the learned behavior, one cannot conclude that the region in question plays no role in learning; parallel circuits may exist. The lesion approach has been used to very good effect in the elegant studies by the Meyers on recovery of function of a brightness discrimination habit following lesions of the cerebral cortex (Meyer & Meyer, 1977).

Another tool often used for localization of the memory trace is disruptive electrical stimulation (see Kesner & Wilbrum, 1974, and Chapter 10, this volume). During the course of acquisition, abnormal activity in a candidate brain structure is induced by electrical stimulation. The consequences are determined by comparing rates of acquisition of the learned response with groups not receiving stimulation or alternatively, stimulation of other structures. The major limitation of this procedure is, of course, that the effective site of action of the disruptive stimulus is not necessarily at the electrode tip; it can be far removed. (Pharmacologically induced seizure activity faces similar problems for localization, as does cortical spreading depression.) Recent findings indicate that electrical stimulation of certain brain structures is much more likely to produce impairment of learning and memory than stimulation of other structures, even though the stimulated structures are not necessary for learning to occur. For example, disruptive electrical stimulation or induced seizures of the hippocampus prevent or severely impair simple conditioned response learning (Thompson, Berger, Berry, Hoehler, Kettner, & Weisz, 1980). Yet the same conditioned response can be learned perfectly well by animals with prior bilateral removal of the hippocampus (Solomon & Moore, 1975). In this case, the simplest inference is that abnormal activation of the hippocampus interferes with development of the memory trace elsewhere in the brain (Isaacson, 1974).

Electrophysiological recording of neural activity has also been a widely used technique for identifying the circuitry involved in generating learned behavior (see also Chapter 9, this volume). The first step is to identify brain structures that show changes in activity that correlate with changes in the learned behavior. However, as Thompson, Patterson, & Teyler (1972) and Tsukahara (1981) have noted, demonstration of a learning-induced change in neuronal activity in a given brain struc-

ture is not in itself sufficient to conclude that the neurons being monitored have changed. Rather, such changes in unit activity indicate only
that the structure is either a part of the normal memory trace circuit or
is influenced by it. Various criteria for identifying sites of plasticity
electrophysiologically have been suggested, including sites showing
learning-induced changes that appear with the shortest latency within
a trial (Olds, Disterhoft, Segal, Hornblith, & Hirsch, 1972) and those
showing the earliest appearance of changed activity over trials (Thompson, Berger, Berry, Cegavske, Patterson, Roemer, Teyler, & Young,
1976). However, the former could be secondary to tonic changes elsewhere (Gabriel, 1976), and the latter may be necessary, but it is not
sufficient.

To determine whether or not a learning-induced change in activity in
a given brain structure develops there, or is simply relayed from elsewhere, one can compare activity of the target structure with activity in
sites afferent to the target structure. Specifically, the activity of output
neurons within a nucleus (as defined by antidromic and collision criteria [Berger, Rinaldi, Weisz, & Thompson, 1983; Fuller & Schlag, 1976])
can be compared with the activity of nuclei providing afferent projections to the target nucleus. If the output of the target nucleus shows
changes over training, but the activity of afferent nuclei does not, then
one has evidence of training-induced neural plasticity within the target
region. Even so, such observations cannot speak to the issue of whether
or not the changes in neural activity play a role in the generation of the
learned behavior. Only if lesions of the same target nucleus selectively
abolish the learned response can one reasonably conclude that the
structure exhibits training-induced plasticity essential for the development and expression of the learned behavior. But, as mentioned earlier,
if destruction of the structure does not impair responding, it does not
mean that the structure plays no role in learning. For example, Cohen
(1982) found that two visual thalamic regions in the pigeon exhibit
learning-induced changes during heart rate conditioning. Lesioning either region alone had no effect, but lesioning both abolished conditioned heart rate responses. Thus, either of the two thalamic regions
can support heart rate conditioning in the pigeon.

A variety of other techniques may also be used within this context.
Localized neurochemical and neuroanatomical changes induced by
learning can also provide evidence for localization of the memory trace
and suggestions about putative mechanisms. Localized intracranial injections of drugs that block or activate neuronal systems permit one to
study selectively the role of particular neurotransmitter–receptor systems. Newer techniques such as 2-deoxyglucose (2-DG), receptor bind-

ing, and in-vitro autoradiography, are promising but have not yet been much applied to the study of neural substrates of learning and memory. It is sufficient to note here that in order to be informative, such structural and biochemical changes or effects must be shown to be specific to the changes in learned behaviors and must be shown to have differential regional distributions to the brain.

It is sometimes argued that one technique reveals "causal" relationships between neural functioning and behavior more readily than another. Actually, all techniques for identifying brain–behavior relations are equally correlational—one simply starts with relationships between experimental manipulations and their consequences (e.g., the relation between locus and extent of a lesion and the effect on behavior, the relation between the type and amount of drug given and the effect on behavior, the relation between training-induced changes in behavior and changes in neuronal activity in a brain structure, etc.). In a fundamental sense, one never observes more than correlation, as David Hume showed so clearly a very long time ago. What should be recognized is that different approaches have particular advantages: Electrophysiological recording is at present the most convenient, relatively noninvasive method for identifying structures in the brain showing learning-produced changes in activity (2-DG ought also to give useful information on this issue); lesions can provide evidence about localization of essential circuitry, as can electrical stimulation; and drug and neurotransmitter studies, microanatomical and electrophysiological approaches provide evidence regarding localization and putative mechanisms.

SOME DEFINITIONS AND ISSUES

Lasting changes in behavior resulting from prior experience can be characterized as the products of learning, memory, and retrieval processes. Most psychologists would agree that there are several forms of learning, but would be less likely to agree on an exact number or the properties that uniquely distinguish them (such problems can arise, in part, as a result of developing explanations of learning at different levels of analysis). At this point, it is useful to keep the basic definition of learning broad. Thus, bacteria show a kind of memory—their behavior can change as a result of experience (e.g., with certain molecules), and this change can persist for a minute or more after the experience. This example does not fit neatly into any of the common categories of learning, but it may well serve as an important model, particularly for mechanisms, and their genetic substrates, by which membranes, receptors, and biochemical processes can be affected by experience, both in terms of effects that persist in time and in terms of receptor–effector processes (Berg, 1975; Koshland, 1980).

In spite of the aforementioned problems in developing a taxonomy of learning, it has been useful to distinguish two basic categories of learning: nonassociative and associative. Nonassociative learning is said to result from experience with one type of event (e.g., as in habituation and sensitization) whereas associative learning is said to result from the conjunction of two or more events (e.g., a CS and US in Pavlovian conditioning, or a response and a reward in instrumental conditioning). In developing neurobiological explanations of learning phenomena observed in invertebrates and vertebrates, the task is one of identifying the essential neural circuitry mediating the learned behavior and localizing and analyzing the cellular mechanisms of information acquisition, storage, and retrieval.

NONASSOCIATIVE LEARNING—HABITUATION AND
SENSITIZATION

Habituation and sensitization are prototypic of nonassociative learning and are perhaps the most ubiquitous forms of behavioral plasticity, occurring at least from hydra (Rushforth, 1965) to human (Sokolov, 1963). A set of properties derived from the behavior of intact organisms have come to define habituation and sensitization (Thompson & Spencer, 1966); a wide range of responses in a variety of preparations exhibit these properties. The primary index of habituation is a decrement in response to repeated stimulation, and it is distinguished from other decremental processes (e.g., receptor adaptation, neuromuscular fatigue) in part by the defining properties (Thompson & Spencer, 1966). Thus, the decrements often observed in responses of the primary auditory system to rapidly repeated acoustic stimuli do not show the properties of habituation. On the other hand, the behavioral startle response to acoustic stimuli does show the properties of habituation (e.g., Davis, 1970). Sensitization, in the simplest sense, is an increase in a response following (usually strong) stimulation, is typically somewhat generalized, and decays passively (Thompson & Spencer, 1966). Short-term habituation has been particularly satisfying in that a common mechanism, synaptic depression, has been found in both invertebrate and vertebrate model systems (Kandel, 1976; Thompson & Spencer, 1966), the neuronal–synaptic events specified in considerable detail in invertebrate models (Kandel, 1976), and it has been shown that this mechanism—together with sensitization—can account for even complex aspects of behavioral habituation in intact mammals, including humans (Groves & Thompson, 1970).

Associative Learning

The two most commonly used procedures for investigating associative learning in infrahuman organisms are Pavlovian and instrumental conditioning.

Classical (Pavlovian) Conditioning

In the broadest terms, Pavlovian (or classical) conditioning is a procedure by which an experimenter presents subjects with stimuli (CS, US) that occur in some prearranged relationship that is independent of the subject's behavior and measures changes in responding to one of them (CS). Changes in the subject's behavior to the CS over the course of training are said to reflect associative learning when it can be shown that the change is due only to the *relationship* between the CS and US, as opposed to sensitization or habituation processes produced by mere exposure to the CS and US, for example, when the correlation between CS and US occurrence is zero (Rescorla, 1967).

From the point of view of neurobiological analysis, Pavlovian conditioning has several advantages over instrumental learning. Perhaps the most important is that the effects of experimental manipulations on learning rather than performance can be more easily evaluated than in instrumental procedures. The problem of learning versus performance has plagued the study of brain substrates of learning from the beginning. For example, does a brain lesion or the administration of a pharmacological agent impair a learned behavior because it damages the memory trace, or because it alters the animal's ability or motivation to respond? By using Pavlovian procedures, one can estimate the relative effects of such manipulations on learning and performance by comparing the subject's ability to generate the conditioned response (CR) and unconditioned response (UR) before and after making a lesion or administering a drug. If the CR is affected and the UR is unaffected, one can reasonably assume that sensory or memory processes are being affected rather than motor processes responsible for generating the behavior. Pavlovian conditioning procedures permit more adequate controls for nonspecific effects of training on biological processes than do instrumental procedures. The same kind and density of stimulation and unconditioned responses can be produced in both experimental and control conditions. With instrumental training procedures, the nature and density of stimulation will differ (except in the yoked control, which can even be confounded by nonassociative factors [Church, 1964]), as will the behavioral responses. Still, another advantage is that conditioned responding is time-locked to the CS. Therefore, neural events can be analyzed relative to known temporal referents. This feature is most helpful when trying to detect correlations between changes in neural events—say through electrophysiological recording—and changes in behavior.

Many years ago, Clark Hull (1934) distinguished two forms of classical conditioning: alpha and beta. In alpha conditioning, the response to be conditioned is initially elicited by the CS and typically has a short latency. As a result of paired training, this response increases in amplitude and/or duration compared to unpaired stimulus presentations. In beta conditioning, the response to be conditioned is not initially elicited by the CS, is said to have a longer latency than the alpha response, develops over training such that its maximum occurs at the time of onset of the US, and its onset latency moves forward in time within the trial. There may be problems with these definitions; for example, the latency of the "alpha" and "beta" responses can be quite similar. Further, whether or not the CS elicits the response to be conditioned may be due in part to the extent to which motor neuron threshold is exceeded prior to training (Patterson, Cegavske, & Thompson, 1973).

For these reasons, and because "alpha" conditioning may have acquired surplus meaning, we suggest Type A and Type B, the key distinctions being: (1) In Type B, the CR amplitude reaches a maximum at the approximate time of the US onset over the range of CS–US onset intervals that conditioning occurs, whereas in Type A, the latency of the maximum amplitude CR remains relatively fixed, and (2) in Type B, the onset latency of the CR begins at about the time of US onset and moves forward in time within the CS–US interval over the course of training, whereas the Type A CR onset latency does not alter appreciably with training. Using these criteria, certain instances of autonomic conditioning (e.g., heart rate change) appear to be Type A (Cohen, 1982; Kapp, Gallagher, Applegate, & Frysinger, 1982; Schneidermann, Smith, Smith, & Gormezano, 1966), as are certain invertebrate examples (Hawkins & Kandel, 1984), conditioning of flexor reflexes in spinal mammals (Patterson, 1980) and certain phasic responses in mammals (e.g., Woody, 1982). Most discrete behavioral CRs in intact mammals are of Type B (Thompson, Berger, & Madden, 1983b), as are certain autonomic responses (salivary response, Pavlov, 1927).

Classically conditioned responses can also differ in terms of CS–US onset intervals necessary for learning, being minutes to hours for taste aversion, seconds to minutes for autonomic responses, and milliseconds to seconds for most striated muscle responses in both invertebrates and vertebrates. Other than the A versus B and effective CS–US interval differences, all these conditioned responses tend to obey the same general "laws." Perhaps the most important is that in almost all response systems, the CS must precede the US for substantial learning to occur—classical conditioning at its most basic level concerns learning about the causal relationships between events occurring in the organism's environment. Regardless of the duration of the effective CS–US interval, all classically conditioned responses, both A and B, show a CS–US interval conditionability function (degree of conditioning as a function of CS–US onset interval duration) that appears to have a relatively rapid rise and a slower decay.

Instrumental Conditioning

Instrumental conditioning (also known as Thorndikian conditioning, operant conditioning, and trial-and-error learning) involves arranging a contingency between the emitted behavior of the organism and the occurrence of some stimulus event, for example, making the presentation of food contingent upon lever pressing or the presentation of footshock contingent upon entering the left arm of a T-maze. Learning about such response-event relationships is indexed by a change in the probability of the response (or latency or magnitude) over training.

The fundamental problem posed by the use of instrumental procedures is that of distinguishing between learning and performance effects of manipulations. For example, passive and active instrumental avoidance tasks are among the most popular paradigms for examining the effects on memory of interventions such as electroconvulsive shock (ECS), lesions, and drug intervention. However, these tasks can pose problems of interpretation (Bolles, 1978). Thus, rats tend to freeze when frightened. This freezing behavior can be induced easily by training procedures involving aversive events, for example, when a rat is placed in a compartment and given a series of unsignalled shocks, it quickly learns to freeze. In this case, the freezing behavior itself results from a Pavlovianly conditioned fear response to the context cues rather than instrumental reinforcement contingencies. As these Pavlovian contingencies are embedded within avoidance learning procedures, disentangling the contribution of each to observed behavior can be difficult.

A different kind of problem exists for biological analysis in more complex learning situations, such as maze learning, where the number of cues that can gain discriminative control over the subject's behavior are often numerous and the stimulus dimensions controlling behavior can change during the course of training as a result of manipulations such as lesions. This problem makes interpretation of the experimental manipulation difficult, as witnessed by Lashley's dilemma (Hunter, 1929; see Rescorla & Holland, 1976, for further consideration of problems of using instrumental conditioning procedures in biological research).

EARLY EXPERIENCE, BRAIN DEVELOPMENT, AND LEARNING

As a result of his 1949 theory, Hebb began work on effects of early enriched experience on behavior. He raised some laboratory rats at home as pets (to his children's delight), and then pitted them against laboratory-reared littermates in learning complex mazes. The pet rats were much superior. Austin Riesen (1947), with Lashley, first looked at effects of visual deprivation on later visual function in primates—a field that was developed at physiological and anatomical levels by Hubel and Wiesel (1962), who showed that normal patterned visual experience was essential for normal development of the visual cortex.

The historical roots of this approach are in significant part in the broad field of developmental biology. As Greenough notes (Chapter 2, this volume), such pioneering neurobiologists as Cajal (1894) and Tanzi (1893) suggested that the processes of growth and development of the embryonic nervous system might in fact continue on a more subtle scale into adulthood and serve as the basic processes underlying learning and memory.

The pioneering work on the general effects of early experience on brain development and behavior was done some years ago (and continues) in the Department of Psychology at the University of California, Berkeley, by Rosenzweig and associates (Bennett, Diamond, Krech, & Rosenzweig, 1964). Rosenzweig and Krech devised a rich environment for rats and raised them together in social groups. Littermate controls (brothers and sisters of the rich rats) were raised individually in standard laboratory cages (poor rats) or in social groups in larger laboratory cages (poor social rats). All these groups, rich rats, poor rats, and poor social rats were given all the food and water they needed and were kept clean, unlike their human counterparts in the real world.

Rosenzweig and his associates measured a number of properties of the brain, particularly the cerebral cortex, and also tested their behavioral capabilities. The results are very clear. Virtually all measures showed increased brain development in the rich rats versus the poor rats. The poor social rats generally were intermediate. Indeed, the effects of early experience are evident just by weighing the brains. The rich rats performed better in a variety of learning tasks in the laboratory.

The two types of measures that have been used most widely in recent work on effects of experience are the number and complexity of neuron dendrites and the number of dendritic spines. The rich rat cerebral cortex has significantly more dendritic complexity and significantly more dendritic spines on certain neurons than does the cortex of the poor rat. Since the spines are synapses (presumably excitatory), it would appear that a rich early environment results in more excitatory synaptic connections in the brain, a seeming verification of Hebb's notions.

Whether the growth of new synaptic connections in the cerebral cortex actually serves to code the memories formed by the rich rats is of course not known. It could be that more excitatory synapses form as a result of greater stimulation and arousal (and more norepinephrine?), but that they are not directly concerned with memory storage. An alternative interpretation is that the rich rats are actually normal rats—rats in the wild live in an environment that is rich in stimuli and stress, if not in food. The poor rats may be abnormally deprived of experience and develop abnormally fewer excitatory synaptic connections in the cerebral cortex. Rosenzweig and associates raised laboratory rats in a semi-natural "wild" environment (on the Berkeley campus outside the psychology building) and found that this may be the case. In these animals the brains were as well or better developed than those of the rich laboratory rats (Bennett et al., 1964).

The effects of a rich environment on the brain are not completely permanent. If rich rats are later returned to a poor environment, the brain development regresses to some degree. Interestingly, the poor rats show some signs of increased brain development when they are run through the mazes and other behavioral tests. The testing and learning experiences can apparently induce some brain development, even in these young adult animals. Stress itself may also be an important factor. Seymour Levine at Stanford University showed that rats who were given electric shock stress experiments as infants performed better on learning tasks than did nonstressed controls (Levine, 1960).

Most of the work on effects of early environmental experience on brain development has been done on rats and mice. William Greenough at the University of Illinois looked at effects of experience on brain development in the monkey (Floeter & Greenough, 1979). One group of monkeys was housed from shortly after birth in individual cages. Another group lived in similar cages but were allowed to play with other monkeys each day. The third group were raised together with other monkeys of all ages in a pair of large adjoining rooms equipped with play objects and structures. The principal neurons of the cerebellum—the Purkinje cells—had significantly greater dendritic complexity in the rich monkeys than in monkeys of the poor and poor social groups. The cerebellum is much involved in the control of movement and recent evidence from our laboratory (see next section) suggests that it may also be much involved in the coding of learned responses.

MEMORY CONSOLIDATION

A basic idea developed in Hebb's 1949 book was that new learning is fragile and well-established memories are not, the notion of memory consolidation (see Chapters 4, 5, & 6, this volume). Gerard (1949) independently suggested the same idea. In the same year, Carl Duncan (1949) published his now classic discovery that the detrimental effect of electroconvulsive shock (ECS) on memory performance in rats was inversely proportioned to the time between the learning trial and the ECS experience—the first clear empirical support for the consolidation hypothesis. This hypothesis was apparently first proposed by Müller and Pilzecker in 1900 to account for the fact that in human verbal learning, interpolation of new information interferes with the retention of previous learning. McDougall (1901) pointed out that this hypothesis provided an explanation for the amnesia often observed with head injuries, where the amnesia is for events that occurred shortly before the injury. An extensive clinical literature developed over the years on amnesia following head injury and following ECS treatment for mental illness (see, e.g., Flescher, 1941). But it was only with Duncan's 1949 study on rats that the phenomenon was brought into the laboratory.

Duncan's study raised many more questions than it answered: Is there a gradient of amnesia? Is the amnesia "really" amnesia or perhaps a learned fear, the learning of competing responses or the incubation of competing emotional responses? These and other controversies led to a large and vigorous literature (see McGaugh & Herz, 1972, for a detailed review). The tentative bottom line from this work is that under certain conditions, ECS or local disruptive brain stimulation can produce amnesia. Indeed, repeated ECS treatments can yield the long-lasting amnesia in animals that is typical of human ECS-treated patients (Squire,

1984). But we do not yet understand the brain mechanisms that underlie ECS-induced amnesia. The patient HM (see below) is perhaps the clearest example of a brain lesion (hippocampus and amygdala) that massively and selectively impaired the "consolidation process" following the lesion. HM is unable to store new verbal–"conscious" material in long-term or permanent memory.

Memory facilitation can be produced by administration of a variety of drugs and hormones. Lashley was apparently the first to observe this effect: Low doses of strychnine given before daily training increased the rate of maze learning in rats (Lashley, 1917). McGaugh and Petrinovich (1959) repeated and extended Lashley's observations. The possibility that the drug was merely acting on performance was then ruled out—post-trial administration also facilitated learning performance (McGaugh, Thompson, Westbrook, & Hudspeth, 1962) and the drug administration was shown to be rewarding, per se (Westbrook & McGaugh, 1964; also see McGaugh & Herz, 1972). Subsequently, a number of different drugs, neurotransmitter substances, and hormones were shown to facilitate learning and memory performance, and others were found to have deleterious effects (McGaugh, 1983).

If memory consolidation is in fact a particular process in the brain that serves to fix memories, then for a given task it ought to have a particular time course, a gradient, that is, a function relating degrees of impairment (e.g., with ECS) or facilitation (e.g., with strychnine) to time of treatment after learning trial. However, this was not the case: The form of the consolidation gradient depends strongly on the type and "intensity" of the post-trial treatment: "The time after training during which a treatment can alter the later retention performance seems to be an indicant of the treatment's effectiveness rather than an indicant of a time constant for memory formation, per se" (Gold & Zornetzer, 1983, p. 156). This kind of evidence led to a major conceptual shift in the field from the notion of "consolidation" to "modulation" (McGaugh & Dawson, 1971; Gold & McGaugh, 1975). The various treatments that influence learning and memory performance modulate the formation and expression of memory. The focus shifted from analysis of the nature and time course of memory formation to analysis of the conditions under which memory storage and performance can be altered. The recently discovered role of the adrenal gland in memory modulation (see below) illustrates the importance of this conceptual shift.

It was earlier assumed that drug and hormone facilitation of memory consolidation occurred directly in the brain. However, recent evidence indicates that many memory facilitating drugs and hormones may actually be acting in part peripherally on the endocrine system, particularly the adrenal gland (Gold & Zornetzer, 1983; McGaugh, 1983). Prior removal of the adrenal medulla eliminates drug faciliation of the memory process and even eliminates some forms of memory interference produced by ECS delivered directly to brain structures. Since the adrenal medulla secretes norepinephrine (NE) [and epinephrine (E)] the memory facilitating drugs and hormones might be acting to modulate this secretion. But NE (and E) in the blood apparently does not cross the blood–brain barrier to any appreciable degree, so it does not seem likely to be acting on the brain directly. Consequently, the remarkable effect of prior removal of the adrenal medulla in preventing memory consolidation and impairment would seem to argue against direct actions on a "consolidation" process in the brain. The adrenal medulla also contains other hormonelike substances, for example, opioids.

A classical theory of emotion, the James–Lange theory, argues that feelings of emotion are due in large part to peripheral action of the sympathetic nervous system and adrenal gland sending back cues through both hormonal and neural routes to the brain about the state of the body. A striking fact about memories is that those learned in a state of extreme emotion, like fear or terror, are never forgotten. Emotional state strongly influences and "stamps in" memories (Gold & Zornetzer, 1983; McGaugh, 1983). By the same token, learning is poorest when done in a state of boredom and inattentiveness. Perhaps the drug and other effects on memory consolidation are acting in part to modulate peripheral emotional cues and producing their effects on memory storage by way of emotional reinforcement. At least this is a current working hypothesis in the field.

THE CHEMISTRY OF MEMORY

It seems self-evident that the memory trace must involve chemical processes in the brain (see Chapters 4, 5, & 6, this volume). The search for chemical substrates of learning and memory has become perhaps the largest aspect of the field. This approach to the psychobiology of learning and memory does not have a long history—biochemical study of the brain is a young discipline. Halstead (1951) was perhaps the first to suggest that engrams might be stored in "template" protein molecules in nerve cells. Hydén was among the first to publish evidence implicating RNA in memory (Hydén & Egyhazi, 1964). In retrospect, it seems surprising that the "specific memories stored in specific molecules" hypothesis could ever have been taken seriously since it ignored the cellular biology and physiology of neurons. An unfortunate blind alley stemming from this hypothesis was memory "transfer."

Memory "transfer" was first reported by James McConnell and colleagues at the University of Michigan in studies where they ground up trained planaria (a flatworm) and fed them to untrained planaria. The untrained planaria were reported to exhibit the trained response (McConnell, 1962). Subsequently, Allen Jacobson and his associates reported a similar finding in rats (Jacobson, Babich, Bubash, & Jacobson, 1965; Jacobson & Schlecter, 1970). We will use Jacobson's study as an example. Rats were trained to approach a food cup upon hearing the click of a food dispenser. Brains from the trained rats and naive control rats were ground up, treated with RNA extraction procedures (RNA is involved in the manufacture of proteins in all cells), and injected into untrained recipient rats. The recipients of trained brain extract were reported to approach the food cup upon presentation of the click more than recipients of untrained brain extract. These experiments were very poorly designed and controlled and it has not been possible for Jacobson or any one else to replicate the observation. As of this writing, there is no evidence whatever for memory transfer. But the possibility of memory transfer led *Time* magazine to its infamous final solution for what to do with old college professors.

If the memory trace has a physical or anatomical basis, as seems very likely, then chemical processes must be involved. In particular, proteins must be manufactured to provide the physical material for the anatomical change. Well-established memories are almost impervious to the interfering effects of ECS, drugs, and other treatments, as we noted earlier. A number of studies have shown that injection of chemicals that stop or inhibit protein synthesis in the brain severely impair the formation of new memories. One of the problems is that such substances also tend to make the animals very sick. Among the earliest and best controlled of these are studies by Bernard Agranoff and his associates at the University of Michigan (Agranoff, 1967; Agranoff, Davis, & Brink, 1966). He used a very hardy animal, the goldfish. The fish is in a 2-part tank. When a light is turned on, the fish must swim to the other part of the tank to avoid shock. Animals are trained and given brain injections of puromyecin, a drug that blocks protein synthesis. Injections just before or within 30 min of the learning experience do not prevent initial learning, but markedly impair retention (long-term memory). However, injections given more than 30 min after learning do not prevent the formation of long-term memory.

A major problem with the idea that protein synthesis inhibition prevents the formation of long-term memories in the brain, as opposed to other less specific actions, is that a variety of treatments (e.g., injecting certain drugs) can, under some conditions, bring back the memories that were supposedly never formed. In fact, first removing the adrenal gland "protects" memories from some effects of protein synthesis inhibition, at least in rats and mice; this is one of the findings that led to exploration of the role of the adrenal gland in memory, as previously noted.

The two major approaches to the biochemistry of memory have often been termed "interventive" and "correlational," interventive meaning attempting to manipulate the chemistry of the brain (e.g., with drugs) and correlational meaning analyzing learning-induced chemical changes in the brain (see, e.g., Dunn, 1980). (These definitions are, of course, oversimplifications; all evidence in science is basically correlational and training is a manipulation, as previously noted). Much of the "interventive" work has been done in the context of memory consolidation. Virtually all putative neurotransmitter systems have been studied in terms of drug actions, with perhaps the greatest emphasis on norepinephrine, stimulated in part by Kety's early suggestion that NE may somehow be involved in reinforcing or "setting" memories (see Gold & Zornetzer, 1983, for a comprehensive review). Dopamine systems have also been studied. Acetylcholine drugs were studied extensively by Deutsch (1973) a few years ago and now enjoy a return to popularity with the new work on Alzheimer's disease implicating forebrain acetylcholine (ACh) systems. Virtually all other known neurotransmitter systems have been studied in terms of drug effects on memory, at least to some degree.

Studies of effects of pituitary peptides began with deWied and Bohus' report in 1966 that a crude posterior pituitary extract ("pitressin") prolonged resistance to extinction of learned responses. Most recent work has focused on vasopressin, ACTH, and endogenous opioid peptides (see Martinez, Jensen, Messing, Rigter, & McGaugh, 1981; also see Chapters 4, 5, & 6, this volume). We summarize this vast literature by quoting from a recent review:

> A wide range of drug and chemical treatments can alter behavioral expression of memory. Those treatments that impair memory include substances known to interfere with protein synthesis, along with other kinds of substances and treatments. However, it is still not known whether such effects are due to impairment of synthesis of particular proteins and at particular places in the brain, or are due to nonspecific biological/behavioral impairments. A number of substances involved in one or more putative neurotransmitter systems also impair memory, and some facilitate the expression of memory. Again, it has not yet been shown that the memorial effects of those substances are due to specific neurochemical transmitter actions or that they occur at specific sites. All this evidence taken

together builds an indirect but nonetheless compelling case that biochemical processes are an essential aspect of the mechanisms of learning and memory storage in the brain (Thompson et al., 1983b).

"Correlational" studies earlier focused on protein and RNA changes induced by training procedures, beginning with Hydén's work noted earlier. The conceptual model shifted from memory molecules to synthetic processes that might result in altered synaptic interactions, either through structural changes (proteins) or "process" changes (enzymes, neurotransmitters, receptors, etc., which of course would likely involve protein synthesis), the current emphasis being more on process changes (see Dunn, 1980, p. 343–90).

Much earlier correlational work focused on global changes in brain chemistry induced by training. Agranoff summarized the difficulties in this approach:

> We are . . . confronted with an enormous haystack that we believe contains a needle of undetermined size, probably miniscule. . . . At present, the approach has an element of "Catch 22"—if a change in labelling pattern is detected in a whole brain extract as a result of training, it can probably safely be ruled out as being a part of an informational process, i.e., related to the learning of a specific new task. Observed changes can more reasonably be attributed to grosser and less specific concomitants of learning related to brain states, such as stress, attentiveness, etc. (Agranoff, Burrell, Dokas, & Springer, 1978, p. 628).

The fundamental problem is localization. Analysis of putative neurochemical changes involved in the coding and storage of memory can only be done when the specific storage sites in the brain have been localized. Otherwise, the signal-to-noise problem is overwhelming, as Agranoff notes above. Indeed, significant progress has been made or appears possible only in these cases where the learned response circuit has to some degree been identified and localized.

Entingh, Dunn, Wilson, Glassman, & Hogan (1975) raise what they consider the fundamental questions to be answered in order to understand the biochemistry of memory:

1. Which neurochemical systems are involved in the formation of memory?
2. When in the learning process do changes in these systems occur?
3. Where in the brain do the neurochemical events occur?
4. What is the behavioral specificity of the changes?

Most work to date has focused on Question #1, and the answer seems to be "all known neurochemical systems." Most work on Question #2 has been in the context of memory consolidation, as previously reviewed. Question #3 has, in general, not been addressed because with the exception of a very few recent discoveries, memory traces have not yet been localized in the mammalian brain. Considerable effort has been devoted to Question #4, that is, in attempting to rule out chemical changes that relate to arousal, activity, stress, and other aspects of behavioral training that may not be a part of the memory process.

COGNITIVE SCIENCE AND NEUROPSYCHOLOGY

Watson and his behaviorist successors forbade appealing to mental or conscious processes in explanations of behavior. However, interest in these phenomena has existed from ancient times. In recent history, there has been a continuous interest in and study of higher mental processes from before the time of Wundt and James.

The experimental study of human learning and memory began with Hermann Ebbinghaus' (1885) heroic experiments on himself. He invented the nonsense syllable, learned thousands of lists of such material, and developed several principles or laws which were not so different from the principles of learning that emerged from animal studies. Another focus was on the learning of motor skills, tasks like telegraphy, typewriting, mirror tracing, tracking (Woodworth, 1938). A great deal was learned about human learning in the systematic parametric studies of Melton (Melton & von Lackum, 1941; Melton, 1970), Underwood (1957), Postman (1971), and others.

The study of human learning and memory was gradually subsumed into what today is called cognitive psychology. However, the term "cognitive" first came into widespread use as a consequence of the establishment of the Center for Cognitive Studies at Harvard in about 1959. According to the story, Jerome Bruner and George Miller presented the Dean, McGeorge Bundy, with a proposal to establish a Center for Cognitive Studies at Harvard (the Dean is said to have replied that Harvard itself was such a center). The Center was established and the term "cognitive" became a rallying point for psychologists interested in studying the human mind. Major traditions that fed into cognitive science include verbal learning (as previously noted), studies on human thinking (e.g., Bartlett, 1932), the ontogeny of human thought and concept formation (Piaget, 1954), the study of language and linguistics (Chomsky, 1968; Brown, 1964), the rapidly developing field of computer science and artificial intelligence (e.g., Newell & Simon's General Problem Solver, 1972), and finally, the study of human intelligence in the context of individual differences, for example, IQ (Binet & Simon, 1905; see Posner & Shulman, 1979).

In its formative years, cognitive psychology was perhaps not greatly interested in brain substrates of cognitive processes. It was sufficient to develop information processing models and computer simulations of the behavioral–experiential aspects of human memory and thought (Atkinson & Shiffrin, 1968; Anderson & Bower, 1973; Newell & Simon, 1972). Indeed, the most explicit formulations of different time course phenomena in memory (iconic, short-term, working, and long-term memory) come from cognitive psychology. From a biological point of view, perhaps the most important contributions of cognitive psychology during this period were the development of objective methods to measure the operations of the machinery of the human mind. Three particularly striking examples are: selective attention (Broadbent, 1971; Treisman, 1969); the search through short-term memory (Sternberg, 1966, 1975); and mental rotation (Sheperd & Metzler, 1971).

The field of neuropsychology, concerned with higher brain functions in humans, treats the same basic subject matter as cognitive science, but from the perspective of human brain injury, and has partly independent origins in the field of clinical neurology.

Neurologists who were key figures in the development of neuropsychology included J. Hughlings Jackson, who in the latter half of the 19th century developed the notion that the nervous system consisted of a hierarchical integration of neural centers with ascending functional organization from the most primitive to the most highly evolved; Sir Henry Head, who completed classic studies on limited brain damage in injuries sustained by soldiers in World War I; and Kurt Goldstein, who also studied this patient population and was heavily influenced by Gestalt psychology, with its emphasis on organizing principles in perceptions.

Perhaps the most influential scientists in the recent development of experimental neuropsychology were Hans-Lukas Teuber and Brenda Milner. Karl Pribram also played an important role. Brenda Milner obtained her PhD at McGill University under Donald Hebb's supervision. Hebb arranged for her to work with Wilder Penfield's neurosurgical patients at the Montreal Neurological Institute. Her work on the psychological effects of temporal lobe removal in humans is classic, as in the case of HM, who, after bilateral removal of his temporal lobes, including the hippocampus, lives forever in the present. Her work stimulated the modern field concerned with human amnesia (Squire, 1982).

Milner's studies of HM had a strong impact on the field of animal learning and led to literally thousands of studies exploring effects of removing the hippocampus on memory functions in animals (Isaacson

& Pribram, 1974). It was learned that, among many other effects, hippo-campal lesions in rats impaired spatial memory (O'Keefe & Nadel, 1978), and working (trial dependent) memory (Olton, 1985), two current theories of hippocampal function in animals. But HM's syndrome could not be modeled in animals until Mishkin showed in 1978 that bilateral removal of the hippocampus and amygdala massively impaired recent visual memory in monkeys in a delayed nonmatching to sample task.

Another very important influence in modern clinical neuropsychology came from the Soviet scientist Alexander Luria. Luria approached detection and evaluation of damage to higher regions of the human brain as a clinician with expertise in neurology, as a psychologist well-versed in the use of psychological tests, and as a scientist interested in higher functions of the nervous system (see, for example, his book on human memory, The Neuropsychology of Memory, 1976).

Another key tradition in neuropsychology, really a field in its own right, concerned the localization of language functions in the human cerebral cortex. Broca's and Wernicke's studies on the types of speech and language deficits shown by patients with localized brain injury were not at first widely accepted in neurology. But evidence accumulated slowly for cerebral localization of language function, and with the advent of computerized tomography, a large-scale data base developed (see Damasio & Geschwind, 1984, for review). There is some recent evidence from neurosurgical studies suggesting an extreme degree of localization of language function in the cerebral cortex (Ojemann & Whitaker, 1978).

THE MODEL BIOLOGICAL SYSTEM APPROACH

Quinn defined the ideal preparation for analysis of neurobiological substrates of learning and memory as follows:

> The organism should have no more than three genes, a generation time of twelve hours, be able to play the cello or at least recite classical Greek, and learn these tasks with a nervous system containing only ten large, differently colored, and therefore easily recognizable neurons (cited as personal communication in Kandel, 1976, p. 45).

Quinn's preparation illustrates a number of features that an ideal model biological system should possess. The model system approach to brain substrates of learning and memory was of course first developed by Pavlov and by Lashley. Lashley states the essence of the approach most simply in the following passage: "In experiments extending over the past 30 years, I have been trying to trace conditioned reflex paths through the brain or to find the locus of specific memory traces." (1950).

At the present time, the model system approach is perhaps the most promising research strategy for investigating the neural bases of behavior and changes in behavior, particularly for dealing with the problem of localization of memory traces (Alkon, 1980; Chang & Gelperin, 1980; Cohen, 1980; Ito, 1982; Kandel & Spencer, 1968; Kandel, 1976; Sahley, Rudy, & Gelperin, 1981; Thompson & Spencer, 1966; Thompson et al., 1983b; Tsukahara, 1981; Woody, 1982; see also Chapter 9, this volume). The strategy of this approach is to select an organism capable of exhibiting a range of behavioral phenomena that one wishes to explain and whose nervous system possesses properties that make neuroanatomical, neuropharmacological, and neurophysiological experimentation tractable. The goal is to work out in detail (to a cellular level) how a nervous system controls some type of behavior. This description then is taken to be a model of how the same and related behavioral phenomena are produced in other species. The trade-off typically encountered is that the more complex the behavior one wishes to explain, the less tractable are the nervous systems of organisms capable of exhibiting such behavior. A chief advantage of model systems is that the facts gained from anatomical, physiological, biochemical, and behavioral investigations for a particular preparation are cumulative and tend to have synergistic effects on theory development and research.

Each approach and model preparation has particular advantages. The unique value of invertebrate preparations as model systems results from the fact that certain behavioral functions are controlled by ganglia containing relatively small numbers of large, identifiable cells—cells which can be consistently identified across individuals of the species (Alkon, 1979, 1980; Davis & Gillette, 1978; Hoyle, 1980; Kandel, 1976; Krasne, 1969). As a result of knowing the architecture of the system, one can begin to determine systematically which neurons of the system are responsible for the behavior under investigation. Upon defining such neural circuits, one can then evaluate how the functioning of the neurons in the circuit are affected by training procedures. Once the neurons exhibiting plasticity are known, it is possible to identify changes in their structure and function that are responsible for the observed changes in behavior (see Chapter 8, this volume).

A model approach that is perhaps even more reductionistic is to use processes of plasticity that can be induced in pieces of tissue, such as long-term potentiation (LTP) in the hippocampal slice, as models of processes that might underlie learning and memory (see Chapter 7, this volume, Lynch & Baudry, 1984).

With intact vertebrate model systems, these goals are considerably more difficult to attain. One uses vertebrates for the simple reason that if one is to understand vertebrate nervous systems, one must at some point study vertebrates. In addition, if the behavior of interest is complex, it might be observed only in vertebrates. It is clear that higher vertebrates have developed increasing capacities for learning and have made use of these capacities in the development of adaptive behavior. It would seem that the evolution of the mammalian brain has resulted in systems especially well adapted for information processing, learning, and memory.

CASE HISTORY OF A MODEL BIOLOGICAL SYSTEM

Some years ago we adopted a particularly clear cut and robust form of associative learning in the intact mammal as a model biological system: Classical conditioning of the rabbit nictitating membrane (NM) and eyelid response to an acoustic or visual CS using a corneal airpuff US.

Classical conditioning of the rabbit NM/eyelid response has a number of advantages for analysis of brain substrates of learning and memory, which have been detailed elsewhere (Thompson et al., 1976). Perhaps the greatest single advantage of this, and classical conditioning paradigms in general, is that the effects of experimental manipulations on learning versus performance can be more easily evaluated than in instrumental procedures, as previously noted.

Another advantage of the conditioned eyelid response is that fact that eyelid conditioning has become perhaps the most widely used paradigm for the study of basic properties of classical or Pavlovian conditioning of striated muscle responses in both humans and infrahuman subjects. It displays the same basic laws of learning in humans and other animals (Hilgard & Marquis, 1940). Consequently, it seems highly likely that neuronal mechanisms found to underly conditioning of the eyelid response in rabbits will hold for all mammals, including humans. We view the conditioned eyelid response as an instance of the general class of discrete, adaptive behavioral responses learned to deal with an aversive stimuli, and we adopt the working assumption that neuronal mechanisms underlying associative learning of the eyelid response will in fact be general for all such learning.

In the rabbit NM conditioning paradigm, considerably more than just NM extension becomes conditioned. Gormezano and associates first showed that eyelid closure, eyeball retraction and NM extension all develop during conditioning in essentially the same manner (Gormezano, Schneiderman, Deaux, & Fuentes, 1962; Schneiderman, Fuentes, & Gormezano, 1962; Deaux & Gormezano, 1963). The efferent limb thus involves several cranial nerve nuclei. The total response is a coordinated defense of the eye involving primarily eyeball retraction (NM extension) and eyelid closure with some contraction of periorbital facial musculature (see McCormick, Lavond, & Thompson, 1982a). Simultaneous recordings from the NM and eyelid during conditioning show essentially perfect correlations in both amplitude and latency of the conditioned responses as they develop over the course of training.

Recordings of neural activity from one of the critical motor nuclei (6th or abducens) simultaneously with measurement of NM extension or eyelid closure show that the pattern of increased neural unit response precedes and closely parallels the amplitude–time course of the behavioral NM response. The cross correlation between the two responses is very high—typically over 0.90 (Cegavske, Thompson, Patterson, & Garmezano, 1976).

The amplitude–time course of the eyelid response thus parallels the pattern of increased neuronal unit activity in the relevant motor nuclei with considerable precision on a trial-by-trial basis, except of course for onset latency differences. This is a great convenience. The extension of the NM eyelid across the eye reflects the change in neural unit activity in the final common path—a learned neuronal response that has the same properties in several motor nuclei. We adopted the working hypothesis that the neuronal system responsible for generation of the learned eyelid response will exhibit this same pattern of increased neuronal activity. Something must drive the several motor nuclei in a synchronous fashion. The amplitude–time course of the learned eyelid response provides a "marker" for the pattern of increased neuronal activity in the memory trace circuit.

In the standard conditioning paradigm, animals with the cerebral neocortex or hippocampus removed are able to learn (Oakley & Russell, 1972; Solomon & Moore, 1975), as are animals with all brain tissue above the level of the thalamus or midbrain removed (Norman, Buchwald, & Villablanca, 1977; see also Chapter 9, this volume). Some caution must be exercised in drawing conclusions regarding the locus of the memory trace in the intact animal from results on reduced preparations. The fact that a decerebrate animal can learn the eyelid response does not necessarily mean that the memory trace is normally established in the intact animal below the level of the thalamus, only that the remaining tissue is capable of supporting learning. Oakley and Russell (1977) addressed this issue for the cerebral cortex by first training the animals, then decorticating them, allowing 5–10 weeks for recovery and then continuing training. They found a transient depression in conditioned responding, but a rapid recovery (marked savings), arguing that a substantial part of the memory trace established in the intact animal is below the level of the cerebral cortex.

Current work by Michael Mauk in our laboratory provides a dramatic demonstration that the essential memory trace for the standard short-delay eyelid conditioned response is in fact established below the level of the thalamus in intact animals. (Our standard conditions are: Tone CS of 1 KHz, 85 dB, duration 350 ms, corneal airpuff US of 100 ms duration, coterminating with CS.) Rabbits were trained and over-trained. At the end of the overtraining session, they were anesthetized (halothane) and decerebrated—all brain tissue above the caudal level of the thalamus was aspirated. They were allowed 3–4 hr of recovery following decerebration and training was continued. The animals retained normal conditioned responses following decerebration!

It seems very likely that memory trace systems develop in higher regions of the brain in classical conditioning. Indeed, evidence to date argues strongly that a memory trace system develops in the hippocampus very early in training in classical conditioning of the rabbit eyelid response (Berger & Thompson, 1978a,b,c; see Chapter 9, this volume). However, this hippocampal memory trace system is not essential for learning or memory of the conditioned response, although it does appear to become more critical when greater demands are placed on the memory system. The development of such "higher order" memory systems in basic learning paradigms may provide simplified models for the study of neuronal substrates of the more complex or cognitive functions of higher regions of the brain like the cerebral cortex and hippocampus.

In a series of studies described elsewhere (Thompson, McCormick, & Lavond, 1985), we have developed evidence against localization of the memory traces for these basic conditioned responses in several brain systems. One must distinguish between the essential memory trace circuit, here from the ear (tone CS) to the eyelid, and the memory traces themselves. In brief, our evidence argues against the memory traces being localized to the primary auditory relay nuclei (CS channel), to the motor nuclei or to the more direct US reflex pathways. But some portions of these nuclei and pathways are of course a part of the essential memory trace circuit.

CEREBELLUM: THE LOCUS OF THE MEMORY TRACE?

From the above findings, the circuitry that might serve to code the primary memory trace for the eyelid CR in the standard delay paradigm could include much of the midbrain and brain stem and the cerebellum, excluding the primary CS channel (here the auditory relay nuclei), the reflex pathways and the motor neurons. Since there was no a priori way of determining which of these regions and structures are involved in the memory trace, we undertook, beginning some years ago, to map the entire midbrain, brain stem, and cerebellum by systematically recording neuronal unit activity (unit cluster recording) in already-trained animals (Cegavske, Patterson, & Thompson, 1979; McCormick & Thompson, 1983; Thompson et al., 1983c). For this purpose we developed a chronic micromanipulator system that permits mapping of unit activity in a substantial number of neural loci per animal. Increases in unit activity that form a temporal model within a trial of the learned behavioral response were prominent in certain regions of the cerebellum, as well as in certain other regions, and of course in the cranial motor nuclei engaged in generation of the behavioral response. The results of the mapping studies pointed to substantial engagement of the cerebellar system in the generation of the conditioned response. An example is shown in Figure 1.1 with unit recordings from the cerebellar interpositus nucleus ipsilateral to the trained eye. This animal was given unpaired training before acquisition began. Average histograms reveal that the unit activity showed only minimal responses to the tone and airpuff during the unpaired day of training. However, during acquisition, as the animal learned, the unit activity developed a model of the conditioned response. Again, there is no clear model of the unconditioned response. The cerebellar unit model of the learned response precedes the behavioral response significantly in time. *A neuronal model of the learned behavioral response appears to develop de novo in the cerebellar deep nuclear region.* The course of development of the conditioned behavioral eyelid response and the concomitant growth in the neuronal unit "model" of the conditioned response in the interpositus nuclear region show very high correlations (e.g., $r = .90$).

In current work, we have found that lesions ipsilateral to the trained eye in the neocerebellum (Figure 1.2) permanently abolish the CR but have no effect on the UR and do not prevent subsequent learning by the contralateral eye (Clark, McCormick, Lavond, Baxter, Gray, & Thompson, 1982; 1984; Lavond, McCormick, Clark, Holmes, & Thompson, 1981; McCormick, Lavond, Clark, Kettner, Rising, & Thompson, 1981; McCormick, Lavond, & Thompson, 1982a; McCormick, Clark, Lavond,

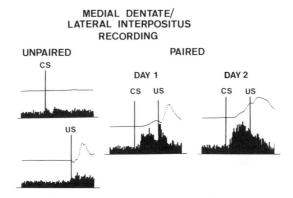

**MEDIAL DENTATE/
LATERAL INTERPOSITUS
RECORDING**

FIGURE 1.1 Histograms of unit recordings obtained from a chronic electrode implanted at the lateral border of the interpositus nucleus. The animal was first given random, unpaired presentations of the tone and airpuff (104 trials of each stimulus) and then trained with 2 days of paired training (117 trials each day). Each histogram is an average over the entire day of training indicated. The upper trace represents movement of the NM. The first vertical line represents the onset of the tone CS, while the second line represents the onset of the corneal airpuff US. Each histogram bar is 9 ms in duration. Notice that these neurons develop a model of the conditioned but not unconditioned response during learning and that this neuronal model precedes the learned behavioral response substantially in time (McCormick & Thompson, 1984b; reproduced by permission).

& Thompson, 1982b; Thompson, 1983; see also Chapter 9, this volume). If the lesion is made before training, no learning occurs (Lincoln, McCormick, & Thompson, 1982). The critical region is the lateral interpositus nucleus. Perhaps most dramatic is a recent study involving kainic acid (it destroys nerve cell bodies but not nerve fibers or terminals)—destruction of neurons in a region as small as a cubic millimeter in the lateral portion of the interpositus causes complete and permanent loss of the learned eyelid response (Lavond, McCormick, & Thompson, 1984b).

Lesions of the cerebellar cortex do not abolish the basic conditioned eyelid response (McCormick & Thompson, 1983). To date, we have removed all lobes of the ipsilateral cerebellar cortex except the flocculus in different groups of animals. However, our results to date do not exclude the possibility of a "multiple trace" in cerebellar cortex represented in several lobes that project to the critical deep nuclear region.

Electrical stimulation through recording microelectrodes in the critical lateral interpositus nuclear region elicits a discrete eyelid response prior to training. Indeed, a range of discrete behavioral responses (eyelid closure, leg flexion, head turning) can be elicited by microstimula-

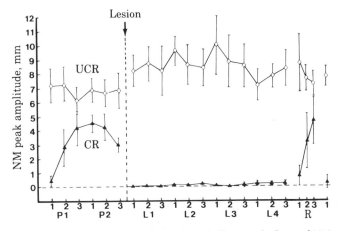

FIGURE 1.2   Effects of ablation of left lateral cerebellum on the learned NM per eyelid response (6 animals). Solid triangles, amplitude of conditioned response (CR); open diamonds, amplitude of unconditioned response (UCR). All training was to left eye (ipsilateral to lesion) except where labeled "R" (for right eye). The cerebellar lesion completely and permanently abolished the CR of the ipsilateral eye but had no effect on the UCR. P_1 and P_2 indicate initial learning on the 2 days prior to the lesion. L_1–L_4 are 4 days of postoperative training to the left eye. The right eye was then trained and learned rapidly (R), thus controlling for nonspecific lesion effects. The left eye was again trained and showed no learning. Numbers on abscissa indicate 40 trial periods, except for right eye, which are 24 trial periods (McCormick et al., 1982a; reproduced by permission).

tion of the interpositus, the type of response depending upon the exact location of the stimulating electrode.

Composite diagrams are shown in Figure 1.3 indicating regions of the ipsilateral cerebellar deep nuclei from which the neuronal unit "model" of the learned behavioral response can be recorded (A = solid dots), regions from which electrical stimulation evokes an eyelid response (B = solid dots), the locus of lesions that permanently abolish the conditioned eyelid response (C) and large cerebellar cortical lesions that do not abolish the conditioned eyelid response (D). Note that the sites of the neuronal model, the sites of effective electrical stimulation and the effective lesion site are essentially identical, involving the lateral portion of the interpositus nucleus. Importantly, a lesion placed more medially in the interpositus nucleus selectively abolishes the learned hind limb flexion response (Donegan, Lowry, & Thompson, 1983).

These results indicate that the essential memory trace circuits for these learned responses are extremely localized in the brain. How general is this finding? Most of our work has been on the learned eyelid response, but as previously noted, we have shown that a different part

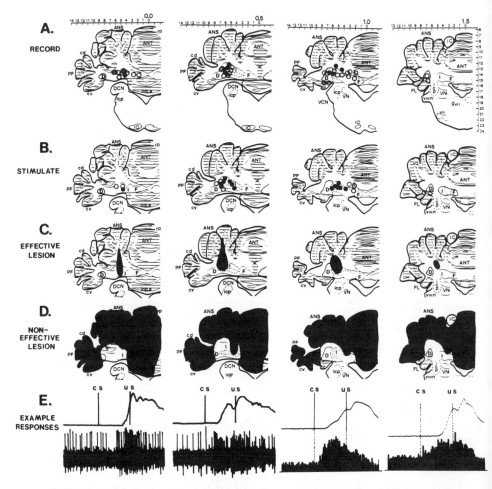

FIGURE 1.3 Summary diagram of the chronic recordings, stimulation, dentate–inter-positus lesions, and noneffective lesions of the cerebellar cortex. A, the recording sites (solid dots) which developed neuronal responses within the CS period which were greater than 2 standard scores (see Figure 1.2 and Part E below), as well as the recording sites (open dots) which did not develop a neuronal response within the CS period. B, the sites at which 60 Hz stimulation at 100 μA or the onset of direct current stimulation at 100 μA produces ipsilateral NM extension and eyelid closure (solid dots). The sites which were ineffective in eliciting eyeblink responses are represented by open dots. C, a typical stereotaxic lesion of the medial dentate/lateral interpositus nuclear region which abolished the conditioned response. D, a composite drawing of aspirations of three animals which were ineffective in abolishing the learned eyeblink response. E, examples of neuronal responses and corresponding histograms recorded from the critical regions indicated in A (see also Figure 1.2). Note that the medial dentate–lateral interpositus region not only develops neuronal responses related to the performance of the learned

of the interpositus is essential for hind limb flexion conditioning. We and our associated laboratories are now exploring the generality of our results across learning paradigms and species. Particularly important are current results in collaboration with Michael Patterson at Ohio University. He developed a procedure for eyelid conditioning in the cat, and has now found that the interpositus nucleus ipsilateral to the trained eye is essential for the learned response in this species, as well as in the rabbit. It would seem that our results may be generalizable to all mammals. In other work, Patterson developed a paradigm for instrumental avoidance learning of the eyelid closure response in the rabbit, where eyelid closure to tone CS before onset of corneal airpuff results in the airpuff not being delivered. He found that lesions of the ipsilateral interpositus nucleus abolish this instrumental avoidance response, as well as the classically conditioned response. Hence, we feel we can generalize our essential cerebellar circuit to discrete, adaptive responses learned to deal with aversive stimuli in both classical and instrumental avoidance learning paradigms in mammals.

In other work we have identified much of the efferent pathway from interpositus nucleus to motor nuclei. Our results indicate that it courses out the superior cerebellar peduncle (McCormick, Guyer, & Thompson, 1982c), crosses to the contralateral side in the peduncle (Lavond et al., 1981), relays in the magnocellular division of the red nucleus (Haley, Lavond, & Thompson, 1983; Madden, Haley, Barchas, & Thompson, 1983), crosses back to the ipsilateral side, and projects to the lower brain stem as a part of the descending rubral pathway. The essential CR circuit we have so far defined could be called the "efferent limb" in that destruction of any part of the circuit abolishes the CR to any CS (e.g., light or tone), but the association between CS and US or UR could very well be formed in the cerebellum. Collectively, these

---

response during training, but, when stimulated, will elicit an eyeblink response which is dependent, as is the learned response, on the intactness of the superior cerebellar peduncle. Furthermore, lesioning of this region of the deep cerebellar nuclei permanently abolished the learned response, while cortical lesions which circumscribe this region do not. Abbreviations are as follows: ANS—ansiform lobule (Crus I and II); ANT—anterior olbe; FL—flocculus; DCN—dorsal cochlear nucleus; IO—inferior olive; Lob. a—Lobulus A (nodulus); Lob. b—Lobulus B (uvula); Lob. c—Lobulus C (pyramis and medius medianus); PF—paraflocculus; VN—vestibular nuclei; cd—dorsal crus; cv—ventral crus; g vii—genu of the tract of the seventh nerve; icp—inferior cerebellar peduncle; vii— seventh (facial) nucleus; vii n—nerve of the seventh nucleus (McCormick & Thompson, 1984a; reproduced by permission).

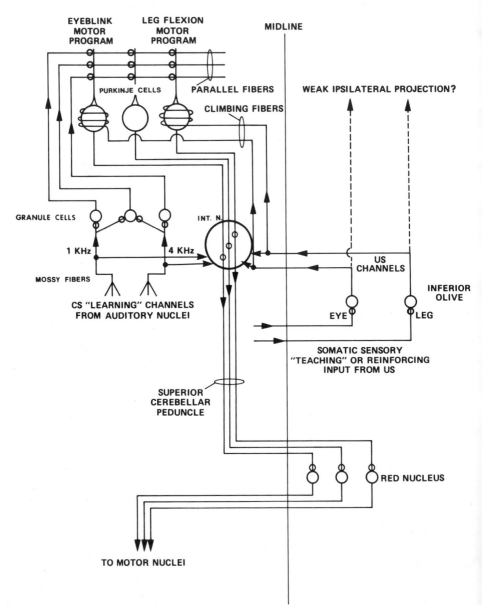

FIGURE 1.4 Scheme of hypothetical memory trace system for associative learning of discrete, adaptive, somatic-motor responses to deal with aversive unconditioned stimuli. Most interneurons are omitted. It is assumed that the site of the memory trace is at the Purkinje cells shown in the upper left under "motor programs" and/or at associated interneurons. The locus of the memory trace is shown as cerebellar cortex, and the basic

results argue strongly for the memory trace being in the cerebellum and/or in structures afferent to it for which the cerebellum is a mandatory efferent.

A Hypothetical Model

In late 1983, we developed a hypothetical schema or model of how the cerebellar memory trace circuit might work (Figure 1.4), based on the well-known anatomy of the system, according to our previously described results, and on theories of how the cerebellum might function as a learning machine. The cerebellar cortex has great appeal to theoreticians and modelers because of its elegant uniformity and simplicity and because of the striking fact of two quite different inputs to each Purkinje cell: a mossy fiber-granule cell-parallel fiber input that is widely distributed and a climbing fiber input that is highly localized. All models, both verbal and computational, have stressed this point, and those that focus on learning and memory have universally hypothesized that the mossy fiber-granule cell-parallel fiber system is the learning input, and the climbing fiber input is the teaching input (Albus, 1971; Brindley, 1964; Eccles, 1977; Gilbert, 1974; Grossberg, 1969; Ito, 1974; Marr, 1969).

In our schema, it is assumed that the site of the memory trace is at the principal neurons (Purkinje cells) shown in the upper left and/or in associated interneurons in the cerebellar cortex (not shown), and/or in the interpositus nucleus. A given CS (1 KHz) is assumed to activate a subset of granule cells and parallel fibers that in turn weakly activate all principal cells. A different tone also activates all principal cells but by a partially different group of parallel fibers. The US pathway is as-

---

notion is very similar to earlier theories of cerebellar plasticity (Albus, Marr, Eccles, Ito), but traces could also or alternatively be formed in the interpositus nucleus (int. n.), we assume by an analogous circuitry. A given CS (1 KHz) activates a subset of parallel fibers that in turn activate weakly all Purkinje cells shown. A different tone also activates all Purkinje cells but by a partially different group of parallel fibers. The US pathway is assumed to be via the inferior olive and climbing fibers. A given US is assumed to activate only a limited group of Purkinje cells coding the motor program for the defensive response that is specific for the US (eyelid closure, leg flexion). When parallel fiber activation occurs at the appropriate time just prior to climbing fiber activation, the connections of the parallel fibers to the Purkinje cells activated by the particular US are strengthened. The efferent pathway from Purkinje cells to motor neurons is by way of the interpositus nucleus, superior cerebellar peduncle, and red nucleus.

sumed to be via the inferior olive and climbing fibers. A given US is assumed to activate only a limited group of principal cells coding the motor program for the defensive response that is specific for the US (e.g., eyelid closure, leg flexion). When parallel fiber activation occurs at the appropriate time just prior to climbing fiber activation, the connections of the parallel fibers to the principal cells activated by the particular US are strengthened. The efferent pathway from principal cells to motor neurons is by way of the superior cerebellar peduncle and red nucleus. The scheme accounts for stimulus specificity, for example, the fact that CRs show a stimulus generalization gradient, for response specificity of learned responses, transfer, and lesion-transfer effects (e.g., training one eye and then the other before or after cerebellar lesion) and is consistent with all our evidence to date.

Although much of this circuit was hypothetical, insofar as it being a substrate for the formation of memories is concerned, each aspect and assumption is testable. Indeed, current work in our laboratory is providing strong new evidence favoring such a schema.

The inferior olive: The necessary and sufficient teaching input for the learning of discrete behavioral responses. A major afferent system that projects to the cerebellum is the inferior olive (IO-climbing fiber system. The dorsal accessory olive (DAO) has a clear somatotopic organization that is maintained in its projection to the interpositus (Gibson, Houk, & Robinson, 1983). In recent work we have found that lesions of the appropriate region of the IO (rostromedial DAO) do not abolish the CR but instead lead to relatively normal *extinction* with continued paired CS–US training (McCormick & Thompson, 1983; Steinmetz, McCormick, Baier, & Thompson, 1984). Lesions of all other regions of the IO do not affect the CR. The DAO appears to be the essential afferent limb for the reinforcing or "teaching" input from the US. The fact that lesions of the DAO do not immediately abolish the CR but instead lead to its eventual extinction argues that the essential memory trace cannot be there.

In current work we find that electrical microstimulation of the DAO can elicit a variety of behavioral responses, including eyelid closure, the nature of the threshold response being determined by the exact location of the stimulating electrode (latency from DAO stimulation ~35 ms). If this is now used as the US, and paired with a tone CS, the *exact response* elicited by DAO stimulation is learned to the tone as a CR, rapidly and with all the properties of a normal CR (Mauk & Thompson, 1984). Lesion in the critical interpositus region abolishes this IO-established CR, *and* abolishes the response elicited by IO stimulation. Control stimulation 1–2 mm dorsal to the DAO in the reticular formation can also elicit movements, presumably by activation of descending reticular pathways, but these elicited movements cannot be trained to a CS.

These IO results strengthen the argument that the IO and its climbing fiber input to the cerebellum is the essential US teaching input and that the trace is localized to the cerebellum. They are also the first clear empirical evidence supporting the pioneering hypothesis and network models of Albus, Eccles, Ito, Marr, and others that the IO-climbing fiber system is the "teaching" input for behavioral learning in the cerebellum. Ito has developed analogous findings in the context of plasticity of the vestibulo-ocular reflex (1984), and Llinas, Walton, Hillman, & Sotelo (1975) report a similar role for the inferior olive-climbing fiber system in recovery from postural abnormalities following vestibular damage.

Creation of a known CS pathway: Mossy fiber projections to cerebellum. The major remaining unknown portion of the essential memory trace circuit concerns how CS information is projected from primary sensory pathways to the essential cerebellar circuit. But we have succeeded in creating a known CS pathway by using electrical microstimulation of mossy fiber projections to the cerebellum as the CS (Steinmetz, Lavond, & Thompson, 1985). Animals rapidly learn normal behavioral conditioned responses to this CS (e.g., eyeblink CR with corneal airpuff US). To date we have successfully used stimulation of mossy fibers from the dorsolateral pontine nucleus and the lateral reticular nucleus as CSs.

Finally, in current pilot work we find that normal behavioral CRs are learned with electrical stimulation of mossy fibers as the CS and of DAO-climbing fibers as the US, thus creating a "reduced" preparation within the intact, behaving animal. This preparation promises much in terms of fine-grained localization of the memory traces and analysis of mechanisms.

Our current working hypothesis is that the essential memory traces are formed in the cerebellum. If this is in fact the case, then the most parsimonious interpretation of our cerebellar recording and lesion results is that memory traces are formed both in cerebellar cortex and interpositus nucleus. Learning-induced increases in neuronal unit activity in cerebellar cortex and interpositus nucleus can precede the onset of the behavioral CR by as much as 60 ms, where the total latency of the CR following CS onset is about 100 ms. Such behavior-predictive unit plasticity must either be formed in the cerebellum or projected there from elsewhere. But if they are formed in the cerebellum, it is likely that they are formed in parallel in cerebellar cortex and interpositus nuclei, or that the cortical traces play a key role in establishing the nuclear traces. The fact that lesions of cerebellar cortex do not abolish the basic CR would simply indicate that the interpositus trace is sufficient for retention of the CR, but does not argue against a parallel trace in the cerebellar cortex.

Results of our recent work have demonstrated quite clearly that the essential memory trace circuits in the brain for the basic category of associative learning we have studied are highly localized. Although we have not yet succeeded in localizing the memory traces themselves beyond doubt, all our evidence to date points to the cerebellum as the locus of memory storage for discrete, adaptive behavioral responses learned to deal with aversive events.

REFERENCES

Agranoff, B. W. (1967). Agents that block memory. In G. C. Quarton, T. Melnechuk, & F. O. Schmitt (Eds.), The neurosciences: A study program (pp. 756–764). New York: Rockefeller University Press.

Agranoff, B. W., Davis, R. E., & Brink, J. J. (1966). Chemical studies on memory fixation in goldfish. Brain Research, 1, 303–309.

Agranoff, B. W., Burrell, H. R., Dokas, L. A., & Springer, A. D. (1978). Progress in biochemical approaches to learning and memory. In M. A. Lipton, A. DiMascio, & K. F. Killam (Eds.), Psychopharmacology: A generation of progress (pp. 623–635). New York: Raven Press.

Albus, J. S. (1971). A theory of cerebellar function. Mathematics and Bioscience, 10, 25–61.

Alkon, D. L. (1979). Voltage-dependent calcium and potassium ion conductances: A contingency mechanism for an associative learning model. Science, 205, 810–816.

Alkon, D. L. (1980). Membrane depolarization accumulates during acquisition of an associative behavioral change. Science, 210, 1375–1376.

Anderson, J. R., & Bower, G. H. (1973). Human associative memory. New York: Wiley.

Atkinson, R. C., & Shiffrin, R. M. (1968). Human memory: A proposed system and its control processes. In K. W. Spence & J. T. Spence (Eds.), The psychology of learning and motivation, vol. 2. New York: Academic Press.

Bartlett, F. C. (1932). Remembering. Cambridge: Cambridge University Press.

Bennett, E. L., Diamond, M. C., Krech, D., and Rosenzweig, M. R. (1964). Chemical and anatomical plasticity of brain. Science, 146, 610–619.

Berg, H. C. (1975). Bacterial behavior. Nature, 254, 389.

Berger, T. W., Rinaldi, P., Weisz, D. J., and Thompson, R. F. (1983). Single unit analysis of different hippocampal cell types during classical conditioning of the rabbit nictitating membrane response. Journal of Neurophysiology, 50(5), 1197–1219.

Berger, T. W., & Thompson, R. F. (1978a). Neuronal plasticity in the limbic system during classical conditioning of the rabbit nictitating membrane response. I. The hippocampus. *Brain Research, 145,* 323–346.

Berger, T. W., & Thompson, R. F. (1978b). Identification of pyramidal cells as the critical elements in hippocampal neuronal plasticity during learning. *Proceedings of the National Academy of Sciences, 75,* 1572–1576.

Berger, T. W., & Thompson, R. F. (1978c). Neuronal plasticity in the limbic system during classical conditioning of the rabbit nictitating membrane response. II. Septum and mamillary bodies. *Brain Research, 156,* 293–314.

Binet, A., & Simon, T. (1905). Methodes nouvelles pour le dignostic du niveau intellectuel des anormaux. *L'Annee Psychologique, 11,* 191–244.

Bolles, R. C. (1978). The role of stimulus learning in defensive behavior. In S. H. Hulse, H. Fowler, & W. K. Honig (Eds.), *Cognitive processes in animal Behavior.* Hillsdale, N.J.: Lawrence Erlbaum Assoc.

Brindley, G. S. (1964). The use made by the cerebellum of the information that it receives from sense organs. *International Brain Research Organization Bulletin, 3,* 30.

Broadbent, D. E. (1971). *Decision and stress.* New York: Academic Press.

Brodgen, W. J., and Gantt, W. H. (1942). Interneural conditioning: Cerebellar conditioned reflexes. *Archives of Neurological Psychiatry, 48,* 437–455.

Brown, R. (1964). The acquisition of syntax. *Monographs of Society for Research in Child Development, 29,* 43–79.

Cajal, S. R. (1894). La fine structure des centres nerveux. *Procedures of the Royal Society London (B), 55,* 444–468.

Cegavske, C. F., Patterson, M. M., and Thompson, R. F. (1979). Neuronal unit activity in the abducens nucleus during classical conditioning of the nictitating membrane response in the rabbit *(Oryctolagus cuniculus). Journal of Comparative and Physiological Psychology, 93,* 595–609.

Cegavske, C. F., Thompson, R. F., Patterson, M. M., and Gormezano, I. (1976). Mechanisms of efferent neuronal control of the reflex nictitating membrane response in the rabbit. *Journal of Comparative Psychology, 90,* 411–423.

Chang, J. J., & Gelperin, A. (1980). Rapid taste aversion learning by an isolated molluscan central nervous system. *Proceedings of the National Academy of Sciences, 77,* 6204.

Chomsky, N. (1968). *Language and mind.* New York: Harcourt Brace Jovanovich.

Church, R. M. (1964). Systematic effect of random error in the yoked control design. *Psychological Bulletin, 62,* 122–131.

Clark, G. A., McCormick, D. A., Lavond, D. G., Baxter, K., Gray, W. J., and Thompson, R. F. (1982). Effects of electrolytic lesions of cerebellar nuclei on conditioned behavioral and hippocampal neuronal responses. *Neuroscience Abstracts, 8,* 22.

Clark, G. A., McCormick, D. A., Lavond, D. G., & Thompson, R. F. (1984). Effects of lesions of cerebellar nuclei on conditioned behavioral and hippocampal neuronal responses. *Brain Research, 291,* 125–136.

Cohen, D. H. (1980). The functional neuroanatomy of a conditioned response. In R. F. Thompson, L. H. Hicks, & V. B. Shvyrkov (Eds.), *Neural mechanisms of goal-directed behavior and learning.* New York: Academic Press.

Cohen, D. H. (1982). Central processing time for a conditioned response in a vertebrate model system. In C. D. Woody (Ed.), *Conditioning: Representation of involved neural functions* (pp. 517–534). New York: Plenum.

Damasio, A. R., & Geschwind, N. (1984). The neural basis of language. *Annual Review of Neuroscience, 7,* 127–147.

Davis, M. (1970). Effects of interstimulus intervals length and variability on startle response habituation in the rat. *Journal of Comparative and Physiological Psychology, 72,* 177–192.

Davis, M., Gendelman, D. S., Tischler, M. D., & Gendelman, P. M. (1982). A primary acoustic startle circuit: Lesion and stimulation studies. *Journal of Neuroscience, 2,* 791–805.

Davis, W. J., & Gillette, R. (1978). Neural correlates of behavioral plasticity in command neurons of *Pleurobranchaea*. *Science, 199,* 801–804.

Deaux, E. G., & Gormezano, I. (1963). Eyeball retraction: Classical conditioning and extinction in the albino rabbit. *Science, 141,* 630–631.

Descartes, R. (1650). *Les passions de l'ame.*

Deutsch, J. A. (1973). The cholingergic synapse and the site of memory. In J. A. Deutsch (Ed.), *The physiological basis of memory.* New York: Academic Press.

Donegan, N. H., Lowry, R. W., & Thompson, R. F. (1983). Effects of lesioning cerebellar nuclei on conditioned leg-flexion responses. *Neuroscience Abstracts, 9,* 331.

Duncan, C. P. (1949). The retroactive effect of electroshock on learning. *Journal of Comparative and Physiological Psychology, 42,* 32–44.

Dunn, A. J. (1980). Neurochemistry of learning and memory: An evaluation of recent data. *Annual Review of Psychology, 31,* 343–390.

De Wied, D., & Bohus, B. (1966). Long term and short term effects on retention of a conditioned avoidance response in rats by treatment with long acting pitnessin and α-MSH. *Nature, 212,* 1484–1486.

Ebbinghaus, H. E. (1964). *Memory: A contribution to experimental psychology.* New York: Dover (Original work published as Über das Gedächtnis, 1885, translated 1913).

Eccles, J. C. (1977). An instruction–selection theory of learning in the cerebellar cortex. *Brain Research, 127,* 327–352.

Entingh, D., Dunn, A., Wilson, J. E., Glassman, E., & Hogan, E. (1975a). Biochemical approaches to the biological basis of memory. *Handbook of Psychobiology,* 201–238.

Estes, W. K. (1959). The statistical approach to learning theory. In S. Koch (Ed.), *Psychology: A study of a science,* vol. 2. New York: McGraw-Hill.

Flescher, G. (1941). I. L'amnesia retrograda dopo l'elettroshock: Contributo allo studio della patogenesi delle amnesie in genere. *Schweiz. Arch. Neurol. Psychiat., 48,* 1–28.

Floeter, M. K., & Greenough, W. T. (1979). Cerebellar plasticity: Modification of Purkinje cell structure by differential rearing in monkeys. *Science, 206,* 227–229.

Fuller, J. H., & Schlag, J. D. (1976). Determination of antidromic excitation by collision test: Problems of interpretation. *Brain Research, 112,* 299–312.

Gabriel, M. (1976). Short latency discriminative unit response: Engram or bias? *Physiological Psychology, 4,* 275–280.

Gerard, R. W. (1949). Physiology and psychiatry. *American Journal of Psychiatry, 106,* 161–173.

Gibson, A. R., Houk, J. C., & Robinson, F. R. (1983). Climbing fiber projections from physiologically identified areas of the cat dorsal accessory olive. *Neuroscience Abstracts, 9,* 869.

Gilbert, P. F. C. (1974). A theory of memory that explains the function and structure of the cerebellum. *Brain Research, 70,* 1–18.

Gold, P. E., & McGaugh, J. L. (1975). A single-trace, two process view of memory storage processes. In D. Deutsch & J. A. Deutsch (Eds.), *Short-Term Memory* (pp. 355–378). New York: Academic Press.

Gold, P. E., & Zornetzer, S. F. (1983). The mnemon and its juices: Neuromodulation of memory processes. *Behavioral and Neural Biology, 38,* 151–189.

Goldman-Rakic, P. (1984). The frontal lobes: Unchartered provinces of the brain. *Trends in Neurosciences*, November.

Gormezano, I., Schneiderman, N., Deaux, E., & Fuentes, I. (1962). Nictitating membrane: Classical conditioning and extinction in the albino rabbit. *Science, 138*, 33–34.

Griffin, D. R. (1981). *The question of animal awareness: Evolutionary continuity of mental experience*, 2nd ed. New York: The Rockefeller University Press.

Grossberg, S. (1969). On learning of spatiotemporal patterns by networks with ordered sensory and motor componenets. I. Excitatory components of the cerebellum. *Studies in Applied Mathematics, 48*, 105–132.

Groves, P. M., & Thompson, R. F. (1970). Habituation: A dual-process theory. *Psychological Review, 77*, 419–450.

Guthrie, E. (1935). *The psychology of learning*. New York: Harper & Row.

Haley, D. A., Lavond, D. G., & Thompson, R. F. (1983). Effects of contralateral red nuclear lesions on retention of the classically conditioned nictitating membrane/eyelid response. *Neuroscience Abstracts, 9*, 643.

Halstead, W. C. (1951). *Cerebral mechanisms for behavior*. New York: Wiley.

Hawkins, R. D., & Kandel, E. R. (1984). Is there a cell-biological alphabet for simple forms of learning? *Psychological Review, 91*(3), 376–391.

Hebb, D. O. (1949). *The organization of behavior*. New York: Wiley & Sons, Inc.

Hilgard, E. R., & Marquis, D. G. (1940). *Conditioning and learning*. New York: Appleton.

Hoyle, G. (1980). Learning, using natural reinforcements, in insect preparations that permit cellular neuronal analysis. *Journal of Neurobiology, 11*, 323–354.

Hubel, D. H., & Wiesel, T. N. (1962). Receptive fields, binocular interaction, and functional architecture in the cat's visual cortex. *Journal of Physiology, 160*, 106–154.

Hull, C. L. (1934). Learning II: The factor of the conditioned reflex. In C. Murchison (Ed.), *Handbook of general experimental psychology*. Worcester: Clark University Press.

Hull, C. L. (1943). *Principles of behavior*. New York: Appleton-Century-Crofts.

Hunter, W. S. (1929). The sensory control of the maze habit in the white rat. *Journal of Genetic Psychology, 36*, 505–537.

Hyden, H., & Egyhazi, E. (1964). Changes in RNA content and base composition in cortical neurons of rats in a learning experiment involving transfer of handedness. *Proc. Natl. Acad. Sci. USA, 52*, 1030–1035.

Isaacson, R. L. (1974). *The limbic system*. New York: Plenum.

Isaacson, R. L., & Pribram, K. H. (1974). *The hippocampus*, vol. 1. New York: Plenum.

Isaacson, R. L., & Pribram, K. H. (1975). *The hippocampus*, vol. 2. New York: Plenum.

Ito, M. (1974). The control mechanisms of cerebellar motor system. In F. O. Schmitt and R. G. Worden (Eds.) *The neurosciences, third study program*. Boston: MIT Press.

Ito, M. (1982). Cerebellar control of the vestibulo-ocular reflex around the flocculus hypothesis. *Annual Review of Neuroscience, 5*, 275–296.

Jacobson, A. L., Babich, F. R., Bubash, S., & Jacobson, A. (1965). Differential approach tendencies produced by injection of ribonucleic acid from trained rats. *Science, 150*, 636–637.

Jacobson, A. L., & Schlecter, J. M. (1970). Chemical transfer of training: Three years later. In K. H. Pribram & D. E. Broadbent (Eds.), *Biology of Memory*. New York: Academic Press.

James, W. (1890). *The principle of psychology*. New York: Holt, Rinehart, & Winston.

John, E. R. (1967). *Mechanisms of memory*. New York: Academic Press.

Kandel, E. R. (1976). *Cellular basis of behavior: An introduction to behavioral neurobiology*. San Francisco, CA: Freeman.

Kandel, E. R., & Spencer, W. A. (1968). Cellular neurophysiological approaches in the study of learning. *Physiological Reviews, 58*, 65–134.

Kapp, B. S., Gallagher, M., Applegate, C. D., & Frysinger, R. C. (1982). The amygdala central nucleus: Contributions to conditioned cardiovascular responding during aversive Pavlovian conditioning in the rabbit. In C. D. Woody (Ed.), *Conditioning: Representation of involved neural functions* (pp. 581–600). New York: Plenum.

Kesner, R. P., & Wilbrum, M. W. (1974). A review of electrical stimulation of the brain in the context of learning and retention. *Behavioral Biology, 10*, 259–293.

Koshland, D. E. (1980). *Bacterial chemotoxis as a model behavioral system.* New York: Raven Press.

Krasne, F. B. (1969). Excitation and habituation of the crayfish escape reflex: The depolarizing response in lateral giant fibers of the isolated abdomen. *Journal of Experimental Biology, 50*, 29–46.

Lashley, K. S. (1917). The effects of strychnine and caffeine upon the rate of learning. *Psychobiology, 1*, 141–170.

Lashley, K. S. (1929). *Brain mechanisms and intelligence.* Chicago: University of Chicago Press.

Lashley, K. S. (1950). In search of the engram. In *Symposium of the Society for Experimental Biology*, No. 4, 454–482. New York: Cambridge University Press.

Lashley, K. S., & Franz, S. I. (1917). The effects of cerebral destruction upon habit-formation and retention in the albino rat. *Psycholobiology*, 71–139.

Lavond, D. G., Lincoln, J. S., McCormick, D. A., and Thompson, R. F. (1984a). Effect of bilateral lesions of the dentate interpositus cerebellar nuclei on conditioning of heart-rate and nictitating membrane/eyelid responses in the rabbit. *Brain Research, 305*, 323–330.

Lavond, D. G., McCormick, D. A., Clark, G. A., Holmes, D. T., & Thompson, R. F. (1981). Effects of ipsilateral rostral pontine reticular lesions on retention of classically conditioned nictitating membrane and eyelid responses. *Physiological Psychology, 9*(4), 335–339.

Lavond, D. G., McCormick, D. A., & Thompson, R. F. (1984b). A nonrecoverable learning deficit. *Physiological Psychology, 12*(2), 103–110.

Levine, S. (1960). Stimulation in infancy. *Scientific American, 202*, 80–86.

Lincoln, J. S., McCormick, D. A., & Thompson, R. F. (1982). Ipsilateral cerebellar lesions prevent learning of the classically conditioned nictitating membrane/eyelid response. *Brain Research, 242*, 190–193.

Llinás, R., Walton, K., Hillman, D. E., & Sotelo, C. (1975). Inferior olive: Its role in motor learning. *Science, 190*, 1230–1231.

Loucks, R. B. (1936). The experimental delimitation of neural structures essential for learning: The attempt to condition striped muscle responses with faradization of the signoid gyri. *Journal of Psychology, 1*, 5–44.

Luria, A. (1976). *The neuropsychology of memory.* Washington, D.C.: Winston.

Lynch, G., & Baudry, M. (1984). The biochemistry of memory: A new and specific hypothesis. *Science, 224*, 1057–1063.

Madden, J. IV, Haley, D. A., Barchas, J. D., & Thompson, R. F. (1983). Micro-infusion of picrotoxin into the caudal red nucleus selectively abolishes the classically conditioned nictitating membrane/eyelid response in the rabbit. *Neuroscience Abstracts, 9*, 830.

Marr, D. (1969). A theory of cerebellar cortex. *Journal of Physiology* (London), *202*, 437–470.

Martinez, J. L., Jr., Jensen, R. A., Messing, R. B., Rigter, H., & McGaugh, J. L. (Eds.) (1981). *Endogenous modulators of learning and memory.* New York: Academic Press.
Mauk, M. D. (1985). Analysis of the neural circuits responsible for classical conditioning of eyelid responses. (Doctoral dissertation, Stanford University).
Mauk, M. D., & Thompson, R. F. (1984). Classical conditioning using stimulation of the inferior olive as the unconditioned stimulus. *Neuroscience Abstracts, 10,* 122.
McConnel, J. V. (1962). Memory transfer through cannibalism in planarians. *Journal of Neuropsychiatry, Suppl. 1* (3), 42–48.
McCormick, D. A., Guyer, P. E., & Thompson, R. F. (1982). Superior cerebellar peduncle lesions selectively abolish the ipsilateral classically conditioned nictitating membrane/eyelid response of the rabbit. *Brain Research, 244,* 347–350.
McCormick, D. A., & Thompson, R. F. (1983). Possible neuronal substrates of classical conditioning within the mammalian CNS: Dentate and interpositus nuclei. *Neuroscience Abstracts, 9,* 643.
McCormick, D. A., & Thompson, R. F. (1984a). Cerebellum: Essential involvement in the classically conditioned eyelid response. *Science, 223,* 296–299.
McCormick, D. A., & Thompson, R. F. (1984b). Neuronal responses of the rabbit cerebellum during acquisition and performance of a classically conditioned nictitating membrane-eyelid response. *Journal of Neuroscience, 4*(11), 2811–2822.
McCormick, D. A., Clark, G. A., Lavond, D. G., & Thompson, R. F. (1982b). Initial localization of the memory trace for a basic form of learning. *Proceedings of the National Academy of Sciences, 79*(8), 2731–2742.
McCormick, D. A., Lavond, D. G., & Thompson, R. F. (1982a). Concomitant classical conditioning of the rabbit nictitating membrane and eyelid responses: Correlations and implications. *Physiology & Behavior, 28,* 769–775.
McDougall, W. (1901). Experimentelle Beiträge zur Lehre vom Gedächtnis by G. E. Müller & A. Pilzecker, *Mind, 10,* 388–394.
McGaugh, J. L., & Dawson, R. G. (1971). Modification of memory storage processes. *Behavioral Science, 16,* 45–63.
Melton, A. W. (1970). The situation with respect to the spacing of repetitions and memory. *Journal of Verbal Learning and Verbal Behavior, 9,* 596–606.
Melton, A. W., & von Lackum, W. J. (1941). Retroactive and proactive inhibition in retention: Evidence for a two-factor theory of retroactive inhibition. *American Journal of Psychology, 54,* 157–173.
Menzel, E. W. (1978). Cognitive mapping in chimpanzees. In S. H. Hulse, H. Fowler, & W. K. Honig (Eds.), *Cognitive processes in animal behavior.* Hillsdale, N.J.: Lawrence Erlbaum Assoc.
Morgan, C. L. (1894). *An introduction to comparative psychology.* London: Scott.
Müller, G. E., & Pilzecker, A. (1900). Experimentelle Beiträge zur Lehre vom Gedächtnis. *Zeitschrift der Psychologie, 1,* 1–288.
Newell, A., & Simon, H. A. (1972). *Human problem solving.* Englewood Cliffs, N.J.: Prentice Hall.
Norman, R. J., Buchwald, J. S., & Villablanca, J. R. (1977). Classical conditioning with auditory discrimination of the eyeblink in decerebrate cats. *Science, 196,* 551–553.
Oakley, D. A., & Russell, I. S. (1972). Neocortical lesions and classical conditioning. *Physiology & Behavior, 8,* 915–926.
Oakley, D. A., & Russell, I. S. (1977). Subcortical storage of Pavlovian conditioning in the rabbit. *Physiology & Behavior, 18,* 931–937.
Ojemann, G. A., & Whitaker, H. A. (1978). The bilingual brain. *Archives of Neurology, 35,* 409–412.

O'Keefe, J., & Nadel, L. (1978). The hippocampus as a cognitive map. Oxford: Clarendon Press.

Olds, J., Disterhoft, J. F., Segal, M., Hornblith, C. L., & Hirsch, R. (1972). Learning centers of rat brain mapped by measuring latencies of conditioned unit responses. Journal of Neurophysics, 35, 202–219.

Olton, D. S. (1985). Learning and memory: Neural and ethological approaches to its classification. In L. G. Nilsson & T. Archer (Eds.), Perspectives in learning and memory. Hillsdale, N.J.: Lawrence Erlbaum Assoc.

Patterson, M. M. (1980). Mechanisms of classical conditioning of spinal reflexes. In R. F. Thompson, L. H. Hicks, V. V. Shvyrkov (Eds.), Neural mechanisms of goal-directed behavior and learning (pp. 263–272). New York: Academic Press.

Patterson, M. M., Cegavske, C. F., & Thompson, R. F. (1973). Effects of a classical conditioning paradigm on hindlimb flexor nerve response in immobilized spinal cat. Journal of Camparative & Physiological Psychology, 84, 88–97.

Pavlov, I. (1927). Conditioned reflexes. London: Oxford University Press.

Piaget, J. (1954). The construction of reality in the child. New York: Basic Books.

Posner, M. I., & Schulman, G. L. (1979). Cognitive science. In E. Hearst (Ed.), The first century of experimental psychology. Hillsdale, N.J.: Lawrence Erlbaum Associates.

Postman, L. (1971). Organization and interference. Psychological Review, 78, 290–302.

Pribram, K. H. (1971). Languages of the brain. Englewood Cliffs, N.J.: Prentice-Hall.

Rescorla, R. A. (1967). Pavlovian conditioning and its proper control procedures. Psychological Review, 74, 71–80.

Rescorla, R. A., & Holland, P. C. (1976). Some behavioral approaches to the study of learning. In M. R. Rosenzweig & E. L. Bennett (Eds.), Neural mechanisms of learning and memory. Cambridge, MA: MIT Press.

Riesen, A. (1947). The development of visual perception in man and chimpanzee. Science, 106, 107–108.

Rommanes, G. J. (1881). Animal intelligence. London: Kegan Paul.

Rushforth, N. B. (1965). Behavioral studies of the coelenterate Hydra pirardi. Animal Behavior Suppl., 1, 30–42.

Sahley, C. L., Rudy, J. W., & Gelperin, A. (1981). An analysis of associative learning in the terrestrial mollusk. I. Higher-order conditioning, blocking, and a US-preexposure effect. Journal of Comparative Physiology, 144, 1–8.

Schneiderman, N., Fuentes, I., & Gormezano, I. (1962). Acquisition and extinction of the classically conditioned eyelid response in the albino rabbit. Science, 136, 650–652.

Schneiderman, N., Smith, M. C., Smith, A. C., & Gormezano, I. (1966). Heart rate classical conditioning in rabbits. Psychonomic Science, 6, 241–242.

Sechenov, I. M. (1965). Reflexes of the brain. (S. Belsky, trans.). Cambridge, MA: Cambridge University Press. (Original work published 1863).

Shepard, R. N., & Metzler, J. (1971). Mental rotation of three-dimensional objects. Science, 171, 701–703.

Skinner, B. F. (1938). The behavior of organisms: An experimental analysis. New York: Aplleton-Century-Crofts.

Sokolov, Y. N. (1963). Perception and the conditioned reflex. New York: Pergamon.

Solomon, P. R., & Moore, J. W. (1975). Latent inhibition and stimulus generalization for the classically conditioned nictitating membrane response in rabbits following dorsal hippocampal ablation. Journal of Comparative and Physiological Psychology, 89, 1192–1203.

Squire, L. (1982). The neurophysiology of human memory. Annual Review of Neuroscience, 5, 241–273.

Squire, L. R., & Spains, C. W. (1984). Long gradient of retrograde amnesia in mice: Continuity with findings in humans. *Behavioral Neuroscience, 98*, 345–348.

Steinmetz, J. E., Lavond, D. G., & Thompson, R. F. (1985). Classical conditioning of the rabbit eyelid response with mossy fiber stimulation as the conditioned stimulus. *Bulletin of the Psychonomic Society, 23*(3), 245–248.

Steinmetz, J. E., McCormick, D. A., Baier, C. A., & Thompson, R. F. (1984). Involvement of the inferior olive in classical conditioning of the rabbit eyelid. *Neuroscience Abstracts, 10*, 122.

Sternberg, S. (1966). High-speed scanning in human memory. *Science, 153*, 652–654.

Sternberg, S. (1975). Memory scanning: New findings and current controversies. *Quarterly Journal of Experimental Psychology, 27*, 1–32.

Tanzi, E. (1893). I fatti e le induzioni nell'odierna istologia del sistema nervoso. *Riv. sper. Freniat. Med. Leg Alien. ment., 19*, 419–472.

Thompson, R. F. (1975). *Introduction to Physiological Psychology*. Harper & Row, New York.

Thompson, R. F. (1983). Neuronal substrates of simple associative learning: Classical conditioning. *Trends in Neuroscience, 6*(7), 270–275.

Thompson, R. F., Berger, T. W., Berry, S. D., Hoehler, F. K., Kettner, R. S., & Weisz, D. J. (1980). Hippocampal substrates of classical conditioning. *Physiological Psychology, 8*(2), 262–279.

Thompson, R. F., Berger, T. W., Cegavske, C. F., Patterson, M. M., Roemer, R. A., Teyler, T. J., & Young, R. A. (1976). The search for the engram. *American Psychologist, 31*, 209–227.

Thompson, R. F., Berger, T. W., & Madden, J. IV. (1983c). Cellular processes of learning and memory in the mammalian CNS. *Annual Review of Neuroscience, 6*, 447–491.

Thompson, R. F., Donegan, N. H., Clark, G. A., Lavond, D. G., Lincoln, J. S., Madden, J. IV, Mamounas, L. A., Mauk, M. D., & McCormick, D. A. (in press). Neuronal substrates of discrete, defensive conditioned reflexes, conditioned fear states, and their interactions in the rabbit. In I. Gormezano, W. F. Prokasy, *Physiological and neurochemical studies in the rabbit*, I. Hillsdale, NJ: Erlbaum.

Thompson, R. F., McCormick, D. A., & Lavond, D. G. (in press). Localization of the essential memory trace system for a basic form of associative learning in the mammalian brain. In S. Hulse (Ed.), *G. Stanley Hall Centennial Volume*.

Thompson, R. F., McCormick, D. A., Lavond, D. G., Clark, G. A., Kettner, R. E., & Mauk, M. D. (1983a). The engram found? Initial localization of the memory trace for a basic form of associative learning. In J. M. Sprague & A. N. Epstein (Eds.), *Progress in psychobiology and physiological psychology* (pp. 167–196). Academic Press: New York.

Thompson, R. F., Patterson, M. M., & Teyler, T. J. (1972). The neurophysiology of learning. *Annual Review of Psychology, 23*, 73–104.

Thompson, R. F., & Spencer, W. A. (1966). Habituation: A model phenomenon for the study of neuronal substrates of behavior. *Psychological Review, 173*, 16–43.

Thorndike, E. L. (1898). Animal intelligence: An experimental study of the associative processes in animals. *Psychological Review, Monograph Supplement, 2*(8), 1–109.

Treisman, A. M. (1969). Strategies and models of selective attention. *Psychological Review, 76*, 282–299.

Tsukahara, N. (1981). Synaptic plasticity in the mammalian central nervous system. *Annual Review of Neuroscience, 4*, 351–379.

Underwood, B. J. (1957). Interference and forgetting. *Psychological Review, 64*, 49–60.

Watson, J. B. (1913). Psychology as the behaviorist views it. *Psychological Review, 20,* 158–177.

Westbrook, W. H., & McGaugh, J. L. (1964). Drug facilitation of latent learning. *Psychopharmacologia, 5,* 440–446.

Woodworth, R. S. (1938). *Experimental psychology.* New York: Holt.

Woody, C. D. (Ed.) (1982). *Conditioning: Representation of involved neural function.* New York: Plenum.

II

ANATOMICAL APPROACHES

2

DEVELOPMENTAL APPROACHES TO THE MEMORY PROCESS*

James E. Black and William T. Greenough

INTRODUCTION

Tinbergen (1951) suggested that the question: "Why does the animal behave as it does?" (p.1) requires four related answers: (1) the immediate causal control of the behavior, (2) the animal's developmental history, or *ontogeny*, (3) the behavior's contribution to survival, and (4) the evolution, or *phylogeny*, of the species trait. In asking, "Why does the animal learn and remember?" scientists have concentrated primarily on the immediate causes (both biological and psychological). This chapter focuses upon the developmental perspective in the context of some ethological and evolutionary concerns.

SOME HISTORICAL ASPECTS OF MEMORY ONTOGENY RESEARCH

In the last half of the 19th century, scientists in fields ranging from histology to psychiatry were proposing that memory and development were intimately linked to subtle movements of neural processes. Because synapses were not visible with light microscopy, these connections between neurons became the focus of much speculation. Ramon y

* This work was supported by NSF BNS 82-16916, NIMH 35321, and the Retirement Research Foundation.

Cajal (1893) suggested that learning might involve the formation of new synaptic connections between neurons. Tanzi (1893), noting that the resistance to transmission between neurons might vary with the size of the connection, proposed that frequent use of a synapse might produce growth similar to that produced by exercising a muscle, thereby strengthening preexisting connections. Both theories assumed that the structural plasticity seen in development extended into adulthood, a concept which has been demonstrated only recently.

Little theoretical or empirical progress was made along this line for half a century, until Hebb (1949) suggested how experience could be represented in new or modified neural organizations. Rejecting the "one memory—one neuron" concept, Hebb proposed that memory involved large intergrative structures, termed cell assemblies. These were hierarchically organized into larger systems called phase sequences, controlling the activation of cell assemblies, a concept resembling that of a computer program which coordinates the use of simpler subroutines. Memory thus became a process more than a place, since encoding and retrieval depended on the cooperation of many neurons rather than a small subset. Hebb, who also felt that developmental plasticity and adult memory might share mechanisms, proposed what is now termed the "Hebb synapse," a model synapse with a rule that simultaneous pre- and postsynaptic activity increases synaptic efficacy.

Another line of interest in memory ontogeny and evolution began with the neural maturationist group. For example, Flechsig (1927) observed that the myelin which wraps mature axons apparently develops in the order of a structure's phylogenetic appearance, suggesting that the brain components most crucial for survival of the young organism correspond to those most crucial for the survival of its ancestors. From this argument, memory was expected to mature in young animals when it became useful for survival, as determined by their phylogenetic history. Thus, the maturationist approach led to the concept of a memory "organ," a neural system insensitive to experience, only needing to ripen on a phylogenetically determined schedule.

In contrast, early experience was important in psychoanalytic theory and had a substantial influence on studies of memory ontogeny. Freud suggested that early childhood memories are retained by the adult, still powerful but repressed from consciousness. Schactel (1947) reviewed studies of childhood memory and concluded that very few events from early childhood could be recalled. In general, investigators had tried to explain this infantile amnesia in cognitive, neural, or psychoanalytic terms: (1) children process information too differently to access it as adults, (2) some area of the child's brain is too immature to consolidate memory, and (3) the adult represses information that is stressful to recall (Allport, 1937). The last explanation has remained outside the domain of memory research, but the others are still actively disputed.

Although few events are recalled, children do remember things, such as language and social order. Continued practice may preserve some memories, or changes in processing (e.g., verbal coding) may selectively disrupt other kinds of memory. One of the first systematic investigations of this issue was that of Campbell and Campbell (1962), where rats ranging in age from 18 to 100 days old were conditioned to avoid one compartment of a shuttle box. The young rats initially learned the task, but showed no memory 21 days later while the older rats remembered well when tested 42 days later. This suggested that the ability to retain or recall developed as the animal grew older. We should note that some types of memories persist from much earlier, such as taste aversions learned *in utero* (e.g., Stickrod, Kimble, & Smotherman, 1982).

The history of work in memory ontogeny demonstrates the importance of an integrated, interdisciplinary approach. The tradition of Tanzi and Cajal focused on how memory is related to other developmental processes sensitive to experience. The maturationists sought to explain memory as a separate component insensitive to experience. The psychoanalytic approaches favored changes in information processing independent of neural maturation. Fundamental issues still largely unresolved after a century of research include: (1) whether adult memorial processes are related to developmental plasticity, (2) whether memory development is restricted by neural maturation or by development of new ways of processing information, and (3) whether memory mechanisms have remained stable with evolutionary changes of the brain.

EXPERIENCE-EXPECTANT AND EXPERIENCE-DEPENDENT NEURAL PLASTICITY

Piaget (1980) stressed that information storage depends both on the amount of information available in experience (termed "contrast" here) and the quality of it (termed "coherence" here). Contrast is not an external, environmental quality, but is based rather on the organism's access to the environmental information. For example, a kitten's mastery of locomotion can greatly increase contrast although the environment itself need not change. Coherence is also an organism-centered quality, reflecting the stability and reliability of experience. For example, the clumsy movements of an infant initially provide incoherent and inconsistent feedback from reaching for an object. After basic sensory-motor skills are established, experience becomes more coherent as stable and repeatable relationships between movement and perception are established.

Piaget argued from an ethological perspective that two types of information were acquired from the environment: (1) general information acquired by all species members from common features of their environments ("expected" environmental features) and (2) idiosyncratic information ("unexpected" environmental features) that the individual uses to adapt to its own unique environment. The first type of information storage (termed "experience-expectant" here) allows a simplification and reduction in the information the genome must carry. For example, if the developmental mechanisms can expect visual edges of all orientations to be in the environment, then this information can be used to fine-tune genetically predisposed edge detectors in the visual system. That is, the information necessary to specify edge detectors need not be entirely provided by genes if it can be expected in the normal environment of all species members. (Chickens and other prococial animals that must use vision immediately after hatching may establish a system largely insensitive to experience, possibly at some cost in operating precision.) Experience-expectant information storage typically involves a brief time span, termed a "critical" or "sensitive" period, when the organism is maximally ready (i.e., expects) to receive the information. The second type of information storage (termed "experience-dependent" here) optimizes individual adaptation to specific and possibly unique features of the individual organism's environment, and includes what we call learning. Experience-dependent information storage does not involve sensitive periods, although there may be sequential dependencies, such as the need to recognize letters before recognizing printed words. Even though these two types of information storage may share neural mechanisms, memory recall for these two may differ in the adult. For example, specific retrieval strategies may not be available until the content of general adaptive memory is largely complete.

Recent work in evolutionary theory has noted that phylogenetic changes are primarily accomplished by altering the developmental program (Bonner, 1982). Altering the sensitivity of a developmental process to environmental influences is one way in which change can occur. In the nervous system, we might expect successful, phylogenetically older adaptations to be preserved, while more recent

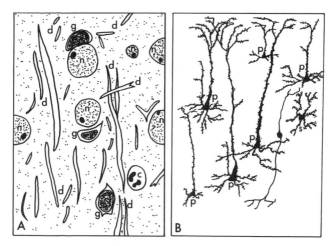

FIGURE 2.1 (A) Drawing of a cortical section stained with toluidine blue. Note the tangled packing of glial somata (g), neuronal somata (n), dendrites (d), and capillaries (c). The density and size of the neuronal somata allow the cortex to be divided into six layers. (B) Drawing at lower magnification of a Golgi-stained cortical section. Fewer pyramidal (p) and stellate (s) neurons are stained, with complete dendrites reaching across cortical layers. Unstained tissue is relatively transparent.

adaptations would add new sensitivity in other brain areas. Mechanisms underlying phylogenetically older sensitivity might be preserved to subserve newer sensitivity, and new or altered mechanisms might arise. Thus the brain substrates of experience-expectant and experience-dependent information storage might differ, although it seems likely that some mechanisms would be shared. We will discuss what is known about these mechanisms following a brief description of the methods used in this research.

QUANTITATIVE METHODS IN DEVELOPMENTAL NEUROBIOLOGY

Nerve cell bodies and processes, glial cells, vasculature, and so on, are tightly packed and intertwined in all brain regions. Figure 2.1A is a drawing of a thin section of rat visual cortex in which all tissue components were stained. Figure 2.1B is a drawing from a similar section stained with the *Golgi method*, which stains only a few neurons in a region, allowing their dendrites (and their axons to varying degrees) to be viewed. To obtain accurate light microscopic measurement of neuron morphology, the dendritic field must be traced completely without becoming lost in the tangle of other neural processes. A camera lucida

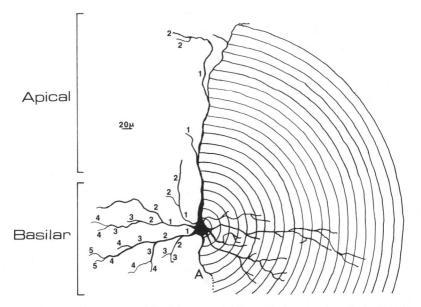

FIGURE 2.2   The amount of dendritic material for cortical neurons can be analyzed in two ways: (1) The intersections between dendrites and a series of concentric rings are counted. Here there are six basilar intersections at the 4th ring on the right. (2) The number and length of dendrites at each order are measured. Here there are six basilar segments of third order on the left.

can be used to make two-dimensional drawings of neurons by superimposing the slide image onto that of the investigator's pencil. A computer-aided microscope can also be used to record the three-dimensional coordinates of points on the dendritic branches, storing a mathematical representation of the neuron.

Dendritic branches are commonly described in terms of order of bifurcation, as indicated in Figure 2.2. A first order segment is defined as originating from the soma (cell body), and a second order segment has its root in the forked end of a first order segment. Another method of measuring dendritic trees uses a two-dimensional transparent overlay of concentric rings (Sholl, 1956), or concentric spheres for three-dimensional computer-microscope data. The frequency of ring intersections indicates dendritic volume distribution.

Golgi methods also allow analysis of dendritic spine frequency, approximate size, and shape. *Spines* are small postsynaptic extensions on many kinds of neurons (e.g., see Figures 2.1B and 2.3). While the stain is assumed to fill all the spines, two major problems exist in estimating their frequency: Some spines may be hidden by the dendrite or other

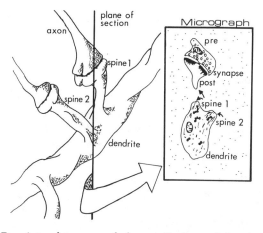

FIGURE 2.3 Drawings of a synapse before sectioning and the electron microscope image of it. One can count and classify synapses from micrographs, as well as measure the synaptic cleft, postsynaptic thickening, and pre- or postsynaptic areas. Note how difficult it would be to identify which axon and dendrite a synapse belongs to.

spines, and some spines may be too small to detect or may resemble small dendritic bumps. Nonetheless, combined quantification of spine frequency and dendritic length can provide a good estimate of synaptic frequency per neuron based upon comparisons with other methods involving electron microscopy (Turner & Greenough, 1983; see the following discussion).

Electron microscopic studies are useful for measurement of synapse frequency, size, and other characteristics, as summarized in Figure 2.3. Since the section cuts randomly through synapses, statistical corrections of size must be made for the probability of cutting a true diameter or just hitting the edge. Corrections of apparent synapse density (counts on photomicrographs) must also be made to account for the synapse size distribution, failure to recognize synapses just barely in the section plane, and other distorting factors. The result of these corrections, an accurate density estimate (i.e., number of synapses per unit volume) may still be misleading, since various manipulations may change the volume of a brain region such as visual cortex. For comparison with Golgi data, the best measure is probably the ratio of synapses-per-unit-volume to neurons-per-unit-volume, or synapses per neuron. In this chapter, we largely restrict our discussion to data indicating changes in numbers of synapses. Potential changes in structural characteristics of existing synapses have been reviewed elsewhere (Greenough & Chang, 1985).

NEUROBIOLOGICAL CORRELATES OF
MEMORY ONTOGENY

Use of these techniques following early visual deprivation, enrichment of the general environment, and learning tasks has provided evidence that changes in both numbers of synapses and structural characteristics of synapses may be involved in the storage of experiential information. Remarkably similar but still distinct effects have been seen with manipulations directed at the experience-expectant and experience-dependent types of information storage.

STUDIES OF EARLY VISUAL DEPRIVATION

Early visual development appears to be a case of experience-expectant neural processes which are normally guided by visual stimulation. Behavioral and structural effects of early light and pattern deprivation have been reported in most mammalian species tested. The effects are most pronounced with monocular deprivation in species with binocularly overlapping visual systems, such as cats, but significant effects also occur in largely nonoverlapping species such as rats. In fact, the studies of monocular deprivation in animals with binocularly overlapping visual systems constitute a special case and will be discussed separately.

Behavioral and Neural Effects of
Early Deprivation

Dark-reared animals are impaired in visual behavior. Walk and Walters (1973) showed that dark-reared animals have long-lasting deficits on a shallow visual cliff, where animals can unwisely choose to step off a small platform. Cats reared in darkness or unpatterned illumination are slower to learn complex discriminations, such as an X versus an N (Riesen, 1965). Tees (1968b) found that dark-reared rats learned simple pattern discriminations as well as normal rats, but that dark-reared animals were slower in learning the more complex X–N task. However, the dark-reared animals could learn very difficult brightness discrimination tasks as well as normal rats (Tees, 1968a), suggesting that the inherent difficulty of the task was not the primary determinant of poor performance of the dark-reared rats. Tees and Cartwright (1972) demonstrated that this learning deficit was related to effects on visual processing rather than some general learning disability. They found that dark-reared animals had no deficiency in associating two auditory stimuli, but did have difficulty with an auditory–visual stimulus pair.

These studies suggest that visual learning of adult animals is impaired if early visual experience has not established effective information processing schemes.

Initial attempts to find neural correlates of visual deprivation were disappointing. Ramon y Cajal (1893) investigated whether neural junctions would grow closer together. He found no apparent differences between the optic lobes of amphibians raised in the light for one month and those raised in the dark. Later work suggests that amphibians were a poor choice for this work, a fact that leads us to question the importance of experience in the development of simpler nervous systems. Lower orders with phylogenetically older developmental mechanisms may be inappropriate models for mammalian plasticity, both experience-expectant and experience-dependent. In general, it appears that vertebrate orders other than mammals and birds (as well as perhaps all but the most complex invertebrates) have evolved nervous systems that employ stereotyped routines designed for expected environments. Mammalian and a few other refined nervous systems, in contrast, are designed to adapt to meet the particular idiosyncratic contingencies of individual experience.

Mammalian nervous system studies have been more consistent in revealing morphological effects of visual deprivation. Coleman and Riesen (1968) found smaller dendritic fields in primary visual cortex neurons of 2 of 3 dark-reared cats. Similarly, Valverde (1970) found reduced basilar dendritic branching of pyramidal neurons in visual cortex of dark-reared mice. Borges and Berry (1976, 1978) found changes in the orientation, but not the number or length of dendrites in a small sample of cells in rat visual cortex. Schwartz and Rothblat (1980) reared monocularly deprived rats in bright light, so that the retina of the sutured eye received unpatterned illumination at levels comparable to an open eye in normal light. They found that spine frequency on dendrites in the contralateral visual cortex was comparable in both cases, but behavioral measures of visual ability indicated a functional impairment of vision using the deprived eye. These results suggest that some spine density changes may require only a certain level of illumination, while neural organization underlying functional vision may require patterned visual experience. Aside from actual changes in the frequency of spines, another interesting possibility is that dark-rearing simply slows down their development. Freire (1978) examined the spines of apical dendrites in Layer IV of occipital cortex of 19-day old dark-reared and normal mice with serial-section electron microscopy. The 3-dimensional reconstructions indicated that spine development progressed from small spines with no spine apparati and small heads to large spines with extensive spine apparati. Dark-reared mice had more of the small-type spines, while normally reared animals had more of the large-type spines. Freire suggested that the spine frequency differences observed by other investigators may reflect a maturational delay of spines in the dark-reared animals, since their relatively immature spines would be easy to miss in Golgi studies, distorting their frequency estimates. Since the maturational lag would eventually fade away as the dark-reared animals caught up, the smaller differences between òlder animals (Cragg, 1967; Valverde, 1971) probably reflect actual and long-lasting frequency changes.

Electron microscopy studies also suggest substantial changes in synaptic frequency after visual deprivation. Cragg (1975b) found that light-experienced kittens had about 40% more synapses per neuron than binocularly deprived kittens. These findings are compatible with the Golgi studies of Coleman and Riesen (1968), Rothblat and Schwartz (1979), and Valverde, (1970), which suggest a reduction in the number of synapses per neuron with visual deprivation. It is possible in some cases that the formation of synapses is delayed and can later catch up. For example, Winfield (1981) showed that binocularly sutured cats eventually catch up with normally reared cats in synapses per neuron, although this study used few animals and they received some eyelid-filtered illumination.

Selective Deprivation in Species with Stereoscopic Vision

For binocularly overlapping species such as cats and monkeys, the electrophysiological effects of visual deprivation are clearly related to the behavioral effects. In general, deprivation of one eye leads to a drastic reduction in its control over visual cortex neurons, while the nondeprived eye correspondingly gains in control. Binocular deprivation leads to a loss in precision of neuronal response properties, but balance in eye dominance is retained. The degree of recovery from deprivation depends on the species and the onset and duration of deprivation. In binocularly overlapping species, it is clear that inhibition from the nondeprived eye's activity is involved, since its removal prompts rapid recovery of the other eye (Smith & Loop, 1978).

Monocular deprivation studies in animals with extensive binocular overlap of the visual fields have indicated involvement of competitive processes in establishing synaptic connections (LeVay, Wiesel, & Hubel, 1980). In monkeys, for example, binocular regions of the visual cortex receive input from the eyes in adjacent bands, also termed columns, about 400 μm wide. After monocular deprivation, the functional blindness of the deprived eye is associated with a narrowing of its cortical bands, while the cortical bands of the nondeprived eye expand in width (LeVay et al., 1980). The establishment of the ocular dominance columns apparently involves regression of axon terminal branches. Axons associated with both eyes initially have overlapping terminal fields in Layer IV, so that the cortical columns are indistinct, but the adult has columns with sharpened borders. If one eye is deprived early, the axon terminations in its ocular dominance columns regress, while the axon terminations of the columns for the other eye do not regress to the normal degree. LeVay et al. (1980) attribute this shift in column width to competition between the axon terminal fields, with the more active connections winning out over the deprived.

In a more selective type of visual deprivation, kittens exposed only to horizontal or vertical stripes during development have visual cortex neurons which respond selectively to visual stimuli of the exposure orientation (Hirsch & Spinelli, 1970). To study anatomical correlates, Coleman, Flood, Whitehead, and Emerson (1981) raised six kittens in horizontal, vertical, and nonstriped cylinders. Layer IV stellate cells of visual cortex from the horizontal- and vertical-stripe groups did not differ in dendritic length or number of branches, but the angular distribution of distal dendritic segments were at approximately 90 degrees from each other, just as their stimuli were at right angles. Tieman and Hirsch (1982) similarly reported that stripe-rearing modifies dendrite orientation of Layer III pyramidal cells of kitten visual cortex. They raised five cats viewing only vertical lines and three cats viewing only horizontal lines. The horizontal-stripe cats and vertical-stripe cats had approximately perpendicular distributions of dendritic orientation. The dendritic fields were generally perpendicular to the representation of the stripe stimuli in the cortex, suggesting a specific relationship between the morphology of Layer III pyramidal cells, their physiological orientation, and their early experience.

Summary of Visual Deprivation Effects

These studies of visual deprivation collectively indicate that early visual experience substantially affects experience expectant neural plasticity and that these effects impair later experience-dependent visual learning. It is clear that experience-expectant mechanisms have a complex role. For example, the simple presence of light does not trigger complete maturation of visual systems in the mammals studied. Instead, these species need coherent experience of a range of features and relationships. Furthermore, low-level, diffuse light filtered through sutured eyelids may inhibit recovery in cats of the other, previously deprived eye receiving normal stimulation (Smith & Loop, 1978). The requirement for early coherent experience ultimately affects experience-dependent processes, since young animals deprived of it have impaired visual learning ability in maturity.

STUDIES OF DIFFERENTIAL REARING

The effects of differential experience are not limited to early sensory development or to relatively extreme manipulations. Studies manipulating the complexity of the housing environment have indicated both microscopic and macroscopic experiential effects on brain structure. Most of the work has used three basic types of environments, although different research groups have sometimes defined them differently. *Environmental Complexity (EC)* involves housing rats in large groups in a large cage with various toys changed daily. *Isolation Cage (IC)* animals are individually housed in standard laboratory cages. *Social Cage (SC)* animals are housed as pairs in cages comparable to those of IC rats.

Behavioral Effects of Differential Rearing

The behavioral effects of differential rearing are profound. One of the earliest studies was that of Hebb (1949), who reported that rats raised as pets at home were superior to laboratory rats in learning the Hebb–Williams maze. In general, rats raised in complex laboratory environments have been found superior to isolated or socially raised rats in complex, appetitively motivated learning tasks (reviewed in Greenough, 1976). The superior performance of EC animals is not simply due to more visual experience, since Krech, Rosenzweig, and Bennett (1962) found blind EC rats superior to blind IC rats in maze performance. Greenough, Wood, and Madden (1972) argued that the information processing capability of EC mice was superior to that of IC or SC mice because they were uniquely capable of mastering the difficult Lashley III maze in a massed-trial situation. While learning a Hebb–Williams maze, EC rats make fewer errors than IC rats, but that superiority vanishes if the maze is rotated, effectively disrupting extramaze cues (Brown, 1968; Hymovitch 1952). Ravizza and Herschberger (1966) found EC rats better at maze learning even if extra-maze cues were hidden by a curtain, suggesting that intramaze cues are better utilized by EC's in the absence of extramaze cues.

Effects of Differential Rearing on the Brain

Bennett, Diamond, Krech, and Rosenzweig (1964) reported that several regions of the dorsal neocortex were heavier and thicker in EC rats than IC rats, particularly the occipital cortex. Values in SC rats were intermediate but generally closer to those of the IC rats. It is interesting to note that Krech et al. (1962) found changes in visual cortex of blinded rats comparable to those of intact EC rats. In addition, EC's have larger neural somata and more glial cells in the occipital cortex (Diamond, 1967).

Holloway (1966) first reported that ring analysis (Fig. 2.2) of visual cortex neurons indicated larger dendritic fields in rats reared in EC. Greenough and Volkmar (1973) placed rats in the EC, SC, and IC conditions at 23–25 days of age for 30 days. Pyramidal neurons from Layers II, IV, and V and Layer IV stellates in the visual cortex had more ring intersections in EC's than IC's. These effects were most pronounced in higher-order branches—the outer part of the dendritic field. To confirm that these dendritic differences reflected synapse number differences, Turner and Greenough (1983) have recently used electron microscopy in the upper visual cortex and found that EC rats exceeded IC rats in synapses per neuron by roughly the amount predicted from the Golgi studies, with SC's intermediate but somewhat closer to the IC's. Thus quantitative Golgi procedures appear to accurately indicate differences in synaptic numbers.

Greenough, Volkmar, and Juraska (1973) found that EC rats also had more dendritic material than their IC counterparts in some types of neurons in the temporal (auditory) cortex but not in the frontolateral (somatosensory–somatomotor) cortex. This suggests that the effects do not merely result from visual stimulation. The lack of frontolateral cortex effects suggests that general hormonal or metabolic factors, which would be expected to affect all cortical areas, do not play a significant role. Different effects of EC rearing are also observed in noncortical areas such as juvenile rat hippocampus (Fiala, Joyce, & Greenough, 1978) and monkey cerebellar cortex (Floeter & Greenough, 1979). Thus the experience-dependent effects of rearing complexity are not restricted to phylogenetically newer brain structures.

Effects of Adult Animals

The neocortex retains considerable structural plasticity in response to such differential housing into adulthood. Riege and Morimoto (1970) reported cortical.weight differences between groups placed in different environments at one year of age. Correspondingly, Uylings, Kuypers, and Veltman (1978) and Juraska, Greenough, Elliott, Mack, and Berkowitz (1980) found that EC rats' dendritic fields exceeded those of IC rats by 10% or more in two of three visual cortex cell populations, nearly equivalent in magnitude to those described in animals exposed as weanlings (Greenough & Volkmar, 1973). Green, Greenough, and Schlumpf (1983) reported somewhat larger differences between middle-aged (450-day-old) EC and IC rats. The environmental complexity studies in adult animals clearly suggest that experience alters the adult neocortex in a similar way to that seen in young animals, although some neuron types affected at weaning may not be affected later (Juraska et al., 1980).

Principal Conclusions from Environmental Complexity Studies

The changes resulting from rearing complexity should not be considered a simple extension of those found in the visual deprivation studies. While the latter studies demonstrated that a drastic but simple manipulation of experience can modify connectivity and subsequent learning ability, visual experience is definitely expected during ontogeny. The types of visual experience described in the section entitled "Studies of Early Visual Deprivation" are normally quite uniform for all species members in their timing (i.e., after eye-opening) and quality (e.g., all visual angles present). Visual deprivation at later ages, once the animals have had experience, has minimal lasting effect. On the other hand, the modification of experience in the environmental complexity research has a character that is much less expected from the phylogenetic perspective. The timing and character of individual experience in the EC environment cannot be uniformly predicted for all species members. The specific experiences of animals raised in EC differ from those of rats raised in IC primarily in the complexity of experience available, so that self-initiation of experience (e.g., exploratory activity) is a key determinant of the timing or quality of experience. The connectivity modifications observed in the EC animals appear more related to *how* information is processed than to *what* information is processed. For example, both EC and IC animals use approximately the same amount of light (average intensity on the retina) quite differently, one with self-initiated activity and its visual consequences, the other with dull routine. The importance of active involvement is particularly evident in the finding that there is essentially no effect on the brain of rearing rats within a small cage inside the EC environment (Ferchmin, Bennett, & Rosenzweig, 1975). The mechanism underlying the effects of the EC environment on the brain may be useful in the natural environment, since the specific pattern of connectivity changes appears related to specific changes in later learning ability.

The distinction between visual deprivation and rearing complexity is further justified by the clear differences between their structural consequences. First, the differences in Golgi-based estimates of synapses per neuron appear to be considerably greater between EC and IC rats than between visually experienced and deprived rats. This may indicate that the complex environment paradigm approximates stimulation levels nearer the dynamic range of neural plasticity mechanisms. Alternatively, it could indicate that early visual experience might primarily affect experience-expectant neural mechanisms, while postweaning EC experience may affect experience-dependent mechanisms. Two findings support this view:

1. The effects of environmental complexity are apparently more widespread in the brain. This phenomenon has not been studied in detail in the visual deprivation paradigms, but where it has, visual deprivation has resulted in increases in measures related to synapses per neuron in the auditory cortex (Gyllensten, Malmfors, & Norrlin, 1966; Ryugo, Ryugo, Globus, & Killackey, 1975) and no effect in the somesthetic cortex whereas the EC rats exceed IC rats in all three regions (Diamond, Rosenzweig, Bennett, Lindner, & Lyon, 1972).
2. The effects of EC versus IC housing are relatively independent of age, as we would expect for experience-dependent neural plasticity of the sort related to memory, whereas visual deprivation involves an experience-expectant period shortly after birth or eye-opening.

Structural Effects of Training

If the dendritic synaptic alterations seen after EC experience are related to experience-dependent mechanisms such as learning, then we would expect similar structural changes after training on traditional psychological tasks. Greenough, Juraska, and Volkmar (1979) used the Hebb–Williams maze, which has moveable barriers allowing a large variety of problems. Adult rats received extensive training for 25–26 days on a new problem plus several old problems each day for water reward. Littermate control rats were allowed to drink water several times daily while held by the investigator. Trained animals had more dendritic material along distal apical dendrites of Layer IV and V pyramidal cells in the occipital cortex. Similarly, Bennett, Rosenzweig, Morimoto, and Hebert (1979) exposed rats to complex mazes in their cages which were changed daily for 30 days, while their littermates were kept in IC. The maze-reared animals had heavier visual cortices. The complexity of the environment is a factor in the effect, since rats housed with a single, simple maze for 30 days had brain weights between EC and IC rats. Cummins, Walsh, Budtz–Olsen, Konstantinos, and Horsfall (1973) similarly found that extensive Hebb–Williams maze training of 500-day-old rats otherwise kept in IC increased forebrain weight and cortical area relative to baseline groups remaining in the IC cages. However, littermates from an EC condition showed no effect of maze training, suggesting that additional effects were small or were obscured by the neural effects of EC exposure.

To further examine the specificity of training effects, Chang and Greenough (1982) studied monocular maze training effects on visual cortex of split-brain rats. Since about 90% of visual afferents in the rat cross to the contralateral cortex, use of an opaque contact lens over one eye of a split-brain rat can effectively isolate one occipital area from the other. Split-brain littermate triplets were placed in one of four conditions: (1) the left and right eyes were occluded on alternate days during successive training periods, (2) the same eye was occluded during all training periods, and (3) alternating or (4) unilateral occlusion of both eyes with no training at all. The occluders were worn for about four hours daily during the training period. There was no effect of fixed versus alternating occluder position in the nontrained rats (Group 3 versus 4), indicating that occluder insertion alone did not affect the brain measures. Figure 2.4 summarizes the comparison of the distal region of the apical dendrites of Layer V pyramidal cells in the hemispheres receiving or not receiving visual input from maze training. The apical dendrites of cells in the trained visual cortex were more extensive both within the fixed occluder rats (Group 2, comparing adjacent hemispheres) and between the alternating occluder and nontrained rats (Group 1 vs. 3 and 4, comparing two trained to two nontrained hemispheres). This finding indicates that the effects of training are relatively restricted to the side of the brain most involved in learning the task.

These learning tasks produced localized effects on cortical tissue that resembled (but were not identical to) those found in the differential rearing experiments. Since the effects were localized to the hemisphere most involved in learning, it is not likely that they were the result of general hormonal or metabolic processes. That different experiences affect different parts of the dendritic tree suggests that the effects are related to differences in information processing.

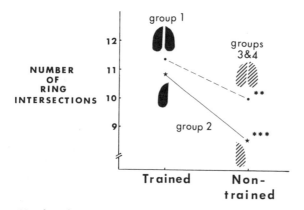

FIGURE 2.4   Number of apical dendrites intersecting distal spheres beyond 250 μm of the cell body in nerve cells from trained and untrained brain areas. $**$, $p < .025$; $***$, $p < .01$ (after Chang & Greenough, 1982).

IMPLICATIONS FOR THE NEUROBIOLOGICAL STUDY OF MEMORY

The evidence is strong for experience-induced changes in the number of synapses in many brain regions of both young and mature animals. The fact that several potentially independent structural effects are seen across a number of mammalian species, and across types of experience from light deprivation to maze learning, and are correlated with changes in neuronal function and behavior suggests that evolution may not have established one simple mechanism for developmental plasticity and another for memory. Rather, there may be a set of mechanisms upon which the organism can draw for the incorporation of information from a wide variety of experiences, and it is probably the case that we have not discovered all of the types of changes involved in encoding experience. Some mechanisms may not even be stucturally detectable, at least with the current techniques. At this point, however, the most consistently reported effect of various experiences is upon the number, and presumably the pattern, of synapses.

The consistency of this effect across visual deprivation, environmental complexity and training paradigms may lead one to question whether our distinction between experience-expectant and experience-dependent neural plasticity is biologically meaningful, despite differences in the timing of susceptibility, response pattern across brain regions, and relative magnitude of effects. We suggest that the distinction is meaningful and that different neural mechanisms underlie these two forms of neural plasticity.

EXPERIENCE-EXPECTANT PLASTICITY

The context in which experience-expectant neural plasticity often (perhaps always) arises is one of synapse overproduction. For example, Cragg (1975a) reported that the number of synapses per neuron in cat visual cortex reached a peak at about 5 weeks of age and then fell to lower levels in adulthood. Similarly, Boothe, Greenough, Lund, and Wrege (1979) reported that spine frequency on some types of monkey visual cortex neurons reached an early peak and later declined to adult values. The peak values are reached, in both cases, at about the time that sensitivity to gross manipulations of visual experience, such as monocular pattern deprivation, is also maximal. In both species, afferent axonal terminal fields overlap during early development, segregating through the elimination of overlapping synapses as development progresses (e.g., LeVay et al., 1980), and in both species, occlusion of one eye causes more of its connections to be lost and more of the open eye's connections to be preserved (LeVay et al., 1980; Hubel & Wiesel, 1969). Similar phenomena are seen in other developing sensory projection systems, and entire dendritic or axonal branches regress in some cases (e.g., Falls & Gobel, 1979; Feng & Rogowski, 1980; Mariani & Changeaux, 1981).

It thus appears that the nervous system may become ready for expected experience by overproducing connections on a sensory system-wide basis, such that experience-related neural activity can select a functionally appropriate subset of connections. The proposals of Changeaux and Danchin (1977), Greenough (1978), and Purves and Lichtman (1980) presume that synaptic contacts are initially transient and require some type of confirmation, perhaps by use, for their survival. If not confirmed or stabilized, these synapses regress according to a developmental schedule and/or due to competition from confirmed synapses. Overproduction is not evident in development of some sensory systems or in some species (e.g., Valverde, 1971), but it is quite possible that if some synapses are being generated as others are being lost, then the process could be masked in quantitative studies. (Moreover, in the Valverde, 1971, case, an excess of small spines may have gone unobserved, as noted above; Freire, 1978).

The electron microscopic study of Winfield (1981) indicated a slower approach to a peak in binocularly deprived cats rather than a greater drop after the peak in synaptic frequency. While both groups showed a peak followed by a loss, the binocularly deprived group peaked at a lower level and showed less loss than the experienced group. This finding suggests that functional activity may be responsible for stimulating a proportion of synapse formation, although the alternative hypothesis, that it reduces synapse elimination earlier, before the peak is achieved, cannot be ruled out by this experiment alone.

EXPERIENCE-DEPENDENT PLASTICITY

In contrast, for experience-dependent neural information storage, neither the timing nor the specific nature of the information can be anticipated by the nervous system and there is little evidence for system-wide overproduction in these cases (although low-level constitutive system-wide turnover cannot be ruled out; Sotelo & Palay, 1971; Greenough & Green, 1981). The metabolically most efficient way to generate synapses locally within the system would be for activity, perhaps combined with some neuromodulatory signal (Kasamatsu & Pettigrew, 1979) to trigger local synaptogenesis from which activity-dependent stabilization might further select an appropriate subset. Thus new synapses would be formed only when they are needed to incorporate new information.

SYNAPSE FORMATION OR SYNAPSE SELECTION?

Sotelo and Palay (1971) and others (see Cotman, Nieto–Sampedro, & Harris, 1981) have interpreted signs of degeneration such as enlarged mitochondria, irregular vacuoles, and membrane whorls in adult presynaptic elements as signs of a continuing synapse turnover or replacement process which may be modulated by neural activity, availability of axonally transported factors, and postsynaptic factors. The implication of this interpretation is that the nervous system continues to constituitively generate connections on a nonsystematic basis. The data, however, are equally compatible with the hypothesis that synaptogenesis and stabilization occur in response to neural activity. Until recently, there was very little evidence that synapse formation could be triggered in the adult brain, and data compatible with that idea could also be explained by selective stabilization of a subpopulation of constitutively generated synapses. Evidence that neural activity may cause the rapid formation of synapses in the adult brain has come from studies of *long term potentiation (LTP)* in the rat hippocampus and hippocampal slice *in vitro*. LTP is a long-lasting increase in the postsynaptic response to one or a series of high frequency stimulus trains delivered to the afferent fibers. Lee, Schottler, Oliver, and Lynch (1980; Lee, Oliver, Schottler, & Lynch, 1981) have reported an increased frequency of certain synapse types in the hippocampus after LTP. Moreover, this synaptogenesis is quite rapid. Chang and Greenough (1984) found synaptic number to increase within 10 to 15 min following stimulation (possibly earlier as this was the shortest time studied). These results indicate that synapses form in response to neural activity on a time scale compatible with that of long-term memory and provide significant support for the idea that experience-dependent information storage could involve local, activity-dependent synaptogenesis.

A further test of the possible role of activity-dependent synaptogenesis in EC rats is made possible by the Steward (1983) finding that aggregates of ribosomes, the cells' protein producing structures, collect in spines during synaptogenesis. Interpreting these ribosomal aggregates as possible markers of newly forming synapses, Greenough, Hwang, and Gorman (1985) asked whether they were more frequent in the visual cortex of EC rats, as might be expected if synapses were forming actively in response to experience. Spines were much more likely to contain these aggregates in EC rats than in SC or IC rats, further supporting the hypothesis that activity-dependent synaptogenesis plays a role in the larger number of synapses per neuron found in EC rats' visual cortex.

CONNECTIONS PATTERNED BY EXPERIENCE

A major question that may apply to both types of information storage is the manner in which new connections could be appropriately patterned by experience. Drawing in part upon the suggestions of many, Hebb (1949) and Arbib (1975) for example, a very simple and hypothetical process is presented in Figure 2.5. In this example, a specific pattern of connections arises through patterned experience acting upon a spatially organized substrate. The developmental biology of the nervous system lays down accurate sensoritopic mappings between a sensory surface (e.g., retina) and its cortical representation (e.g., retinotopic cortex) without the aid of experience. Normal experience has an intrinsic order, so that, for example, points A and B are much more likely to be simultaneously stimulated than points A and D. If sensory neuron B can drive its central neuron B*, then simultaneous stimulation of neurons A and B will result in simultaneous pre- and postsynaptic activity in region 1 (where A and B* connect). If such activity can stimulate synapse formation or preservation, then area 1 will be affected more than area 2, which requires the less-likely simultaneous activity of neurons A and D. This simplistic model does not require directed growth of neural processes, since even random blooming of synapses (either generated or preserved by activity) within area 1

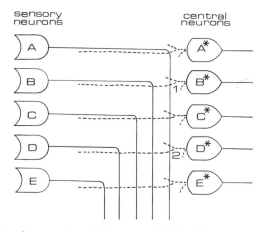

FIGURE 2.5   In this simple model, axons (solid lines) from sensory neurons project onto the dendrites (dashed lines) of central neurons. Area 1 is where the axon of sensory neuron A meets the dendrites of central neuron B*. Similarly, area 2 is where the axon of A meets the dendrites of D*.

would allow for the same result. This model illustrates how order in the environment (coherence) might induce ordered patterns in central connectivity. The Hebb synapse could be involved in the selection of appropriate synapses from inappropriate ones. In this model close temporal association between pre- and postsynaptic activity is required for changes. Recent CNS data which fit the Hebb synapse model (e.g., Levy & Steward, 1979; Blasdel & Pettigrew, 1979; Rauschecker & Singer, 1981) have increased the attractiveness of Hebb's model of synaptic plasticity.

Furthermore, the above model of patterning neural connections requires both contrast and coherence in experience. The coherence is necessary to maintain stable patterns of concordant activity, and the contrast is needed to segregate connections. For example, if the sensory surface in Figure 3.5 is the retina of stripe-reared kitten, then differential synapse effects at 1 but not 2 would only occur if the stripes were perpendicular to the receptor line A–E. If the stripes were parallel to A–E, then all their activities would always be concordant (either all on or all off), and synapses would be affected at all the intersections. In this example, the requirement of order is met if the probability for adjacent receptors to fire simultaneously is stable and higher than that for nonadjacent ones. An experimental example of experience-induced patterns in central connectivity is the work by Tieman and Hirsch (1982), where the lack of contrast along one visual axis in stripe-reared kittens produced corresponding dendritic changes in one axis of visual cortex neurons.

SUMMARY AND CONCLUSIONS

Experience-expectant processes have been described here in terms of the species-wide reliability of some experience. We suggested that species survival may be facilitated by information storage processes anticipating an experience with identical timing and features for all juvenile members. A structural correlate of "expectation" may be a temporary overproduction of synapses during the sensitive period, with a subsequent pruning back of inappropriate synapses. This experience-expectant blooming of new synapses is distributed uniformly across the entire population of homologous cells (although not necessarily uniformly distributed along their dendrites). The neuromodulatory trigger may be under maturational control or may be activity-dependent (as after eye-opening), but it is diffuse and pervasive. The expected experience produces patterned activity of neurons, effectively targeting which synapses will be selected, as illustrated for monocular deprivation in binocular species.

Experience-dependent mechanisms, on the other hand, may utilize synapse generation and preservation in different balance for quite different effect. Because the phylogenetic adaptations of neural plasticity cannot anticipate the timing nor specific features of such idiosyncratic experience, the "sensitive period" is necessarily left wide open. Here synapses are generated locally, upon demand. The nature of the demand, perhaps requiring stable patterns of neural activity arising directly from experience, possibly with an experience-contingent modulatory signal, has to be left an open question. We suggest that active participation by the animal is necessary for it to obtain the necessary coherent relationship between responses and their consequences. The organism's attempts to make its experience coherent could generate specific and stable patterns of neural activity. For example, juvenile play or adult attention may serve both to extract new information (increase contrast) and help repeat it or stabilize it without distraction (increase coherence). This experience-dependent localized shaping of connectivity suggests that very general experience (as in EC) would produce a widespread increase in synaptic frequency, but that relatively specific experience (as in training tasks) would produce localized increases.

In describing information storage mechanisms, we have tried to break down some of the distinctions between maturation, experience-sensitive development, and learning. Some aspects of experience (such as juvenile EC versus IC rearing) may influence both experience-expectant and experience-dependent processes. In fact, these processes probably cannot be entirely isolated, since they have substantial interactive consequences for how the brain processes information and they share mechanisms at a neural level. The evidence that different species have different susceptibility to experience and that brain areas are differentially influenced by experience suggests that information storage mechanisms have not remained stable through evolution. We suggest that, as more complicated sensory, motor and information processing schemes evolved, experience was utilized in two ways: (1) to shape common features of the nervous system through experiences common to members of the species, and (2) to provide for storage of information about the unique environment of the individual. The underlying mechanisms may have diverged to meet these separate needs, such that system-wide overproduction at a specific maturational stage, followed by selection subserves storage of common information, while local activity-dependent synaptogenesis, again followed by selection, subserves later storage of unique information.

REFERENCES

Allport, G. W. (1937). *Personality: A psychological interpretation*. New York: Holt.

Arbib, M. (1975). From automata theory to brain theory. *International Journal of Man–Machine Studies, 7*, 279–295.

Bennett, E. L., Diamond, M. C., Krech, D., & Rosenzweig, M. R. (1964). Chemical and anatomical plasticity of brain. *Science, 146*, 610–619.

Bennett, E. L., Rosenzeig, M. R., Morimoto, H., & Hebert, M. (1979). Maze training alters brain weights and cortical RNA/DNA ratios. *Behavioral and Neural Biology, 26*, 1–22.

Blasdel, G. G., & Pettigrew, J. D. (1979). Degree of interocular synchrony required for maintenance of binocularity in kitten's visual cortex. *Journal of Neurophysiology, 42*, 1692–1710.

Bonner, J. T. (Ed.). (1982). *Evolution and development*. Dahlem Konferenzen, No. 22.

Boothe, R. G., Greenough, W. T., Lund, J. S., & Wrege, K. (1979). A quantitative investigation of spine and dendritic development of neurons in visual cortex (Area 17) of *Macaca nemistrina* monkeys. *Journal of Comparative Neurology, 186*, 473–490.

Borges, S., & Berry, M. (1976). Preferential orientation of stellate cell dendrites in the visual cortex of the dark-reared rat. *Brain Research, 112*, 141–147.

Borges, S., & Berry, M. (1978). The effects of dark rearing on the development of the visual cortex of the rat. *Journal of Comparative Neurology, 180*, 277–300.

Brown, R. T. (1968). Early experience and problem solving ability. *Journal of Comparative and Physiological Psychology, 65*, 433–440.

Campbell, B. A., & Campbell, E. H. (1962). Retention and extinction of learned fear in infant and adult rats. *Journal of Comparative and Physiological Psychology, 55*, 1–8.

Chang, F.-L. F., & Greenough, W. T. (1982). Lateralized effects of monocular training on dendritic branching in adult split-brain rats. *Brain Research, 232,* 283–292.

Chang, F.-L. F., & Greenough, W. T. (1984). Transient and enduring morphological correlates of synaptic activity and efficacy changes in the rat hippocampal slice. *Brain Research, 309,* 35–46.

Changeaux, J.-P., & Danchin, A. (1977). Biochemical models for the selective stabilization of developing synapses. In G. A. Cottrell & P. M. Usherwood (Eds.), *Synapses* (pp. 705–712). New York: Academic Press.

Coleman, P. D., Flood, D. G., Whitehead, M. C., & Emerson, R. C. (1981). Spatial sampling by dendritic trees in visual cortex. *Brain Research, 214,* 1–21.

Coleman, P. D., & Riesen, A. H. (1968). Environmental effects on cortical dendritic fields: I. Rearing in the dark. *Journal of Anatomy, 102,* 363–374.

Cotman, C. W., Nieto–Sampedro, M., & Harris, E. W. (1981). Synapse replacement in the nervous system of adult vertebrates. *Physiological Reviews, 61,* 684–784.

Cragg, B. G. (1967). Changes in visual cortex on first exposure of rats to light. Effect on synaptic dimensions. *Nature, 215,* 251–253.

Cragg, B. G. (1975). The development of synapses in the visual system of the cat. *Journal of Comparative Neurology, 160,* 147–166. (a)

Cragg, B. G. (1975). The development of synapses in kitten visual cortex during visual deprivation. *Experimental Neurology, 46,* 445–451. (b)

Cummins, R. A., Walsh, R. N., Budtz–Olsen, O. E., Konstantinos, T., & Horsfall, C. R. (1973). Environmentally-induced changes in the brains of elderly rats. *Nature, 243,* 516–518.

Diamond, M. C. (1967). Extensive cortical depth measurements and neuron size increases in the cortex of environmentally enriched rats. *Journal of Comparative Neurology, 131,* 357–364.

Diamond, M. C., Rosenzweig, M. R., Bennett, E. L., Lindner, B., & Lyon, L. (1972). Effects of environmental enrichment and impoverishment on rat cerebral cortex. *Journal of Neurobiology, 3,* 47–64.

Falls, W., & Gobel, S. (1979). Golgi and EM studies of the formation of dendritic and axonal arbors: The interneurons of the substantia gelatinosa of Rolando in newborn kittens. *Journal of Comparative Neurology, 187,* 1–18.

Feng, A. S., & Rogowski, B. A. (1980). Effects of monaural and binaural occlusion on the morphology of neurons in the medial superior olivary nucleus of the rat. *Brain Research, 189,* 530–534.

Ferchmin, P. A., Bennett, E. L., & Rosenzweig, M. R. (1975). Direct contact with enriched environments is required to alter cerebral weights in rats. *Journal of Comparative and Physiological Psychology, 88,* 360–367.

Fiala, B. A., Joyce, J. N., & Greenough, W. T. (1978). Environmental complexity modulates growth of granule cell dendrites in developing but not adult hippocampus of rats. *Experimental Neurology, 59,* 372–383.

Flechsig, P. (1927). *Meine Myelogenetische Hirnlehre mit Biographischer Einleitung.* [My theory of brain myelinization with a biographical introduction.] Berlin: Springer.

Floeter, M. K., & Greenough, W. T. (1979). Cerebellar plasticity: Modification of Purkinje cell structure by differential rearing in monkeys. *Science, 206,* 227–229.

Freire, M. (1978). Effects of dark rearing on dendritic spines in Layer IV of the mouse visual cortex. A quantitative electron microscopical study. *Journal of Anatomy, 126,* 193–201.

Green, E. J., Greenough, W. T., & Schlumpf, B. E. (1983). Effects of complex or isolated environments on cortical dendrites of middle-aged rats. *Brain Research, 264,* 233–240.

Greenough, W. T. (1976). Enduring brain effects of differential experience and training. In M. R. Rosenzweig & E. L. Bennett (Eds.) *Neural mechanisms of learning and memory* (pp. 255–278). Cambridge: MIT Press.

Greenough, W. T. (1978). Development and memory: The synaptic connection. In T. Teyler (Ed), *Brain and learning* (pp. 127–145). Stamford, Connecticut: Greylock Publishers.

Greenough, W. T. & Chang, F.-L. F. (1985). Anatomically detectable correlates of brain plasticity. In C. Cotman (Ed.), *Synaptic plasticity and recovery of function* (pp. 335–372). New York: Guilford Press.

Greenough, W. T., & Green, E. J. (1981). Experience and the changing brain. In J. L. McGaugh, J. G. March, & S. B. Kiesler (Eds.) *Aging: Biology and behavior* (pp. 159–200). New York: Academic Press.

Greenough, W. T., Hwang, H.-M., & Gorman, C. (1985). Evidence for active synapse formation, or altered postsynaptic metabolism, in visual cortex of rats reared in complex environments. *Proceedings of the National Academy of Sciences (U.S.A.), 82,* 4549–4552.

Greenough, W. T., Juraska, J. M., & Volkmar, F. R. (1979). Maze training effects on dendritic branching in occipital cortex of adult rats. *Behavioral and Neural Biology, 26,* 287–297.

Greenough, W. T., & Volkmar, F. R. (1973). Pattern of dendritic branching in occipital cortex of rats reared in complex environments. *Experimental Neurology, 40,* 491–504.

Greenough, W. T., Volkmar, F. R., & Juraska, J. M. (1973). Effects of rearing complexity on dendritic branching in frontolateral and temporal cortex of the rat. *Experimental Neurology, 41,* 371–378.

Greenough, W. T., Wood, W. E., & Madden, T. C. (1972). Possible memory storage differences among mice reared in environments varying in complexity. *Behavioral Biology, 7,* 717–722.

Gyllensten, L., Malmfors, T., Norrlin, M.-L. (1966). Growth alteration in the auditory cortex of visually deprived mice. *Journal of Comparative Neurology, 126,* 463–470.

Hebb, D. O. (1949). *The organization of behavior.* New York: Wiley.

Hirsch, H. V. B., & Spinelli, D. N. (1970). Visual experience modifies distribution of horizontally and vertically oriented receptive fields in cats. *Science, 168,* 869–871.

Holloway, R. L. (1966). Dendritic branching: Some preliminary results of training and complexity in rat visual cortex. *Brain Research, 2,* 393–396.

Hubel, D. H., & Wiesel, T. N. (1969). Anatomical demonstration of columns in the monkey striate cortex. *Nature, 221,* 747–750.

Hymovitch, B. (1952). The effects of experimental variations on problem solving in the rat. *Journal of Comparative and Physiological Psychology, 45,* 313–321.

Juraska, J. M., Greenough, W. T., Elliott, C., Mack, K. J., & Berkowitz, R. (1980). Plasticity in adult rat visual cortex: An examination of several cell populations after differential rearing. *Behavioral and Neural Biology, 29,* 157–167.

Kasamatsu, T., & Pettigrew, J. D. (1979). preservation of binocularity after monocular deprivation in the striate cortex of kittens treated with 6-hydroxydopamine. *Journal of Comparative Neurology, 185,* 139–162.

Krech, D., Rosenzweig, M. R., & Bennett, E. L. (1962). Relations between brain chemistry and problem-solving among rats raised in enriched and impoverished environments. *Journal of Comparative and Physiological Psychology, 55,* 801–807.

Lee, K. S., Schottler, F., Oliver, M., & Lynch, G.,(1980). Brief bursts of high-frequency stimulation produce two types of structural change in rat hippocampus. *Journal of Neurophysiology, 44,* 247–258.

Lee, K. S., Oliver, M., Schottler, F., & Lynch, G. (1981). Electron microscopic studies of brain slices: The effects of high-frequency stimulation on dendritic ultrastructure. In G. A. Kerkut & H. V. Wheal (Eds.), *Electrophysiology of isolated mammalian CNS preparations* (pp. 189–211). New York: Academic.

Levay, S., Wiesel, T. N., & Hubel, D. H. (1980). The development of ocular dominance columns in normal and visually deprived monkeys. *Journal of Comparative Neurology, 191,* 1–51.

Levy, W. B., & Steward, O. (1979). Synapses as associative memory elements in the hippocampal formation. *Brain Research, 175,* 233–245.

Mariani, J., & Changeaux, J.-P. (1981). Ontogenesis of olivocerebellar relationships: I. Studies by intracellular recording of the multiple innervation of Purkinje cells by climbing fibers in the developing rat. *Journal of Neuroscience, 1,* 696–702.

Piaget, J. (1980). *Adaptation and intelligence: Organic selection and phenocopy.* (S. S. Eames, Trans.) Chicago: University of Chicago Press.

Purves, D., & Lichtman, J. W. (1980). Elimination of synapses in the developing nervous system. *Science, 210,* 153–157.

Ramon y Cajal, S. (1893). Neue Darstellung vom histologischen Bau des Central nerven-system [New findings about the histological structure of the central nervous system]. *Archiv fur Anatomie und Physiologie (Anatomie)* (pp. 319–428).

Ravizza, R. J., & Herschberger, A. C. (1966). The effect of prolonged motor restriction upon later behavior of the rat. *Psychological Record, 16,* 73–80.

Rauschecker, J. P., & Singer, W. (1981). The effects of early visual experience on the cat's visual cortex and their possible explanation by Hebb synapses. *Journal of Physiology, 310,* 215–239.

Riege, W. H., & Morimoto, H. (1970). Effects of chronic stress and differential environments upon brain weights and biogenic amine levels in rats. *Journal of Comparative and Physiological Psychology, 71,* 396–404.

Riesen, A. H. (1965). Effects of visual deprivation on perceptual function and the neural substrate. In J. DeAjuriaguerra (Ed.), *Symposium bel air II. desafferentation experimentale et Clinique* (pp. 47–66). Geneva: George & Cie.

Rothblat, L. A., & Schwartz, M. L. (1979). The effect of monocular deprivation on dendritic spines in visual cortex of young and adult albino rats: Evidence for a sensitive period. *Brain Research, 161,* 156–161.

Ryugo, D. K., Ryugo, R., Globus, A., & Killackey, H. P. (1975). Increased spine density in auditory cortex following visual or somatic deafferentation. *Brain Research, 90,* 143–146.

Schactel, E. G. (1947). On memory and childhood amnesia. *Psychiatry, 10,* 1–26.

Schwartz, M. L., & Rothblat, L. A. (1980). Behavioral and dendritic spine deficits in monocularly deprived rats: The role of reduced photic stimulation. *Society for Neuroscience Abstracts, 6,* 635.

Sholl, D. A. (1956). *Organization of the Cerebral Cortex.* London: Methuen.

Smith, D. C., & Loop, M. S. (1978). Rapid restoration of visual abilities in the monocularly deprived adult cat. *Investigative Opthalmology and Visual Science Supplement, 17,* 294.

Sotelo, C., & Palay, S. L. (1971). Altered axons and axon terminals in the lateral vestibular nucleus of the rat: Possible example of axonal remodeling. *Laboratory Investigation, 25,* 653–671.

Steward, O. (1983). Polyribosomes at the base of dendritic spines of CNS neurons: Their possible role in synapse construction and modification. *Cold Spring Harbor Symposium on Quantitative Biology, 48*, 745–759.

Stickrod, G., Kimble, D. P., & Smotherman, W. P. (1982). In utero taste/odor aversion conditioning in the rat. *Physiology and Behavior, 28*, 5–7.

Tanzi, E. (1893). I fatti e le induzioni nell'odierna istologia del sistema nervoso. [The facts and the inductions in current histology of the nervous system]. *Rivista sperimentale di freniatria e medicina legale delle mentali alienazioni, 19*, 419–472.

Tees, R. C. (1968). Effect of early visual restriction on later visual intensity discrimination in rats. *Journal of Comparative and Physiological Psychology, 66*, 224–227. (a)

Tees, R. C. (1968). Effect of early restriction on later form discrimination in the rat. *Canadian Journal of Psychology, 22*, 294–298. (b)

Tees, R. C., & Cartwright, J. (1972). Sensory preconditioning in rats following early visual deprivation. *Journal of Comparative and Physiological Psychology, 81*, 12–20.

Tieman, S. B., & Hirsch, H. V. B. (1982). Exposure to lines of only one orientation modifies dendritic morphology of cells in the visual cortex of the cat. *Journal of Comparative Neurology, 211*, 353–362.

Tinbergen, N. (1951). *The study of instinct.* London: Oxford University Press.

Turner, A. M., & Greenough, W. T. (1983). Synapses per neuron and synaptic dimensions in occipital cortex of rats reared in complex, social, or isolation housing. *Acta Stereologica, 2/Suppl. I*, 239–244.

Uylings, H. B. M., Kuypers, K., & Veltman, W. A. M. (1978). Environmental influences on neocortex in later life. In M. A. Corner, R. E. Baker, N. E. van de Poll, D. F. Swabb, & H. B. M. Uylings (Eds.), *Maturation of the nervous system: Progress in brain research: Vol. 48* (pp. 261–274). Amsterdam: Elsevier.

Valverde, F. (1970). The Golgi method: A tool for comparative structural analyses. In W. J. H. Nauta & S. O. E. Ebbesson (Eds.), *Contemporary Research Methods in Neuroanatomy* (pp. 12–31). New York: Springer-Verlag.

Valverde, F. (1971). Rate and extent of recovery from dark rearing in the mouse. *Brain Research, 33*, 1–11.

Walk, R. D., & Walters, C. P. (1973). Effect of visual deprivation on depth discrimination of hooded rats. *Journal of Comparative and Physiological Psychology, 85*, 559–63.

Winfield, D. A. (1981). The postnatal development of synapses in the visual cortex of the cat and the effects of eyelid closure. *Brain Research, 206*, 166–171.

ANATOMICAL CORRELATES OF NEURONAL PLASTICITY

Keith A. Crutcher

INTRODUCTION

This chapter deals with anatomical correlates of neuronal plasticity. The rationale for including this information in a book on learning and memory is that the mechanisms underlying normal developmental plasticity, as well as neuronal rearrangements that occur following damage to the nervous system, may also be involved in mediating long-lasting changes in behavior. Although it is obvious that behavior is a product of the nervous system, the correlation between specific changes in behavior and alterations in the structure and connectivity of specific neurons has been elusive. This is due, in part, to the technical difficulty of the necessary experiments as well as our ignorance of how to ask the right questions. However, recent advances have been made in identifying neuroanatomical changes that accompany normal development as well as rearrangements that occur following injury of the nervous system. These sometimes dramatic changes in neuronal morphology and connectivity reveal a capacity for anatomical plasticity that may underlie certain forms of behavioral plasticity.

To identify the anatomical or physiological basis of learning and memory we must have some idea of where and when to look. One approach is to remove specific brain regions and test the effect this has on an animal's ability to learn or to remember a previously learned task (see Chapters 1, 11, and 12, this volume). Another approach is to measure anatomical, biochemical or physiological changes in brain regions that might be expected to be involved in learning or remembering a particular task (See Chapters 5, 7, and 9, this volume). A third approach, the one covered here, is to ask what kinds of changes in connectivity (anatomical plasticity) the nervous system is capable of.

This chapter first reviews some of the anatomical changes that occur during normal development as well as in response to experimental manipulations. A brief review of the evidence for anatomical plasticity associated with learning in maturity will then be followed by a detailed discussion of injury-induced anatomical plasticity including possible mechanisms that might be involved. Finally, some reference will be made to the proposed functional significance of anatomical rearrangements. The intention is not to prove that anatomical plasticity directly correlates with behavioral plasticity but, rather, to present information from anatomical studies that may provide clues to mechanisms which mediate long-term changes in behavior. Unless stated otherwise, the information that is covered in this chapter is derived from studies of the mammalian nervous system.

FOCUS ON THE SYNAPSE

The Neuron Doctrine

The concept of separate nerve cells communicating through synapses, which came to be referred to as the neuron doctrine, was only slowly accepted during the first half of the twentieth century. It was difficult with early anatomical techniques to determine where one nerve cell ended and another began due to the close apposition of axons and dendrites. In fact, the term synapse was first proposed by Sherrington (1906) based on electrophysiological results obtained in 1897. Many scientists initially believed that the nervous system was a mass of protoplasm (a syncytium) with cell nuclei embedded in it here and there. The arguments for and against the neuron doctrine are summarized by Ramon y Cajal (1928) who is usually credited with establishing the validity of the neuron doctrine. His account is worth reading not just for historical interest but also for the different interpretations of the same data that were used to support opposite points of view.

For students of learning and memory, the identification of the synapse as the point of interneuronal communication provided a likely candidate for a modifiable element in the formation of memory. For example, Hebb (1949) proposed that selective activation of afferent fibers in synchrony with the postsynaptic neuron could lead to long-lasting changes in the effectiveness of specific synaptic connections.

Such changes in synaptic efficacy would be expected to occur with associative forms of learning. Hebb's hypothesis emphasized the synapse as the likely point of modification during learning. A related hypothesis has been proposed to explain the establishment of synapses during development (Changeux & Danchin, 1976). It is beyond the scope of this chapter to review the many theories of learning that are based on changes in synaptic function, but most neuroscientists currently agree that changes in synaptic connections are likely to be involved in the phenomena of learning and memory.

APPROACHES TO STUDYING THE SYNAPSE

Although the synapse occupies the center of attention for theories of learning and memory, different levels of analysis lead to different emphases as to which specific events are the most important. Biochemists make an effective case for the study of changes in molecules and proteins associated with learning and memory. A synapse may become more effective, for example, by releasing more of its transmitter or the activity of released transmitter may be prolonged by changing the rate at which it is inactivated, either through enzymatic degradation or reuptake by the terminal. Postsynaptic targets may also become more responsive to a transmitter by increasing the number or affinity of transmitter receptors in the postsynaptic membrane (Lynch & Baudry, 1984). All of these changes can theoretically be measured with sensitive biochemical techniques.

The physiologist, on the other hand, views the synapse as a sensitive transducer whose changes in efficacy are measured with refined electrophysiological techniques. Such fascinating phenomena as long-term potentiation (LTP), desensitization, habituation and unmasking of ineffective synapses (Wall, 1977) have been fully documented with this approach. Even more exciting is the realization that some changes in synaptic function correlate, in many ways, with certain types of learning and memory.

The anatomist approaches the synapse in terms of its morphology and develops increasingly sensitive techniques to visualize the synapse and quantify changes in its structure. Such parameters as the number of synaptic vesicles, the length of membrane apposition between pre- and postsynaptic elements, the number of dendritic spines, the number of synapses, or the number of dendritic branches have been shown to change during normal development and in response to experimental manipulations (Greenough, 1984). However, with few exceptions, the anatomist is confined to a static view of the nervous system and must infer dynamic processes from sequential snapshots.

Clearly all of these views of the synapse are correct to some degree but reflect the different levels of analysis and techniques used. The current challenge is to unify the information obtained from each view in order to obtain a complete picture. Such unification is slowly being accomplished, as the contributions to this volume reveal. Contemporary neuroscientists try to incorporate neurochemical, neurophysiological and neuroanatomical results in their analysis. The phenomenon of long-term potentiation, to take one example, has now been approached with biochemical, physiological and anatomical techniques (Lynch & Baudry, 1984; Teyler, Chapter 7, this volume).

Although changes in synaptic connections may reasonably be expected to correlate with long-term changes in behavior, a major unanswered question is to what extent existing synapses are modified as opposed to changes occurring in the number and pattern of synapses that is, the formation and loss of synaptic contacts. The answer appears to be that both types of plasticity exist and, in many cases, it is difficult to distinguish between them, particularly using electrophysiological techniques (Mendell, 1984). Some of the most dramatic changes in neuronal connectivity occur during development and these changes are often responsive to experimental manipulations as will be discussed in the next section.

ANATOMICAL PLASTICITY DURING DEVELOPMENT

Anatomical Changes During Normal Development

Anatomical change (plasticity) is characteristic of all developing organisms and of all systems within an organism. Morphogenesis involves dramatic changes in the shape and constituents of organs and tissues. During development, neurons undergo the same fundamental series of transformations that cells forming other tissues go through. That is, there is a period during which the cells that will form the nervous system divide, migrate, and differentiate in order to establish the specific populations of neurons that comprise the mature tissue (Jacobson, 1978). However, nerve cells become specialized in ways not shared by most other cell types. One obvious morphological specialization is the extension of axons and dendrites, collectively called neurites, and the formation of synaptic contacts with each other as well as with other cell types. In addition, and presumably as a result of the latter, mature neurons lose their ability to divide, although there are a few examples of neurogenesis continuing in maturity both in mammals (Bayer, Yackel, & Puri, 1982; Kaplan & Bell, 1983, 1984) and in birds (Goldman & Nottebohm, 1983).

It is reasonable to assume that the ontogeny of particular behaviors correlates with the maturation of specific neural centers even if such correlations are often difficult to make (Oppenheim, 1982). The ability to perform coordinated movements, to cite but one example, is dependent on the development of specific neuronal connections (Bekoff, 1982). In this sense, at least, changes in neuronal connectivity directly determine behavioral competence. But this is true only in the most obvious sense that information is processed in specific ways by specific connections in the nervous system. What about the ongoing changes in behavior that occur as development continues?

Although there are examples of neurogenesis continuing in maturity in restricted brain regions (Bayer et al., 1982; Kaplan & Bell, 1983, 1984; Goldman & Nottebohm, 1983), the generalization that the vast majority of neurons are generated prenatally is still valid. Therefore, the fact that few neurons are formed after a certain stage in development means that subsequent changes in behavior are likely to be due to alterations in the connections of existing neurons. It is not clear, however, to what extent the connectivity of the mature nervous system is static or whether processes underlying development, to be discussed shortly, persist in maturity (Greenough, 1984). The mature nervous system may be static only in the sense that a dynamic equilibrium is established between the rates at which synaptic connections are formed and lost. Lasting changes could be due to a change in this equilibrium. If learning, for example, involves the stabilization or loss of a small percentage of synapses that are otherwise turning over, identifying that subpopulation may be beyond the realm of contemporary technology. This question of synaptic changes in maturity will be discussed further. For now we are concerned with changes which occur during development.

Although mature neurons cannot proliferate, one surprising feature of normal development is that many more neurons are produced than survive to maturity. This overproduction and subsequent death of nerve cells was recently reviewed by Oppenheim (1981a) and the reader is referred to this scholarly and thorough paper for details. The development of the nervous system not only involves the death of many neurons but also the overproduction and elimination of axons and synaptic connections (Cowan, Fawcett, O'Leary, & Stanfield, 1984). For example, many neurons in the cerebral cortex have axons which project to other areas of the central nervous system only during a restricted period in development, indicating that extensive loss of axons occurs (Stanfield, 1984). Furthermore, there is a period of synapse proliferation followed by synapse elimination as maturation proceeds in many neuronal systems (see the following discussion). Although this process may seem wasteful, the overproduction and subsequent elimination of neurons and their connections appears to provide the basis for the selective connectivity which is ultimately attained in the mature organism. In other words, this reduction in neuronal connectivity leads to a subset of the initial set of connections established during development. Which subset of possible connections an organism maintains may depend on environmental conditions.

Once axons arrive in a target area, they must form synaptic contacts with specific cells or parts of cells. It is during this period that neuronal death occurs, but cell death does not appear to account for the subsequent elimination of synapses and the development of specific connections (Purves & Lichtman, 1980; Oppenheim, 1981b; Van Essen, 1982; Landmesser, 1984). Some synapses are lost because their target cells die (Knyihar, Sillik, & Rakic, 1978). The neurons which survive the period of cell death initially form synapses with many postsynaptic targets (polyneuronal innervation) and then undergo a period of synapse elimination resulting in the mature pattern of connectivity. Although a neuron may reduce the number of target cells it innervates, the total number of synapses it makes may actually increase (Purves & Lichtman, 1980). This is due to the increase in synaptic contacts made by any one neuron on each of its final target cells. Thus, developing neurons undergo dramatic transformations in the pattern of connections they make even if there is no decrease in the total number of synaptic contacts they form.

Competition between axons has been observed during development of neuromuscular synapses (Van Essen, 1982) as well as in the development of connections within the autonomic nervous system (Purves & Lichtman, 1980). Purves and coworkers correlated the functional and morphological development of synaptic connections in mammalian autonomic ganglia, including the hamster superior cervical ganglion (Lichtman & Purves, 1980) and the rabbit ciliary ganglion (Purves & Hume, 1981). In addition, Lichtman (1977, 1980) performed similar studies of the rat submandibular ganglion. The major conclusion reached is that there is a positive correlation between the number of different axons ultimately innervating a postsynaptic cell and the number of dendrites present on the postsynaptic neuron. These results led to the suggestion that the ability of a neuron to accept synapses from different axons is based upon the extent and form of its dendritic tree

(Purves & Hume, 1981). In other words, individual axons may compete for their own spatial domains. This is consistent with the idea that axons compete during development for synaptic space or some other attribute of a target such as the presence of a growth factor.

Crepel, Mariani, and Delhaye-Bouchard (1976) and Crepel, Delhaye-Bouchard, and Dupont (1981), as well as Mariani and Changeux (1981) found that there is a developmental loss of climbing fiber input to the Purkinje cells of the developing rat cerebellum. This extended the concept of synapse elimination to the central nervous system (CNS). Jackson and Parks (1982) found that functional synapse elimination during development of primary afferent (auditory nerve) input in the chick auditory system was due to decreased branching of individual axons. It seems likely, therefore, that the loss of neurons, axons and synapses is characteristic of developing neuronal connections throughout the peripheral and central nervous systems.

Although the loss of neurons and connections in the developing nervous system has been proposed to represent a means of correcting errors (Cowan et al., 1984), the criteria for determining what constitutes a fundamental error in neuronal development have not been established. The assumption that developing connections which do not persist into maturity represent mistakes, does not take into account the possibility that such connections serve a transient purpose. Ebbesson has proposed a novel theory that transient projections in ontogeny reflect the phylogenetic origin of mature connections (Ebbesson, 1980). Thus, transient projections may represent an obligatory stage in the development of specific pathways as opposed to errors arising from imprecision in developmental mechanisms. A similar suggestion has been made by Oppenheim (1982) regarding the ontogeny of certain behaviors.

MANIPULATIONS DURING DEVELOPMENT

The production of more neurons and synapses during development than are retained in the mature organism provides a dramatic example of anatomical change or plasticity. Furthermore, there are numerous experiments demonstrating that the developmental loss of nerve cells and connections can be modified. Hamburger and Levi–Montalcini (1949) observed that removing limb target tissue during development resulted in greater cell death than normal in the chick spinal cord. Increasing the target size of developing motor neurons in the chick spinal cord, by grafting an additional target limb, resulted in less nerve cell death than would normally occur (Hollyday & Hamburger, 1976).

The specific mechanism by which the size of the neuron population is matched to its target is unknown but the amount and pattern of activity may play a critical role. Oppenheim and Nunez (1982) found that stimulation of the developing hindlimb increases the naturally occurring cell death in the spinal cord. On the other hand, paralysis of the target muscles resulted in less cell death than normal (Pittman & Oppenheim, 1979). Although other interpretations are possible, one hypothesis which is consistent with this data is that developing motor neurons require a target substance for survival (trophic factor), and the availability of the putative factor is inversely related to the amount of target activity. The requirement of developing motor neurons for target trophic support is thought to be a general mechanism underlying the extensive cell death that occurs in most systems (Cowan et al., 1984). This hypothesis is consistent with the observation that some developing neuronal populations, such as dorsal root ganglion neurons, exhibit transient survival requirements for specific growth factors in culture (Barde, Edgar, & Thoenen 1980).

In addition to the problem of matching the size of the innervating neuronal population with the target size, the developing nervous system also exhibits tremendous specificity in the connections it ultimately makes. For example, developing axons must find their appropriate target area by selecting appropriate pathways and subsequently form synapses with specific portions of that target, such as a certain part of a dendrite.

The question of pathway selection by developing axons has been addressed by several investigators and has been reviewed in detail by Landmesser (1980, 1984). In work done by Landmesser and her colleagues, segments of the embryonic chick spinal cord were removed, reversed, and put back into the spinal cord. The subsequent development of motor connections was observed. Normally, motor neurons at any particular level in the chick spinal cord send axons only to muscles appropriate for that level. Thus, an individual nerve cell only innervates certain muscles. Following anterior–posterior rotation of spinal cord segments, motor neurons were still able to find their appropriate targets even though some of the axons had to take abnormal routes to reach them. Similar results were obtained with dorsal–ventral rotations of the target tissue that is, developing limb-buds (Ferguson, 1983). However, motor neurons did not innervate appropriate targets if the limbs were transplanted several segments away from their normal location.

These results show that developing neurons are partly, although not completely, dependent on local cues for finding their normal targets.

Part of the mechanism must involve the initial spatial relationship between the developing neuron and its target since there is a limit to the amount of displacement that will still permit appropriate innervation. The means by which growing axons initially select appropriate pathways, or correct their trajectory from an incorrect pathway *in vivo*, are still unknown. However, considerable information is now available on the behavior of growing axons in culture (reviewed by Letourneau, 1982). Collins and Garrett (1980), for example, demonstrated that factors bound to a narrow strip of substratum can guide axonal growth *in vitro*. The role of intermediate target cells (landmark or guidepost cells) in the development of connections in certain invertebrates may also provide clues as to how axons find their ultimate targets in more complex organisms (Ho & Goodman, 1982).

As previously discussed, activity seems to play a role in the developmental loss of neurons even though the general pattern of connectivity is not dependent on activity (Oppenheim, 1981b). Evidence that competition between developing axons for specific target sites is regulated, in part, by neuronal activity is provided by studies of the mammalian visual system. In the mature nervous system of cats and some monkeys, information from each eye is segregated into specific areas (columns) that alternate within the visual cortex. If the connections from one eye are removed or visual input is reduced to one eye, there is apparent expansion of the connections from the remaining eye into the columns that would normally be occupied by the removed eye (Hubel, Wiesel, & LeVay, 1977; LeVay, Wiesel, & Hubel, 1980; Blakemore, Vital–Durand, & Garey, 1981). The conclusion that physiological activity is important in the development of these ocular dominance columns, as they are called, is underscored by the observation that cats raised in the dark do not develop such columns (Swindale, 1981). Suppression of neuronal activity through injections of tetrodotoxin produce a similar result (Stryker, 1981). The presence of prolonged activity does not seem to be required since the inhibition of column development can be reversed by brief visual experience during the sensitive period (Mower, Christen, & Caplan, 1983). In the monocular deprivation studies the expanded innervation seems to be due, in part, to the retention of connections from the unaffected eye that would normally retract during development (Rakic, 1976; LeVay, Stryker, & Shatz, 1978; LeVay et al., 1980; Swindale, 1981). This example of activity-dependent influences on development is covered in depth in Chapter 2, this volume, by Black and Greenough who consider this to be an example of experience-dependent development.

The observation that altering visual input results in alteration of the development of the visual pathways provides strong evidence for a role of activity in axonal competition for synaptic targets and subsequent synapse elimination. It is not clear if the amount of activity directly affects the ability of axons to compete for synaptic space or to take up a growth factor, or if this effect is due to changes in the target which subsequently affect competition, such as the amount of growth substance produced (see the previous discussion).

The changes in connectivity which occur during development may also be related to sensitive or critical periods for the development of certain behaviors (Clopton & Silverman, 1977; Erzurumlu & Killackey, 1982). The existence of critical periods emphasizes the strict correlation between the development of specific brain regions and the emergence of a particular behavior (Oppenheim, 1982). For example, imprinting appears to be a dramatic example of specific learning occurring only during a restricted period of development (Horn, 1981). There is little flexibility in whether or not the animal will imprint at a particular age, and the stimulus to which imprinting occurs may be quite variable. As a result, one might expect this kind of learning to be dependent on the development of specific connections which are reserved to learn a particular aspect of the environment (see Chapter 2, this volume).

The major conclusion that can be made from the preceding discussion is that development involves a tremendous amount of anatomical plasticity in terms of the number and pattern of synaptic connections that are made. The competition between axons for targets may be regulated to a certain extent by the amount of activity in that system. The tremendous loss of synapses which characterizes normal development indicates that the initial formation of synapses is not sufficient to establish a permanent innervation. Additional information must be exchanged to determine which connections will be maintained (stabilization). This information is determined, in part, by the environment, as evidenced by the effect on certain anatomical parameters of raising animals under different environmental conditions (Chapter 2, this volume; Greenough, Hwang, & Gorman, 1985).

Although anatomical plasticity characterizes the developing nervous system, to what extent does such plasticity extend into maturity? As we shall see in the following sections, anatomical changes continue to occur in mature organisms in response to environmental manipulations as well as following injury. To what extent the mechanisms that operate during development are also active in these situations remains to be determined.

ANATOMICAL CORRELATES OF LEARNING IN MATURITY

EXAMPLES OF CHANGES IN MATURE ORGANISMS

Some of the best examples of synaptic changes accompanying learning are provided by studies of relatively simple invertebrate nervous systems which, nevertheless, exhibit basic forms of learning. Some of these systems also exhibit morphological changes (Bailey & Chen, 1983). Chapter 8, this volume, as well as a recent review by Kandel and Schwartz (1982) deal with these topics in detail, so they will not be covered here. The study of invertebrates is useful to the extent that similar synaptic mechanisms are likely to operate in all nervous systems. However, the specific mechanisms underlying learning in more complex nervous systems, such as in mammals, may be qualitatively, as well as quantitatively, different (Thompson & Doneyon, Chapter 1, this volume; Lynch & Baudry, 1984). In addition, as the contributions to this book reveal, there are different kinds of learning, only the simplest of which are exhibited by invertebrates.

Some approaches to simplifying the study of learning in the mammalian nervous system include the electrophysiological analysis of single cells *in vivo* as well as the study of slices of brain tissue *in vitro* (see Chapter 7, this volume). In these studies, synapses exhibit habituation and sensitization, and there is some *in vivo* evidence for the kind of enhancement of synaptic efficacy proposed by Hebb (Levy & Steward, 1979). Some of the electrophysiological changes such as long-term potentiation, which is enhanced sensitivity to a synaptic input and thought by some to represent a good model for learning and memory, have also been correlated with morphological changes in dendritic spines (Fifkova & Van Harreveld, 1977; Lee, Schottler, Oliver, & Lynch, 1980). In fact, a very specific hypothesis has recently been proposed to account for the biochemical, physiological and anatomical changes occurring in long-term potentiation (LTP) (Lynch & Baudry, 1984).

Other morphological changes that are probably related to learning are found in specific brain regions of animals exposed to different environmental conditions (Greenough, 1984, and Chapter 2, this volume). Synaptic shape, the number of dendritic spines, the pattern of dendritic branches and/or the distribution of synapses are affected by the type of environment to which an organism is exposed. Many of these effects appear to be specific to the brain regions affected by the experimental stimuli. For example, visual cortical areas are primarily affected by visual deprivation. Such correlations support the concept that the environment alters the quantity and quality of neuronal connections which, in turn, are reflected in the organism's behavior, including learning and memory.

One of the most dramatic examples of morphological changes accompanying behavior in maturity is in the song control nuclei of certain birds. Nottebohm and co-workers demonstrated a striking change in the size of brain nuclei that control song production in the male canary. This change in size is due, in part, to the growth of dendrites, but has also recently been shown to involve the addition of new, functional neurons (Goldman & Nottebohm, 1983; Paton & Nottebohm, 1984). This example of anatomical and behavioral plasticity is under seasonal hormonal control. Anatomical changes correlating with the presence of a certain behavior thus occur in some cases in adult vertebrate animals and may correspond to the kind of changes which occur throughout development. Even so, the production of new neurons is thought to occur only rarely in mature brains so that other types of anatomical plasticity are thought to underly learning and memory.

There are other examples of morphological changes correlated with learning in mature organisms. For example, behavioral conditioning affects the number of dendritic spines on cortical pyramidal neurons (Rutledge, Wright, & Duncan, 1974). Also, training on a pattern-discrimination task results in changes in synaptic morphology (surface area, length) in the visual cortex (Vrensen & Cardozo, 1981). Wenzel, Kammerer, Kirsche, Matthies, & Wenzel (1980) reported an increase in the number of synapses on hippocampal neurons following training on a brightness-discrimination task. All of these studies provide evidence for anatomical plasticity of the mature nervous system. No direct causality has been demonstrated between such anatomical plasticity and behavior, but such observations suggest that this correlation may exist.

THE PARADOX OF MEMORY

One definition of behavioral plasticity is the ability of an organism to remember something that was experienced before or to alter its behavior in response to such experience. However, memory is a reflection of the stability of neuronal connectivity and not its plasticity! Here we are confronted with an apparent contradiction. The ability of an organism to learn a new behavior probably involves changes in connectivity (anatomical plasticity) since there is an obvious change in the function of the nervous system over the period during which the learning occurs. On the other hand, the ability of the organism to remember requires that such a change be relatively permanent (stabile), which is the opposite of plasticity. Furthermore, the ability of an organism to forget a previous response and to learn a new response or behavior, may be considered as evidence of further plasticity. This sequence of plasticity followed by stability is characteristic of development in general. Therefore, the assumption that mechanisms underlying development persist in learning in mature organisms is not unreasonable.

This contradiction is also evident in the evolutionary distribution of learning and memory. As a rule, invertebrate organisms exhibit very little plasticity in their behavior compared to vertebrates. Invertebrates do demonstrate a remarkable complexity in their behavior and exhibit certain types of learning that seem remarkable, such as the oft-cited example of honeybees which can remember and communicate the location of nectar sites (Menzel, 1983). In general, such learning in insects appears to involve eidetic images (Collett & Cartwright, 1983) and may be similar to immature forms of learning in vertebrates, such as imprinting, since there is little flexibility in the kind of information that is learned. Vertebrates exhibit all of the forms of learning that invertebrates do, yet demonstrate additional adaptability when confronted with new environments, something invertebrates cannot generally do. Does this difference in behavioral plasticity reflect itself in the repertoire of anatomical changes that occur during development or following injury? Such correlations have not been made, but it is possible that the mechanisms involved in examples of higher learning are restricted to higher vertebrates and to certain brain regions within those organisms. A prediction of this sort has recently been proposed by Lynch & Baudry (1984) in relation to their model of memory formation.

Another way to view behavioral plasticity is to distinguish between those behaviors which are rigidly determined by the inherited genetic program for development and those behaviors which can be modified by experience within limits set by the genetic program. Thus, the behavioral repertoire of an organism can be thought of in terms of those behaviors that are rigidly determined by the genome and those which arise through interaction with the environment. This distinction correlates with the experience-independent and experience-dependent behaviors discussed by Greenough in Chapter 2 of this volume but again, it is not clear if this classification reflects differences in anatomical plasticity.

Similarly, the ability of an organism to accomplish a task in a new way following injury to the nervous system is an example of behavioral plasticity (Marshall, 1985). Such recovery of function may involve anatomical plasticity (Loesche & Steward, 1977; Goldberger & Murray, 1978), but it may also involve other mechanisms such as the substitution of a different behavioral strategy (Goldberger & Murray, 1978) or the recovery of certain brain regions transiently affected by a lesion (Finger & Stein, 1982). Conversely, there are examples of anatomical changes following injury which may or may not result in measurable recovery of function. Yet such rearrangements reveal the potential of the nervous system to change its connectivity. Such anatomical rearrangements include regeneration and collateral sprouting and are covered in detail in the following sections.

ANATOMICAL REARRANGEMENTS FOLLOWING INJURY

FACTORS AFFECTING PLASTICITY

Severe damage to the nervous system usually results in death, but less serious injury produces varying degrees of behavioral impairment depending on several variables including the location and size of the injury, the rate at which the injury occurs and the age of the organism at the time of injury (Finger & Stein, 1982; Marshall, 1985). The importance of injury location is directly related to the specialization of brain regions. For example, lower brain stem centers control vital functions and damage to this region is usually fatal. On the other hand, localized injury to certain cortical areas may be difficult to detect behaviorally. This is particularly true if the injury is inflicted slowly, as a result of a tumor for example. Finally, the age of the organism at the time of injury determines to a large degree how successful recovery will be (Stelzner, Ershler, & Weber, 1975; Bregman & Goldberger, 1982). The exact reason for this is not known but the fact that the developing nervous system is less compromised by injury than the mature nervous system (with a few exceptions) may relate to the fact that anatomical plasticity also changes with age (Lynch, Stanfield, & Cotman, 1973; Scheff, Bernardo, & Cotman, 1978; Gall & Lynch, 1981; Jackson & Diamond, 1984; West, 1984).

During the early phase of development, as previously mentioned, there is an abundance of neurons and synaptic connections. In addition, injuring the nervous system at an early age may alter the normal development of connections (Schneider, 1970; Lynch, Stanfield, & Cotman, 1973; Lund & Lund, 1973; Crain & Hall, 1980a,b). On the other hand, it is not clear when development ends, particularly if defined on the basis of synaptic stability. In addition to the evidence for a certain amount of neurogenesis continuing into maturity (see previous discussion) axonal growth or synaptic turnover may be a normal occurrence

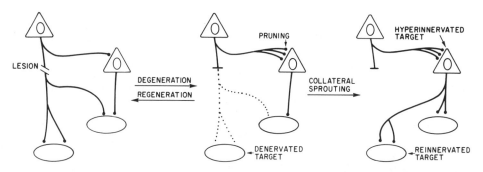

FIGURE 3.1   This series of drawings illustrates the basic types of anatomical plastic-ity that have been described. On the left are shown a pair of neurons which innervate unspecified targets within the peripheral or central nervous system. The left neuron of the pair provides innervation to both targets as well as to the other neuron. The changes which occur subsequent to a lesion of the left neuron are shown in the center. That portion of the axon distal to the injury undergoes Wallerian degeneration leaving a completely denervated target and a partially denervated target. The surviving collaterals may undergo a pruning response, expanding their innervation pattern (middle drawing). If the injured neuron regrows its axon, then regeneration has occurred to restore the original innervation. In the central nervous system, a more common response is that the surviving axons of uninjured neurons undergo collateral sprouting thus reinnervating the denervated target (right drawing). The expanded innervation resulting from the pruning response is called a hyperinnervation.

in the adult nervous system, albeit at a reduced rate compared to youn-ger ages (Cotman, Nieto–Sampedro, & Harris, 1981; Wernig, Carmody, Anzil, Hansert, Marcimak, & Zucker, 1984). The possibility that devel-opmental processes extend into maturity is important in assessing the possible mechanisms which account for anatomical plasticity, a topic we will return to later.

TERMINOLOGY

To discuss different types of anatomical plasticity it is helpful to review some terms (Fig. 3.1). A neuron which makes synaptic contact with another neuron, or other cell type, is said to *innervate* the target. An innervation that is greater than normal is referred to as *hyperinner-vation*. The term hyperinnervation may not be appropriate when refer-ring to the transient proliferation of synaptic contacts which occurs in development since such an innervation is only *hyper* when compared to the adult situation. The term *exuberance* has been applied to the developmental production of synapses.

If a target loses synaptic contacts it is said to be *denervated* of its input and such denervation may be partial or complete. In some peripheral organs, synaptic contacts do not exhibit membrane specializations characteristic of classical synapses such as membrane thickening. As a result, the anatomical criteria that are used to establish the presence of innervation are not hard and fast. In fact, during development of the peripheral nervous system (PNS) there are examples of functional innervation being established before evidence of anatomical synapses is obtained (Landmesser & Pilar, 1978). To what extent neuronal communication in the CNS may also occur without the presence of morphological synapses is unknown.

Regrowth of damaged axons is referred to as *regeneration*, and if the axons succeed in reaching the denervated target and form synapses then they have *reinnervated* the target. Undamaged axons may also grow in response to damage of other axons. Such growth is referred to as *collateral sprouting*. (Some authors refer to regeneration as regenerative sprouting). Depending on the source of the new axons, collateral sprouting has been classified as *homotypic,* when the sprouting neuron arises from the same region (Field & Raisman, 1983) or is of the same transmitter type (Zhou & Azmitia, 1984) as the degenerated neuron, or *heterotypic,* when sprouting occurs from a different class of neurons. Of course this definition is only useful if the criteria used to define neuronal similarity is relevant to the sprouting mechanism (Cotman et al., 1981). As will be discussed later, attributes other than origin or transmitter identity may be more important when trying to explain the specificity of some examples of anatomical plasticity.

New synaptic contacts may also be formed without true axonal growth. Existing synaptic boutons may form additional appositions (active sites) or membrane specializations may form where close association between an axon and a target cell already exists (Carlin & Siekevitz, 1983; Dyson & Jones, 1984). Some investigators refer to any example of new synapse formation, regardless of whether it involves axonal growth, as *reactive synaptogenesis* (Cotman & Nadler, 1978). This term is useful in that no assumption is made concerning the mechanism underlying synapse formation; however, it is limited to the extent that axonal sprouting and regeneration may occur without synapse formation.

Still another form of reactive growth occurs from undamaged axons of a neuron which has sustained damage to other axonal branches. This *pruning* response, as it has been referred to (Schneider, 1970, 1973), is commonly observed during development but may also occur in adult nervous tissue (Pickel, Segal, & Bloom, 1974). The pruning response underscores the difficulty in any classification scheme applied to anatomical plasticity, since it is not clear if pruning reflects a regenerative response on the part of an injured neuron or if sprouting is induced by other effects of the lesion such as target denervation.

INJURY DURING DEVELOPMENT

There are several examples of successful target innervation in both the central and peripheral nervous systems when damage is made during development (Schneider, 1970; Lund & Lund, 1973; Crain & Hall, 1980a,b; Cowan & Finger, 1982; Castro & Mihailoff, 1983). In many of these cases, it is not clear if damaged axons have regenerated, collateral sprouting has occurred, or if uninjured axons arriving later account for the innervation. Anatomical plasticity during development is, to a certain extent, a consequence of the fact that the nervous system is already growing (see previous discussion), and some systems are later to mature than others. One apparent corollary of this phenomenon is that functional recovery following injury is often, although not always, better in young organisms (Bregman & Goldberger, 1982; Finger & Stein, 1982; Passingham, Perry, & Wilkinson, 1983).

In addition to successful reinnervation of targets following axonal injury during development, removal of a target area will often result in rerouting of axons to a new target or hyperinnervation of other normally innervated targets (Schneider, 1970). This latter response may reflect the pruning effect described earlier.

REGENERATION

The ability of peripheral nerves to regenerate following injury is a dramatic demonstration that certain mature nerve cells can exhibit growth. Following damage to an axon in the PNS, the portion beyond the point of damage degenerates and is phagocytized, a process referred to as Wallerian degeneration. The axonal segment which remains connected to the nerve cell body may survive and within a few days new extensions (sprouts) emerge from the damaged tip (Carbonetto & Muller, 1982). These axonal sprouts continue to elongate and in many cases manage to reach (reinnervate) the original target sites from which the axons were disconnected. Such regenerated connections exhibit selectivity (Guth & Bernstein, 1961) and clearly underly functional recovery in many cases.

This process of regeneration has been studied for a century or more (Guth, 1975) and is understood in some detail. When a neuron sustains injury to its axon, its success in regrowing depends on several factors including the age of the organism, the proximity of the injury to the neuronal cell body, and the environment in which it must regrow. This last part appears to be critical in accounting for differences in the regenerative ability of central and peripheral neurons (see following discussion). Axonal injury initially leads to a series of morphological and biochemical changes in the nerve cell body known as chromatolysis (Lieberman, 1971). In many cases the injury is too severe and the neuron dies. Developing neurons appear to be particularly susceptible to axotomy. In other circumstances, however, the neuron is able to redirect is synthetic machinery to form additional axonal components and regrowth occurs.

Regeneration of damaged axons readily occurs in the invertebrate nervous system (Mason & Muller, 1983). In fact, unlike most vertebrate neurons, when an invertebrate axon is transected the distal portion may survive for long periods without the cell body. Vertebrate neurons, on the other hand, usually undergo dramatic degeneration in that portion of the axon that is separated from the cell body (Wallerian degeneration). Yet, proximal axons in the vertebrate peripheral nervous system can exhibit regeneration.

Axonal damage within the mammalian CNS was initially thought to result only in abortive attempts at regrowth (Ramon y Cajal, 1928). However, there have been reports of successful regeneration in the mammalian CNS (Clemente, 1964). For example, Björklund and coworkers demonstrated that by implanting different tissues, such as the iris, into the CNS they were able to elicit regenerative growth of certain axons (reviewed in Björklund & Stenevi, 1979). Even so, there does appear to be a fundamental difference in the regenerative capacity of axons within the central nervous system compared to those in the periphery (Kiernan, 1979). The reasons for this difference in regenerative ability between central and peripheral neurons have been the subject of intense debate for many years. For the most part, the explanations for this difference fall into two major classes. The first is that central neurons are intrinsically unable to regenerate axons for long distances. The second general hypothesis is that the CNS environment is less conducive to axonal growth than the PNS environment.

The regenerative ability of CNS tissue has also been demonstrated by transplanting fetal brain regions (Björklund, Segal, & Stenevi, 1979; Lund & Harvey, 1981). In addition, Kromer, Björklund, & Stenevi (1981) found that embryonic hippocampal implants promote the regeneration of septohippocampal axons in adult rats. However, it is not clear whether the transplant contributes to or induces a more favorable environment in the host tissue or whether the fetal neurons simply exhibit a greater intrinsic growth potential compared to mature neurons.

Another way to test the environmental hypothesis is to provide central neurons an opportunity to grow within a favorable environment such as the one to which peripheral neurons are normally exposed. Using segments of peripheral nerve grafted to the brain or spinal cord, neurons within the CNS extend axons for long distances within such peripheral bridges (David & Aguayo, 1981; Richardson, McGuinness, & Aguayo, 1982).

The demonstration that central axons will regenerate under favorable conditions indicates that there is no intrinsic inability of central neurons to grow axons, suggesting that the axonal environment determines whether successful regeneration will occur. The fact that central neurons can regenerate in certain circumstances provides some hope for the study of recovery from brain injury. However, the mechanism by which regenerative axonal growth is initiated clearly involves damage to the axon and, even so, for most mature central neurons, successful regeneration following injury to the CNS is a rare event. In many cases, for example, there is considerable cell death following axonal injury, limiting the potential for regeneration. Therefore, in terms of understanding anatomical correlates of learning and memory, the study of rearrangements involving interactions between uninjured neurons is more relevant. In other words, under what conditions will undamaged mature neurons form additional axons and/or synapses?

COLLATERAL SPROUTING

The second major type of anatomical plasticity, first documented in the PNS, was first referred to as collateral regeneration (Edds, 1953). Since then, it has also been observed in the CNS, but has come to be referred to as collateral sprouting since it does not require the regrowth of injured axons. As with regeneration, new axons (sprouts) are produced but, unlike regenerative growth, collateral sprouting occurs without direct injury to the neuron. This also means that the initiation of sprouting is due to changes in the neuron's environment. There are many examples of this kind of sprouting within both the peripheral and central nervous system (Cotman et al., 1981; Cotman & Nieto–Sampedro, 1984).

Before a damaged peripheral nerve regenerates, sprouting often occurs from adjacent, undamaged nerves. These nerves will send collateral axons to the denervated tissue and establish functional connections before the regenerating axons have arrived. Such collateral sprouting occurs in muscle (Brown, Holland, & Hopkins, 1981), skin (Diamond, Cooper, Turner, & Macintyre, 1976; Diamond, 1982), and other peripheral organs (Murray & Thompson, 1957), although not all types of peripheral axons exhibit this response (Horch, 1981; Jackson & Diamond, 1983). Often, the regenerating axons will displace the sprouted connections.

The possibility of collateral sprouting occurring within the CNS was suggested in a study by Liu and Chambers (1958) on the deafferented (denervated) cat spinal cord. The spinal cord receives sensory information by way of the dorsal roots and transmits information to the muscles and organs by way of the ventral roots. Thus the dorsal (sensory) roots can be transected without injuring the ventral (motor) roots. In the Liu and Chambers experiment, all but one of the dorsal roots entering the cat lumbar spinal cord were cut on one side. Several weeks later the remaining dorsal root and the corresponding root on the opposite side were cut. When the spinal cord was examined for signs of degeneration, more was found on the side of the isolated root compared to the side that had been left intact. These observations suggested that the uninjured axons of the spared root on the denervated side extended their innervation by collateral sprouting. Further characterization of this response was undertaken by Goldberger and Murray (1978), but not all attempts to reproduce this finding have been successful (Rodin, Sampogna & Kruger, 1983).

Although the Liu and Chambers experiment was limited by technical considerations, it certainly stimulated interest in this area. A more dramatic and convincing demonstration of collateral sprouting within the CNS was provided by Raisman (1969) and Raisman & Field (1973). Using electron microscopic techniques, which allowed for direct visualization of the synaptic contacts on nerve cells in the septal region of the rat brain, they showed that loss of synaptic connections to the dendrites of septal neurons, by cutting major pathways, resulted in the formation of new connections from axons that normally formed synapses only on the neuronal cell body. The new synapses presumably arose from initially undamaged neurons since they were identified by their subsequent degeneration following damage to a pathway that was not included in the original injury. This elegant demonstration that connectivity within the CNS is altered by injury, provided the first ultrastructural evidence that axons can be induced to make additional synaptic contacts in the adult mammalian CNS.

Since these pioneering observations in the septum, there have been several more demonstrations of collateral sprouting within other brain regions. Extensive studies have been performed of sprouting within the red nucleus, a group of large neurons within the midbrain which projects to the spinal cord and receives connections from the cerebral cortex and the cerebellum. Loss of the cerebellar connections results in the sprouting of undamaged cortical axons which form synaptic contacts on areas of the neurons denervated by the cerebellar lesion. In addition to the morphological evidence for new synaptic contacts (Nakamura, Mizuno, Konishi, & Sato, 1974), Tsukahara and co-workers have shown that the sprouted connections are functional when assessed with electrophysiological techniques (Tsukahara, 1981; Murakami, Tsukahara, & Fujito, 1977). Furthermore, similar changes have been found to occur in response to cross-reinnervation (switching nerves from one muscle to another) of muscles in the leg (Tsukahara & Fujito, 1976; Murakami, Katsumaru, Maeda, & Tsukahara, 1984) and to conditioning of a behavioral response (Tsukahara, 1981).

There are other examples of apparent collateral sprouting in the CNS (Goodman & Horel, 1966; Moore, Björklund, & Stenevi, 1971; Murray, Zimmer, & Raisman, 1979; Zimmer, Lawrence, & Raisman, 1982), but one region has been the focus of extensive studies of such anatomical plasticity namely, the hippocampal formation. This brain region is unique in that the major cell populations, as well as axonal projections, are separated into discrete layers or laminae which facilitates the detection of changes in connectivity. Figure 3.2 shows a schematic diagram of one portion of the hippocampal formation known as the dentate gyrus where many examples of collateral sprouting have been observed. The distribution of the major axonal populations which make synaptic connections with one of the major cell types, the dentate granule cell, is also shown.

The granule cells are grouped in a V-shaped layer (the V lying on its side) with dendrites extending outside the V in the molecular layer and their axons extending from within it (an area called the hilus) over to the layer of pyramidal cells (CA_3 zone). The major input to the granule cell dendrites is from neurons in a cortical region called the entorhinal cortex which make synapses along the outer two-thirds of the dendritic tree. Cells within the hilus (the inside of the V) and CA_3 zone also send axons to the inner third of the granule cell dendrites in the molecular layer of the same, or associational, and the opposite, or commissural, sides of the brain. For simplicity the projection is referred to as commissural/associational or, simply, C/A innervation.

In addition to these major inputs, the granule cells receive less numerous connections from other brain regions. These include a cholinergic innervation from the septal region, a noradrenergic input from the locus coeruleus and a serotonergic (5-HT) input from the raphe nuclei

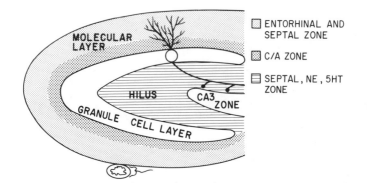

FIGURE 3.2   This drawing illustrates the terminal zones of the major inputs to the dentate gyrus of the rat hippocampal formation. The major cell type is the granule cell which occupies the V-shaped layer and has dendrites extending into the molecular layer. The granule cell axon (mossy fiber) extends through the hilus into the CA3 zone of the hippocampus where it innervates the pyramidal cell. The major inputs to the granule cells are from the entorhinal cortex (outer two-thirds of the molecular layer) and the hilus-CA3 area of the contralateral (commissural) and ipsilateral (associational) sides which occupy the inner third of the molecular layer (C/A zone). The hilus also receives input from the medial septal nucleus and from noradrenergic (NE) and serotonergic (5-HT) nuclei in the brain stem. The autonomic sympathetic innervation is normally restricted to blood vessels outside the dentate gyrus (shown at bottom of figure). However, following loss of the cholinergic innervation from the septum, the sympathetic fibers invade the hippocampal formation along branches of the blood vessels which they normally innervate and appear in association with the granule cells and their axons.

in the brain stem. These axons also have a characteristic distribution within the dentate gyrus with a particularly dense innervation of the hilus where many different cell types are found (Amaral, 1978).

Some of the first examples of collateral sprouting in the hippocampal formation (HF) were described by Cotman, Lynch, and co-workers (Cotman, Matthews, Taylor, & Lynch, 1973; Lynch, Matthews, Mosko, Parks, & Cotman, 1972; Lynch, Stanfield, Parks, & Cotman, 1974) as well as by Zimmer (1973). Removal of the major entorhinal input to the dentate granule cells resulted in proliferation of terminals from other afferent inputs including the contralateral entorhinal input, the C/A input, and the septal cholinergic input. Although much of the analysis was done at the light microscopic level, electron microscopic studies confirmed that synaptic contacts reappear in normal numbers following removal of the entorhinal input (Matthews, Cotman, & Lynch, 1976a,b; Steward & Vinsant, 1983). In addition, such contacts appear to be functional since electrophysiological recordings from the dentate molecular layer showed that stimulation of the contralateral entorhinal input, which contributes to the sprouting response, resulted in enhanced responses compared to controls (Steward, Cotman, & Lynch, 1973).

One of the interesting features of sprouting in the hippocampal formation is that only certain axons sprout in response to specific denervations. For example, the C/A axons sprout in response to loss of the entorhinal input, but the entorhinal axons do not sprout following loss of the C/A terminals. Sympathetic axons, which are normally confined to blood vessels outside the hippocampal formation, sprout in response to loss of the septal input and septal fibers respond to entorhinal lesions, but sympathetic fibers do not respond to entorhinal lesions (Crutcher & Davis, 1981). Specificity of sprouting has also been observed in the septum (Field, 1980; Field, Coldham, & Raisman, 1980). The observed hierarchy of sprouting has led to several hypotheses to account for the specificity of such growth. For example, the spatial or temporal sequence in which connections develop may determine subsequent rules for sprouting such as the proximity to denervated target sites (Zimmer, 1974). It is possible that axons within the hippocampal formation continually attempt to form additional synapses and loss of adjacent axons permits such contacts to be made or stabilized. In a sense, this would reflect prolonged developmental processes, which would be consistent with the cases in which sprouting seems to be most successful on the part of axons in the immediate vicinity of the denervation.

Although the sprouting of contralateral entorhinal axons following removal of the ipsilateral entorhinal input was initially thought to represent a new innervation (Steward et al., 1973, 1974), subsequent work established the presence of a normally sparse contralateral entorhinal input (Steward, Cotman, & Lynch, 1976). Thus, the sprouting response of the contralateral entorhinal projection is an example of hyperinnervation. In fact, most examples of collateral sprouting appear to represent hyperinnervations. This makes sense if sprouting is an attempt to replace lost inputs with inputs normally received by the denervated targets. However, if the sprouted connections provide an input that is functionally antagonistic to the lost input, such sprouting may be maladaptive.

SYMPATHETIC SPROUTING—A UNIQUE SPROUTING RESPONSE

An example of collateral sprouting in the hippocampal formation which appears to involve the growth of axons into a region they do not normally innervate is sympathetic ingrowth following septal denervation. This was first reported as an anomalous response to damage of the hippocampal formation or following septal lesions (Loy & Moore, 1977; Stenevi & Björklund, 1978). Subsequent work established that uninjured sympathetic fibers would grow into the hippocampal formation specifically following loss of septal (presumably cholinergic) fibers (Crutcher, Brothers, & Davis, 1979; Loy, Milner, & Moore, 1980; Crutcher, Brothers, & Davis, 1981; Crutcher & Davis, 1981). Loss of any other input did not elicit or enhance the sympathetic sprouting response (Loy et al., 1980; Crutcher et al., 1981). In addition to representing an apparent example of neoinnervation, this sprouting response is unique for several reasons. First of all, it appears to be an example of peripheral axons growing into the central nervous system. Second, it appears to be a heterotypic response since the sprouting neurons arise from a different location and since the transmitter present in sympathetic axons, norepinephrine, is different from that released by the septal fibers, acetylcholine. Thirdly, the sympathetic axons, which normally innervate extracerebral vascular targets, may be seeking neuronal targets, implying the presence of a powerful sprouting signal released by the denervation.

Studies of this sprouting response support the hypothesis that the mechanism initiating sprouting involves the release of a growth factor. Disconnecting the superior cervical ganglion, the source of the sprouting axons, from the rest of the nervous system did not prevent the sprouting (Crutcher et al., 1979). Destruction of the dentate granule cells, however, did prevent sprouting (Crutcher & Davis, 1982). In addition, the sympathetic fibers grew into the hippocampal formation even if the septal lesion was placed before the cholinergic innervation had completely developed (Crutcher, 1982). Taken together, these results suggest that target cells of the septohippocampal projection, perhaps the dentate granule cells, normally provide a growth factor to septal cholinergic neurons. When granule cells are denervated of septal input, or the input is prevented from developing, sympathetic fibers sprout in response to the putative growth factor.

Although this hypothesis is speculative, increasing evidence supports the basic idea that sympathetic sprouting is regulated by a growth factor released by the denervated hippocampal formation. Sympathetic ganglia transplanted to the region of the hippocampal formation exhibit enhanced innervation and survival if the septal input is removed (Björklund & Stenevi, 1981; Gage, Björklund, & Stenevi, 1984). The identity of the putative growth factor is unknown but there are several theoretical and experimental reasons for expecting the active substance to be similar to nerve growth factor (NGF). First, medial septal neurons exhibit specific retrograde transport of radioactive NGF injected into the hippocampal formation (Schwab, Otten, Agid, & Thoenen, 1979). Second, sympathetic neurons will respond to intracerebral injections of NGF, by growing into the CNS of chick embryos and neonatal rats (Levi–Montalcini, Chen, & Chen, 1978). Third, NGF has recently been shown to affect some cholinergic neurons in vivo (Gnahn, Hefti, Heuman, Schwab, & Thoenen, 1983; Hefti, Dravid, & Hartikka, 1984) and in vitro (Honegger & Lenoir, 1982; Collins, 1984). Fourth, NGF-like material has been detected in extracts of the rat hippocampal formation (Crutcher & Collins, 1982).

Perhaps the most convincing evidence for a role of NGF-like material in sympathetic sprouting was recently reported by Collins and Crutcher (1985). Slices of the rat hippocampal formation were used to condition medium that was then applied to embryonic chick sympathetic ganglia in vitro. Medium exposed to slices from rats receiving medial septal lesions elicited greater growth from sympathetic ganglia than did medium exposed to control slices. More importantly, the majority of the activity was inhibited by affinity-purified antibodies to NGF demonstrating that the active material is antigenically and biologically similar to mouse submaxillary gland NGF. If this in vitro data reflects a similar increase in vivo, it seems very likely that an NGF-like substance is involved in this sprouting response.

This example of collateral sprouting dramatically emphasizes the plasticity of the mature nervous system and provides support for the growth-factor regulation of at least one anatomical rearrangement. The fact that sprouting continues without neuronal input to the sprouting neurons emphasizes the preeminence of the denervated target in initiating the response. Furthermore, the growing axons appear to depend on the presence of a particular target cell population, namely the dentate granule cells, for successful sprouting to occur. Whether this target cell population actually represents the source of the putative growth factor can only be determined through additional experimentation. Other mechanisms have also been proposed to account for other examples of collateral sprouting, and these will be examined in more detail in the following section.

PROPOSED MECHANISMS UNDERLYING ANATOMICAL PLASTICITY

The relative importance of the intrinsic growth potential of neurons versus the role of their target in development, regeneration and collateral sprouting is at the heart of the debate on mechanisms. Even though a target growth factor seems to be involved in the sympathetic sprouting response, no single mechanism is likely to underly the diverse examples of anatomical plasticity that have been observed. Damage to an axon appears to be sufficient to elicit the growth response that characterizes regeneration and may also account for the pruning response. Thus, a neuronal cell body has some means of detecting injury to its axon. However, the initiation of collateral sprouting, which does not necessarily involve injury to the reactive neurons, must involve other interactions. These other interactions can be grouped into two general classes. The first class of mechanisms involves changes in the neuronal environment that allow for the stabilization of ongoing axonal growth and/or synaptogenesis. The second class includes all mechanisms involving the initiation of growth as a result of the lesion, such as the release of a growth factor from the target or from the injured axons. Although the distinction between these two classes of mechanisms is not always clear, this categorization is useful when discussing neuronal interactions underlying anatomical plasticity.

The possibility that axons are always in a state of growth, or, in other words, development never really stops, was raised by Sotelo and Palay (1971) from electron microscopic observations of degeneration and apparent growth in the lateral vestibular nucleus of the adult rat. This hypothesis also received support from other investigators (Goodman, Bogdasatrian, & Horel, 1973; Cotman et al., 1981). If axons are normally trying to expand their territory, then something must normally prevent such expansion. Thus, neurons attempt to expand their territory but may be prevented from doing so by neighboring axons (Diamond, Cooper, Turner, & Macintyre, 1976) or the lack of some requirement such as synaptic space, trophic support, or absence of a suitable substrate for growth. Removal of adjacent axons or partial target denervation could alter any, or all, of these factors and allow for expansion of the axonal projection.

The possibility that collateral sprouting is initiated by growth factors released from the denervated target is an extension of the idea that similar growth substances (trophic factors) underly the normal development of connections in the nervous system. This concept is supported by observations such as those made by Ebendal, Olson, Seiger, & Hedlund (1980), who showed that the iris produces nerve growth factor following denervation of its sympathetic innervation. There is also evidence for the presence of growth factors within the peripheral and central nervous systems and a growth factor is thought to be involved in the sympathetic sprouting response previously described. However, it is not clear how such factors could regulate synaptogenesis once axonal sprouting occurs. Competition of some sort must be involved in axonal sprouting following selective denervation since the lamination of axons within a dendritic region, such as the dentate molecular layer, is retained even following massive denervation (Lynch et al., 1972).

Once axonal growth or synaptogenesis is underway, other factors appear to be involved in the ultimate success or failure of the rearrangement. For example, as in development, the amount of activity of the neuron has been proposed to regulate axonal growth and synaptogenesis (Diamond, 1982). This concept is reminiscent of Hebb's idea but extends to the level of the control of growth. Thus, the amount of activity within a set of axons will determine its effectiveness in establishing target connections. This idea is appealing, since it is consistent with the loss of synapses during development and the reported effects of environmental manipulation on synaptogenesis.

There have been suggestions that specific rules apply to collateral sprouting within the CNS (Schneider, 1973; Cotman et al., 1981). For instance, most examples of sprouting involve an expansion of a previous innervation (hyperinnervation). The several examples of collateral sprouting which have been documented in the hippocampal formation, do involve the formation of additional synaptic contacts with neurons that are normally contacted by those axons. One possible exception is the case of sympathetic sprouting described above since sympathetic fibers are not normally present in the hippocampal formation. The same principal applies to the examples of sprouting in the septum and red nucleus. However, one could argue that the sprouted connections are fundamentally different, because they are made with portions of the postsynaptic cell which do not normally receive such contacts. Certainly in the case of sprouting in the red nucleus, the new synapses are functional but their effect is different from that in normal animals. It is not clear, therefore, if this is an adaptive or maladaptive response.

Another general rule that has been proposed to apply to sprouting is that the transmitter of the lost synapses is functionally similar to the transmitter used by the sprouted terminals (homotypic sprouting). This certainly is the case when the sprouting axons arise from neurons which are of the same type as those which were destroyed. For example, Gage, Björklund, & Stenevi (1983a) reported that partial noradrenergic or cholinergic denervation of the hippocampal formation results in sprouting of the remaining corresponding fibers. However, in most other cases of sprouting, it is not known what transmitter is used by either the degenerated or sprouted afferents. Certainly in the case of sympathetic sprouting previously described, a different transmitter is present in the sprouting neurons compared to the removed input. Thus, the validity of the hypothesis that most sprouting is homotypic (Cotman et al., 1981) depends on identifying the transmitters used by the axonal systems that are involved. It may also be necessary to establish different criteria for determining whether two inputs are homotypic or heterotypic. For example, although sympathetic neurons are heterotypic as far as transmitter identity is concerned, when compared to septohippocampal neurons, they may be homotypic in their responsiveness to NGF.

It is possible that the conditions which allow for maintenance of synaptic connections are also necessary for alterations in their efficacy. If synapses are continually turning over, then it is easy to conceive of a mechanism whereby behavioral plasticity would be based on the selective stabilization of specific synaptic connections similar to processes occurring in development (Greenough, 1984). A postsynaptic neuron could produce more recognition sites for a particular kind of synapse or more growth factor which would increase the probability of maintaining a synaptic connection. There could be as many different kinds of membrane markers or trophic molecules as there are different classes of synapses. The production of such factors could be related to the amount of activity (transmitter or other substances released) of the presynaptic terminals (a Hebb synapse). Such interactions could be limited to the specific pathways involved in learning a particular behavior thus making detection of such changes difficult, although not necessarily impossible.

Another hypothesis that explains the specificity of synaptic connections is that learning and memory arises through the loss of synaptic connections. Although this notion is intuitively less appealing, it is consistent with the overall process of development previously described. The net result is the same as that obtained in the selective stabilization hypothesis, namely the formation of specific connections, but the fundamental process differs in that synapses are lost instead of formed. This hypothesis is related to the parcellation theory of Ebbesson (1980) who proposed that the specificity of connections in mature organisms is obtained through the loss of pathways and synapses.

Assessing the validity of the various proposed mechanisms depends on what kind of plasticity, such as regeneration or collateral sprouting, one is discussing. Even so, it is very difficult to compare the plasticity of one brain region to another, because the connections vary widely, as does the architecture of the nervous tissue. One of the reasons that studies of anatomical plasticity within the hippocampal formation have been so successful is that the discrete lamination and segregation of cells and axons allows for relatively easy detection of changes in the pattern of connections.

The hippocampal formation exhibits tremendous anatomical plasticity and is thought to be directly involved in certain forms of learning and memory. Although the changes in hippocampal anatomy and the organism's behavior are difficult to correlate directly, it seems likely that there is some relationship between them. Whether these correlations will involve mechanisms that are thought to operate in the rearrangements described here remains to be determined.

FUNCTIONAL SIGNIFICANCE OF ANATOMICAL PLASTICITY

The demonstration of plasticity within the adult nervous system provides for the possibility that learning and memory may involve similar rearrangements. The other side of the coin is to ask whether examples of plasticity have behavioral significance. There is relatively little information on this subject and there are many pitfalls associated with the experimental approaches used to study this question (Steward, 1982; Marshall, 1985). Nevertheless, there have been studies which assess the functional significance of anatomical rearrangements.

There is little doubt that regeneration or collateral sprouting of peripheral nerves leads to recovery of function to varying degrees (Weddell, Cuttmann, & Gutman, 1941; Edds, 1953). One of the earliest suggestions that collateral sprouting in the CNS also has functional significance was that of McCouch, Austin, Liu, & Liu (1958) who proposed that the sprouting of the spared dorsal root preparation studied by Liu and Chambers led to spasticity. Detailed studies of the behavioral consequences of this procedure were performed by Goldberger and Murray (1978, 1982). They found that the rules governing sprouting in the spinal cord seem to correlate with the recovery of the affected limb or the absence of recovery, such as spasticity.

Loesche and Steward (1977) as well as Scheff and Cotman (1977) examined the behavioral consequences of sprouting in the hippocampal formation and found that animals regained performance on a spontaneous alternation task that correlated with the growth of synapses in the dentate gyrus. Gage et al. (1983a) found a correlation between collateral sprouting and behavioral recovery in studies of adrenergic and cholinergic inputs to the hippocampal formation. Azmitia, Buchan, & Williams (1978) found evidence for behavioral recovery correlating with collateral sprouting of serotonergic axons in the hippocampal formation. An even more dramatic demonstration that a sprouted pathway can be functional is the finding that kindling (stimulation-induced seizures) could be elicited from the sprouted pathway but not from the normally sparse contralateral entorhinal projection (Messenheimer, Harris, & Steward, 1979). There is also evidence that restoration of certain behaviors may occur following transplantation of neural tissue (Dunnett, Low, Iversen, Stenevi, & Björklund, 1982; Low et al., 1982; Gage, Dunnett, Stenevi, & Björklund, 1983). The restoration of certain learning behaviors was also recently found to correlate with the amount of innervation provided by septal grafts to aged rats (Gage, Björklund, Stenevi, Dunnett, & Kelly, 1984).

Other attempts to identify functional significance for rearrangements in the CNS have not been as successful. In the case of sympathetic invasion of the CNS, there was a clear correlation between the recovery of performance on a radial-arm maze task and the time course of sprouting (Crutcher, Kesner, & Novak, 1983). However, removal of the superior cervical ganglion, which results in selective removal of the sprouted projection, did not affect the recovered behavior. This does not mean that such sprouting is not functional since there are other potential functions that have not been measured. The failure to identify functional significance for this and other anatomical rearrangements emphasizes the difficulty in establishing the correlation between morphological changes and functional plasticity, including behavior. The reverse correlation between behavioral plasticity and anatomical changes, is equally difficult, as is hopefully evident from the information presented in this chapter.

SUMMARY AND CONCLUSIONS

This brief excursion into the realm of anatomical plasticity should convince the reader that the nervous system is not a static hard-wired structure but, rather, exhibits considerable lability which, for lack of a better term, has been called plasticity. This does not mean that neuronal rearrangements underlie every example of behavioral modification. There is no reason to expect that all forms of learning require the formation or loss of synapses. Changes in the efficacy of synapses are adequate to account for certain forms of learning. On the other hand, it is not clear when development ends. Synaptic turnover may continue in the mature organism perhaps at a higher rate in some brain regions than in others. Memory, on the other hand, implies a long-lasting change in neuronal function that may be associated with the stabilization of synapses.

There are many mechanisms, including those outlined above, which could underlie connections established during development but not be necessary for the turnover of synapses in the mature state. Mechanisms not covered in this chapter such as the unmasking of silent synapses (Wall and Egger, 1971; Merrill & Wall, 1978) or changes in the amount or effectiveness of released transmitter would be effective in changing the functional connectivity of the CNS without altering the anatomy (Mendell, 1984; Marshall, 1985).

It seems likely that several mechanisms are all operating to some extent in different kinds of plasticity, including learning and memory. For example, the short-term changes in synaptic efficacy may relate to short-term memory, whereas longer traces may require more permanent changes in connectivity, perhaps even involving the establishment of new synaptic contacts (Hebb, 1949).

The main conclusions that are reached in this chapter can be summarized as follows:

1. Neuronal development is characterized by a period of overproduction of neurons, axons, and synapses with subsequent loss of a certain proportion of all of these elements.
2. The development of specific neuronal connections appears to depend on several factors such as appropriate pathway selection, target identification, and synapse formation and elimination.
3. Although there is some evidence for anatomical correlates of behavioral plasticity in mature organisms, the most dramatic correlations between anatomical and behavioral changes occur during development.
4. Evidence that connectivity in the adult nervous system is "plastic" comes mainly from studies of rearrangements following injury. The major type of anatomical plasticity observed in the CNS is collateral sprouting which, in some cases, appears to involve the release of growth factors, but is also regulated by the availability of suitable substrates for growth and the amount of neuronal activity.
5. The correlation between behavioral plasticity and anatomical changes still awaits direct confirmation but the neuronal plasticity exhibited by an injured nervous system may well signify the kinds of mechanisms underlying nontraumatic influences of the environment on neuronal connectivity.

REFERENCES

Amaral, D. G. (1978). A golgi study of cell types in the hilar region of the hippocampus in the rat. *Journal of Comparative Neurology, 182*, 851–914.

Azmitia, E. C., Buchan, A. M., & Williams, J. H. (1978). Structural and functional restoration by collateral sprouting of hippocampal 5-HT axons. *Nature, 274*, 374–376.

Bailey, C. H., & Chen, M. (1983). Morphological basis of long-term habituation and sensitization in Aplysia. *Science, 220*, 91–93.

Barde, Y.-A., Edgar, D. & Thoenen, H. (1980). Sensory neurons in culture: Changing requirements for survival factors during embryonic development. *Proceedings of the National Academy of Sciences, 77*, 1199–1203.

Bayer, S. A., Yackel, J. W., & Puri, P. S. (1982). Neurons in the rat dentate gyrus granular layer substantially increase during juvenile and adult life. *Science, 216*, 890–892.

Bekoff, A. (1981). Embryonic development of the neural circuitry underlying motor coordination. In W. M. Cowan (Ed.) *Studies in Developmental Neurobiology* (pp. 134–170). New York: Oxford University Press.

Björklund, A., Segal, M., & Stenevi, U. (1979). Functional reinnervation of rat hippocampus by locus coeruleus implants. *Brain Research, 170*, 409–426.

Björklund, A., & Stenevi, U. (1979). Regeneration of monoaminergic and cholinergic neurons in the mammalian central nervous system. *Physiological Reviews, 59*, 62–100.

Björklund, A., & Stenevi, U. (1981). In vivo evidence for a hippocampal adrenergic neuronotrophic factor specifically released on septal deafferentation. *Brain Research, 229*, 403–428.

Blakemore, C., Vital–Durand, F., & Garey, L. J. (1981). Recovery from monocular deprivation in the monkey: I. Reversal of physiological effects in the visual cortex. *Proceedings of the Royal Society of London* (Series B) **213**, 399–423.

Bregman, B. S., & Goldberger, M. E. (1982). Anatomical plasticity and sparing of function after spinal cord damage in neonatal cats. *Science, 217*, 553–555.

Brown, M. C., Holland, R. L., & Hopkins, W. G. (1981). Motor nerve sprouting. *Annual Review Neuroscience, 4*, 17–42.

Carbonetto, S., & Muller, K. J. (1982). Nerve fiber growth and the cellular response to axotomy. *Current Topics in Developmental Biology, 17*, 33–76.

Carlin, R. K. & Siekevitz, P. (1983). Plasticity in the central nervous system: Do synapses divide? *Proceedings of the National Academy of Sciences, 80*, 3517–3521.

Castro, A. J., & Mihailoff, G. A. (1983). Corticopontine remodelling after cortical and/or cerebellar lesions in newborn rats. *Journal of Comparative Neurology, 219*, 112–123.

Changeux, J. P., & Danchin, A. (1976). Selective stabilization of developing synapses as a mechanism for the specification of neuronal networks. *Nature, 264*, 705–711.

Clemente, C. D. (1964). Regeneration in the vertebrate central nervous system. *International Review of Neurobiology, 6*, 257–301.

Clopton, B. M., & Silverman, M. S. (1977). Plasticity of binaural interaction: 2. Critical period and changes in midline response *Journal Neurophysiology, 40*, 1275–1280.

Collett, T. S., & Cartwright, B. A. (1983). Eidetic images in insects: Their role in navigation. *Trends in Neuroscience, 6*, 101–105.

Collins, F. & Garrett, J. E., Jr. (1980). Elongating nerve fibers are guided by a pathway of material released from embryonic nonneuronal cells. *Proceedings of the National Academy of Sciences, 77*, 6226–6228.

Collins, F. (1984). An effect of nerve growth factor on the parasympathetic ciliary ganglion. *Journal of Neuroscience, 4*, 1281–1288.

Collins, F. & Crutcher, K. A. (1985). Neurotrophic activity in the adult rat hippocampal formation: Regional distribution and increase after septal lesion. *Journal of Neuroscience, 5*, 2809–2814.

Cotman, C. W., Matthews, D. A., Taylor, D., & Lynch, G. S. (1973). Synaptic rearrangement in the dentate gyrus: Histochemical evidence of adjustments after lesions in premature and adult rats. *Proceedings of the National Academy of Sciences, 70*, 3473–3477.

Cotman, C. W., & Nadler, V. G. (1978). Reactive synaptogenesis in the hippocampus. In C. W. Cotman (Ed.), *Neuronal Plasticity* (pp. 227–271). New York: Raven Press.

Cotman, C. W., Nieto–Sampedro, M., & Harris, E. W. (1981). Synapse replacement in the nervous system of adult vertebrates. *Physiological Reviews, 61*, 684–784.

Cotman, C. W., & Nieto–Sampedro, M. (1984). Cell biology of synaptic plasticity. *Science, 225*, 1287–1299.

Cowan, W. M., & Finger, T. E. (1982). Regeneration and regulation in the developing central nervous system. In N. C. Spitzer (Ed.), *Neuronal Development* (pp. 377–415). New York: Plenum Press.

Cowan, W. M., Fawcett, J. W., O'Leary, D. D. M. & Stanfield, B. B. (1984). Regressive events in neurogenesis. *Science, 225*, 1258–1265.

Crain, B. J., & Hall, W. C. (1980a). The organization of the lateral posterior nucleus of the golden hamster after neonatal superior colliculus lesions. *Journal of Comparative Neurology, 193*, 383–401.

Crain, B. J., & Hall, W. C. (1980b). The organization of afferents to the lateral posterior nucleus in the golden hamster after different combinations of neonatal lesions. *Journal of Comparative Neurology, 193*, 403–412.

Crepel, F., Mariani, J., & Delhaye–Bouchaud, N. (1976). Evidence for a multiple innervation of Purkinje cells by climbing fibers in the immature rat cerebellum. *Journal of Neurobiology, 7*, 567–578.

Crepel, F., Delhaye–Bouchoud, N., & Dupont, J. L. (1981). Fate of the multiple innervation of cerebellar Purkinje cells by climbing fibers in immature control, X-irradiated, and hypothyroid rats. *Developmental Brain Research, 1*, 59–71.

Crutcher, K. A., Brothers, L. & Davis, J. N. (1979). Sprouting of sympathetic nerves in the absence of afferent input. *Experimental Neurology, 66*, 778–783.

Crutcher, K. A., Brothers, L., & Davis, J. N. (1981). Sympathetic noradrenergic sprouting in response to central cholinergic denervation: A histochemical study of neuronal sprouting in the rat hippocampal formation. *Brain Research, 210*, 115–128.

Crutcher, K. A., & Davis, J. N. (1981). Sympathetic noradrenergic sprouting in response to central cholinergic denervation. *Trends in Neurosciences, 4*, 70–72.

Crutcher, K. A., & Collins, F. (1982). In vitro evidence for two distinct hippocampal growth factors: Basis of neuronal plasticity? *Science, 217*, 67–68.

Crutcher, K. A. (1982). Neonatal septal lesions result in sympathohippocampal innervation in the adult rat. *Experimental Neurology, 76*, 1–11.

Crutcher, K. A., & Davis, J. N. (1982). Target regulation of sympathetic sprouting in the rat hippocampal formation. *Experimental Neurology, 75*, 347–359.

Crutcher, K. A., Kesner, R. P., & Novak, J. M. (1983). Medial septal lesions, radial arm maze performance, and sympathetic sprouting: A study of recovery of function. *Brain Research, 262*, 91–98.

David, S., & Aguayo, A. J. (1981). Axonal elongation into peripheral nervous system "bridges" after central nervous system injury in adult rats. *Science, 214*, 931–933.

Diamond, J., Cooper, E., Turner, C., & Macintyre, L. (1976). Trophic regulation of nerve sprouting. *Science, 193*, 371–377.

Diamond, J. (1982). Modeling and competition in the nervous system: Clues from the sensory innervation of skin. *Current Topics in Developmental Biology, 17*, 147–205.

Dunnett, S. B., Low, W. C., Iversen, S. D., Stenevi, U., & Bjorklund, A. (1982). Septal transplants restore maze learning in rats with fornix-fimbria lesions. *Brain Research, 251*, 335–348.

Dyson, S. E., & Jones, D. G. (1984). Synaptic remodeling during development and maturation: Junction differentiation and splitting as a mechanism for modifying connectivity. *Development Brain Research, 13*, 125–137.

Ebbesson, S. O. E. (1980). The parcellation theory and its relation to interspecific variability in brain organization, evolutionary and ontogenetic development, and neuronal plasticity. *Cell and Tissue Research, 213*, 179–212.

Ebendal, T., Olson, L., Seiger, A., & Hedlund, K.-O. (1980). Nerve growth factors in the rat iris. *Nature, 286*, 25–28.

Edds, M. V., Jr. (1953). Collateral regeneration. *Quarterly Review of Biology, 28*, 260–276.

Erzurumlu, R. S., & Killackey, H. P. (1982). Cortical and sensitive periods in neurobiology. In A. A. Moscona & A. Monroy (Eds.), *Current Topics in Developmental Biology Vol. 17* (pp. 207–240). New York: Academic Press.

Ferguson, B. A. (1983). Development of motor innervation of the chick following dorsal-ventral limb-bud rotations. *Journal of Neuroscience, 3*, 1760–1772.

Field, P. M. (1980). Synapse reinnervation after injury in the adult rat brain: Failure of fimbrial axons to reinnervate the bed nucleus or the stria terminalis. *Brain Research, 189*, 91–101.

Field, P. M., Coldham, D. E., & Raisman, G. (1980). Synapse formation after injury in the adult rat brain: Preferential reinnervation of denervated fimbrial sites by axons of the contralateral fimbria. *Brain Research, 189*, 103–113.

Field, P. M., & Raisman, G. (1983). Relative slowness of heterotypic synaptogenesis in the septal nuclei. *Brain Research, 272*, 83–99.

Fifkova, E., & Van Herreveld, A. (1977). Long-lasting morphological changes in dendritic spines of dentate granular cells following stimulation of the entorhinal area. *Journal of Neurocytology, 6*, 211–230.

Finger, S., & Stein, D. G. (1982). *Brain Damage and recovery. Research and clinical perspectives.* New York: Academic Press.

Gage, F. H., Björklund, A. & Stenevi, U. (1983a). Reinnervation of the partially deafferented hippocampus by compensatory collateral sprouting by aminergic and cholinergic afferents in the hippocampal formation. *Brain Research, 268*, 27–37.

Gage, F. H., Bjorklund, A., Stenevi, U., & Dunnett, S. B. (1983b). Functional correlates of compensatory collateral sprouting by aminergic and cholinergic afferents in the hippocampal formation. *Brain Research, 268*, 39–47.

Gage, F. H., Dunnett, S. B., Stenevi, U., & Björklund, A. (1983). Aged rats: Recovery of motor impairments by intrastriatal nigral grafts. *Science, 221*, 55–959.

Gage, F. H., Björklund, A., Stenevi, U., Dunnett, S. B., & Kelly, P. A. T. (1984). Intrahippocampal septal grafts ameliorate learning impairments in aged rats. *Science, 225*, 533–536.

Gage, F. H., Björklund, A., & Stenevi, U. (1984). Denervation releases a neuronal survival factor in adult rat hippocampus. *Nature, 308*, 637–639.

Gall, C., & Lynch, G. (1981). Fiber architecture of the dentate gyrus following ablation of the entorhinal cortex in rats of different ages: Evidence for two forms of axon sprouting in the immature brain. *Neuroscience, 6*, 903–910.

Gnahn, H., Hefti, F., Heuman, R., Schwab, M. E., & Thoenen, H. (1983). NGF-mediated increase of choline acetyltransferase (CHAT) in the neonatal rat forebrain: Evidence for a physiological role of NGF in the brain? *Developmental Brain Research, 9*, 45–52.

Goldberger, M. E., & Murray, M. (1978). Recovery of movement and axonal sprouting may obey some of the same laws. In C. W. Cotman (Ed.), *Neuronal Plasticity* (pp. 73–96). New York: Raven Press.

Goldberger, M. E., & Murray, M. (1982). Lack of sprouting and its presence after lesions of the cat spinal cord. *Brain Research, 241*, 227–239.

Goldman, S. A., & Nottebohm, F. (1983). Neuronal production, migration, and differentiation in a vocal control nucleus of the adult female canary brain. *Proceedings of the National Academy of Sciences, 80*, 2390–2394.

Goodman, D. C. & Horel, J. A. (1966). Sprouting of optic tract projections in the brain stem of the rat. *Journal of Comparative Neurology, 127*, 71–88.

Goodman, D. C., Bogdasatrian, R. S., & Horel, J. A. (1973). Axonal sprouting of ipsilateral optic tract following opposite eye removal. *Brain, Behavior and Evolution, 8*, 27–50.

Greenough, W. T. (1984). Structural correlates of information storage in the mammalian brain: A review and hypothesis. *Trends in Neurosciences, 7*, 229–233.

Greenough, W. T., Hwang, H. F. & Gorman, C. (1985). Evidence for active synapse formation or altered postsynaptic metabolism in visual cortex of rats reared in complex environments. *Proceedings of the National Academy of Sciences, 82*, 4549–4552.

Guth, L., (1975). History of central nervous system regeneration research. *Experimental Neurology, 48*, 3–15.

Guth, L., & Bernstein, J. J. (1961). Selectivity in the re-establishment of synapses in the superior cervical sympathetic ganglion of the cat. *Experimental Neurology, 4*, 59–69.

Hamburger, V., & Levi–Montalcini, R. (1949). Poliferation, differentation and degeneration in the spinal ganglia of the chick embryo under normal experimental conditions. *Journal of Experimental Zoology, 11*, 457–501.

Hebb, D. O. (1949). *The organization of behavior.* New York: Wiley.

Hefti, F., Dravid, A., & Hartikka, J. (1984). Chronic intraventricular injections of nerve growth factor elevate hippocampal choline acetlytransferase activity in adult rats with partial septo-hippocampal lesions. *Brain Research, 293*, 305–311.

Ho, R. K., & Goodman, C. (1982). Peripheral pathways are pioneered by an array of central and peripheral neurons in grasshopper embryos. *Nature, 297*, 404–406.

Hollyday, M., & Hamburger, V. (1976). Reduction of the naturally occurring motor neuron loss by enlargement of the periphery. *Journal of Comparative Neurology, 170*, 311–320.

Honegger, P., & Lenoir, D. (1982). Nerve growth factor (NGF) stimulation of cholinergic telencephalic neurons in aggregating cell cultures. *Developmental Brain Research, 3*, 229–238.

Horch, K. W. (1981). Absence of functional collateral sprouting of mechanoreceptor axons into denervated areas of mammalian skin. *Experimental Neurology, 74*, 313–317.

Horn, G. (1981). Neural mechanisms of learning: An analysis of imprinting in the domestic chick. *Proceedings of the Royal Society of London* (Series B), *213*, 101–137.

Hubel, D. H., Wiesel, T. N., & LeVay, S. (1977). Plasticity of ocular dominance columns in monkey striate cortex. *Philosophical Transactions of The Royal Society of London* (Series B), *278*, 371–409.

Jackson, P. C., & Diamond, J. (1983). Failure of intact cutaneous mechanosensory axons to sprout functional collaterals in skin of adult rabbits. *Brain Research, 273*, 277–283.

Jackson, P. C., & Diamond, J. (1984). Temporal and spatial constraints on the collateral sprouting of low-threshold mechanosensory nerves in the skin of rats. *Journal of Comparative Neurology, 226*, 336–345.

Jackson, H., & Parks, T. N. (1982). Functional synapse elimination in the developing avian cochlear nucleus with simultaneous reduction in cochlear nerve axon branching. *Journal of Neuroscience, 2*, 1736–1743.

Jacobson, M. (1978). *Developmental neurobiology*. New York: Plenum.

Kaplan, M. S., & Bell, D. H. (1983). Neuronal proliferation in the 9-month-old rodent—radioautographic study of granule cells in the hippocampus. *Experimental Brain Research, 52*, 1–5.

Kaplan, M. S., & Bell, D. H. (1984). Mitotic neuroblasts in the 9-day-old and 11-month-old rodent hippocampus. *Journal of Neuroscience, 4*, 1429–1441.

Kandel, E., & Schwartz, J. H. (1982). Molecular biology of learning: Modulation of transmitter release. *Science, 218*, 433–443.

Kiernan, J. A. (1979). Hypotheses concerned with axonal regeneration in the mammalian nervous system. *Biological Reviews, 54*, 155–197.

Knyihar, E., Csillik, B., & Rakic, P. (1978). Transient synapses in the embryonic primate spinal cord. *Science, 202*, 1206–1209.

Kromer, L. F., Björklund, A., & Stenevi, U. (1981). Regeneration of the septohippocampal pathways in adult rats is promoted by utilizing embryonic hippocampal implants as bridges. *Brain Research, 210*, 173–200.

Landmesser, L. T., & Pilar, G. (1978). Interactions between neurons and their targets during in vivo synaptogenesis. *Federation Proceedings*, 2016–2022.

Landmesser, L. T. (1980). The generation of neuromuscular specificity. *Annual Review of Neurosciences, 3*, 279–302.

Landmesser, L. (1984). The development of specific motor pathways in the chick embryo. *Trends in Neurosciences, 7*, 336–339.

Lee, K. S., Schottler, F., Oliver, M., & Lynch, G. (1980). Brief bursts of high-frequency stimulation produce two types of structural change in rat hippocampus. *Journal of Neurophysiology, 44*, 247–258.

Letourneau, P. C. (1982). Nerve fiber growth and its regulation by extrinsic factors. In N. C. Spitzer (Ed.), *Neuronal Development* (pp. 213–254). New York: Plenum Press.

LeVay, S., Stryker, M. P., & Shatz, C. J. (1978). Ocular dominance columns and their development in layer IV of the cat's visual cortex: A quantitative study. *Journal of Comparative Neurology, 179*, 223–244.

LeVay, S., Wiesel, T. N., & Hubel, D. H. (1980). The development of ocular dominance columns in normal and visually deprived monkeys. *Journal of Comparative Neurology, 191*, 1–51.

Levi–Montalcini, R., Chen, M. G. M., & Chen, J. S. (1978). Neurotropic effects of the nerve growth factor in chick embryos and in neonatal rodents. *Zoon, 6*, 201–212.

Levy, W. G., & Steward, O. (1979). Synapses as associative memory elements in the hippocampal formation. *Brain Research, 175*, 233–245.

Lichtman, J. W. (1977). The reorganization of synaptic connexions in the rat submandibular ganglion during postnatal development. *Journal of Physiology, 273*, 155–177.

Lichtman, J. W., & Purves, D. (1980). The elimination of redundant preganglionic innervation to hamster sympathetic ganglion cells in early postnatal life. *Journal of Physiology, 301*, 213–228.

Lichtman, J. W. (1980). On the predominantly single innervation of submandibular ganglion cells in the rat. *Journal of Physiology, 302*, 121–130.

Lieberman, A. R. (1971). The axon reaction: A review of the principal features of perikaryal responses to axon injury. *International Review of Neurobiology, 14*, 49–124.

Liu, C–N., & Chambers, W. W. (1958). Intraspinal sprouting of dorsal root axons. *Archives of Neurology and Psychiatry, 79*, 46–61.

Loesche, J., & Steward, O. (1977). Behavioral correlates of denervation and reinnervation of the hippocampal formation of the rat: Recovery of alternation performance following unilateral entorhinal cortex lesions. *Brain Research Bulletin, 2*, 31–39.

Low, W. C., Lewis, P. R., & Bunch, S. T., Dunnett, S. B., Thomas, S. R., Iversen, S. D., Björklund, A., & Stenevi, U. (1982). Functional recovery following neural transplantation of embryonic septal nuclei in adult rats with septohippocampal lesions. *Nature, 300*, 260–262.

Loy, R., Milner, T. A., & Moore, R. Y. (1980). Sprouting of sympathetic axons in the hippocampal formation: Conditions necessary to elicit ingrowth. *Experimental Neurology, 67*, 399–411.

Loy, R., & Moore, R. Y. (1977). Anomalous innervation of the hippocampal formation by peripheral sympathetic axons following mechanical injury. *Experimental Neurology, 57*, 645–650.

Lund, R. D., & Lund, J. S. (1973). Reorganization of the retinotectal pathway in rats after neonatal retinal lesions. *Experimental Neurology, 40*, 377–390.

Lund, R. D., & Harvey, A. R. Transplantation of tectal tissue in rats: I. Organization of transplants and pattern of distribution of host afferents within them. *Journal of Comparative Neurology, 201*, 191–209.

Lynch, G., Deadwyler, S., & Cotman, C. (1973). Postlesion axonal growth produces permanent functional connections. *Science, 180*, 1364–1366.

Lynch, D., Matthews, D., Mosko, S., Parks, T., & Cotman, C. (1972). Induced acetylcholinesterase-rich layer in rat dentate gyrus following entorhinal lesions. *Brain Research, 842*, 311–318.

Lynch, G., Stanfield, B., & Cotman, C. W. (1973). Developmental differences in postlesion axonal growth in the hippocampus, *Brain Research, 59*, 155–168.

Lynch, G., Stanfield, B., Parks, T., & Cotman, C. W. (1974). Evidence for selective postlesion axonal growth in the dentate gyrus of the rat. *Brain Research, 69*, 1–11.

Lynch, G., & Baudry, M. (1984). The biochemistry of memory: A new and specific hypothesis. *Science, 224*, 1057–1063.

Mariani, J., & Changeux, J.-P. (1981). Ontogenesis of olivocerebellar relationships. I. Studies by intracellular recordings of the multiple innervation of Purkinje cells by climbing fibers in the developing rat cerebellum. *Journal of Neuroscience, 1*, 696–702.

Marshall, J. F. (1985). Neural plasticity and recovery of function after brain injury. *International Review of Neurobiology, 26*, 201–247.

Mason, A., & Muller, K. J. (1983). Regeneration and plasticity of neuronal connections in the leech. *Trends in Neurosciences, 6*, 172–176.

Matthews, D. A., Cotman, C. W., & Lynch, G. (1976a). An electron microscopic study of lesion-induced synaptogenesis in the dentate gyrus of the adult rat. I. Magnitude and time course of the degeneration. *Brain Research, 115*, 1–21.

Matthews, D. A., Cotman, C., & Lynch, G. (1976b). An electron microscopic study of lesion-induced synaptogensis in the dentate gyrus of the adult rat. II. Reappearance of morphologically normal synaptic contacts. *Brain Research, 115*, 23–41.

McCouch, G. P., Austin, G. M., Liu, C. N., & Liu, C. Y. (1958). Sprouting as a cause of spasticity. *Journal of Neurophysiology, 21*, 205–216.

Mendell, L. M. (1984). Modifiability of spinal synapses. *Physiological Reviews, 64*, 260–324.

Menzel, R. (1983). Neurobiology of learning and memory: The honeybee as a model system. *Naturwissenschaften, 70,* 504–511.

Merrill, E. G., & Wall, P. D. (1978). Plasticity of connections in the adult nervous system. In C. W. Cotman (Ed.), *Neuronal plasticity* (pp. 97–111). New York: Raven Press.

Messenheimer, J. A., Harris, E. W., & Steward, O. (1979). Sprouting fibers gain access to circuitry transsynaptically altered by kindling. *Experimental Neurology, 64,* 469–481.

Moore, R. Y., Björklund, A., & Stenevi, U. (1971). Plastic changes in the adrenergic innervation of the rat septal area in response to denervation. *Brain Research, 33,* 13–35.

Mower, G. D., Christen, W. G., & Caplan, C. J. (1983). Very brief visual experience eliminates plasticity in the cat visual cortex. *Science, 221,* 178–180.

Murakami, F., Tsukahara, N., & Fujito, Y. (1977). Properties of the synaptic transmission of the newly formed corticorubral synapses after lesion of the nucleus interpositus of the cerebellum. *Experimental Brain Research, 30,* 245–258.

Murakami, F., Katsumaru, H., Maeda, J., & Tsukahara, N. (1984). Reorganization of corticorubral synapses following cross-innervation of flexor and extensor nerves of adult cat: A quantitative electron microscopic study. *Brain Research, 306,* 299–306.

Murray, J. G., & Thompson, J. W. (1957). The occurrence and function of collateral sprouting in the sympathetic nervous system of the cat. *Journal of Physiology, 135–*162.

Murray, M., Zimmer, J., & Raisman, G. (1979). Quantitative electron microscopic evidence for reinnervation in the adult rat interpenduncular nucleus after lesions of the fasciulus retroflexus. *Journal of Comparative Neurology, 187,* 447–468.

Nakamura, Y., Mizuno, N., Konishi, A., & Sato, M. (1974). Synaptic reorganization of the red nucleus after chronic deafferentation from cerebellorubal fibers: An electron microscope study in the cat. *Brain Research, 298–301.*

Oppenheim, R. W. (1981a). Neuronal cell death and some related phenomena during neurogenesis: A selective historical review and progress report. In W. M. Cowman (Ed.), *Studies in Developmental Neurobiology* (pp. 74–133). New York: Oxford University Press.

Oppenheim, R. W. (1981b). Cell death of motoneurons in the chick embryo spinal cord: V. Evidence on the role of cell death and neuromuscular function in the formation of specific peripheral connections. *Journal of Neuroscience, 1,* 141–151.

Oppenheim, R. W., & Nunez, R. (1982). Electrical stimulation of hindlimb increases neuronal cell death in chick embryo. *Nature, 295,* 57–59.

Oppenheim, R. W. (1982). The neuroembryological study of behavior: Progress, problems, perspectives. *Current Topics in Developmental Biology, 17,* 257–309.

Passingham, R. E., Perry, V. H., & Wilkinson, F. (1983). The long-term effects of removal of sensorimotor cortex in infant and adult rhesus monkeys. *Brain, 106,* 675–705.

Paton, J. A., & Nottebohm, F. N. (1984). Neurons generated in the adult brain are recruited into functional circuits. *Science, 225,* 1046–1048.

Pickel, V. M., Segal, M. & Bloom, F. E. (1974). Axonal proliferation following lesions of cerebellar peduncles. A combined fluorescence microscopic and radioautographic study. *Journal of Comparative Neurology, 155,* 43–60.

Pittman, R., & Oppenheim, R. W. (1979). Cell death of motoneurons in the chick embryo spinal cord: IV. Evidence that a functional neuromuscular interaction is involved in the regulation of naturally occuring cell death and the stabilization of synapses. *Journal of Comparative Neurology, 187,* 425–446.

Purves, D., & Lichtman, J. W. (1980). Elimination of synapses in the developing neurons system. *Science, 210,* 53–157.

Purves, D., & Hume, R. I. (1981). The relation of postsynaptic geometry to the number of presynaptic axons that innervate autonomic ganglion cells. *Journal of Neuroscience,* 1, 441–452.

Rakic, P. (1976). Prenatal genesis of connections subserving ocular dominance in the rhesus monkey. *Nature, 261,* 467–471.

Ramon y Cajal, S. (1968). Degeneration and regeneration of the nervous system. New York: Hafner Publ. Comp. (Fascimile of 1928 edition).

Raisman, G. (1969). Neuronal plasticity in the septal nuclei of the adult brain. *Brain Research, 14,* 25–48.

Raisman, G., & Field, P. M. (1973). A quantitative investigation of the development of collateral reinnervation after partial deafferentation of the septal nuclei. *Brain Research, 50,* 241–264.

Richardson, P. M., McGuinness, U. M., & Aguayo, A. J. (1982). Peripheral nerve autografts to the rat spinal cord: Studies with axonal tracing methods. *Brain Research, 237,* 147–162.

Rodin, G. E., Sampogna, S. L., & Kruger, L. (1983). An examination of intraspinal sprouting in dorsal root axons with the tracer horseradish peroxidase. *Journal of Comparative Neurology, 215,* 187–198.

Rutledge, L. T., Wright, C., & Duncan, J. (1974). Morphological changes in pyramidal cells of mammalian neocortex associated with increased use. *Experimental Neurology,* 44, 209–228.

Scheff, S. W., & Cotman, C. W. (1977). Recovery of spontaneous alternation following lesion of entorhinal cortex in adult rats: Possible correlation to axon sprouting. *Behavioral Biology, 21,* 286–293.

Scheff, S. W., Bernardo, L. S. & Cotman, C. W. (1978). Decrease in adrenergic axon sprouting in the senescent rat. *Science, 202,* 775–778.

Schwab, M. E., Otten, U., Agid, Y., & Thoenen, H. (1979). Nerve growth factor (NGF) in the rat CNS: Absence of specific retrograde transport and tyrosine hydroxylase induction in locus coeruleus and substantia nigra. *Brain Research, 168,* 473–483.

Schneider, G. E. (1970). Mechanisms of functional recovery following lesions of visual cortex or superior colliculus in neonate and adult hamsters. *Brain, Behavior, and Evolution,* 3, 295–323.

Schneider, G. E. (1973). Early lesions of superior colliculus: Factors affecting the formation of abnormal retinal projections. *Brain Behavior and Evolution, 8,* 73–109.

Sherrington, C. S. (1906). *The integrative action of the nervous system.* New Haven: Yale University Press.

Sotelo, C., & Palay, S. L. (1971). Altered axons and axon terminals in the lateral vestibular nucleus of the rat. Possible example of neuronal remodelling. *Laboratory Investigation, 25,* 633–672.

Stanfield, B. (1984). Postnatal reorganization of cortical projections: The role of collateral elimination. *Trends in Neurosciences, 7,* 37–41.

Stelzner, D. J., Ershler, W. B., & Weber, E. D. (1975). Effects of spinal transection in neonatal and yearling rats: Survival of function. *Experimental Neurology, 46,* 156–177.

Stenevi, U., & Björklund, A. (1978). Growth of vascular sympathetic axons into the hippocampus after lesions of the septohippocampal pathway: A pitfall in brain lesion studies. *Neuroscience Letters, 7,* 219–224.

Steward, O. (1982). Assessing the functional significance of lesion-induced neuronal plasticity. *International Review of Neurobiology, 23,* 197–253.

Steward, O., Cotman, C. W., & Lynch, G. S. (1973). Re-establishment of electrophysiologically functional entohinal cortical input to the dentate gyrus deafferented by ipsilateral entorhinal lesions: Innervation by the contralateral entorhinal cortex. *Experimental Brain Research, 18,* 396–414.

Steward, O., Cotman, C. W. & Lynch, G. S. (1974). Growth of a new fiber projection in the brain of adult rats: Reinnervation of the dentate gyrus by the contralateral entohinal cortex following ipsilateral entorhinal lesions. *Experimental Brain Research, 20,* 45–66.

Steward, O., Cotman, C. W., & Lynch, G. S. (1976). A quantitative autoradiographic and electrophysiological study of the reinnervation of the dentate gyrus by the contralateral entorhinal cortex following ipsilateral entorhinal lesions. *Brain Research, 114,* 181–200.

Steward, O. & Vinsant, S. L. (1983). The process of reinnervation in the dentate gyrus of the adult rat: A quantitative electron microscopic analysis of terminal proliferation and reactive synaptogenesis. *Journal of Comparative Neurology, 214,* 370–386.

Stryker, M. P. (1981). Late segregation of geniculate afferents to the cat's visual cortex after recovery from binocular impulse blockade. *Society for Neuroscience Abstracts, 7,* 842.

Swindale, N. V. (1981). Absence of ocular dominance patches in dark-reared cats. *Nature, 290,* 332–333.

Tsukahara, N., & Fujito, Y. (1976). Physiological evidence of formation of new synapses from cerebrum in the red nucleus neurons following cross-union of forelimb nerves. *Brain Research, 106,* 184–188.

Tsukahara, N. (1981). Synaptic plasticity in the mammalian central nervous system. *Annual Review of Neuroscience, 4,* 351–379.

Van Essen, D. C. (1982). Neuromuscular synapse elimination. In N. C. Spitzer (Ed.), *Neuronal Development* (pp. 333–376). New York: Plenum Press.

Wall, P. D. (1977). The presence of ineffective synapses and the circumstances which unmask them. *Philosophical Transactions of the Royal Society of London* (Series B), *278,* 361–372.

Wall, P. D., & Egger, M. D. (1971). Formation of new connections in adult rat brains after partial deafferentation. *Nature, 232,* 542–545.

Weddell, G., Cuttmann, L., & Gutman, E. (1941). The local extension of nerve fibers into denervated areas of skin. *Journal of Neurology and Psychiatry, 4,* 206–225.

Wernig, A., Carmody, J. J., Anzil, A. P., Hansert, E., Marcimak, M. & Zucker, H. (1984). Persistence of nerve sprouting with features of synapse remodelling in soleus muscles of adult mice. *Neuroscience, 11,* 241–253.

Wenzel, S., Kammerer, E., Kirsche, W., Matthies, H., & Wenzel, M. (1980). Electron microscopic and morphometric studies on synaptic plasticity in the hippocampus of the rat following conditioning. *Journal of Hirnforschung, 21,* 647–654.

West, J. R. (1984). Age-dependent sprouting in the dentate gyrus demonstrated with anterograde HRP. *Brain Research Bulletin, 12,* 323–330.

Vrensen, G., & Cardozo, J. N. (1981). Changes in size and shape of synaptic connections after visual training: An ultrastructural approach of synaptic plasticity. *Brain Research, 218,* 79–97.

Zhou, F.-C., & Azmitia, E. C. (1984). Induced homotypic collateral sprouting of serotonergic fibers in the hippocampus of rat. *Brain Research, 308,* 53–62.

Zimmer, J., Lawrence, J., & Raisman, G. (1982). A quantitative electron microscopic study of synaptic reorganization in the rat medial habenular nucleus after transection of the stria medullaris. *Neuroscience, 7,* 1905–1928.

Zimmer, J. (1973). Extended commissural and ipsilateral projections in postnatally deentorhinated hippocampus and fascia dentata demonstrated in rats by silver impregnation. *Brain Research, 64,* 293–311.

Zimmer, J. (1974). Proximity as a factor in the regulation of aberrant axonal growth in postnatally deafferented fascia dentata. *Brain Research, 78,* 137–142.

III

PHARMACOLOGY AND BIOCHEMISTRY

4

MEMORY: DRUGS AND HORMONES*

Joe L. Martinez, Jr.

INTRODUCTION

Behavior is a phenomenon we all take for granted, because we and other animals are capable of it. Sometimes, in a chapter such as this, we pause to consider the complexity of nervous and hormonal function that certainly underlies all behavior. The body has resorted to a simple principle for organizing behavior: Its elements communicate by means of messenger molecules, virtually throughout all of its parts. Yet, the complexity of the connections that establish this system of communicating molecules is staggering. Thompson, Patterson, and Berger (1978) suggest that the potential number of interconnections (not the actual number) among neurons in a single human brain is greater than the total number of atomic particles that comprise the entire known universe. It is this principle of communication, through messenger molecules, that makes drug research interesting and valuable. For with careful design, scientists are able to communicate with the brain and hormonal systems using drug molecules to gain a better understanding of how they operate to influence behavior.

* Supported by Office of Naval Research Contract N00014-83-K-0408. The author wishes to thank Mark R. Rosenzweig, Edward Bennett, Seth Roberts, and Adrian Dunn for their helpful comments on initial drafts of this paper.

All messenger molecule systems have a source and a site of action. Sometimes the source and site of action are only micrometers apart, as in the case of neurons, or they may be many centimeters away as in the case of hormones (see Rosenzweig & Leiman, 1982, Chapters 4 & 5). Krieger (1983) classifies cell-to-cell communication into three basic types: (1) autocrine where the secreted product acts on the cell of origin, (2) paracrine where the secretory product acts on neighboring cells, and (3) endocrine where a product is secreted into the blood stream to affect distant targets. Thus, the strategy for investigating how these messenger molecule systems affect behavior is based on their design to some degree, but basically is directed to the source or the site of action. For example, in the case of the source it is common to try to remove it through a lesion, or to change in some way the metabolism of the secretory product, or to prevent its release. In the case of the site of action, known as receptors (see Cooper, Bloom, & Roth, 1982), it is common to stimulate the receptor with an agonist drug that mimics the action of a messenger molecule, or to prevent it from acting at the receptor through the use of an antagonist drug. These are the basic strategies adopted by researchers investigating learning and memory.

The area of drug research is too broad to cover exhaustively in a chapter such as this. Therefore, no attempt is made to do so. However, major issues such as time-dependency, U-shaped curves, memory modulation, and central versus peripheral actions of drugs are covered. Traditional topics such as the identification of neurotransmitter systems that are involved in learning and memory are briefly discussed. Another traditional topic that is covered in this chapter is antibiotic protein synthesis inhibitors and what they tell us about memory formation. The following sections deal with hormones, and which hormones affect learning and memory, such as vasopressin, epinephrine, ACTH, and many opioid peptides. A James–Lange view of memory is presented as is the possibility that memory modulatory hormones exist and that they are part of the normal machinery of learning and memory. One nontraditional issue, discussed in the final section, is the use of "Drugs to Understand or to Alter Learning and Memory."

Before moving on to a discussion of drug and hormone actions on learning and memory, it is important to realize that many things determine how a drug affects the body, and consequently, behavior. Some of these variables are species or even strain of animal, age, sex, body size, transport, metabolism, time of day, and the stress state of the organism. A more complete discussion of these issues may be found in Feldman and Quenzer (1984) or Leavitt (1982).

TIME DEPENDENCY REVISITED

Duncan (1949) provided the first experimental demonstration of a retrograde amnesia gradient. Rats trained in an active avoidance task were found to be amnesic, if electroconclusive shock (ECS) was given close in time, but following, the training trial. If the ECS was delayed by only a few minutes, then it no longer produced amnesia. It is also possible to facilitate an animal's memory by stimulating the brain or by giving drugs following training, and the effectiveness of these facilitating treatments also produces a retrograde gradient (see Martinez, Jensen, & McGaugh, 1983). McGaugh and Herz (1972) propose that the time-dependent nature of amnesia and enhancement gradients show that the memory of an experience is not fixed or consolidated at the time the experience occurs. Thus, memory storage involves a time-dependent process.

It is also true that gradients can be anterograde. Excellent examples are provided by Karpiak and Rapport (1979) and Haycock, van Buskirk, and McGaugh (1977), shown in Figure 4.1 below. Both of these studies found that amnestic agents, antiserum to brain gangliosides, in one case, and diethyldithiocarbamate (DDC), an inhibitor of norepinephrine biosynthesis, in the second case, produced amnesia for a passive avoidance response when administered either before or after training. Thus, time dependency is both antero- and retrograde for at least some treatments that affect learning and memory in animals (Martinez et al., 1983). In fact, the strict contiguity between the experimental treatment and the training experience evident in Figure 4.1 is quite striking. Furthermore, treatment with the antiserum or the DDC either before or after training leads to qualitatively the same result; both produce amnesia, even though the two curves are accelerated at different rates. Thus, it is possible that the administration of an experimental treatment produces an effect on learning and memory by the same mechanism, regardless of whether it is given before or after training. Thus, the demonstration of time dependency may not be evidence of an endogenous storage process, because in the case of pretraining treatment there is no experience to store. Rather, the gradient may reveal the temporal domain within which the function of any particular neural or hormonal system may be altered to affect learning and memory. This phenomena would explain why each experimental treatment appears to produce its own unique time gradient (Chorover, 1976), rather than each treatment producing the same gradient, because each would be affecting the same biological process, memory storage.

Yet, it seems intuitively true that different processes are affected by

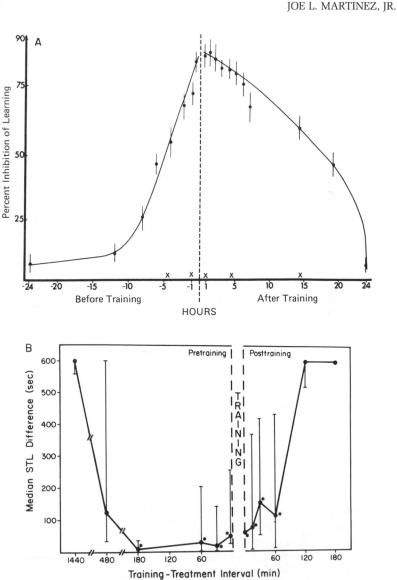

FIGURE 4.1   (A) Inhibition of learning (+/− SEM) following intraventricular injection of antiserum to brain gangliosides into groups of mice (n = 12) at varying intervals before and after training in a step-through passive avoidance task. Control groups of mice injected with the antiserum previously absorbed with pure G_{M1} ganglioside to remove antibodies (X) demonstrated no inhibition of learning (from Karpiak & Rapport, 1979). (B) Median step-through latencies (STL) (Day 2–Day 1) for mice trained in a passive avoidance task. Diethyldithiocarbamate was administered at varying times before or after training. From Haycock et al. (1977).

pre- or posttraining treatment. If a drug is given before training it can influence behavior through actions on other variables such as attention, motivation, or arousal (McGaugh, 1973). For example, consider trying to memorize a poem in two different situations. First, drink six cans of beer and study the poem, or study the poem first and then drink six cans of beer. The result may be the same the next morning, one may not remember the poem, but the mechanism responsible for the amnesia *seems* different. Also, there are cases where drugs are effective if given before training and not following training, and vice versa (see Martinez et al., 1983), indicating that drugs administered either before or after training affect fundamentally different mechanisms. However, little careful research has been conducted to correlate the time course of drug action to its purported effect on behavior. Thus, a drug may be administered close to the training trial, but its time course of effectiveness, due to factors such as uptake, metabolism, and so on, may not be within the proper time frame to affect learning and memory. Recall (Figure 4.1) that there is a strict relationship between the effectiveness of a drug and the time of administration relative to the training trial. Also, drugs that are administered before training may actually have their important effects after training. A good example of this problem is found with antibiotic protein synthesis inhibitors (PSI), which are known to produce experimental amnesia in a variety of learning tasks. Some PSIs have a slow onset of action and it is difficult to produce any amnesic effect if these drugs are given after training. Thus, it is common to administer them shortly before training assuming they will have an action following training (Barraco & Stettner, 1976).

The major question that arises from this discussion is why should an animal possess internal mechanisms that would be expressed as a learning and memory gradient? A plausible but unproven answer is that it reflects the function of endogenous hormonal mechanisms that influence learning and memory in a way that exhibits strict contiguity. That is, the learning experience and the hormonal response have to occur within certain temporal limits for the hormonal response to influence the learning and memory.

Taking these considerations together it appears that time dependency is a concept that is still central to those interested in studying drug effects on learning and memory. At the very least, a demonstration of time dependency will insure that the observed actions of the drug are on the particular learning being studied, and not some proactive effect of the drug on performance of the learned response.

DOSE RESPONSE

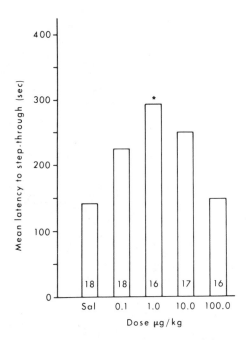

FIGURE 4.2   A dose of 1.0 μg/kg γ-endorphin administered to rats (i.p.) significantly enhanced retention performance measured 72 hr later in a step-through passive avoidance task. From Martinez & Rigter (1980).

U-SHAPED CURVES

It is common in the scientific literature on drug effects on learning and memory to find U-shaped dose response curves. For example, Martinez and Rigter (1980) reported that γ-endorphin, administered to rats prior to training in a passive avoidance task, enhanced retention performance measured 24 hr later. As can be seen in Figure 4.2, the shape of the dose response function is clearly U-shaped. The facilitatory dose was found to be 1.0 μg per kg while doses on either side (0.1 or 10.0 μg per kg) were not found to be effective. This phenomenon is paradoxical, because in classic pharmacology the ideal relationship between the concentration of a drug and the magnitude of the response to it is a hyperbolic function when dose is plotted on a linear scale (Gilman, Mayer, & Melman, 1980). This relationship could also be true for drugs that affect learning and memory, if they act through a direct action on receptors. According to Gilman et al., in this situation where there are a finite number of receptors the drug effect should be proportional to the fraction of receptors occupied by the drug, and a maximal effect should occur when all of the receptors are occupied. However, there is one receptor phenomenon that will explain U-shaped curves. If the receptor, because of its constant occupation by agonist drugs, shows tachyphylaxis or fatigue, then greater activity should lead to greater fatigue, hence larger doses should produce less of an effect than some optimal dose (Day, 1979).

Another explanation of U-shaped curves is provided by considering the ascending and descending parts of the curves to represent opposing processes. For example, Mueller, Palmer, Hoffer, & Dunwiddie, (1982) found a U-shaped dose response curve for the effect of norepinephrine on evoked potentials in the *in vitro* rat hippocampus. Low doses of norepinephrine increased the magnitude of the evoked response, while high doses inhibited the response. Mueller et al. showed that this dose response function is due to the fact that norepinephrine is both an α- and a β-agonist; it acts at two different kinds of adrenergic receptors, which mediate opposite actions in the hippocampus. This dual action was shown by blocking the action of norepinephrine in the hippocampus by using selective α- or β-antagonists. The α-antagonist blocked the ascending portion of the curve while the β-antagonist blocked the descending portion of the curve.

Unfortunately, in drug-related research in learning and memory there is little or no research directed toward understanding U-shaped functions, even though receptor tachyphylaxis or contributions of receptor populations could provide ready explanations. Alternatively U-shaped dose response functions might also be the manifestation of an unknown biological process or of an interaction of known processes that is waiting to be elucidated.

MODULATION OF LEARNING AND MEMORY

Modulation is easily described. Whether enhancement or impairment of retention performance is observed following an experimental treatment is dependent on the strength of the experimental treatment, the strength of the training experience, and the interaction between the two (Martinez et al., 1983). An excellent example of modulation is provided by the research of Gold and van Buskirk (1976). In this study groups of rats were trained in a passive avoidance task at different footshock intensities and given either 3 or 6 international units (IU) of ACTH immediately following training. The rats were given a retention test 24 hr later. At the lowest footshock level used (0.4 mA) both doses of ACTH enhanced memory. At the next lowest level (0.5 mA) only the 3 IU dose was enhancing, and as the footshock was increased to 0.7 and 2.0 mA, both doses of ACTH produced retrograde amnesia. Thus, whether enhancement or impairment is observed depends on the level of the training footshock and on the strength of the experimental treatment.

Similarly, the strength of the experimental treatment can also be varied to produce either enhancement or impairment. Castellano (1982), for example, found that a dose of 5.0 mg per kg of FK 33-824 (a Met-enkephalin analog) enhanced later retention of a passive avoidance response when the drug was injected immediately following training. If the dose of the drug was increased to 40.0 mg per kg, then a retention impairment was observed. Another example is provided by Soumireu–Mourat, Destrade, and Cardo (1975) who found that subseizure stimulation of the hippocampus enhanced retention of an operant response for food, but supraseizure stimulation produced a retention impairment. One counter-intuitive prediction that arises from the concept of modulation of learning and memory is that ECS under appropriate experimental conditions should produce retrograde enhancement of memory. Interestingly, Sternberg, Gold, and McGaugh (1983) recently reported that frontal cortex stimulation which produces tonic–clonic convulsions enhances retention of an active avoidance response if the animals are trained with a weak footshock. However, if a strong footshock is used, then normal retrograde amnesia is observed. Thus, manipulation of the strength of the experimental treatment may lead to either enhancement or impairment (Martinez et al., 1983). This is analogous to the phenomenon of U-shaped curves previously described, except that in this case the dose response function is biphasic.

CENTRAL VERSUS PERIPHERAL ACTIONS OF DRUGS

As noted in the Introduction, each messenger molecule system has its appropriate field of receptors. If a drug alters learning and memory by acting on some set of receptors, then this is considered to be presumptive evidence that the whole messenger molecule system, of which the receptors are only a part, may normally be involved in the acquisition and storage of information in the brain. More often than not, the set of receptors that the drug acts upon are present both in the brain and periphery. Thus, one inescapable question that arises from drug research is what are the contributions of central and peripheral processes to learning and memory as revealed by drug treatment? Another related problem encountered in interpreting drug effects is that drugs themselves are more or less permeable to the brain through the blood–brain barrier, and various parts of the brain lie outside the blood–brain barrier (see Feldman & Quenzer, 1984, for a discussion), and are therefore more or less accessible to drugs. Thus, the question of central versus peripheral actions of drugs is not easy to answer.

However, there are good examples of clear central and peripheral drug actions on learning and memory; two will be considered. First, Mauk, Warren, & Thompson (1982a) reported that intravenous administration of morphine abolished a simple learned response, a classically conditioned nictitating membrane extension in the rabbit. Importantly, the morphine had no effect on the unconditioned response, and the action of morphine was completely reversible by naloxone. The next study reported by this group (Mauk, Madden, Barchas, & Thompson, 1982b) found that morphiceptin, an opioid peptide derived from milk protein, produced the same action as morphine on the conditioned response, if the peptide was infused directly into the fourth ventricle. Moreover, the effect of the morphiceptin was readily reversed by naloxone given peripherally, but not by a quaternary form of naloxone, which does not pass the blood brain barrier. Thus, the morphiceptin almost certainly produces its effects on conditioning through a central mechanism. It also seems likely that the peripherally administered morphine, which produces the same qualitative effect as morphiceptin given centrally, is acting through a central mechanism. However, the evidence that this assertion is true would be stronger if Mauk et al. (1982a) had tried to antagonize the morphine effect on conditioning with the quaternary form of naloxone. Nevertheless, these data provide a good demonstration of a drug effect on conditioning that is most probably central in origin.

In the second example, Rigter, Jensen, Martinez, Messing, Vasquez, Liang, and McGaugh (1980) found that the opioid peptides, Met-enkephalin and Leu-enkephalin, administered intraperitoneally, impaired acquisition of an active avoidance response in rats. Rigter et al. suggested that this effect was mediated by a peripheral mechanism, because in general, peptides of peripheral origin enter the brain poorly, if at all (Pardridge, 1983). As in the case of Mauk et al. (1982a), the opioid effects are antagonized by naloxone (Rigter et al., 1980b). However, in contrast Figure 4.3 shows that the quarternary form of naloxone, known as methylnaloxonium (naloxonium) also antagonizes the Leu-enkephalin effect. In this study mice were injected with Leu-enkephalin or with a combination of Leu-enkephalin and naloxonium

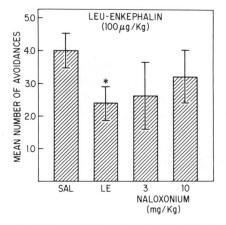

FIGURE 4.3   Leu-enkephalin administered to mice 5 min before training in a 1-way active avoidance task significantly decreases the number of avoidances observed in the peptide-treated group. Naloxonium (10 mg per kg) administered as a mixture with the Leu-enkephalin partially attenuates the action of Leu-enkephalin. From Martinez et al. (1984a).

before training in a one-way active avoidance response. Leu-enkephalin impaired acquisition of the response and this effect was blocked by the high dose of naloxonium (Martinez, Conner, Dana, Chaukin, Bloom, & de Graaf, 1984a). Thus, enkephalin actions on avoidance conditioning appear to be mediated through an opioid receptor somewhere outside of the blood–brain barrier.

Another way to distinguish between central and peripheral actions of drugs is to compare the dose effectiveness of drugs administered both centrally and peripherally. Bohus and de Wied (1981) suggest that $ACTH_{4-10}$ delays extinction of avoidance behavior through a direct action on the brain following peripheral administration, because 100 times less drug is needed to produce this effect following central administration. However, this strategy can lead to ambiguous results. For example, Melegini, Ledergerber, and McGaugh (1978) tested the hypothesis that peripherally administered DDC produces memory impairment through an action on central norepinephrine pathways. Importantly, DDC inhibits norepinephrine and epinephrine biosynthesis throughout the central and peripheral nervous systems, as well as the adrenal medulla, where norepinephrine and epinephrine hormones are made and released. As expected, DDC injected intraperitoneally (i.p.) produced amnesia for a passive avoidance response, and replacement in the brain of norepinephrine attenuated the amnesia produced by the DDC. Norepinephrine was injected peripherally in some animals that received DDC as a control procedure. Surprisingly, the peripherally administered norepinephrine also attenuated the DDC-induced amnesia. The effective peripheral dose was between 5 and 500 times greater than the effective central dose depending on which effective doses are compared. Thus, Meligini et al. interpret their data to suggest that the norepinephrine acted at a peripheral site because the low dose was effective; yet by the criterion stated by Bohus and de Wied, these data also suggest that at the high dose the norepinephrine acted centrally to attenuate the DDC-induced amnesia. Of course, the possibility exists that both sets of scientists are correct and norepinephrine may attenuate DDC-induced amnesia by either a central or a peripheral action, or both. Thus, this strategy would not distinguish between parallel systems, one in the brain, one in the autonomic nervous system, that operated to produce effects at roughly equivalent doses.

A final method that is commonly used to try to distinguish central from peripheral actions is to produce the same qualitative effect by both a central and a peripheral route of administration (Bohus & de Wied, 1981). Thus, if an effect on learning and memory that is originally produced with a systemic injection can be reproduced by a more local administration in the brain, then this is evidence that both effects were produced through an action at the same site in the brain. For example Messing et al. (1979) found that naloxone-administered i.p. to rats enhanced retention of either a passive or active avoidance task. Gallagher and Kapp (1978) reported that naloxone injected directly into the amygdala enhanced retention of a similar passive avoidance response. Viewed together these two studies suggest that naloxone, regardless of the route of administration, affects memory through an action on the amygdala. Yet this strategy does not distinguish between parallel central and peripheral systems either. For example, Martinez and de Graaf (1985) reported that naloxonium (which does not cross into the brain) enhances acquisition of an active avoidance response in mice, much as naloxone is reported to enhance this same response in rats (Messing et al., 1979). Furthermore, naloxonium and naloxone enhance acquisition of a discriminated shock escape task in mice at equivalent doses (Martinez, 1983). Thus, antagonism of peripheral opioid receptors with naloxonium produces an effect on learning that is qualitatively the same as that produced by naloxone, which acts both in the periphery and the brain. There are at least two possible solutions to this puzzle. First, since both forms of naloxone act on peripheral opioid receptors, the most simple explanation is that naloxone and naloxonium produce their actions on learning and memory through peripheral opioid receptors. Second, the naloxones may affect learning through an action on central opioid systems in rats and peripheral opioid systems in mice. As this second solution seems unlikely, and as Gallagher and Kapp did show that central administration of naloxone affects conditioning, it is probable that both central and peripheral opioid systems may affect conditioning. Hence, trying to reproduce a systemic effect by more local brain administration in order to distinguish central from peripheral actions may be misleading. In some sense the distinction between the central and peripheral nervous systems is arbitrary because they are interconnected and certainly have to function cooperatively to produce behavior.

Yet, the importance of drugs having either a peripheral or central action can be appreciated by considering the belladona alkaloid, atropine, which is derived from the plant named the deadly nightshade. This drug is a cholinergic antagonist and high doses produce central nervous system depression that can lead to death. However, quaternary ammonium derivatives of the belladona alkaloids are commonly used to inhibit gastrointestinal activity and respiratory secretion in humans as cold remedies without significant effects on the central nervous system, because these drugs do not readily cross the blood–brain barrier (Weiner, 1980).

WHICH NEUROTRANSMITTER SYSTEMS ARE IMPORTANT FOR LEARNING AND MEMORY?

Probably the best way to ask the question is, which neurotransmitter systems are not important for learning and memory? Extensive evidence exists that the more classic neurotransmitters such as acetylcholine, norepinephrine, dopamine, and serotonin all influence learning and memory (for reviews see Dunn, 1980; Hunter, Zornetzer, Jarvik, & McGaugh, 1977). However, as new neurotransmitters and neuromodulators are continually discovered, such as β-endorphin, the enkephalins, vasopressin, and substance P, a literature supporting their role in learning and memory also develops (see Koob & Bloom, 1983; Huston & Staubli, 1981; Martinez, Rigter, Jensen, Messing, Vasquez, & McGaugh, 1981; and Van Wimersma Greidanus, Bohus, & de Wied, 1981). This vast literature seems to suggest that the expression of learning and memory, which is always inferred through performance, is dependent on the functioning of the central, peripheral, and associated endocrine systems in a rather global fashion. The attribute of memory in an organism may be something like the quality of speed in a car (an analogy borrowed from John Garcia). Speed is the result of most of the parts of the car functioning together. Damage to any number of parts, such as wheels, axles, drive shaft, and so on, will lead to less speed. Similarly, memory results from the simultaneous functioning of many neurotransmitter systems, and alteration of the functioning of any one will alter learning and memory, usually measured as experimental amnesia. Thus, Zornetzer (1978) cautioned scientists not to develop a phrenology of memory based on neurotransmitters, because it is possible that "no single neurochemical . . . explains the complexity of memory" (p. 647). With this caveat in mind some basic findings regarding the involvement of major neurotransmitter systems in learning and memory will be reviewed.

The question then becomes, how is the involvement of any particular neurotransmitter system in learning and memory determined? If it is understood that no neurotransmitter system functions in isolation, and actions on one system must necessarily have ramifications on many neurotransmitter systems, then the strategy is straightforward. Experiments are performed to alter the source or site of action of one neurotransmitter system through the use of a drug and then observe the effect on behavior by comparison to a control group that did not receive the drug. An important assumption of this research strategy is that the drug in question has a unitary or specific action on the messenger molecule system under study. The transmitters that are specifically discussed are acetycholine, the catecholamines, and serotonin.

ACETYLCHOLINE

Studies beginning in 1966 by Deutsch and colleagues (for review see Deutsch, 1983) suggested that alteration of cholinergic systems affected learning and memory. In these studies rats were trained to discriminate a lighted from a dark arm of a Y-maze in order to escape shock. At various times following training the animals were injected with an anticholinesterase drug (diisopropyl fluorophosphate or DFP) directly into the brain. Animals that received injections close to the time of training showed poor performance, which is interpreted as retrograde amnesia. However, Stratton and Petrinovitch (1963) found that another anticholinesterase, physostigmine, both enhanced and impaired acquisition of an appetitive maze task in rats depending on dose. Thus, antagonizing cholinergic systems with enzyme inhibitors produces bidirectional effects, and this is another instance of modulation. Predictably, then, stimulation of cholinergic systems with agonist drugs, such as nicotine, produces either impairment (Garg & Holland, 1969) or enhancement (Battig, 1970) depending on the strength of the experimental treatment and the training experience.

Recently, there has been renewed interest in cholinergic systems, because of their apparent involvement in memory deficits in aged subjects and Alzheimer's disease (see Gold & Zornetzer, 1983; Squire & Davis, 1981; also Zornetzer, Chapter 6, this volume). For example, Bartus, Dean, Goas, & Lippa (1980) reported that 13-month-old mice show a deficit in retention of a passive avoidance response compared to young 3-month-old mice. However, mice kept for some months on a choline-enriched diet showed no deficit. Presumably, choline, the amino acid necessary to make acetylcholine, somehow increased the activity of this neurotransmitter system to alleviate the memory deficit.

In the case of Alzheimer's disease it is now known that one manifestation is a severe reduction of choline acetyltransferase in the cortex that may be greater than 80% (Davies & Maloney, 1976). Since acetylcholine is synthesized from acetyl CoA and choline by choline acetyltransferase (Cooper et al., 1982), it was to be expected that Alzheimer's patients would have compromised cholinergic neurotransmitter function. Furthermore, one salient symptom of this disease is profound deficits in learning and memory. Thus, even though treatment of Alzheimer's disease with cholinergic drugs has not been very successful to date, it is hoped that better understanding of the disease may lead to treatment through intervention in cholinergic systems (Squire & Davis, 1981).

CATECHOLAMINES

Kety (1970) first proposed that catecholamines might be involved in learning and memory, because of the diffuse nature of the noradrenergic projections arising from locus coeruleus. Norepinephrine synapses are virtually everywhere in the brain and are positioned to influence the storage of information in a number of places. Thus, Kety's notion was not that norepinephrine projections systems were the substrate of learning and memory, but that they influenced the neural substrate. However, another catecholamine system comprised of dopamine neurons is more complex in its organization than norepinephrine projection systems and contains more cells. These are the nigrostriatal and mesolimbic systems (Cooper et al., 1982). More recently, a rather extensive epinephrine containing system projecting from the lateral tegmental system (C-1) and the dorsal medulla (C-2) to hypothalamus has been identified (Cooper et al., 1982). Thus, catecholamine is probably not a proper rubric to consider drug effects on learning and memory, and norepinephrine, dopamine, and epinephrine should be considered in turn. Yet, most drugs that affect catecholamines will affect all three of these neurotransmitter systems, and specific actions on one or the other system are frequently impossible to determine.

The state of drug research into catecholamines and learning and memory was summarized by Dunn (1980). "In general, antagonists of catecholamine metabolism interfere with learning and memory, whereas agonists can improve it" (p. 376; see also reviews by Beninger, 1983; Gold & Zornetzer, 1983; Hunter et al., 1977; Squire & Davis, 1981). However, modulatory effects have been reported as well. For example, Karpiak, Kirchmer, and Rapport (1976) reported that reserpine, a catecholamine antagonist, given to mice following training in a passive avoidance task produced retrograde amnesia. In contrast Martinez, Vasquez, Jensen, & McGaugh (1977) found that reserpine enhanced later retention performance. Thus, as with drugs affecting cholinergic systems, the observation of enhancement or impairment is dependent on the strength of the experimental treatment and training experience.

An interesting development in catecholamine research on learning and memory is the apparent involvement of peripheral adrenergic systems in mediating drug effects on conditioning. In fact only one year after Kety (1970) proposed his hypothesis, Orshinger and Fulginiti (1971) reported that removal of the adrenal medulla blocked the enhancing actions of both amphetamine and nicotine in an avoidance conditioning paradigm. This result may seem a little paradoxical as amphetamine is an adrenergic agonist and nicotine is a cholinergic agonist. Yet, release of adrenal catecholamine hormones is mediated by nicotinic–cholinergic receptors located in splanchnic nerve terminals on adrenal chromaffin cells (see Day, 1979). Thus, if the action of nicotine on conditioning was mediated by adrenal catecholamines, then adrenal medullectomy would abolish this action. In any case, the fact that adrenal medullectomy would abolish the actions of either nicotine or amphetamine was startling, because most would have thought these drugs directly affected conditioning through brain neurotransmitter systems. Importantly, the early work of Orshinger and Fulginiti was replicated (Martinez, Vasquez, Rigter, Messing, Jensen, Liang, & McGaugh, 1980), and it is apparently true that amphetamine influences conditioned avoidance behavior through an action on adrenal medullary catecholamine systems.

In related work it was found that either norepinephrine or epinephrine administered systemically to rats would alter avoidance conditioning (Gold & van Buskirk, 1975; 1976b). In contrast syrosingopine, a peripherally acting adrenergic antagonist, produced retention deficits in mice for a passive avoidance response, but not for a discriminated escape reversal task (Palfai, Wichlinski, & Brown, 1983; Walsh & Palfai, 1979). Thus, it is not yet clear whether Dunn's (1980) conclusion, that agonists improve while antagonists impair learning and memory, applies equally well to drugs that alter peripheral catecholamine function. However, it is apparent that dramatic alterations of learning and memory can be observed by altering the function of peripheral catecholamine systems.

SEROTONIN

This neurotransmitter has received less attention than acetylcholine or the catecholamines, probably because the drugs that affect serotonergic systems have less specificity than drugs which affect other neurotransmitter systems (Gold & Zornetzer, 1983; Hunter et al., 1977). However, Essman (1973) reported that intrahippocampal injections of serotonin produced amnesia for a passive avoidance response. Also, Church and Sprott (1979) found that genetically different strains of mice learned a passive avoidance response with different facility. And, the ability of the mice to learn the response was related in a general way to serotonin levels detected in the hippocampus. Thus, there is every reason to suspect that when new drugs are developed, which affect serotonergic systems more specifically, that a complex literature will develop regarding serotonin and learning and memory.

Taken together it does appear that manipulation of classic neurotransmitter systems such as acetylcholine, catecholamines, including norepinephrine, epinephrine, dopamine, and serotonin will dramatically alter learning and memory of conditioned responses in animals. It appears that there is some generality to these effects as many different kinds of conditioning situations were investigated. Yet, none of these systems seems essential for learning and memory to occur, because frequently enhancement of learning is observed when antagonists are used. These results suggest that learning and memory result from the cooperative operation of many neurotransmitter and neuroendocrine systems.

PROTEIN SYNTHESIS INHIBITORS

Learning is the property of the individual organism; it occurs through experience. At a biological level, learning must be represented by a physical change in some tissue, probably nervous and endocrine tissues. All eukaryotic cells have three fundamental synthetic properties. They can synthesize complex nucleic acids, polysaccharides, and proteins. Proteins are the most complex biological chemicals known, and it must be true that learning and memory involves protein function in some way. An important question for learning and memory researchers is whether the development of long-term memory involves the synthesis of new proteins. This question is based on the logic that short-term memory develops quickly, almost instantaneously, and then decays over time. Since protein synthesis requires time, it follows that short-term memory is not dependent on the synthesis of new proteins. It is postulated that the converse is true for long-term memory; it develops slowly over time (minutes to hours) and is rather permanent. Since long-term memory is relatively permanent, it is suspected that some structural change occurs in the nervous system that requires protein synthesis (see Rosenzweig & Leiman, 1982, Chapter 15). The possible ways in which new proteins could be involved in long-term memory were outlined by Squire (1975). A learning experience could cause the synthesis of: (1) unique proteins (or peptides) that would themselves encode the experience, (2) new enzymes, (3) receptor molecules, (4) structural proteins (for example in new synapses), or (5) some synaptic regulatory protein.

A reasonable test of the hypothesis that new proteins are necessary for long-term memory would be to substantially prevent the expression of new proteins using drugs. Thus, a vast literature has developed using many drugs that inhibit protein synthesis, but primarily antibiotic protein synthesis inhibitors (see Barraco & Stettner, 1976; Chapouthier, 1983). Early studies (Barondes & Jarvik, 1964; Cohen & Barondes, 1966) showed that actinomycin D could produce impairments in learning and memory, but the results were never generally accepted, because of the severe toxicity of the drug (most of the drug-treated animals died). However, this objection has been overcome with the introduction of new, less toxic drugs, particularly anisomycin (Rosenzweig, 1984). The most convincing research, to date, demonstrating that protein synthesis inhibitors prevent the formation of long-term memory is that of Flood, Bennett, Orme, & Rosenzweig (1975) and Flood, Bennett, Rosenzweig, and Orme (1973). These researchers found that the stronger the training, and consequently the greater the amount of learning, the greater had to be the duration of inhibition of protein synthesis in order to produce experimental amnesia. Increased duration of inhibition was accomplished with multiple injection of anisomycin at 2-hour intervals.

Squire and Davis (1981, p. 331) note that the work with these drugs can be summarized into a few basic findings. First, protein synthesis has to be inhibited up to a level of 90–95% to observe the development of amnesia. Second, if inhibition is established 30 or more minutes after training, no amnesia develops. Third, these basic findings have been observed in rodents, birds, and fish in a wide variety of conditioning situations. Interestingly, there is even one report of tetracycline, a common antibiotic protein synthesis inhibitor, producing impairment of memory in humans (Idzilowski & Oswald, 1983).

However, there is some skepticism regarding the conclusion that treatment with protein synthesis inhibitors demonstrates that synthesis of new proteins is required for long-term memory. Importantly, it is not the concept that proteins are required for long-term memory that is in doubt, only whether antibiotic protein synthesis inhibitors demonstrate this notion (Barraco & Stettner, 1976). Besides being toxic, protein synthesis inhibitors produce a variety of side effects, some of which could explain their effects on conditioned behavior. Moreover, major problems reside in the fact that puromycin, a drug that causes release of shortened polypeptide chains from the ribosome with puromycin attached, produce effects on learning and memory that are qualitatively different from drugs such as acetoxycycloheximide, cycloheximide, and anisomycin, which inhibit peptide bond synthesis (see Dunn, 1980). For example, Flexner and Flexner (1968) found that NaCl injected into the brains of mice some days after training reversed the amnesia produced by puromycin given at the time of training, suggesting that puromycin did not prevent the formation of long-term memory, but only its expression. On the other hand Rosenbaum, Cohen, and Barondes (1968), while replicating this unusual finding of the Flexner's, found that NaCl did not have an effect on amnesia produced by acetoxycycloheximide, suggesting that this drug prevented the formation of a long-term memory trace. Yet, both puromycin and acetoxycycloheximide inhibit protein synthesis up to the criterion level of 90–95%, suggested by Squire and Davis (1981) among others to be important.

Also, many other drugs and treatments will attenuate the amnesic effects of all protein synthesis inhibitors while not affecting the rate of protein synthesis (see Dunn, 1980; Martinez et al., 1981). For example, Flood, Bennett, Orme, Rosenzweig, & Jarvik (1978) found that amnesia induced by anisomycin could be attenuated by either amphetamine, strychnine, or picrotoxin if these attenuating drugs were given at the time of training; none of these drugs significantly reversed the inhibition of protein synthesis induced by anisomycin. It seems that drugs such as amphetamine, strychnine, and picrotoxin which enhance learning and memory (McGaugh, 1973) act in this manner when pitted against amnestic agents such as protein synthesis inhibitors (Martinez et al., 1981). These studies therefore, provide a paradox. If protein synthesis is necessary for long-term memory, and protein synthesis inhibitors reduce synthesis by 90–95%, then how could any drug that does not affect protein synthesis reverse the amnesia produced by anisomycin? Rosenzweig, Bennett, and Flood (1981) suggest that the answer lies in the arousing properties of drugs such as amphetamine on the brain. If such a drug were to substantially alter neural processing, then this could alter the formation of long-term memory. Thus, there is evidence both pro and con that protein synthesis inhibitors prevent the formation of long-term memory, and that by implication proteins are necessary for the formation of long-term memory.

HORMONES AND LEARNING AND MEMORY

The juxtaposition of the words *hormones* and *learning and memory* immediately raises two questions. In fact, do hormones influence complex cognitive processes such as learning and memory, and if so, why? For the time being, let us assume the answer to the first question is affirmative, although the evidence will be reviewed, and proceed to the second question. Gold and McGaugh (1977) and later Martinez (1983; see also Leshner, Merkle, & Mixon, 1981) suggested that hormonal responses following a particular environmental event serve to establish the importance of the event. In analogy with the James–Lange theory of emotion, we can suggest a James–Lange view of memory; we meet a bear, run, and most likely remember in vivid detail many aspects of the encounter. In this view, hormonal responses, which are massive following the bear encounter, modify some brain process to help store information on the size of the bear, its particularly bad smell, its large, glistening sharp teeth, and so on. This hypothesis also provides a physiological explanation of what Brown and Kulik (1977) referred to as flashbulb memories. For example, most remember the circumstances in which one first heard of John Kennedy's assassination. Most not only remember the fact that he was assassinated, but also many details surrounding one's particular circumstance, such as where you were, who was with you, and so on. Thus, the similarity between the bear encounter and John Kennedy's death is massive autonomic and hormonal activation, which serves to mark the importance of the event for the individual organism. Importantly, flashbulb memories

(strongly stored memories) should only represent one end of a contin-
uum of hormonal modulation of learning and memory. It should be
possible to demonstrate that hormonal systems, depending on the state
of activation, only slightly increase the strength of stored information,
or perhaps even produce the opposite effect of decreasing the strength
of storage. Thus, this is essentially a restatement of modulation. Recall
the experiment of Gold and van Buskirk (1976) reviewed earlier in
which ACTH was found to enhance or impair training performance
based on the dose used and the magnitude of the training footshock.
Finally, consideration of the issue of time dependency should also lead
to the expectation that modification of hormonal states before learning
should modulate the strength of a learned response. As discussed earlier, Karpiak and Rapport (1979) and Haycock et al. (1977) found both
antero- and retrograde amnesia gradients.

An example of the power of hormones to influence learning and
memory was recently provided in an interesting experiment conducted
by Weinberger, Gold, & Sternberg (1984). They trained rats to associate
a white noise with a leg shock, and later showed that turning on the
white noise inhibited drinking behavior. This is a common form of
Pavlovian fear conditioning. What is notable about this experiment is
that the rats that learned the association were deeply anesthetized at
the time, and learning only took place if the adrenal hormone epinephrine was injected into the rats at the time of the training. Importantly,
epinephrine apparently did not reduce the depth of anesthesia, so that
the effect was not due to the hormone-treated rats being less anesthetized.

LEARNING MODULATORY HORMONES

Levine (1968) and de Wied (1964) were among the first to suggest that
hormones might influence learning and memory. The list of hormones
that might influence learning and memory is impressively long and
includes ACTH, various forms of melanocyte stimulating hormone
(MSH), corticosterone, epinephrine, norepinephrine, oxytocin, vasopressin, Substance P, and several opioid peptides including various
endorphins, and enkephalins (see Martinez et al., 1981). Since it is
possible that a primary function of all of these hormones is to influence
learning and memory, McGaugh and Martinez (1981) proposed that
these substances collectively be named learning modulatory hormones.

De Wied (1974) further suggested that many peptide hormones, such
as ACTH, vasopressin, oxytocin, and endorphins, have a behavioral

message encoded into certain of their amino acid sequences, as well as an endocrinological message. The parent molecule, when released, would be metabolized to produce a behaviorally active learning modulatory hormone. Evidence for this position is discussed below.

ACTH

It was known as early as 1955 that ACTH delayed extinction of, and hypophysectomy impaired acquisition of, an avoidance response (Applezweig & Baudry, 1955; Murphy & Miller, 1955). Much later de Wied (see de Wied, 1974) showed that the impaired acquisition of an avoidance response produced by adenohypophysectomy could be restored by ACTH or a small fragment of the whole hormone molecule $ACTH_{4-10}$, which does not have any corticotrophic action. These were the first data to indicate that ACTH might have both a behavioral and an endocrinological message. However, there are no known mechanisms by which $ACTH_{4-10}$ may be produced in sufficient concentrations within an organism to affect behavior (Witter, Gispen, & de Wied, 1981). Also, the deficit induced by hypophysectomy is reversed by a posterior pituitary hormone, vasopressin, indicating that the reversal of the learning deficit is not specific to ACTH (Bohus, Gispen, & de Wied, 1973; de Wied, 1969).

Considered as a pharmacological agent, the range of conditioned behaviors that are affected by $ACTH_{4-10}$ is impressive. For example, $ACTH_{4-10}$ affects extinction of pole-jumping (de Wied, 1966), of appetitively motivated behavior in a T-maze (Leonard, 1969), of conditioned taste aversion (Rigter & Popping, 1976), and of sexually motivated behavior (Bohus, Hendricx, van Kolfschoter, & Kredit, 1975). $ACTH_{4-10}$ also enhances acquisition (Martinez, Vasquez, Jensen, Soumireu–Mourat, & McGaugh, 1979) and retention (Flood, Jarvik, Bennett, & Orme, 1976) of a passive avoidance response and acquisition of complex maze task (O'Reilly, Coleman, & Ng, 1983) (for reviews see Beckwith & Sandman, 1978; de Wied & Jolles, 1982). It appears that even though $ACTH_{4-10}$ affects a number of conditioned behaviors, it is not a naturally occurring peptide of consequence. However, since $ACTH_{4-10}$ is part of the whole ACTH molecule, and the effects of ACTH on behavior are similar to those produced by $ACTH_{4-10}$ (Gold & Zornetzer, 1983; Riccio & Concannon, 1981), it is possible that $ACTH_{4-10}$ represents a sequence important for behavior contained within ACTH. If this is true, then there must be a receptive site for ACTH somewhere within the organism that is distinct from the classic adrenal cortical ACTH receptor. Interestingly, the little research conducted in this area shows that $ACTH_{4-10}$ and the much longer peptide, $ACTH_{1-28}$ have considerable affinity for opioid receptors in brain tissue (Terenius 1976).

VASOPRESSIN

The story for vasopressin unfolded much as it did for ACTH. De Wied (1965) found that rats with the neural lobe of their pituitaries removed extinguished an avoidance response faster than normal rats. This deficit was restored by synthetic vasopressin (Bohus et al., 1973). As with $ACTH_{4-10}$, a fragment of vasopressin, des glycinamide lysine vasopressin (DGLVP), which has little or no endocrine activity, reversed the behavioral deficit produced by neurohypophysectomy. The behavioral deficit was also reversed by other hormones such as ACTH and alpha-melanocyte-stimulating hormone (de Wied, 1969), suggesting the deficit induced by the lesion was not specific to vasopressin being removed.

Interestingly, there is a homozygous variant of the Brattleboro rat strain which lacks vasopressin and consequently expresses hypothalamic diabetes insipidus. These animals reportedly have an impaired ability to learn a passive avoidance response that is restored by DGLVP, and de Wied, Bohus and Wimersma Greidanus (1975) suggest that this is evidence that vasopressin is a hormone that is important for learning. An alternative view is that these diabetic animals are indeed poor at passive avoidance, but that this is the reflection of other anomalies of lacking vasopressin, such as reduced pituitary-adrenal response to stress or perhaps an altered electrolyte balance (Bailey & Weiss, 1981). On the other hand, some investigators have not been able to find any learning deficits in Brattleboro rats (Brito, Thomas, Gingold, & Gash, 1980; Williams, Carey, & Miller 1983). In any case the Brattleboro rat has not convinced the majority of scientists that vasopressin is important for learning and memory (see Gash & Thomas, 1983).

A more recent development is the report that vasopressin may be a prohormone for a smaller behaviorally active fragment named [pGlu⁴, Cyt⁶]AVP-(4–9). When injected directly into the brain this substance enhances passive avoidance learning, is a thousand times more potent than the parent molecule, vasopressin, and has a U-shaped dose response function (Burbach, Kovacs, de Wied, van Nispen, & Greven, 1983). Thus, the search for learning modulatory hormones may well be directed in the future to metabolic products of more classical endocrine hormones such as vasopressin.

Finally, there are those who think that vasopressin effects learning and memory, but not through a direct action of the hormone on the brain substrate of these processes. Rather, it is suspected that the peripheral autonomic sequelae of vasopressin administration, such as increased blood pressure, in turn affect brain function to alter conditioning (Le Moal, Koob, Koda, Bloom, Manning, Sawyer, & Rivier, 1981; Ettenberg, van der Kooy, Le Moal, Koob, & Bloom, 1983). This position is similar to the James–Lange view of memory described earlier (Martinez, 1983), except that the action of the hormone to influence learning is indirect. What does seem clear is that vasopressin affects conditioning in a number of different tasks, and by either central or peripheral administration. Future research will determine whether endogenous vasopressin systems normally function to influence learning and memory, and whether hormonal and/or central vasopressin systems are involved (Iverson, 1981).

EPINEPHRINE AND NOREPINEPHRINE

The role of peripheral catecholamines in mediating certain drug actions was discussed earlier (see section entitled "Catecholamines"). However, the possibility that epinephrine and norepinephrine may be learning modulatory hormones deserves some discussion. The influence of hormonal adrenergic systems on conditioning is more difficult to study than is the case with other hormones, because major stores of norepinephrine are found in two places, the sympathetic terminals and adrenal medulla. On the other hand, epinephrine is found mainly in the adrenal medulla. Early studies indicated that either sympathectomy or removal of a source of norepinephrine produced a deficit in the acquisition of an avoidance response (Wynne & Solomon, 1955), while administration of epinephrine produced the opposite result (Latane & Schacter, 1962). In the intervening years these finding have been extended to indicate that no part of the adrenergic system appears necessary for avoidance conditioning to occur, although deficits are sometimes seen, particularly in tasks that require high levels of stress suggesting that a stress system impaired by a lesion or some other means has a limited capacity or respond to challenge (see Martinez, 1983).

Administration of the hormones themselves is now known to be modulatory. Either enhancement or impairment of conditioning may be observed depending on the strength of the experimental treatment and the training parameters (see Di Giusto, Cairncross, & King, 1971; Leshner, 1978; Gold & Zornetzer, 1983). Important evidence that epinephrine may be a learning modulatory hormone was provided by Gold

& McCarty (1981; and McCarty & Gold, 1981). They showed that good retention of a passive avoidance response in rats is associated with a measurable high plasma concentration of epinephrine. This high plasma level of epinephrine may be achieved in one of two ways: (1) either by the animal itself, if it is intensely shocked, or (2) by injecting the animal with the hormone and giving it a mild footshock. These findings agree with the idea expressed earlier that the hormonal response, in this case the adrenergic response, serves to establish the importance of the event for the organism. Interestingly, the animal may not even have to be conscious for this process to occur, as epinephrine promotes conditioning in an anesthetized animal (Weinberger et al., 1984).

OPIOID PEPTIDES

It is now known that there are at least three great families of opioid peptides: (1) the proopiomelanocortins (β-endorphin, α-endorphin, and γ-endorphin), (2) preproenkephalin A (Met-enkephalin, Met-enkephlain-Arg-Phe, Leu-enkephalin), and (3) preproenkephalin B (dynorphin A, dynorphin B, α- and β-neoendorphin) to name the best characterized (see Bloom, 1983). Identification of new opioid peptides has outstripped the ability of behavioral scientists to characterize the actions of each, particularly as these peptides may have a relationship to learning and memory (see Martinez, Jensen, Messing, Rigter, & McGaugh, 1981). Nevertheless, an impressive literature concerning opioid peptides and learning and memory has developed in recent years, and it will be briefly summarized here (see Koob & Bloom, 1983).

The enkephalins were the first opioid peptides to be identified (Hughes, 1975). Within a year of this discovery, Kastin, Scollan, King, Schally, & Coy (1976) reported that Met-enkephalin given systemically to rats enhanced acquisition of a complex maze. This group also reported that an analog (D-Phe[4])-Met-enkephalin, which does not have opiate receptor activity, enhanced acquisition of the response, much as did Met-enkephalin. This peculiar feature of enkephalin action on conditioning was again reported by Izquierdo, Perry, Dias, Souza, Elisabetsky, Carrasco, Orshinger, & Netto (1981) who found that Met-enkephalin and des-Tyr-Met-enkephalin, a metabolite of Met-enkephalin without opioid activity, both impaired conditioning. In contrast Linden and Martinez (1985, in press) reported that Leu-enkephalin impaired retention of an appetitive maze response, but des-Try-Leu-enkephalin, which is a nonopioid peptide, was without effect. Izquierdo et al. also report that the actions of Met-enkephalin and des-

Tyr-Met enkephalin are reversible by naloxone, which is a standard test and definition of opioid activity (Hughes & Kosterlitz, 1983). Thus, the data suggest two opposite and conflicting conclusions: Enkephalin actions on conditioning are mediated by opioid receptors, and enkephalin actions on conditioning are not mediated by opioid receptors. The solution to this puzzle awaits further research, but nonopioid analogs such as des-Tyr-Met-enkephalin need to be better characterized in more behavioral conditioning situations before the second conclusion can be accepted with any generality. As regards naloxone most researchers have reported that it blocks the effects of enkephalins on aversive conditioning (Izquierdo et al., 1981; Martinez, Olson, & Hilston, 1984b; Rigter, Hannan, Messing, Martinez, Vasquez, Jensen, Veliquette, & McGaugh, 1980b), although there are important exceptions (Rigter, Dekker, & Martinez, 1981).

As noted earlier (see section entitled "Central versus Peripheral Actions of Drugs"), it is likely that enkephalins affect avoidance conditioning through a peripheral mechanism when they are injected systemically, because they probably do not cross the blood-brain barrier (Pardridge, 1983). Also, it is known that adrenal medullary integrity is necessary for enkephalin effects to be evident on avoidance conditioning (Martinez & Rigter, 1982), and naloxonium, which only acts on peripheral opioid receptors, attenuates the actions of enkephalin on conditioning (Martinez et al., 1984a). Thus, even though it is likely that enkephalins exert their primary action to influence aversive conditioning through a receptive site somewhere in the periphery, the location and nature of this receptor is unknown.

Finally, as regards the enkephalins, recent evidence suggests that these substances may be part of the normal machinery of learning and memory. As discussed in the Introduction, the fact that an agonist, such as enkephalin, influences conditioning is taken as evidence that enkephalinergic systems may be involved in learning and memory. However, a better experiment would be to manipulate the endogenous system by preventing the enkephalins circulating in the plasma from reaching their receptive sites, and demonstrating that this alters learning in a predictable way. This is akin to the lesion method where the hormone is also prevented from reaching its receptive sites, but the many side effects of gland removal are not present. Thus, Martinez and de Graaf (1985) and Martinez et al. (1984a) recently reported that naloxonium and an antiserum to Leu-enkephalin both produced an effect on conditioning that was the same; these substances enhanced acquisition of an avoidance response. The direction of the effect of the antagonists was the opposite to that seen with Leu-enkephalin alone. Importantly, both the naloxonium and the antiserum prevent Leu-enkephalin from reaching its receptor, but do so by quite different mechanisms. Taken together these data suggest that enkephalins in the periphery may act as learning modulatory hormones, particularly since the source and site of enkephalins can be manipulated to produce predictable behavioral results.

β-Endorphin was first isolated a year after the enkephalins and was also shown to be an opioid peptide (Goldstein, 1976). Two years later, de Wied, Bohus, van Ree, & Urban (1978) reported that both β-endorphin and α-endorphin, a probable metabolite (see following discussion) of β-endorphin, delayed extinction of a pole jump response and enhanced retention of a passive avoidance response in rats. Others find that β-endorphin impairs avoidance conditioning (Izquiredo, Paiva, & Elisabetsky, 1980; Martinez & Rigter, 1980), suggesting that the actions of β-endorphin are most likely modulatory. Kovacs and de Wied (1981) propose that β-endorphin may be a parent molecule for the degradation products α- and γ-endorphin (Burbach, Loeber, Verhoef, Wiegant, de Kloet, & de Wied, 1980; Burbach & de Kloet, 1982) which they suggest, may be learning modulatory hormones, since they reportedly affect conditioning (Kovacs & de Wied, 1981; Martinez & Rigter, 1980). Izquierdo (1982) has a different idea. He proposes that there is an endogenous amnestic mechanism whose function is mediated by β-endorphinergic systems in the brain. Izquierdo feels that most information we learn "is completely useless or becomes obsolete very soon, like most of the telephone numbers we learned last year." Thus, an endogenous amnestic mechanism helps us to keep our mind uncluttered.

Conceptually, Izquierdo's (1982) idea of an amnestic mechanism is quite different from the ideas of hormonal modulation of memory discussed earlier. First, the proposed mechanism is not the same, peripheral versus central, as regards the primary site of action of the opioid peptide or hormone. Second, hormonal modulation could also be used to explain the poor recollection of incidental learning, but only because the original information was stored with more or less strength or fidelity, not because it was actively destroyed by an amnestic process. Third, Izquierdo has picked a single opioid peptide system to be the final common pathway, whereas hormonal modulation would suggest multiple, parallel, and perhaps even independent actions on the brain and ultimately on learning and memory (see Kastin, Olson, Sandman, & Coy, 1981).

In retrospect is appears that hormones are capable of altering learning and memory in many species and varieties of conditioning situations, when given exogenously. It is not clear whether hormones in this situation are acting like drugs. That is, the hormonal system is no doubt mediating the effect, but only because it was artificially stimulated through injection. Does the hormonal system normally participate in the behavior in a normal intact animal? This question is harder to answer, but correlational (Gold & McCarty, 1981; McCarty & Gold, 1981) and other studies using strategies to abolish the source of the hormone other than lesions (Martinez et al., 1984a) are beginning to provide additional positive evidence. Thus, it may be that endocrine hormones, a most highly evolved messenger molecule system, which exist rather exclusively in vertebrates (Krieger, 1983), may participate and even be part of the normal machinery of a complex cognitive process such as learning and memory (Martinez, 1983).

DRUGS TO UNDERSTAND OR TO ALTER
LEARNING AND MEMORY?

The discussion, so far, had centered around the use of drugs to understand learning and memory. Yet, some space should be given to a discussion of drugs to affect learning and memory. Certainly, this is a societal issue as well as a scientific one. Should drugs be developed that accelerate learning and improve memory? In some sense the question is moot, because efforts have been and are currently underway to develop such drugs. Interestingly, there is a discernable pattern in the manner and type of experiments that lead to the development of a drug that alters cognitive functioning in humans. First the drug is shown to reverse experimental amnesia, then to enhance learning and memory in the absence of any amnestic treatment. Finally, if the drug is nontoxic it is brought to limited clinical trials in humans. For example Plotnikoff (1966) reported many years ago that magnesium pemoline attenuated ECS-induced amnesia for an avoidance response in rats, and that this drug enhanced performance of various learning tasks (Plotnikoff, 1971). The reversal of ECS effects was also found in humans. Small, Sharpley, and Small (1968) found that magnesium pemoline attenuated the deleterious effects of ECS therapy on memory as measured on the Weschler Memory scale. Today magnesium pemoline is sold under the trade name Cylert; it is considered to be a mild CNS stimulant, and it is used to treat minimal brain dysfunction in children (Franz, 1980). A similar series of studies led to the development of Piracetam (1-acetamine-2-pyrrolidone) (Giurgea, 1976), a nootropic drug that purportedly enhances the efficiency of brain integrative mechanisms (see Nicolaus, 1982). Piracetam in not currently sold in the U.S.A.

Other drugs that may soon appear on the shelves that were discovered in animal laboratories to reverse experimental amnesia and facilitate avoidance conditioning include an analog of adrenocorticotrophic hormone, $ACTH_{4-9}$ (Organon 2766) that appears to increase sustained attention in humans (Gaillard, 1981), vasopressin which has been reported to have clinical efficacy in alleviating posttraumatic amnesia, (see Jolles, 1983), and surprisingly naloxone, an opioid antagonist, that was recently reported to improve selective attention in humans (Arnsten, Segal, Neville, Hillyard, Janowsky, Judd, & Bloom, 1983) and to ameliorate some of the memory deficit associated with Alzheimer's disease (Reisberg, Ferris, Anand, Pervez Mir, Geibel, de Leon, & Roberts, 1983). Finally, it is a good bet that many of the drugs of the future that will be found to influence complex cognitive processing in humans will be derived from endogenous peptides presently known and soon to be discovered (see Tiklenberg & Thornton, 1983).

CONCLUSIONS

Several major points have emerged in this discussion of interventional approaches to learning and memory: drugs and hormones. These points are briefly detailed below.

1. All messenger molecule systems have a source and site of action, and it is either the source or the site that is altered in some way to understand the role of the particular messenger system in learning and memory.
2. Time dependency is both an anterograde and a retrograde phenomenon. It is likely that these gradients reveal the temporal domain within which the function of any particular neural or hormonal system may be altered to affect learning and memory.
3. It is common in the scientific literature on drug effects on learning and memory to find U-shaped dose response curves. The biological mechanism(s) responsible for U-shaped curves are not currently understood.
4. Most drugs and hormones affect learning and memory in a modulatory fashion. Whether enhancement or impairment of retention performance is observed following treatment with a drug or hormone is dependent on the strength of the experimental treatment, the strength of the training experience, and the interaction between the two.

5. Many drugs and hormones do not easily cross the blood–brain barrier, if they cross at all. This fact has generated a controversy about the primary site of action, either central or peripheral, for a good many drugs but in particular the neuropeptides.

6. Evidence was reviewed showing that many neurotransmitter systems seem to be involved in learning and memory. The neurotransmitter systems that were examined include those whose primary neurotransmitter is acetylcholine, norepinephrine, and serotonin.

7. Learning and memory no doubt involves the function of proteins in some way. Evidence obtained with antibiotic protein synthesis inhibitors supports this view. Yet, toxic and other anomolous findings generated with the use of these antibiotics have led some to question whether protein synthesis inhibitors provide hard evidence concerning the role of proteins in learning and memory.

8. Hormones appear to affect complex cognitive processes such as learning and memory. The fact that the hormonal response often follows the environmental event to be remembered has led to a James–Lange view of hormones and learning and memory. We meet a bear, run, and most likely remember in vivid detail many aspects of the encounter.

9. It is possible that many hormones are part of the normal machinery of learning and memory. Such hormones are called learning modulatory hormones and include as candidates, ACTH, MSH, corticosterone, epinephrine, norepinephrine, oxytocin, vasopressin, Substance P, and several opioid peptides.

10. Drugs are used both to understand and to alter learning and memory. Currently, there is research devoted to developing drugs that will affect learning and memory in humans.

REFERENCES

Applezweig, M. H., & Baudry, F. D. (1955). The pituitary adrenocoritcal system in avoidance learning. *Psychological Reports, 1,* 417–420.

Arnsten, A. F. T., Segal, D. S., Neville, H. J., Hillyard, S. A., Janowsky, D. S., Judd, L. L., & Bloom, F. E. (1983). Naloxone augments electrophysiological signs of attention in man. *Nature, 304,* 725–727.

Bailey, W. H., & Weiss, J. M. (1981). Avoidance conditioning and endocrine function in Brattleboro rats. In J. L. Martinez, Jr., R. A. Jensen, R. B. Messing, H. Rigter, & J. L. McGaugh (Eds.), *Endogenous Peptides and learning and memory processes* (pp. 371–395). New York: Academic Press.

Barondes, S. H., & Jarvik, M. E. (1964). The influence of actinomycin D on brain RNA synthesis and on memory. *Journal of Neurochemistry, 11*, 187–189.

Barraco, R. A., & Stettner, L. J. (1976). Antibiotics and memory. *Psychological Bulletin, 83*, 242–302.

Bartus, R. T., Dean, R. L., Goas, J. A., & Lippa, A. S. (1980). Age-related changes in passive avoidance retention: Modulation with dietary choline. *Science, 209*, 301–303.

Battig, K. (1970). The effect of pre- and post-trial application of nicotine on the 12 problems of the Hebb–Williams test in the rat. *Psychopharmacologia, 18*, 68–76.

Beckwith, B. E., & Sandman, C. A. (1978). Behavioral influences of the neuropeptides ACTH and MSH: A methodological review. *Neuroscience and Biobehavioral Reviews, 2*, 311–338.

Beninger, R. J. (1983). The role of dopamine in locomotor activity and learning. *Brain Research Reviews, 6*, 173–196.

Bloom, F. E. (1983). The endorphins: A growing family of pharmacologically pertinent peptides. *Annual Review of Pharmacology and Toxicology, 23*, 151–170.

Bohus, B., & de Wied, D. (1981). Actions of ACTH- and MSH-like peptides on learning, performance, and retention. In J. L. Martinez, Jr., R. A. Jensen, R. B. Messing, H. Rigter, & J. L. McGaugh (Eds.), *Endogenous peptides and learning and memory processes* (pp. 59–77). New York: Academic Press.

Bohus, B., Gispen, W. H., & de Wied, D. (1973). Effect of lysine vasopressin and ACTH$_{4-10}$ on conditioned avoidance behavior of hypophysectomized rats. *Neuroendocrinology, 11*, 137–143.

Bohus, B., Hendricx, H. H. L., van Kolfschoten, A. A., & Kredit, T. G. (1975). The effect of ACTH$_{4-10}$ on copulatory and sexually motivated approach behavior in the male rat. In M. Sandler & G. L. Gessa (Eds.), *Sexual behavior: pharmacology and biochemistry* (pp. 269–275). New York: Raven.

Brito, G. N., Thomas, G. J., Gingold, S. I., & Gash, D. M. (1980). Behavioral characteristics of vasopressin-deficient rats (Brattleboro strain). *Brain Research Bulletin, 6*, 71–75.

Brown, R., & Kulik, J. (1977). Flashbulb memories, *Cognition, 5*, 73–99.

Burbach, J. P. H., & de Kloet, R. (1982). Proteolysis of β-endorphin in brain tissue. *Peptides, 3*, 451–453.

Burbach, J. P. H., Kovacs, G. L., de Wied, D., van Nispen, J. W., & Greven, H. M. (1983). A major metabolite of arginine vasopressin in the brain is a highly potent neuropeptide. *Science, 221*, 1310–1312.

Burbach, J. P. H., Loeber, J. G., Verhof, J., Wiegant, V. M., de Kloet, E. R., & de Wied, D. (1980). Selective conversion of β-endorphin into peptides related to γ- and α-endorphin. *Nature, 283*, 96–97.

Castellano, C. (1982). Dose-dependent modulation of memory by the enkephalin analog FK 33-824 in C57BL/6 mice. *Behavioral and Neural Biology, 36*, 189–196.

Chapouthier, G. (1983). Protein synthesis and memory. In J. A. Deutsch (Ed). *The physiological basis of memory* (pp. 1–47; 2nd ed.). New York: Academic Press.

Chorover, S. (1976). An experimental critique of "consolidation studies" and an alternative "model-systems" approach to the biophysiology of memory. In M. R. Rosenzweig & E. L. Bennett (Eds.), *Neural mechanisms of learning and memory* (pp. 561–582). Cambridge: The MIT Press.

Church, A. C., & Sprott, R. L. (1979). The influence of mouse genotype on passive avoidance learning in subsequent concentrations of norepinephrine and serotonin in the hypothalamus and hippocampus. *Physiological Psychology, 7*, 84–88.

Cohen, H. D., & Barondes, S. H., (1966). Further studies on learning and memory after intracerebral actinomycin D. *Journal of Neurochemistry, 13*, 207–211.

Cooper, J. R., Bloom, F. E., & Roth, R. H. (1982). *The biochemical basis of neuropharmacology.* (4th ed.). New York: Oxford University.

Davies, P., & Maloney, A. J. F. (1976). Selective loss of central cholinergic neurons in Alzheimer's disease. *Lancet, 2,* 1403.

Day, M. D. (1979). *Autonomic pharmacology. Experimental and clinical aspects.* New York: Churchill Livingston.

Deutsch, J. A. (1983). The cholinergic synapse and the site of memory. In J. A. Deutsch (Ed.), *The physiological basis of memory* (pp. 367–386). (2nd ed.) New York: Academic Press.

DiGiusto, E. L., Cairncross, K., & King, M. G. (1971). Hormonal influences on fear-motivated responses. *Psychological Bulletin, 75,* 432–444.

Duncan, C. P. (1949). The retroactive effect of electroshock on learning. *Journal of Comparative and Physiological Psychology, 42,* 32–44.

Dunn, A. J. (1980). Neurochemistry of learning and memory: An evaluation of recent data. *Annual Review of Psychology, 31,* 343–390.

Essman, W. B. (1973). Age-dependent effects of 5-hydroxytryptamine upon memory consolidation and cerebral protein synthesis. *Pharmacology Biochemistry and Behavior, 1,* 7–14.

Ettenberg, A., van der Kooy, D., Le Moal, M., Koob, G. F., & Bloom, F. E. (1983). Can aversize properties of (peripherally-injected) vasopressin account for its putative role in memory? *Behavioural Brain Research, 7,* 331–350.

Feldman, R. S., & Quenzer, L. F. (1984). *Fundamentals of neuropsychopharmacology.* Sunderland, MA: Sinauer Associates.

Flexner, L. B., & Flexner, J. B. (1968). Intracerebral saline: Effect on memory of trained mice treated with puromycin. *Science, 159,* 330–331.

Flood, J. F., Bennett, E. L., Orme, A. E., & Rosenzweig, M. R. (1975). Relation of memory formation to controlled amounts of brain protein synthesis. *Physiology and Behavior, 15,* 97–102.

Flood, J. F., Bennett, E. L., Rosenzweig, M. R., & Orme, A. E. (1973). The influence of duration of protein synthesis inhibition on memory. *Physiology and Behavior, 10,* 555–562.

Flood, J. F., Jarvik, M. E., Bennett, E. L., & Orme, A. E. (1976). Effects of ACTH peptide fragments on memory formation. *Pharmacology, Biology, and Behavior, 5,* (1), 41–51.

Flood, J. F., Bennett, E. L., Orme, A. E., Rosenzweig, M. R., & Jarvik, M. E. (1978). Modifications of anisomycin-induced amnesia by stimulants and depressants. *Science, 199,* 324–326.

Franz, D. N. (1980). Central nervous system stimulants. In A. Goodman Gilman, L. S. Goodman, & A. Gilman (Eds.), *Goodman and Gilman's the pharmacological basis of therapeutics* (pp. 585–591; 6th ed.). New York: Macmillan.

Gaillard, A. W. K. (1981). ACTH analogs and human performance. In J. L. Martinez, Jr., R. A. Jensen, R. B. Messing, H. Rigter, & J. L. McGaugh (Eds.), *Endogenous peptides and learning and memory processes* (pp. 181–196). New York: Academic Press.

Gallagher, M., & Kapp, B. S. (1978). Manipulation of opiate activity in the amygdala alters memory processes. *Life Sciences, 23,* 1973–1978.

Garg, M., & Holland, H. C. (1969). Consolidation and maze learning: A study of some strain/drug interactions. *Psychopharmacologia, 14,* 426–431.

Gash, D. M., & Thomas, G. J. (1983). What is the importance of vasopressin in memory processes. *Trends in Neurosciences, 6,* 197–198.

Gilman, A. G., Mayer, S., & Melman, K. L. (1980). Pharmacodynamics: Mechanisms of

drug action and the relationship between drug concentrations and effect. In A. Goodman Gilman, L. S. Goodman, & A. Gilman (Eds.), *Goodman and Gilman's the pharmacological basis of therapeutics* (pp. 28–39). (6th ed.) New York: Macmillan.

Giurgea, C. (1976). Piracetam: Nootropic pharmacology of neurointegrative activity. In W.
B. Essman, & L. Valzelli (Eds.), *Current developments in psychopharmacology* (Vol.
3; pp. 221–273). New York: Spectrum.

Gold, P. E., & McCarty, R. (1981). Plasma catecholamines: Changes after footshock and
seizure-producing frontal cortex stimulation. *Behavioral and Neural Biology, 31,*
247–260.

Gold, P. E., & McGaugh, J. L. (1977). Hormones and memory. In L. H. Miller, C. A.
Sandman, & A. J. Kastin (Eds.), *Neuropeptide influences on the brain and behavior*
(pp. 127–143). New York: Raven.

Gold, P. E., & van Buskirk, R. B. (1975). Facilitation of time-dependent memory processes
with post-trial epinephrine injections. *Behavioral Biology, 13,* 145–153.

Gold, P. E., & van Buskirk, R. (1976a). Effects of post-trial hormone injections on memory
processes. *Hormones and Behavior, 7,* 509–517.

Gold, P. E., & van Buskirk, R. B. (1976b). Enhancement and impairment of memory
processes with post-trial injections of adrenocorticotrophic hormone. *Behavioral
Biology, 16,* 387–400.

Gold, P. E., & Zornetzer, S. F. (1983). The mnemon and its juices: Neuromodulation of
memory processes. *Behavioral and Neural Biology, 38,* 151–189.

Goldstein, A. (1976). Opioid peptides (endorphins) in pituitary and brain. *Science, 193,*
1081–1083.

Haycock, J. W., van Buskirk, R., & McGaugh, J. L. (1977). Effects of catecholaminergic
drugs upon memory storage processes in mice. *Behavioral Biology, 20,* 281–310.

Hughes, J. (1975). Isolation of an endogenous compound from the brain with pharmacological properties similar to morphine. *Brain Research, 88,* 295–308.

Hughes, J., & Kosterlitz, H. W. (1983). Introduction (to Opioid Peptides). *British Medical
Bulletin, 39,* 1–3.

Hunter, B., Zornetzer, S. F., Jarvik, M. E., & McGaugh, J. L. (1977). Modulation of learning
and memory: Effects of drugs influencing neurotransmitters. In L. Iverson, S. Iverson,
& S. Snyder (Eds.), *Handbook of psychopharmacology* (pp. 531–577). (Vol. 8, Drugs,
Neurotransmitters and Behavior). New York: Plenum.

Huston, J. P., & Staubli, U. (1981). Substance P and its effects on learning and memory. In
J. L. Martinez, Jr., R. A. Jensen, R. B. Messing, H. Rigter, & J. L. McGaugh (Eds.),
Endogenous modulators of learning and memory processes (pp. 521–540). New
York: Academic Press.

Idzikowski, C., & Oswald, I. (1983). Interference with human memory by an antibiotic.
Psychopharmacology, 79, 108–110.

Iverson, I. (1981). Neuropeptides: Do they integrate body and brain? *Nature, 291,* 454.

Izquierdo, I. (1982). β-endorphin and forgetting. *Trends in Pharmacological Sciences, 15,*
119–121.

Izquierdo, I., Paiva, A. C. M., & Elisabetsky, E. (1980). Post-training intraperitoneal administration of leu-enkephalin and β-endorphin causes retrograde amnesia for two
different tasks in rats. *Behavioral and Neural Biology, 28,* 246–250.

Izquierdo, I., Perry, M. L., Dias, R. D., Souza, D. O., Elisabetsky, E., Carrasco, M. A.,
Orshinger, O. A., & Netto, C. A. (1981). In J. L. Martinez, Jr., R. A. Jensen, R. B.
Messing, H. Rigter, & J. L. McGaugh (Eds.), *Endogenous peptides and learning and
memory processes* (pp. 269–290). New York: Academic Press.

Jolles, J. (1983). Vasopresin-like peptides and the treatment of memory disorders in man.

In B. A. Cross & G. Leng (Eds.), *The neurohypophysis: Structure, function and control, progress in brain research* (pp. 169–182). (Vol. 60). Amsterdam: Elsevier Science Publishers, B. V.

Karpiak, S. E., & Rapport, M. M. (1979). Inhibition of consolidation and retrieval stages of passive-avoidance learning by antibodies to gangliosides. *Behavioral and Neural Biology, 27,* 146–156.

Karpiak, S. W., Kirchmer, M., & Rapport, M. M. (1976). Reserpine inhibition of passive avoidance behavior: Time and dose responses. *Research Communications Psychology Psychiatry Behavior,* 149–154.

Kastin, A. J., Olson, R. D., Sandman, C. A., & Coy, D. H. (1981). Multiple independent actions of neuropeptides on behavior. In J. L. Martinez, Jr., R. A. Jensen, R. B. Messing, H. Rigter, & J. L. McGaugh (Eds.), *Endogenous peptides and learning and memory processes* (pp. 563–577). New York: Academic Press.

Kastin, A. J., Scollan, E. L., King, M. G., Schally, A. V., & Coy, D. H. (1976). Enkephalin and a potent analog facilitate maze performance after intraperitoneal administration in rats. *Pharmacology, Biochemistry & Behavior, 5,* 691–695.

Kety, S. S. (1970). The biogenic amines in the central nervous system: Their possible roles in arousal, emotion, and learning. In F. O. Schmitt (Ed.), *The neurosciences* (pp. 324–336). New York: The Rockefeller University.

Koob, G. F., & Bloom, F. E. (1983). Behavioural effects of opioid peptides. *British Medical Bulletin, 39,* 89–94.

Kovacs, G. L., & de Wied, D. (1981). Endorphin influences on learning and memory. In J. L. Martinez, Jr., R. A. Jensen, R. B. Messing, H. Rigter, and J. L. McGaugh (Eds.), *Endogenous peptides and learning and memory processes* (pp. 231–247). New York: Academic Press.

Krieger, D. T. (1983). Brain peptides: What, where, and why? *Science, 222,* 975–985.

Latane, B., & Schacter, S. (1962). Adrenaline and avoidance learning. *Journal of Comparative and Physiological Psychology, 55,* 369–372.

Leavitt, F. (1982). *Drugs and behavior.* New York: John Wiley & Sons.

Le Moal, M., Koob, G. F., Koda, L. Y., Bloom, F. E., Manning, M., Sawyer, W. H., & Rivier, J. (1981). Vasopressor receptor antagonists effects of vasopressin. *Nature, 291,* 491–493.

Leonard, B. E. (1969). The effect of sodium-barbitone, alone and together with ACTH and amphetamine, on the behavior of the rat in the multiple "T" maze. *International Journal of Neuropharmacology, 8,* 427–435.

Leshner, A. I. (1978). *An introduction to behavioral endocrinology.* New York: Oxford University, 249–277.

Leshner, A. I., Merkle, D. A., & Mixon, J. F. (1981). Pituitary-adrenocortical effects on learning and memory in social situations. In J. L. Martinez, Jr., R. A. Jensen, R. B. Messing, H. Rigter, & J. L. McGaugh (Eds.), *Endogenous peptides and learning and memory processes* (pp. 159–179). New York: Academic Press.

Levine, S. (1968). Hormones and conditioning. In W. J. Arnold (Ed.), *Nebraska symposium and motivation* (pp. 85–101). Lincoln: University of Nebraska.

Linden, D., & Martinez, Jr., J. L. (1985). Leu-enkephalin impairs memory of an appetitive maze response in mice. *Behavioral Neuroscience, 100,* in press.

Martinez, Jr., J. L. (1982). Conditioning: Modification by peripheral mechanisms. In C. D. Woody (Ed.), *Conditioning: Representation of involved neural functions* (pp. 601–623). New York: Plenum.

Martinez, Jr., J. L. (1983). Endogenous modulators of learning and memory. In S. Cooper

(Ed.). *Theory in psychopharmacology* (pp. 47–74). (Vol. 2). London: Academic Press.

Martinez, Jr., J. L., & de Graaf, J. S. (1985). Quaternary naloxone enhances acquisition of a discriminated y-maze and a one-way active avoidance task in mice. *Psychopharmacology, 87*, 410–413.

Martinez, Jr., J. L., & Rigter, H. (1980). Endorphins alter acquisition and consolidation of an inhibitory avoidance response in rats. *Neuroscience Letters, 18*, 197–201.

Martinez, Jr., J. L., & Rigter, H. (1982) Enkephalin actions on avoidance conditioning may be related to adrenal medullary function, *Behavioural Brain Research, 6*, 289–299.

Martinez, Jr., J. L. Conner, P., Dana, R., Chavkin, C., Bloom, F., & de Graaf, J. (1984a). Endogenous modulation of peripheral Leu-enkephalin (LE) systems affects avoidance conditioning. *Society for Neuroscience Abstracts, 10*, 176.

Martinez, Jr., J. L., Jensen, R. A., & McGaugh, J. L. (1981). Attenuation of experimentally-induced amnesia. *Progress in Neurobiology, 16*, 155–186.

Martinez, Jr., J. L., Jensen, R. A., & McGaugh, J. L. (1983). Facilitation of memory consolidation. In J. A. Deutsch (Ed.), *The physiological basis of memory* (pp. 49–70). New York: Academic Press.

Martinez, Jr., J. L., Jensen, R. A., Messing, R. B. Rigter, H., & McGaugh, J. L. (1981). (Eds.), *Endogenous modulators of learning and memory*. New York: Academic Press.

Martinez, Jr., J. L., Olson, K., & Hilston, C. (1984b). Opposite effects of Met-enkephalin and Leu-enkephalin on a discriminated shock-escape task. *Behavioral neuroscience, 98*, 487–495.

Martinez, Jr., J. L., Rigter, H., Jensen, R. A., Messing, R. B., Vasquez, B. J. & McGaugh, J. L. (1981). Endorphin and enkephalin effects on avoidance conditioning: The other side of the pituitary-adrenal axis. In J. L. Martinez, Jr., R. A. Jensen, R. B. Messing, H. Rigter, & J. L. McGaugh (Eds.), *Endogenous peptides and learning and memory processes* (pp. 305–324). New York: Academic Press.

Martinez, Jr., J. L., Vasquez, B. J., Jensen, R. A., & McGaugh, J. L. (1977). Facilitation by reserpine in an inhibitory avoidance task in mice. *Behavioral Biology, 21*, 139–144.

Martinez, Jr., J. L., Vasquez, B. J., Jensen, R. A., Soumireu–Mourat, B., & McGaugh, J. L. (1979). $ACTH_{4-9}$ analog (ORG 2766) facilitates acquisition of an inhibitory avoidance response in rats. *Pharmacology, Biochemistry, and Behavior, 10*, 145–147.

Martinez, Jr., J. L., Vasquez, B. J., Rigter, H., Messing, R. B., Jensen, R. A., Liang, K. C., & McGaugh, J. L. (1980). Attenuation of amphetamine-induced enhancement of learning by adrenal demedullation, *Brain Research, 195*, 433–443.

Mauk, M. D., Warren, J. T., & Thompson, R. F. (1982). Selective, naloxone-reversible morphine depression of learned behavioral and hippocampal responses. *Science, 216*, 434–436.

Mauk, M. D., Madden, J., Barchas, J. D., & Thompson, R. F. (1982). Opiates and classical conditioning: Selective abolition of conditioned responses by activation of opiate receptors within the central nervous system. *Proceedings of the National Academy of Science, USA, 79*, 7598–7602.

McCarty, R. & Gold, P. E. (1981). Plasma catecholamines: Effects of footshock level and hormonal modulators of memory storage. *Hormones and Behavior, 15*, 168–182.

McGaugh, J. L. (1973). Drug facilitation of learning and memory. *Annual Review of Pharmacology, 13*, 229–241.

McGaugh, J. L., & Herz, M. J. (1972). *Memory consolidation*. San Francisco: Albion Publishing Co.

McGaugh, J. L., & Martinez, Jr., J. L. (1981). Learning modulatory hormones: An introduction to endogenous peptides and learning and memory processes. In J. L. Martinez,

Jr., R. A. Jensen, R. B. Messing, H. Rigter, & J. L. McGaugh (Eds.), *Endogenous peptides and learning and memory processes* (pp. 1–3). New York: Academic Press.

Meligeni, J. A., Ledergerber, S. A., & McGaugh, J. L. (1978). Norepinephrine attenuation of amnesia produced by diethyldithiocarbamate. *Brain Research, 149,* 155–164.

Messing, R. B., Jensen, R. A., Martinez, Jr., J. L., Spiehler, V. R., Vasquez, B. J., Soumireu–Mourat, B., Liang, K. C., & McGaugh, J. L. (1979). Naloxone enhancement of memory. *Behavioral and Neural Biology, 27,* 266–275.

Mueller, A. L., Palmer, M. R., Hoffer, B. J., & Dunwiddie, T. V. (1982). Hippocampal noradrenergic responses in vivo and in vitro characterization of alpha and beta components. *Naunyn–Schmiedeberg's Archives of Pharmacology, 318,* 259–266.

Murphy, J. V., & Miller, R. E. (1955). The effect of adrenocorticotrophic hormone (ACTH) on avoidance conditioning in the rat. *Journal Comparative and Physiological Psychology, 48,* 47–49.

Nicolaus, B. J. R. (1982). Chemistry and pharmacology of nootropics. *Drug Development Research, 2,* 463–474.

O'Reilly, H. M., Coleman, G. J., & Ng, K. T. (1983). The role of adrenocorticotrophin and norepinephrine in appetitive learning in the rat. *Physiology and Behavior, 30,* 253–258.

Orsingher, O. A., & Fulginiti, S. (1971). Effects of alpha-methyl tyrosine and adrenergic blocking agents on the facilitating action of amphetamine and nicotine on learning in rats. *Psychopharmacologia, 19,* 231–240.

Palfai, T., Wichlinski, L., & Brown, O. M. (1983). The effect of reserpine, syrosingapine, and guanethidine on the retention of discriminated escape reversal: Peripherally administered catecholamines cannot reverse the reserpine amnesia in this situation. *Behavioral and Neural Biology, 38,* 120–126.

Pardridge, W. M. (1983). Neuropeptides and the blood-brain barrier. *Annual Review of Physiology, 45,* 73–82.

Plotnikoff, N. (1966). Magnesium pemoline: Enhancement of memory after electroconvulsive shock in rats. *Life Science, 5,* 1495–1498.

Plotnikoff, N. (1971). Pemoline: A review of performance. *Texas Reports Biology Medicine, 29,* 467–479.

Reisberg, B., Ferris, S. H., Anand, R., Pervez Mir, M. A., Geibel, V., de Leon, M. J., & Roberts, E. (1983). Effects of naloxone in senile dementia: A double-blind trial. *New England Journal of Medicine, 308,* 721–722.

Riccio, D. C., & Concannon, J. T. (1981). ACTH and the reminder phenomena. In J. L. Martinez, Jr., R. A. Jensen, R. B. Messing, H. Rigter, & J. L. McGaugh (Eds.), *Endogenous peptides and learning and memory processes* (pp. 117–142). New York: Academic Press.

Rigter, H., & Popping, A. (1976). Hormonal influences on the extinction of conditioned taste aversion. *Psychopharmacologia, 46,* 255–261.

Rigter, H., Dekker, I., & Martinez, Jr., J. L. (1981). A comparison of the ability of opioid peptides and opiates to affect active avoidance conditioning in rats. *Regulatory Peptides, 2,* 317–322.

Rigter, H., Jensen, R. A., Martinez, Jr., J. L., Messing, R. B., Vasquez, B. J., Liang, K. C. & McGaugh, J. L. (1980a). Enkephalin and fear-motivated behavior. *Proceedings of the National Academy of Sciences USA, 77,* 3729–3732.

Rigter, H., Hannan, T. J., Messing, R. B., Martinez, Jr., J. L., Vasquez, B. J., Jensen, R. A., Veliquette, J., & McGaugh, J. L. (1980b). Enkephalins interfere with acquisition of an active avoidance response. *Life Sciences, 26,* 337–345.

Rosenbaum, M., Cohen, H. D., & Barondes, S. H. (1968). Effect of intracerbral saline on amnesia produced by inhibitors of cerebral protein synthesis. *Communications in Behavioral Biology, Part A, 2,* 47–50.

Rosenzweig, M. R. (1984). Experience, memory, and the brain. *American Psychologist, 39,* 365–376.

Rosenzweig, M. R., & Leiman, A. L. (1982). *Physiological psychology.* Lexington, MA: D.C. Health and Co.

Rosenzweig, M. R., Bennett, E. L., & Flood, J. F. (1981). Pharmacological modulation of formation of long-term memory. In G. Adam, I. Meszaros, & E. I. Benyai (Eds.), *Brain and behavior advances in physiological science: Vol. 17.* (pp. 101–111). London: Pergamon.

Small, J. G., Sharpley, P., & Small, I. F. (1968). Influences of Cylert upon memory changes with ECT. *American Journal of Psychiatry, 125,* 837–840.

Stratton, L. O., & Petrinovich, L. F. (1963). Postrial injection of an anticholineterase drug on maze learning in two strains of mice. *Psychopharmacologia, 5,* 47–54.

Soumireu–Mourat, B., Destrade, C., & Cardo, B. (1975). Effects of seizure and subseizure posttrial hippocampal stimulation on appetitive operant behavior in mice. *Behavioral Biology, 15,* 303–316.

Squire, L. R. (1975). Short-term memory as a biological entity. In D. Deutsch & J. A. Deutsch (Eds.), *Short-term memory* (pp. 1–40). New York: Academic Press.

Squire, L. R., & Davis, H. P. (1981). The pharmacology of memory: A neurobiological perspective. *Annual Review of Pharmacology and Toxicology, 21,* 323–356.

Sternberg, D. B., Gold, P. E., & McGaugh, J. L. (1983). Memory facilitation and impariment with supra-seizure electrical brain stimulation: Attenuation with pretrial propranolol injections. *Behavioral and Neural Biology, 38,* 261–268.

Terenius, L. (1976). Somatostatin and ACTH are peptides with partial antagonist-like selectivity for opiate receptors. *European Journal of Pharmacology, 38,* 211–213.

Thompson, R. F., Patterson, M. M., & Berger, T. (1978). Associative learning in the mammalian nervous system. In T. Teyler (Ed.), *Brain and learning* (pp. 51–90). Stamford: Greylock.

Tiklenberg, J. R., & Thornton, J. E. (1983). Neuropeptides in geriatric psychopharmacology. *Psychopharmacology Bulletin, 19,* 198–211.

van Wimersma Greidanus, T. J. B., Bohus, B., & de Wied, D. (1981). Vasopressin and oxytocin in learning and memory. In J. L. Martinez, Jr., R. A. Jensen, R. B. Messing, H. Rigter, & J. C. McGaugh (Eds.), *Endogenous peptides and learning and memory processes.* (pp. 413–427). New York: Academic Press.

Walsh, T. J., & Palfai, T. (1979). Memory storage impairment or retrieval failure: Pharmacologically distinguishable processes. *Pharmacology Biochemistry & Behavior, 11,* 453–456.

Weinberger, N. M., Gold, P. E., & Sternberg, D. B. (1984). Epinephrine enables Pavlovian fear conditioning under anesthesia. *Science, 223,* 605–607.

Weiner, N. (1980). Atropine, scopolamine, and related antimuscarinic drugs. In A. Goodman Gilman, L. S. Goodman, & A. Gilman (Eds.), *Goodman and Gilman's the pharmacological basis of therapeutics* (pp. 120–137). (6th ed.) New York: Macmillan.

de Wied, D. (1964). Influence of anterior pituitary on avoidance learning and escape behavior. *American Journal of Physiology, 207,* 255–259.

de Wied, D. (1965). The influence of the posterior and intermediate lobe of the pituitary and pituitary peptides on the maintenance of a conditioned avoidance response in rats. *International Journal of Neuropharmacology, 4,* 157–167.

de Wied, D. (1966). Inhibitory effect of ACTH and related peptides on extinction of conditioned avoidance behavior in rats. *Proceedings Society Experimental Biology Medicine, 122,* 28–32.

de Wied, D. (1969). Effects of peptide hormones on behavior. In W. F. Ganong & L. Martini (Eds.), *Frontiers in neuroendocrinology* (pp. 97–140). New York: Oxford University.

de Wied, D. (1974). Pituitary-adrenal system hormones and behavior. In F. O. Schmitt & F. G. Worden (Eds.), *The neurosceinces third study program* (pp. 653–666). Cambridge: MIT Press.

de Wied, D. & Jolles, J. (1982). Neuropeptides derived from pro-opiocortin: Behavioral, physiological, and neurochemical effects. *Physiological Reviews, 62,* 976–1059.

de Wied, D., Bohus, B., & Wimersma Greidanus, Tj. B. (1975). Memory deficit in rats with hereditary diabetes insipidus. *Brain Research, 85,* 152–156.

de Wied, D., Bohus, B., van Ree, J. M., & Urban, I. (1978). Behavioral and electrophysiological effects of peptides related to lipotropin (β-LPH). *Journal of Pharmacology Experimental Therapeutics, 204,* 570–580.

Williams, A. R., Carey, R. J., Miller, M. (1983). Behavioral difference between vasopresin-deficient (Brattleboro) and normal Long–Evans rats. *Peptides, 4,* 711–716.

Witter, A., Gipsen, W. H., & de Wied, D. (1981). Mechanisms of action of behaviorally active ACTH-like peptides. In J. L. Martinez, Jr., R. A. Jensen, R. B. Messing, H. Rigter, & J. L. McGaugh (Eds.), *Endogenous peptides and learning and memory processes* (pp. 37–57). New York: Academic Press.

Wynn, L. C., & Solomon, R. L. (1955). Tramatic avoidance learning: Acquisition and extinction in dogs deprived of normal peripheral autonomic function. *Genetic Psychology Monographs, 52,* 241–284.

Zornetzer, S. F. (1978). Neurotransmitter modulation and memory: A new neuropharmacological phrenology? In M. A. Lipton, A. DiMascio, & K. F. Killam (Eds.), *Psychopharmacology: A generation of progress* (pp. 637–649). New York: Raven.

5

BIOCHEMICAL CORRELATES OF LEARNING AND MEMORY

Adrian J. Dunn

INTRODUCTION

The durability of memory strongly suggests that it has a chemical or structural basis. The ephemeral nature of electrophysiological activity, even in reverberating circuits, and the persistence of memory after gross disruption of the ongoing electrophysiological activity either by seizures (McGaugh, 1966) or by flattening of the electroencephalogram (Baldwin & Soltysik, 1969) support this notion. Nevertheless, the precise nature of the chemical or structural changes that form the basis of memory remains elusive.

A large number of reviews of the biochemistry of memory exists. Some of these (e.g., Agranoff, 1981; Agranoff, Burrell, Dokas, & Springer, 1978; Dunn, 1976b; Entingh, Dunn, Glassman, Wilson, Hogan & Damstra, 1975; and Rose, 1981, 1984) carefully analyzed potential experimental approaches for determining the biochemical bases for memory. The reader interested in a detailed analysis of the published experiments in this area is encouraged to consult one of the several reviews that have concentrated on this aspect (e.g., Agranoff et al., 1978; Dunn, 1976b, 1980; Rose, Hambley, & Haywood, 1976). The purpose of this chapter is to discuss the important issues in the research, the directions the research taken, and the reasons for these directions.

Most authors distinguish two approaches: *correlative* and *interventive*. In the correlative approach, neurochemical changes occurring subsequent to learning are studied, the problem being to demonstrate that the changes are specific for the learning. In the interventive approach, agents with presumed specific molecular or cellular actions are used to alter the processing of memory, the problem being to prove that the effects of the agent are truly on learning, and are specific for the intended process.

The shortcomings of the strict correlational approach are many and are discussed in detail by Dunn (1976b), Agranoff et al. (1978), Rose et al. (1976), and Rose (1981, 1984), and others. First, one has to guess which neurochemicals will be involved, and as if that were not enough, in which cells the changes will occur and when. When a consistent and reproducible effect is demonstrated, one must begin the painstaking task of determining its behavioral specificity, to prove that it is related to learning. The problems of interventive studies are just as great. Results have a high probability of being trivial because any treatment that impairs cerebral function is likely to influence a sophisticated process such as learning, yet not be in any way specific for it. For example, interfering with an animal's ability to see or move would undoubtedly impair its ability to learn many tasks, but would tell us little about learning. False negatives are also possible, because redundancy in the central nervous system (CNS) is such that when one brain system is impaired, another one may be able to take over the same function. It may seem more advantageous to seek treatments that improve learning, but, in order to observe an improvement, the particular process affected by the treatment must have been functioning less than optimally before. Of the many processes involved in learning, only one or a few will be operating in a rate-limiting fashion, and only treatments affecting these processes can produce improvement. It is also possible that improving performance for one kind of task may impair it for another.

For these reasons most reviewers have concluded that a combination of interventive and correlational approaches is necessary for success. Although it is certainly true that such an approach, which is modelled on that used to determine biochemical pathways, may identify biochemical processes important in learning, it is by no means clear that the combined approach can identify the chemical basis of memory. For example, let us assume that a particular biochemical pathway is critical for the storage of the memory, but is not associated with the memory per se. Then inhibition of this biochemical process would impair memory. But, this does not mean that the particular biochemical involved is the memory. A good example is protein synthesis. A variety of excellent data suggest that protein synthesis inhibitors can impair acquisition of memory (Dunn, 1980; Davis & Squire, 1984; see Chapter 4, this volume). This finding suggests that protein synthesis is necessary for the formation of at least some types of memory. There may also be an increase in cerebral protein synthesis associated with some types of learning. However, this does not establish that the memory is a protein. It might well be that it is a product of the protein functioning as an enzyme that is the real memory.

It is possible to combine interventive and correlational approaches in the same experiment. The first example of this was the experiment of Shashoua (1968) who reported that a biochemical change in RNA metabolism following training of goldfish could be prevented by posttraining treatment with puromycin, which also induced amnesia for the task. Thus the correlation between the learning and the biochemical change was strengthened by this demonstration of the absence of the biochemical change in an animal that had been rendered amnesic. A more elaborate example of the same design is provided by the experiments of Rose and Harding (1984). Here, electroconvulsive shock (ECS) was used to induce amnesia in the chick for a passive avoidance task. An increase in the incorporation of [^{3}H]fucose into glycoproteins of the forebrain base and anterior roof, which was normally observed in trained chicks, was not found in chicks subjected to ECS immediately after training. This biochemical change was, however, observed if the ECS was delayed until 10 minutes posttraining, a treatment that did not result in significant amnesia. Other examples have involved measurement of protein or catecholamine synthesis after treatment with inhibitors to establish a correlation between the biochemical process and the retention (see Dunn, 1980). Although this integrated approach is more powerful than either approach alone, it is not definitive. Many of the agents used to induce amnesia may have such widespread effects (e.g., puromycin or ECS; see Dunn, 1976b) that the disruption of both the formation of memory and the biochemical consequences of training may be coincidental and not causally related.

In their classic analysis, Entingh et al. (1975) indicated that to understand the biochemistry of memory one needed to answer four questions:

1. Which neurochemical systems are involved in the formation of memory?
2. When in the learning process do changes in these systems occur?
3. Where in the brain do the neurochemical events occur?
4. What is the behavioral specificity of the changes?

These are still the crucial questions, and I shall discuss them each in turn.

WHICH NEUROCHEMICAL SYSTEMS?

In approaching the biochemistry of memory, it is appropriate first to ask what kind of biochemistry is to be expected. The immediate inclination is to focus on the particular chemical entity that is responsible for the memory, or what is often referred to as the engram. But what form should the engram take? Jim McGaugh was fond of asking, how would you recognize an engram if you saw one? It seemed to the early memory biochemists that the chemical engram should be a stable molecule, at least as enduring as memories were known to be. For this reason the emphasis was on macromolecules, because most small molecules in cells are in a state of rapid turnover, which is to say that they are being synthesized and replaced frequently (i.e. they have a short half-life). Neurotransmitters were considered far too ephemeral to be the basis of memory. By contrast, many macromolecules had considerably longer half-lives. In the brain, most neurons do not divide, so that their DNA must have a life span similar to that of the organism itself, although some replacement of damaged components may occur. Also, it is known that certain of the structural proteins of myelin have a half-life of the order of months. Thus, most early studies were concerned with nucleic acids and proteins, the major kinds of macromolecules considered stable enough to encode memory.

Even though the focus of early research was on finding the neurochemical engram, it was realized that many other biochemical processes were likely to be involved in the formation of this engram. The learning process was believed to set off a whole chain of biochemical events which would ultimately result in the formation of the tangible engram. These are the cellular events that presumably occur during the period of consolidation, and can account for the retrograde amnesia gradients observed with (ECS) and other inhibitors of memory formation (see Chapter 4, this volume). Thus, the simplest interpretation of differing retrograde amnesia gradients is that the agents affect different biochemical or cellular processes which occur at different times in the formation of the memory. The problem is that there are likely to be a whole host of biochemical changes associated with memory formation, each of which plays an important role in the process, but most of which are not directly involved in the formation of the engram. The experimental results are consistent with this picture.

What form should the engram take? The idea that the information content of a memory might be stored in the structure of a particular molecule arose from the excitement generated by the discoveries of the 1950s and 1960s that genetic information was stored chemically in the structure of DNA and that the amino acid sequences of proteins are encoded in the base sequences of nucleic acids (DNA and RNA). Hence, the early research on the biochemistry of memory focused on nucleic acids, because these molecules were the only ones considered to have a complexity adequate to encode the information, combined with the stability necessary for memory. DNA was neglected, in part because it was thought to be the repository of genetic information, and because it was known to be metabolically stable in the brain. However, the pioneering work of Hydén (1943) indicated that the metabolism of RNA in neurons was rather sensitive to neuronal activity. So the spotlight was on RNA.

A major problem was the lack of a mechanism for translating the RNA code into an electrical one, thought to be the major mode of interneuronal communication in the brain. Such a mechanism, if it existed, ought to be specific to the brain. For a while, consideration was given to various models for reading RNA sequences rather like a magnetic tape recorder reading an RNA tape. However, biochemical studies of cerebral RNA metabolism (Mahler, 1981) failed to reveal any features that were different from those of other tissues, such as the liver, which is not noted for its learning ability. Therefore, if RNA did in fact play a particular role in memory, it had to be consistent with its conventional role in the synthesis of protein, most probably as a messenger RNA (mRNA). Further details of this research will be discussed below, but currently this area of research is unfashionable, largely because it is considered to have been unproductive.

The focus then shifted from RNA to proteins. This occurred not only because of the technical problems of analyzing RNA, but also because it was believed that if the engram resided in RNA it would most likely be decoded into protein, and knowing the nature of the proteins could facilitate understanding of the mechanisms. This trend also paralleled a shift from thinking of neurochemical engrams as special molecules with properties unique to the brain, to mechanisms consistent with the known principles of cell biology. It was still possible that the kinds of proteins synthesized were specific to the brain, and even specific to memories, but it was just as likely that the new mRNA's might be involved in the synthesis of increased amounts of existing proteins, for example, enzymes or structural proteins. This was consistent with the thinking of neuroanatomists and electrophysiologists, who had always thought of changes in synaptic connections as underlying the behavioral plasticity associated with learning (see Greenough [1984] for a recent review).

This evolution involved important conceptual changes in the thinking of memory biochemists. First, it was no longer necessary to think of unique memory molecules, so that the search now was not for molecules of a type that had not existed before learning occurred, rather the new molecules might be identical to many molecules already existing in the brain. Second, it was no longer necessary that the stability of the chemical engram itself parallel that of the memory. It was perfectly possible, for example, for all the structural components of a synapse to be replaced (by turnover), yet the synapse itself could still exist, and therefore also the functions associated with it. Third, the focus need not be on synthesis. Just as adaptation could involve either the addition or the removal of synapses, so could memory involve either the addition or the removal of molecules. Proteins in axons must be synthesized in the cell bodies of neurons and transported to presynaptic terminals by axoplasmic transport, a process that could take hours, days, or even months in the case of very long axons. This situation is analogous to the problem of getting spare parts for machinery to distant parts of the world. To make sufficient proteins readily available to presynaptic terminals for the replacement of enzymes or structural proteins, it must be necessary to transport axonally a full spectrum of such proteins on a continuous basis. Proteins that are not needed would simply be degraded at the terminals. If this is true, then it would imply that the specificity of new proteins incorporated into structural components of axons would be determined by degradation, not synthesis. Thus, I have previously suggested that protein degradation must be an important, if not a critical, aspect of metabolism in presynaptic terminals (Dunn, 1982).

Although the focus of so much neuroscience research is on the synapse, it should not be assumed that this is the only site at which plastic changes can occur. It can readily be appreciated that changes in axonal or dendritic branching could profoundly alter the electrical properties of the cell. Also, more subtle changes in the morphology, such as, for example, the dimensions of dendritic spines, could alter the postsynaptic response to synaptic input, or a simple change in the diameter of the axon could alter its threshold for firing.

More recently, protein derivatives, such as phosphoproteins and glycoproteins have drawn attention, because it was realized that the removal or addition of the nonprotein moieties could be performed very rapidly, substantially altering the properties of the molecule. Thus protein derivatives were good candidates for early stages in the formation of memory, and could even be the basis of short-term memory.

Little attention was initially given to neurotransmitters, because the biological turnover of these molecules was very rapid, and they were regarded merely as chemical messengers, which although possessing specificity, could not be as specific as memories. Furthermore, the available technology was only capable of measuring amounts or providing crude estimates of turnover rate. However, the possibility is very real that proteins associated with neurotransmitter metabolism, such as synthetic or degradative enzymes, or neurotransmitter receptors, are involved in learning.

The problem of identifying a neurochemical engram has been compared with searching for a needle in a haystack (Agranoff et al., 1978; Dunn, 1976b); if there were such a molecule, how could it ever be discovered among all the other molecules that comprise the mass of brain tissue? Even if one were to use methods for determining the synthesis of new molecules, how would it ever be possible to identify the engram molecules in the presence of the overwhelming mass of general brain metabolism? Agranoff et al. (1978) considered this to be a *Catch 22* situation, namely, that any change large enough to be detected was almost certainly too large to be associated with memory per se. And conversely, any change specifically associated with memory was likely to be too small to be detectable.

BIOCHEMICAL PROBLEMS

Although the recent major advances in neurochemical analysis have permitted exciting findings, it is not always appreciated how limited are our current techniques. In principle, neurochemists are able to make only three kinds of measurement: the content of neurochemicals, the activity of enzymes, and certain kinetic parameters.

Chemical Content

Assays exist for most chemicals in the brain, but an important technical problem is whether the quantities measured in tissue samples accurately reflect *in vivo* concentrations. The problem is most obvious with molecules that have high metabolic activity, such as glucose or adenosine triphosphate (ATP), which are degraded very rapidly after brain death, but it also applies to neurotransmitters, such as acetylcholine, and molecules like cyclic adenosine monophosphate (AMP). Special techniques such as freezing in liquid nitrogen or microwave fixation have been developed, but even so the time taken for fixation is finite, and a residual uncertainty exists. Unfortunately also, these techniques preclude good regional analyses, and the opportunity to perform cellular or subcellular fractionation. Although most macromolecules are considered to be very stable, some important ones may not be. For example, there is good evidence that the turnover of some types of brain RNA is very rapid (see following discussion). Moreover, potentially very important changes in protein derivatives, such as phosphoproteins, occur extremely rapidly (see following discussion).

For learning and memory studies, the major problem with measures of chemical content is accuracy. The best neurochemical assays would probably not detect changes of less than 5%, and most are less reliable than that. Do we really expect a change of this magnitude in the brain content of a chemical during learning? Anatomical localization can help, but then problems may be incurred with the sensitivity of the chemical assays.

Enzyme Assays

Sensitive assays exist or can be devised for any cerebral enzyme. The use of radioisotopes or ingenious techniques such as enzymatic recycling (see Lowry, 1963) enables assay of a single cell, or even of a single enzyme molecule. However, enzymes are most often assayed in cell-free preparations, in which the conditions have been designed to maximize activity. In this state, the enzyme is free of many if not all of the regulatory factors that control its activity *in vivo*. Thus, what is normally measured is the *capacity* of the enzyme to perform a reaction with optimal amounts of cofactors. The capacity may not be related to its *in vivo* activity, which is probably rarely maximal. The problem is compounded for membrane-bound enzymes which may work poorly, if at all, unless they are in the correct membrane environment. Furthermore, membranes in the brain have quite different concentrations of metabolites on either side, a situation difficult to reproduce *in vitro*. Thus, measurements of enzyme activity are most useful for studies of long-term adaptation, and have found relatively little use in studies of learning and memory.

Kinetic Measures

It may be unreasonable to expect detectable changes in the content of a particular brain protein, but at crucial times the rate of synthesis or degradation may be markedly changed, and thus readily detected. The aim of kinetic studies is to determine the rate of ongoing processes in the brain. Generally a tracer technique is used in which a small amount of labeled material (normally radioactive) is introduced into the system and its disposition followed. The principle is straightforward; if the tracer is a good one it will be converted into metabolic products at the same rate as the endogenous compounds, allowing estimates of rate to be made. There has been much discussion on the problems of interpreting labeling data from the brain (see for example, Oja, 1967; Dunlop, Lajtha, & Toth, 1977; Dunn, 1977). First, it is important that the metabolic product be stable so that other reactions do not confound the results; the product is frequently stable for the synthesis of macromolecules, but rarely so for small molecules. Second, for accurate estimation it is necessary to know the concentration of the labeled tracer relative to that of the endogenous compound (i.e. its specific activity) in the appropriate place at the appropriate time. However, during the experiment the size of the pool of metabolic precursor and its specific activity may change, so that these changes must be taken into account for correct interpretation of the data. A further important problem is compartmentation. This term refers to the fact that the metabolic activity of interest may occur in only one cell or cell type, or one subcellular compartment, but the neurochemical analyses often measure the net specific activities in all the cellular compartments. Unfortunately, specific activities and synthesis rates may differ in the various cellular compartments. The problems are such that it is probably not possible to measure accurately and unequivocally metabolic rates in brain cells using the tracer technique (Dunn, 1977). Nevertheless, the method is extremely sensitive and at the very least can detect metabolic changes, although it may be difficult to ascertain the precise nature of these changes. Also with a suitable choice of precursor, the biochemistry can often be simplified, enabling the analysis of large numbers of samples.

WHERE IN THE BRAIN?

The molecular changes associated with learning are likely to be associated with small populations of cells. Inclusion of unrelated uninvolved cells dilutes the magnitude of the changes, thus rendering them less detectable. Neurochemists have frequently been criticized for grinding up whole brains or very large regions with little regard for their intricate anatomy. Ideally, if the expected location of the change is unknown, a large number of small samples should be analyzed. However, the assay may not only lack sensitivity for this, but processing even 20 samples from the brain of each animal can be a formidable problem for many if not most assays. There may also be statistical problems in analyzing the data. If alpha is set at 0.05 as an acceptable level of statistical significance (i.e., $p < .05$), then 5% of the samples will yield significant results by chance alone. Thus, of every 20 regions analyzed, one will falsely appear statistically significant (so-called

Type I error). Nevertheless, histochemical analysis using autoradiography has proved useful. Thus the hyperstriatum ventrale was identified as the crucial brain site involved in imprinting in the chick, because it was the major region showing increased incorporation of [^{3}H]uracil into RNA (Horn, McCabe, & Bateson, 1979) and increasing glucose utilization, as determined by the deoxyglucose procedure (see following discussion; Kohsaka, Takamatsu, Aoki, & Tsukada, 1979).

Theoretically, it should be easiest to determine the crucial anatomical sites associated with learning by classical lesioning and stimulation techniques. However, these techniques have their own drawbacks. If lesioning a particular structure disrupts learning, it does not necessarily follow that the structure was essential for learning. The lesion could have caused secondary trans-synaptic degeneration in other structures, which resulted in the behavioral change. Likewise, the failure of a lesion to affect learning does not prove that the lesioned site was not involved. Redundancy in many parts of the brain is such that another intact structure may have assumed the function. It is notable that after more than 50 years, the effects of lesions on learning and memory are still controversial (see for example, Horel, 1978) and we still have no consensus on the structures involved.

Of course if we had a good handle on learning biochemistry, neurochemical techniques could be used to localize behaviorally relevant sites in the brain. Unfortunately, the biochemical techniques are often too cumbersome to be used as a screening technique. However, some recently developed histological techniques may be usable, including measurement of cerebral blood flow and the deoxyglucose procedure (see following discussion).

WHEN?

Because learning is a time-dependent process, the time at which the biochemical studies are performed in relation to learning is obviously critical (see discussion in Chapter 4, this volume). Because the interventive studies suggested that the critical events take place shortly after learning, most studies focused on this period. Nevertheless, given that a chain of biochemical events is likely to be involved in the consolidation process, the precise time in the consolidation period may be critical. In agreement with this, several studies found that the metabolic changes accompanying learning vary in the immediate postlearning period (Matthies, 1982; Rose, 1986; Morgan & Routtenberg, 1979). In general, changes associated with learning should not be evident when memory is retrieved, thus examination of metabolic changes when memory is tested can be a useful control for performance aspects of the task.

BEHAVIORAL SPECIFICITY

Having discovered a neurochemical correlate of learning, it is important to analyze its behavioral specificity. Clearly the effect is of interest only if it is specifically associated with learning. Most experimental systems for the study of learning introduce a variety of other factors, including those affecting the performance and motivation of the subjects, stress, and a variety of sensory stimuli and motor activities. It is now clear that these factors, which are often termed *nonspecific* (probably incorrectly), can produce large changes in cerebral metabolism which could easily obscure any specific learning-related neurochemical changes.

A variety of authors attempted to define clear criteria for distinguishing neurochemical changes that are associated with the memory per se, from those that occur during learning but are not associated with the nonspecific aspects of the experience (e.g., Entingh et al., 1975; Rose, 1981, 1984a). Indeed there has been considerable ingenuity used in the design of experimental paradigms to eliminate such factors.

The work of the Glassman–Wilson group provides an early example of the behavioral analysis of a neurochemical response. Initial studies indicated an increase in the incorporation of labeled uridine into RNA in mice trained in a conditioned avoidance task relative to untrained mice (Zemp, Wilson, Schlesinger, Boggan, & Glassman, 1966). This task used a light and a buzzer as the conditioned stimulus (CS), and electric footshock as the unconditioned stimulus (UCS). To escape the footshock the mice could jump to a shelf a few inches above the grid floor. However they could avoid it by jumping to the shelf within 3 s after presentation of the CS. Trained mice clearly differ from quiet mice (i.e., those left in their home cages and not exposed to the training apparatus) in a number of respects. An important control was the so-called yoked animal. Yoked mice were treated like trained mice but placed in an adjacent compartment of the jumpbox that lacked a shelf. Thus the yoked mouse received all the handling and the conditioning stimuli (including the footshock) that the trained mouse did, but could not learn to avoid the shock, because there was no shelf to jump to. (It is not claimed that the yoked mouse did not learn anything.) Because the footshock was turned off as soon as the trained mouse jumped, the yoked mouse received the same amount of shock as did the trained mouse. Trained mice showed increased incorporation of [^{3}H]uridine into RNA compared with yoked mice.

In other experiments, mice that had previously learned the task and were performing it competently were studied. Mice that were trained for four successive days did not show RNA labeling significantly different from quiet mice (Adair, Wilson, & Glassman, 1968). A further control was to study extinction of the training. Mice were trained in the task for five successive days, but on the sixth day the footshock was no longer presented. The mouse now learned that it need no longer avoid. During extinction mice showed increased incorporation of [^{3}H]uridine into RNA compared with quiet mice (Coleman, Wilson, & Glassman, 1971a). When mice that had learned and extinguished the task were retrained, there was again an increased incorporation of [^{3}H]uridine into RNA compared to quiet mice (Coleman et al., 1971). Other results, showed that classically conditioned mice (i.e., mice that received CS–UCS pairings but could not avoid or escape) did not differ from quiet mice in their [^{3}H]uridine incorporation into RNA (Adair et al., 1968). It was apparently necessary for the mice to learn to avoid the footshock, for the neurochemical response to appear. These studies strongly suggested that the changes of brain RNA labeling were specifically related to the learning of the active avoidance task.

A similar behavioral analysis of the neurochemical responses has been carried out using the chick imprinting model (Horn, Rose, Bateson, 1973b; Rose et al., 1976). Because most chicks exposed to the imprinting stimulus imprint, it is difficult to control for the effects of the stimulus per se. One control used by this group was based on the observation that late-hatching chicks had a far lower probability of imprinting than early-hatching chicks; and indeed it was found that late-hatching chicks did not display the increased incorporation of [^{3}H]lysine into protein that early hatching birds did (Bateson, Horn, & Rose, 1972). The problem with this control is that whatever was different about the brains of late-hatching chicks may have caused them to respond differently to the stimulus. A much more sophisticated control was to sever the corpus callosum to split the brain, and then expose the chick to the imprinting stimulus with only one eye and hence only one half of the brain. In this case, incorporation of [^{3}H]uracil into RNA of the forebrain roof was increased only on the (contralateral) side corresponding to the imprinting stimulus (Horn, Rose, & Bateson, 1973a). This experiment rules out systemic factors, such as hormones, as mediators of the response. A further control was the so-called 2-day experiment, in which chicks were exposed to the imprinting stimulus on two consecutive days for complementary periods, such that their total exposure was constant. In this case, the [³H]uracil incorporation into the forebrain roof was correlated with the length of the training period on the second day (Bateson, Rose, & Horn, 1973).

Various factors may be eliminated from the behavioral paradigm one at a time to determine which is responsible for the neurochemical response. The problem with this kind of analysis is that the whole may be more than the sum of the parts. Each time the behavioral paradigm is changed the brain will respond differently. While light stimuli will produce one response and stress another, it is not necessarily true that the responses can simply be added and subtracted so that what is left over is the memory. Memory results from the combination of various stimuli, if any one is absent, the memory is changed or does not appear. This point was made earlier by Greenough (1976) and is also pertinent to environmental enrichment paradigms as pointed out in the excellent analysis by Uphouse (1980).

SPECIFIC MOLECULES

THE RNA STUDIES

As previously discussed, many of the early studies of the biochemistry of memory focused on RNA. This was largely because of the work of Hydén (1943) who showed that stimulation could alter the RNA content of rat spinal motor neurons measured by cytospectrophotometry, a quantitative light absorption technique used on histological sections. These changes occurred with either stress or direct electrical stimulation of the spinal roots. Hydén concluded that mild stimulation would increase the neuronal content, whereas stronger or excessive stimulation would decrease it. He conceived that the stimulation of the neurons somehow increased the use and hence the degradation of RNA. In the short term, the net RNA content increased because its synthesis was enhanced. However, with excessive or prolonged stimulation, degradation exceeded synthesis and the neuronal RNA content fell. Later, Hydén became convinced that the reason for the initial rise in RNA content was the transfer of RNA from glial to neuronal cells, and that the eventual decline signaled the exhaustion of the stores of both the neurons and their associated glia in the neuronal-glial unit. He set about proving this hypothesis using elegant techniques for the microdissection of individual neurons, and quantification of the RNA in individual cells. In 1964, Hydén and Egyházi reported results from a paradigm in which rats learned to change the paw they used to retrieve food pellets (so-called transfer of handedness). The RNA content of cortical pyramidal neurons increased in the trained animals, correlated quantitatively with a decrease in the associated glia. Changes in the base composition of the RNA were consistent with the transfer from the glia to the neurons of RNA with a base composition resembling that of mRNA (i.e., low guanine and cytidine content relative to the total cellular RNA). Unfortunately, no replication of this type of experiment was ever reported from outside Hydén's laboratory. In addition, the experiments were criticized on a number of methodological grounds including the choice of cells, their purity, the methods for determining the base composition of the RNA, the consistency of the results, and the nature of the learning involved (Dunn, 1976b; Rose 1968).

The evidence from interventive studies for the involvement of RNA in learning is equivocal, largely because of the high toxicity of RNA synthesis inhibitors in mammals (Dunn, 1976b, 1982). Most studies other than those of Hydén attempted to correlate learning with changes in RNA synthesis measured using labeled precursors. Unfortunately, RNA labeling data are very difficult to interpret. This difficulty is not just because of the problems of accurately determining the specific radioactivity of the precursor in the appropriate pool at the appropriate time (see previous discussion). In mammalian cells, the rate of RNA labeling is known to be exceedingly fast, and the so-called *rapidly labeled* RNA has a half-life of 10 min or less (Dunn, 1976a; Harris, 1963). This means that the newly synthesized RNA has a half-life considerably shorter than the labeling times normally used. Under these circumstances, it is clearly not possible to estimate synthesis rates, because the product RNA is degraded too rapidly. Thus, experiments that have used pulses longer than a few minutes cannot be used to estimate rates of synthesis. Furthermore, most of the RNA labeled in less than 1 hour is heterogeneous nuclear RNA (hnRNA), a type of RNA whose function is incompletely understood, although a part of it is undoubtedly a precursor to mRNA (see Perry, 1976). Much of this RNA never enters the cytoplasm and cannot therefore be considered mRNA in the classical sense (Dunn, 1976a; Harris, 1964). To reiterate, RNA labeling studies in mammalian cells, at least as currently performed, cannot accurately measure synthesis rates, and the function of much of the RNA that is labeled is not known.

The studies of the Glassman–Wilson group measured the incorporation of [³H]uridine into brain RNA over a 45-min period (Zemp et al., 1966). This is equivalent to several half-lives of the rapidly labeled RNA, but even at this time the RNA labeled is primarily nuclear (Dunn, 1976a). In these studies, the behavioral treatments were not initiated until 30 min after [³H]uridine administration. This delay was to allow time for the mice to recover from the intracranial injections of [³H]uridine which were stressful. Thus, trained and yoked mice were treated differently for only the last 15 min of the labeling period. When the RNA was analyzed, the incorporation that occurred in this period was averaged in with the previous 30 min incorporation. Thus, the percentage changes determined over the entire 45 min must be less than those that occur in the last 15 min of labeling. Zemp et al. (1966) reported increases in RNA labeling following training as high as 100% or more, and *averaging* 25%, therefore the behaviorally induced changes in RNA synthesis would have to be dramatic indeed. The explanation lies in the correction factors used. To correct for variations in the uptake of [³H]uridine into the brain following the intracranial injections, the radioactivity in cerebral uridine monophosphate (UMP) was determined (UTP was not used because it did not survive the subcellular fractionation procedures used in these experiments). The estimate of RNA synthesis was thus: (radioactivity in RNA) or (radioactivity in UMP). Clearly, this ratio could increase either because the numerator increased or because the denominator decreased (or of course both). Large changes may more easily derived from the latter, because of the timing factors used in these experiments (see previous discussion). Subsequent experiments in which quantitative techniques were used indicated that following training the radioactivity in the RNA did not change significantly, whereas that of UMP actually decreased (Entingh, Damstra–Entingh, Dunn, Wilson, & Glassman, 1974). This change of nucleotide labeling seems to be a reproducible finding, and does not preclude a change in RNA synthesis even as a cause of the change of nucleotide labeling. However, an adequate biochemical explanation of it has not been presented.

PROTEINS

Agents that inhibit protein synthesis interfere with the formation of memory but have little or no effect on ongoing behavior (see reviews by Dunn, 1980 and Davis & Squire, 1984, for details). The latter is remarkable considering the high rate of protein synthesis in the brain (Mahler, 1981). Changes in the total content of proteins would only be expected in the long term. Nevertheless, we might expect to observe changes in the rate of protein sysnthesis associated with learning. The experimental data on such changes have been extensively reviewed previously (Agranoff, 1981; Dunn, 1976b, 1980; Rose & Haywood, 1977).

Some experiments suggest that there may be a general increase in the rate of cerebral protein synthesis associated with stress. Studies in the jumpbox conditioned avoidance task previously described indicated that there was an increase in the incorporation of radiolabeled amino acids into brain protein in trained mice relative to quiet mice in the period immediately following training (Rees, Brogan, Entingh, Dunn, Shinkman, Damstra–Entingh, Wilson, & Glassman, 1974). However, yoked mice or mice exposed to the CS or UCS exhibited the same biochemical response as did trained mice. Thus, the metabolic change was probably not associated with learning the avoidance task, but rather with the stimuli used in the conditioned avoidance training (e.g., light, buzzers, shock) and most likely is a stress response. Consistent with this, repeated training or presentation of the stimuli resulted in a decreased biochemical response (Rees et al., 1974). The increased amino acid incorporation into protein thus appears to be a stress response. As such, the changes may be due to the release of one or another of the hormones known to respond during stress (e.g., adrenocorticotropic hormone [ACTH], corticosterone, see Dunn & Kramarcy, 1984). This idea was supported by the observation that the increased amino acid incorporation into protein was not regionally specific, several gross brain regions showed the change; nor was it tissue specific— the liver also showed a response (Rees et al., 1974). Adrenal hormones, such as corticosterone and the catecholamines, were ruled out as mediators of the response, because adrenalectomized mice showed biochemical responses to footshock stress like those of intact mice, and administration of corticosterone did not alter amino acid incorporation into brain and liver protein (Rees & Dunn, 1977). However, the brain response was absent in hypophysectomized mice (see Dunn & Schotman, 1981), and could be mimicked by administration of ACTH (Dunn, Rees, & Iuvone, 1978). A variety of other data suggest that ACTH increases cerebral protein synthesis; Dunn and Schotman (1981) reviewed the data suggesting that the increased amino acid incorporation into brain protein observed following ACTH administration (or stress) truly reflects an increased rate of cerebral protein synthesis.

These results strongly suggest that ACTH released in response to stress causes the increased labeling of brain protein. This conclusion may explain many earlier data indicating increased cerebral protein synthesis in response to environmental stimulation (e.g., Appel, Davis, & Scott, 1967). Studies from three different laboratories failed to find evidence that the effect of ACTH on cerebral protein synthesis is specific for any particular protein (Dunn & Gildersleeve, 1980; Pavlík, Jakoubek, Burešová, & Hájek, 1971; Reith, Schotman, & Gispen, 1975). Earlier I had speculated that this increased cerebral protein synthesis during stress might facilitate learning (Dunn, 1976a). The generalized nature of the response could be explained by suggesting that the proteins would only be used in locations where the prevailing conditions were right. This scheme avoids the need to duplicate the anatomical specificity already present in the neuronal firing pattern. Clearly, this same rationale could be used to explain the lack of molecular specificity of the increased protein synthesis. Increased amounts of all proteins would be available for use either as enzymes or as building blocks for synapses or whatever. Note that this explanation is also consistent with the idea previously discussed that the crucial factors in consolidating a memory (or making a new synapse for that matter) might be which proteins are degraded, rather than which ones are synthesized, because they are all being synthesized continually.

PROTEIN DERIVATIVES

As previously indicated, the attraction of protein derivatives as substrates for memory is that a variety of chemical groups can be added to or subtracted from the proteins very rapidly, resulting in major changes in the properties of the molecule. Thus they have been touted as a potential basis for short-term memory (Agranoff, 1980; Dunn, 1976b).

Glycoproteins

Glycoproteins became of interest because of the potential complexity of their structure, which made them candidates for determinants of the specificity of intercellular interactions (Irwin, 1974). Also, the changes of uridine nucleotide metabolism discovered by Entingh et al. (1974, see previous discussion), suggested the possibility that there might be changes in uridine nucleotide derivatives used as building blocks for glycoprotein (and glycolipid) synthesis. Nevertheless, there have been relatively few experiments conducted on glycoproteins (see Dunn, 1980, 1982; Matthies, 1982; Rose, 1984b, for details), although some of those reported have potentially interesting results (Popov, Pohle, Schulzeck, Matthies, Brodemann, & Matthies, 1983; Sukumar, Rose, & Burgoyne, 1980; Rose & Harding, 1984).

Phosphoproteins

Phosphate groups on proteins are metabolically active, and there has been much interest in phosphoproteins, because of the hypothesis of Kuo and Greengard (1969) that the intracellular actions of cyclic AMP (and cyclic guanosine monophosphate [GMP] are mediated through phosphorylation of proteins. In its simplest form the hypothesis states that an extracellular messenger (e.g., a hormone or neurotransmitter) binds to a receptor on the outside of the cell membrane, thereby activating an adenylate cyclase molecule on the inner surface of the membrane, so that it synthesizes $3',5'$-cyclic AMP (cAMP) from ATP. This intracellular cAMP can then activate one or more protein kinases, enzymes that can transfer phosphate groups from ATP to proteins. Cyclic AMP achieves this by binding to the *regulatory* subunit of the protein kinase molecule, thus freeing the *catalytic* subunit to phosphorylate a protein substrate. Most cells contain more than one type of protein kinase some of which are activated by cAMP (kinase A) and others by cGMP, Ca^{2+}, diacylglycerol (kinase C), or other unknown factors. The protein kinases have high (tissue) specificity and will only phosphorylate certain protein substrates.

The first indication that the phosphorylation of cerebral proteins was sensitive to behavioral manipulations came from the work of Machlus, Wilson, & Glassman (1974) on nuclear proteins, but subsequently the emphasis has been on synaptic or membrane proteins. There is now widespread evidence for an important role of phosphoproteins in synaptic function (see Kennedy, 1983; Nestler & Greengard, 1983). Gispen, Perumal, Wilson, & Glassman (1977) demonstrated a change in a synaptosomal protein phosphorylation associated with active avoidance training in mice). These early experiments used ^{32}P labeling *in vivo*; [^{32}P]orthophosphate was injected into the animal, and the labeled phosphoproteins were extracted and separated. Most subsequent experiments have used an *in vitro* labeling technique (sometimes known as the "post hoc" assay), which is in effect a back-titration of sites available for phosphorylation on the proteins. That is, the proteins are extracted and incubated *in vitro* with ATP labeled with ^{32}P in its terminal (gamma) phosphate, so that protein kinases transfer this labeled phosphate group to the protein. Labels will not be added to sites that already contain a phosphate group (unless of course it is cleaved *in vitro*), thus the procedure gives a negative image of the phosphorylation state *in situ*.

Routtenberg's group has shown changes in the *in vitro* phosphorylation of proteins of the synaptic plasma membrane fraction from the frontal cortex of rats trained in inhibitory avoidance or exposed to unavoidable footshock (Routtenberg & Benson, 1980). The particular protein band (F2) whose phosphorylation changed was a 41,000 dalton protein, subsequently identified as a subunit of pyruvate dehydrogenase (PDH, Morgan & Routtenberg, 1980). Following avoidance training, there was an increase in PDH activity, and a concomitant increase in the ability of PDH to undergo phosphorylation *in vitro,* implying decreased phosphorylation *in vivo* (Morgan & Routtenberg, 1981). Lyn-Cook and Wilson (1983) also observed increased *in vitro* phosphorylation of PDH following avoidance training in rats, but in their studies, the phosphorylation of three synaptic plasma membrane protein bands (19,000, 21,000, and 24,000 daltons) was also increased.

These results closely parallel those of Browning, Dunwiddie, Bennett, Gispen, & Lynch (1979) who found a specific increase in the phosphorylation of a synaptic plasma membrane protein in the hippocampal slice after long-term potentiation (LTP). LTP is a long-lasting change in the physiological response of the hippocampal tissue observed following repetitive stimulation, and is considered by some to be a potential basis for memory (see Chapter 7, this volume). The protein had a molecular weight of 40,000 daltons, and as in Routtenberg's work, appeared to be identical with the alpha-subunit of PDH (Browning, Bennett, Kelly, & Lynch, 1981). Phosphorylation of PDH was known to inactivate the enzyme, so increased labeling in the post hoc assay indicated decreased *in vivo* phosphorylation and hence increased activity. Because inhibition of PDH phosphorylation by dichloroacetate increased the enzyme's activity and the uptake of Ca^{2+} by mitochondria, Browning, Baudry and Lynch (1982) suggested that PDH might play an important role in the regulation of intracellular Ca^{2+}, which might in turn account for LTP. One problem with this hypothesis was that whereas LTP affected only a small population of cells in the slice, the phosphorylation changes were observed in the total PDH of the slice, including that in nonneuronal cells. It was also surprising that such a crucial glycolytic enzyme as PDH should in addition be the regulator of intraneuronal Ca^{2+}. Furthermore, studies by Bar, Schotman, Gispen, Tielen, & Lopes da Silva (1980), Hoch, Dingledine, and Wilson (1984), and Routtenberg, Lovinger, and Steward (1985) found a poor correlation between phosphorylation of PDH and LTP. Hoch et al. (1984) suggested that changes of PDH phosphorylation may be associated with changes in PDH kinase, and they concluded that it was unlikely that changes in PDH activity regulated intraneuronal Ca^{2+}, but that the reverse was possible. The new hypothesis of Lynch and Baudry (1984) (see following discussion) suggests that the Ca^{2+}-influx associated with depolarization may be sufficient to trigger the LTP.

More recent work on hippocampal LTP by Routtenberg et al. (1985) has shown that LTP in the hippocampus *in vivo* is correlated with *in vitro* phosphorylation of a 47,000 dalton protein, F1. This protein appears to be identical with the brain-specific protein, B-50, which had previously been identified as a synaptic plasma membrane protein whose phosphorylation state was sensitive to ACTH in vitro (Zwiers, Wiegant, Schotman & Gispen, 1978) and also with an axon growth-related protein, GAP-43. This protein appears to be phosphorylated by protein kinase C, a kinase whose activity is independent of cAMP, but which is activated by Ca^{2+} or phospholipids. The results of Routtenberg et al. contrast with earlier work on LTP in the slice preparation, in which no changes were found in the phosphorylation of F1 or B-50 (Browning et al., 1979; Bar et al., 1980). Routtenberg (1985) considers the increased phosphorylation of F1 to reflect an activation of kinase C, rather than an increase of available phosphorylation sites on the protein. Some recent evidence (cited in Routtenberg, 1984b) suggests that radial maze training may also alter in vitro phosphorylation of F1. Because protein F1 is phosphorylated by protein kinase C, Routtenberg (1984b) has suggested that LTP may be effected by activation of this enzyme to phosphorylate F1. In the short term, this activation would involve an increase in intracellular Ca^{2+}, and in the long term, a Ca^{2+}-activated protease, which can permanently activate kinase C. Thus the Routtenberg (1984b) hypothesis resembles that of Lynch and Baudry (1984, see following discussion) in that Ca^{2+} influx during LTP activates a protease, but in Routtenberg's hypothesis, the substrate for the protease is kinase C, rather than glutamate receptors.

Another mechanism for electrophysiological adaptation could involve phosphorylation of the proteins of ion channels, perhaps mediated by cyclic nucleotides (Levitan, Lemos, & Novak–Hofer, 1983). Changes of protein phosphorylation have also been found associated with learning in so-called simple nervous sytems from invertebrates. The marine snail, Hermissenda crassicornis can apparently learn to associate a light stimulus (CS) paired with a presumed aversive rotation (UCS). After three days training (50 trials per day), incubation of the eyes, statocysts, and ganglia with [^{32}P]orthophosphate resulted in an increase in the labeling of one particular band (molecular weight 20,000) with no change in the total incorporation of ^{32}P into phosphoproteins (Neary, Crow, & Alkon, 1981). This change was specifically associated with pairing of the stimuli; unpaired or random stimuli did not change the labeling of any of the protein bands, nor was learning observed in these conditions. Other work from this group has indicated that the learning is correlated with changes in a specific voltage-dependent K^+-current in Type B photoreceptor cells (Farley, Richards, Ling, Liman, & Alkon, 1983; see also Chapter 8, this volume). Moreover, this change can be mimicked by injection into the cells of the catalytic subunit of either a cAMP-dependent or a Ca^{2+}-calmodulin-dependent protein kinase (Acosta-Urquidi, Alkon, & Neary, 1984). However, pharmacological manipulations of Hermissenda eyes and ganglia that alter the K^+-currents, appear to be associated with changes in the phosphorylation of two phosphoproteins of molecular weight 25,000 and 23,000, distinct from the 20,000 dalton protein affected in the learning task (Neary & Alkon, 1983).

Perhaps the most detailed example of the association of a molecular with a behavioral change is to be found in the work of Kandel and colleagues in Aplysia californica. This group has succeeded in identifying the neural circuitry associated with the gill and syphon-withdrawl reflex in Aplysia (Kandel & Schwartz, 1982). This reflex exhibits habituation to repeated stimulation, but can be sensitized by other sensory stimuli—an effect that can be mimicked by direct electrical stimulation of certain cells (L28 & L29) of the abdominal ganglia. The sensitization is apparently associated with an increased release of neurotransmitter, caused by an increased influx of Ca^{2+}, which in turn depends upon a prolongation of the depolarization of the presynaptic terminal by inhibiting a K^+-current (Klein & Kandel, 1980). Serotonin applied directly to the ganglion induces sensitization and, like electrical stimulation, increases its content of cAMP. Moreover, dibutyryl cAMP applied to the ganglion, or cAMP itself injected directly into the sensory neurons increased the synaptic facilitation. Injection of the catalytic subunit of cAMP-dependent protein kinase (from bovine heart) increased Ca^{2+} influx, decreased the K^+ current, and increased the amount of neurotransmitter released by the cell (Castellucci, Kandel, Schwartz, Wilson, Nairn, & Greengard, 1980). These results suggest that the sensitization can be explained by a synaptic facilitation induced by serotonergic neurons that act via an adenylate cyclase in the presynaptic terminal, increasing cAMP and the release of neurotransmitter (Fig. 5.1).

Kandel and Schwartz (1982) postulate that this change in the K^+-channel is caused by the phosphorylation of one of its components, triggered by a cAMP-dependent activation of a protein kinase. In support of this, incubation of the ganglia with serotonin increases the phosphorylation of several proteins in the ganglion. The hypothetical sequence is thus: serotonergic neurons synapse presynaptically on terminals instrumental in withdrawing the gill and syphon. The released serotonin activates an adenylate cyclase, which increases the intraterminal content of cAMP. This cAMP in turn activates a protein kinase which phosphorylates a component of a particular K^+-channel, inhibiting the influx of K^+ after depolarization of the terminal. This in turn prolongs the inward Ca^{2+}-current, increasing the intracellular Ca^{2+} and thereby the amount of neurotransmitter released.

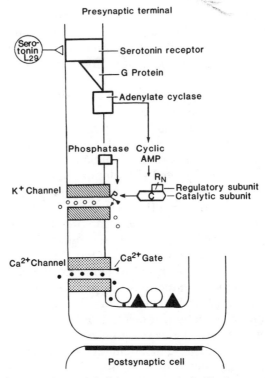

FIGURE 5.1   A molecular model of the presynaptic facilitation proposed to underlie
sensitization in *Aplysia*. Serotonin acts on a receptor on the presynaptic terminal activating adenylate cyclase, thus increasing the intraterminal content of cAMP. The cAMP
binds to the regulatory subunit of a protein kinase, freeing the catalytic subunit to phosphorylate a protein of a novel type of K+-channel. Phosphorylation inactivates the channel, thereby slowing the repolarization of the presynaptic terminal membrane after the
arrival of an action potential. The prolonged depolarization in turn allows a greater influx
of Ca2+ causing a greater release of neurotransmitter. From Kandel and Schwartz (1982).
Copyright 1982, by the AAAS.

On the basis of these data, Kandel and Schwartz (1982) consider that
the elevation of cAMP is sufficient to account for the short-term memory of the sensitization, because the time courses of both effects are
parallel. They also speculate that long-term memory may be initiated
by the same serotonin-activated adenylate cyclase, but which, via
changes in gene expression, ultimately results in structural changes in
the synapse. Some morphological changes have already been characterized (Bailey & Chen, 1983). There is some question regarding the serotonergic nature of the input, and some biochemical steps in this sequence are poorly substantiated, chiefly because the phosphorylation

studies were carried out with whole ganglia rather than individual cells, (Routtenberg, 1984a). Now that Lemos, Novak–Hofer, and Levitan (1984) have shown that it is possible to analyse the phosphoproteins of a single neuron after intracellular injection of labeled ATP, these problems should be accessible to study.

Nevertheless, this is a very impressive series of studies and is a beautiful example of the analysis of a behavioral response at anatomical, physiological and biochemical levels. But is it relevant to more complex forms of learning, or to learning in any kind of mammal? Kandel and Schwartz (1982) argue that their reductionist approach is reasonable, and they may well be right. Only time will tell. Certainly those who work on more complex systems have a model to look to.

Further indications that learning may involve phosphoproteins come from intriguing studies with *Drosophila melanogaster*. Flies of this species can be trained to learn an odor discrimination in which electric shock is used as a UCS (Quinn, Harris, & Benzer, 1974). Memory for this task decays with time, and its strength is dependent on the intensity of training. It can also be disrupted by cold narcosis, but only within the first few minutes following training (Dudai & Quinn, 1980). Memory can also be extinguished by exposing the flies to the previously paired odor in the absence of the shock. Thus for these behavioral characteristics, *Drosophila* resembles rodents. *Drosophila* mutants that show abnormalities in learning have been bred. One such mutant, *Dunce*, fails to learn the task even though it can sense both the odors and the shock (Dudai, Jan, Byers, Quinn, & Benzer, 1976). Dunce has a specific deficiency in a cyclic AMP phosphodiesterase isoenzyme (Byers, Davis, & Kiger, 1981). This molecular deficiency may underlie the learning deficit because administration of phosphodiesterase inhibitors to normal flies causes poor learning.

Another mutant, *Rutabaga*, has a deficiency in adenylate cyclase (Dudai, Uzzan, & Zvi, 1983). Like Dunce, Rutabaga shows a rapid decay of memory following training in the olfactory discrimination task (Dudai, 1983). Thus genetic deficits in the cAMP system are associated with learning abnormalities in fruit flies.

Unfortunately, the deficiencies in these mutants generalize to some but not all forms of learning. Dunce performs poorly in the Horridge leg-lifting paradigm, which is learned well by normal *Drosophila*. Dunce shows a slowness to habituate to presented stimuli, but does not exhibit any deficit in a visual task (Dudai & Quinn, 1980). Nevertheless, the approach is a novel one and may well provide important information complementary to that deriving from the *Aplysia, Hermissenda*, and hippocampal studies.

CEREBRAL BLOOD FLOW AND GLUCOSE UTILIZATION

Because changes in neural activity are associated with changes in the rate of cerebral blood flow (CBF) or energy utilization (Sokoloff, 1977), measurement of these parameters could provide important clues to the structures involved in learning. Most techniques for the measurement of CBF are not readily adaptable for histological use, because the tracers used are by design too readily diffusible. However, recent studies suggest that isopropyliodoamphetamine or iodoamphetamine may be usable for such studies even in humans (Lassen, Henriksen, Holm, Barry, Paulson, Vorstrup, Rapin, Le Poncin–Lafitte, Marretti, Askienazy, & Raynaud, 1983; Rapin, LePoncin–Lafitte, Duterte, Rips, Morier, & Lassen, 1984). Studies with isopropyliodoamphetamine indicate that apomorphine may induce parallel increases in maze learning performance CBF and glucose utilization (Le Poncin–Lafitte, Lamproglou, Duterte, & Rapin, 1984).

Sokoloff, Reivich, Kennedy, des Rosiers, Patlak, Pettigrew, Sakurada, and Shinohara (1977) devised a technique to measure cerebral glucose utilization. Glucose is almost the exclusive energy source for normal brain tissue, so that net glucose uptake is closely related to total energy use, and extensive evidence suggests that the major use of energy in the brain is to transport ions across membranes (Sokoloff, 1977). Therefore, changes of net glucose uptake will largely reflect changes of neural activity. The technique of Sokoloff et al. (1977) uses radioactively labeled 2-deoxyglucose, an analogue of glucose which is taken up by brain cells and phosphorylated by hexokinase. The 2-deoxyglucose 6-phosphate thus formed is not a substrate for any of the enzymes that normally metabolize glucose 6-phosphate, so that it accumulates and is trapped, and can be used as a measure of past glucose uptake. Using quantitative autoradiography of the trapped [^{14}C]deoxyglucose 6-phosphate, and knowing the specific activity of the plasma deoxyglucose–glucose mixture, it is possible to calculate absolute rates of glucose uptake for particular cerebral structures (Sokoloff et al., 1977). The technique has had an important impact on neuroscience research and has even been adapted for human use (Phelps, Huang, Hoffman, Selin, Sokoloff, & Kuhl, 1979).

For determining changes of neural activity during learning, there are two problems with the technique. For technical reasons it is necessary to use a labeling period of 30–60 min, so that the results reflect a weighted integral of the metabolism during that period. Thus if the changes associated with learning are transient, or a sequence of events occurs, they may not be detected. The second problem is whether the technique is sensitive enough to detect behaviorally significant changes. Published results have shown a dramatic ability to highlight localized changes (See Sokoloff, 1977), but to date these have been primarily in sensory systems very sensitive to external stimuli, or following systemic drug treatments. Quantitative autoradiography has a high inherent variance, and in results published so far, only changes that exceed 20% have been found statistically significant. It is not at all clear that changes of this magnitude are likely to be associated with normal changes of ongoing behavior. A further disadvantage of the classical Sokoloff procedure is that subjects are restrained during the deoxyglucose uptake period because of the intravenous cannula necessary to inject the deoxyglucose and to measure the plasma-specific activity of the glucose. This is clearly undesirable for behavioral experiments because of the stress of restraint, and because it is desirable to record behavioral measures during the deoxyglucose accumulation period, to be correlated later with the uptake pattern. Nevertheless, Kohsaka et al. (1979) using subcutaneous injections were able to use the technique to determine the locus of imprinting-induced changes in chick brain, and very recently, Kossut and Rose (1984) found significant changes in the brains of chicks following passive-avoidance training.

The above problems have led others to devise modifications of Sokoloff's procedure, using scintillation counting of free-hand dissected brain structures to determine deoxyglucose accumulation (Dunn, Steelman, & Delanoy, 1980; Meibach, Glick, Ross, Cox, & Maayani, 1980). These variations substitute subcutaneous or intraperitoneal injections of label, and economize by substituting [^{3}H]deoxyglucose for the more expensive ^{14}C. They also forgo measurement of plasma glucose and determine relative changes between brain regions, or as a function of the whole brain. This procedure is adequate to determine behaviorally relevant structures, although a major disadvantage is that the anatomical resolution is poor. The techniques have proved capable of identifying small (i.e., < 10%) regional changes in glucose utilization, for example, following footshock treatment or peptide-induced behaviors (Delanoy & Dunn, 1978; Dunn et al., 1980), or Y-maze acquisition in mice (Martinez, Petty, & Messing, 1982).

Altenau and Agranoff (1978) devised a means of improving the anatomical resolution and the sensitivity. Their method uses micropunches of tissue from frozen sections. The tissue is labeled for a long control period (1–3 hours) with [^{3}H]deoxyglucose, and for a short (30–60 min) experimental period with [^{14}C]deoxyglucose, during which the experimental manipulation is performed. Experiment-related changes are then determined by the alterations in the $^3H:^{14}C$ ratio of the sample. The technique appears to be very sensitive and applicable to very small pieces of tissue, but few data have yet been published using it.

RECEPTOR ADAPTATION

Alterations of the sensitivity of receptors for various neurotransmitters and hormones appear to be a major mechanism of cellular adaptation, and this is currently an important area of research. Receptor *supersensitivity* means that there is an exaggerated response to a given quantity of neurotransmitter or hormone. Receptor *subsensitivity* means that there is a diminished response to the neurotransmitter or hormone. In either case, the change in sensitivity may result from alterations in the number of receptors, their affinity for the neurotransmitter or hormone, or in the coupling of the receptor to cellular responses.

It is important to understand the distinction between a *receptor* and a *binding site;* a distinction confused by the current terminology "receptor-binding." The receptor is by definition the site of action of an *effector* (i.e., a neurotransmitter, hormone, or drug) for producing a cellular response. In binding studies, the quantity of a radiolabeled *ligand* that binds to cellular components is determined. The binding sites so determined may include more than one type of receptor, and even binding sites with no biological significance. Receptors cannot be determined by binding studies per se, but only by a cellular response which could be the release of a hormone, the contraction of a muscle, or the activation of adenylate cyclase, or a specific ion channel. Whereas, it is the aim of binding studies to determine characteristics of receptors, the important distinction between a receptor and a binding site must always be borne in mind.

The classical example of receptor supersensitivity is the supersensitivity to acetylcholine that follows denervation of skeletal muscle (see Changeaux & Danchin, 1976). Receptor sensitivity changes occur in response to a variety of chronic treatments; for example, chronic neuroleptic treatment induces supersensitivity to dopamine (Burt, Creese, & Snyder, 1977), chronic tricyclic antidepressant treatment results in subsensitivity to norepinephrine (Crews & Smith, 1978), and chronic footshock stress results in subsensitivity to norepinephrine (Stone, 1979; for a review see Schwartz, Constentin, Martres, Protais, & Baudry, 1978). Changes of this type have been suggested to underlie diseases such as depression (see Bunney, Post, Anderson, & Kopanda, 1977) and schizophrenia (Owen, Crow, Poulter, Cross, Longden, & Riley, 1978). Such adaptations could clearly provide a mechanism for learning.

Currently, we know little of the mechanism of receptor sensitivity changes. In most of the cases previously mentioned, the sensitivity change is accomplished by changes in the number of binding sites, suggesting changes in receptor number. The change in receptor sensitivity is generally a slow process and is often sensitive to inhibitors of protein synthesis (Schwartz et al., 1978). The mechanisms probably vary widely, because rapid changes are seen in muscarinic binding sites following imprinting (Rose, Gibbs, & Hambley, 1980), and in benzodiazepine binding sites following seizures (Paul & Skolnick, 1978) and stress.

There are few studies indicating changes in the number of binding sites during learning (Rose et al., 1980), however, a recent hypothesis uses this as its focus. Based on their earlier work with LTP in the hippocampus, Lynch and Baudry (1984) proposed a detailed model which proposes changes in glutamate receptors as the basis of LTP and perhaps learning in the hippocampus (Figure 5.2). The occurrence of LTP in hippocampal slices has previously been correlated with an increase in the number of glutamate binding sites (Lynch, Halpain, & Baudry, 1982). LTP can be prevented by the injection into target neurons of the Ca^{2+}-chelating agent, EGTA (Lynch, Larson, Kelso, Barrionuevo, & Schottler, 1983). A similar increase in glutamate binding sites can be produced by low concentrations of Ca^{2+} (10^{-5} M) in vitro, a change which is irreversible (Baudry, Kramer, & Lynch, 1983). Baudry and Lynch postulated that the change in presumed glutamate receptors was caused by Ca^{2+}-dependent acitivation of a protease. In support of this hypothesis, leupeptin, an inhibitor of Ca^{2+}-activated neutral thiol proteases, antagonizes the effect of Ca^{2+} on glutamate binding sites (Baudry, Bundman, Smith, & Lynch, 1981). Ca^{2+} increases the breakdown of a synaptic plasma membrane polypeptide which may be identical with fodrin, a protein that lines the inner face of neuronal membranes. Lynch and Baudry (1984) hypothesize that brief periods of high-frequency activity cause a transient elevation of Ca^{2+} within dendritic spines. The Ca^{2+} activates a membrane-associated protease, calpain, which locally breaks up the fodrin network, producing structural and chemical changes in the region of the postsynaptic membrane. This rearrangement exposes previously occluded glutamate receptors, thus producing LTP.

Rats infused with leupeptin on a continuous basis from osmotic minipumps were impaired in the performance of a radial maze (Staubli, Baudry, & Lynch, 1984), and in the acquisition of an olfactory discrimination task for water reward, providing behavioral evidence for this hypothesis (see Lynch & Baudry, 1984). Furthermore, rabbits

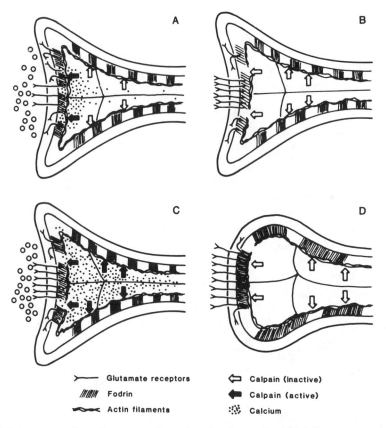

>——— Glutamate receptors   ⇐ Calpain (inactive)

/////// Fodrin   ◀ Calpain (active)

~~◀ Actin filaments   :⋰: Calcium

FIGURE 5.2   A hypothesis to indicate how brief periods of high-frequency activity could produce long-lasting changes of synaptic efficacy. A. Neurotransmitter release causes an increase in Ca^{2+} in the subsynaptic zone of a dendritic spine. This Ca^{2+} activates calpain which degrades fodrin uncovering occluded glutamate receptors. B. Ca^{2+} is removed from the spine inactivating calpain, but the changes in glutamate receptors persist. C. Subsequent episodes of high-frequency activity produce a larger postsynaptic response and a larger influx of Ca^{2+} because of the greater number of receptors. The increased Ca^{2+} stimulates calpain throughout the spine and leads to widespread degradation of the fodrin network permitting a shape change to occur. D. Ca^{2+} is again eliminated from the spine, but the structural and receptor changes produced by transient activation of calpain remain. From Lynch and Baudry (1984). Copyright 1984, by the AAAS.

trained in a conditioned eyeblink paradigm show significantly increased glutamate binding to hippocampal membranes (Mamounas, Thompson, Lynch, & Baudry, 1984). These data are very exciting, but it will be extraordinarily difficult to prove such a hypothesis, both because of the ubiquity of Ca^{2+}-mediated effects in cellular metabolism, and because of all the problems inherent in demonstrating that hippocampal LTP can be the basis for learning.

CONCLUSIONS

In the past few years, there has been a substantial shift in the nature of experiments performed on biochemical correlates of learning and memory. The number of experiments in which biochemical events have been monitored following training in rodents has declined dramatically. Also, there has been a large contribution from invertebrate systems and model systems, such as the hippocampal slice. Thus data gleaned from biochemical correlates of LTP in the hippocampus have been extrapolated to learning in the intact animal (Routtenberg, 1984b; Lynch & Baudry, 1984).

At least for short-term memory, there has been a shift away from mechanisms of storage involving synthesis, toward those involving degradation, especially of proteins and their derivatives. While memory biochemists have long been aware of this possibility, fewer biochemical techniques are available for studying degradation and they are less sophisticated than those for studying synthesis. This progression could perhaps have been predicted from the ease and rapidity of degradative processes, and from the unusual features of protein metabolism of neurons, in which most synthesis must occur in the perikaryon (see Dunn, 1982). Ca^{2+} influx into cells has been suggested to activate cellular proteases, to initiate the mechanism underlying hippocampal LTP. In one case, the protease is postulated to act on glutamate receptors (Lynch & Baudry, 1984) and in the other on protein kinase C (Routtenberg, 1984b). Hence electrophysiological events can be coupled with biochemical ones.

The focus has also shifted away from RNA and proteins, and toward glycoproteins and phosphoproteins. Changes in the sensitivity of receptors have also received attention as potential mechanisms for behavioral adaptation. There is a remarkable consensus from a variety of systems that phosphoproteins may play an important role in adaptation, both electrophysiological and behavioral (Gispen & Routtenberg, 1982). Although this resembles superficially the picture obtained in the late 1960s and early 1970s on the role of RNA in learning and memory (see Dunn, 1976b), the phosphoprotein hypothesis appears to be on a firmer cell biological basis. The possibility of rapid addition and removal of phosphate groups make phosphoproteins attractive candidates for substrates of memory. Also, the possibility of activation of specific kinases by cyclic AMP or Ca^{2+} provides a link with well-characterized cellular mechanisms. Changes in the phosphoproteins are capable of altering the activity of enzymes, opening or closing ion channels, and activating or inhibiting gene expression.

Possibilities for the links between electrophysiology and neurochemistry have also been established. Thus the Ca^{2+}-activated proteases previously mentioned may provide a mechanism for linking an electrophysiological event to a more permanent biochemical change. On the other hand, changes in protein derivatives, particularly phosphoproteins, may regulate ion channels (Levitan et al., 1983). Thus interactions between ions and macromolecules may provide mechanisms for memory and a link between electrophysiological and neurochemical events.

Finally, there has been a trend for autoradiographic techniques, based on biochemical findings, to be used to identify the cerebral location of behavior-related changes. Particular examples have involved application of Sokoloff's deoxyglucose procedure for the estimation of glucose utilization (e.g., Kohsaka et al., 1979; Kossut & Rose, 1984), but labeling of RNA has also been used (Horn et al., 1979).

In a previous review, I criticized the lack of attempts to replicate experiments between laboratories. While precise replications are still rare, the avenues of research being pursued in several laboratories are close enough that essential confirmation often occurs with the added advantage of generalization to several systems and organisms. This is particularly true for the phosphoprotein work. Now that models of mammalian learning are becoming more dependent on models such as LTP in the hippocampus and various synaptic phenomena in invertebrate ganglia, the important question is whether the extrapolation is valid, and whether we will miss forms and mechanisms of learning in higher organisms by adopting such a reductionist approach. At least the answers to these questions seem more accessible experimentally than they were only a few years ago.

ACKNOWLEDGMENTS

The research form the author's laboratory cited in this chapter was supported by a grant from the U.S. National Institute of Mental Health (MH 25486). I am grateful to Steven Rose and Aryeh Routtenberg for the provision of unpublished manuscripts, and to Joe Martinez for useful input to this chapter.

REFERENCES

Acosta–Urquidi, J., Alkon, D. L., & Neary, J. T. (1984). Ca^{2+}-dependent protein kinase injection in a photoreceptor mimics biophysical effects of associative phenomena. Science, 224, 1254–1257.

Adair, L. B., Wilson, J. E., & Glassman, E. (1968). Brain function and macromolecules: IV. Uridine incorporation into polysomes of mouse brain during different behavioral experiences. Proceedings of the National Academy of Sciences, U.S.A., 61, 917–922.

Agranoff, B. W., Burrell, H. R., Dokas, L. A., & Springer, A. D. (1978). Progress in biochemical approaches to learning and memory. In M. A. Lipton, A. DiMascio, & K. F. Killman (Eds.), Psychopharmacology: A generation of progress (pp. 623–635). New York: Raven Press.

Agranoff, B. W. (1981). Learning and memory: Biochemical approaches. In G. J. Siegel, R. W. Albers, B. W. Agranoff, & R. Katzman (Eds.), Basic neurochemistry (pp. 801–820). (3rd ed.) Boston: Little Brown.

Agranoff, B. W. (1980). Biochemical events mediating the formation of short-term and long-term memory. In Y. Tsukada & B. W. Agranoff (Eds.), Nuerological basis of learning and memory (pp. 138–147). New York: John Wiley.

Altenau, L. L., & Agranoff, B. W. (1978). A sequential double-label 2-deoxyglucose method for measuring regional cerebral metabolism. Brain Research, 153, 375–381.

Appel, S. H., Davis, W., & Scott, S. (1967). Brain polysomes: Response to environmental stimulation. Science, 157, 836–838.

Bailey, C. H., & Chen, M. (1983). Morphological basis of long-term habituation and sensitization in aplysia. Science, 220, 91–93.

Baldwin, B. A., & S. S. Soltysik. (1969). The effect of cerebral ischaemia or intracarotid injection of methohexitone on short-term memory in goats. Brain Research, 16, 105–120.

Bar, P. R., Schotman, P., Gispen, W. H., Tielen, A. M., & Lopes da Silva, F. H. (1980). Changes in synaptic membrane phosphorylation after tetanic stimulation in the dentate area of the rat hippocampal slice. Brain Research, 198, 478–484.

Bateson, P. P. G., Horn, G., & Rose, S. P. R. (1972). Effects of early experience on regional incorporation of precursors into RNA and protein in the chick brain. Brain Research, 39, 449–465.

Bateson, P. P. G., Rose, S. P. R., & Horn, G. (1973). Imprinting: Lasting effects on uracil incorporation into chick brain. Science, 181, 576–578.

Baudry, M., Bundman, M. C., Smith, E. K., & Lynch, G. S. (1981). Micromolar calcium stimulates proteolysis and glutamate binding in rat brain synaptic membranes. Science, 212, 937–938.

Baudry, M., Kramer, K., & Lynch, G. (1983). Irreversibility and time course of calcium stimulated [^{3}H]glutamate binding to rat hippocampal membranes. Brain Research, 270, 142–145.

Browning, M., Dunwiddie, T., Bennett, W., Gispen, W., & Lynch, G. (1979). Synaptic phosphoproteins: Specific changes after repetitive stimulation of the hippocampal slice. Science, 203, 60–62.

Browning, M., Bennett, W. F., Kelly, P., & Lynch, G. (1981). Evidence that the 40,000 Mr phosphoprotein influenced by high frequency synaptic stimulation is the alpha subunit of pyruvate dehydrogenase. Brain Research, 218, 255–266.

Browning, M., Baudry, M., & Lynch, G. (1982). Evidence that high frequency stimulation influences the phosphorylation of pyruvate dehydrogenase and that the activity of this enzyme is linked to mitochondrial calcium sequestration. *Progress in Brain Research, 56*, 317–337.

Bunney, W. E., Jr., Post, R. M., Anderson, A. E., & Kopanda, R. I. (1977). A neuronal receptor sensitivity mechanism in affective illness (a review of evidence). *Communications in Psychopharmacology, 1*, 393–405.

Burt, D. R., Creese, I., & Snyder, S. H. (1977). Antischizophrenic drugs: Chronic treatment elevates dopamine receptor binding in brain. *Science, 196*, 326–328.

Byers, D., Davis, R. L., & Kiger, J. A., Jr. (1981). Defect in cyclic AMP-phosphodiesterase due to the dunce mutation of learning in Drosophila melanogaster. *Nature, 289*, 79–81.

Castellucci, V. F., Kandel, E. R., Schwartz, J. H., Wilson, F. D., Nairn, A. C., & Greengard, P. (1980). Intracellular injection of the catalytic subunit of cyclic AMP-dependent protein kinase simulates facilitation of transmitter release underlying behavioral sensitization in Aplysia. *Proceedings of the National Academy of Sciences, U.S.A., 77*, 7492–7496.

Changeux, J. P., & Danchin, A. (1976). Selective stabilization of developing synapses as a mechanism for the specification of neuronal networks. *Nature, 264*, 705–712.

Coleman, M. S., Wilson, J. E., & Glassman, E. (1971). Incorporation of uridine into polysomes of mouse brain during extinction. *Nature, 229*, 54–55.

Crews, F. T. & Smith, C. B. (1978). Presynaptic alpha-receptor subsensitivity after long-term antidepressant treatment. *Science, 202*, 322–324.

Davis, H. P., & Squire, L. R. (1984). Protein synthesis and memory: A review. *Psychological Bulletin, 96*, 518–559.

Delanoy, R. L., & Dunn, A. J. (1978). Mouse brain deoxyglucose uptake after footshock, ACTH analogs, α-MSH, corticosterone or lysine vasopressin. *Pharmacology Biochemistry and Behavior, 9*, 21–26.

Dudai, Y., & Quinn, W. G. (1980). Genes and learning in Drosophila. *Trends in Neurosciences, 2*, 28–30.

Dudai, Y., Uzzan, A., & Zvi, S. (1983). Abnormal activity of adenylate cyclase in the drosophila memory mutant rutabaga. *Neuroscience Letters, 42*, 207–212.

Dudai, Y., Jan, Y. N., Byers, D., Quinn, W. G., & Benzer, S. (1976). Dunce, a mutant of Drosophila deficient in learning. *Proceedings of the National Academy of Sciences, U.S.A., 73*, 1684–1688.

Dudai, Y. (1983). Mutations affect storage and use of memory differentially in Drosophila. *Proceedings of the National Academy of Sciences, U.S.A., 80*, 5445–5448.

Dunlop, D. S., Lajtha, A., & Toth, J. (1977). Measuring brain protein metabolism in young and adult rats. In S. Roberts, A. Lajtha, & W. H. Gispen (Eds.), *Mechanisms, regulations and special functions of protein synthesis in the brain* (pp. 79–96). Amsterdam: Elsevier.

Dunn, A. J. (1976a). Biochemical correlates of training: A discussion of the evidence. In M. Rosenzweig & E. L. Bennett (Eds.), *Neural mechanisms of learning and memory* (pp. 311–320). Boston: M.I.T. Press.

Dunn, A. J. (1976b). The chemistry of learning and the formation of memory. In W. H. Gispen (Ed.), *Molecular and functional neurobiology* (pp. 347–387). Amsterdam: Elsevier.

Dunn, A. J. (1977). Measurement of the rate of brain protein synthesis. In S. Roberts, A. Lajtha, & W. H. Gispen (Eds.), *Mechanisms, regulations and special functions of protein synthesis in the brain* (pp. 97–105). Amsterdam: Elsevier.

Dunn, A. J. (1980). Neurochemistry of learning and memory: An evaluation of recent data. *Annual Reviews of Psychology, 31*, 343–390.

Dunn, A. J. (1982). Macromolecules and behavior. In I. R. Brown (Ed.), *Molecular approaches to neurobiology* (pp. 317–340). New York: Academic Press.

Dunn, A. J., & Kramarcy, N. R. (1984). Neurochemical responses in stress: Relationships between the hypothalamic-pituitary-adrenal and catecholamine systems. In L. L. Iversen, S. D. Iversen, & S. H. Snyder (Eds.), *Handbook of psychopharmacology* (pp. 455–515). (Vol. 18). New York: Plenum Press.

Dunn, A. J., Steelman, S., & Delanoy, R. L. (1980). Intraventricular ACTH and vasopressin cause regionally specific changes in cerebral deoxyglucose uptake. *Journal of Neuroscience Research, 5*, 585–595.

Dunn, A. J., & Schotman, P. (1981). Effects of ACTH and related peptides on cerebral RNA and protein synthesis. *Pharmacology and Therapeutics, 12*, 353–372.

Dunn, A. J., Rees, H. D., & Iuvone, P. M. (1978). ACTH and the stress-induced changes of lysine incorporation into brain and liver protein. *Pharmacology Biochemistry and Behavior, 8*, 455–464.

Dunn, A. J., & Gildersleeve, N. B. (1980). Corticotropin-induced changes in protein labelling: Lack of molecular specificity. *Pharmacology Biochemistry and Behavior, 13*, 823–827.

Entingh, D., Damstra–Entingh, T., Dunn, A. J., Wilson, J. E., & Glassman, E. (1974). Brain uridine monophosphate: Reduced incorporation of uridine during avoidance learning. *Brain Research, 70*, 131–138.

Entingh, D., Dunn, A. J., Glassman, E., Wilson, J. E., Hogan, E., & Damstra, T. (1975). Biochemical approaches to the biological basis of memory. In M. S. Gazzaniga & C. Blakemore (Eds.), *Handbook of psychobiology* (pp. 201–238). New York: Academic Press.

Gispen, W. H., Perumal, R., Wilson, J. E., & Glassman, E. (1977). Phosphorylation of proteins of synaptosome-enriched fractions of brain during a short-term training experience: The effects of various treatments. *Behavioral Biology, 21*, 358–363.

Gispen, W. H., & A. Routtenberg. (1982). Brain phosphoproteins: Characterization and function. *Progress in Brain Research*, Vol. 56.

Greenough, W. T. (1976). Enduring brain effects of differential experience and training. In M. Rosenzweig & E. L. Bennett (Eds.), *Neural mechanisms of learning and memory* (pp. 255–278). Boston: M.I.T. Press.

Greenough, W. T. (1984). Structured correlates of information storage in the mammalian brain: A review and hypothesis. *Trends in Neurosciences, 7*, 229–233.

Harris, H. (1963). Nuclear ribonuclear acid. *Progress in Nucleic Acid Research, 2*, 20–59.

Harris, H. (1964). Function of the short-lived ribonucleic acid in the cell nucleus. *Nature, 201*, 863–867.

Hoch, D. B., Dingledine, R. J., & Wilson, J. E. (1984). Long-term potentiation in the hippocampal slice: Possible involvement of pyruvate dehydrogenase. *Brain Research, 302*, 125–134.

Horel, J. A. (1978). The neuroanatomy of amnesia (a critique of the hippocampal memory hypothesis). *Brain, 101*, 403–445.

Horn, G., Rose, S. P. R., & Bateson, P. P. G. (1973a). Monocular imprinting and regional incorporation of tritiated uracil into the brains of intact and 'split-brain' chicks. *Brain Research, 56*, 227–237.

Horn, G., Rose, S. P. R., & Bateson, P. P. G. (1973b). Experience and plasticity in the central nervous system. Is the nervous system modified by experience? Are such modifications involved in learning? *Science, 181*, 506–514.

Horn, G., McCabe, B. J., & Bateson, P. P. G. (1979). An autoradiographic study of the chick brain after imprinting. *Brain Research, 168*, 361–373.

Hydén, H. (1943). Protein metabolism in the nerve cell during growth and function. *Acta Physiologica Scandinavica* (suppl.), *17*, 1–136.

Hydén, H., & Egyházi, E. (1964). Changes in RNA content and base composition in cortical neurons of rats in a learning experiment involving transfer of handedness. *Proceedings of the National Academy of Sciences, U.S.A., 52*, 1030–1035.

Irwin, L. N. (1974). Glycolipids and glycoproteins in brain function. *Reviews of Neuroscience, 1*, 137–182.

Kandel, E. R., & Schwartz, J. H. (1982). Molecular biology of learning: Modulation of transmitter release. *Science, 218*, 433–443.

Kennedy, M. B. (1983). Experimental approaches to understanding the role of protein phosphorylation in the regulation of neuronal function. *Annual Reviews of Neuroscience, 6*, 493–525.

Klein, M. & Kandel, E. R. (1980). Mechanism of calcium current modulation underlying presynaptic facilitation and behavioral sensitization in Aplysia. *Proceedings of the National Academy of Sciences, U.S.A., 77*, 6912–6916.

Kohsaka, S., Takamatsu, K., Aoki, E., & Tsukada, Y. (1979). Metabolic mapping of chick brain after imprinting using [^{14}C]2-deoxyglucose technique. *Brain Research, 172*, 539–544.

Kossut, M., & Rose, S.P.R. (1984). Differential 2-deoxyglucose uptake into chick brain structures during passive avoidance training. *Neuroscience, 12*, 971–978.

Kuo, J. F., & Greengard, P. (1969). An adenosine 3′,5′-monophosphate-dependent protein kinase from Escherichia coli. *Journal of Biological Chemistry, 244*, 3417–3419.

Lassen, N. A., Henriksen, L., Holm, S., Barry, S. I., Paulson, D. B., Vorstrup, S., Rapin, J., Le Poncin–Lafitte, M., Moretti, J. L., Askienazy, S., & Raynaud, C. (1983). Cerebral blood-flow tomography: Xenon-133 compared with isopropyl-amphetamine-iodine-123. *Journal of Nuclear Medicine, 24*, 17–21.

Lemos, J. R., Novak–Hofer, I., & Levitan, I. B. (1984). Synaptic stimulation after protein phosphorylation *in vivo* in a single *Aplysia* neuron. *Proceedings of the National Academy of Sciences, U.S.A., 81*, 3233–3237.

Levitan, I. B., Lemos, J. R., & Novak–Hofer, I. (1983). Protein phosphorylation and the regulation of ion channels. *Trends in Neuroscience, 6*, 496–499.

Lowry, O. H. (1963). The chemical study of single neurons. *Harvey Lectures, 58*, 1–19.

Lynch, G., Halpain, S., & Baudry, M. (1982). Effects of high-frequency synaptic stimulation of glumate receptor binding studied with a modified *in vitro* hippocampal slice preparation. *Brain Research, 244*, 101–111.

Lynch, G., Larson, J., Kelso, S., Barrionuevo, G., & Schottler, F. (1983). Intracellular injections of EGTA block induction of hippocampal long-term potentiation. *Nature, 305*, 719–721.

Lynch, G., & Baudry, M. (1984). The biochemistry of memory: A new and specific hypothesis. *Science, 224*, 1057–1063.

Lyn-Cook, B. D., & Wilson, J. E. (1983). Effects of experiences on synaptic protein phosphorylation *in vitro*. *Pharmacology Biochemistry and Behavior, 18*, 949–952.

McGaugh, J. L. (1966). Time-dependent processes in memory storage. *Science, 153*, 1351–1358.

Machlus, B., Wilson, J. E., & Glassman, E. (1974). Brain phosphoproteins: The effect of short experiences on the phosphorylation of nuclear proteins of rat brain. *Behavioral Biology, 10*, 43–62.

Mahler, H. (1981). Nucleic acid and protein metabolism. In G. J. Siegel, R. W. Albers, B. W. Agranoff, & R. Katzman (Eds.), *Basic neurochemistry* (pp. 371–400). (3rd ed.) Boston: Little Brown.

Mamounas, L. A., Thompson, R. F., Lynch, G., & Baudry, M. (1984). Classical conditioning of the rabbit eyelid response increases glutamate receptor binding in hippocampal synaptic membranes. Proceedings of the National Academy of Sciences USA, 81, 2548–2552.

Martinez, J. L., Petty, C., & Messing, R. B. (1982). Regional brain uptake of 2-deoxy-D-glucose following training in a discriminated Y-maze avoidance task. Journal of Comparative and Physiological Psychology, 96, 721–724.

Matthies, H. (1982). Plasticity in the nervous system—an approach to memory research. In C. Ajmone Marsan & H. Matthies (Eds.), Neuronal plasticity and memory formation (pp. 1–15). New York: Raven Press.

Meibach, R. C., Glick, S. D., Ross, D. A., Cox, R. D., & Maayani, S. (1980). Intraperitoneal administration and other modifications of the 2-deoxy-I-D-glucose technique. Brain Research, 195, 167–176.

Morgan, D. G., & Routtenberg, A. (1979). Incorporation of intrastriatally injected [³H]fucose into electrophoretically separated synaptosomal glucoproteins: II. the influence of passive avoidance training. Brain Research, 179, 343–354.

Morgan, D. G., & Routtenberg, A. (1980). Evidence that a 41,000 dalton brain phosphoprotein is pyruvate dehydrogenase. Biochemistry Biophysical Research Communications, 95, 569–576.

Morgan, D. G., & Routtenberg, A. (1981). Brain pyruvate dehydrogenase: Phosphorylation and enzyme activity altered by a training experience. Science, 214, 470–471.

Neary, J. T., Crow, T., & Alkon, D. L. (1981). Change in a specific phosphoprotein band following associative learning in Hermissenda. Nature, 293, 658–660.

Neary, J. T., & Alkon, D. L. (1983). Protein phosphorylation/dephosphorylation and the transient, voltage-dependent potassium conductance in Hermissenda crassicornis. Journal of Biological Chemistry, 258, 8979–8983.

Nestler, E. J., & Greengard, P. (1983). Protein phosphorylation in the brain. Nature, 305, 583–588.

Oja, S. S. (1967). Studies on protein metabolism in developing rat brain. Annales Academiae Scientiarum Fennicae AV, 131, 1–81.

Owen, F., Crow, T. J., Poulter, M., Cross, A. J., Langden, A., & Riley, G. J. (1978). Increased dopamine-receptor sensitivity in schizophrenia. Lancet, ii, 223–226.

Paul, S. M., & Skolnick, P. (1978). Rapid changes in brain benzodiazepine receptors after experimental seizures. Science, 202, 892–894.

Pavlík, A., Jakoubek, J., Burešová, M., & Hájek, I. (1971). The effect of ACTH on the synthesis of acidic proteins in brain cortical slices. Physiologia Bohemoslavica, 20, 399–400.

Perry, R. P. (1976). Processing of RNA. Annual Reviews of Biochemistry, 45, 605–630.

Phelps, M. E., Huang, S. C., Hoffman, E. J., Selin, C., Sokoloff, L., & Kuhl, D. E. (1979). Tomographic measurement of local cerebral glucose metabolic rate in humans with (F-18) 2-fluoro-2 deoxy-D-glucose: Validation of method. Annals of Neurology, 6, 371–388.

Le Poncin–Lafitte, M., Lamproglou, Y., Duterte, D., & Rapin, J. R. (1984). Simultaneous study of learning, cerebral hemodynamics, and metabolism in aged rats: Effects of a dopaminergic agonist. Monographs in Neural Science, 11, 68–77.

Popov, N. Pohle, W., Schulzeck, S., Matthies, H. K., Brodemann, R., & Matthies, H. (1983). PAGE-autoradiography of fucose incorporation into rat hippocampal glycoproteins after acquisition of a brightness discrimination. Biochimica Biophysica Acta 42, 6, 763–776.

Quinn, W. G., Harris, W. A., & Benzer, S. (1974). Conditioned behavior in *Drosophila melanogaster*. *Proceedings of the National Academy of Sciences, 71*, 708–712.

Rapin, J. R., Le Poncin–Lafitte, M., Duterte, D., Rips, R., Morier, E., & Lassen, N. A. (1984). Iodoamphetamine as a new tracer for local cerebral blood flow in the rat: Comparison with isopropyliodoamphetamine. *Journal of Cerebral Blood Flow and Metabolism, 41*, 270–274.

Rees, H. D., Brogan, L. L., Entingh, D. J., Dunn, A. J., Shinkman, T., Damstra–Entingh, Wilson, J. E., & Glassman, E. (1974). Effect of sensory stimulation on the uptake and incorporation of radioactive lysine into protein of mouse brain and liver. *Brain Research, 68*, 143–156.

Rees, H. D., & Dunn, A. J. (1977). The role of pituitary-adrenal system in the footshock-induced increase of [³H]lysine incorporation into mouse brain and liver proteins. *Brain Research, 120*, 317–325.

Reith, M. E. A., Schotman, P., & Gispen, W. H. (1975). Incorporation of [³H]leucine into brain stem protein fractions: The effect of a behaviorally active, N-terminal fragment of ACTH in hypophysectomized rats. *Neurobiology, 5*, 355–368.

Rose, S. P. R. (1968). The biochemistry of neurons and glia. In A. N. Davison & J. Dobbing (Eds.), *Applied neurochemistry* (p. 351). Oxford: Blackwell Scientific Publishers.

Rose, S. P. R. (1981). What should a biochemistry of learning and memory be about? *Neuroscience, 6*, 811–821.

Rose, S. P. R. (1984a). Strategies in studying the cell biology of learning and memory. In L. R. Squire & N. Butters (Eds.), *The neurpsychology of memory* (pp. 547–554). New York: Guilford Press.

Rose, S. P. R. (1986). Passive avoidance training in the chick: A model for the analysis of the cell biology of memory storage. In D. L. Alkon & C. D. Woody (Eds.), *Neural mechanisms of conditioning*. New York: Plenum Press.

Rose, S. P. R., Gibbs, M. E., & Hambley, J. W. (1980). Transient increase in forebrain muscarinic cholinergic receptors following passive avoidance learning in the young chick. *Neuroscience, 5*, 169–172.

Rose, S. P. R., Hambley, J., & Haywood, J. (1976). Neurochemical approaches to developmental plasticity and learning. In E. L. Bennett & M. R. Rosenzweig (Eds.), *Neural mechanisms of learning and memory* (pp. 293–310). Boston: M.I.T. Press.

Rose, S. P. R., & Harding, S. (1984). Training increases [³H]fucose incorporation in chick brain only if followed by memory storage. *Neuroscience, 12*, 663–667.

Rose, S. P. R., & Haywood, J. (1977). Experience, learning and brain metabolism. In A. N. Davidson (Ed.), *Biochemical correlates of brain structure and function* (pp. 249–292). New York: Academic Press.

Routtenberg, A. (1984). Brain phosphoproteins, kinase C and protein F1: Protagonists of plasticity in particular pathways. In G. Lynch, J. L. McGaugh, & N. Weinberger, (Eds.), *Neurobiology of Learning and Memory* (pp. 479–490). New York: Guilford Press.

Routtenberg, A. (1985). Phosphoprotein regulation of memory formation: Enhancement and control of synaptic plasticity by protein kinase-C and protein-F1. *Annals of the New York Academy of Sciences, 444*, 203–211.

Routtenberg, A., & Benson, G. E. (1980). In vitro phosphorylation of a 41,000-MW protein band is selectivity increased 24 hr after footshock or learning. *Behavioral and Neural Biology, 29*, 168–175.

Routtenberg, A., Lovinger, D. M., & Steward, O. (1985). Selective increase in phosphorylation state of a 47 kD protein (F1) directly related to long-term potentiation. *Behavioral Neural Biology, 43*, 3–11.

Schwartz, J. C., Constentin, J., Martres, M, P., Protais, P., & Baudry, M. (1978). Modulation of receptor mechanisms in the CNS: Hyper and hyposensitivity to catecholamines. *Neuropharmacology, 17,* 665–685.

Shashoua, V. E. (1968). RNA changes in goldfish brain during learning. *Nature, 217,* 238–240.

Sokoloff, L. (1977). Relation between physiological function and energy metabolism in the central nervous system. *Journal of Neurochemistry, 29,* 13–26.

Sokoloff, L., Reivich, M., Kennedy, C., des Rosiers, M. H., Patlak, C. S., Pettigrew, K. D., Sakurada, O., & Shinohara, M. (1977). The [^{14}C]deoxyglucose method for the measurement of local cerebral glucose utilization: Theory, procedure and normal values in the conscious and anesthetized albino rat. *Journal of Neurochemistry, 28,* 897–916.

Staubli, U., Baudry, M., & Lynch, G. (1984). Leupeptin, a thiol proteinase inhibitor, causes a selective impairment of spatial maze performance in rats. *Behavioral and Neural Biology, 40,* 58–69.

Stone, E. A. (1979). Subsensitivity to norepinephrine as a link between adaptation to stress and antidepressant therapy: A hypothesis. *Research Communications Psychology, Psychiatry, and Behavior, 4,* 241–255.

Sukumar, R., Rose, S. P. R., & Burgoyne, R. D. (1980). Increased incorporation of [^{3}H]fucose into chick brain glycoproteins following training on a passive avoidance task. *Journal of Neurochemistry, 34,* 1000–1006.

Uphouse, L. L. (1980). Reevaluation of mechanisms that mediate brain differences between enriched and impoverished animals. *Psychological Bulletin, 88,* 215–232.

Zemp, J. W., Wilson, J. E., Schlesinger, K., Boggan, W. O., & Glassman, E. (1966). Brain function and macromolecules: I. Incorporation of uridine into RNA of mouse brain during short-term training experience. *Proceedings of the National Academy of Sciences, U.S.A., 55,* 1423–1431.

Zwiers, H., Wiegant, V. M., Schotman, P., & Gispen, W. H. (1978). ACTH-induced inhibition of endogenous rat brain protein phosphorylation *in vitro:* Structure activity. *Neurochemical Research, 3,* 455–463.

6

APPLIED ASPECTS OF MEMORY RESEARCH: AGING

Steven F. Zornetzer

PROLOGUE

The uncharted rocky road (should we be so prosaic and call it "memory lane"?) upon which memory researchers must travel is filled with conceptual hazards and empirical pot holes. Unpleasant as these are, we must additionally prepare for a long and uncertain trip. Between us today and our final destination lie many dead ends and side roads leading nowhere. The astute student of course would (should) ask at this point, "Why even attempt to make such a journey since there are many other available destinations in psychobiology accessible by high speed comfortable freeways?"

The answer to this question (forgive me the use of this metaphor for a few more lines) is that to most memory researchers, there is a scientific daring in this journey, motivating them to endure the uncertainties and unpleasantries of their quest. To these intrepid researchers sheer adventurism coupled with the scenic view of the journey more than justifies the scientific perils of the trip.

One such "scenic view" of contemporary memory research that may prove fruitful in helping us to better understand some basic features of memory is the role of the aging process upon memory function. Underlying such changes in memory are, of course, age-related changes in the brain substrates responsible for the various component processes mediating memory.

INTRODUCTION

This chapter considers some of the evidence from both infrahuman and human subjects regarding memory decline in aging. Following a brief overview of the behavioral evidence for such a decline, the chapter focuses on the possible etiological factors contributing to senescent memory decline in both normal and pathological conditions. There is a large and growing literature describing the many age-related psychobiological changes associated with memory decline in aging (cf. Bartus, Dean, Beer, & Lippa, 1982; Dean, Scozzafava, Goas, Reagan, Beer, & Bartus, 1981; Jensen, Messing, Martinez, Vasquez, Spiehler, & McGaugh, 1981; Kubanis & Zornetzer, 1981). The reader interested in delving further into these topics should additionally consider these excellent reviews.

Pioneering studies by Ruch (1934) and Gilbert (1941) demonstrated clearly that, relative to young adults, the aged exhibit a decline in performance on tests of learning and memory capabilities. Once age-related performance deficits were established, experimental attention focused on identifying the particular aspects of cognitive functioning that are impaired with aging. There has been, and continues to be, a decided lack of agreement on this matter. In particular, changes in both nonspecific processes and in memory-specific processes have been invoked to account for the same behavioral performance deficits (see Gold & McGaugh, 1975). The complicated task of localizing the source of cognitive impairment associated with aging is our goal as students of brain and behavior.

What do we mean by "old"? In human studies, the aged group has generally included subjects older than 60 years (with a variable upper age limit), ostensibly in good health. The average age group in young control groups is usually between 20 and 30, although subjects in their 40s are occasionally included. Since this is a relatively consistent practice, the exact ages of subjects in the discussion of individual studies is generally omitted.

More variability is found in the animal literature. It is generally conceded that at 24 months, rodents are old. Young comparison groups most often consists of animals between 2 and 6 months of age. In the behavioral section of this paper, the ages are provided for all subjects used in primate research, as well as in those rodent studies using less typical age categorizations. For most neurobiological research, specific age comparisons are indicated.

BEHAVIORAL STUDIES: MEMORY DEFICITS
WITH NORMAL AGING

SHORT-TERM MEMORY: HUMAN STUDIES

The effect of aging on short-term memory (STM) in humans has been studied extensively. The principal finding concerning the deterioration of STM with age is that it is task-dependent. Several investigators have reported no significant age differences in performance on simple tasks such as serial recall of a list of digits (Bromley, 1958; Drachman & Leavitt, 1972) or words (Talland, 1965). Others have reported small (.5–1.0 digit) but reliable deficits in digit span in older subjects (e.g., Botwinick & Storandt, 1974; Gilbert, 1941; Mueller, Rankin, & Carlomusto, 1979). Using the free recall paradigm, Craik (1968) and Raymond (1971) supported intact STM capacity in the elderly by demonstrating normal recall of the last five items presented, commonly inferred to reflect STM.

On other tests of STM capacity, large age-related impairments have been reported. Aged subjects show deficits on tests of backward span (Bromley, 1958; Meuller et al., 1979), a task requiring repetition of a list of items in reverse order that are larger than deficits reported for forward span.

Dichotic listening is a task in which subjects are simultaneously presented with a separate set of stimuli to each ear, and are subsequently tested on recall for each half-set. Inglish and Caird (1963) reported no effect of aging on recall for the first half-set reported, but impaired second half-set recall in elderly subjects. Other investigators have reported impairment in recall for both the first and second half-sets (Clark & Knowles, 1973; Schonfield, Trueman, & Kline, 1972).

In an experiment by Kay (1953, cited by Welford, 1958), subjects were presented with an array of twelve lights, each with an associated key. Older subjects performed well when instructed to press each key as its respective light came on. However, when asked to press the key corresponding to the light that had flicked on one, two, or three trials previously, performance of aged subjects showed a dramatic and progressive decline. Broadbent and Gregory (1965) found that elderly subjects were impaired on a task in which visual and auditory items were presented simultaneously, but subjects were required to recall stimuli from the modalities separately.

Age-related performance impairments were originally attributed to a faster rate of STM decay in older subjects (Fraser, 1958). The passive

decay theory of short-term forgetting has not withstood vigorous experimental testing (see Murdock, 1974, for a review), and it is now generally accepted that interference by intervening material, rather than time
per se, is responsible for forgetting. Welford (1958) suggested that STM
deficits in the elderly could be explained by a progressive increase in
susceptibility to retroactive interference with age. This influential hypothesis is compatible with Kay's (1953) key press results and is also
supported by age-related dichotic listening deficits. However, numerous other interference paradigms, each using an interpolated distractor
task between stimulus presentation and response opportunity, have
shown equivalent rate of forgetting for young and aged subjects (e.g.,
Craik, 1971; Schonfield, 1969; Wickelgren, 1975). Thus, neither accelerated decay nor Welford's interference hypothesis appears to account
for the task-selective decline in STM in aged subjects.

What then is the critical factor in this task-dependent aging effect? In
a review of age difference in short-term retention, Craik (1977) concluded that the situation in which older subjects are impaired are those
which require (1) division of attention, either between two input
sources, between input and holding, or between holding and responding and/or (2) reorganization of the input prior to responding. Craik's
categorization incorporated the available data particularly well. Most
of the studies cited above, in which deficits were found, employed
tasks requiring either division of attention or reorganization of cue
categories by subjects. These include backward span, the key press
experiment, visual–auditory recall, and dichotic listening. Thus, it appears that aging results in a slight decrement in STM as measured by
digit span, with a more severe impairment on tasks requiring division
of attention or reorganization of stimuli.

SHORT-TERM MEMORY: ANIMAL STUDIES

Goodrick found that older rats were impaired in acquisition of a 14-
choice maze under distributed practice conditions, although no impairment was observed under massed practice conditions. He attributed
this effect to a short-term memory deficit in the old rats. Using a delayed discrimination task, in which a 3-s delay was imposed between a
conditioned stimulus and an avoidance response, Doty (1966a) reported an age-related short-term retention deficit in rats.

Conflicting evidence has been reported by Wallace, Krauter, and
Campbell (1980) in a systematic study of Fischer rats ranging in age
from 6 to 26 months. The first task involved retention of previous

choices in a radial arm maze after a 0–15 min delay. A second experiment utilized a modification of Konorski's (1959) discriminated delay response task with delay intervals of 0, 2, and 5 s. No age-related deficit was observed on either task.

In a recent study, Zornetzer, Thompson, and Rogers (1982) investigated the time course of forgetting in aged (24–26 months) Sprague–Dawley rats. Three different tasks were used to access memory decay. The task most sensitive to accelerated forgetting from STM was spontaneous alternation. Accordingly, young rats (6 months) persisted to spontaneously alternate at above chance level for at least 10 min after an initial trial. Aged rats approached chance levels of alternation by 4 min. This accelerated age-related decay in alternation behavior suggests a more rapid forgetting of the relevant maze cues in aged rats.

The results of studies of aging and STM in nonhuman primates have been more consistent than in rodents. Several laboratories have examined STM differences using delayed-response discrimination paradigms. Riopelle and Rogers (1965) first reported impaired performance by older chimpanzees on a task in which food was placed under one of five identical stimuli, and a delay was imposed before allowing the animal an opportunity to respond. Since old animals were impaired in an 0-s delay condition, in addition to longer delays, the effect was attributed to a defect in attention, rather than in memory. Differences in visual acuity or psychomotor coordination could also account for these results.

A well-controlled study by Bartus, Fleming, and Johnson (1978) replicated and extended earlier findings of Medin (1969) using the aged rhesus monkey. Use of an automated apparatus with an observation window for viewing stimuli eliminated distracting influences and possible experimenter bias. Extensive pretraining and self-pacing by subjects precluded differential effects of test situation novelty and time pressure. In addition to 0-, 15- and 30-s retention intervals, monkeys were tested on a continuous information condition in which the stimulus remained lighted during the response period. This condition was included as a control for possible age differences in sensory-perceptual abilities and psychomotor coordination. Bartus et al. found that 18–20-year-old monkeys performed comparably to 3–4-year-old subjects on both the 0-delay and continuous information conditions. Older monkeys were significantly impaired on the two longer retention intervals (15 s and 30 s), such that there was no overlap between the two groups. A subsequent experiment manipulating deprivation level ruled out age-related difference in motivation as an explanation for the results.

Conclusions on Short-Term Memory

In combination, human and animal studies are providing useful information about STM and aging. Human research is providing a careful characteristic of the kinds of tasks on which there are age-related impairments of STM. On the other hand, these studies are plagued by problems of interpretation since age difference in health, motivation, and sensory-motor variables are difficult to exclude. Such research has demonstrated that there is a relatively minor decrement with age in digit span performance and related simple tasks. Older subjects are substantially impaired only on more complex tasks requiring divided attention or reorganization of stimulus materials.

Animal research is playing an important role in determining the generality of age-related short-term performance deficits, and in refuting some nonmemorial alternative explanations for these deficits.

Only a few rodent studies investigating STM and aging have been reported in the literature, and the results are conflicting. If there is a STM deficit in aged rodents (e.g., Zornetzer et al., 1982), the Wallace et al. (1980) study suggests that the deficit does not generalize to all STM tasks. Primate studies, however, have consistently shown age-related deficits in STM, as measured by delayed-response discrimination problems. In general, the animal literature corroborates age-related declines in STM capacity, and suggests that there may be species differences in the magnitude of the aging effect.

LONG-TERM MEMORY: HUMAN STUDIES

The human literature on aging and long-term memory (LTM) is both voluminous and controversial. Adherents may be found to every conceivable position on this issue, including one which perceives age-related LTM deficits as cultural artifacts (e.g., Labouvie–Vief, Hoyer, Baltes, & Baltes, 1974). Nevertheless, most investigators concur that there is a genuine impairment of some aspects of LTM with aging. Much of the disagreement concerns the relative importance of acquisition versus retrieval processes in accounting for the observed deficits.

Paired-associate learning and tests of recall or recognition of word lists are the most commonly used tests of LTM capabilities of the elderly. Gilbert (1941) first reported paired-associate learning impairments in aged subjects. Free recall, but not recognition, of a word list was found to be impaired in older subjects by Schonfield and Robertson (1966). Other investigators have reported age-related deficits in word list recognition as well (e.g., Botwinick & Storandt, 1974; Erber,

1974, 1978). Arenberg (1978) has shown that aging impairs performance on the Benton Revised Visual Retention Test, which is a recall test of memory for designs. This result indicates that age-related recall deficits are not restricted to the verbal–memory domain. Typically, performance levels on paired-associate and recognition tasks are considered to reflect acquisition strength, while tests of recall ability are considered to reflect adequacy of retrieval which may be impaired with advancing age.

Pacing

Pacing, the rate of stimulus presentation and time allowed for response, is one situational variable that differentially influences the performance of older subjects on LTM tasks. Canestrari (1963) showed that older subjects benefitted more than younger subjects when they were allowed to work at a slower pace or set their own pace on a paired-associate task. In a more recent study (Monge & Hultsch, 1971), increasing the inspection interval (time allowed to learn the association) improved the performance of young and old subjects equally. Increasing the anticipation interval (time allowed for response production) was selectively beneficial to older subjects, suggesting that retrieval and/or response production take longer for the elderly.

Older subjects make more errors of commission and also more errors of omission compared to young subjects (Canestrari, 1968; Eisdorfer, 1968). Eisdorfer (1968) found that the effect of pacing on performance could be attributed to a change in the number of errors of omission, and he hypothesized that such errors were related to heightened situational anxiety in the elderly.

Factors like pacing and test anxiety appear to have important effects on performance by the elderly. Several possible reasons for this phenomenon can be postulated. One possibility is that neural processing of information per se in the elderly is equivalent to that in younger adults, but that older subjects require more time to acclimate to the situation before demonstrating their true capabilities. In this case, unpaced conditions should reveal the actual memory processing abilities of older subjects. If, on the other hand, adjustment of environmental demands compensates for actual biological deficits in LTM, then making these environmental adjustments might mask a real aging deficit. The role of pacing in determining LTM recall has been and will continue to be debated, but neither of the two possibilities previously mentioned can account for all of the data on aging and LTM. Even under self-paced conditions with considerable practice, age-related differences on LTM tasks persist. These deficits are discussed below.

Acquisition-Encoding Deficits

There is considerable evidence that some of the deficits in LTM reported under optimal conditions are due to age-related decrements in effective encoding of information. Organization of material to be remembered is one factor which facilitates retention. Hultsch (1969) found that when subjects of different ages were given a word list to learn, older subjects benefitted disproportionately when instructed to organize the list or associate each word with its first letter, rather than simply to remember the words. In other experiments reporting recall deficits, organization differences have not been found (e.g., Hultsch, 1971; Laurence, 1966). These studies were based on sorting behavior, which according to several investigators (Craik, 1977; Hultsch, 1974), may not accurately represent organization. Using a more appropriate measure of organization (from Bousfield & Bousfield, 1966), Hultsch (1974) reported that elderly subjects exhibited both recall and organization defects.

Another age-related difference in encoding concerns the use of mnemonics. Elderly subjects do not spontaneously use effective mediators for encoding information, but are able to utilize mnemonics if specifically instructed to do so. In addition, there appear to be qualitative differences in the relative usefulness of mediators developed.

Retrieval Deficits

Many of the age-related decrements in LTM are eliminated on tests of recognition as opposed to recall. However, as previously mentioned, deficits have been reported in both situations. Recall impairments are usually greater than recognition deficits (e.g., Erber, 1974; Harwood & Naylor, 1969), but age differences in recognition are pronounced in complex tasks (Erber, 1974) and tasks including difficult distractor items (Smith, 1975). Conversely, age-related recall differences can be attenuated under cued conditions in which categories for list items are provided (Laurence, 1967). These data are all consistent with the idea that aids to retrieval can mitigate age decrements in LTM.

Craik and Masani (1969) examined retrieval capabilities with a "chunking" experiment. Subjects were presented with word lists differing in order of approximation to English, and a chunk was defined (Tulving & Patkau, 1962) as a string of words recalled in the same order as presented. No age difference was found in the size of chunks recalled, although older subjects recalled fewer chunks. These results were interpreted to represent intact encoding (size of chunks) but impaired retrieval (number of chunks) in the elderly.

Acquisition vs. Retrieval

The acquisition–retrieval controversy will undoubtedly continue among investigators of age-related memory dysfunction. It is probable that both processes are involved and that the cause–effect relationships are difficult to disentangle. The capability for adequate encoding of information is relatively preserved, although the elderly tend not to spontaneously utilize the most effective strategies. Providing encoding strategies or retrieval cues can dramatically improve the performance of the elderly.

The contrast between intentional and incidental learning by older subjects is relevant to this point. Craik (1977) has discussed the rationale for incidental learning paradigms and described the methodological requirements for clear interpretation of their results. Essentially, the idea is that if older subjects are capable of efficient encoding but ordinarily fail to use optimal strategies, then by specifically instructing subjects to perform certain operations on the material and testing them unexpectedly, acquisition should be equivalent at all ages. Differences which remain under incidental conditions may be attributed to sources other than acquisition strategy. Johnson (1973), as one example of these studies, reported no age differences under incidental learning conditions in recognition, free recall, or cued recall.

Zelinski, Walsh, and Thompson (1978) trained young and old subjects under a variety of conditions, including intentional memorization and three incidental tasks: semantic, nonsemantic, and passive listening. Recall testing commenced 2 min or 48 hr later. Recognition was not tested. Older subjects had poorer recall at both time points. Nevertheless, at 2 min both groups demonstrated similar patterns of performance according to task, that is, intentional or semantic incidental training resulted in better recall than did nonsemantic incidental training or passive listening. At 48 hours, however, the older subjects' performance was not influenced by different learning conditions, even though young subjects retained the same performance pattern as at 2 min. Presumably, retrieval demands are low 2 min after training and much higher 48 hr later. Zelinski et al. interpreted their findings to indicate that older subjects are capable of adequate encoding but are impaired in retrieval processes. Interestingly, these authors ignored the possibility that their data could be equally well explained if an ineffective transfer into LTM or a LTM storage failure occurred.

A model of memory processing which is relevant to the international–incidental contrast in performance is the "depth of processing" view proposed by Craik and Lockhart (1972). According to this model, the durability of memory is determined by the degree to which elaborate, semantic (deep) processing of stimuli occurs. Shallow encoding, that is, attending to nonsemantic, sensory features of stimuli, is presumed to result in inferior retention. Craik (1977) applied this model to age-associated memory impairments, hypothesizing that older subjects fail to engage spontaneously in deep processing. Incidental semantic training conditions would be predicted to improve the performance of elderly subjects. Thus, the contrast between intentional and incidental recognition performance in the elderly is consonant with this view.

Since Craik's (1977) review, several studies have tested the "depth of processing" hypothesis. Rankin and Kausler (1979) tested subjects of different ages for phonological and semantic false recognitions on a continuous recognition memory procedure. Older subjects displayed a significantly higher false recognition effect for both rhymes and synonyms. The depth of processing view predicts this effect for rhymes only. Older subjects also made fewer correct recognitions of previously presented stimuli. Rankin and Kausler suggested that the degree of elaboration within a given processing domain, rather than a semantic–sensory dichotomy, could better account for their results.

In conclusion, it appears that young subjects spontaneously adopt strategies for acquisition that generally improve their performance relative to older subjects. The results of most incidental learning studies indicate that older subjects continue to demonstrate retrieval deficits (as reflected by recall testing), even when acquisition strategies are presumably identical.

Long-Term Memory: Animal Studies

Acquisition Deficits

A number of investigators have reported the absence of age-related performance impairments on both appetitive and shock-motivated tasks. Doty (1966b) reported equivalent acquisition by young and old rats of simple shock avoidance and discriminated shock avoidance with distributed practice. Straight runway learning of 1-choice T-maze and 4-choice T-maze problems for food reward presented no particular difficulty for old rats (Goodrick, 1972). Old and middle-aged rhesus monkeys were compared on concurrent discrimination learning in a study by Medin, O'Neal, Smeltz, and Davis (1973). Although older monkeys made more errors on the first trial of each day of training, on subsequent trials and overall, the two groups performed comparably.

In other cases, aging appears to have a deleterious effect on acquisition. Older rats were deficient in learning simple shock avoidance and discriminated shock avoidance if trials were massed, rather than distributed (Doty, 1966b). Several studies have indicated that shuttle box acquisition declines with aging in mice (Freund & Walker, 1971; Oliverio & Bovet, 1966). Using a shock-motivated brightness discrimination task, Thompson and Fitzsimons (1976) found that aged rats were slower to reach criterion levels of performance than were young adult control rats.

Goodrick has done a series of studies examining the effect of aging on acquisition of 1-, 4-, and 14-choice mazes by rats. In addition to finding an age-related impairment in acquisition on the 14-choice maze (1968), and showing that the effect was related to the number of choices (1972), as previously mentioned, he also reported that young animals performed "better" on a schedule of distributed trials, while older animals were benefitted by massed trials (1968, 1973). This last finding contrasts with the adverse effect of massed trials on shock avoidance (Doty, 1966b). Old rats consistently made more perseverative errors in these maze studies. In a further experiment, Goodrick (1975) gave rats forced-correct-choice training on the 14-choice maze, hypothesizing that old rats were more rigid in their behavior and would benefit from this training. The results supported this hypothesis. Performance by older rats on test trials was selectively faciliated by the training when compared to younger control rats.

Bartus, Dean, and Fleming (1979) investigated visual discrimination learning in rhesus monkeys of different ages. Using a subject-paced, automated procedure, they found no age deficit in acquisition of color and pattern discrimination problems to an 18/20 criterion. However, when monkeys were subsequently trained to reverse one of their previous discriminations, aged subjects were significantly slower to extinguish the first habit and learn the reversal problem. Bartus et al. interpreted this finding as evidence for "behavioral rigidity" and/or increased susceptibility to proactive interference in older monkeys.

It may be concluded that aged animals are equivalent to young animals in acquisition of some tasks but impaired on other tasks. Task complexity, determined, for example, by number of choice points in a maze, appears to be one factor in this distinction. A higher incidence of

persistent errors and difficulty on reversal tasks may also be characteristic of older animals' performance.

Retention Deficits

Retention in aging animals has been less thoroughly studied than has
acquisition ability. The usual method of assessing retention has been to
train animals to an equal criterion of acquisition, and test them or
retrain them following a specified time interval. Most of these studies
have been limited by the use of only one training–test interval.

In their review chapter, Arenberg and Robertson–Tchabo (1977) concluded that there is evidence for a retention deficit in old rats. They
cited relearning studies by Goodrick (1968) and Doty (1966a), in which
young and old rats were able to relearn a multiple T-maze and discriminated avoidance test respectively in a comparable number of trials.
However, they also reported Doty's (1968) study, in which aged rats
(421–621-days-old) performed relatively poorly on relearning of discriminated avoidance 2 and 4 months· after initial training. Interestingly, handling prior to initial training greatly attenuated the relearning
deficit of older animals.

Several recent studies have provided evidence for age-related retention impairments. Thompson and Fitzsimons (1976) reported that relearning time on discriminated avoidance after an 8-day interval increased linearly with age. In another study using a 30-day training-test
interval, old rats demonstrated retention impairments for both passive
and active avoidance compared to younger adult rats (McNamara,
Benignus, Benignus, & Miller, 1977). Sherman, Dallob, Dean, Bartus,
and Friedman (1980) reported a significant performance impairment of
24-month-old Fischer rats compared to 6-month-old rats on a single-
trial passive avoidance task. Brizzee and Ordy (1979) reported significantly lower 2- and 6-hr retention in older Fischer rats of a passive
avoidance task in which they were shocked as they approached a food
reward.

Gold and colleagues have reported data on single-trial step-through
passive avoidance retention of 60-day, 1-year, and 2-year Fischer rats at
several training–test intervals. Young animals performed well after 1-,
7-, or 21-day intervals with retention declining at 6 weeks. One-year-
old rats showed good retention at 1 day, but showed a performance
drop at intervals of 7 days or longer. Retention in 2-year-old rats was
preserved at a 2-hour training-test interval but declined within a 6-hour
interval (Gold & McGaugh, 1975; Gold, McGaugh, Hankins, Rose, &
Vasquez, 1980). Preliminary data reported by Gold and McGaugh on

discriminated avoidance also suggested that rate of forgetting increases with advancing age. Kubanis, Gobbel, and Zornetzer (1981) reported age-related deficits in performance of the inhibitory avoidance step-down response. Young mice (3–5 months) displayed good avoidance behavior at both 2 hr and 24 hr after training. Aged mice (20–21 months) had good avoidance behavior 2 hr after training, suggesting good short- or intermediate-term memory, but had impaired performance 24 hr after training. These findings agree with those of Gold and McGaugh (1975) and suggest an impaired memory function for LTM.

Several investigators have reported age-related deficits on spatial memory tasks. Barnes (1979) reported inferior performance by 28–34-month-old Long–Evans hooded rats compared to 10–16-month-old rats on a task which utilized the rodent's innate preference for dark enclosed places. Animals were trained on a circular platform to go to a particular place, through which they could escape to a dark box. On subsequent testing days, the number of errors made by the older group of rats was larger. Wallace, Krauter, and Campbell (1980), who found no deficit on STM of senescent Fischer rats, reported an overall LTM performance deficit on an 8-choice radial arm maze. Thus, it may be concluded that spatial memory, as well as retention on some discriminated avoidance tasks, active avoidance, and passive avoidance, is disrupted by aging in animals.

Conclusions on Long-Term Memory

Like STM impairments, age-related impairments in human LTM are task-dependent. Deficits on tests of both acquisition and retrieval capabilities have been found among older subjects. Age-related performance differences are generally larger on tests of recall than on tests of recognition, although elderly subjects perform well on cued recall tasks and show deficits on complex recognition tasks. Task complexity appears to be a critical factor in determining whether age differences will affect performance in a particular situation.

Animal studies corroborate age-related impairments in retention, as well as acquisition deficits. Performance decrements are found on both appetitive and shock-motivated tasks, including active and passive avoidance and tests of spatial memory. The animal literature also supports the importance of task complexity in age-related mnemonic deficits.

Certain situational variables appear to particularly influence the performance of older subjects. Pacing is the most obvious of these variables. When older subjects are allowed more time to learn associations and/or to respond, their performance is selectively improved. Organizational strategies and mnemonics appear to be used less effectively by older subjects. Specific instructions regarding organization of stimulus materials and development of mediators can disproportionately improve the performance of the elderly. Incidental learning conditions, in which acquisition strategies are equalized, generally eliminate recognition deficits, but not recall deficits, indicating a persistent memory retrieval deficit with aging.

Now we will shift our focus from the behavioral literature to the literature dealing with age-related neurobiological changes. Our challenge is to demonstrate important potential linkages between changing events at the biological level and changing behavior. Clearly, the eventual goal in such an undertaking is to understand better the causal relationships between altered neural function and behavior.

NEUROBIOLOGICAL STUDIES

The Search for a Neurobiological Substrate

The remainder of this chapter focuses upon a narrow consideration of the possible etiological factors underlying senescent memory decline. For purposes of contemporary interest, we will evaluate the so-called "cholinergic hypothesis" of age-related memory decline as an anchor point for our discussion.

There is an important caveat that needs to be mentioned from the outset. The study of neurobiological and associated behavioral changes occurring with normal aging is often blurred by the study of these same phenomena in age-related "pathological" conditions. This phenomena is best illustrated by the recent proliferation of interest in, and new data pertaining to, Senile Dementia of the Alzheimer's type (SDAT). If, as some have suggested (see following discussion), SDAT is nothing more than an acceleration of normal aging processes, then data obtained from normal aging animals (which do not develop SDAT) may indeed be a valid model for studying some aspects of human SDAT. Conversely, clinical–pathological correlates of human SDAT may provide important insights into normal aging. Of course, we should keep in mind that this need not be the case at all, and that the basic assumption may be faulty, that is, data obtained from normal aged organisms might have little or no relationship to SDAT and vice versa.

SDAT AS A RESEARCH FOCAL POINT

A common impairment in both normal aging and SDAT is a decline in memory. The dramatic loss of cholinergic neurons observed in Senile Dementia of the Alzheimer's type (SDAT) has led to the hypothesis that degeneration of cholinergic systems may be responsible for the loss of higher-order function in these individuals. Recent data suggest that there is a relation between the severity of the clinical expression of SDAT and transmitter-specific changes in cholinergic neurons located in the basal forebrain (Bowen, Smith, White, Goodhart, Spillane, Flack, & Davison, 1977; Davies & Maloney, 1976; Perry, Perry, Blessed, & Tomlinson 1977). These cholinergic neuron changes are believed to occur specifically in magnocellular cholinergic basal forebrain systems located in the medial septum, the diagonal band of Broca, and the nucleus basalis of Meynert. These data, coupled with the recent hypothesis (Price, Whitehouse, Struble, Clark, Coyle, Delong, & Hedreen, 1982) that degenerating cholinergic neurons and terminals originating in the basal forebrain give rise to neuritic plaques, support the growing conventional wisdom that pathogenetic processes primary to the basal forebrain cholinergic system are closely associated with SDAT.

Since SDAT is thought to represent an acceleration of normal aging processes, it has been proposed that cholinergic dysfunction may underlie normal age-related memory deficits (Drachman & Leavitt, 1974; Drachman & Sahakian, 1980). The finding that, in young subjects, blockage of cholinergic systems results in interruption of normal memory processes (Drachman, 1977) has strengthened this hypothesis. Disturbingly, however, interventive strategies designed to stimulate cholinergic systems have not resulted in significant generalized improvement in age-related memory loss (Ferris, Sathananthan, Reisberg, & Gershon, 1979; Mohs, Davis, Tinklenberg, Hollister, Yesavage, & Kopell 1979; Mohs, Davis, & Tinklenberg, 1980; Vroulis & Smith, 1981).

MULTIPLE NEUROTRANSMITTER INVOLEMENT

Although basal forebrain cholinergic activity has taken "center stage" with respect to its pathogenetic importance in age-related memory loss, it is very unlikely, given our current knowledge of brain complexity, that any single neurotransmitter would selectively and exclusively be involved in disorders of cognitive function and memory (cf. Gold & Zornetzer, 1983; Zornetzer, 1978). Other neurotransmitter systems have been implicated in normal memory processes, particularly catecholamines and opioids (Gallagher & Kapp, 1978; Messing, Jensen, Martinez, Spiehler, Vasquez, Soumireu–Mourat, Liang, & McGaugh, 1979; Stein, Belluzzi, & Wise, 1975; Zornetzer, Abraham, & Appleton, 1978). A growing literature has also described multiple neurochemical (Finch, 1978; Maggi, Schmidt, Ghetti, & Enna, 1979; Ponzio, Brunello, & Algeri, 1978; Simpkins, Mueller, Huang, & Meites, 1977), neuroanatomical (Landfield, Rose, Sandles, Wohlstadter, & Lynch, 1977; Rogers, Silver, Shoemaker, & Bloom, 1980), and behavioral (Barnes, 1979; Bartus, 1979; Bartus, Dean, & Flemming, 1979; Gold & McGaugh, 1975; Kubanis, Gobbel, & Zornetzer, 1981; Zornetzer, Thompson, & Rogers, 1982) changes in aged animals. It is therefore possible that age-related memory deficits may result from concurrent changes in several neurotransmitter systems. This point can be made even more strongly in the case of SDAT, in which there is widespread degeneration and cell loss seen in postmortem tissue (cf. Brody, 1970, 1976). Rather than review the entire morphologic and neurotransmitter literature on age-related brain changes, let us focus upon available data for noncholinergic neuronal systems believed to employ primarily a single neurotransmitter. For purposes of both example and personal interest, the paragraphs below will focus on the noradrenergic nucleus locus coeruleus (LC).

Vijayashankar and Brody (1979) were the first to report significant cell loss of LC neurons in senescent human brain. These data were extended by Bondereff, Mountjoy, and Roth (1982), who recently reported that in patients with SDAT, cell loss in LC was significantly greater than that which occurred with normal aging. Furthermore, two subclasses of Alzeheimer's patients could be identified: a group having severe cognitive impairment and 80% cell loss in LC, and a less impaired group with correspondingly less LC cell loss. These data are particularly exciting for a number of reasons. First, this system, like the basal forebrain cholinergic system, constitutes a neurotransmitter-specific (norepinephrine) brain region which shows significant cell loss with both normal aging and SDAT. Second, and importantly, the extent of cell loss in LC appears directly correlated with the degree of impaired cognitive function. This second point is interesting in that it parallels the observations and speculations that the four major pathomnemonic findings in Alzheimer's disease (neurofibrillary tangles, senile plaques, granulo-vacuolar degenertion, and Hirano bodies) are similarly related in prevalence to the severity of impaired cognitive function. Accordingly, all of these changes are also found in normal aged brains, but they are quantitatively more frequent in brains from SDAT patients (Appel, 1981). These data from the noradrenergic LC suggest that age-related cognitive decline may be quantitively related to transmitter-specific dysfunction(s).

Other, more functional data support these morphological findings regarding catecholamine-specific cell loss in normal aging and SDAT. Several investigations have reported reduced activity of catecholamine systems in aged rat brain (Algeri, 1978; Finch, 1973, 1976). Furthermore, a reduced activity with age of tyrosine hydroxylase, the rate-limiting enzyme in the synthesis of catecholamines, has been reported for humans (Cote & Kremzner, 1974; McGeer, Fibiger, McGeer, & Wickson, 1971; McGeer & McGeer, 1973) and rodents (Algeria, 1978). Postmortem studies in humans have reported reduced levels of dopamine (DA) and norepinephrine (NE) related to age (Adolfsson, Goffries, Roos,& Winblad, 1979; Carlsson & Winblad, 1976).

Clearly, from this brief discussion of the data describing age-related changes in the catecholamine system, there is good reason for us to consider the possibility that these systems, particularly the noradrenergic nucleus locus coeruleus, may be as important as the age-related changes occurring in basal forebrain cholinergic systems, which have received greater attention. Further, there is considerable additional support for the idea that the LC system plays an essential modulatory role in metabolic (Abraham, Delanoy, Dunn, & Zornetzer, 1979), sensorimotor (Aston–Jones & Bloom, 1981), attentional (Mason, 1981), and higher-order (memory) functions (Zornetzer et al., 1978), in normal-aged subjects. These data, coupled with both published and new data (see following discussion) from my own laboratory strongly reinforces the hypothesis that functional decline of the noradrenergic LC system may be directly implicated in normal age-related cognitive decline and the more precipitous functional decline observed in SDAT.

Recent anatomical studies have suggested that there are several brain loci where functional interactions could occur between the locus coeruleus, nucleus basalis, and other neurotransmitter-defined systems of interest (e.g., the dopamine cells of the substantia nigra-ventral tegmental area and the widespread opiate-containing systems). Of particular interest in this chapter are the interactions between noradrenergic (NE) neurons of the locus coeruleus and cholinergic neurons (ACh) of the nucleus basalis. Although it is known that LC axons traverse the basal forebrain regions that contain nucleus basalis neurons (Fallon & Moore, 1978; Fallon, Kozrell, & Moore, 1978) there has not been convincing evidence that LC innervates these neurons. Based on the density of the LC fibers in these regions, such a projection would be sparse as best. Likewise, a projection from nucleus basalis neurons to the locus coeruleus has not been demonstrated. The presence of moderately dense AChE-positive neuropil in and around the LC could be the dendrites of AChE-positive cells (cholineceptive but not cholinergic) or another cholinergic input. A more likely site of noradrenergic–cholinergic interaction is in the cerebral cortex, where dense noradrenergic (Morrison, Grzanna, Molliver, & Coyle 1978) and cholinergic (Jacobowitz & Palkovitz, 1974) innervation overlaps, especially in Layer I and II. A more isolated, but nonetheless dense, catecholamine innervation of Layer II of supragenual cortex arises in the central tegmental area (Lindvall, Bjorkland, Moore, & Stenevi, 1974; Moore & Bloom, 1978). Connections between the two major catecholamine cell groups could provide a second level of interaction. These include the innervation of the LC by the ventral tegmental area and a possible reciprocal innervation of the ventral tegmental area by the LC (Jones & Moore, 1977).

Another important consideration to keep in mind is the role of opiate interactions with the catecholamine and cholinergic systems. In this regard, there is some evidence for anatomical projections of opiate-containing neurons to cholinergic neurons of the basal forebrain (Fallon, 1983, personal communication) and locus coeruleus (Herkenham & Pert, 1982). Reciprocal projections of the cell groups to opiate-containing cells are unknown, but based on the widespread localization of opiate cell bodies and terminals, such connections may exist and could be significant in the etiology of SDAT.

As an interim summary, it can be concluded that a number of projections could account for interactions between cholinergic, catecholaminergic and opiate systems as they relate to SDAT. The regions of greatest potential for interaction of cholinergic and catecholaminergic systems are the superficial layers of the cerebral cortex.

THE LOCUS COERULEUS AND
AGE-RELATED MEMORY DECLINE

In 1976, studies were begun in young adult rodents which implicated an important role of the nucleus locus coeruleus in memory processes (Zornetzer & Gold, 1976; Zornetzer, Abraham, & Appleton, 1978). These studies were amplified and further supported by others (see Zornetzer, 1978, and Gold & Zornetzer, 1983, for reviews). One particularly interesting study (Stein et al., 1975) reported that pharmacological inhibition of brain NE synthesis resulted in impaired memory. Administration of NE directly into forebrain ventricular systems, thereby bypassing synthesis inhibition, restored normal memory function.

Interest in relating information regarding the LC and memory function to problems of age-related decline were further stimulated with reports indicating that significant functional and morphological impairment of the LC occurs with both normal aging and SDAT (vida supra).

Of particular interest is whether experimental manipulation of the LC-originating NE system results in functional changes in the basal forebrain cholinergic system. In support of this possibility is the finding that LC terminals share common postsynaptic targets with basal forebrain cholinergic neurons in the diagonal band of Broca, medial septal area, and hippocampal formation (Segal, 1976). Additionally, large regions of cerebral cortex receive NE and ACh terminal field projections from the LC and basal forebrain, respectively. Is is possible that LC-derived NE serves as a chemical modulator of cholinergic function in the forebrain and, in turn, modulates memory function as well?

Direct Electrical Activation of LC Cell Bodies Results in Prevention of Age-Related Memory Loss

As previously discussed, aged organisms, ranging from humans to mice, develop memory dysfunction. Recently, my laboratory has begun studying these age-related memory impairments in aged rats and mice (Kubanis, Gobbel, Zornetzer, 1981; Kubanis, Zornetzer, & Freund, 1982; Zornetzer et al., 1982). One conclusion from the data obtained to date is that, generally, aged rodents do not have severe acquisition or learning impairments. Rather, they have an accelerated loss of recently acquired information, that is, they forget faster then do young rodents. This accelerated loss of recently acquired information appears quite general to a variety of learning-memory situations (i.e., short-term, intermediate-term, and long-term memory, Zornetzer et al., 1982).

Considerable interest and effort has been (and is being) devoted to developing effective interventive, usually pharmacologic, strategies to ameliorate these age-related memorial and cognitive deficits (Etienne, Gauthier, Johnson, Collier, Mendis, Dastoor, Cole, & Muller, H. F., 1978). In general, two main thrusts are being used. The first involves administration of agents which increase the efficacy of the cholinergic system in the brain. Such treatments include precursor loading with lecithin and/or choline (Boyd, Grahan–White, Blockwood, Glen, & McQueen, 1977; Mohs, Davis, Tinklenberg, 1980). The second thrust has led to the development of a new class of pharmacologic agents, the nootropics, believed to improve cognitive function in the aged. Accordingly, agents such as piracetam, hydergine, vincamine, centrophenoxine, and so on, which have varied actions on brain-blood flow and/or metabolism (see Ban, 1978), are being tested. To date, their efficacy in improving cognitive function in the elderly is not convincing.

A careful evaluation of each of these research thrusts leads to two observations: (1) there has been an excessively narrow and exclusive focus upon the cholinergic system and memory impairment and (2) the data reported thus far are collectively neither convincing nor impressive (with occasional notable exception, cf. Bartus & Dean, 1980). Perhaps the latter observation is derived from the former observation?

Manipulation of central catecholamines in aging brain represents an additional strategy to supplement the two research strategies previously briefly described. The NE-containing locus coeruleus (LC) is certainly another candidate transmitter-specific system likely to be involved in cognitive function (vida supra). The fact that LC neurons and their terminal field receptors show widespread age-related changes makes it an ideal system to study. Accordingly, the hypothesis tested in the study reported below was, "Can experimental manipulation of the LC alter normally-expected age-related memory decline?" The results provide exciting new data suggesting that age-related memory failure in senescent rodents can be significantly retarded as a result of direct LC activation. A brief description of these experiments follows.

The initial phase of the experiment merely demonstrated that aged (24 months) male C57BL/6J mice, remember more poorly than young (5 months) controls. To demonstrate this, we used a single-trial step-down inhibitory avoidance apparatus (see Kubanis, Gobbel, & Zornetzer, 1981, for details). The results are shown in Figure 6.1.

The second phase of the experiment was designed to test directly, the hypothesis stated above. Groups of mice, either 5-months-old or 18-months-old at the start of the experiment, were surgically prepared, using stereotaxic procedures, with chronic indwelling electrodes targeted bilaterally for the LC. This is a well-established procedure in my laboratory (cf. Prado de Carvalho & Zornetzer, 1981).

Following a 10-day postsurgical recovery period, the mice began an electrical stimulation regimen consisting of regular stimultion of the LC at 48-hour intervals for a period of 6 months. Thus, at the termination of this prolonged intermittent electric stimulation period, mice were either 11 months or 24 months of age. Stimulation parameters were either 100uA or 50uA current at 60HZ using 0.1 ms biphasic pulses. Each stimulation session lasted 10 min, with stimulation actually administered intermittently during this period.

The third phase of the experiment began one week after the last electrical stimulation was administered. All mice were trained in the step-down inhibitory avoidance task. Mice were then tested 24 hr later

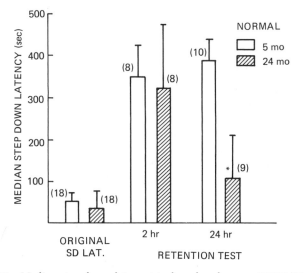

FIGURE 6.1   Median step-down latency(s) of aged and young C57BL/67 male mice. The figure indicates that original step-down latencies in naive mice did not differ between young and aged groups. When tested 2 hr after training, both young and aged mice had a long step-down latency suggesting good memory of the inhibitory avoidance response. Independent groups of mice tested 24 hr after training indicated that aged, but not young, mice now had a significant (p < .02) performance impairment, suggesting memory loss.

for retention of the shock avoidance response. As the results shown in Figure 6.2 indicate, 24-month-old sham-stimulated mice typically forget (i.e., have a shorter step-down latency) the inhibitory avoidance response when tested 24 hr after learning. The data from the 24-month-old mice having had received chronic and repeated LC electrical stimulation are shown in Figure 6.2.

As these data indicated in Figure 6.2, regular repeated prior electrical stimulation of the LC resulted in an improved performance compared to aged controls, when tested 24 hr after learning. In fact, performance of the LC-stimulated aged mice were indistinguishable from that of young controls.

Pharmacological Activation of the LC Results in Prevention of Age-Related Memory Loss

Surgical intervention and electrode implantation in the brain represents a rather extreme procedure for ameliorating age-related memory decline. In an attempt to circumvent this problem a pharmacological approach seemed more desirable. Accordingly, our first pharmacologi-

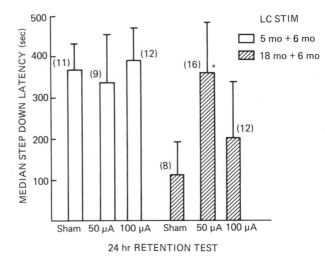

FIGURE 6.2   The effects of prior 6-month intermittent electrical stimulation of the LC upon memory of the inhibitory avoidance response. All stimulation was ended 1 week prior to training. The data indicate that stimulation at 50µA current resulted in significant facilitation in performance in aged mice. Young mice, curiously, were not affected by the treatment. The higher current level (150µA) did not result in significant facilitation of performance.

cal approach to LC activation involved the use of piperoxane, an α_2-noradrenergic receptor blocking agent shown to have an excitatory action upon LC neurons (Ceaderbaum & Aghajanian, 1976) when administered systemically. Piperoxane is believed to activate LC neurons by directly blocking auto- and collateral inhibition in the nucleus of the LC. These intranuclear inhibitory projections utilize the α_2-receptor. Thus, α_2 blockade results in release from inhibition and greater LC cell firing (Ceaderbaum and Aghajanian, 1976). Presumably, elevated LC cell firing would result in correspondingly greater synaptic release of NE at the many terminal fields of the LC in forebrain and other brain regions.

The experimental protocol was designed to parallel the electrical stimulation experiment just described. Mice, 5 months and 18 months of age, at the start of the experiment were divided into independent groups. Animals received either 0.5 or 1.5 mg/kg piperoxane or saline i.p. Injections were given once every 48 hr for 6 months. Injection sites were systematically varied to produce peritoneal irritation or infection.

At the end of the 6-month drug administration period, all mice had a 1 week drug-free period prior to behavioral training and memory test-

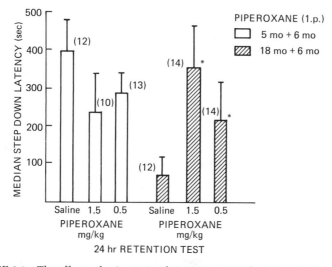

FIGURE 6.3   The effects of prior 6 month injection, at 48 hr intervals, of piperoxane upon memory of the inhibitory avoidance response. Drug administration was ended 1 week prior to training. The data indicate that both doses of piperoxane (0.5 and 1.5 mg/kg, i.p.) resulted in significant improvement of aged, but not young, mice.

ing. At the end of this week, mice were trained and tested on the step-down inhibitory avoidance task, as described previously.

The results of this experiment are shown in Figure 6.3. Twenty-four month old mice who had received repeated administration of piperoxane showed no performance impairment compared to young controls. Aged saline control mice performed as expected, that is, these mice had a significant age-related performance impairment when tested 24 hr after training. It should be noted that prior long-term piperoxane treatment did not appear to alter initial step-down latencies in the mice. This observation would argue against the possibility that the piperoxane effect was due merely to altered activity or anxiety levels. These data are interpreted to suggest that piperoxane, a pharmacological agent capable of increasing LC cell activity, is also capable of significantly reducing age-related memory impairment.

SUMMARY AND CONCLUSIONS

The implications of these new findings are very important. First, the data suggest that age-related memory loss need not be inevitable. Appropriate interventive strategies can at least delay their onset. The extent to which this delay can be maintained relative to life-span is not

understood at present. Many more careful experiments need to be conducted. Second, activation of LC electrical activity appears to be an
important condition leading to the persistence of youthful memory
function into senescence. The result of both the electrical stimulatin
and the piperoxane treatments would suggest the locus coeruleus is a
common target for the site of action of the two treatments. The question
of what is necessary versus sufficient LC activation, vis a vis memory
function, is not presently understood. The 6-month protocol used in
the two experiments previously described was chosen based upon the
assumption that if LC cell function was normally diminished during
aging, the point of onset for such diminished function would likely be
during middle age, which for the C57BL/67 mouse is about 18 months
(Finch, 1978). Accordingly, long-term artificial activation of the LC was
provided in an attempt to sustain and/or mimic greater LC functional
output.

At this juncture, it is important to determine (1) the mechanism
through which LC activation serves to sustain youthful memory function in aged rodents and (2) the optimal parameters for obtaining improved memory function. Presumably the effect is in some way related
to cellular changes occurring, or perhaps not occurring, at distant terminal projection fields receiving LC synaptic endings. One very interesting possibility is that NE-containing LC terminals and/or postsynaptic receptors modulate basal forebrain cholinergic activity directly.
Alternatively, LC terminals may interact at common cortical postsynaptic target sites with cholinergic terminals. In either case, loss of normal LC function with aging might result in diminished cholinergic
efficacy. This testable hypothesis awaits further study.

REFERENCES

Abraham, W. C., Delanoy, R. L., Dunn, A. J., & Zornetzer, S. F. (1979). Locus coeruleus
    stimulation decreases deoxyglucose uptake in mouse cerebral cortex. Brain Re-
    search, 172, 387–392.
Adolfsson, R., Gottfries, C. G., Roos, B. E., & Windblad, B. (1979). Postmortem distribu-
    tion of dopamine and homovanillic acid in human brain, variations related to age
    and a review of the literature. Journal of Neural Transmission, 45, 81–105.
Algeri, S. (1978). Biochemical changes in central catecholaminergic neurons of the senes-
    cent rat. In P. Deniker, C. Radiuco, T. A. Villeneuve (Eds.), Neuro-psychopharmacol-
    ogy: Proceedings of the 10th Congress of the Colleguim International Neuropsy-
    chopharmacologicum, Quebec, July 1976 (Vol. II. pp. 1647–1654). New York: Perga-
    mon Press.
Appel, S. H. (1981). Alzheimer's disease. In S. J. Enna et al. (Eds.), Brain Neurotransmit-
    ters and Receptors in Aging and Age-Related Disorders, 17, New York: Raven Press.

Arenberg, D. (1978). Differences and changes with age in the Benton Visual Retention Test. *Journal of Gerontology, 33,* 534–540.

Arenberg, D., & Robertson–Tchabo, E. A. (1977). Learning and aging. In R. E. Birren & K. W. Schaie (Eds.), *Handbook of the Psychology of Aging* (pp. 421–449). New York: Van Nostrand Reinhold Company.

Aston–Jones, G., & Bloom, F. E. (1981). Norepinephrine-containing locus coeruleus neurons in behaving rats exhibit pronounced responses to non-noxious environmental stimuli. *The Journal of Neuroscience, 1,* 887–900.

Ban, T. A. (1978). Vasodilators, stimulants and anabolic agents in the treatment of geropsychiatric patients. In M. A. Lipton, A. Dimascio, & K. F. Killam, *Psychopharmacology: A generation of progress* (pp. 535–541). New York, Raven Press.

Barnes, C. A. (1979). Memory deficits associated with senescence: A neurophysiological and behavioral study in the rat. *Journal of Comparative and Physiological Psychology, 93,* 74–101.

Bartus, R. T. (1979). Physostigmine and recent memory: Effects in young and aged non-human primates, *Science, 206,* 1087–1089.

Bartus, R. T., & Dean, R. L. (1980). Facilitation of aged primate memory via pharmacological manipulation of central cholinergic activity, *Neurobiology of Aging, 1,* 145–152.

Bartus, R. T., Dean, R. L., III, & Flemming, D. L. (1979). Aging in the rhesus monkey: Effects on visual discrimination learning and reversal learning. *Journal of Gerontology, 34,* 209–219.

Bartus, R. T., Dean, R. L., Beer, B., & Lippa, A. S. (1982). The cholinergic hypothesis of geriatric memory dysfunction. *Science, 217,* 408–417.

Bartus, R., Fleming, D., & Johnson, H. (1978). Aging in the rhesus monkey: Debilitating effects on short-term memory. *Journal of Gerontology, 33,* 858–871.

Bondareff, W., Mountjoy, C. Q., & Roth, M. (1982). Loss of neurons of origin of the adrenergic projection to cerebral cortex (nucleus locus coeruleus) in senile dementia. *Neurology, 32,* 164–168.

Botwinick, J., & Storandt, M. (1974). *Memory related functions and age.* Springfield, IL: Charles C. Thomas.

Bousfield, A. K., & Bousfield, W. A. (1966). Measurement of clustering and of sequential constancies in repeated free recall. *Psychological Reports, 19,* 935–942.

Bowen, D. M., Smith, C. B., White, P., Goodhart, M. J., Spillane, J. A., Flack, R. H. A., & Davison, A. N. (1977). Chemical pathology of the organic dementias. *Brain, 100,* 397–426.

Boyd, W. D., Graham–White, J., Blockwood, G., Glen, I., & McQueen, J. (1977). Clinical effects of choline in Alzheimer senile dementia, *Lancet, 2,* 711.

Brizzee, K. R., & Ordy, J. M. (1979). Age pigments, cell loss and hippocampal function. *Mechanisms of Ageing and Development, 9,* 143–162.

Broadbent, D. E., & Gregory, M. (1965). Some confirmatory results on age differences in memory for simultaneous stimulation. *British Journal of Psychology, 56,* 77–80.

Brody, H. (1970). Structural changes in the aging nervous system. In H. T. Blumenthal (Ed.), *Interdisciplinary topics in gerontology* (pp. 9–21). 7, New York: Basel/Munchen, Karger.

Brody, H. (1976). An examination of cerebral cortex and brain stem aging. In R. D. Terry & S. Gershon (Eds.), *Aging: Neurobiology of aging.* New York: Raven Press.

Bromley, D. E. (1958). Some effects of age on short-term learning and memory. *Journal of Gerontology, 13,* 398–406.

Canestrari, R. E. (1963). Paced and self-paced learning in young and elderly adults. *Journal of Gerontology, 18,* 165–168.

Canestrari, R. E. (1968). Age changes in acquisition. In G. A. Talland (Ed.), *Human aging and behavior*, New York: Academic Press. 169–187.

Carlsson, A., & Winblad, B. (1976). The influence of age and time interval between death and autopsy on dopamine and 3-methoxytryramine levels in human basal ganglia. *Journal of Neural Transmission, 83,* 271–276.

Cedarbaum, J. M., & Aghajanian, G. K. (1976). Noradrenergic neurons of the locus coeruleus: Inhibition by epinephrine and activation by the α_2-antagonist piperoxane. *Brain Research, 112,* 413–419.

Clark, L., & Knowles, J. (1973). Age differences in dichotic listening performance. *Journal of Gerontology, 28,* 173–178.

Cote, L. J., & Kremzner, L. T. (1974). Changes in neurotransmitter systems with increasing age in human brain. In *Transactions of the American Society for Neurochemistry, 5th Annual Meeting* (p. 83). 1978, New Orleans, LA.

Craik, F. I. M. (1968). Two components in free recall. *Journal of Verbal Learning and Verbal Behavior, 7,* 996–1004.

Craik, F. I. M. (1971). Age differences in recognition memory. *Quarterly Journal of Experimental Psychology, 23,* 316–323.

Craik, F. I. M. (1977). Age differences in human memory. In J. E. Birren & K. W. Schaie (Eds.), *Handbook of the psychology of aging* (pp. 348–420). New York: Van Nostrand Reinhold Company.

Craik, F. I. M., & Lockhart, R. S. (1972). Levels of processing: A framework for memory research. *Journal of Verbal Learning and Verbal Behavior, 11,* 671–684.

Craik, F. I. M., & Masani, P. A. (1969). Age and intelligence differences in coding and retrieval of word lists. *British Journal of Psychology, 60,* 315–319.

Craik, F. I. M., & Tulving, E. (1975). Depth of processing and the retention of words in episodic memory. *Journal of Experimental Psychology: General, 104,* 268–294.

Crowder, R. G. (1976). *Principles of learning and memory.* Hillsdale, New Jersey: Lawrence Erlbaum Associates.

Davies, P., & Maloney, A. (1976). Selective loss of central cholinergic neurons in Alzheimer's disease. *Lancet, ii,* 1403.

Dean, R. L., Scozzafava, J., Goas, J. A., Regan, B., Beer, B., & Bartus, R. T. (1981). Age-related differences in behavior across the life-span of the C57BL/6J mouse. *Experimental Aging Research, 7,* 427–451.

Doty, B. A. (1966a). Age and avoidance conditioning in rats. *Journal of Gerontology, 21,* 287–290.

Doty, B. A. (1966b). Age differences in avoidance conditioning as a function of distribution of trials and task difficulty. *Journal of Genetic Psychology, 109,* 249–254.

Doty, B. A. (1968). Effects of handling on learning of young and aged rats. *Journal of Gerontology, 23,* 142–144.

Doty, B. A., & Doty, L. A. (1966). Facilitative effects of amphetamine on avoidance conditioning in relation to age and problem difficulty, *Psychopharmacologia, 9,* 234–241.

Drachman, D. A. (1977). Memory and cognitive function in man: Does the cholinergic system have a specific role? *Neurology, 27,* 783–790.

Drachman, D. A., & Leavitt, J. (1972). Human memory and the cholinergic system: A relationship to aging? *Archives of Neurology, 30,* 113–121.

Drachman, D. A., & Sahakian, B. J. (1980). Memory and cognitive function in the elderly. *Archives of Neurology, 37,* 674–675.

Eisdorfer, C. (1968). Arousal and performance: Experiments on verbal learning and a tentative theory. In G. A. Talland (Ed.), *Human Aging and Behavior* (pp. 189–216). New York, Academic Press.

Erber, J. T. (1974). Age differences in recognition memory. *Journal of Gerontology, 29,* 177–181.

Erber, J. T. (1978). Age differences in a controlled-lag recognition memory task. *Experimental Aging Research, 4,* 195–205.

Etienne, P., Gauthier, S., Johnson, G., Collier, B., Mendis, T., Dastoor, D., Cole, M., & Muller, H. F. (1978). Clinical effects of choline in Alzheimer's disease. *Lancet, 1,* 500–509.

Eysenck, M. W. (1974). Age differences in incidental learning. *Developmental Psychology, 10,* 936–941.

Fallon, J. H., & Moore, R. Y. (1978). Catecholaine innervation of the basal forebrain III, olfactory tubercle, and piriform cortex. *Journal of Comparative Neurology, 180,* 533–544.

Fallon, J. H., Kozrell, D. A., & Moore, R. Y. (1978). Catecholamine innervation of the basal forebrain II, Amygdala, suprarhinal cortex and entorhinal cortex. *Journal of Comparative Neurology, 180,* 509–532.

Finch, C. E. (1973). Catecholamine metabolism in the brains of aging male mice. *Brain Research, 52,* 267–276.

Finch, C. E. (1976). The regulation of physiological changes during mammalian aging. *The Quarterly Review of Biology, 51,* 49–83.

Finch, C. E. (1978). Age-related changes in brain catecholamines: A synopsis of findings in C57BL/6J mice and other rodent models. In C. E. Finch, D. E. Potter, & A. D. Kenny (Eds.), *Advances in experimental medicine and biology, 113,* Parkinson's Disease-II, pp. 15–39. New York: Plenum Press.

Fraser, D. C. (1958). Decay of immediate memory with age. *Nature, 182,* 1163.

Freund, G., & Walker, D. W. (1971). The effects of aging on acquisition and retention of shuttle box avoidance in mice. *Life Sciences, 10,* 1343–1349.

Gallagher, M., & Kapp, B. S. (1978). Manipulation of opiate activity in the amygdala alters memory processes. *Life Sciences, 23,* 1973–1978.

Gilbert, J. G. (1941). Memory loss in senescence. *Journal of Abnormal and Social Psychology, 36,* 73–86.

Gold, P. E., & McGaugh, J. L. (1975). Changes in learning and memory during aging. In J. M. Ordy, & K. R. Brizzee (Eds.), *Neurobiology of Aging* (pp. 145–158). New York, Plenum Press.

Gold, P. E., & Zornetzer, S. F. (1983). The mnemon and its juices: Neuromodulation of memory processes. *Behavioral and Neural Biology, 38,* 151–189.

Gold, P. E., McGaugh, J. L., Hankins, L. L., Rose, R. P., & Vasquez, B. J. (1981). Age-dependent changes in retention in rats. *Experimental Aging Research, 81,* 53–58.

Goodrick, C. L. (1968). Learning, retention, and extinction of a complex maze habit for mature-young and senescent Wistar albino rats. *Journal of Gerontology, 23,* 298–304.

Goodrick, C. L. (1972). Learning by mature–young and aged Wistar albino rats as a function of test complexity. *Journal of Gerontology, 27,* 353–357.

Goodrick, C. L. (1973). Maze learning of mature-young and aged rats as a function of distribution of practice. *Journal of Experimental Psychology, 98,* 344–349.

Goodrick, C. L. (1975). Behavioral rigidity as a mechanism for the facilitation of problem solving for aged rats. *Journal of Gerontology, 30,* 181–184.

Harwood, E., & Naylor, G. F. K. (1969). Recall and recognition in elderly and young subjects. *Australian Journal of Psychology, 21,* 251–257.

Herkenham, M., & Pert, C. G. (1982). Light microscopic localization of brain opiate receptors: A general autoradiographic method which preserves tissue quality. *The Journal of Neuroscience, 2,* 1129–1149.

Hier, D. B., & Caplan, L. R. (1980). Drugs for senile dementia. *Drugs, 20,* 74–80.

Hughes, J. R., Williams, J. G., & Currier, R. D. (1976). An ergot alkaloid preparation (hydergine) in the treatment of dementia: Critical review of the clinical literature. *Journal of the American Geriatric Society, 24,* 490–497.

Hultsch, D. F. (1969). Adult age differences in the organization of free recall. *Developmental Psychology, 1,* 673–678.

Hultsch, D. F. (1974). Learning to learn in adulthood. *Journal of Gerontology, 29,* 302–308.

Inglis, J., & Caird, W. K. (1963). Age differences in successive responses to simultaneous stimulation. *Canadian Journal of Psychology, 17,* 98–105.

Jacobowitz, D. M., & Palkovitz, M. (1974). Topagraphic atlas of catecholamine and acetylcholinesterase-containing neurons in the rat brain I: Forebrain (telencephalon, diencephalon). *Journal of Comparative Neurology, 157,* 13–28.

Jensen, R. A., Messing, R. B., Martinez, J. L., Vasquez, B. J., Spiehler, V. R., & McGaugh, J. L. (1981). Changes in brain peptide systems and altered learning and memory processes in aged animals. In J. L. Martinez, R. A. Jensen, R. B. Messing, H. Rigter, & J. L. McGaugh (Eds.), *Endogenous peptides and learning and memory processes* (pp. 463–477). New York: Academic Press.

Johnson, L. K. (1973). *Changes in memory as a function of age.* Doctoral dissertation, University of Southern California.

Jones, B. E., & Moore, R. Y. (1977). Ascending projections of the locus coeruleus in the rat II: Autoradiographic study. *Brain Research, 127,* 23–53.

Konorski, J. (1959). A new method of physiological investigations of recent memory in animals. *Bulletin de L'Acaemie Polonaise des Sciences, 7,* 115–117.

Kubanis, P., & Zornetzer, S. F. (1981). Age-related behavioral and neurobiological changes: A review with an emphasis on memory. *Behavioral and Neural Biology, 31,* 115–172.

Kubanis, P., Gobbel, G., & Zornetzer, S. F. (1981). Age-related memory deficits in Swiss mice. *Behavioral and Neural Biology, 32,* 241–247.

Kubanis, P., Zornetzer, S. F., & Freund, G. (1982). Memory and postsynaptic cholinergic receptors in aging mice. *Pharmacology, Biochemistry, and Behavior, 17,* 313–322.

Labouvie-Vief, G., Hoyer, W. J., Baltes, M. M., & Baltes, P. B. (1974). Operant analysis of intellectual behavior in old age. *Human Development, 17,* 259–272.

Landfield, P. W., Rose, G., Sandles, L., Wohlstadter, T., & Lynch, G. (1977). Patterns of astroglial hypertrophy and neuronal degeneration in the hippocampus of aged, memory-deficient rats. *Journal of Gerontology, 32,* 3–12.

Laurence, M. W. (1966). Age differences in performance and subjective organization in the free recall of pictorial material. *Canadian Journal of Psychology, 20,* 388–399.

Laurence, M. W. (1967). Memory loss with age: A test of two strategies for its retardation. *Psychonomic Science, 9,* 209–210.

Lindvall, O., Bjorkland, A., Moore, R. Y., & Stenevi, J. (1974). Mesencephalic dopamine neurons projecting to neocortex. *Brain Research, 81,* 325–331.

Loew, D. M. (1980). Pharmacological approaches to the treatment of senile dementia. In L. Amaducci, A. N. Davidson, & P. Antuono (Eds.), *Aging of the brain and dementia* (Vol. 13) (pp. 127–139). New York, Raven Press.

Maggi, A., Schmidt, M. J., Ghetti, B., & Enna, S. J. (1979). Effect of aging on neurotransmitter receptor binding in rat and human brain. *Life Sciences, 24,* 367–374.

Mason, S. T. (1981). Noradrenaline in the brain: Progress in theories of behavioral function. *Progress in Neurobiology, 16,* 263–303.

McGeer, E. G., & McGeer, P. L. (1973). Some characteristics of brain tyrosine hydroxylase. In A. J. Mandell (Ed.), *New concepts in neurotransmitter regulation* (pp. 151–164.) New York, Plenum Press.

McGeer, E. G., Fibiger, H. C., McGeer, P. L., & Wickson, V. (1971). Aging and brain enzymes. *Experimental Gerontology, 6,* 391–396.

Medin, D. L. (1969). Form perception and pattern reproduction by monkeys. *Journal of Comparative and Physiological Psychology, 68,* 412–419.

Medin, D. L., O'Neil, P., Smeltz, E., & Davis, R. T. (1973). Age differences in retention of concurrent discrimination problems in monkeys. *Journal of Gerontology, 28,* 63–67.

Mohs, R. C., Davis, K. L., Tinklenberg, J. R., Hollister, L., Yesavage, J. A., & Kopell, B. S. (1979). Choline chloride treatment of memory deficits in the elderly. *American Journal of Psychiatry, 136,* 1275–1277.

Mohs, R. C., Davis, K. L., Tinklenberg, J. R. (1980). Choline chloride effects on memory in the elderly. *Neurobiology of Aging, 1,* 21–25.

Monge, R., & Hultsch, D. (1971). Paired associate learning as a function of adult age and length of anticipation and inspection intervals. *Journal of Gerontology, 26,* 157–162.

Moore, R. Y., & Bloom, F. E. (1978). Central catecholamine neurone systems: Anatomy and physiology of the dopamine systems. *Annual Review of Neuroscience, 1,* 129–169.

Morrison, J., Grzanna, R., Molliver, M., & Coyle, J. (1978). The distribution and orientation of noradrenergic fibers in neocortex of the rat: An immunofluorescence study. *Journal of Comparative Neurology, 181,* 17–40.

Mueller, J. H., Rankin, J. L., & Carlomusto, M. (1979). Adult age differences in free recall as a function of basis of organization and method of presentation. *Journal of Gerontology, 34,* 375–380.

Murdock, B. B. (1974). *Human memory: Theory and data.* Potomac, MD: Lawrence Erlbaum Associates.

Oliverio, A., & Bovet, D. (1966). Effects of age on maze learning and avoidance conditioning of mice. *Life Sciences, 5,* 1317–1324.

Perry, E., Perry, R., Blessed, G., & Tomlinson, B. (1977). Necropsy evidence of central cholinergic deficits in senile dementia. *Lancet, 1,* 189.

Ponzio, F., Brunello, N., & Algeri, S. (1978). Catecholamine synthesis in brain of aging rats. *Journal of Neurochemistry, 30,* 1617–1620.

Prado de Carvalho, L., & Zornetzer, S. F. (1981). The involvement of the locus coeruleus in memory. *Behavioral and Neural Biology, 31,* 173–186.

Price, D. L., Whitehouse, P. J., Struble, R. G., Clark, A. W., Coyle, J. T., Delong, M. R. and Hedrenn, J. C. (1982). Basal forebrain cholinergic systems in Alzheimer's disease and related dementias. *Neuroscience Commentaries, 1,* 84–92.

Rankin, J. L., & Kaulser, D. H. (1979). Adult age differences in false recognitions. *Journal of Gerontology, 34,* 58–65.

Raymond, B. (1971). Free recall among the aged. *Psychological Reports, 29,* 1179–1182.

Riopelle, A. J., & Rogers, C. M. (1965). Age changes in chimpanzees. In A. M. Schrier, H. F. Harlow & F. Stollnitz (Eds.), *Behavior in nonhuman primates.* New York: Academic Press. 449–462.

Rogers, J., Silver, M. A., Shoemaker, W. J., & Bloom, F. E. (1980). Senescent changes in a neurobiological model system: Cerebellar Purkinje cell electrophysiology and correlative anatomy. *Neurobiology of Aging, 1,* 3–11.

Ruch, F. L. (1934). The differentiative effects of age upon human learning. *Journal of Genetic Psychiatry, 11,* 261–286.

Schonfield, D. (1969). *Age and remembering* (pp. 228–236). Duke University Council on Aging and Human Development. Proceedings of seminars.

Schonfield, D., & Robertson, B. A. (1966). Memory storage and aging. *Canadian Journal of Psychology, 20,* 228–236.

Schonfield, D., Trueman, V., & Kline, D. (1972). Recognition tests of dichotic listening and age variable. *Journal of Gerontology, 27,* 487–493.

Scott, F. L. (1979). A review of some current drugs used in the pharmacotherapy of organic brain syndrome. In A. Cherkin, C. E. Finch, N. Kharasch, T. Makinodon, F. L. Scott, & B. S. Strehler, *Aging, Vol. 8: Physiology and Cell Biology of Aging* (pp. 93–104). New York, Raven Press.

Segal, M. (1976). Brain stem afferents to the rat medial system. *Journal of Physiology, 261,* 617–631.

Sherman, K., Dallob, A., Dean, R. L., Bartus, R. T., & Friedman, E. (1980). Neurochemical and behavioral deficit in aging rats. *Federation Proceedings, 39,* 508.

Simpkins, J. W., Mueller, G. P., Huang, H. H., & Meites, J. (1977). Evidence for depressed catecholamine and enhanced serotonin metabolism in aging male rats: Possible relation to gonadotrophin secretion. *Endocrinology, 100,* 1672–1678.

Smith, A. D. (1975). Partial learning and recognition memory in the aged. *International Journal of Aging and Human Development, 6,* 359–365.

Stein, L., Belluzzi, J. D., & Wise, C. D. (1975). Memory enhancement by central administrations of norepinephrine. *Brain Research, 84,* 329–335.

Talland, G. A. (1965). Three estimates of the word span and their stability over the adult years. *Quarterly Journal of Experimental Psychology, 17,* 301–307.

Thompson, C. I., & Fitzsimons, T. R. (1976). Age differences in aversively motivated visual discrimination learning and retention in male Sprague–Dawley rats. *Journal of Gerontology, 31,* 47–52.

Tulving, E., & Patkau, J. E. (1962). Concurrent effects of contextual constraint and word frequency on immediate recall and learning of verbal material. *Canadian Journal of Gerontology, 16,* 83–95.

Vijayashankar, N., & Brody, H. (1979). A quantitative study of the pigmental neurons in the nuclei locus coeruleus and subcoeruleus in man as related to aging. *Journal of Neuropathology and Experimental Neurology, 38,* 490–497.

Vroulis, G. A., & Smith, R. C. (1981). Cholinergic drugs and memory disorders in Alzheimer's type dementia. In S. J. Enna, T. Samorajski, & B. Beer (Eds.), *Brain neurotransmitter and receptors in aging and age-related disorders* (pp. 195–208). New York: Raven Press.

Wallace, J. E., Krauter, E. E., & Campbell, B. A. (1980). Animal models of declining memory in the aged: Short-term and spatial memory in the aged rat. *Journal of Gerontology, 35,* 355–363.

Welford, A. T. (1958). *Aging and human skills.* London: Oxford University Press.

Wickelgren, W. A. (1975). Age and storage dynamics in continuous recognition memory. *Developmental Psychology, 11,* 165–169.

Zelinski, E. M., Walsh, D. A., & Thompson, L. W. (1978). Orienting task effects on EDR and free recall in three age groups. *Journal of Gerontology, 33,* 239–245.

Zornetzer, S. F. (1978). Neurotransmitter modulation and memory: A new pharmacological phrenology? In M. A. Lipton, A. DiMascio & K. F. Killam (Eds.), *Psychopharmacology: A generation of progress* (pp. 637–649). New York: Raven Press.

Zornetzer, S. F., & Gold, M. (1976). The locus coeruleus: Its possible role in memory consolidation. *Physiology and Behavior*, 16, 331–336.

Zornetzer, S. F., Abraham, W. C., & Appleton, R. (1978). Locus coeruleus and labile memory. *Pharmacology Biochemistry and Behavior*, 9, 227–234.

Zornetzer, S. F., Thompson, R., & Rogers, J. (1982). Rapid forgetting of aged rats. *Behavioral and Neural Biology*, 36, 49–60.

IV

MODEL SYSTEMS

7

MEMORY: ELECTROPHYSIOLOGICAL ANALOGS*

Timothy J. Teyler

INTRODUCTION

What is memory? While intuitively familiar to all, it is surprisingly difficult to define. Memory cannot be measured directly, it is always inferred as a result of a change in the behavior of the organism or a change in some physiological response. However, in order to study the neuronal basis of memory it is necessary to define it in terms useful to the neuroscientist.

For our purposes, memory shall refer to the relatively enduring neural alterations induced by the interaction of an organism with its environment. Further, the memory store or engram, to be useful, must be accessible to the nervous system to alter future behavior. The process of laying down the memory trace in the first place is usually termed *learning*, although some would argue that learning implies a change in overt *behavior* as a result of experience—not merely the laying down of an engram in the brain. There can be no memory, however, without altering the behavior of the nervous system, whether or not the organism's overt behavior reflects that neural change at that time. This alteration in the behavior of the nervous system is often termed *plasticity*. Presum-

* Supported in part by research grants from NSF and NIH.

ably much of the information entering the nervous system is capable of altering overt behavior under some future conditions and therefore the process of encoding that information into memory can be considered as a form of learning, albeit covert learning.

Since we cannot measure memory directly, we must rely upon observed correlations between treatments and behaviors. As always, one must guard against immediately assuming that correlation means causation. Just because a neuron increases its firing rate in response to a well-learned conditioned stimulus does not mean that the neural response caused the behavioral response. We shall encounter a good example of just this case later in the chapter when considering hippocampal unit activity increases to a conditioned stimulus (work of R. F. Thompson and colleagues).

ELECTROPHYSIOLOGICAL APPROACHES

Two general experimental approaches have dominated the study of the electrophysiological basis of memory. The first, and oldest, has sought to localize the critical brain structures involved in memory. Typically, recording electrodes are placed in a variety of brain regions of the behaving animal to sample neural activity correlated with performance on learning or memory tasks. A second approach attempts to simplify the experimental situation in order to better control the variables capable of influencing the activity of neurons. This approach, often termed the *model systems* approach, seeks to study simpler nervous systems engaged in relatively simple learned behaviors. Samples include invertebrate nervous systems, some of which have thousands as opposed to billions of neurons and are, relatively speaking, simpler and easier to study. Invertebrate neurons are generally larger than their mammalian counterparts and are thus easier to study with intracellular techniques. Other model systems employ surgically simplified portions of the mammalian brain—the hippocampal slice being an example. In all model systems, the goal is to uncover the mechanisms underlying the changes in order to explain the observed behavior or in order to extrapolate observations to more complex systems.

In recent years, tremendous advances have been made in the invertebrate preparations. Largely the work of two investigators working on the marine mollusks *Aplysia* (Kandel & Schwartz, 1982) and *Hermissenda* (Alkon, 1983), these preparations have proven amenable to an analysis of the mechanisms underlying associative learning and memory. In both preparations, it has been possible to further simplify these nervous systems until only a handful of interconnected cells remain. Although dramatically reduced, these model systems continue to display appropriate plastic changes. Such simplification facilitates the search for the responsible mechanisms at the level of conductance changes of individual ionophore species.

In the vertebrate central nervous system, neuroscientists have widely employed the intact preparation to search for the critical circuits involved in learning and memory. Among the early experiments are those reported by Adey (1966) wherein the hippocampal EEG systematically changed in response to a probe stimulus introduced when the cat was performing a learned discrimination or at other times. John, Bartlett, Shimokochi, & Kleinman (1973) observed that the EEG evoked by two stimuli (lights) flashing at different rates, each associated with a particular response, consistently differed. When the cats were presented with an ambiguous stimulus (flashing at an intermediate rate) they sometimes responded one way and sometimes the other. Interestingly, the evoked EEG was correlated with how the cat responded to the ambiguous stimulus suggesting to John that the responses represented a form of neural readout from memory.

Many brain regions may give rise to responses that are correlated with learned behavior, particularly in the early stages of memory formation. Halas, Beardsley, & Sandlie (1970) showed that activity in the brain was relatively widespread and changed as a function of additional training. In their review, Thompson, Patterson, & Teyler (1972) observed that as training proceeds, activity becomes restricted to the relevant sensory and motor areas of neocortex associated with the response. The work of Olds, Disterhoft, Segal, Hornblith, & Hirsch (1972) extended these experiments to the level of single cells in many areas of the brain. They observed that neurons whose activity was correlated with memory retrieval were widespread in the brain, but that the hippocampus and frontal neocortex were likely places to encounter such cells.

The work of R. F. Thompson (1976) and Thompson, Berger, Berry, Clark, & Kettner (1983) provides a clear example of the utility of the intact animal approach in discovering the neural mechanisms of learning and memory. Employing a well-defined learned response (nictitating membrane conditioning in rabbits), Thompson set out to find the critical brain loci involved in this learned behavior. As reviewed in Thompson (1976), the search began with the motor and sensory relays involved in the response. Responses more closely related to the learned response were, however, recorded from the hippocampus. So faithful were these hippocampal unit discharges that Thompson referred to them as forming a neural "template" of the subsequent behavioral response. The activity of these hippocampal units in the delayed-conditioning paradigm, however, is not essential to the behavioral response which survives bilateral lesion of hippocampus. As mentioned earlier, this is a good example of correlation not implying causation. Thompson and colleagues (1983) have succeeded, however, in identifying the critical pathway involved in this delayed-conditioning response. Lesions to restricted portions of the deep cerebellar nuclei, cerebellar cortex or the superior cerebellar peduncle will abolish the learned (but not the unlearned) response. This pathway which is essential to the learned response presumably contains plastic synapses that are changed during training.

Given the demonstrated critical contribution of the cerebellar circuit, what role are the hippocampal neurons playing and why do they so accurately reflect the learned behavioral response? The answer to this question remains to be discovered, but may reflect the existence of multiple memory systems in the brain. The hippocampus may be involved in the storage of the more cognitive aspects of the situation, aspects more related to time, space, and affect than to the mechanics of the behavioral response per se.

Electrophysiological studies of memory have, in recent years, focused upon the phenomenon of long-term potentiation (LTP) as a promising electrophysiological correlate of information storage in the mammalian brain. In this chapter we shall see what LTP is, where it is observed, what might be its underlying mechanism of action and how it might relate to memory storage and retrieval.

THE HIPPOCAMPUS

The hippocampus has been the focal point of memory studies in the mammalian brain since the reports by the Canadian neuropsychologists led by Wilden Penfield and Brenda Milner some 25 years ago (Scoville & Milner, 1957; Penfield & Milner, 1958). Subsequent electrophysiological studies by such workers as Olds, Vinogradova, and Thompson, to be reviewed later in this chapter, have done much to further implicate the hippocampus in learning and memory. Much of the interest in the hippocampus comes from an appreciation of the anatomy of the hippocampus. On the phylogenetic level, the hippocampus only clearly appears in the mammalian brain, although hippocampal homologs can be found in the brains of amphibians, reptiles, and birds (Angevine, 1975).

HIPPOCAMPAL ANATOMY

The geometry of the hippocampus is unique in the mammalian CNS. The hippocampus is a bilaterally symmetrical structure shaped somewhat like a cashew nut (Fig. 7.1A, B). The hippocampus comprises two interdigitating archicortical fields: the hippocampus proper (cornu ammonis) and the dentate gyrus (fascia dentata). Both fields are folded into a shape reminiscent of the letter "C." Each field contains a densely packed sheet of cells, pyramidals and granules, respectively, which are the principal cell type of their respective field. Within each sheet of cells, the dendrites possess the same orientation, that is, normal to the plane of the sheet. In addition to the principal cells, each field contains a variety of interneurons, or local circuit neurons.

One striking feature of hippocampal circuitry is the pattern of afferent termination. Major hippocampal afferents originating from the entorhinal cortex and contralateral and ipsilateral hippocampal subfields synapse on the dendrites of the principal cells in a laminated pattern (Raisman, Cowan, & Powell, 1965). The dentate gyrus provides an illustration of this pattern of laminated afferent inputs. Hippocampal commissural and associational fibers synapse within the proximal one-third of the granule cell dendritic field (dendritic surface closest to the cell body layer) (Blackstad, 1956; Zimmer, 1971). The massive entorhinal cortex projections from the perforant path terminate topographically in the outer two-thirds of the dendritic field; the lateral entorhinal cortex projects most distally, the medial entorhinal cortex, most proximally and the intermediate entorhinal area projects to a position between the medial and lateral entorhinal termination zones (Hjorth–Simonsen, 1972; Steward, 1976). Other granule cell afferents display lamination and/or dispersion to varying degrees. Afferent lamination is also an organizing principal in the hippocampus proper.

Another important feature of the hippocampus is the manner in which units within the sheets of cells are functionally connected—their intrinsic circuitry. Contained within the sheets of cells is a functional circuit (Fig. 7.2), oriented transverse to the longitudinal (or septo-temporal) axis of the hippocampus. This has become known as the principal trisynaptic circuit, and the hippocampus has been described as possessing a lamellar organization (Andersen, Bliss & Skede, 1971). The transverse system may be thought of as strips of cells that form a functional circuit. The transverse system emerges as a function of the connectivity patterns of the trisynaptic circuitry. Thus, the entorhinal projections onto dentate granule cells, the granule cell projections onto CA3 pyramidal cells—the mossy fiber system, and the effer-

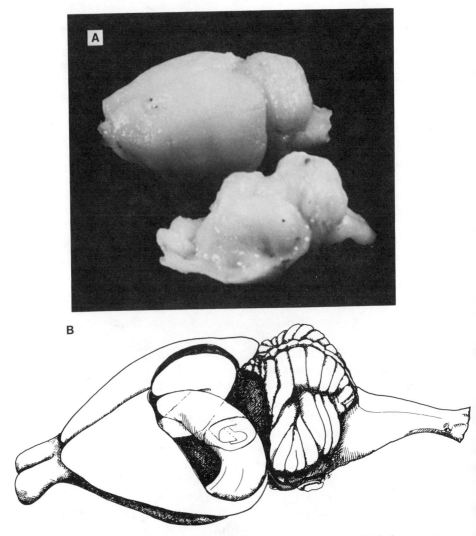

FIGURE 7.1   A. Photograph of an intact rat brain (top) and one in which the neocortex and corpus callosum has been removed (bottom) to reveal the hippocampus. B. Phantom drawing of the hippocampus, outlining the transverse circuit and cell sheets comprising the CA3/CA1 (anterior) and dentate gyrus (posterior) subdivisions. (Adapted from Teyler & DiScenna, 1984.)

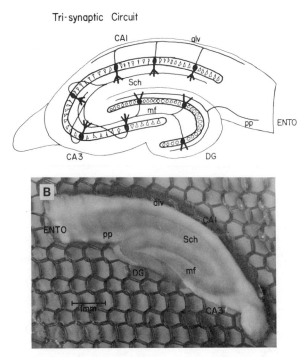

FIGURE 7.2   A. Diagrammatic representation of the transverse or trisynpatic circuit of
the hippocampus. pp = perforant path; DG = dentate gyrus; mf = mossy fibers; Sch =
Schaffer collaterals; Alv = alveus. B. Photograph of a hippocampal slice prepared to
preserve the transverse circuitry.

ents of CA1 pyramids into the alveus demonstrate a transverse, or
lamellar orientation. One circuit component, the CA3 pyramidal cell
projection to area CA1, via the Schaffer collaterals, is an exception to
this organization in that it displays relatively wider (in terms of septo-
temporal spread) distribution (Rawlins & Green, 1977).

To appreciate the geometry of this structure it is useful to construct
an equivalent circuit of the hippocampus (Fig. 7.3). A two-dimensional
equivalent circuit of the transverse system is depicted in Fig. 7.3A.

Coursing in the septo-temporal plane of the hippocampus lies an
incompletely studied, but nevertheless extensive, fiber system serving
to interconnect the transverse system. These fibers, known as the hippocampal longitudinal association fibers (Swanson, Wyss, & Cowan,
1978), are thought to be involved in interlamellar communication. Superimposed, in turn, upon this system is the hippocampal commissural

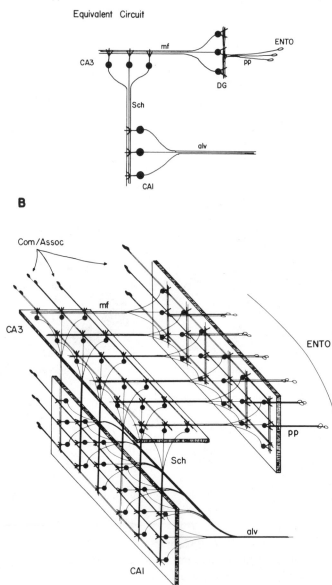

FIGURE 7.3   A. A planar equivalent circuit of the transverse hippocampal trisynaptic circuit. Abbreviations as in Fig. 7.2. B. The equivalent circuit of A with the addition of the associational and commissural pathways. With the addition of the temporal parameter, the hippocampus represents a four-dimensional array (from Teyler & DiScenna, 1984).

system—a series of fibers that serve to link homologous and nonhomologous portions of the hippocampus proper and dentate gyrus (Gottlieb & Cowan, 1973). The degree of independence or interdependence of these three systems has received little study.

Graphically depicted, the pattern of connectivity previously described might appear as shown in Figure 7.3B. Here the hippocampal trisynaptic circuit appears as one of two major orthogonal fiber systems within the hippocampus. The other is composed of both the longitudinal associational and commissural fiber systems. The existence of two roughly orthogonal fiber systems within the system of laminated dendritic afferents provides for a three-dimensional representation of information on the dendritic surface of the hippocampus. When the aspect of time is taken into consideration, another dimension is added to the geometrical representation of hippocampus, such that a four-dimensional array is apparent. The four dimensions are: (1) the laminated afferent terminations on dendritic surfaces, (2) the transverse system, (3) the longitudinal/commissural fiber systems, and (4) time.

While there may be many possibilities with respect to the functional significance of such a four-dimensional system, it could be utilized as a coordinate system. The unique features of hippocampal geometry have been appreciated for some time and enter quite prominently in the theories of O'Keefe and Nadel (1978). In their formulation, hippocampal neuronal geometry specifies cognitive space, which is a transformation of Euclidian space. While the view of the hippocampus as a cognitive map has been highly productive from both empirical and theoretical points of view, it is possible to arrive at alternative conceptions of this hippocampal mapping potential. After considering hippocampal electrophysiology we will consider an alternative role for the hippocampus as a brain coordinate system.

HIPPOCAMPAL ELECTROPHYSIOLOGY

HIPPOCAMPAL THETA

Investigations attempting to relate the dominant EEG rhythm of the hippocampus (4–8 Hz, termed theta) to behavior have inferred theta to be associated with processes including: orienting responses (Grastyán, Lissák, Madarász, & Donhoffer, 1959); information processing (Elazar & Adey, 1967); response inhibition (Bennett & Gottfried, 1970) and voluntary movement (Vanderwolf, 1969). Unfortunately, the diversity of behavioral paradigms and recording sites make difficult the assessment of the functional significance of this rhythm. In addition, insufficient attention has been given to the cytoarchitectural differences in the hippocampus.

The physiological basis of the theta rhythm has been studied in regard to its hippocampal distribution (Bland, Anderson, & Ganes, 1975; Fox & Ranck, 1975) and in relation to medial septal nucleus neuronal activity (Apostol & Creutzfeldt, 1974; Ranck, 1976). These workers found a close relationship between septal and hippocampal activity, suggesting a possible driving source for the theta rhythm. Theta rhythms can be recorded from both dentate gyrus and hippocampus (Bland et al., 1975) and may represent the activity of local circuit neurons (Fox & Ranck, 1975). Thus while evidence is accumulating regarding the physiology of the theta rhythm its functional relation to behavior and memory has remained elusive.

HIPPOCAMPAL UNIT ACTIVITY

Numerous reports have appeared dealing with single- or multiple-unit recordings made in chronically implanted animals during various behavioral tasks. Data from the laboratories of Olds (Olds et al., 1972) and Thompson (Berger & Thompson, 1977, 1978a–c; Thompson, 1976; Thompson et al., 1983) consist of single- and multiple-unit records from identified regions of the hippocampus and elsewhere obtained during the acquisition of a learned behavior. Both groups find that hippocampal neurons, as assessed by the latency criterion of Olds or the correlational criterion of Thompson, participate in the earliest stages of behavioral acquisition of the learned task. The latency criterion identifies those neurons which first change their activity following the stimulus. Later firing neurons may also participate in learning and memory but their role is more difficult to assess since they may be driven by the earlier firing cells. The correlation criterion focuses upon the moment-to-moment correlations between the response topography and the form of the neural response. When they accurately map onto one another, the correlation is high and suggests a functional relationship between them. While multiple-unit studies can be criticized in terms of the confounding of individual neuronal differences in the overall record, the plastic nature of single units have been demonstrated by Vinogradova (1970, 1975) and Mays and Best (1975). These workers observed habituation of hippocampal unit discharge patterns to peripheral stimuli in intact rats.

These studies have focused upon the plastic nature of stimulus-evoked hippocampal activity. A different approach was taken by Ranck (1973) who reported the existance of two classes of hippocampal cells based upon their firing patterns: *complex spike* cells and *theta* cells. He provided evidence that the former are the principal cells of the hippocampus and the latter are local circuit neurons (Fox & Ranck, 1975), although the classes overlap considerably. He notes also that the two cell classes are differentially activated. Complex spike cells are activated by voluntary movement, whereas theta cells are activated by novel stimuli. Based in part on single-unit recordings from rats freely moving in patterned space, O'Keefe and Nadel (1978) provide data which they interpret to reflect the existence of a spatial or cognitive mapping of the animal's environment onto the hippocampus.

Most of the theoretical descriptions of the role of the hippocampus have not achieved broad acceptance by the scientific community, although some, like that of O'Keefe and Nadel, have attracted considerable interest. The reasons for this are: (1) the nonobvious role of the hippocampus in relation to behavioral and neural processes, (2) methodological differences evident in the hippocampal literature, and (3) the apparently ubiquitous involvement of the hippocampus in a variety of situations.

The experiments discussed below deal with several varieties of response plasticity in the hippocampus and dentate gyrus, and in particular long-term potentiation (LTP). LTP represents a dramatic and enduring increase in postsynaptic responsivity following a brief and physiologically realistic period of afferent stimulation. Studies have shown that LTP can influence synaptic transmission at monosynaptic junctions in the hippocampus by several hundred percent and that in living animals the change can endure for periods of weeks. In short, LTP is a form of long-term information storage prominently displayed by the hippocampus—a tissue that has been repeatedly implicated in learning and memory.

HIPPOCAMPAL RESPONSE PLASTICITY

Much of the pioneering electrophysiological work on the hippocampus was done by Andersen, Lømo, Kandel, and Spencer, and their co-workers on the intact preparation. Andersen and Lømo took advantage of the high density of principal cells and their uniform cytoarchitectonic arrangements to demonstrate, as verified with intracellular recordings, that the extracellular population field potentials (Fig. 7.4) recorded at various depths reflected excitatory postsynaptic potential (EPSP) and cell body spike discharges (Andersen & Lømo, 1966; Lømo, 1971a,b). A single weak stimulation of an orthodromic fiber pathway

TIMOTHY J. TEYLER

HIPPOCAMPAL FIELD POTENTIAL

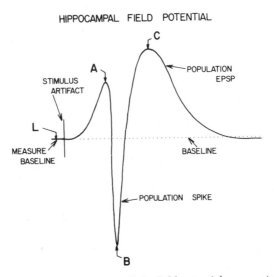

FIGURE 7.4   The hippocampal extracellular field potential represents a population of synchronously active neurons. The sharp negative-going population spike is superimposed on a slower positive-going population EPSP in this response recorded at the cell body layer.

was shown to evoke a short-latency negative potential in the synaptic layer of the apical dendrites (Fig. 7.5) which reversed in the proximal dendritic layer and cell body layer (Lømo, 1971a). This potential was termed the *extracellular population EPSP*. More intense stimulation evoked a similar potential with a superimposed short-duration positive potential recorded at the synaptic layer which reversed to become a negative potential with a maxima in the cell body layer. This potential was termed the *extracellular population spike*. The case has been made that field potentials are reliable indicators of massed single unit activity based on intracellular recordings from dentate granule cells in response to perforant path stimulation (Andersen et al., 1971; Lømo 1971a,b). Similar analyses have been made for other hippocampal regions (Andersen & Lømo, 1966). Also, the amplitude and latency of the extracellular population spike was found to be closely related to the number and temporal distribution of synchronously activated units (Andersen et al., 1971).

The first evidence of the plastic properties of hippocampal synapses came from the work of Lømo (1971a,b). Using conditioning-test stimulation of the perforant path in the intact rabbit, he reported a facilitation of the dentate granule cell test response. The response could be sup-

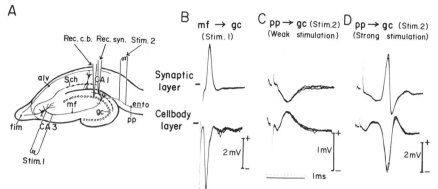

FIGURE 7.5   A. The extracellular field potential recorded from the cell body layer (Rec. c.b.) and the synaptic zone in the molecular layer (Rec. syn.) of the dentate gyrus. Stimulation delivered to the mossy fibers (MF) (Stim. 1) to antidromically activate the dentate granule cells (GC) and to fibers of the perforant path (pp) (Stim. 2) to synaptically activate the same population of granule cells. B. Synaptic layer and cell body layer recordings to antidromic activation of granule cells. Antidromic invasions of the granule cells results in a sharp negativity recorded at the cell body and a mirror-image positivity recorded in the synaptic layer reflecting the current sink and source, respectively. C. Weak stimulation of perforant path fibers elicits a population EPSP seen as a slow negativity in the synaptic layer and a mirror-image positivity in the cell body layer. D. Stronger stimulation of perforant path fibers results in a population EPSP with a superimposed action potential. ento = entorhinal cortex, alv = alveus, Fim = fimbria (from Skrede & Westgaard, 1973, unpublished observations).

pressed by stronger stimulation acting through recurrently activated inhibitory basket cells (Kandel & Spencer, 1961; Andersen & Lømo, 1967). On the basis of latency and frequency following criteria, Lømo (1971a) argues that this is a monosynaptic junction. The duration of suppression was on the order of 10 ms and cannot be accounted for by the refractory properties of the cells. Conditioning-test stimulation at the optimal interval indicated that the reduction of the test population spike developed in conjunction with the growth of the conditioning population spike. This observation also implicates the operation of recurrent inhibitory mechanisms. Spencer and Kandel (1961) found that antidromic stimulation of deafferented CA3 axons resulted in an inhibitory postsynaptic potential (IPSP) following the antidromic response, showing that the IPSP was due to collaterals of the CA3 axons acting via inhibitory local circuit neurons. Similar observations have been reported by Teyler (1976), Schwartzkroin (1975), and Alger and Nicoll (1980).

FREQUENCY POTENTIATION

The phenomena of frequency potentiation, an augmented postsynaptic response to orthodromic stimulation with a relatively narrow band of frequencies, was demonstrated by Andersen & Lømo (1967). They observed that dentate extracellular population EPSPs and population spike potentials were markedly potentiated at frequencies between 8–25 Hz. During frequency potentiation the intracellularly recorded EPSP was enhanced and the subsequent IPSP depressed. The EPSP was briefly potentiated following termination of the low-frequency tetanic stimulus. These results have been duplicated in the hippocampal slice preparation (Fig. 7.6) (Schwartzkroin, 1975; Deadwyler, Dudex, Cotman, & Lynch, 1975; Dudek, Deadwyler, Cotman, & Lynch, 1976). The role of the afferent fibers in this phenomena is not clear. Deadwyler et al. (1975) suggest that current spread to adjacent axons accounts for the effect, the evidence of Lømo (1971b) indicates otherwise. It has been proposed that the phenomenon is either an increased presynaptic release of transmitter (Lømo, 1971b) or altered postsynaptic membrane conductance (Schwartzkroin, 1975), perhaps limited to the dendritic synaptic region (Andersen & Lømo, 1966). Many of the hypotheses offered to explain frequency potentiation are also suggested for the other forms of response plasticity displayed by the hippocampus.

LONG-TERM POTENTIATION

The most dramatic form of plasticity seen in the hippocampus, and the one with most presumed relevance to the phenomena underlying memory storage in the brain, is the phenomenon of LTP. This was first shown in the dentate gyrus of the in vivo rabbit preparation by Bliss and Gardner–Medwin (1973) and in the unanesthetized rabbit by Bliss and Lømo (1973). LTP is characterized by a stable, relatively long-lasting increase in the magnitude of a postsynaptic response to a constant afferent volley, following brief tetanic stimulation of the same

---

FIGURE 7.6 Frequency potentiation in area CA1 of the hippocampal slice to stimulation of Schaffer collateral afferents at various stimulus frequencies. A. The amplitude of the synaptic responses are facilitated between 10 and 30 stimulations per second, whereas the antidromic response declines monotonically as a function of frequency. B. The latency of the synaptic responses is shortest between 10 and 30 stimulations per second, whereas the antidromic response is relatively invariant across frequency (from Skrede & Teyler, 1973 unpublished observations).

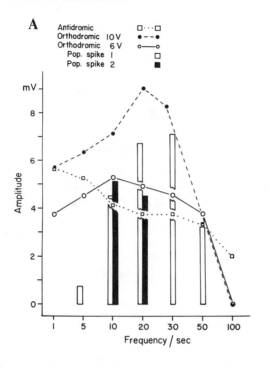

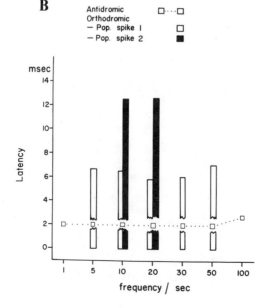

afferents. Thus LTP is an increase in synaptic efficacy, at monosynaptic junctions, occurring as the result of afferent fiber tetanization.

LTP was first described in the rabbit hippocampal formation. Subsequently it has been observed in a variety of other species and brain structures (Fig. 7.7). In hippocampus, the postsynaptic response to a constant afferent input, following induction of LTP, is about 250% of the amplitude of the pre-LTP population spike. The amplitude of the population EPSP is increased about 50% over the pre-LTP baseline. LTP develops to an appreciable degree within 5 min and is asymptotic in about an hour. Thus, the magnitude of change in synaptic efficacy is substantial and the change develops quickly.

Most of our knowledge of the properties and potential mechanisms of LTP comes from studies of rodent and rabbit hippocampal formation. Similar phenomena are described in other brain regions and in other

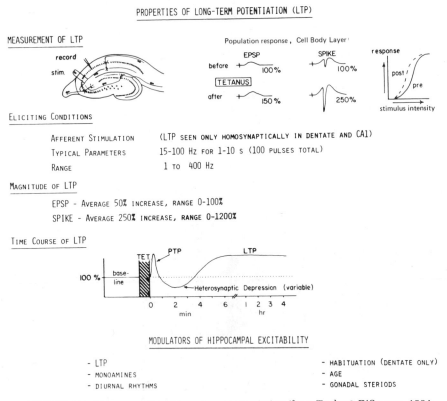

FIGURE 7.7   The properties of long-term potentiation (from Teyler & DiScenna, 1984; Swanson et al., 1982).

species, however their characteristics are somewhat different (Gerren & Weinberger, 1983; Lewis, Teyler, & Shashoua, 1981). It is not clear if these nonhippocampal forms should be considered as variations of a common phenomenon - LTP, or if they represent different phenomena. For the present, we shall adopt the simplifying assumption that they are alternate forms of the same phenomenon. Obviously this assertion is subject to change if it develops that different mechanisms underlie the alternate forms of LTP seen in other tissues and other species.

The neuronal mechanisms underlying LTP are currently unknown (Swanson, Teyler, & Thompson, 1982), but are being actively sought. Presynaptic and postsynaptic models have been proposed to explain LTP, based on LTP-associated changes seen at anatomical (Desmond & Levy, 1983; Lee, Schottler, Oliver, & Lynch, 1980; van Harreveld & Fifkova, 1975), physiological (Alger & Teyler, 1976; Andersen, Sundberg, Sveen, Swann, & Wigstrom, 1980; Douglas & Goddard, 1975) and biochemical (Baudry & Lynch, 1980; Dolphin, Errington, & Bliss, 1982; Duffy, Teyler, & Shashoua, 1981; Skrede & Malthe–Sorenssen, 1981) levels. At the anatomical level it has been reported that there is a change in spine shape (Fifkova & Anderson, 1981; van Harreveld & Fifkova, 1975) such that one could predict an increased postsynaptic effect for a constant presynaptic input. Others report more subtle morphological correlates of LTP (Lee et al., 1980). At the physiological and biochemical level it has been suggested that a local increase in dendritic membrane resistance could account for LTP (Andersen et al., 1980). Others have suggested a role for postsynaptic receptor changes (Baudry & Lynch, 1980), changes in transmitter release (Skrede & Malthe–Sorenssen, 1981), involvement of local circuit neurons (Yamamoto & Chujo, 1978) and protein synthesis (Duffy et al., 1981). Presumably some, if not all, of these observations are related to the mechanism(s) underlying LTP. It is evident that LTP induction is associated with an array of presynaptic and postsynaptic changes, demonstrable at multiple levels of analysis. However, the necessary and sufficient conditions for LTP induction are not known. A more complete discussion of LTP, its parameters, possible mechanisms and behavioral variables, can be found in Swanson et al. (1982) and Teyler and DiScenna (1987).

Teyler and DiScenna (1984) have examined the evidence supporting the hypothesis that LTP is a viable candidate for a mnemonic device in the vertebrate nervous system. Arguments supporting this hypothesis include: (1) the time-course and magnitude of LTP, (2) the induction of LTP by physiologically reasonable treatments, (3) its distribution in the brain relative to structures previously implicated in learning and memory, (4) the observation that hippocampal LTP can result from behavioral learning experiences, and (5) the parallels between certain pharmacologic manipulations upon LTP and behavioral learning and memory. On the basis of these arguments, they conclude that LTP represents the best current candidate for the neural basis of memory.

LTP AS A SUBSTRATE FOR MEMORY

The demonstration of LTP in the hippocampus and elsewhere has, in the minds of many, been a startling and potentially very important discovery. It seems possible that information storage in the CNS is accomplished by a mechanism such as LTP operating at countless synaptic junctions as part of an unknown and presumably complex pattern of information flow through the brain. It is likely that the long-term information storage system of the brain involves alterations in synaptic coupling between communicating neurons. It is difficult to imagine systems of permanent information storage that do not involve alterations in input or output functions between communicating neurons. The fascination that many have with LTP and with a search for the mechanism(s) that underlie it is not without problem. The problem manifests itself in the form of a paradox.

Monosynaptic junctions of the vertebrate hippocampus are capable of modifying their synaptic coupling such that following afferent stimulation they show a pronounced and enduring increase in synaptic efficacy. The difficulty with such an enduring system is that once a monosynaptic junction has "learned something" it would appear incapable of learning anything further. In other words, once LTP has been established to its maximal degree at a synaptic junction, further information storage is no longer possible at that junction. One can imagine that the information coding capacity of the rat hippocampus could be saturated in a short period of time if, for example, the function of the hippocampus is to encode information regarding the spatial world (O'Keefe & Nadel, 1978). The paradox thus presents itself since we have, at the same time, an apparently very plastic and enduring phenomenon, yet one that may be difficult to fit into a behavioral or information processing scheme.

It may be that the hippocampus is a site of long-term information storage in the mammalian brain. Such storage could occur either exclusively in the hippocampus or in coordination with storage in other structures. Such a hypothesis is not unreasonable if one refers to human clinical data on hippocampal damage (Milner, 1968). If this is the case, then the observation of an enduring alteration in synaptic efficacy is not surprising. With respect to this hypothesis, however, the results of scores of lesion studies do not support the thesis that, in the rodent, memory storage occurs in the hippocampus (Thompson et al., 1983). This statement must be qualified, however, because the effects of hippocampal lesions have differential effects depending upon the nature of the behavioral taks. Hippocampal lesions do not impair learning and recall in simple testing paradigms (O'Keefe & Nadel, 1978). However, a significant impairment is observed in tasks that are judged to require more processing, such as trace classical conditioning, serial position learning and discrimination reversals (Berger & Orr, 1983; Kesner & Novak, 1982; O'Keefe & Nadel, 1978).

If the hippocampus is involved in the acquisition and storage of experiential events associated with more demanding tasks, the question can be asked if LTP is the neural mechanism underlying the hippocampal plasticity. Despite the fact that LTP has been known since the early 1970s, there is limited data showing that LTP results as a consequence of behavioral learning paradigms.

If LTP is involved in information storage, it must be elicitable by naturally occurring patterns of afferent activity. A critical question regarding LTP is if it can be measured in the behaving animal. One attempt to investigate this relationship (Barnes, 1979) demonstrated a correlation between the magnitude of LTP produced in a chronically implanted animal and the level of retention of a behavioral task. A more direct relationship was shown by Thompson and colleagues utilizing the rabbit nictitating membrane paradigm. These workers earlier demonstrated that hippocampal unit activity was correlated with the development of the conditioned nictitating membrane response. Specifically, the pattern of multiple and single unit activity created a template of the behavioral response (Hoehler & Thompson, 1980).

Using the same rabbit nictitating membrane paradigm, Thompson and colleagues implanted animals with stimulating electrodes in afferent fibers of the dentate gyrus (perforant path) and recorded the postsynaptic response from dentate granule cells. In this experiment, single test stimuli were given at various points throughout behavioral training. The results indicated that synaptic efficacy, as measured in the dentate granule cells' response to constant intensity afferent stimulation, increased as function of training, increased in parallel with the acquisition of the behavioral response and was limited to the CS+ (Weisz, Clark, Yang, & Thompson, 1982). This was an important indication that hippocampal LTP can be observed as a correlate of the behavioral learning process. Similar results have been obtained in a tone-footshock conditioning paradigm (Laroche & Bloch, 1982), a brightness discrimination task (Ruthrich, Matthies, & Ott, 1982) and following exposure to an enriched and complex spatial environment (Sharp, McNaughton, & Barnes, 1983).

Since behavioral learning experiences have been shown to result in LTP, it is of interest to see what the effect of establishing LTP *before* learning would be. Using the rabbit nictitating membrane preparation, Berger (1984) established maximal LTP over much of the dentate gyrus before instituting behavioral training. The effect of the LTP was to facilitate the learning process with the animals acquiring the response quicker and with fewer errors. Barnes & McNaughton (1983), using a circular platform maze, found that the rats receiving LTP were impaired in their ability to learn a new spatial location, but had no difficulty in the retention of a previous spatial location. Since the LTP procedures in the Berger and the Barnes and McNaughton studies were similar, the marked differences in outcome probably reflect task differences. In the nictitating membrane experiment, the hippocampus is clearly nonessential for learning this task whereas hippocampal lesions impair the acqusition of spatial behavior. Thus, the differences may reflect what Squire, Cohen, & Nadel (1982) have referred to as "knowledge-about" as opposed to "knowledge-how." In this context, the hippocampus may be active in acquiring information "about" with respect to the conditioning experiment and in acquiring information "how" to with respect to spatial behavior.

It is possible that the large LTP increases in synaptic efficacy observed in the laboratory are not produced under natural conditions. Rather, small changes might be produced as a result of local dendritic activity and these small changes might influence the pattern of *throughput* in the hippocampus. These small changes might then modulate other brain regions giving rise to a distributed store of information storage within the CNS. Such a system of throughput modulations can be viewed in terms of a multipath maze wherein information is stored at multiple locations (redundancy) and is represented by the pattern over which information flows. The latter is determined by the relative synaptic efficacies at numerous synaptic junctions. The pattern of information flow is thus the representation of information stored within the brain. Such a conceptualization does not require that exactly the same information be stored in the multiple loci. Rather, it is probable that some brain circuits operate the muscular apparatus associated with the response (as in Thompson's hippocampal template). All, however, are part of the same experience and are learned changes in brain and thus are learned changes in behavior. While admittedly speculative, such a system may be realistic in terms of the known dynamics of brain function.

In April of 1977 two papers appeared in Nature relating to the issue of the permanence of LTP. Lynch and colleagues presented evidence that when LTP is established in one of two independent afferent inputs to the CA1 region the response to test stimulation of the nontetanized (control) pathway is depressed. Lynch, Dunwiddle, & Gribkoff (1977a) and Lynch, Gribkoff, & Deadwyler (1977b) claimed that the depression of the control pathway was as persistent as the LTP produced by the tetanized pathway. The same workers have shown that tetanic stimulation leads to a persistent and generalized depression of postsynaptic excitability as measured by a decrease in cell firing to the iontophoretic application of glutamic acid (Lynch et al., 1977b). The hypothesis is that when one synaptic region on a neuron is activated the other synaptic inputs on that neuron are depressed. With such a phenomenon one can reverse the stimulus parameters to the two sets of afferents and can eliminate the LTP produced by the prior stimulation.

As exciting and potentially meaningful as these results were, the second paper in the same issue of Nature by Andersen, Sundberg, Sveen, & Wigstrom (1977) doing a similar experiment, provided evidence that when the tetanized pathway exhibits LTP, the control pathway does not change. This careful experiment monitored the size of the afferent volley and concluded that LTP is an input-specific process and fails to produce systematic changes in the excitability of the neuron as a whole. The same conclusion was reached by Alger, Megela, and Teyler (1978) in a more extensive study of what has become known as heterosynaptic depression. They took advantage of the independence of two afferent fiber systems to area CA1 (Alger & Teyler, 1976), produced LTP in either of the pathways, and observed a transient depression in the other pathway. The depression was of the same magnitude seen by Lynch and colleagues, but was maximal at three minutes post tetanus, then declined to baseline levels within five minutes post tetanus. Alger et al. (1978) observed that similar transient depression could be elicited by antidromic stimulation of the CA1 cells. They conclude that heterosynaptic depression is a nonspecific effect of neuronal activation, distinct from synaptic activation or LTP. Thus, Alger et al. would concur with Anderson in stating that LTP in CA1 hippocampus appears to be an input specific alteration with no long-term heterosynaptic effects.

LTP AS A CANDIDATE
MEMORY MECHANISM

A major difficulty with the hypothesis that LTP is a mechanism of information storage relates to the time-course of LTP. While dramatically lengthy from a neurobiological standpoint, LTP does not appear to have the longevity to account for truly long-term information storage that may span decades in some species (Teyler & DiScenna, 1984). While there are technical limitations that hinder the measurement of the actual duration of LTP, it is probable that LTP is not a permanent alteration in synaptic efficacy. Until more is known about the induction and parameters of LTP in behavioral situations we may not feel confident in ascribing to it the role of long-term information storage. The alternatives are several. First, LTP may be only a first stage in laying down a permanent engram. Second, the induction of behavioral LTP may be sufficiently different from the laboratory induction of LTP to alter the time-course of the potentiation. In behavioral situations, for example, learning generally occurs over a longer time course than does the electrical induction of LTP in the laboratory. Also spaced behavioral trials yield longer retention than does massed practice. Perhaps the same is true of LTP.

As mentioned earlier another problem with considering LTP as a mnemonic device is that it appears that an organism could well use up all of its available potential for information storage. Once a maximal LTP has been produced no further increments are possible (Goddard, 1982). Conceivably, an organism might run out of the potential for LTP and thus further information storage, given a unique set of environmental circumstances, although this result has not been reported in the behavioral literature. Part of this criticism stems from the consideration of LTP induction via the simultaneous electrical stimulation of a group of afferents. Given this mode of LTP induction it is easy to imagine using up the potential for LTP. Behavioral LTP induction, however, may not involve the synchronous activation of a large number of afferents. Again, we must await the results of behavioral LTP experiments and experiments investigating the question of coactivation among afferents to help answer this question.

It is generally agreed that LTP is a homosynaptic phenomenon, as opposed to being a cell-wide phenomenon. If so, what sorts of synaptic modifications might underlie LTP? One possibility is that LTP stimulates the generation of new synaptic contacts. Evidence is now accumulating that synaptogenesis is not limited to the early development of the brain, but continues even in the senescent brain (Buell & Coleman,

1979). More startling is the observation that neurogenesis in the dentate gyrus of rats continues during adulthood (Bayer, 1982). These factors may compensate for the synapses effectively used up by the process of LTP. A similar conclusion was reached by Harris and Teyler (1984) regarding LTP production in developing animals. Their data suggested that two pools of synapses exist at hippocampal pyramidal cells; a pool of *plastic* synapses, which diminishes as more synapses become part of the *consolidated* pool by the production of LTP. One possibility is that as synapses become consolidated via LTP, more plastic synapses are formed by the cell and/or additional neurons are formed, thus preserving a pool of plastic synapses for future use. One means by which such an increase in synapses could be effected is by a division of preexisting synapses. Such a possibility has been considered by Carlin & Siekevitz (1983) and evidence supporting the notion of synapse turnover has been reported by Nieto–Stampedro, Hoff, and Cotman (1982).

THE HIPPOCAMPAL MEMORY INDEXING THEORY

Clearly it is not possible to assert that LTP is a mnemonic device in the brain. However, the available evidence suggests that LTP should be considered the leading candidate at present for such a role. Significant gaps remain in our knowledge about LTP and its functional significance. While numerous theories exist (Swanson et al., 1982), the neuronal mechanism(s) underlying LTP remain unknown. In addition, little is known about the necessary and sufficient conditions to induce LTP in a behavioral setting. As these questions are addressed, answers will begin to emerge regarding the question of the functional significance of LTP and whether it merits continued consideration as a mnemonic device. Beyond this, one must begin to ponder the nature of the distributed information store. What is it that is stored, how is it represented, and how is it addressed?

One such attempt to consider the larger question of memory processing has recently been formalized by Teyler and DiScenna (1986). This theory, termed the *hippocampal memory indexing theory*, asserts that the interaction between neocortex and hippocampus is involved in memory storage and retrieval.

The theory asserts that experiential information is registered and understood primarily by multiple, specialized neocortical analyzers. In order for an experiential event to be identified as one previously experienced (e.g., a memory) the neocortical analyzers must be utilized.

The theory proposes that the initial storage of information occurs in the hippocampus, but not in the form of the iconic storage of the neural code of the event. Rather, the hippocampus stores the spatiotemporal pattern of neocortical analyzers, perhaps at the cortical module level, activated by the experiential event. This information, which is an index of neocortical activation, is stored via LTP in specific hippocampal loci. Thus, the hippocampus stores not a neural representation of the memory, but rather the neocortical loci, which, when reactivated in the correct sequence, will recreate a representation of the initial experiential event.

Once the neocortical index is stored in the hippocampus, a reoccurrence of the experiential event will be registered in the same neocortical loci, whose activation will imfringe upon previously potentiated hippocampal loci and will be interpreted as a memory. A partial activation of a previously indexed constellation of cortical loci may be recognized as a memorial event if a suprathreshold subset of loci is achieved. If threshold is achieved, the entire neocortical constellation may be reactivated and the event recognized in its original context. In this formulation, incoming experiential events are continually and automatically tested to determine if they match a previously stored pattern. In behavioral terms, this is analogous to recognition memory.

The hippocampal memory indexing theory, while consistent with experimental data, is by no means established in fact and represents one plausible idea for memory processing in the mammalian brain. It is an interesting comment on the rapid advances within the neurosciences that such ideas can be seriously put forth today when only a decade ago such theorizing would have seemed very far off.

REFERENCES

Adey, W. R. (1966). Neurophysiological correlates of information transaction and storage in brain tissue. In E. Stellar & J. M. Sprague (Eds.), Progress in Physiological Psychology NY: Academic Press.

Alger, B. E., Megela, A. L., & Teyler, T. J. (1978). Transient heterosynaptic depression in the hippocampal slice. Brain Research Bulletin, 8, 64–69.

Alger, B. E., & Nicoll, R. A. (1980). Spontaneous inhibitory postsynaptic potentials in hippocampus: Mechanism for tonic inhibition. Brain Research, 200, 195–200.

Alger, B. E., & Teyler, T. J. (1976). Long-term and short-term plasticity in the CA1, CA3 and dentate region of the rat hippocampal slice. Brain Research, 110, 463–480.

Alkon, D. L. (1983). Learning in a marine snale. Scientific American, 249, 70–84.

Andersen, P., Bliss, T. V. P., Skrede, K. K. (1971a). Lamellar organization of hippocampal excitatory pathways. Experimental Brain Research, 13, 222–238.

Andersen, P., Bliss, T. V. P., Skrede, K. K. (1971b). Unit analysis of hippocampal population spikes. Experimental Brain Research, 13, 222–238.

Andersen, P., & Lømo, T. (1966). Mode of action of population spikes. *Experimental Brain Research, 2,* 247–260.

Andersen, P., & Lømo, T. (1967). Control of hippocampal output by afferent volley frequency. In W. R. Adey & T. Tokizane (Eds.), *Progress in brain research: Vol. 27. structure and function of the limbic system* (pp. 400–412). Amsterdam: Elsevier.

Andersen, P., Sundberg, S. H., Sveen, O. & Wigstrom, H. (1977). Specific long-lasting potentiation of synaptic transmission in hippocampal slices. *Nature, 266,* 736–737.

Andersen, P., Sundberg, S. H., Sveen, O., Swann, J. W. & Wigstrom, H. (1980). Possible mechanisms for long-lasting potentiation of synaptic transmission in hippocampal slices from guinea-pigs. *Journal of Physiology, 302,* 463–482.

Angevine, J. (1975). Development of the Hippocampal Region. In R. L. Isaacson & K. H. Pribram (Eds.), *The hippocampus: Vol. 1. Structure and development* (pp. 61–94). New York: Plenum Press.

Apostol, G., & Creutzfeldt, O. D. (1974). Cross correlation between the activity of septal units and hippocampal EEG during arousal. *Brain Research, 67,* 65–75.

Barnes, C. A. (1979). Memory deficits associated with senescence: A neurophysiological and behavioral study in the rat. *Journal of Comparative and Physiological Psychology, 93,* 74–104.

Barnes, C. A., & McNaughton, B. L. (1983). Where is the cognitive map? *Neuroscience Abstracts, 9,* 191.16.

Baudry, M., & Lynch, G. (1980). Hypothesis regarding the cellular mechanisms responsible for long-term synaptic potentiation in the hippocampus. *Experimental Neurology, 68,* 202–204.

Bayer, S. A. (1982). Changes in the total number of dentate granule cells in juvenile and adult rats: A correlated volumetric and 3H/thymidine autoradiographic study. *Experimental Brain Research, 46,* 315–323.

Bennett, T. L., & Gottfried, J. (1970). Hippocampal theta activity and response inhibition. *Electroencephalography and Clinical Neurophysiology, 29,* 196–200.

Berger, T. W. (1984) Long-term potentiation of hippocampal synaptic transmission affects rates of behavioral learning. *Science, 224,* 627–629.

Berger, T. W., & Orr, W. B. (1983). Role of the hippocampus in reversal learning of the rabbit nictitating membrane response. In C. P. Woody (Ed.), *Conditioning: Representation of involved neural functions.* New York: Plenum.

Berger, T. W., & Thompson, R. F. (1977). Limbic system interrelations: Functional division among hippocampal-septal connections. *Science, 197,* 587–589.

Berger, T. W., & Thompson, R. F. (1978a). Neuronal plasticity in the limbic system during classical conditioning of the rabbit nictitating membrane response. I. The hippocampus. *Brain Research, 145,* 323–46.

Berger, T. W., & Thompson, R. F. (1978b). Neuronal plasticity in the limbic system during classical conditioning of the rabbit nictitating membrane response. II. Septum and mammillary bodies. *Brain Research, 156,* 293–314.

Berger, T. W., & Thompson, R. F. (1978c). Identification of pyramidal cells as the critical elements in hippocampal neuronal plasticity during learning. *Proceedings of the National Academy of Sciences, USA, 75,* 1572–76.

Blackstad, T. W. (1956). Commissural connections of the hippocampal region of the rat, with special reference to their mode of termination. *Journal of Comparative Neurology, 105,* 417–538.

Bland, B. H., Andersen, P., & Ganes, T. (1975). Two generators of hippocampal theta in rabbits. *Brain Research, 94,* 199–218.

Bliss, T. V. P., & Gardner–Medwin, A. R. (1973). Long-lasting potentiation of synaptic transmission in the dentate area of the unanesthetized rabbit following stimulation of the perforant path. *Journal of Physiology, 232,* 357–374.

Bliss, T. V. P., & Lømo, T. (1973). Long-lasting potentiation of synaptic transmission in the dentate area of the anesthetized rabbit following stimulation of the perforant path. *Journal of Physiology, 232,* 331–356.

Buell, S. J., & Coleman, P. D. (1979). Dendritic growth in the aged human brain and failure of growth in senile dementia, *Science, 206,* 854–856.

Carlin, R., & Siekevitz, P. (1983). Plasticity in the central nervous system: Do synapses divide? *Proceedings of the National Academy of Sciences, USA, 80,* 3517–3521.

Deadwyler, S. A., Dudek, F. E., Cotman, C. W., & Lynch, G. (1975). Intracellular responses of rat dentate gyrus granule cells *in vitro:* Posttetanic potentiation to perforant path stimulation. *Brain Research, 88,* 59–65.

Desmond, N. L., & Levy, W. B. (1983). Synaptic correlates of associative potentiation/depression: An ultrastructural study in the hippocampus, *Brain Research, 265,* 21–30.

Dolphin, A. C., Errington, M. L., & Bliss, T. V. P. (1982). Long-term potentiation of the perforant path *in vivo* is associated with increased glutamate release, *Nature, 297,* 496–497.

Douglas, R. M., & Goddard, G. V. (1975). Long-term potentiation of the perforant path-granule cell synapse in the hippocampus, *Brain Research, 86,* 205–215.

Dudek, F. E., Deadwyler, S. A., Cotman, C. W., & Lynch, G. (1976). Intracellular responses from granule cell layer in slices of rat hippocampus: Perforant path synapses. *Journal of Neurophysiology, 39,* 384–393.

Duffy, C. F., Teyler, T. J., & Shashoua, V. E. (1981). Long-term potentiation in the hippocampal slice: Evidence for stimulated secretion of newly synthesized proteins. *Science, 212,* 1148–1151.

Elazar, Z., & Adey, W. R. (1967). Spectra analysis of low frequency components in the electrical activity of the hippocampus during learning. *Electroencephalography and Clinical Neurophysiology, 23,* 225–240.

Fifkova, E., & Anderson, C. L. (1981). Stimulation-induced changes in dimensions of stalks of dendritic spines in the dentate molecular layer. *Experimental Neurology, 74,* 621–627.

Fox, S. E., & Ranck, J. B., Jr. (1975). Localization and anatomical identification of theta and complex spike cells in dorsal hippocampal formation of rats. *Experimental Neurology, 49,* 299–313.

Gerren, R. A., & Weinberger, N. M. (1983). Long-term potentiation in the magnocellular medial geniculate nucleus of the anesthetized cat. *Brain Research, 265,* 138–142.

Goddard, G. V. (1982). Figure 15. In L. W. Swanson, T. J. Teyler, & R. F. Thompson (Eds.), Hippocampal long-term potentiation: Mechanisms and implications for memory, *Neurosciences research program bulletin* (Vol. 20, p. 649). Cambridge: MIT Press.

Gottlieb, D. E., & Cowan, W. M. (1973). Autoradiographic studies of the commissural and ipsilateral association connections of the hippocampus and dentate gyrus of the rat. The commissural connections. *Journal of Comparative Neurology, 149,* 393–422.

Grastýan, E., Lisśak, K., Madaŕasz, I., & Donhoffer, H. (1959). Hippocampal electrical activity during the development of conditioned reflexes. *Electroencephalography and Clinical Neurophysiology, 11,* 409–430.

Halas, E. S., Beardsley, J. V., & Sandlie, M. E. (1970). Conditioned neuronal responses at various levels in conditioning paradigms. *Electroencephalography and Clinical Neurophysiology, 28,* 468–477.

Harris, K. M., & Teyler, T. J. (1984). Developmental onset of long-term potentiation in area CA1 of the rat hippocampus. *Journal of Physiology, 346,* 27–48.

Hjorth–Simonsen, A. (1972). Projection of the lateral part of the entorhinal area to the hippocampus and fascia dentata. *Journal of Comparative Neurology, 146,* 219–232.

Hoehler, F. K., & Thompson, R. F. (1980). Effect of the interstimulus (CS-UCS) interval on hippocampal unit activity during classical conditioning of the nictitating membrane response of the rabbit (*Oryctolagus cuniculus*). *Journal of Comparative and Physiological Psychology, 94,* 201–215.

John, E. R., Bartlett, F., Shimokochi, M., & Kleinman, D. (1973). Neural readout from memory. *Journal of Neurophysiology, 36,* 893–924.

Kandel, E. R., & Schwartz, J. H. (1982). Molecular biology of learning: Modulation of transmitter release. *Science, 218,* 433–443.

Kandel, E. R., & Spencer, W. A. (1961). Electrophysiology of hippocampal neurons. II. After-potentials and repetetive firing. *Journal of Neurophysiology, 24,* 243–259.

Kesner, R. P., Novak, J. M. (1982). Serial position curve in rats: Role of the dorsal hippocampus. *Science, 218,* 173–175.

Laroche, S., & Bloch, V. (1982). Conditioning of hippocampal cells and long-term potentiation: An approach to mechanisms of posttrial memory formation. In C. Ajmone Marsan & H. Matthies, (Eds.), *Neuronal plasticity and memory formation* (pp. 575–587). New York: Raven Press.

Lee, K. S., Schottler, F., Oliver, M., & Lynch, G. (1980). Brief bursts of high-frequency stimulation produce two types of structural change in the hippocampus. *Journal of Neurophysiology, 44,* 247–258.

Lewis, D., Teyler, T. J., & Shashoua, V. (1981). Development of long-term potentiation in the *in vitro* goldfish optic tectum. *Neuroscience Abstracts, 7,* A23.13.

Lømo, T. (1971a). Patterns of activation in a monosynaptic cortical pathway: The perforant path input to the dentate area of the hippocampal formation. *Experimental Brain Research, 12,* 18–45.

Lømo, T. (1971b). Potentiation of monosynaptic EPSPs in the perforant path-dentate granule cell synapse. *Experimental Brain Research, 12,* 46–63.

Lynch, G. S., Dunwiddie, T., & Gribkoff, V. (1977a). Heterosynaptic depression: A postsynaptic correlate of long-term potentiation. *Nature, 266,* 737–739.

Lynch, G., Gribkoff, V. K., & Deadwyler, S. A. (1977b). Long term potentiation is accompanied by a reduction in dendritic responsiveness to glutamic acid. *Nature, 263,* 151–153.

Mays, L. E., & Best, P. J. (1975). Hippocampal unit activity to tonal stimuli during arousal from sleep and in awake rats. *Experimental Neurology, 47,* 268–279.

Milner, B. (1968). Disorders of the brain lesions in man. *Neuropsychologia, 6,* 175–179.

Nietro–Stampedro, M., Hoff, S. F., & Cotman, C. W. (1982). Perforated postsynaptic densities: Probable intermediaries in synapse turnover. *Proceedings of the National Academy of Sciences, USA, 79,* 5718–5722.

O'Keefe, J., & Nadel, L. (1978). *The hippocampus as a cognitive map.* New York: Oxford University Press.

Olds, J., Disterhoft, J. F., Segal, M., Hornblith, C. L., & Hirsch, R. (1972). Learning centers of rat brain mapped by measuring latencies of conditioned unit responses. *Journal of Neurophysiology, 35,* 202–19.

Penfield, W., & Milner, B. (1958). Memory deficit produced by bilateral lesions in the hippocampal zone. *American Medical Association Archives of Neurology and Psychiatry, 79,* 475–97.

Raisman, G., Cowan, W. M., & Powell, T. P. S. (1965). The extrinsic afferent, commissural and association fibres of the hippocampus. Brain, 88, 963–996.

Ranck, J. B., Jr. (1973). Studies on single neurons in dorsal hippocampal formation and septum in unrestrained rats. Experimental Neurology, 41, 461–555.

Ranck, J. B., Jr. (1976). Behavioral correlates and firing repertoires of neurons in septal nuclei in unrestrained rats. In J. DeFrance (Ed.), The Septal Nuclei. Detroit: Wayne State University Press.

Rawlins, J. N. P., & Green, K. F. (1977). Lamellar organization in the rat hippocampus. Experimental Brain Research, 28, 335–344.

Ruthrich, H., Matthies, H., & Ott, T. (1982). Long-term changes in synaptic excitability of hippocampal cell populations as a result of training. In C. Ajmone Marsan & H. Matthies (Eds.), Neuronal plasticity and memory formation (pp. 589–594). New York: Raven Press.

Schwartzkroin, P. A. (1975). Characteristics of CA1 neurones recorded intracellularly in the hippocampal in vitro slice preparation. Brain Research, 85, 423–432.

Scoville, W. B., & Milner, B. (1957). Loss of recent memory after bilateral hippocampal lesions. Journal of Neurology & Psychiatry, 20, 11–21.

Sharp, P. E., McNaughton, B. L. & Barnes, C. A. (1983). Spontaneous synaptic enhancement in hippocampi of rats exposed to a spatially complex environment. Neuroscience Abstracts, 9, A191.7.

Skrede, K. K., & Malthe–Sorenssen, D. (1981). Increased resting and evoked release of transmitter following repetitive electrical tetanization in hippocampus: A biochemical correlate to long-lasting synaptic potentiation, Brain Research, 208, 436–441.

Skrede, K., & Teyler, T. J. (1973). Unpublished observations.

Skrede, K., & Westgaard, R. (1973). Unpublished observations.

Spencer, W. A., & Kandel, E. R. (1961). Electrophysiology of hippocampal neurons. IV. fast prepotentials. Journal of Neurophysiology, 24, 272–285.

Squire, L. R., Cohen, N. J., & Nadel, L. (1983). The medial temporal region and memory consolidation: A new hypothesis. In H. Weingartner & E. Parker (Eds.), Memory consolidation, Hillsdale NJ: Lawrence Erlbaum.

Steward, O. (1976). Topographic organization of the projections from the entorhinal area to the hippocampal formation of the rat. Journal of Comparative Neurology, 167, 285–314.

Swanson, L. W., Teyler, T. J., & Thompson, R. F. (1982). Hippocampal long-term potentiation: Mechanisms and implications for memory. Neurosciences Research Program Bulletin, 20, 613–769.

Swanson, L. W., Wyss, J. M., & Cowan, W. M. (1978). An autoradiographic study of the organization of intrahippocampal association pathways in the rat. Journal of Comparative Neurology, 181, 681–716.

Teyler, T. J. (1976). Plasticity in the hippocampus: A model systems approach. In A. H. Riesen & R. F. Thompson (Eds.), Advances in psychobiology: Vol. III (pp. 301–326). New York: Wiley.

Teyler, T. J., & DiScenna, P. (1984). Long-term potentiation as a candidate mnemonic device. Brain Research Review, 7, 15–28.

Teyler, T. J., & DiScenna, P. (1986). The hippocampal memory indexing theory. Behavioral Neuroscience, 100, in press.

Teyler, T. J., & DiScenna, P. (1987). Long-term potentiation. Annual Review of Neuroscience, 11, in press.

Thompson, R. F. (1976). The search for the engram. American Psychologist, 31, 209–227.

Thompson, R. F. (1983). Neuronal substrates of simple associative learning: Classical conditioning. Trends in Neuroscience, 6, 270–275.

Thompson, R. F., Berger, T. W., Berry, S. D., Clark, G. A., & Kettner, R. E. (1983). Neuronal substrates of learning and memory: Hippocampus and other structures. In C. D. Woody (Ed.), Conditioning: Representation of involved neural functions. New York: Plenum.

Thompson, R. F., Patterson, M. M., & Teyler, T. J. (1972). Neurophysiology of learning. Annual Review of Psychology, 23, 73–104.

Vanderwolf, C. H. (1969). Hippocampal electrical activity and voluntary movement in the rat. Electroencephalography of Clinical Neurophysiology, 26, 407–418.

van Harreveld, A., & Fifkova, E. (1975). Swelling of dendritic spines in the fascia dentata after stimulation of the perforant fibers as a mechanism of post-tetanic potentiation. Experimental Neurology, 49, 736–749.

Vinogradova, O. S. (1970). Registration of information and the limbic system. In M. Gittorn & R. A. Hinde (Eds.), Short-term changes in neural activity in behavior, Cambridge: Cambridge University Press.

Vinogradova, O. S. (1975). The hippocampus and the orienting reflex. In E. Sokolov & N. M. Weinberger (Eds.), Neuronal mechanism of the orienting reflex, Hillsdale, NJ: Lawrence Earlbaum.

Weisz, D. J., Clark, G. A., Yang, B. & Thompson, R. F. (1982). Activity of dentate gyrus during NM conditioning in rabbit. Asilomar conference. Hillsdale, NJ: L. Erlbaum Associates.

Yamamoto, C., & Chujo, T. (1978). Long-term potentiation in thin hippocampal sections studied by intracellular and extracellular recordings. Experimental Neurology, 58, 242–250.

Zimmer, J. (1971). Ipsilateral afferents to the commissural zone of the fascia dentata, demonstrated in decommissurated rats by silver impregnation. Journal of Comparative Neurology, 142, 393–416.

8

INVERTEBRATE MODEL SYSTEMS*

W. Jackson Davis

INTRODUCTION

The brain is in a constant state of flux with respect to information processing and storage. Throughout the lifetime of an organism, new experiences are continually stamped on the slate of the nervous system, and are later recalled as appropriate to the survival needs of the organism. The process by which such experiential information is entered for storage and later retrieval is termed *associative learning*, defined formally as a modification in behavior that is acquired because of reinforced experience. The reinforcement can be positive (reward) or negative (punishment), and it can be delivered according to any of several paradigms, including classical conditioning (Type I or Pavlovian), operant conditioning (Type II or instrumental), or avoidance conditioning (a blend of Types I and II).

As previously defined, learning is a behavioral phenomenon. Underlying learned behavioral modifications, however, must be a definable set of physiological rules addressable in neurophysiological and ultimately molecular terms. Beginning with the work of the Soviet scientist Pavlov, psychologists and physiologists attempted to define the behavioral and cellular rules by which associative learning takes place. The task is among the most challenging that ever faced modern science, in

* Studies are identified by the genus used according to the following abbreviations: Ap = *Aplysia*; He = *Hermissenda*; Li = *Limax*; Pl = *Pleurobranchaea*.

large part owing to the complexity of the mammalian brain. Packed within the skull of even the simplest vertebrate is a biological computer composed of trillions of individual neurons, connected together in complex and shifting patterns and capable of tasks far beyond the most sophisticated computer that humans have created.

In the face of this complexity, many neuroscientists have turned in the last two decades to simpler invertebrate animals that are nonetheless capable of associative learning. These animals have fewer, larger, and reidentifiable neurons, making their nervous systems more tractable to detailed cellular analysis. Consequently invertebrates offer the promise of an immediate and comprehensive understanding of the physiological processes underlying associative learning, which may in turn provide insights into mammalian learning. This approach has come to be known as the *model systems* approach, although the name is somewhat of a misnomer since all animal preparations, vertebrate and invertebrate alike, are equally deserving of this status.

My purpose in the present review is to exemplify the model systems approach by selectively highlighting some of the best available examples drawn from the invertebrates. For technical reasons, gastropod molluscs are favorite subjects for the model systems approach. These organisms have large, pigmented nerve cells with electrically active cell bodies (somata) that are electrically close to synaptic processes. Therefore the cell bodies furnish easily accessible electrical windows through which the integrative activity of the nervous system may be conveniently and accurately viewed. Moreover in the last decade several laboratories have made significant progress toward understanding the cellular mechanisms of learning in gastropods, providing a critical mass of information on the subject. For these reasons the present review will be restricted to studies of gastropods that provided or promise cellular insights into the learning process.

THE NEED FOR UNIFYING PRINCIPLES

In this review I wish to focus not only on the wealth of experimental detail generated during the past decade of research on gastropod learning, but also on the principles and generalities that emerged as a consequence. Only when such principles are identified can we feel confident that a branch of knowledge is approaching intellectual maturity. Moreover such principles will hopefully help our colleagues who study the immensely more complex vertebrate systems to understand the cellular nature of learning in these higher animals. If this can be accomplished, then the invertebrates will have fulfilled their promise as model systems.

Toward this end, in preparing this review I asked each of my colleagues, whose work I shall summarize to ennumerate the general principles of learning that emerge from their investigations (see the section entitled "General Principles of Learning in Invertebrate Model Systems"). In arriving at these principles, I shall first review the studies on which they are based, in alphabetical order of the genus used.

APLYSIA

The studies of Kandel and his collaborators on the marine gastropod *Aplysia* provided among the first cellular explanations of nonassociative learning, including habituation and sensitization (for a review see Kandel & Schwarz, 1982). More recently, *Aplysia* also proved fruitful for investigation of associative learning, including both physiological and psychological aspects (Carew, Abrams, Hawkins, & Kandel, 1983a).

BEHAVIOR

Progress on the physiological aspects of associative learning in *Aplysia* have been based on conditioning of the siphon withdrawal reflex. To condition specimens, a weak tactile conditioned stimulus (CS) was delivered to the siphon, eliciting a weak reflex contraction of the gill and siphon. When the CS was paired with a strong electric shock to the tail (the unconditioned stimulus or US), the CS alone subsequently elicited a strong reflex contraction of the gill and siphon. The response following pairing was significantly larger than when the US and CS were presented randomly, when they were specifically unpaired or when presented alone (Carew, Walters, & Kandel, 1981). Thus, the animal learns to withdraw more strongly from a tactile stimulus that has previously been associated with an aversive stimulus.

The siphon withdrawal reflex can also be differentially conditioned (Carew et al., 1983a; Carew, Hawkins, & Kandel, 1983b). Toward this end, two tactile CS's were employed, one delivered to the siphon and the other to the mantle shelf. When the US (tail shock) was paired with one CS (defined as the CS+) but not the other (the CS−), only the CS+ subsequently showed the capacity to elicit enhanced contractions of the gill and siphon (Fig. 8.1).

What is the behavioral relevance of this form of learning? The demonstrated learning capacity could in principle enable *Aplysia* to effectively avoid the tactile stimulation associated with predators. As in all

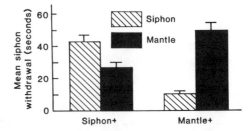

FIGURE 8.1 Behavioral effects of differential classical conditioning in *Aplysia*. The histograms show mean durations of siphon withdrawal in response to tactile stimulation of the siphon and mantle, 30 min after the conclusion of 15 trials in which tactile stimulation (CS) and tail shock (US) were paired. When shock was paired with touching the siphon during training (siphon+), subsequent withdrawal responses to siphon touch were greater than to mantle touch. When shock was paired with touching the mantle during training (mantle+), the converse was true. (From Carew, Hawkins, & Kandel, 1983.)

laboratory studies involving artificial stimuli such as electric shock, such a teleology is unavoidably speculative. However, even in the unlikely extreme that these forms of learning have no behavioral counterpart, they are nonetheless capable of revealing the neurophysiological processes that could in principle underlie the formation of learned associations by the nervous system.

NEUROPHYSIOLOGY

The discriminative classical conditioning described above presumably occurs within the neural circuitry mediating the siphon-withdrawing reflex. The known neural circuitry of this reflex includes approximately 24 sensory neurons that are directly connected with 13 motor neurons, and indirectly connected with the same motor neurons through several identified interneurons (Carew et al., 1983a). This neural circuitry has been subjected to analog conditioning paradigms (Hawkins, Abrams, Carew, & Kandel, 1983). For example, intracellular stimulation of the tactile sensory neurons was substituted for the conditioned stimuli used in the behavioral conditioning. Microelectrodes were inserted into two sensory neurons and also into a common withdrawal motoneuron innervated by both sensory neurons. In unconditioned specimens, single action potentials in a sensory neuron cause an excitatory postsynaptic potential (EPSP) in a withdrawal motoneuron. Pairing the US (tail shock) with driven spike activity in one sensory neuron (CS+ analog) doubled the amplitude of the EPSP caused by that sensory neuron, but did not increase the EPSP induced by the other

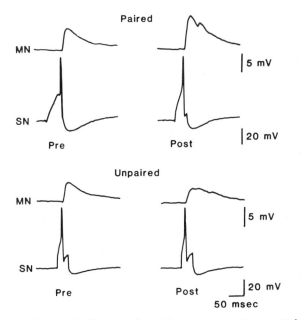

FIGURE 8.2   Differential facilitation of excitatory postsynaptic potentials (EPSPs) after associative training in reduced preparation of *Aplysia*. When tail shock and touch were paired (upper records), the EPSP induced in a motor neuron (MN) by an action potential in a sensory neuron (SN) was greater 1 hour after training (post) than before training (pre). The effects were absent when the CS and US were unpaired (lower records). (From Hawkins, Abrams, Carew, & Kandel, 1983.)

sensory neuron (CS− analog) (Fig. 8.2). Comparable results using a similar paradigm are reported independently by Walters and Byrne (1983).

What is the mechanism of the enhanced EPSP following conditioning? Hawkins et al. (1983) report that action potentials in the sensory neurons increase in duration as a function of simultaneous pairing of their activity with the US, causing the sensory neurons to release more synaptic transmitter substance onto their postsynaptic targets, the motor neurons. This form of learning in *Aplysia* may therefore be based on an elaboration of heterosynaptic facilitation, in which the activity of one presynaptic pathway facilitates transmitter release within a second pathway. In this case input from the tail shock would heterosynaptically facilitate the sensory neurons for the CS. Interestingly, this mechanism is also suggested to underlie a form of nonassociative learning (sensitization) in the same system (Castellucci & Kandel, 1976). Further, broadened action potentials in molluscan somata are in turn caused by increased calcium influx (Gillette, Kovac, & Davis, 1982;

Meech, 1972, 1974; Meech & Standen, 1975), suggesting eventual bio-physical analysis of this learning analog. Walters and Byrne (1983) enumerate several additional or complementary models that are capable of explaining these results.

Conclusions

As these extremely interesting experiments indicate, *Aplysia* furnishes a relatively simple preparation in which physiological analogs to behavioral learning can be studied at the cellular level. Moreover the training-induced broadening of action potentials in tactile sensory neurons lends itself to biophysical analysis. The striking similarities between the temporal dynamics of behavioral learning and conditioning of the nervous system analog (Hawkins et al., 1983; Carew et al., 1983b) support the hypothesis that the underlying physiological processes are similar. The connection between the demonstrated physiological analog to learning and the demonstrated behavioral learning remains to be definitively established.

HERMISSENDA

Behavior

An extensive investigation has been undertaken on the cellular mechanisms of an associative training paradigm using the marine nudibranch *Hermissenda*. These intertidal gastropods are normally attracted to light: They exhibit positive phototaxis. When specimens are exposed to 150 trials of light (CS) paired with rapid rotation on a turntable (US) spaced over a three day period, their subsequent behavior to light is modified. If their heads were pointed *toward* the center of rotation during training, then they move more slowly toward light than they did before training (Alkon, 1974; Crow & Alkon, 1978; Crow & Offenbach, 1979; Farley & Alkon, 1980). If their heads were pointed *away* from the center of rotation during training, then they move more quickly toward light after training (Farley & Alkon, 1980). The modification of this phototactic behavior is apparently greater if specimens are tested in the vertical rather than the horizontal plane (Farley & Alkon, 1982).

Is this behavioral modification representative of associative learning? In some cases the altered phototactic behavior is reported to appear following paired CS–US, but not following various control procedures such as unpaired CS–US (Alkon, 1974). In this case the behavioral modifications would be ascribable to associative processes. In other cases there appears to be no significant difference in the behavior of experimental (paired CS–US) and control (random CS–US) animals (Table 1 in Farley & Alkon, 1982). Independent studies, however, would appear to definitively establish this behavioral modification as associative (Crow & Offenbach, 1983).

The behavioral significance of the altered phototactic behavior of Hermissenda is unknown. The physical conditions required for its manifestation, such as intense unidirectional rotation of the animal and vertical test orientation, probably do not occur in nature. Behavioral significance, however, may not be prerequisite to cellular relevance in laboratory studies of learning.

NEUROPHYSIOLOGY

As in the preceding example drawn from Aplysia, understanding the cellular basis of this form of learning required mapping the wiring diagram of the relevant portions of Hermissenda's nervous system. Alkon and his collaborators began in the periphery with the sensory systems that are responsible for transducing the CS and the US, namely the visual system and the statocysts, respectively. The visual system had been studied earlier by Dennis (1967), who found that the eye is composed of a primitive lens overlying two Type A and three Type B photoreceptors. The five photoreceptors are individually identifiable on the basis of several anatomical and physiological criteria. Light stimuli cause depolarization of these neurons, which is in turn transmitted to the central nervous system (CNS) in the form of a conventional action potential frequency code. This and subsequent studies (Alkon, 1973a,b; Alkon & Fuortes, 1972; Alkon & Grossman, 1978) showed the 3 Type B photoreceptors are inhibitory to themselves and also to the other 2 Type A receptors in each eye. The primary photoreceptors also interact synaptically with neurons in the optic ganglion and in the CNS (Akaike & Alkon, 1980).

The rotation of the animal that serves as the US in the previously mentioned training paradigm is transduced by the bilateral statocyst organs described by German anatomists 150 years ago. Each statocyst consists of 13 concave cells bearing motile sensory cilia that project into the central lumen formed by the hair cells (Kuzirian, Alkon, & Harris, 1981). The lumen is filled with fluid that contains 150–200 solid crystals of calcium carbonate in contact with the sensory hairs. When the animal is tilted to one side, the crystals impinge upon the motile cilia, which transmit the stimulus to the corresponding hair cell, which in turn relays the signal to the CNS (Detwiler & Alkon, 1973; Grossman, Alkon, & Heldman, 1979; Stommel, Stephens, & Alkon, 1980). Thus, this primitive vestibular system informs the CNS of the rotation used as the US in the conditioning paradigm (Alkon, 1979).

The behavioral modifications observed following training in this model system probably result from synaptic interactions between the eyes and the statocysts. Individual statocyst receptor cells deliver synaptic excitation to the Type B photoreceptor cells, by direct projection and by means of complex and only partially understood interneuronal systems (Alkon, 1973; Alkon, Akaike, & Harrigan, 1978; Tabata & Alkon, 1982). When the statocyst receptors are activated by rotation, they furnish intersensory cross-talk that is proposed to influence the subsequent excitability of the Type B photoreceptor, and hence the organism's subsequent response to light. Specifically, following associative training in the above paradigm, the Type B photoreceptors respond to light with larger and longer depolarizations than in naive or control animals (Alkon, 1975, 1976, 1979, 1980a,b; Alkon, Lederhendler, & Shoukimas, 1982; Crow & Alkon, 1980). As a consequence the Type B photoreceptors inhibit Type A photoreceptors, which are hypothesized to indirectly excite motor neurons that cause the animal to turn toward light (Fig. 8.3). This model assumes that Type B photoreceptors indirectly inhibit the neural machinery responsible for positive phototaxis. Increases in Type B photoreceptor excitability correlated with conditioning would, by this model, lead to the reduction in positive phototactic behavior.

BIOPHYSICS

Potassium Currents

Increases in Type B photoreceptor excitability might be expected a priori to be manifest at the membrane level as decreases in currents that repolarize the membrane. These are potassium currents. Imposed depolarization of the Type B photoreceptors revealed two types of voltage-dependent potassium currents (Alkon et al., 1982; Shoukimas & Alkon, 1980). One current appears immediately after depolarization and decays (inactivates) rapidly, to half its initial amplitude in less than 1 s. This potassium current therefore exhibits the properties of an A-current (I-A). The second potassium current appears only after several seconds, and decays with a time course of many seconds, and therefore has the properties of a B-current (I-B) (Thompson, 1977).

What happens to these membrane potassium currrents as a conse-

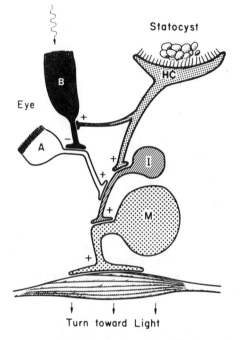

FIGURE 8.3   Hypothetical model of training-induced behavioral modification in *Her-missenda*. By this model statocyst hair cells (HC) excite Type B photoreceptors (B), increasing their subsequent excitability. The Type B photoreceptors in turn inhibit the neural machinery that turns the animal toward light, beginning with the Type A photoreceptors. I = interneurons; M = motor neurons. Some components of this simplified schema have been identified (see text).

quence of training in the above paradigm? This question has been addressed by comparing I-A in the Type B photoreceptors of trained and control animals (Alkon et al., 1982; Shoukimas & Alkon, 1980). It was found that I-A in medial Type B photoreceptors removed from trained animals, given paired light and rotation, was reduced by approximately 30% from that seen in animals given random light–rotation (controls) or untrained animals (Figure 8.4). In contrast, I-B was not affected by training. The authors propose that this training-induced reduction in I-A is adequate to account for the enhanced excitability of the photoreceptors of conditioned animals (Alkon, 1980; Crow & Alkon, 1980).

Calcium Currents

In addition to the reduction of fast transient potassium current (I-A) following associative conditioning, evidence of calcium involvement

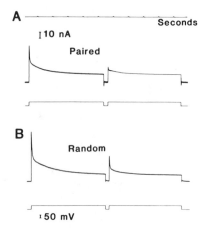

FIGURE 8.4   Potassium currents in axotomized Type B photoreceptor cells of *Hermissenda* following associative training. The records show outward membrane currents elicited by command pulses at the beginning and in the middle of the records. The currents are smaller for the paired CS–US (A) than for random CS–US presentation (B). (From Alkon, Lederhendler, & Shoukimas, 1982.)

has been reported (Alkon, 1979, 1983; Alkon, Lederhendler, & Shoukimas, 1982). As a consequence of associative training, there is a light-induced voltage-dependent inward calcium current (Grossman, Schmidt, & Alkon, 1981) increases (Alkon, 1979), which results in the accumulation of intracellular calcium. As might be expected, direct injection of calcium into the Type B photoreceptor transiently reduces the A current (Alkon, Shoukimas & Heldman, 1982). This reduction of Ca-current is of short duration (<10 min), however, in comparison with training-induced changes in I-A (24–72 hours). Moreover, in a separate series of experiments evidence was obtained that intracellular calcium increases potassium conductance (Grossman et al., 1981). Therefore the connection, if any, between calcium current and the biophysical correlates of training is unclear.

BIOCHEMISTRY

Studies on associative training in *Hermissenda* have been extended to the biochemical level by Neary, Crow, & Alkon (1981). They report that following conditioning but not following unpaired presentation of CS and UCS that there is a significant increase in incorporation of radioactive phosphorous into a 20,000 Dalton phosphoprotein within the whole eye. Neary et al. think that changes in potassium currents which are observed following associative training may be related to this biochemical change. Injection of Ca^{++}-calmodulin-dependent protein kinase into single Type B photoreceptors also selectively affects I-A, but not I-B potassium currents (Alkon et al., 1982; Alkon, 1983). Therefore Ca^{++}-calmodulin-dependent phosphorylation of membrane proteins may be involved in altering the I-A channels, although the connection between these biophysical and biochemical phenomena is far from established.

CONCLUSIONS

Studies on *Hermissenda* indicate that exposure of animals to an associative training procedure is correlated with subsequent biophysical and biochemical changes in peripheral sense organs. Whether these changes result from associative processes, and how they relate to the modified behavior (see section entitled "Correlation versus Causality in Cellular Studies of Learning"), remains to be shown.

LIMAX

BEHAVIOR

Psychological aspects of invertebrate learning have been studied most extensively and exactly in the giant garden slug *Limax maximus* by Gelperin, Sahley and their associates (Gelperin, 1975; Sahley, Hardison, Hsuan and Gelperin, 1982a; Sahley, Gelperin, & Rudy, 1981a; Sahley, Rudy, & Gelperin, 1981b; Sahley, Rudy and Gelperin, 1983). Gelperin (1975) first showed that *Limax* can learn in a single trial to suppress feeding responses to formerly preferred food following pairing of this food (the CS) with carbon dioxide toxocis (US). That this form of operant learning conforms to a true associative process was shown by extensive control experiments, none of which yielded the same behavioral modifications as the paired presentation of CS–US. Sahley et al. (1981a,b) extended this paradigm by substituting exposure to quinine, a bitter plant substance, as the US. Slugs normally prefer potato as a food source, but after one exposure to paired quinine and potato, they show a strong aversion to potato (Fig. 8.5).

Remarkably, once these creatures have been aversively conditioned against potato, this stimulus can be successfully employed as the US in place of quinine. Thus, *Limax* is capable of second-order conditioning. Pairing multiple attractive food odors with quinine renders all of the

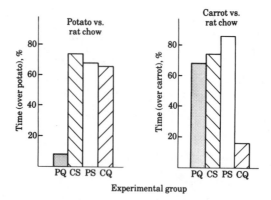

FIGURE 8.5   Behavioral manifestation of food aversion learning in *Limax*. Histograms
show the mean amount of time (%) the animals spent over potato (left histogram) or carrot
(right histogram) when given a choice between potato and rat chow, after a single pairing
of potato with quinine (PQ), carrot with saline (CS), potato with saline (PS) or carrot with
quinine (CQ). The learned aversion is selective to the punished food odor. (From Sahley,
Gelperin, & Rudy, 1981.)

odors aversive; this is an example of compound conditioning. Finally,
pairing an already aversively conditioned odor with quinine and a
third, unconditioned odor does not yield an aversion to the third odor,
which is identical to blocking of conditioning as documented in mammals (Kamin, 1969). Recent studies revealed further learning parallels
with vertebrates (Sahley et al., 1983) and also documented instances of
appetitive conditioning (Sahley et al., 1982). Finally, extensive and
well-designed control procedures have excluded nonassociative contributions to learning in *Limax*.

Compared with other invertebrate model systems, the behavioral significance of this form of learning in *Limax* seems especially clear, owing both to sound paradigm design and to the wealth of data available
on the natural history of this commercially significant gastropod. *Limax* is a generalized herbivore that is strongly nocturnal and heavily
reliant on chemosensation for homing (Gelperin, 1974), food localization and evaluation (Kittel, 1956), and consummatory feeding. Certain
plants in *Limax*'s natural habitat are toxic, and *Limax* normally avoids
these (Cates, 1975; Cates & Orians, 1975). It seems possible that these
food preferences observed under natural conditions reflect to some
degree associative learning of the type demonstrated by the previously
stated laboratory studies.

NEUROPHYSIOLOGY

Food aversion learning presumably is manifest in the neural circuitry that mediates feeding behavior. Gelperin and his colleagues studied a presumed feeding motor program in Limax. They accomplished this by developing a reduced preparation, consisting of the nearly isolated nervous system with bilateral flaps of the chemosensory lip tissue still attached by the appropriate nerves. Application of liquefied food stimuli to the two halves of the lips causes rhythmic motor output recorded from buccal motoneurons (Gelperin, Chang, and Reingold, 1978; Prior & Gelperin, 1977). This cyclic motor program is accompanied by vigorous discharge in the salivary duct (Copeland & Gelperin, 1982), shown in Pleurobranchaea to occur only during feeding (Croll & Davis, 1981, 1982; Croll, Kovac, & Davis, 1984a; Croll, Kovac, & Davis, 1984b; Croll, Kovac, Davis, & Matera, 1984c). Therefore, by analogy this motor program is probably that which normally underlies ingestion (feeding) and not egestion (rejection).

Sensory modulation of Limax's feeding motor program has been analyzed by Reingold and Gelperin (1980). Filling the crop with saline to the volume normally attained at the end of meals suppresses the feeding motor output elicited by chemostimulation. Therefore an excellent quantitative control of feeding motivation exists and furnishes a potentially useful control for nonassociative motivational variables in future studies of the cellular mechanisms underlying learning in Limax.

The prospect of understanding associative learning at the cellular level in Limax has been greatly enhanced by the discovery that the isolated CNS-lip preparation can be associatively trained. Pairing potato (CS) with colchicine (US), a bitter plant substance, leads to subsequent suppression of the feeding motor program in response to potato in one trial (Fig. 8.6). Moreover, this learning is selective. Following training with potato as the CS, the feeding motor program can still be elicited using other food substances that were not paired with the US (Chang & Gelperin, 1980). In an ingenious series of experiments, Culligan and Gelperin (1982) conditioned preparations with one half of the lip, and tested them with the other. Blind scoring of the motor responses revealed selective suppression of the feeding motor program when the CS was subsequently applied to either lip. This observation suggests that the underlying cellular modifications take place inside the CNS, rather than in the periphery as in Hermissenda. Indeed, retention of a previously learned food avoidance task by the subsequently

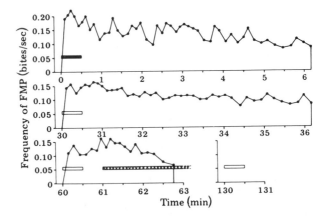

FIGURE 8.6   Food aversion learning in the isolated central nervous system of *Limax*. The motor correlate of the presumed feeding motor program (FMP) is graphed against cumulative time after exposure of the lip to potato extract alone (solid bar in upper graph), mushroom extract alone (open bar in middle graph), paired mushroom extract (open bar) and colchicine (hatched bar) in lower left graph, and subsequent mushroom extract alone (lower right graph). Before (but not after) "training" mushroom extract elicited the FMP, suggestive of food aversion learning of the same type as seen in the intact animal. (From Chang & Gelperin, 1980.)

isolated CNS has recently been demonstrated in *Limax* (Gelperin & Culligan, 1982, 1983).

Intracellular studies on the feeding neural circuitry of *Limax* are in an early stage. Published studies to date have been confined to buccal motoneurons and the metacerebral giant neuron (MCG), a characteristic brain neuron that has been studied across several species of molluscs. The MCG of *Limax* excites the feeding motor program (Gelperin, 1981), and is itself excited by food stimuli (Egan & Gelperin, 1981). The role of this identified neuron in learning, if any, has not been studied in *Limax*.

CONCLUSIONS

The previously discussed studies on *Limax* provide a persuasive behavioral analysis of learning in an invertebrate system. There is no question regarding the basic learning phenomenon; parallels with vertebrates are numerous and striking; *in vitro* learning has been demonstrated; and *in vitro* retention of *in vivo* learning has been documented. As in *Aplysia* it remains to be demonstrated that the *in vitro* learning is indeed homologous with the documented *in vivo* learning in the whole animal.

PLEUROBRANCHAEA

Pleurobranchaea is a large and comparatively active carnivorous genus of marine gastropod. Studies on learning have been conducted using P. californica, which may be found off the California coast. Other members of the genus are distributed along the eastern seaboard of the U.S. (P. pileus), in European waters (P. meckelii), and in coastal zones of Australia and New Zealand (P. novaezelandiae). This global distribution of the genus encourages comparative studies of learning in Pleurobranchaea.

BEHAVIOR

The study of associative learning in Pleurobranchaea began with classical conditioning of feeding behavior (Mpitsos & Davis, 1973). Pairing of touch (CS) and food (US) yielded, after many trials, a learned feeding response to touch alone. The same behavioral modification did not result following touch alone, food alone, nor unpaired food and touch. The classically conditioned feeding behavior could then be suppressed by avoidance conditioning (touch paired with shock). Subsequent studies of reduced preparations made from classically conditioned specimens showed enhanced buccal motor output induced by brain nerve stimulation in conditioned but not control or naive animals (Mpitsos & Davis, 1973).

A similar avoidance conditioning paradigm was subsequently developed in which food (CS) and aversive electric shock (US) were paired (Davis, Villet, Lee, Rigler, Gillette, & Prince, 1980; Mpitsos & Collins, 1975; Mpitsos, Collins, & McClellan, 1978). Specimens learned rapidly (1–10 trials separated by 1 hour) to suppress feeding behavior in response to the CS alone (passive avoidance learning) and to withdraw from the CS (active avoidance learning). Control procedures (random CS–US, explicitly unpaired CS–US, CS alone, US alone) did not cause a comparable behavioral modification. This form of learning is rapid and robust, with approximately 85% of conditioned animals reaching a demanding learning criterion, and is retained for days to weeks. The learned aversion to food is selective to the specific food stimulus used as the CS, and specimens have been differentially conditioned under this paradigm using two different but distinguishable food substances (Davis et al., 1980).

What is the behavioral significance of this form of associative learning? Field studies have shown that Pleurobranchaea is a scavenging carnivore, feeding on dead and live conspecifics, other gastropods

(Hirsch, 1915) and on living sea anemones (Ottoway, 1977). Although the US employed in laboratory studies (electric shock) is artificial and learning has not been studied in nature, it seems plausible that the demonstrated capacity for food aversion learning underlies learned avoidance of toxic or harmful food substances, such as sea anemones having especially objectionable stinging cells, the nematocysts.

NEUROPHYSIOLOGY

What is the neural basis of this form of associative learning in Pleuro-branchaea? As in the case of previous model systems reviewed, addressing this question required first mapping the neural circuitry of the conditioned response, namely the feeding behavior. This has proved a difficult undertaking, because the feeding circuitry of this simple animal has proved to be extraordinarily complex. However, several years of circuit analysis have now furnished a detailed picture of the peripheral pathways and central neural circuits that mediate feeding behavior in Pleurobranchaea.

The feeding behavior is initiated by peripheral "discociliated" putative chemoreceptors located on anterior sensory structures (Davis & Matera, 1982; Matera & Davis, 1982). These primary afferents project without interruption to two peripheral ganglia (tentacle and rhinophore ganglia), where they synapse with a population of about 100 sensory interneurons (Bicker, Davis, Matera, Kovac, & Stormo–Gipson, 1982a; Bicker, Davis, & Matera, 1982b). Here mechanical and chemical information about the food stimulus is integrated and then relayed to the brain (cerebropleural ganglion).

Within the brain lies a complex but well-analyzed circuitry that includes feeding command interneurons and their many excitatory and inhibitory inputs, as well as neural oscillator(s) and motoneurons (Croll & Davis, 1981, 1982; Croll et al., 1985a–c; Davis, Siegler, and Mpitsos, 1973; Davis, Mpitsos, Siegler, Pinneo, & Davis, 1974; Davis, Kovac, Croll, & Matera, 1984; Gillette and Davis, 1977; Gillette, Kovac, & Davis, 1978; Gillette, Kovac, & Davis, 1982a; Kovac, Davis, Matera & Gillette, 1982; Kovac, Davis, Matera, & Croll, 1983a,b; Siegler, Mpitsos, & Davis, 1974). The command neurons also play a pattern-generating role for the feeding motor program, and perhaps also a coordinating role for the independent feeding oscillators located in the brain and buccal ganglion (Davis et al., 1984; Gillette et al., 1982a). Within the buccal ganglion, which is attached to the brain by the paired cerebro-buccal connectives, lies a redundant pattern-generating network and also many of the sensory and motor neurons that innervate the buccal mass and its musculature (Davis et al., 1973, 1974; Gillette, Gillette, &

Davis, 1980; Gillette, Gillette, & Davis, 1982b,c; Siegler, 1977; Siegler et al., 1974).

That these neurons mediate feeding, rather than some other buccal behavior such as egestion of unpalatable objects, is known from recordings made from the buccal muscles of intact specimens during the respective behaviors (Croll & Davis, 1981) and from identifying the feeding motor program in the reduced preparation (Croll & Davis, 1982) and in the isolated CNS (Croll et al., 1985a). The same pattern-generating machinery may be utilized for both feeding and egestion (Croll et al., 1985a; McClellan, 1982a,b), but separate central command pathways have been demonstrated for the two behaviors (Croll et al., 1985b,c). This distinction is important, since learned modifications have been shown only for feeding behavior in the whole animal.

How does this complex and distributed neural circuitry mediate learned modifications of feeding behavior? The answer lies in part within the command circuitry of the brain, which is responsible for initiating the feeding behavior (Croll et al., 1985c; Gillette et al., 1978, 1982a). Intracellular recordings from one subset of the command system, the phasic paracerebral command neurons (PCP's) (Kovac et al., 1982), has shown that in whole animal preparations, food stimuli normally excite these neurons. In contrast, responses from trained specimens showed decreased excitation and increased tonic inhibition of the PCP's in response to the conditioned food stimulus (Davis & Gillette, 1978; Davis, Gillette, Kovac, Croll, & Matera, 1983). Importantly, responses from control animals given explicitly unpaired CS and US were excitatory and indistinguishable from those of naive animals. These studies thus established a neurophysiological correlate to learning in behaving, whole animal preparations.

As noted earlier, in identifying the cellular mechanisms of learning it is imperative to distinguish between specific cellular correlates of associative processes and more general cellular correlates of motivation. Toward this end, the responses of feeding command neurons (PCP's) were examined in whole animal preparations that had been previously satiated with food. Such animals show suppressed feeding responses as in trained animals (Davis, Mpitsos, Pinneo, & Ram, 1977), but the underlying physiological processes are motivational and nonassociative, rather than associative. These control experiments showed that the PCP's of satiated whole animal preparations were inhibited by food stimuli, as found also for trained animals. Therefore, associative processes (avoidance learning) and nonassociative motivational processes (food satiation) are identical at the command neuron level and are manifest as depressed excitation and enhanced synaptic inhibition. These data provide a neurophysiological explanation of behavioral mo-

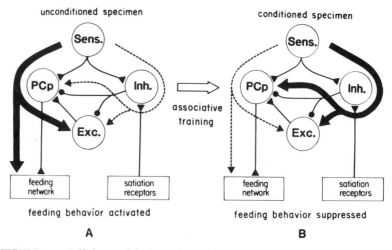

FIGURE 8.7   Cellular model of avoidance learning in *Pleurobranchaea*, based upon the identified neural circuitry of the feeding motor system. Before training, neural information regarding food is routed through predominantly excitatory pathways to activate feeding (A). After training, information is routed through preexisting inhibitory pathways in the same neural network. (From Davis, Gillette, Kovac, Croll, & Matera, 1983.)

tivation, namely synaptic modulation of central command interneurons. They also illustrate the need to design experiments on the cellular mechanisms of learning so as to exclude general motivational influences. Finally, these results showed that the search for the neural causes of learning must be carried to neurons that are presynaptic to the command interneurons, since no differentiation exists at the command neuron level.

To pursue such studies, an isolated CNS–lip preparation analogous to that described above for *Limax* was developed (Kovac, Davis, Matera, Morielli, & Croll, 1984). These reduced preparations were made from animals that were previously trained in the avoidance learning paradigm. Remarkably, the nearly isolated CNS remembers the task taught previously to the whole animal, as evidenced by reduced excitation and increased inhibition of the feeding command interneurons in response to the CS (Fig. 8.7A). In contrast, command interneurons from control and naive animals were excited by application of the CS (Fig. 8.8, B & C). Unlike the finding in the whole animal preparation, however, the command interneurons of animals that had been satiated with food before removing their nervous system were excited, rather than inhibited, by the food stimulus, presumably because inhibitory feedback pathways from satiation receptors were cut by isolating the CNS. This finding provides the crucial demonstration that the CS-induced inhibition in nervous systems taken from trained animals is ascribable specifically to associative learning rather than to a general motivational process such as satiation.

How does the central nervous system of Pleurobranchaea orchestrate the reduced excitation and increased inhibition of feeding command interneurons in response to associative training? To answer this question, intracellular studies were performed on neurons that are presynaptic to the command interneurons, in reduced preparations made from previously trained animals (Kovac et al., 1984). These experiments showed that the reduced excitation of command interneurons caused by training has at least two causes: (1) decreased transmission efficacy through an identified chemical polysynaptic pathway that is presynaptic to the command interneurons; and (2) increased inhibition of central neurons that normally excite the command interneurons.

With regard to decreased excitation, the participating polysynaptic pathway begins with the identified polysynaptic excitor neurons of the brain (PSE's), which are also capable of initiating the feeding motor program (Croll et al., 1984c; Kovac, Davis, Matera, & Croll, 1983a), and ends with the PCPs. Interposed between these neurons is a neuron located in the buccal ganglion that sends an ascending axon to the brain via the cerebrobuccal connectives (Davis et al., 1984, and unpublished). Intracellular stimulation of a single PSE in an untrained animal causes the polysynaptic response in the PCP's at a presynaptic spike threshold of approximately 15 Hz. After training, however, the threshold for the same postsynaptic response is significantly increased, to nearly double the pretraining value. The finding that this increase in threshold persists in the isolated CNS demonstrates that these neurophysiological changes attendant to learning occur centrally. The cellular mechanisms of the demonstrated reduced transmission efficacy in the command pathway are unknown, but since the neurons composing the pathway are now identified (Davis et al., 1984) it should be possible to determine the mechanism of learning at the synaptic and subcellular level.

In addition to the decrease in excitation of feeding command interneurons that accompanies learned suppression of feeding, the same command interneurons show an increase in synaptic inhibition in response to the CS following training. The neurons mediating this inhibition appear to be identical with those that normally supply cyclic inhibition to the command interneurons during feeding behavior. These neurons are known as the cyclic inhibitory network (CIN) (Davis, Gillette, Kovac, Croll, & Matera, 1983a; Gillette et al., 1982a). These data collectively provide partial confirmation of a cellular model of avoidance learning in Pleurobranchaea (Fig. 8.8), in which the flow of neural information through a preexisting network of central neurons is shifted

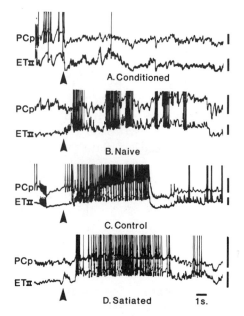

FIGURE 8.8 Neurophysiological correlates to avoidance learning in feeding command interneurons of the isolated brain of *Pleurobranchaea* following training of the intact animal. Shown are the responses to food stimuli applied to anterior chemosensory structures of conditioned (A), naive (B), control (unpaired CS–US; C) and satiated (D) animals. Inhibition of the feeding command interneurons (corresponding to suppression of feeding) is seen only in the brains of trained animals. PC$_P$, phasic paracerebral command interneuron; ET$_{II}$, Type II electrotonic neuron. (From Kovac, Davis, Matera, Morielli, & Croll, 1983.)

from excitatory to inhibitory pathways by associative training. Increased inhibition is accomplished by the conversion of the CIN from a pacemaker to a tonic inhibitor of the feeding motor program (Davis et al., 1983).

Recent studies show that the learning-induced decline in command neuron respones is mediated by postsynaptic modulation of neurotransmitter responsiveness (Morielli et al., 1986). Food detection is mediated normally by muscarinic acetylcholine (ACh) receptors. Following food avoidance training, however, this muscarinic ACh response is strongly suppressed, causing the learned suppression of feeding behavior. This learning-induced postsynaptic modulation of neurotransmitter-gated ion channels in central interneurons of *Pleurobranchaea* contrasts with the presynaptic modulation of voltage-gated channels in sensory neurons of *Aplysia*, and modulation of non-synaptic voltage-gated ion channels in sensory neurons of *Hermissenda*.

CONCLUSIONS

Studies on learning in *Pleurobranchaea* have established a cellular neurophysiological correlate to avoidance learning. Because the isolated CNS remembers the avoidance task taught previously to the whole animal, it is possible to investigate the central neural correlates of true associative learning, rather than a learning analog in a nearly isolated brain. Analyses to date indicate that learning in *Pleurobranchaea* is based on an entirely different mechanism from those reported in *Aplysia* and *Hermissenda*. Modulation of neurotransmitter responsiveness could represent a general model of learning in mammals, where the involvement of ACh in learning has long been known.

CORRELATION VERSUS CAUSALITY IN CELLULAR STUDIES OF LEARNING

The model systems approach has clearly enabled rapid and immense progress toward a cellular understanding of associative learning. The central issue, however, remains unanswered: how does peripheral sensory contiguity (paired stimuli) cause the formation of new and persistent central neural associations? Answering this question will first require overcoming a significant conceptual hurdle, namely, distinguishing between correlation and causality. The model systems approach seeks to uncover the causative agents of learning; it is insufficient to determine merely the cellular correlates of learning, since these may represent a secondary effect rather than a primary cause. As yet, there exists no consensus regarding the operational criteria that must be satisfied before causation has been established.

To date the problem has been addressed independently by the individual laboratories working in the field. Alkon (1983a,b), for example, argues that the observed sensory correlates of learning in *Hermissenda* are causal, since: (1) the correlation is strong; (2) the modified sensory pathways (eyes) are necessary for the conditioned behavior (phototaxis); and (3) pairing the injection of current into the photoreceptors with a light step is sufficient to modify the subsequent phototactic behavior. These tests are certainly useful, but are they conclusive? Independent experiments have in fact shown that other correlates of learning in *Hermissenda*, such as the enhanced photoresponse and light-produced photoreceptor desensitization, cannot be explained by a decrease in the A-current. Moreover, as reported earlier, the onset of a potassium current (I-A) is claimed to underlie learning in this preparation, but blocking A-current (with 4-aminopyridine) does not mimic the effects of conditioning on Type B photoreceptors (Alkon 1983, Alkon et al., 1982).

Standards of causality derived from a related field, namely motor control, are more demanding. A neuron is considered causal to a behavior if: (1) it is *sufficient* to produce the behavior; (2) it is *necessary* to produce the behavior (Kupferman & Weiss, 1978); and (3) its activity pattern (both sensory and motor) is *appropriate* to the behavior (Parsons, Ter Maat, & Pinsker, 1983). To this list we might add *temporal primacy*, since the most directly causal event in a sequence by definition occurs first in time.

These four criteria have the advantages that they are systematic and they imply operational tests for causality. Thus a neuron or a neurophysiological process is *sufficient* for a behavior or its modification if, when activated, it causes that behavior or its modification; a neuron or neurophysiological process is *necessary* for a behavior or its modification if, when eliminated, the behavior or its modification is eliminated, and so on. These criteria suffer the disadvantage, however, that they are often technically and/or conceptually difficult to apply or inappropriate owing to intrinsic organizational features of the nervous system (e.g., Davis, 1978). The challenge facing those who seek to understand the causative agents of learning is to formulate criteria for causality that are logically rigorous, while at the same time operationally plausible. Without such a formulation, progress toward our common goal of understanding the cellular causes of learning will be slower.

GENERAL PRINCIPLES OF LEARNING IN INVERTEBRATE MODEL SYSTEMS

Several general principles are emerging from the model systems approach as it enters its adolescence. In this section I will synthesize several such principles, identify the studies that support them by the abbreviation of the species used (Ap = *Aplysia;* He = *Hermissenda;* Li = *Limax;* and Pl = *Pleurobranchaea*), and offer a brief commentary. This synthesis is based upon input from several of the principal investigators whose work is reviewed here (see the section entitled "Acknowledgments"). Some of these colleagues suggested, quite correctly, that such principles may be premature, inasmuch as the studies on which they are based are incomplete and ongoing. The following principles, therefore, are offered as working hypotheses that appear consistent with available data. These principles will no doubt require modification as this exciting field continues its dramatic progress.

The Principle of Behavioral Generality

Invertebrate learning follows the same behavioral and psychological laws as established for vertebrates (Ap, He, Li, Pl).

Psychologists once questioned, quite legitimately, whether invertebrate animals were capable of any type of learning. Model systems research has conclusively answered this question in the affirmative, and in the process shown that invertebrate learning follows the same basic rules established for vertebrates. Learning phenomena common to both invertebrates and vertebrates include: classical, operant, avoidance, alpha, and trace conditioning; increased strength of learning with increased training; stronger effect of spaced than massed training; temporal specificity; one trial learning; lack of backward conditioning (generally but not always); effect of motivational state and age on learning; capacity for selective learning; capacity for differential learning; higher order conditioning; block of conditioning; long-term retention; extinction; forgetting; and savings on retraining. Evolution has clearly been conservative with respect to the laws of learning.

The Principle Of Engram Localization

Learning entails functional modification of the neural circuitry that mediates the unconditioned/conditioned response (Ap, He, Li, Pl).

The details in support of this principle vary depending upon the nature of the behavioral modification. In *Pleurobranchaea*, for example, avoidance learning entails functional modification of command and pattern-generating circuitry, while in *Aplysia* and *Hermissenda*, changes in sensory neurons are implicated. The latter strategy would seem less flexible and selective than the former, but the two strategies are by no means mutually exclusive and may coexist redundantly in any given learning task.

The Principle of Existing Circuit Modification

Learning does not require the formation of new synaptic connections but rather can be explained in terms of functional modification of existing neurons and/or neuronal circuits (Ap, He, Pl).

This principle, which is in fact a corollary of the second principle, addresses the long-standing question of whether learning entails *de novo* formation of synapses. Model systems research has not in fact excluded this possibility, but simply suggests that *de novo* synapse formation is not essential to those forms of learning studied to date. And it should be noted that there is impressive evidence for new synapse formation in vertebrates in association with enriched sensory experience, although a causal role in learning has not been demonstrated (see Chapter 2, this volume).

THE PRINCIPLE OF BIAS TOWARD INPUT MODIFICATION

Learning occurs near the input end of the neuronal circuits controlling the modified behavior (Ap, He, Pl).

This principle, also a corollary of the second principle, derives largely from studies on gastropods. It must be admitted, however, that neurophysiological modifications near the motor end of gastropod circuits have not been pursued as vigorously, and hence the bias may not lie in the design of learning mechanisms but rather in the design of experiments intended to reveal them. Studies of learning in insects implicate changes in motoneuron membrane properties as a possible correlate of avoidance learning (Woollacott & Hoyle, 1977; Hoyle, 1979, 1980, 1982). Indeed, experiments on a primitive insect suggested the muscle tissue itself may be a locus of learning (Hoyle & Field, 1983a,b). Redundancy, a well-known feature of the nervous system, may extend as well to the loci of learning even within a single species in a single learning task.

THE PRINCIPLE OF THE COMMON LOCUS

Learning (acquisition) and memory (retention of information) occur in the same neurons and/or neural circuits (Ap, He, Pl).

Psychologists have often wondered whether the physiological processes underlying learning and memory occupy the same anatomical substrates, and whether short-term and long-term memory occur in the same place. Studies on model systems indicate that learned associations are stored at the same central nervous address as they are entered, namely in a common locus within the neural circuits of the unconditioned or conditioned response. This principle also is a corollary of the second principle.

THE PRINCIPLE OF ENGRAM STABILITY

Both learning and memory of a new task (Ap, Li) and memory of a previously learned task (He, Pl) can be accomplished in vitro by the nearly isolated nervous system.

The finding that acquisition and retention of simple conditioned responses both occur in highly reduced invertebrate preparations is testimony to the physical stability of the engram. It also provides confirmatory support for the S–R model of learning, since cognition is presumably absent in such radically reduced preparations. The discovery that the memory of a previously learned task survives the surgical reduction of the preparation to the isolated CNS promises to facilitate the deeper study of the neurophysiology, biophysics, and molecular biology of associative learning.

THE PRINCIPLE OF SINGLE NEURON MANIFESTATION

Learning and memory can be analyzed at the level of the single, identified neuron (Ap, He, Pl).

Prior to the studies reviewed here, it was possible to imagine that learning is a mass phenomenon, necessarily involving functionally affiliated events in hundreds or even millions of individual neurons. In this case the neurophysiological alterations that accompany learning might well be too small to detect by applying conventional electrophysiological approaches to single neurons. Model systems research has permanently dispelled this gloomy scenario, at least for invertebrate animals. Single invertebrate neurons may not tell the whole story; but they tell enough to justify and permit pursuit of the engram at the level of the individual, identified neuron.

CONCLUSIONS

The ability to formulate general principles, as indicated above, is itself evidence that model systems research has entered its prime. On the other hand, fundamental differences between models, and in particular the discovery of a novel mechanism of learning in *Pleurobranchaea* (postsynaptic modulation of neurotransmitter responsiveness), suggests the need for caution in extrapolation to vertebrate learning. It remains to be established whether presynaptic or postsynaptic models will prove most generalizable to learning in higher animals. The coming decade will no doubt witness the maturing of the model systems approach and the determination of which invertebrate models are most applicable to mammalian learning.

ACKNOWLEDGMENTS

I thank my colleagues Dr. Dan Alkon, Dr. Terry Audesirk, Dr. Gerry Audesirk, Dr. Tom Carew, Dr. Terry Crow, Dr. Alan Gelperin, and Dr. Mark Kovac for their input to this review, although responsibility for any errors or misinterpretations must remain mine. This review was prepared during the tenure of a Senior Scientist Award from the Alexander von Humboldt Foundation of the Federal Republic of Germany. I thank my German hosts, Dr. Hübert Markl (University of Konstanz) and Dr. Franz Huber (Max-Planck Institute, Seewiesen), for hospitality and excellent facilities during the tenure of this award. Original research from our laboratory has been supported by NSF Research Grant BNS–8110235 and NIH Research Grant NS–09050.

REFERENCES

Akaike, T., & Alkon, D. L. (1980). Sensory convergence on central visual neurons in Hermissenda. Journal of Neurophysiology, 44, 501–513.

Alkon, D. L. (1973a). Neural organization of a molluscan visual system. Journal of General Physiology, 61, 444–461.

Alkon, D. L. (1973b). Intersensory interactions in Hermissenda. Journal of General Physiology, 62, 185–202.

Alkon, D. L. (1974). Associative training of Hermissenda. Journal of General Physiology, 64, 70–84.

Alkon, D. L. (1975). Neural correlates of associative training in hermissenda. Journal of General Physiology, 65, 46–56.

Alkon, D. L. (1976). Neural modification by paired sensory stimuli. Journal of General Physiology, 68, 341–358.

Alkon, D. L. (1979). Voltage-dependent calcium and potassium ion conductances: A contingency mechanism for an associative learning model. Science, 205, 810–816.

Alkon, D. L. (1980a). Cellular analysis of a gastropod (Hermissenda crassicornis) model of associative learning. Biological Bulletin, 159, 505–560.

Alkon, D. L. (1980b). Membrane depolarization accumulates during acquisition of an associative behavioral change. Science, 210, 1375–1376.

Alkon, D. L. (1983). Learning in a marine snail. Scientific American, 249, 70–84.

Alkon, D. L., Akaike, T., & Harrigan, J. F. (1978). Interaction of chemosensory, visual and statocyst pathways in Hermissenda. Journal of General Physiology, 71, 177–194.

Alkon, D. L., & Fuortes, M. G. F. (1972). Responses of photoreceptors in Hermissenda, Journal of General Physiology, 60, 631–649.

Alkon, D. L., & Grossman, Y. (1978). Long-lasting depolarization and hyperpolarization in the eye of Hermissenda. Journal of Neurophysiology, 41, 1328–1342.

Alkon, D. L., Lederhendler, I., & Shoukimas, J. L. (1982). Primary changes of membrane currents during retention of associative learning. Science, 215, 693–695.

Alkon, D. L., Shoukimas, J. J., & Heldman, E. (1982). Calcium-mediated decrease of a voltage-dependent potassium current. Biophysical Journal, 40, 245–250.

Bicker, G., Davis, W. J., Matera, E. M., Kovac, M. P., Stormo–Gipsin, J. (1982a). Mechano- and chemoreception in Pleurobranchaea californica. I. Extracellular analysis of afferent responses. Journal of Comparative Physiology, 144, 221–234.

Bicker, G., Davis, W. J., & Matera, E. M. (1982b). Mechano- and chemoreception in Pleurobranchaea californica. II. Neuroanatomical and chemoreception in Pleurobranchaea californica. II. Neuroanatomical and intracellular analysis of centripetal pathways. Journal of Comparative Physiology, 149, 235–250.

Carew, T. J., Abrams, T. W., Hawkins, R. D., & Kandel, E. R. (1983). The use of simple invertebrate systems to explore psychological issues related to associative learning. In D. L. Alkon & J. Farley (Eds.), *Primary neural substrates of learning and behavioral change.* New York: Cambridge University Press. in press. (a)

Carew, T. J., Hawkins, R. D., & Kandel, E. R. (1983b). Differential classical conditioning of a defensive withdrawal reflex in *Aplysia californica. Science, 219,* 397–400. (b)

Carew, T. J., Walters, E. T., & Kandel, E. R. (1981). Classical conditioning in a simple withdrawal reflex in *Aplysia californica. Journal of Neuroscience, 1,* 1426–1437.

Castellucci, V. F., & Kandel, E. R. (1976). Presynaptic facilitation as a mechanism for behavioral sensitization in *Aplysia. Science, 194,* 1176–1178.

Cates, R. G. (1975). The interface between slugs and wild ginger: Some evolutionary aspects. *Ecology, 56,* 391–400.

Cates, R. G., & Orians, G. H. (1975). Successional status and the palatability of plants to generalized herbivores. *Ecology, 56,* 410–418.

Chang, J. J., & Gelperin, A. (1980). Rapid taste-aversion learning by an isolated molluscan central nervous system. *Proceedings of the National Academy of Sciences of the United States of America, 77,* 6204–6206.

Copeland, J., & Gelperin, A. (1982). Feeding and a serotonergic interneuron activate an identified autoactive salivary neuron in *Limax maximus. Comparative Biochemistry and Physiology, 76A,* 21–30.

Croll, R. P., & Davis, W. J. (1981). Motor program switching in *Pleurobranchaea.* I. Behavioral and electromyographic study of ingestion and egestion in intact specimens. *Journal of Comparative Physiology, 145,* 277–287.

Croll, R. P., & Davis, W. J. (1982). Motor program switching in *Pleurobranchaea.* II. Ingestion and egestion in the reduced preparation. *Journal of Comparative Physiology, 147,* 143–154.

Croll, R. P., Davis, W. J., & Kovac, M. P. (1984a). Neural mechanisms of motor program switching in the mollusc *Pleurobranchaea.* I. Central motor programs underlying ingestion, egestion and the "neutral" rhythm(s). *Journal of Neuroscience, 5,* 48–55.

Croll, R. P., Kovac, M. P., & Davis, W. J. (1984b). Neural mechanisms of motor program switching in the mollusc *Pleurobranchaea.* II. Role of the ventral white cell, AV neurons and interneuron B3. *Journal of Neuroscience, 5,* 56–63.

Croll, R. P., Kovac, M. P., Davis, W. J., & Matera, E. M. (1984c). Neural mechanisms of motor program switching in the mollusc *Pleurobranchaea.* III. Role of the paracerebral neurons and other identified brain neurons. *Journal of Neuroscience, 5,* 64–71.

Crow, T. J., & Alkon, D. L. (1978). Retention of an associative behavioral change in *Hermissenda. Science, 201,* 1239–1241.

Crow, T. J., & Alkon, D. L. (1980). Associative behavioral modification in *Hermissenda:* Cellular correlates. *Science, 209,* 412–414.

Crow, T. J., & Offenbach, N. (1979). Response specificity following behavioral training in the nudibranch mollusc *Hermissenda crassicornis. Biological Bulletin, 157,* 364.

Crow, T. J., & Offenbach, N. (1983). Modification of the initiation of locomotion in *Hermissenda:* Behavioral analysis. *Brain Research, 271,* 301–310.

Culligan, N., & Gelperin, A. (1982). One-trial associative learning by an isolated molluscan CNS: Use of different chemoreceptors for training and testing. *Brain Research,* in press.

Davis, W. J. (1978). On the trail of the command neuron. *The Behavioral and Brain Sciences, 1,* 17–19.

Davis, W. J., & Gillette, R. (1978). Neural correlate of behavioral plasticity in command neurons of *Pleurobranchaea. Science, 199,* 801–804.

Davis, W. J., Gillette, R., Kovac, M. P., Croll, R. P., & Matera, E. M. (1983). Organization of synaptic inputs to paracerebral feeding command interneurons of *Pleurobranchaea californica*. III. Modifications induced by experience. *Journal of Neurophysiology*, 49, 1557–1572. (a)

Davis, W. J., Kovac, M. P., Croll, R. P., & Matera, E. M. (1984). Brain oscillator(s) underlying rhythmic buccal motor output in the mollusc *Pleurobranchaea californica*. *Journal of Experimental Biology* (1984).

Davis, W. J., & Matera, E. M. (1982). Chemoreception in gastropod mollusks: Electron microscopy of putative receptor cells. *Journal of Neurophysiology*, 13, 79–84.

Davis, W. J., Mpitsos, G. J., Pinneo, Journal of M. & Ram, J. L. (1977). Modification of the behavioral hierarchy of *Pleurobranchaea*. I. Satiation and feeding motivation. *Journal of Comparative Physiology*, 117, 99–125.

Davis, W. J., Mpitsos, G. J., Siegler, M. V. S., Pinneo, & Davis, K. B. Journal of Neuronal substrates of behavioral hierarchies and associative learning in the mollusk *Pleurobranchaea*. *American Zoologist*, 14, 1037–1050.

Davis, W. J., Siegler, M. V. S., & Mpitsos, G. J. (1973). Distributed neuronal oscillators and efference copy in the feeding system of *Pleurobranchaea*. *Journal of Neurophysiology*, 36, 258–274.

Davis, W. J., Villet, J., Lee, D., Rigler, M., Gillette, R., & Prince, E. (1980). Selective and differential avoidance learning in the feeding and withdrawal behavior of *Pleurobranchaea californica*. *Journal of Comparative Physiology*, 138, 157–165.

Dennis, M. J. (1967). Electrophysiology of the visual system in a nudibranch mollusc. *Journal of Neurophysiology*, 30, 1437–1465.

Detwiler, P. B., & Alkon, D. L. (1973). Hair cell interactions in the statocyst of *Hermissenda*. *Journal of General Physiology*, 62, 618–642.

Egan, M., & Gelperin, A. (1981). Olfactory inputs to a bursting serotonergic interneuron in a terrestrial mollusc. *Journal of Molluscan Studies*, 47, 80–88.

Farley, J., & Alkon, D. L. (1980). Neural organization predicts stimulus specificity for a retained associative behavioral change. *Science*, 210, 1373–1375.

Farley, J., & Alkon, D. L. (1982). Associative neural and behavioral change in *Hermissenda*: Consequences of nervous system orientation for light- and pairing-specificity. *Journal of Neurophysiology*, 48, 785–808.

Gelperin, A. (1974). Olfactory basis of homing behavior in the giant garden slug, *Limax maximus*. *Proceedings of the National Academy of Sciences of the United States of America*, 71, 966–970.

Gelperin, A. (1975). Rapid food-aversion learning by a terrestrial mollusk. *Science*, 189, 567–570.

Gelperin, A. (1981). Synaptic modulation by identified serotonin neurons. In B. Jacobs & A. Gelperin (Eds.), *Serotonin neurotransmission and behavior* (pp. 288–304). Cambridge, MA: MIT Press.

Gelperin, A., Chang, J. J., & Reingold, S. C. (1978). Feeding motor program in *Limax*. I. Neuromuscular correlates and control by chemosensory input. *Journal of Neurobiology*, 9, 285–300.

Gelperin, A., & Culligan, N. (1982). In vitro expression of in vivo learning by the cerebral ganglia of the terrestrial mollusc *Limax maximus*. *Society for Neuroscience Abstract*, 8, 823.

Gelperin, A., & Culligan, N. (1984). In vitro expression of in vivo learning by an isolated molluscan CNS. *Brain Research*, 304, 207–213.

Gillette, R., & Davis, W. J. (1977). The role of the metacerebral giant neuron in the feeding behavior of *Pleurobranchaea*. *Journal of Comparative Physiology*, 116, 129–159.

Gillette, R., Gillette, M. U., & Davis, W. J. (1980). Action potential broadening and endogenously sustained bursting are substrates of command ability in a feeding neuron of *Pleurobranchaea. Journal of Neurophysiology, 43*, 669–685.

Gillette, R., Gillette, M. U., & Davis, W. J. (1982b). Substrates of command ability in a buccal neuron of *Pleurobranchaea*. I. Mechanisms of action potential broadening. *Journal of Comparative Physiology, 146*, 449–459.

Gillette, R., Gillette, M. U., & Davis, W. J. (1982c). Substrates of command ability in a buccal neuron of *Pleurobranchaea*. II. Potential role of cyclic AMP. *Journal of Comparative Physiology, 146*, 461–470.

Gillette, R., Kovac, M. P., & Davis, W. J. (1978). Command neurons in *Pleurobranchaea* receive synaptic feedback from the motor network they excite. *Science, 199*, 798–801.

Gillette, R., Kovac, M. P., & Davis, W. J. (1982a). Control of feeding motor output by paracerebral neurons in the brain of *Pleurobranchaea californica. Journal of Neurophysiology, 47*, 885–908. (a)

Grossman, Y., Alkon, D. L., & Heldman, E. (1979). A common origin of voltage noise and hair cell generator potentials. *Journal of General Psychology, 73*, 23–48.

Grossman, Y., Schmidt, J. A., & Alkon, D. L. (1981). Calcium-dependent potassium conductance in the photoresponse of a nudibranch mollusk. *Comparative Biochemistry and Physiology, 68A*, 487–494.

Hawkins, R. D., Abrams, T. W., Carew, T. J., & Kandel, E. R. (1983). A cellular mechanism of classical conditioning in *Aplysia*: Activity-dependent amplification of presynaptic facilitation. *Science, 219*, 400–405.

Hirsch, G. (1915). Die Ernährungsbiologie fleishfressender Gastropoden. [(transl.)] *Zoologische Jahrbucher Abteilung fur Allgemeine Zoologie und Physiolgie der tiere, 35*, 357–504.

Hoyle, G. (1979). Mechanisms of simple motor learning. *Trends in Neuroscience, 2*, 153–155.

Hoyle, G. (1980). Learning, using natural reinforcements, in insect preparations that permit cellular neuronal analysis. *Journal of Neurobiology, 11*, 323–354.

Hoyle, G. (1982). Pacemaker change in a learning paradigm. In D. O. Carpenter (Ed.), *Cellular Pacemakers* (pp. 3–25, Vol. 2). New York: Academic Press.

Hoyle, G., & Field, L. H. (1983a). Defense posture and leg-position learning in a primitive insect utilize catch-like tension. *Journal of Neurobiology*, in press.

Hoyle, G., & Field, L. H. (1983b). Elicitation and abrupt termination of behaviorally-significant catch-like tension in a primitive insect. *Journal of Neurobiology*, in press.

Kamin, L. J. (1969). Predictability, surprise, attention and conditioning. In R. Church & B. A. Campbell (Eds.), *Punishment and aversive behavior* (pp. 279–296). New York: Appelton-Century-Crofts.

Kandel, E. R., & Schwartz, J. H. (1982). Molecular biology of learning: Modulation of transmitter release. *Science, 218*, 433–442.

Kittel, R. (1956). Untersuchungen uber den Geruchs- und Geschmackssinn bei den Gattungen *Arion* und *Limax. Zoologischer Anzeiger, 157*, 185–195.

Kovac, M. P., Davis, W. J., Matera, E. M., & Croll, R. P. (1983a). Organization of synaptic inputs to paracerebral feeding command interneurons of *Pleurobranchaea californica*. I. Excitatory inputs. *Journal of Neurophysiology, 49*, 1517–1538.

Kovac, M. P., Davis, W. J., Matera, E. M., & Croll, R. P. (1983b). Organization of synaptic inputs to paracerebral feeding command interneurons of *Pleurobranchaea californica*. II. Inhibitory inputs. *Journal of Neurophysiology, 49*, 1539–1556.

Kovac, M. P., Davis, W. J., Matera, E. M., & Gillette, R. (1982). Functional and structural correlates of cell size in paracerebral neurons of *Pleurobranchaea californica. Journal of Neurophysiology, 47*, 909–927.

Kovac, M. P., Davis, W. J., Matera, E. M., Morielli, A., & Croll, R. P. (1984). Cellular mechanisms of avoidance learning studied in the isolated brain of Pleurobranchaea. Brain Research.

Kupfermann, I., & Weiss, K. R. (1978). The command neuron concept. The Behavioral and Brain Sciences, 1, 3–10.

Kuzirian, A. M., Alkon, D. L., & Harris, L. G. (1981). An infraciliary network in statocyst hair cells. Journal of Neurocytology, 10, 497–514.

Matera, E. M., & Davis, W. J. (1982). Paddle cilia (discocilia) in chemosensitive structures of the gastropod mollusk Pleurobranchaea californica. Cell and Tissue Research, 222, 25–40.

McClellan, A. D. (1982a). Movements and motor patterns of the buccal mass of Pleurobranchaea during feeding, regurgitation and rejection. Journal of Experimental Biology, 98, 195–211.

McClellan, A. D. (1982b). Re-examination of presumed feeding motor activity in the isolated nervous system of Pleurobranchaea. Journal of Experimental Biology, 98, 213–228.

Meech, R. W. (1972). Intracellular calcium injection causes increased potassium conductance in Aplysia nerve cells. Comparative Biochemistry and Physiology, 42, 493–499.

Meech, R. W. (1974). The sensitivity of Helix aspersa neurons to injected calcium ions. Journal of Physiology (London), 237, 259–277.

Meech, R. W., & Standen, N. B. (1975). Potassium activation in Helix aspersa under voltage clamp: A component mediated by calcium influx. Journal of Physiology (London), 249, 211–239.

Morielli, A. D., Matera, E. M., Kovac, M. P., McCormack, K. J., & Davis, W. J. (1986). Cholinergic suppression: a postsynaptic mechanism of long-term associative learning. Proceedings of the National Academy of Sciences of the United States of America, in press.

Mpitsos, G. J., & Collins, S. D. (1975). Learning: Rapid aversive conditioning in the gastropod mollusc Pleurobranchaea. Science, 188, 954–957.

Mpitsos, G. J., Collins, S. D., & McClellan, A. D. (1978). Learning: A model system for physiological studies. Science, 199, 497–506.

Mpitsos, G. J., & Davis, W. J. (1973). Learning: Classical and avoidance conditioning in the mollusk Pleurobranchaea. Science, 180, 317–320.

Neary, J. T., Crow, T., & Alkon, D. L. (1981). Change in a specific phosphoprotein band following associative learning in Hermissenda, Nature, 293, 658–660.

Ottoway, J. R. (1977). Pleurobranchaea novaezelandiae preying on Actinia tenebrosa New Zealand Journal of Marine and Freshwater Research, 11, 125–130.

Parsons, D. W., Ter Maat, A., & Pinsker, H. M. (1983). Selective recording and stimulation of individual identified neurons in freely behaving Aplysia. Science (New York), 221, 1203–1206.

Prior, D., & Gelperin, A. (1977). Autoactive molluscan neuron: Reflex function and synaptic modulation during feeding in the terrestrial slug Limax maximus. Journal of Comparative Physiology, 114, 217–232.

Reingold, S. R., & Gelperin, A. (1980). Feeding motor program in Limax. II. Modulation by sensory inputs in intact animals and isolated central nervous system. Journal of Experimental Biology, 85, 1–19.

Sahley, C. L., Gelperin, A., Rudy, J. (1981a). One-trial associative learning modifies food odor preferences of a terrestrial mollusc. Proceedings of the National Academy of Sciences of the United States of America, 78, 640–642.

Sahley, C. L., Hardison, P., Hsuan, A., & Gelperin, A. (1982). Appetitively reinforced odor-conditioning modulates feeding in Limax maximus. Society for Neuroscience Abstract, 8, 823.

Sahley, C. L., Rudy, J. W., & Gelperin, A. (1981). An analysis of associative learning in a terrestrial mollusc: Higher-order conditioning, blocking and a transient US pre-exposure effect. Journal of Comparative Physiology, 144, 1–8.

Sahley, C. L., Rudy, J. W., & Gelperin, A. (1983). Associative learning in a mollusc: A comparative analysis. In D. L. Alkon & J. Farley (Eds.), Primary Neural Substrates of Learning and Behavioral Change. New York: Cambridge University Press.

Shoukimas, J. J., & Alkon, D. L. (1980). Voltage-dependent, early outward current in a photoreceptor of Hermissenda crassicornis. Society for Neuroscience Abstract, 6, 17.

Siegler, M. V. S. (1977). Motor neurone coordination and sensory modulation in the feeding system of the mollusc Pleurobranchaea californica. Journal of Experimental Biology, 71, 27–48.

Siegler, M. V. S., Mpitsos, G. J., & Davis, W. J. (1974). Motor organization and generation of rhythmic feeding output in the buccal ganglion of Pleurobranchaea. Journal of Neurophysiology, 37, 1173–1196.

Stommel, E. W., Stephens, R. E., & Alkon, D. L. (1980). Motile statocyst cilia transmit rather than directly transduce mechanical stimuli. Journal of Cell Biology, 87, 652–662.

Tabata, M., & Alkon, D. L. (1982). Positive synaptic feedback in visual system of nudibranch mollusc Hermissenda crassicornia. Journal of Neurophysiology, 48, 174–191.

Thompson, S. H. (1977). Three pharmacologically distinct potassium channels in molluscan neurons. Journal of Physiology (London), 265, 465–488.

Walters, E. T., & Byrne, J. H. (1983). Associative conditioning of single sensory neurons suggests a cellular mechanism for learning. Science, 219, 405–408.

Woollacott, M. & Hoyle, G. (1977). Neural events underlying learning: Changes in pacemaker. Proceedings of the Royal Society of London (Series B), 195, 395–415.

9

MEMORY: VERTEBRATE MODEL SYSTEMS

Bruce S. Kapp and Jeffrey P. Pascoe

INTRODUCTION

To achieve a more complete understanding of the neural substrates of learning and memory, several goals must be attained. Clearly, it would be necessary to identify critical brain areas which participate in the acquisition, storage and retrieval of information. Having identified these areas, it would then be necessary to determine the exact manner by which they contribute to learning and memory processes. For example, does a particular area represent a sensory input or motor output channel, does it contribute to motivational processes, or is it actually the site of information storage? Ultimately, it would be necessary to provide a precise description of the synaptic and intracellular mechanisms which are the substrates for learning and memory, including possible alterations in synaptic efficacy, the synthesis of new proteins and changes in neuronal membrane structure.

To advanced students of behavioral neuroscience, it should come as no surprise that these goals have not yet been realized. Indeed, considering the staggering complexities of the nervous system as well as the intracacies of behavior, it is a tribute to the ingenuity of many neuroscientists that progress has been made toward understanding the neural bases of learning and memory. Such progress is the result of the adoption of a variety of research strategies including the use of neural analogue and intact invertebrate model systems (see Chapters 7 and 8, this volume). The rationale for the use of these relatively "simple" systems is well justified, and the importance of the results arising from their use cannot be over-emphasized. However, whether the neural substrates of learning and memory in such "simple" systems are similar or identical to the analogous neural substrates in the more complex vertebrate, and in particular the human nervous system, is a matter for speculation that has led to considerable research in the vertebrate.

The analysis of the neural substrates of learning and memory in a brain as complex as that of the vertebrate is, obviously, a formidable task. Nevertheless, the recent adoption of well-characterized, vertebrate behavioral model systems in this analysis has yielded important new insights into the neural substrates of learning and memory, insights which may generalize to the human. In this chapter we review selected examples of the current research efforts of neuroscientists using vertebrate behavioral model systems to investigate the neural substrates of associative learning and memory in the intact, behaving animal. Our discussion focuses on the aforementioned goals, and emphasizes correlational analyses; that is, the measurement of changes in neural events which accompany the acquisition of a conditioned response. Where appropriate, investigations of the effects of various manipulations of the brain on the acquisition of conditioned responding will also be discussed. Finally, our chapter is concerned not only with a review of research results, but also with specific conceptual and problematic issues which are inherent in the analysis of the neural substrates of learning and memory using a model systems approach in the vertebrate. We begin with a discussion of the general characteristics of an appropriate behavioral model system with which to study the neural substrates of learning and memory in the vertebrate.

CHARACTERISTICS OF AN IDEAL
VERTEBRATE BEHAVIORAL MODEL SYSTEM

If we are to elucidate the neural substrates of learning and memory, then a necessary requirement is to fully understand exactly what is learned by the organism. Over the years, a wealth of information has been offered by animal learning theorists which has contributed to this understanding. Emerging from this research has been the use of a variety of experimental procedures which are believed to promote learning, but which differ in the manner by which environmental stimuli are presented to an animal (Rescorla & Holland, 1976). Three types of procedures have predominated and are considered to promote different forms of learning. The first involves the repeated presentation of a stimulus independent of the occurrence of the presentation of other stimuli or of the animal's behavior. This procedure results in either habituation, sensitization, or imprinting—phenomena generally regarded as nonassociative forms of learning. The second procedure involves the presentation of one stimulus which is dependent in time upon the presentation of a second stimulus. This produces Pavlovian or classical conditioning. In the third procedure, the presentation of a stimulus is contingent upon a behavioral response emitted by the organism and the result is operant or instrumental conditioning. Both Pavlovian and instrumental conditioning are considered to be associative forms of learning.

While scientists investigating the neural substrates of vertebrate learning and memory have adopted specific behavioral paradigms which promote each of the above forms of learning, a number of recent research efforts have focused on the use of Pavlovian conditioning procedures. The emphasis on Pavlovian conditioning is for a variety of reasons. First, Pavlovian conditioning represents perhaps the simplest form of associative learning, and a large amount of parametric data exist concerning the stimulus characteristics and procedural details which promote it (Black & Prokasy, 1972). Hence, behavioral scientists have made significant strides in the comprehension of exactly what is learned during Pavlovian conditioning. It is now generally accepted that an animal learns that one stimulus, the conditioned stimulus (CS), provides information about and therefore predicts the imminent occurrence of a second stimulus, the unconditioned stimulus (US) (Rescorla & Wagner, 1972). This associative information is stored such that, upon the subsequent presentation of the CS, an appropriate, adaptive conditioned response (CR) will be emitted for the purpose of enhancing the animal's survival. The probability of the occurrence of this response obviously reflects the extent to which learning has taken place. Second, several Pavlovian conditioned response systems have been extensively investigated, and a large amount of data exist concerning their characteristics under a variety of experimental conditions (Cohen & Goff, 1978; Gormezano, Kehoe, & Marshall, 1983; Schneiderman, 1972). Third, procedures which promote instrumental conditioning typically incorporate procedures for habituation and Pavlovian conditioning. Hence, instrumental conditioning procedures are sufficiently complex such that attempts to determine the exact behavioral source of any observed neural changes are difficult, and thus more simple Pavlovian conditioning procedures have been preferred.

A variety of vertebrate behavioral model conditioned response systems have been used as preparations for analyses of the neural substrates of learning and memory in the intact, behaving animal. The reasons for the choice of each of these response systems are varied, but most investigators would agree that their choice is dictated by several important characteristics, many of which have been previously described (Cohen, 1974; Thompson, 1976). Some of the most important of these are as follows:

1. *The conditioned response should be precisely measurable and quantifiable.* Since we infer learning from a change in the probability of the occurrence of a response as a function of experience, we must be capable of recognizing this change when it occurs. Furthermore, accurate measurement and quantification of the CR (e.g., latency and amplitude) can prove to be an important component in one's analysis. For example, the observation that a neural change grows in amplitude over conditioning trials at the same rate that the behavioral CR increases in amplitude can offer important insights into the significance of the neural change. Without quantification of the behavioral response, the power of the analysis is reduced.

2. *The conditioned response should be well characterized under a variety of stimulus conditions.* It is now well established that variations in stimulus parameters (i.e., intensity, duration, interstimulus interval) alter the rate of acquisition, frequency of occurrence and/or amplitude of the CR. A conditioned response system in which the effects of varying these parameters are known becomes a powerful tool in studies on the neural substrates of learning. If, for example, variations in these parameters result in variations in CR characteristics which covary with neural changes, then such neural changes may well represent fundamental mechanisms which contribute to, or for that matter represent, the neural substrates of information storage.

3. *The conditioned response should be associative in nature and clearly distinguishable from nonassociative forms of learning.* If one's goal is to investigate the neural substrates of Pavlovian associative learning, then it is essential that the procedures used result in this form of learning relatively uncontaminated by such nonassociative phenomena as pseudoconditioning[1] or sensitization[2]. While the neural mecha-

---

[1] The occurrence of a response to a previously neutral stimulus due to random, unpaired presentations of the CS and US.

[2] The increase in a previously habituated response to a CS following presentation of the US.

nisms underlying the occurrence of such nonassociative phenomena are of interest in their own right, their presence during the presumed investigation of associative learning can lead to difficulties of interpretation; any neural changes which emerge over the course of a conditioning procedure could well reflect these nonassociative phenomena rather than associative learning processes. Considerable research has therefore focused on the refinement of control procedures that demonstrate the extent to which a Pavlovian CR is clearly dissociable from nonassociative phenomena (Rescorla, 1967).

4. *The conditioned response should emerge relatively rapidly and should endure.* It is advantageous that the CR emerge relatively rapidly in order to be compatible with neurophysiological recording techniques. Since the use of these techniques is presently limited by the duration of time that electrical activity can be recorded from neurons, a CR which develops within a reasonable number of conditioning trials is desirable, particularly if changes in neural activity are to be assessed during the development of the behavioral CR. It is also advantageous that the CR be retained over time, such that the effects of specific manipulations on the retention of the CR can be tested.

5. *The efferent motor pathway(s) responsible for the expression of the conditioned response should be known or at least amenable to analysis.* From an identification and localization of those motoneurons responsible for the expression of the CR, additional experiments can be performed to determine the structures which project upon these neurons. Hence, important information concerning the critical central circuitry which contributes to the acquisition of the CR, and which may, in fact, contain the cellular substrates of learning, becomes available.

These characteristics are of major importance for an optimal analysis of a behavioral conditioned response system and hence for investigating the neural substrates of learning and memory. It should be emphasized that other characteristics may be desirable, their importance being dependent upon the response system employed, the specific research question to be answered, and the techniques used to address that question.

Vertebrate model response systems used most extensively are listed in Table 9.1, and as previously mentioned, the majority are Pavlovian conditioned responses. Weinberger (1982) has conveniently categorized Pavlovian conditioned responses into two general categories, specific and nonspecific, based on several distinguishing characteristics. *Specific* responses generally include somatic motor responses (e.g., nic-

TABLE 9.1

Vertebrate Model Response Systems Used in the Neural Analysis of Learning and Memory

Response system	Species	Conditioning procedure	Investigators
Nictitating membrane extension	Rabbit	Pavlovian	Thompson et al. (1982) Moore et al. (1982) Berger et al. (1980) Disterhoft et al. (1982) Solomon et al. (1983) Albiniak & Powell (1980)
Limb flexion	Cat	Pavlovian	Patterson et al. (1982) Tsukahara et al. (1981)
Eyelid closure	Cat	Pavlovian	Woody et al. (1982b)
Pupillary dilation	Cat	Pavlovian	Weinberger (1982)
Heart rate	Pigeon	Pavlovian	Cohen (1982)
	Rabbit	Pavlovian	Schneiderman et al. (1974) Powell & Buchanan (1980) Kapp et al. (1982)
Locomotor avoidance	Rabbit	Instrumental	Gabriel et al. (1982)
Head and body orientation	Rat	Pavlovian/ instrumental	Olds et al. (1972)

titating membrane extension, eyelid closure, limb flexion) and are so named because of their specificity to the nature of the US; for example, limb flexion to shock applied to the paw, or eyelid closure to a puff of air applied to the cornea. The acquisition of these specific conditioned responses generally require substantially more conditioning trials than the number necessary for the acquisition of nonspecific conditioned responses. These nonspecific responses include autonomic (e.g., heart rate, pupillary dilation) and diffuse somatic responses (e.g., behavioral immobility or freezing). Furthermore, they are not specific to the nature of the US since they can be elicited by nearly all stimuli, particularly those considered to be aversive. Finally, nonspecific conditioned responses are considered to be a manifestation of a conditioned change in the central activity state of the organism, most frequently described as heightened arousal or, in situations utilizing an aversive US, fear. We shall return to a discussion of the interaction of specific and nonspecific response systems and its implications at the end of our review.

ANALYSIS OF THE NEURAL CIRCUITRY MEDIATING THE ACQUISITION OF NONSPECIFIC MODEL RESPONSE SYSTEMS

Beyond the consideration that a suitable model response system is an important component in the analysis of the physiological substrates of vertebrate learning and memory, an important question to be addressed concerns the various research strategies that may be adopted for the analysis of that model system. The most commonly followed strategy has been to initially localize and identify the brain areas and neuroanatomical pathways that participate in the development of the learned response in question. The identification of the critical circuitry involved will provide us with the opportunity to further investigate components of this circuitry to determine the nature of synaptic and intracellular changes that occur over the course of conditioning, and the degree to which the development of such changes correlates in time with the development of the learned response. Research incorporating this strategy is being conducted by Cohen and his colleagues who are analyzing the neural substrates of Pavlovian conditioned heart rate responding in the pigeon, a nonspecific model response system (Cohen, 1974, 1980, 1982). Cohen's analytic strategy places particular emphasis upon the identification of the sensory, motor, and central neuroanatomical circuitry that conveys information that is necessary for the development of the conditioned response. His strategy is based on the assumption that a systematic analysis of the flow of information, from sensory input to behavioral response output, should eventually reveal sites of afferent and efferent convergence where conditioning-induced neural modifications occur.

CONDITIONED HEART RATE RESPONDING IN THE PIGEON

The Model Response System

Cohen's model response is the pigeon conditioned accelerative heart rate response, which emerges to a CS during a typical Pavlovian aversive conditioning procedure (Cohen & Goff, 1978). Conditioning trials consist of a 6-second light CS, the offset of which is accompanied by a 0.5-second footshock US. The unconditioned response (UR) to the US is also a cardio-acceleration. Over the course of the first 10 conditioning trials a conditioned cardioacceleration to the CS begins to emerge, which asymtotes following approximately 30 conditioning trials (Fig. 9.1). The use of control groups receiving either presentations of the CS alone or unpaired presentations of the CS and US (pseudoconditioning

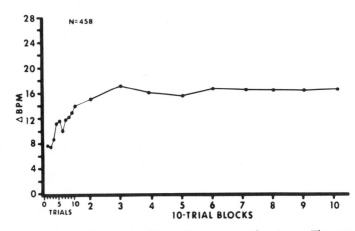

FIGURE 9.1   Acquisition of conditioned heart rate in the pigeon. The curve represents mean heart rate changes in beats per min (BPM) between the 6-s CS and an immediately preceding 6-s control period. Each point represents a group mean for a block of 10
CS–US training trials, with the exception of the first block for which individual trial
means are shown. (Reprinted with permission from Cohen, 1982.)

controls) demonstrated that nonassociative, cardioaccelerative orienting and sensitization responses are small, habituate within the first 10
trials, and do not contribute significantly to the dynamics of the CR.
Furthermore, the CR is a primary response produced by the neural
innervation of the heart and is not secondary to other conditioned
responses (e.g., respiratory, somatic, or hormonal CRs).

Efferent Control of the Conditioned Response

Recall from our discussion in the section entitled "Characteristics of
an Ideal Vertebrate Behavioral Model System" that one important characteristic of a model response system is its suitability for analysis of the
final pathway motoneurons responsible for the expression of the CR.
The conditioned heart rate response in the pigeon meets this requirement. Based upon cardiac denervation and pharmacological blockade
experiments, it has been determined that the motoneurons responsible
for the expression of both the CR and UR are components of the sympathetic, and to a lesser extent, the parasympathetic branches of the autonomic nervous system (Cohen & Pitts, 1968; MacDonald & Cohen, 1970;
Cohen & Schnall, 1970). The postganglionic sympathetic component of
the final pathway is located in the right sympathetic cardiac nerve, the
motoneurons of which originate in a restricted area of the sympathetic
ganglia. The preganglionic sympathetic motoneurons, which project

upon these postganglionic motoneurons, have been traced to the column of Terni in the spinal cord. Electrophysiological recordings from the sympathetic postganglionic cardiomotor neurons revealed a brief, excitatory, phasic discharge to the initial presentation of the CS to a naive animal with a latency of 100 ms following CS onset (Cohen, 1980). Repeated presentations of the CS alone resulted in habituation of this neural response. However, the effect of the presentation of paired CS–US conditioning trials was to sustain and increase the magnitude of this discharge to the CS, thereby contributing to the expression of the conditioned accelerative heart rate response (Fig. 9.2).

The preganglionic parasympathetic component of the final motor pathway is comprised of vagus nerve cardiac neurons, which originate in the dorsal motor nucleus of the vagus nerve situated in the dorsal medulla. These neurons also responded to the initial presentation of the CS with a latency of 100 ms. This response, however, was an inhibition of spontaneous activity, thereby decreasing vagal inhibitory tone on the heart. The effect of the repeated presentation of CS–US conditioning trials was to increase the magnitude and decrease the latency of this initial inhibitory response to 60–80 ms following CS onset. In summary, the final motor pathways for the expression of the CR have been found to be composed of both sympathetic and parasympathetic cardiac neurons. Both components demonstrate training-induced modifications in neural activity in a complimentary manner, leading to a net increase in heart rate to the CS.

Sensory Pathways Conveying CS Information

In keeping with the strategy of identifying the critical circuitry which participates in the development of the learned response, Cohen has also analyzed the afferent pathways which transmit visual CS information (Cohen, 1974, 1984). Starting at the periphery, it was demonstrated that bilateral retinal enucleation rendered pigeons incapable of acquiring the CR, as did combined lesions of the visual Wulst and ecto-striatum, two avian visual telencephalic areas homologous to the mammalian striate and extrastriate visual cortical regions (Fig. 9.3). Additional anatomical, electrophysiological and lesion experiments designed to analyze the critical pathways conveying necessary CS information from the retina to the telencephalon revealed that such information may reach the telencephalic visual areas via three separate pathways (Cohen, 1974). Only combined lesions within all three pathways were found to produce severe deficits in conditioned responding comparable to those observed following combined lesions of the two

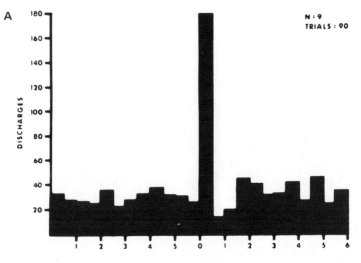

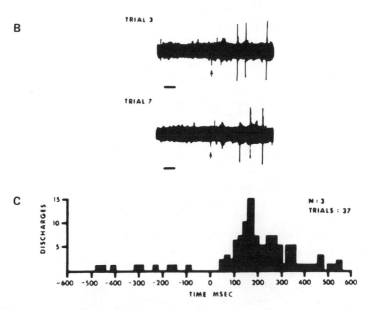

FIGURE 9.2   Discharge of cardiac sympathetic postganglionic neurons during the conditioned heart rate response in the pigeon. Panel A shows a summary peristimulus time histogram of the responses of 9 cardiac postganglionic neurons to 10 CS presentations. Time 0 indicates onset of the 6-s CS; bin width is 500 ms bin. Panel B shows representative responses of one of these neurons on 2 of the 10 CS presentations. The arrows indicate CS onset and the calibration bar represents 50 ms. Panel C shows a peristimulus time histogram of the discharges of three neurons for the 600 ms immediately before and after CS onset. (Reprinted with permission from Cohen, 1980.)

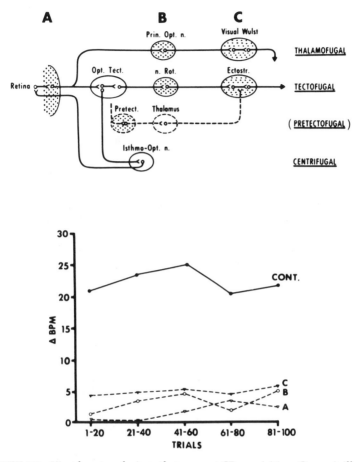

FIGURE 9.3 Visual system lesions that prevent CR acquisition. Curve A illustrates the performance of animals with bilateral enucleation (A in upper panel). Curve B illustrates the performance of animals with a combined lesion of the principal optic nucleus, nucleus rotundus and the pretectal terminal field of the optic tract (B in upper panel). Curve C illustrates the performance of animals with a combined lesion of the visual Wulst and ectostriatum (C in upper panel). For all curves each point represents the mean heart rate change in beats per min (BPM) between the 6-s CS and an immediately preceding 6-s control period. (Reprinted with permission from Cohen, 1982.)

visual telencephalic areas (Fig. 9.3). Hence, it would appear that each of these three ascending visual pathways may convey necessary CS information in a parallel fashion.

With the identification of the afferent sensory and efferent motor pathways critical for the development of the CR, a major question arises. Given that conditioning-induced modifications have been recorded in the activity of the motoneurons, where within the critical circuitry do these modifications initially appear? Are they induced at the level of the motoneurons or are they formed more rostrally along the circuitry, in either sensory or more centrally located structures, and simply relayed to the appropriate cardiac motoneurons? In an analysis designed to address this question, Cohen adopted the use of electro-physiological technqiues to search for alterations in neural activity along the pathway during conditioning. In an investigation of the visual CS pathway, it was found that the neural response of retinal ganglion cells to the CS during conditioning remained invariant with a latency of 18 ms and demonstrated no modifications during the development of the conditioned response. Additional analyses, however, demonstrated that training-induced modifications in the neural response to the CS occurred within at least two of the visual pathways (Cohen, 1984). For example, many retinorecipient neurons of the principal optic nucleus (PON), the avian homologue of the mammalian dorsal lateral geniculate nucleus, show an excitatory, phasic response to the presentation of the CS prior to training. The repeated presentation of paired CS–US conditioning trials resulted in an enhancement of this response whereas repeated CS presentations alone, or unpaired presentations of the CS and US, resulted in habituation of the neural response. Several important features of these training-induced modifications are noteworthy. First, they emerged in parallel with the emergence of the CR—that is, during the first ten conditioning trials, suggesting that they may indeed contribute to the development of the learned heart rate response. Second, the onset latencies of these modified neural responses to the CS were short, suggesting that the observed modifications were not relayed to the nucleus by feedback from more centrally located structures. Third, and perhaps most intriguing, those PON neurons showing training-induced modifications to the CS were initially responsive, not only to the light CS, but also to the footshock US. Furthermore, PON neurons which showed a decreased discharge to the US demonstrated such modification, whereas those which were unresponsive or which showed an increased discharge in response to the US did not (Cohen, 1984). Hence, convergence of CS and US evoked responses, as well as the type of US evoked response, were predictive of the emergence of a conditioned neuronal response to the CS over conditioning trials.

Several more recent findings indicate that the US input to PON neurons originates within the locus coeruleus (LC) and subcoeruleus (SC) (Gibbs, Broyles, & Cohen, 1983; Cohen, 1984). First, stimulation of the LC and SC affects the firing rates of PON neurons in a manner similar to that observed in response to the footshock US. Second, LC and SC cells respond with an increased discharge to footshock. Third, lesions of the

LC eliminate the US-evoked decrease in discharge of PON neurons. Fourth, the LC and SC send direct projections to the PON. Finally, using standard Pavlovian conditioning procedures, presentation of a light CS paired with electrical stimulation of the LC as a US resulted in a rapid training-induced modification of those PON neurons which demonstrated a decreased discharge to stimulation of the LC. This finding is strikingly similar to that observed using footshock as the US. Hence, LC stimulation-induced activation of PON neurons is a sufficient condition for training-induced modification of PON neurons in response to CS presentation. These results suggest that the CS pathway and US pathway may converge at the first visual relay, a convergence which may underlie training-induced plasticity of neuronal responses within the critical learning circuit.

The finding that training-induced modifications of neural activity occur in sensory pathways is not restricted to the avian heart rate conditioned response system. Indeed, Weinberger and his associates (Oleson, Ashe, & Weinberger, 1975; Ryugo & Weinberger, 1978; Weinberger, 1982) demonstrated similar changes in the auditory system of the cat during aversive Pavlovian conditioning of pupillary dilation, a nonspecific response, using an auditory CS and a pawshock US. Their analysis revealed that while no systematic training-induced changes in neuronal activity occurred at the level of the cochlea (as measured by the cochlear microphonic), such changes were present in the cochlear nucleus, medial geniculate, and auditory cortex. Furthermore, in a detailed analysis of the response properties of neurons of the magnocellular division of the medial geniculate nucleus, Weinberger (1982) found that many neurons which demonstrated training-induced modifications to the CS were initially responsive to the CS, but then showed habituation during unpaired presentations of the CS and US prior to the presentation of paired CS–US conditioning trials. The effect of the presentation of paired conditioning trials was to increase the response to the CS. This increase emerged within the first ten conditioning trials and paralleled the emergence of the conditioned pupillary response. Thus, the results of Cohen and Weinberger are similar in many respects and point to the generality of training-induced modifications in sensory system neurons during the conditioning of nonspecific responses.

Central Circuitry Contributing to Response Acquisition

What is the significance of these training-induced changes in sensory pathway neuronal responses within the context of the overall circuitry mediating the CR? Are these changes, for example, initially established in the sensory pathways and subsequently relayed to more centrally located structures over the course of conditioning? The answer to this question depends, at least in part, upon a delineation and analysis of the central circuitry which is located between the afferent sensory and efferent motor pathways, and which contributes to the development of the CR. Cohen has attempted to identify some of this central circuitry (Cohen, 1974, 1975, 1980). The initial strategy involved the use of electrical stimulation to extensively map the pigeon central nervous system to identify brain regions capable of influencing heart rate and blood pressure, regions which might be involved in the mediation of the CR. Several areas identified in this manner were then lesioned in order to evaluate the effects of such lesions on the acquisition of the CR. In some areas, such as the septum, marked cardiovascular effects were elicited by stimulation, and yet lesions of these areas had no effect on the development of the CR. In contrast, striking alterations in heart rate were observed following stimulation of a continuous region extending from the posteromedial archistriatum (the avian amygdaloid homologue), through the medial hypothalamus (upon which the archistriatum projects) and descending through the ventromedial mesencephalon, the pons, and medulla (Fig. 9.4). Lesions along the course of these continuous brain regions, including those of the posteromedial archistriatum, the medial hypothalamus and ventromedial mesencephalon, resulted in severe conditioning deficits. These data, then, provide an initial analysis of the components of some of the central circuitry which might contribute to the mediation of the CR. It will be of interest to determine if training-induced modifications in neural activity occur in these more central regions, and the extent to which such changes develop with a similar time-course and latency as those occurring in the sensory pathways. Such data will be pertinent to the question of whether training-induced changes develop in series or parallel within the various components of the critical circuitry.

CONDITIONED HEART RATE RESPONDING IN THE RABBIT:
CONTRIBUTIONS OF THE AMYGDALA

The work of Cohen and his associates implicated the contribution of several centrally-located structures in the development of the CR, including the posteromediale archistriatum, the avian homologue of the mammalian amygdala. Our own recent work has been concerned with the contributions of the mammalian amygdala to learning and memory processes. Our analysis reflects a somewhat different strategy from that of Cohen in that our efforts have been devoted primarily to a thorough

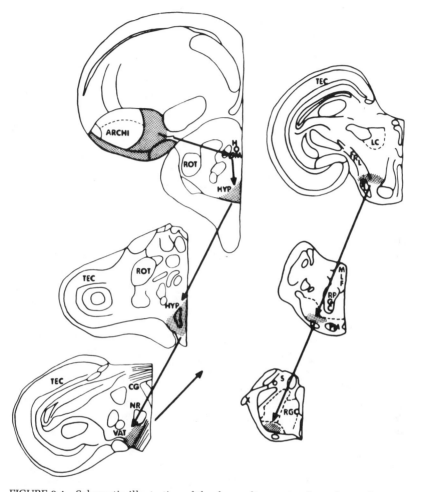

FIGURE 9.4   Schematic illustration of the descending system hypothesized to mediate expression of the conditioned heart rate response in the pigeon. This system is shown on schematic sections by the stippled areas joined across successively caudal sections by arrows. Relevant abbreviations: ARCHI = archistriatum; CG = central gray; HOM = tractus occipitomesencephalicus, pars hypothalami; HYP = hypothalamus; LC = locus coeruleus; NR = red nucleus; VAT = ventral area of Tsai; X = vagal rootlets. (Reprinted with permission from Cohen, 1974.)

analysis of one central structure long implicated in learning and memory processes (Ben–Ari, 1981). The complexity of the mammalian amygdala, a heterogeneous structure composed of a variety of nuclei, each processing its own unique afferent and efferent projection systems, dictated that a thorough investigation of the exact amygdaloid circuitry contributing to the acquisition of the conditioned response be undertaken. Such an analysis is a necessary prerequisite not only for determining the role of the amygdala in learning and memory, but also for the identification of a more extensive central circuit involved in these processes.

For our analysis we chose the conditioned heart rate response in the rabbit during Pavlovian fear conditioning as a model response. Our choice was guided by several factors. First, the parameters of this rapidly conditioned, cardiodecelerative (bradycardia) response are well defined in the rabbit (Fredericks, Moore, Metcalf, Schwaber, & Schneiderman, 1974; Powell & Kazis, 1976; Schneiderman, 1972). Second, the final pathway for the expression of the CR is primarily via the vagus nerves (Fredericks et al., 1974) and the cell bodies of preganglionic cardioinhibitory neurons are known to lie within the nucleus ambiguus and dorsal motor nucleus of the vagus nerve in this species (Jordan, Khalid, Schneiderman, & Spyer, 1982; Schwaber & Schneiderman, 1975). Third, electrical stimulation of the mammalian amygdala, as well as its avian homologue, produces cardiovascular alterations (Hilton & Zbrozyna, 1963). These findings, taken together with the observations of Cohen (1975) that lesions of the avian amygdaloid homologue produced profound deficits in heart rate conditioning, suggested that the heart rate CR would be an appropriate model response system for an analysis of the contributions of the mammalian amygdala to the acquisition of conditioned responding.

Of the various amygdaloid nuclei, we began the analysis by focusing on the amygdaloid central nucleus for several reasons which have been detailed elsewhere (Kapp, Gallagher, Applegate, & Frysinger, 1982). Initially, we sought to determine the effects of various manipulations of the central nucleus on the acquisition of the bradycardia CR using a standard Pavlovian aversive conditioning procedure in which the offset of a 5-s tone CS was coincident with the onset of a 0.5-s shock US. In our first experiment (Kapp, Frysinger, Gallagher, & Haselton, 1979) both large and small lesions of the central nucleus significantly attenuated the magnitude of the CR to the CS (see Fig. 9.5). No significant effects were observed on pre-CS baseline heart rate, nor on the heart rate orienting response to a novel tone stimulus, nor could the results be explained as a lesion-induced attenuation of the unconditioned response to the US. The possibility existed, however, that the effects were a function of lesion-induced damage to fibers passing through and near the central nucleus rather than to the central nucleus per se. This limitation of the interpretation of the lesion technique can be addressed by using specific receptor agonists and antagonists applied to the region of

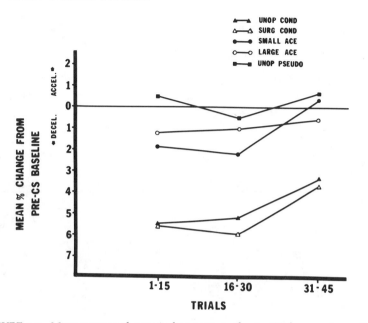

FIGURE 9.5   Mean percent change in heart rate to the 5-s CS from an immediately preceding 5-s baseline period for groups (n's = 8) receiving 45 conditioning trials. Abbreviations: Unop Cond, Surg Cond = Unoperated and surgical control groups receiving 45 paired conditioning trials. Small ACE, Large ACE = groups with small (<50% damage) and large (>50% damage) lesions of the central nucleus and receiving 45 paired conditioning trials; Unop Pseudo = unoperated control group receiving 45 unpaired presentations of both the CS and US. Data points represent group means for 15 trial blocks. (Reprinted with permission from Kapp et al., 1982.)

the central nucleus. These agents exert their effects on synaptic functioning and not on conduction along the axon. Hence, any effects observed following their application to the region of the central nucleus should reflect an interference with synaptic transmission within the nucleus rather than with conduction in fibers passing through the nucleus. Therefore, in additional experiments receptor agonists and antagonists of the β-adrenergic and opioid systems, systems richly concentrated within the central nucleus, were injected into the central nucleus immediately prior to conditioning, and the effects on the acquisition of the CR were assessed (Gallagher, Kapp, Frysinger, & Rapp, 1980; Gallagher, Kapp, McNall, & Pascoe, 1981). Such injections produced either decreases or increases in the magnitude of the CR when compared to vehicle-injected and unoperated control groups, depending upon the agent administered. These results support the interpreta-

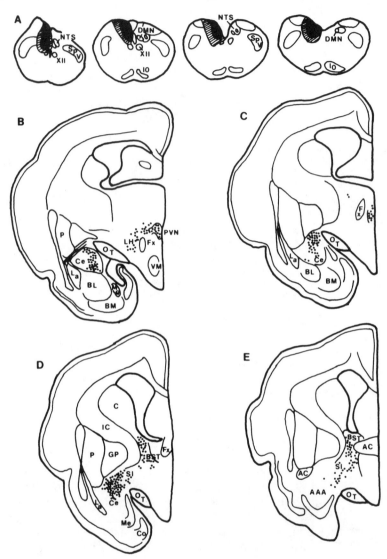

FIGURE 9.6   Labeled neurons in the amygdaloid central nucleus from a representative case in which four injections of horseradish peroxidase (HRP) were made at different
levels along the rostral–caudal extent of the nucleus of the solitary tract and dorsal motor
nucleus of the vagus (A). Each dot represents one retrogradely labeled neuron from that
section alone. B–E, caudal–rostral levels through the amygdaloid complex. Abbreviations: AAA = anterior amygdaloid area; AC = anterior commissure; BL = amygdaloid
basolateral nucleus; BM = amygdaloid basomedial nucleus; BST = bed nucleus of the

tion that damage to the central nucleus per se, rather than to fibers of passage, contributed to the effects observed in our lesion study. The results of these initial experiments were similar to those reported by Cohen (1975) in the pigeon, and although they were indicative of a central nucleus contribution to the acquisition of the CR, the specific nature of this contribution remained unknown. An important anatomical finding, however, yielded an insight. A direct anatomical projection was found to exist in the cat extending from the region of the central nucleus to autonomic regulatory nuclei in the dorsal medulla; the nucleus of the solitary tract and the vagal dorsal motor nucleus (Hopkins & Holstege, 1978). Since the bradycardia CR in rabbit is primarily under vagal control, and since preganglionic cardioinhibitory neurons that serve as the origin of the final pathway for the expression of the CR are located within the vagal dorsal motor nucleus and nucleus ambiguus in the rabbit, we sought to determine if such a projection existed in the rabbit. Using retrograde and anterograde axonal transport techniques we found that the central nucleus projected directly to the vagal dorsal motor nucleus, the nucleus ambiguus and the nucleus of the solitary tract (Schwaber, Kapp, & Higgins, 1980; Schwaber, Kapp, Higgins, & Rapp, 1982) (see Fig. 9.6). A similar projection has also recently been demonstrated in the primate (Price & Amaral, 1981).

Our anatomical findings suggested that the central nucleus possessed the potential to exert a rather direct influence on the autonomic nervous system and particularly upon cardioinhibitory neurons which may mediate the expression of the bradycardia CR. On the basis of these observations, taken together with our findings that manipulations of the central nucleus affected the magnitude of the conditioned response, we proposed the working hypothesis that the central nucleus may function, at least in part, in the motoric expression of the CR (and perhaps other nonspecific autonomic and somatomotor responses) to the CS (Kapp, Gallagher, Frysinger, & Applegate, 1981). This function could be mediated by either a direct or indirect (e.g., via the nucleus of the solitary tract) excitation of vagal cardioinhibitory neurons in the vagal dorsal motor nucleus and/or nucleus ambiguus.

Consistent with this hypothesis are the results of additional experiments. First, electrical stimulation of the central nucleus in both anes-

---

stria terminalis; C = caudate nucleus; Ce = amygdaloid central nucleus; Co = amygdaloid cortical nucleus; DMN = dorsal motor nucleus of the vagus; La = amygdaloid lateral nucleus; NTS = nucleus of the solitary tract; OT = optic tract; P = putamen; SI = substantia innominata.

thetized and awake rabbits produced short-latency vagally mediated bradycardia accompanied by decreases in arterial blood pressure and alterations in respiration, most frequently an increased frequency and decreased depth (Kapp, Gallagher, Underwood, McNall, & Whitehorn, 1982; Applegate, Kapp, Underwood, & McNall, 1983). Of significance was the finding that these responses were of the same pattern as those observed in response to the CS during aversive Pavlovian conditioning (Powell & Kazis, 1976; Yehle, Dauth, & Schneiderman, 1967). Furthermore, the stimulation-induced bradycardia may result from excitation of central nucleus descending projection neurons which may directly, or indirectly (via the activation of neurons within the nucleus of the solitary tract), activate vagal preganglionic cardioinhibitory neurons of the vagal dorsal motor nucleus. Second, in a recent experiment in which we recorded multiple unit neuronal activity from the central nucleus in the rabbit during Pavlovian fear conditioning (Applegate, Frysinger, Kapp, & Gallagher, 1982), a significant increase in short-latency multiple unit activity developed to the CS during the course of conditioning in a number of cases (see Figs. 9.7, 9.8). This increased activity emerged at the time when the bradycardia CR emerged to the CS, and in some instances the magnitude of the increase in neuronal activity to the CS was significantly correlated with the magnitude of the bradycardia CR to the CS over the course of the conditioning session. However, only approximately one-third of the placements within the central nucleus demonstrated significant short-latency increases in multiple unit activity which emerged to the CS during conditioning. Hence, not all central nucleus neuronal elements responded in a unitary fashion during the conditioning procedure, a finding which may indicate a heterogeneity of function for this nucleus. Nevertheless, the emergence of short-latency increases in neuronal activity to the CS and the fact that the magnitude of the neuronal response in some cases correlated significantly with the magnitude of the bradycardia CR to the CS is consistent with the hypothesis that the central nucleus functions in the motoric expression of the CR to the CS. Whether such neuronal activity reflects the activity of central nucleus projection neurons to cardioregulatory nuclei of the dorsal medulla, however, has yet to be determined. Such an analysis is now a focus of our ongoing research, the results of which should yield further evidence concerning the validity of our hypothesis.

In summary, our analysis to date offers insight into the critical central circuitry which may contribute to the acquisition of conditioned bradycardia (and perhaps other nonspecific responses), and which lies

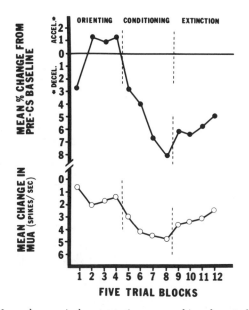

FIGURE 9.7   Mean changes in heart rate (upper graph) and central nucleus multiple unit activity (MUA) (lower graph) to the CS during orienting (20 CS-alone trials), conditioning (20 paired CS–US conditioning trials) and extinction (20 CS-alone trials) components of a conditioning session for a single animal. Each data point represents the mean for a block of five trials. Note the increase in multiple unit activity which parallels the emergence of the conditioned bradycardia response during the conditioning and extinction components of the session. (Adapted with permission from Applegate et al., 1982.)

in proximity to final pathway motoneurons responsible for the expression of the CR. It must be emphasized, however, that extending our analysis to the delineation of the entire central forebrain circuitry critical for the acquisition of the CR, particularly those loci lying more distant from final pathway motoneurons, will be a difficult undertaking. For example, a further identification of this circuitry would initially involve a detailed neuroanatomical analysis of the regions anatomically connected with the central nucleus. We are presently engaged in such an analysis and our own emerging observations, as well as those of others, indicate that the central nuclues possesses a complex afferent and efferent projection system (Fig. 9.9). Hence, considerable effort will be necessary to define the critical interactions and components of this system necessary for the acquisition of the CR. The difficulty of this task is perhaps as expected, given the complexities of the vertebrate brain and the intracacies of the phenomenon of learning.

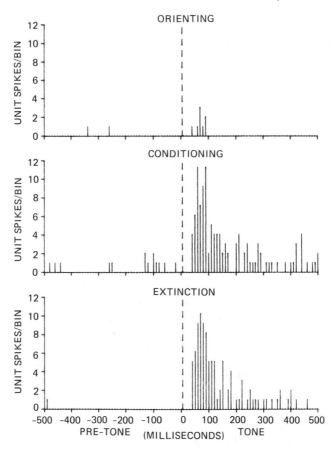

FIGURE 9.8   Peristimulus time histograms of multiple unit activity for the case de-picted in Figure 9.7. Shown are unit spikes/10-ms bin, summed across the 20 trials of the orienting, conditioning and extinction components of the session for the 500 ms preced-ing and the first 500 ms of the CS. Note the increase in activity that develops during the conditioning component of the session. (Reprinted by permission from Kapp et al., 1982.)

ANALYSIS OF THE NEURAL CIRCUITRY MEDIATING THE ACQUISITION OF SPECIFIC MODEL RESPONSE SYSTEMS

Thus far in our discussion we have concentrated upon research de-signed to define the circuitry which contributes to the acquisition of what have been classified by Weinberger (1982) as nonspecific condi-tioned responses. Recall from our earlier discussion that these nonspe-cific CRs may be considered to reflect the conditioning of an emotional

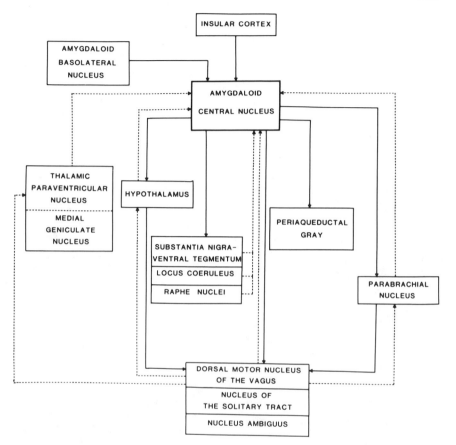

FIGURE 9.9   A schematic representation of some of the major afferent and efferent projections of the amygdaloid central nucleus based on observations in the rat and rabbit. For clarity, some suspected projection systems have been omitted. Dotted lines represent major ascending projections, either direct or indirect, to the central nucleus. Many of these indirect, ascending projections arise from cardioregulatory nuclei of the dorsal medulla and project to structures which in turn project to the central nucleus.

state, and in the case of aversive conditioning procedures, conditioned fear. In the context of traditional two-process learning theory (Mowrer, 1947), the conditioning of fear is a necessary condition for the subsequent acquisition of more specific adaptive responses. Recall that such specific responses are a function of the nature of the unconditioned stimulus and require more conditioning trials than are necessary for the conditioning of nonspecific responses. A number of investigators have adopted the use of specific model response systems in their analysis of the neural substrates of learning and memory. It is to a discussion of investigations incorporating one such extensively studied system, the conditioned nictitating membrane (NM) response system in the rabbit, that we now turn.

CONDITIONED NICTITATING MEMBRANE RESPONDING IN THE RABBIT

The Model Response System

Over the last twenty years the Pavlovian conditioned nictitating membrane response in the rabbit has been the focus of an extensive behavioral analysis (Gormezano et al., 1983). Hence, the behavioral parameters of this response system are particularly well characterized, and the system meets the requirements of a model behavioral response system as described previously (see Thompson, 1976). The CR is an extension of the nictitating membrane across the cornea in response to a CS paired with a noxious US such as an airpuff to the cornea or a brief electric shock to the eyelid. The UR is also an extension of the membrane to the US. The membrane extension occurs largely as a passive consequence to retraction of the eyeball and is but one component of a coordinated defensive response including eyeball retraction, eyelid closure, and contraction of the periorbital facial musculature (McCormick, Lavond, & Thompson, 1982). Eyeball retraction, and hence extension of the NM, is primarily a function of contraction of the retractor bulbi muscles. It is now generally agreed that the accessory abducens nucleus is the primary site of origin of final pathway motoneurons responsible for this contraction, although some motoneurons may lie within the abducens nucleus (Berthier & Moore, 1983; Disterhoft, Shipley & Kraus, 1982; Gray, McMaster, Harvey, & Gormezano, 1981).

The Critical Circuitry

In an extensive series of experiments Thompson, Berger, and colleagues have attempted to identify the brain structures which demonstrate associative neuronal changes to a tone CS over the course of NM conditioning and hence identify those which may be critical for the acquisition of the CR (Berger & Thompson, 1978a,b; Thompson, 1976; Thompson, Berger, Berry, Hoehler, Kettner, & Weisz, 1980; Thompson, McCormick, Lavond, Clark, Kettner, & Mauk, 1983; Thompson, Clark, Donegan, Lavond, Madden, Mamounas, Mauk, & McCormick, 1984). One aspect of this analysis concerned an investigation of the primary auditory relay nuclei which convey CS information, including the anteroventral cochlear nucleus, the central nucleus of the inferior colliculus and the ventral division of the medial geniculate body. Using an elegant signal detection analysis and multiple- and single-cell recording techniques, no evidence was found which suggested that training-induced changes in neuronal activity occurred in the CS sensory channel (Kettner & Thompson, 1982), leading to the conclusion that "the primary auditory relay nuclei from the cochlear nucleus through the medial geniculate body are not a part of the engram—the neuronal plasticity that codes learning and memory" (Thompson et al., 1983). Recall, however, that Cohen (1984) found training-induced neuronal modifications in the first visual relay nucleus during Pavlovian heart rate conditioning in the pigeon, and Weinberger and colleagues (Oleson et al., 1975) found similar training-induced changes in the anteroventral cochlear nucleus during Pavlovian pupillary conditioning to a tone CS in the cat. A variety of factors may contribute to these disparate results and the identification of these factors is deserving of further research.

The Hippocampus. While the research of Thompson and colleagues suggests that training-induced changes do not occur in primary sensory nuclei during Pavlovian conditioning of the NM response, such changes are found when one records from more centrally located structures. A dramatic example is the hippocampus, a structure long implicated in learning and memory processes (see Chapters 10 and 11, this volume). Multiple unit recording from the hippocampus during NM conditioning revealed a profound training-induced alteration in neuronal activity (Berger & Thompson, 1978a). As is apparent from Figure 9.10, during paired CS–US conditioning trials the neuronal activity within the hippocampal CA1 pyramidal cell layer rapidly develops an excitatory response which grows in amplitude over conditioning and which forms a temporal model of the amplitude and time course of the behavioral NM response. This neuronal response models the behavioral UR in response to the US early during conditioning (Fig. 9.10A), but over trials it emerges to the CS at the time when conditioned NM responses occur to the CS (Fig. 9.10B). The neuronal response precedes the NM response by some 40 ms and does not develop in control animals receiving unpaired presentations of the CS and US (Fig. 9.10C–F). Furthermore, not only does the neuronal response serve as a temporal model of the behavioral response during any one trial, it is also predictive of the occurrence of the CR over a variety of conditions. For example, procedural manipulations which produce no behavioral CRs, such as a decrease in the CS–US interstimulus interval, likewise produce no associative hippocampal neuronal response (Thompson et al., 1980).

PAIRED CONDITIONING

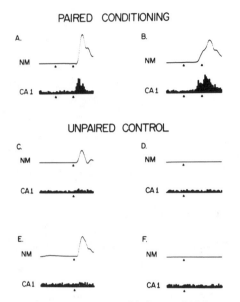

UNPAIRED CONTROL

FIGURE 9.10 Examples of 8-trial averaged behavioral NM responses and associated multiple-unit histograms of hippocampal CA1 activity for a conditioning (A, B) and a control (C–F) animal at the beginning and end of training. Note the very large increase in hippocampal unit activity that develops in the conditioning animal. Upper trace: Average nictitating membrane response for one block of eight trials. Lower trace: Hippocampal unit poststimulus histogram (15-ms time bins) for one block of eight trials. (A) First block of eight paired-conditioning trials, Day 1. (B) Last block of eight paired conditioning trials, Day 1, after conditioning has occurred. First cursor represents onset of the 350-ms tone CS, second cursor that of the 100-ms airpuff US. (C) First block of eight unpaired US-alone trials, Day 1. (D) First block of eight unpaired CS-alone trials, Day 1. (E) Last block of eight unpaired US-alone trials, Day 2. (F) Last block of eight unpaired CS-alone trials, Day 2. (Reprinted with permission from Thompson et al., 1980.)

Similarly, intraperitoneal injections of morphine, which abolish the occurrence of the behavioral CR in trained animals, also abolish the conditioned hippocampal neuronal response, while leaving the unconditioned behavioral and neuronal responses unaffected (Mauk, Warren, & Thompson, 1982) (Fig. 9.11). Thus, those conditions which affect the occurrence of the learned behavioral response also affect that of the learned neuronal response in a predictive manner.

The previous observations suggest that the hippocampus may play a rather direct role in simple Pavlovian associative learning. Such an interpretation is supported by the generality of the training-induced neuronal changes within the hippocampus; these changes occur to a light as well as to a tone CS, and emerge during Pavlovian conditioning

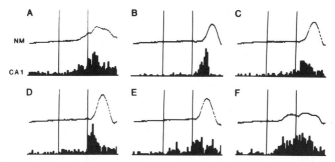

FIGURE 9.11   Examples of 8-trial averaged behavioral nictitating membrane (NM) responses (upper trace) and associated multiple unit histograms of hippocampal CA1 activity (lower trace, 12-ms time bins) for a single animal. The early vertical line indicates tone onset, and the later line, airpuff onset. (A) Block of eight trials immediately preceding the injection of morphine. Note the increase in hippocampal activity in the CS period, which is completely absent immediately after the systemic injection of morphine (B). The unit increase begins to redevelop in the later blocks (C–E). Both the behavioral and unit conditioned responses recover fully after an injection of naloxone (F). (Reprinted with permission from Mauk et al., 1982. Copyright 1982 with permission of the AAAS.)

of the cat as well as the rabbit NM response. Furthermore, they emerge during Pavlovian conditioning of a hindlimb flexor muscle using a hindlimb footshock US and appear to form a temporal model of the conditioned increase in hindlimb EMG activity (Thompson et al., 1980).

It was important to determine if neuronal changes in the hippocampus were initiated within the hippocampus, or were simply relayed to this structure from other areas which project upon the hippocampus. Experiments during which multiple unit recordings were obtained from the entorhinal cortex and medial septum, two regions from which the hippocampus receives most of its afferent innervation, directly addressed this question (Berger, Clark, & Thompson, 1980). Neuronal activity in the medial septum, while demonstrating stimulus-evoked increases to initial presentations of the CS and US, demonstrated no associative increases over training and the evoked activity habituated over repeated conditioning trials. Unit activity in the entorhinal cortex demonstrated training-induced increases early during conditioning in a manner similar to that recorded from the hippocampus. Unlike the hippocampal unit response, however, entorhinal neuronal activity did not grow in amplitude over the course of conditioning. These results suggested that while it is possible that the training-induced increase in unit activity may be projected to the hippocampus from the entorhinal cortex, the growth in amplitude of the hippocampal response over the course of conditioning develops within the hippocampus itself.

The observations by Thompson and his associates suggest an important contribution for the hippocampus in the acquisition of a simple Pavlovian conditioned response. But what is the nature of this contribution? Certainly, the fact that the neuronal response is a function of procedures which promote associative learning and that the neuronal response is predictive of the behavioral response suggest that the hippocampus may function in the formation and/or storage of the association necessary for the acquisition of the CR. If this were indeed one of the functions of the hippocampus, then it might be predicted that lesions of the hippocampus would produce deficits in the acquisition of the CR. This, however, appears not to be the case: Lesions of the hippocampus do not produce deficits in the acquisition of the conditioned NM response in a simple delay Pavlovian conditioning procedure in which the CS and US occur contiguously in time (Solomon & Moore, 1975). However, with the use of procedures which dictate a more rigorous analysis of the stimulus contingencies appropriate for optimal conditioned responding, lesions of the hippocampus produce severe deficits in the acquisition of the conditioned NM response (Berger & Orr, 1982; Solomon & Moore, 1975; Solomon, Vander Schaaf, Nobre, Weisz, & Thompson, 1983). For example, rabbits with lesions of the hippocampus which are subjected to a trace conditioning procedure in which the CS terminates 0.5 s prior to US onset are severely deficient in the acquisition of the conditioned NM response (Solomon et al., 1983). Such a procedure requires the animal to retain the memory of the CS during the interval between CS offset and US onset, and requires more conditioning trials for normal, nonlesioned animals to acquire the CR than for animals subjected to a delay conditioning procedure. Thus, while apparently not essential for the acquisition of the CR in a simple delay Pavlovian procedure, the hippocampus becomes necessary for optimal acquisition as the situation places increasing demands upon the organism. Exactly how the hippocampus is engaged, as well as its exact role in the acquisition of the CR during more complex procedures, is an area for further research.

The Cerebellum. Is there a brain circuit which is critical for the acquisition of the conditioned NM response in a simple delay Pavlovian conditioning procedure? While it has been observed that rabbits with most of the neocortex removed demonstrate relatively normal acquisition of the CR (Moore, Yeo, Oakley, & Steele–Russell, 1980; Oakley & Russell, 1975, 1977), recent experiments indicate that cere-

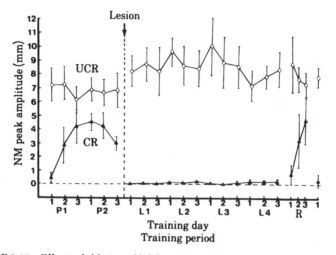

FIGURE 9.12   Effects of ablation of left lateral cerebellum on the learned NM response (six animals). ▲, Amplitude of conditioned response (CR); ◇, amplitude of unconditioned response (UCR). All training was to the left NM (ipsilateral to lesion), except where labeled *right NM* (R). The cerebellar lesion completely and permanently abolished the CR of the ipsilateral NM but had no effect on the UCR. P1 and P2, initial learning on the two days prior to the lesion; L1–L4, four days of postoperative training to the left NM; R, right NM training (rapid learning). After training the right NM, the left NM was again trained and it showed no learning. Left NM, 40-trial training periods; right NM, 24-trial training periods. (Reprinted with permission from McCormick et al., 1982).

bellar lesions produce total deficits in conditioned NM responding (McCormick, Clark, Lavond, & Thompson, 1982). Ablation of the lateral cerebellum ipsilateral to the trained NM completely and permanently abolished the CR in a previously trained rabbit, while producing no effect on the UR. When training was subsequently administered to the untrained NM contralateral to the lesion, the CR developed rapidly (Fig. 9.12). Subsequent analyses revealed that localized electrolytic lesions confined to the dentate and interpositus nuclei and surrounding fibers, as well as lesions of the superior cerebellar peduncle, the major efferent cerebellar pathway, produced similar effects (Clark, McCormick, Lavond, Baxter, Gray, & Thompson, 1982). Such effects have also been observed in the classical conditioning of the hind-limb flexion reflex demonstrating the generality of the contribution of the cerebellum to more than one CR system. Finally, bilateral ablations of the lateral cerebellum permanently abolish the previously acquired conditioned NM response and prevent its reacquisition (Thompson et al., 1983).

The effects of cerebellar lesions are consistent with multiple unit

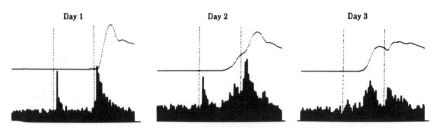

FIGURE 9.13   Unit histograms obtained from the medial dentate nucleus of the cerebellum of a rabbit during classical conditioning of the NM response. Each histogram bar
is 15-ms wide, and each histogram is summed over an entire day of training. The first
vertical line represents the onset of the tone and the second vertical line represents the
onset of the air puff. The trace above each histogram represents the averaged movement
of the animal's NM for an entire day. (Reprinted with permission from McCormick et al.,
1982.)

recording data from the cerebellar dentate and interpositus nuclei with
demonstrated training-induced changes in neuronal activity (McCormick et al., 1982; Thompson et al., 1983). The data from one such
recording are depicted in Figure 9.13. Both the CS and US produced
evoked responses, but unlike the hippocampal response, a temporal
model of the UR was not evident. With the emergence of the conditioned NM response to the CS over the course of conditioning, a temporal neuronal model of the CR emerged which preceded the CR in time
by about 50 ms. Hence, in contrast to the hippocampus, cerebellar unit
activity at some sites was restricted to a model of the CR and preceded
in time both the behavioral response and the hippocampal neuronal
response, suggesting that the hippocampal response may be dependent
upon the development of this cerebellar response. In support of this
notion, it was demonstrated that unilateral lesions of the dentate and
lateral interpositus nuclei abolish not only the ipsilateral conditioned
NM response to the CS, but also the ipsilateral hippocampal neuronal
response to the CS (Clark et al., 1982). In summary, the suggestion has
been offered that the memory trace necessary for the acquisition of the
conditioned NM response, and possibly of other simple adaptive somatomotor responses, may be localized to the cerebellum and its associated circuitry (Thompson et al., 1983).

More recent experiments have indicated that this circuitry may include the red nucleus, which is recipient of direct projections from the
dentate and interpositus nuclei, and which in turn sends direct projections to the accessory abducens nuclei, a site of origin of the motoneurons responsible for the CR (Desmond, Rosenfield, & Moore, 1983).
Lesions of the red nucleus following acquisition of the conditioned NM

response abolish the CR, while multiple unit activity recorded from this nucleus responds in a manner similar to that observed from the dentate and interpositus nuclei (Haley, Lavond, & Thompson, 1983; McCormick & Thompson, 1983). Whether the dentate and interpositus nuclei of the cerebellum are the essential sites of associative change or whether these nuclei and the red nucleus are part of the essential efferent circuitry for the expression of the conditioned response is the subject of current research. Such research should yield important insights into the entire circuitry critical to the acquisition of simple conditioned somatomotor responses and the manner by which this circuitry interacts with other structures, such as the hippocampus, during conditioning.

CONDITIONED EYEBLINK RESPONDING IN THE CAT:
CELLULAR CORRELATES

As is evident from the previous discussion, by utilizing vertebrate model systems considerable progress continues to be realized in defining the critical circuitry which contributes to learning and memory processes. It is apparent, however, that analyses using such model systems generally have not been extended to incorporate an analysis of exact cellular physiological mechanisms, such as alterations in synaptic efficacy or membrane structure, which may underlie the training-induced changes in neuronal activity during conditioning. An exception in this regard is exemplified by the research of Woody and colleagues who have extensively investigated Pavlovian conditioned eyeblink responding in the cat as a vertebrate model system (Woody, 1974; 1982b).

Woody's conditioning procedure incorporates the use of a click CS which is paired with a glabella (forehead) tap US. The glabella tap reliably elicits an unconditioned blink response, which is easily measured by recording EMG activity from the eye muscle that mediates the response (the orbicularis oculi). After a considerable number of paired conditioning trials (up to 900) the click itself comes to elicit an eyeblink CR. While the large number of trials required for response acquisition can be a disadvantage for neurophysiological analysis (see the section entitled "Characteristics of an Ideal Vertebrate Behavioral Model System"), this disadvantage has been overcome to a considerable degree by the incorporation of an appropriate experimental design and control groups.

Focusing initially upon the final pathway for the expression of the blink response, Woody and Brozek (1969) observed that initial presen-

tations of the CS produced evoked potentials in the brainstem facial
nucleus that were closely related to EMG activity recorded from the
orbicularis oculi. These evoked potentials preceded EMG activity by
approximately 3 ms, the time required for an action potential to travel
along the facial nerve to the muscle. Paired CS–US conditioning trials
significantly increased the magnitude of the CS-evoked potentials in
the facial nucleus. The subsequent presentation of backward conditioning trials (reversing the order of the CS and US while continuing to
present them in a paired manner) produced extinction of both the behavioral CR and the augmented facial nucleus neuronal response to the
CS, demonstrating the associative nature of both the behavioral and the
neuronal responses. Additional experiments revealed the dependence
of the behavioral CR and the facial nucleus neuronal CR on the integrity
of the motor cortex. Depression of the neuronal activity of the motor
cortex by the application of potassium chloride abolished both of these
CRs, but not the URs, while lesions of the motor cortex, but not of more
posterior cortical areas, rendered animals virtually unable to acquire
these CRs despite prolonged training (Woody, Yarowsky, Owens,
Black–Cleworth, & Crow, 1974).

In the first of a series of experiments aimed at more precisely determining the nature of the cortical involvement in the acquisition of the
CR, Woody and colleagues (Woody, Vassilevsky, & Engel, 1970) recorded from single neurons in the motor cortex before and after
eyeblink conditioning. Many neurons were responsive to the click CS
prior to conditioning, and the effect of conditioning was to significantly
increase and prolong the click-evoked response of a particular subpopulation of these neurons. Furthermore, electrical stimulation of the
areas where these particular neurons were located reliably elicited an
eye muscle EMG response. These neurons were considered to be located in an area which mediates blinking and were classified as projective neurons. Other neurons, however, showed no augmented response
to the CS as a function of conditioning, and stimulation of the area in
which these neurons were located produced no eye muscle EMG response. Hence, neurons in these areas were considered to be unprojective. Of particular interest was the additional finding that conditioning
significantly lowered the stimulation threshold for the elicitation of the
eye muscle EMG response from projection neuron areas, and that this
decrease in threshold was specific to the cortical areas which ultimately projected to the muscle mediating the eyeblink CR. Further
evidence for the specificity of this effect was provided when additional
animals were trained to twitch their nose to the CS. Such training
selectively reduced the stimulation threshold of cortical areas ulti-

mately projecting to the muscle mediating the nose twitch CR (Woody & Engel, 1972).

Using more refined techniques, Woody and Black–Cleworth (1973) sought to determine the nature of this conditioning-induced threshold decrease in projection neuron areas. Single projection neurons were identified by intracellular recording and microstimulation techniques in which a single neuron was stimulated by passing a minute stimulation current through an intracellular microelectrode, while recording the eye muscle EMG response. Consistent with earlier experiments it was found that in animals receiving eyeblink conditioning, the amount of current required to produce an action potential in single neurons ultimately projecting to the eye muscle was significantly lower than for neurons ultimately projecting to the nose muscle or elsewhere. Projective and unprojective neurons could not be distinguished on the basis of spontaneous rates of discharge, resting membrane potential, or spike potential amplitude, seemingly excluding the possibility that threshold changes were mediated synaptically. Rather, the decreased threshold of projective neurons appeared to be postsynaptically mediated and to result from an increase in the neuronal membrane resistance (recall Ohm's law, which predicts that with increased membrane resistance an equivalent depolarization will be produced by a smaller current). In a more recent investigation (Brons & Woody, 1980), it was found that the alterations of intracellular stimulation thresholds were maximal in animals receiving paired conditioning trials and minimal in animals receiving CS alone presentations. Although it was found that presentations of the US alone resulted in lower stimulation thresholds, the effect was less than that observed following paired conditioning trials and rapidly diminished over time (Fig. 9.14). Hence, the maximal effects were clearly a function of associative learning processes. Finally, it was found that these training-induced threshold changes persisted for several weeks or more following conditioning.

Woody, having identified training-induced increases in the neuronal membrane resistance of motor cortex neurons which ultimately influence the final pathway for the expression of the eyeblink CR, has directed recent efforts toward identifying the cellular mechanisms which contribute to these alterations (Woody, 1982a; 1982b). Several procedures were used in attempts to produce increases in cortical neuronal membrane resistance (and the resulting decrease of intracellular stimulation threshold) comparable to those produced as a function of conditioning. Increases in membrane resistance were found to occur in some cortical pyramidal neurons following iontophoretic application of acetylcholine (ACh), but such increases lasted only for a few minutes.

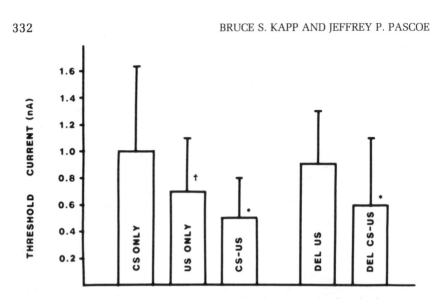

FIGURE 9.14   Mean (±SD) threshold current levels (nA) required to discharge cortical projective neurons. Data are shown for cats that were presented with CS-alone (CS
ONLY), US-alone (US ONLY), or paired CS-US conditioning trials (CS-US). Also shown
are data from cats presented with the US-alone and tested from 25–100 days later (DEL
US), and cats given paired conditioning trials and tested from 3–28 days later (DEL CS-
US). Asterisks indicate significant decreases ($p < 0.05$) in thresholds compared to the CS-
only group. The US-only group exhibited only moderate decreases in thresholds ($p <$
0.10). (Adapted with permission from Brons & Woody, 1980.)

However, when the iontophoresis of ACh was combined with depolarizing   intracellular stimulation, producing repetitive discharge, increases in membrane resistance persisted for at least one hour, the
longest period during which recordings were made. Repetitive discharge alone was not sufficient to produce the effect, nor was the application of saline. Atropine blocked the effect of ACh on membrane resistance (Fig. 9.15). The intracellular application of cyclic guanosine
3',5'-monophosphate (cGMP), which is thought to act as a second messenger for ACh in some cortical neurons, produced effects that were
essentially the same as those produced by ACh—a transient increase in
membrane resistance occurred following application of cGMP alone,
and the increase persisted if cGMP application was combined with
repetitive discharge. The possibility exists that the persistent alterations in membrane resistance produced in these experiments may be
analogous to those observed in conditioned animals.

In summary, the results of the research conducted by Woody and his
associates demonstrated that the physical properties of cortical pyrami-

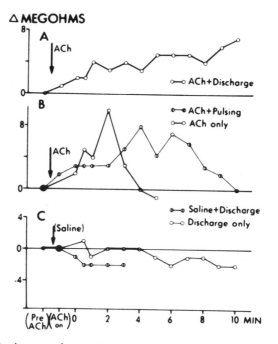

FIGURE 9.15 Average changes in membrane resistance in cells given: (A) ionto-phoresis of ACh plus deplorarizing current sufficient to repeatedly discharge the cell (ACh plus discharge); (B) iontophoresis of ACh alone (ACh only) or iontophoresis of ACh plus depolarizing current insufficient to repeatedly discharge the cell (ACh plus pulsing); A and B are data from cells that responded with some increase in input resistance; (C) iontophoresis of saline plus current-induced discharge (saline plus discharge) and injection of depolarizing current sufficient to produce repeated discharge (discharge only). Ordinate shows mean differences in membrane resistance (Rm) in megohms from initial value, the latter set to zero. Abscissa: pre-ACh—before administration of ACh; ACh on—during iontophoresis of acetylcholine; 0—immediately after cessation of iontophoresis of ACh; remaining numbers—time in minutes after cessation of ACh. (Reprinted with permission from Woody, 1982.)

dal neurons located within the circuitry mediating the eyeblink CR are altered as a function of procedures which promote associative learning. The significance of this finding, particularly with respect to its relationship to the cellular processes which contribute to the storage of the association necessary for the acquisition of the CR, is at present a matter for speculation. Nevertheless, the results of further research should yield additional clues to the significance of these findings; research made possible by the use of a vertebrate model system.

CONCLUDING REMARKS

Some of the current research efforts which have incorporated the use of vertebrate model response systems to investigate the neural substrates of learning and memory were reviewed. Various response systems can be categorized as either specific or nonspecific. Furthermore, while the sensory and motor pathways that mediate the acquisition of different responses obviously differ, an important question remains concerning whether a critical central circuitry exists that is necessary for the normal acquisition of all responses, both specific and nonspecific. In this context recall that nonspecific CRs are considered to be reflective of a central state of conditioned arousal, and in the case of aversive conditioning procedures this state is commonly referred to as conditioned fear. Fear, as indexed by nonspecific responses, is conditioned far more rapidly than are specific CRs. Indeed, the conditioning of fear is believed to be necessary for the initial acquisition of specific responses (Mowrer, 1947; Thompson et al., 1984). It follows, therefore, that the normal acquisition of both nonspecific and specific responses during aversive conditioning procedures may be dependent upon a critical neural system that is necessary for the conditioning of fear. Is there evidence that such a system exists? We believe so (Kapp, Pascoe, & Bixler, 1984). Specifically, a substantial body of evidence suggests that the amygdaloid complex, including the central nucleus, is part of a neural system that is necessary for normal fear conditioning, and without which the conditioning of specific responses is retarded. For example, lesions and other manipulations of the amygdala not only interfere with the acquisition of nonspecific conditioned responses indicative of fear (e.g., freezing, heart rate), but also with the acquisition of specific responses (Ben-Ari, 1981), including the nictitating membrane response (Kapp, Frysinger, Gallagher, & Bretschneider, 1977). Hence, the amygdaloid complex appears to be a component of a neural system, the normal functioning of which is required for the normal acquisition of both nonspecific and specific responses during aversive conditioning procedures. It should be noted, however, that neural systems which appear to be necessary for the acquisition of specific responses may not be necessary for the acquisition of nonspecific responses. For example, lesions of the cerebellum that prevent NM conditioning do not affect the acquisition of conditioned bradycardia in the rabbit (Thompson et al., 1984). Of great interest will be an analysis of the manner by which the neural system(s) necessary for the acquisition of nonspecific conditioned fear responses interacts with systems necessary for the acquisition of specific conditioned responses.

SUMMARY

Significant progress has been realized toward our understanding of the neural substrates of learning and memory with the use of well-characterized vertebrate model response systems. Using a number of neurobiological techniques, the neural circuits which contribute to the acquisition of a variety of CRs are now being identified. Of importance is the observation that different central neural systems may, at least in part, form the circuitry which is responsible for the acquisition of different response categories. In addition, the cellular changes (e.g., changes in membrane resistance) which occur as a function of procedures that promote associative learning in the vertebrate, are beginning to be understood. Our knowledge, however, is still vastly incomplete, and the task which lies ahead will be difficult. Nevertheless, the use of vertebrate model systems will continue to facilitate our efforts to understand the neural substrates of learning and memory processes.

REFERENCES

Albiniak, B. A., & Powell, D. A. (1980). Peripheral autonomic mechanisms and Pavlovian conditioning in the rabbit (Oryctolagus cuniculus). Journal of Comparative and Physiological Psychology, 94, 1101–1113.

Applegate, C. D., Frysinger, R. C., Kapp, B. S., & Gallagher, M. (1982). Multiple unit activity recorded from amygdala central nucleus during Pavlovian heart rate conditioning in rabbit. Brain Research, 238, 457–462.

Applegate, C. D., Kapp, B. S., Underwood, M. D., & McNall, C. L. (1983). Autonomic and somatomotor effects of amygdala central n. stimulation in awake rabbits. Physiology and Behavior, 31, 353–360.

Ben–Ari, Y. (Ed.). (1981). The amygdaloid complex: INSERM symposium no. 20. Amsterdam: Elsevier/North Holland Biomedical Press.

Berger, T. W., & Orr, W. B. (1982). Role of the hippocampus in reversal learning of the rabbit nictitating membrane response. In C. D. Woody (Ed.), Conditioning: Representation of involved neural functions (pp. 1–12). New York: Plenum Press.

Berger, T. W., Clark, G. A., & Thompson, R. F. (1980). Learning-dependent neuronal responses recorded from limbic system brain structures during classical conditioning. Physiological Psychology, 8, 155–167.

Berger, T. W., & Thompson, R. F. (1978a). Neuronal plasticity in the limbic system during classical conditioning of the rabbit nictitating membrane response. I. The hippocampus. Brain Research, 145, 323–346.

Berger, T. W., & Thompson, R. F. (1978b). Neuronal plasticity in the limbic system during classical conditioning of the rabbit nictitating membrane response. II. Septum and mammillary bodies. Brain Research, 156, 293–314.

Berthier, N. E., & Moore, J. W. (1983). The nictitating membrane response: An electrophysiological study of the abducens nerve and nucleus and the accessory abducens nucleus in the rabbit. Brain Research, 258, 201–210.

Black, A., & Prokasy, W. F. (Eds.). (1972). *Classical conditioning II: Current research and theory.* New York: Appleton-Century-Crofts.

Brons, J. F., & Woody, C. D. (1980). Long-term changes in excitability of cortical neurons after Pavlovian conditioning and extinction. *Journal of Neurophysiology, 44,* 605–615.

Clark, G. A., McCormick, D. A., Lavond, D. G., Baxter, K., Gray, W. J., & Thompson, R. F. (1982). Effects of electrolytic lesions of cerebellar nuclei on conditioned behavioral and hippocampal neuronal responses. *Neuroscience Abstracts, 8,* 22.

Cohen, D. H. (1974). The neural pathways and informational flow mediating a conditioned autonomic response. In L. V. DiCara (Ed.), *Limbic and autonomic nervous systems research* (pp. 223–275). New York: Plenum Press.

Cohen, D. H. (1975). Involvement of the avian amygdalar-homologue (archistriatum posterior and mediale) in defensively conditioned heart rate change. *Journal of Comparative Neurology, 160,* 13–36.

Cohen, D. H. (1980). The functional neuroanatomy of a conditioned response. In R. F. Thompson, L. H. Hicks, & V. B. Shvyrkov (Eds.), *Neural mechanisms of goal directed behavior and learning* (pp. 283–302). New York: Academic Press.

Cohen, D. H. (1982). Central processing time for a conditioned response in a vertebrate model system. In C. D. Woody (Ed.), *Conditioning: Representation of involved neural functions* (pp. 517–534). New York: Plenum Press.

Cohen, D. H. (1984). Identification of vertebrate neurons modified during learning: Analysis of sensory pathways. In D. L. Alkon & J. Farley (Eds.), *Primary neural substrates of learning and behavioral change* pp. 129–154. Cambridge: Cambridge University Press.

Cohen, D. H., & Goff, D. M. (1978). Conditioned heart rate changes in the pigeon: Analysis and prediction of acquisition patterns. *Physiological Psychology, 6,* 127–141.

Cohen, D. H., & Pitts, L. H. (1968). Vagal and sympathetic components of conditioned cardioacceleration in the pigeon. *Brain Research, 9,* 15–31.

Cohen, D. H., & Schnall, A. M. (1970). Medullary cells of origin of vagal cardio-inhibitory fibers in the pigeon. II. Electrical stimulation of the dorsal motor nucleus. *Journal of Comparative Neurology, 140,* 321–342.

Desmond, J. E., Rosenfield, M. E., & Moore, J. W. (1983). Red nucleus and supratrigeminal reticular formation: Brain stem components of the conditioned nictitating membrane response. *Neuroscience Abstracts, 9,* 331.

Disterhoft, J. F., Shipley, M. T., & Kraus, N. (1982). Analyzing the rabbit NM conditioned reflex arc. In C. D. Woody (Ed.), *Conditioning: Representation of involved neural functions* (pp. 433–449). New York: Plenum Press.

Fredericks, A., Moore, J. W., Metcalf, F. U., Schwaber, J. S., & Schneiderman, N. (1974). Selective autonomic blockade of conditioned and unconditioned heart rate changes in rabbits. *Pharmacology, Biochemistry and Behavior, 2,* 493–501.

Gabriel, M., Orona, E., Foster, K., & Lambert, R. W. (1982). Mechanism and generality of stimulus significance coding in a mammalian model system. In C. D. Woody (Ed.), *Conditioning: Representation of involved neural functions* (pp. 535–566). New York: Plenum Press.

Gallagher, M., Kapp, B. S., Frysinger, R. C., & Rapp, P. R. β-adrenergic manipulation in amygdala central n. alters rabbit heart rate conditioning. *Pharmacology, Biochemistry and Behavior, 12,* 419–426.

Gallagher, M., Kapp, B. S., McNall, C. L., & Pascoe, J. P. (1981). Opiate effects in the amygdala central nucleus on heart rate conditioning in rabbits. *Pharmacology, Biochemistry and Behavior, 14,* 497–505.

Gibbs, C. M., Broyles, J. L., & Cohen, D. H. (1983). Further studies of the involvement of locus coeruleus in plasticity of avian lateral geniculate neurons during learning. *Neuroscience Abstracts, 9,* 641.

Gormezano, I., Kehoe, E. I., & Marshall, B. S. (1983). Twenty years of classical conditioning research with the rabbit. In A. N. Epstein (Ed.), *Progress in psychobiology and physiological psychology* (pp. 197–275). New York: Academic Press.

Gray, T. W., McMaster, S. E., Harvey, J. A., & Gormezano, I. (1981). Localization of retractor bulbi motoneurons in the rabbit. *Brain Research, 226,* 93–106.

Haley, D. A., Lavond, D. G., & Thompson, R. F. (1983). Effects of contralateral red nuclear lesions on retention of the classically conditioned nictitating membrane/eyelid response. *Neuroscience Abstracts, 9,* 643.

Hilton, S. M., & Zbrozyna, A. W. (1963). Amygdaloid region for defense reactions and its efferent pathway to the brainstem. *Journal of Physiology, 165,* 160–173.

Hopkins, D. A., & Holstege, G. (1978). Amygdaloid projections to the mesencephalon, pons and medulla oblongata in the cat. *Experimental Brain Research, 32,* 529–547.

Jordan, D., Khalid, M. E. M., Schneiderman, N., & Spyer, K. M. (1982). The location and properties of preganglionic vagal cardiomotor neurones in the rabbit. *Pflügers Archiv, 395,* 244–250.

Kapp, B. S., Frysinger, R., Gallagher, M., & Bretschneider, A. (1977). Effects of amygdala and stria terminalis lesions on aversive conditioning in the rabbit. *Neuroscience Abstracts, 3,* 236.

Kapp, B. S., Frysinger, R. C., Gallagher, M., & Haselton, J. R. (1979). Amygdala central nucleus lesions: Effects on heart rate conditioning in the rabbit. *Physiology and Behavior, 23,* 1109–1117.

Kapp, B. S., Gallagher, M., Applegate, C. D., & Frysinger, R. C. (1982). The amygdala central nucleus: Contributions to conditioned cardiovascular responding during aversive Pavlovian conditioning in the rabbit. In C. D. Woody (Ed.), *Conditioning: Representation of involved neural functions* (pp. 581–600). New York: Plenum Press.

Kapp, B. S., Gallagher, M., Frysinger, R. C., & Applegate, C. D. (1981). The amygdala, emotion and cardiovascular conditioning. In Y. Ben-Ari (Ed.), *The amygdaloid complex: INSERM symposium no. 20* (pp. 355–366). Amsterdam: Elsevier/North Holland Biomedical Press.

Kapp, B. S., Gallagher, M., Underwood, M. D., McNall, C. L., & Whitehorn, D. (1982). Cardiovascular responses elicited by electrical stimulation of the amygdala central nucleus in the rabbit. *Brain Research, 234,* 251–262.

Kapp, B. S., Pascoe, J. P., & Bixler, M. A. (1984). The amygdala: A neuroanatomical systems approach to its contribution to aversive conditioning. In L. Squire & N. Butters (Ed.), *The neuropsychology of memory* (pp. 473–488). New York: The Guilford Press.

Kettner, R. E., & Thompson, R. F. (1982). Auditory signal detection and decision processes in the nervous system. *Journal of Comparative and Physiological Psychology, 96,* 328–331.

MacDonald, R. L., & Cohen, D. H. (1970). Cells of origin of sympathetic pre- and postganglionic cardioacceleratory fibers in the pigeon. *Journal of Comparative Neurology, 140,* 343–358.

Mauk, M. D., Warren, J. T., & Thompson, R. F. (1982). Selective, naloxone-reversible morphine depression of learned behavioral and hippocampal responses. *Science, 216,* 434–435.

McCormick, D. A., Clark, G. A., Lavond, D. G., & Thompson, R. F. (1982). Initial localization of the memory trace for a basic form of learning. *Proceedings of the National Academy of Science, 79,* 2731–2742.

McCormick, D. A., Lavond, D. G., & Thompson, R. F. (1982). Concomitant classical conditioning of the rabbit nictitating membrane and eyelid responses: Correlations and implications. *Physiology and Behavior, 28,* 769–775.

McCormick, D. A., & Thompson, R. F. (1983). Possible neuronal substrate of classical conditioning within the mammalian CNS: Dentate and interpositus nuclei. *Neuroscience Abstracts, 9,* 643.

Moore, J. W., Desmond, J. E., & Berthier, N. E. (1982). The metencephalic basis of the conditioned nictitating membrane response. In C. D. Woody (Ed.), *Conditioning: Representation of involved neural functions* (pp. 459–482). New York: Plenum Press.

Moore, J. W., Yeo, C. H., Oakley, D. A., & Steele–Russell, I. S. (1980). Conditioned inhibition of the nictitating membrane response in decorticate rabbits. *Behavioral Brain Research, 1,* 397–409.

Mowrer, O. H. (1947). On the dual nature of learning—A reinterpretation of "conditioning" and "problem solving." *Harvard Educational Review, 17,* 102–148.

Oakley, D. A., & Russell, I. S. (1975). Role of cortex in Pavlovian discrimination learning. *Physiology and Behavior, 15,* 315–321.

Oakley, D. A., & Russell, I. S. (1977). Subcortical storage of Pavlovian conditioning in the rabbit. *Physiology and Behavior, 18,* 931–937.

Olds, J., Disterhoft, J. F., Segal, M., Kornblith, C. L., & Hirsh, R. (1972). Learning centers of the brain mapped by measuring latencies of conditioned unit responses. *Journal of Neurophysiology, 35,* 202–219.

Oleson, T. D., Ashe, J. H., & Weinberger, N. M. (1975). Modification of auditory and somatosensory system activity during pupillary conditioning in the paralyzed cat. *Journal of Neurophysiology, 38,* 1114–1139.

Patterson, M. M., Steinmetz, J. E., Beggs, A. L., & Romano, A. G. (1982). Associative processes in spinal reflexes. In C. D. Woody (Ed.), *Conditioning: Representation of involved neural functions* (pp. 637–650). New York: Plenum Press.

Powell, D. A., & Buchanan, S. (1980). Autonomic-somatic relationships in the rabbit (*Oryctolagus cuniculus*): Effects of hippocampal lesions. *Physiological Psychology, 8,* 455–462.

Powell, D. A., & Kazis, E. (1976). Blood pressure and heart rate changes accompanying classical eyeblink conditioning in the rabbit (*Oryctolagus cuniculus*) *Psychophysiology, 13,* 441–447.

Price, J. L., & Amaral, D. G. (1981). An autoradiographic study of the projections of the amygdala central nucleus of the monkey amygdala. *The Journal of Neuroscience, 1,* 1242–1259.

Rescorla, R. A. (1967). Pavlovian conditioning and its proper control procedures. *Psychological Review, 74,* 71–80.

Rescorla, R. A., & Holland, P. C. (1976). Some behavioral approaches to the study of learning. In M. R. Rosenzweig & E. L. Bennett (Eds.), *Neural mechanisms of learning and memory* (pp. 165–192). Cambridge, MA: MIT Press.

Rescorla, R. A., & Wagner, A. R. (1972). A theory of Pavlovian conditioning: Variations in the effectiveness of reinforcement and nonreinforcement. In A. H. Black & W. F. Prokasy (Eds.), *Classical conditioning II: Current research and theory* (pp. 64–99). New York: Appleton-Century-Crofts.

Ryugo, D. K., & Weinberger, N. M. (1978). Differential plasticity of morphologically

distinct neuron populations in the medical geniculate body of the cat during classical conditioning. *Behavioral Biology, 22,* 275–301.

Schneiderman, N. (1972). Response system divergencies in aversive classical conditioning. In A. H. Black & W. F. Prokasy (Eds.), *Classical conditioning Vol. II: Current
research and theory* (pp. 341–378). New York: Appleton-Century-Crofts.

Schneiderman, N., Francis, J., Sampson, L. D., & Schwaber, J. S. (1974). CNS integration
of learned cardiovascular behavior. In L. V. DiCara (Ed.), *Limbic and autonomic
nervous systems research* (pp. 277–309). New York: Plenum Press.

Schwaber, J. S., Kapp, B. S., & Higgins, G. A. (1980). The origin and extent of direct
amygdala projections to the region of the dorsal motor nucleus of the vagus and the
nucleus of the solitary tract. *Neuroscience Letters, 20,* 15–20.

Schwaber, J. S., Kapp, B. S., Higgins, G. A., & Rapp, P. R. (1982). Amygdaloid and basal
forebrain direct connections with the nucleus of the solitary tract and the dorsal
motor nucleus. *The Journal of Neuroscience, 2,* 1424–1438.

Schwaber, J. S., & Schneiderman, N. (1975). Aortic nerve activated cardioinhibitory
neurons and interneurons. *American Journal of Physiology, 299,* 783–790.

Solomon, P. R., & Moore, J. W. (1975). Latent inhibition and stimulus generalization for
the classically conditioned nictitating membrane response in rabbits (*Oryctolagus
cuniculus*) following dorsal hippocampal ablation. *Journal of Comparative and
Physiological Psychology, 89,* 1192–1203.

Solomon, P. R., Solomon, S. D., Vander Schaaf, E., & Perry, H. E. (1983). Altered activity
in the hippocampus is more detrimental to classical conditioning than removing the
structure. *Science, 220,* 329–331.

Solomon, P. R., Vander Schaaf, E. R., Nobre, A. C., Weisz, D. J., & Thompson, R. F. (1983).
Hippocampus and trace conditioning of the rabbit's nictitating membrane response.
Neuroscience Abstracts, 9, 645.

Thompson, R. F. (1976). The search for the engram. *American Psychologist, 31,* 209–227.

Thompson, R. F., Berger, T. W., Berry, S. D., Clark, G. A., Kettner, R. N., Lavond, D. G.,
Mauk, M. D., McCormick, D. A., Solomon, P. R., & Weisz, D. J. (1982). Neuronal
substrates of learning and memory: Hippocampus and other structures. In C. D.
Woody (Ed.), *Conditioning: Representation of involved neural functions* (pp. 115–
129). New York: Plenum Press.

Thompson, R. F., Berger, T. W., Berry, S. D., Hoehler, F. K., Kettner, R. E., & Weisz, D. J.
(1980). Hippocampal substrate of classical conditioning. *Physiological Psychology,
8,* 262–279.

Thompson, R. F., Clark, G. A., Donegan, N. H., Lavond, D. G., Madden, J., Mamounas, L.
A., Mauk, M. D., & McCormick, D. A. (1984). Neuronal substrates of basic associative
learning. In L. R. Squire & N. Butters (Eds.), *The neuropsychology of memory.* (pp.
424–442). New York: The Guildford Press.

Thompson, R. F., McCormick, D. A., Lavond, D. G., Clark, G. A., Kettner, R. E., & Mauk,
M. D. (1983). The engram found? Initial localization of the memory trace for a basic
form of associative learning. In A. N. Epstein (Ed.), *Progress in psychobiology and
physiological psychology* (pp. 167–196). New York: Academic Press.

Tsukahara, N., Oda, Y., & Notsu, T. (1981). Classical conditioning mediated by the red
nucleus in the cat. *The Journal of Neuroscience, 1,* 72–79.

Weinberger, N. M. (1982). Effects of conditioned arousal on the auditory system. In A. L.
Beckman (Ed.), *The Neural Basis of Behavior* (pp. 63–91). Jamaica, NY: Spectrum
Publications, Inc.

Woody, C. D. (1974). Aspects of the electrophysiology of cortical processes related to the development and performance of learned motor response. *The Physiologist, 17*, 49–69.

Woody, C. D. (1982a). Neurophysiologic correlates of latent facilitation. In C. D. Woody (Ed.), *Conditioning: Representation of involved neural functions* (pp. 233–248). New York: Plenum Press.

Woody, C. D. (1982b). Acquisition of conditioned facial reflexes in the cat: Cortical control of different facial movements. *Federation Proceedings, 41*, 2160–2168.

Woody, C. D., & Black–Cleworth, P. (1973). Differences in excitability of cortical neurons as a function of motor projection in conditioned cats. *Journal of Neurophysiology, 36*, 1104–1116.

Woody, C. D., & Brozek, G. (1969). Changes in evoked responses from facial nucleus of cat with conditioning and extinction of an eyeblink. *Journal of Neurophysiology, 32*, 717–726.

Woody, C. D., & Engel, J. (1972). Changes in unit activity and thresholds to electrical microstimulation at coronal-pericruciate cortex of cat with classical conditioning of different facial movements. *Journal of Neurophysiology, 35*, 230–241.

Woody, C. D., Vassilevsky, N. N., & Engel, J. (1970). Conditioned eye blink: Unit activity at coronal-precruciate cortex of cat. *Journal of Neurophysiology, 33*, 851–864.

Woody, C. D., Yarowsky, P., Owens, J., Black–Cleworth, P., & Crow, T. (1974). Effect of lesions of cortical motor areas on acquisition of conditioned eye blink in the cat. *Journal of Neurophysiology, 37*, 385–394.

Yehle, A., Dauth, G., & Schneiderman, N. (1967). Correlates of heart-rate classical conditioning in curarized rabbits. *Journal of Comparative and Physiological Psychology, 64*, 98–104.

10

STUDIES OF MEMORY PROCESSES USING ELECTRICAL BRAIN STIMULATION

Robert F. Berman

INTRODUCTION

The technique of electrical brain stimulation (EBS) is more than 100 years old. Its use originated in the early work of John Walsh in 1774 on animal electricity in electric eels, and in the work of Galvani and Volta on the nature of electricity. By the 1800's, physiologists were regularly using electrical stimulation to explore the nervous system. Johannes Müller postulated his law of specific nerve energies in part, from his observations that the sensory perception induced by electrical brain stimulation was in keeping with the system's physiological function. Students of Müller, including DuBois–Reymond, Virchov, and Helmholtz, dominated German physiology during the latter half of the 19th century and used electrical stimulation extensively in their studies of the brain and nerves. Several years later in 1870 Fritsch, who had worked in Dubois–Reymond's laboratory, and Hitzig demonstrated specific muscle contractions elicited by localized electrical stimulation of dog cerebral cortex. With the development of the Horsley–Clark stereotaxic apparatus it became possible to position stimulating electrodes in virtually any region of the brain with a relatively high degree of accuracy. Thus, development of the stereotaxic instrument, along with refinements in electrode construction and electrical stimulating and recording techniques contributed to the widespread acceptance of EBS as a fundamental tool for the study of brain function.

The technique involves the surgical implantation of electrodes onto the surface of the cortex or into subcortical regions. Stimulation is delivered through wires attached to the implanted electrodes. While current is flowing, the stimulation is able to disrupt the normal spatio–temporal firing patterns of neurons near the electrode tip (Doty, 1969). Presumably, the nonsensical patterns of neuronal activity at the stimulation site alter activity in remote brain regions leading to a modification of behavior, including sleeping, fighting, feeding, drinking, vocalization, arrest reactions, and fear. EBS can also have reinforcing, positive or negative, properties so that animals will work to deliver EBS to such regions as the medial forebrain bundle or learn to escape aversive EBS delivered to other regions. Finally, EBS can also block neuronal input to the focus of stimulation. The behavioral effects of stimulation are generally reversible as long as current levels are kept low (typically between 50 and 500 μA), and stimulation durations are kept relatively short (typically between 0.5 and 15 s). Many details and parameters of EBS can be varied, and the reader is referred to several recent reviews for more information (Berman & Kesner, 1981; Kesner, 1982).

In memory and learning research, electrical brain stimulation is used to produce reversible, localized disruption of neural activity at or around the time of learning or retention testing. The rationale is that, to the extent that a given brain region is involved in some aspect of memory processing (e.g., storage or retrieval), appropriately applied EBS will modify memory. In the pages that follow, EBS experiments in both laboratory animals (i.e., rodents, primates) and humans will be described that demonstrate amnesia or memory facilitation depending upon the brain region studied, when EBS is applied, and the nature of the specific memory task employed. Many of our current ideas concerning basic brain mechanisms of memory and learning have evolved from consideration of the results of such studies.

ADVANTAGE OF THE TECHNIQUE

The major advantage of EBS is the ability too reversibly disrupt activity in specific brain locations, a feature not shared by brain lesioning techniques. Furthermore, the EBS can be imposed any time during a learning experience so that it is possible to investigate the effects of stimulation on specific stages of memory formation. That is, stimulation can be given during initial acquisition, sometime after learning or just before tests of memory retrieval. This degree of control is an important advantage of the technique. Finally, EBS can be used to explore the functional circuitry in the human brain during neurosurgical procedures as described in this chapter. Thus it is possible to compare results from human studies with data gathered in the laboratory using research animals.

LOCALIZATION OF EFFECTS

Experimental evidence indicates that if care is taken to keep the stimulation current below the level producing epileptiform after discharges, then the effects of stimulation on behavior can be quite localized. Ojemann (1982) reports that in human brain the effects of EBS frequently change in nature as the site of stimulation is moved a few millimeters. Wyers, Peeke, Williston, and Herz (1968) demonstrated that single-pulse stimulation of the caudate nucleus of rats results in amnesia, while stimulation of structures also activated by caudate stimulation (e.g., frontal cortex, corpus callosum, or internal capsule) do not. Such results suggest that the effects of EBS can, indeed, be quite localized. Furthermore, the sites where stimulation disrupts behavior appear to closely parallel sites where lesions have also been found to be effective. However, it is clear that disruption of neuronal activity in one region can alter activity in interconnected regions, and this downstream activity could also influence behavior. Caution is therefore required in the interpretation of stimulation studies. Data gathered from lesion, electrophysiological, anatomical and pharmacological studies should be considered along with those from stimulation studies when making inferences about functional relationships among brain structures that may underlie memory. However, the same cautions are required in the interpretation of lesion studies, where activity downstream is also unquestionably altered by removal of interconnected sites.

MECHANISM OF ACTION OF EBS

Electrical stimulation can directly block or excite neural activity (Ranck, 1981). Axons and cell bodies may be directly depolarized by imposed electrical currents, resulting in antidromic and orthodromic propagation of electrical signals to distal brain regions. Stimulation may also affect the storage, release, and synthesis of neurotransmitters. In fact, several studies report that one can reverse experimentally induced amnesia in rats following EBS by pharmacological means. For example, Gold and Sternberg (1978) demonstrated that amnesia following electrical brain stimulation can be reversed by noradrenergic antagonists (e.g., propranalol) and suggest that disruption of noradrenergic activity may underlie most examples of experimentally induced amnesia. While such a mechanism is possible, it does not appear to be able to account for all forms of amnesia (Ellis, Berman, & Kesner, 1983).

LONG-TERM EFFECTS OF EBS

Goddard, McIntyre, and Leech (1969) reported that repeated, low-level, subconvulsive stimulation of the amygdala can lead to the evolution of electrical afterdischarges and behavioral convulsions. The severity of seizures continues to increase until generalized seizures are observed both behaviorally and electrographically. The phenomenon is known as kindling, and kindled seizures can be produced from stimulation of several structures including the amygdala, hippocampus, caudate nucleus, and frontal cortex. Clearly, care must be used in interpreting studies in which the possibility of seizures, kindled or otherwise elicited, exists. Even chronic electrode implantation has been reported to produce sufficient damage to neural tissue to affect behavior (Boast, Reid, Johnson, & Zornetzer, 1976). This fact necessitates the use of electrode-implanted but not stimulated control groups for most studies using EBS to explore complex behaviors such as memory and learning.

EXPERIMENTAL DESIGN CONCERNS

EBS can be delivered either during learning, immediately after learning, or just before memory retention is tested (usually within 30 min of testing). The time-point chosen depends upon whether the investigator is interested in examining the effects of EBS of a particular brain region on initial acquisition, memory storage, or retrieval of memory, respectively. In practice, a combination of time-points is usually incorporated into the experimental design and examined (see Kesner, 1982, for a description of the various paradigms).

Several studies have examined the effects of EBS given only during initial learning. Such studies are typically difficult to interpret because such stimulation can interfere with memory processing directly, or indirectly by altering sensory, perceptual, or selective attention processes active during learning. Another problem is that learning that occurs during EBS may not be observable unless the animal is also tested for memory under EBS. This phenomenon is called state-dependent learning and has been well described by Overton, 1977.

As a result, in many studies EBS is given immediately after learning so that initial registration of information (sensory, perceptual, attentional) during acquisition can be assumed to have occurred normally. This is often referred to as *posttrial* EBS. Memory disruption can then be attributed to postacquisitional processing of experiential information, including consolidation and retrieval processes. As is described later in this chapter, electrical brain stimulation of a number of neural regions (amygdala, hippocampus, caudate nucleus, frontal cortex) delivered immediately after training can result in amnesia when animals are later tested for memory. Memory is typically tested within a few minutes of training if short-term memory is of interest or after 24 hr or more if long-term memory is beng studied.

Electrical stimulation delayed after training by more than a few minutes is typically less effective in interfering with memory. These observations have been used as primary support for the *consolidation hypothesis* of memory (McGaugh, 1966). According to the hypothesis, initial memory processing, or the memory trace itself, is labile and subject to interference and rapid decay. This form of memory is typically referred to as short-term memory (STM). If, however, information remains in short-term stores through rehearsal, then a relatively stable long-term memory (LTM) trace evolves. The nature of this evolution of LTM is the subject of considerable debate, ranging from simple sequential models in which memory is directly transferred from STM to LTM (Hebb, 1949; McGaugh, 1966), to parallel models that envision STM and LTM as being activated in parallel (Kesner, 1973). A more recent formulation (Gold & McGaugh, 1975) suggests that there may be only a single memory system, with the strength, stability, and duration of specific memories modulated by arousal levels in the central nervous system. Regardless of model, each predicts that memories are consolidated over time from an initially labile into a relatively stable long-term trace. They also predict that experimental treatments, such as localized brain stimulation that disrupts memory when given to critical brain regions immediately after learning, should become less effective as the passage of time leads to consolidation of the memory trace. This, then is the framework within which most theorists interpret studies of experimental amnesia, as will be later described in this chapter. However, it should be kept in mind that others (DeVietti & Kirkpatrick, 1976; Lewis, 1976) have provided strong support for a retrieval hypothesis to account for examples of experimental amnesia. According to "retrieval" theorists, amnesia results from interference with specific processes necessary to retrieve memory, not from interference in consolidation processes. At present no experimental paradigm has been proposed that appears to clearly resolve this issue.

MEMORY IMPAIRMENT PRODUCED BY
ELECTRICAL BRAIN STIMULATION

Most studies with EBS have found that stimulation delivered to various brain regions during or shortly after learning impairs subsequent memory of training.

STIMULATION DURING LEARNING

In one of the first studies of the effects of EBS on memory, Goddard (1964) applied low-intensity, unilateral electrical stimulation to the amygdala of rats during acquisition of a number of tasks. Goddard noted that studies on the effects of amygdaloid lesions on learning were inconclusive and attempted to determine the nature of the psychological deficit following amygdala disruption by using localized amygdala stimulation to produce a functional, reversible lesion. He reported that acquisition of signaled fear conditioning was disrupted by unilateral EBS of the amygdala, whereas maze learning was unaffected. On the basis of these studies Goddard was among the first to suggest that the amygdaloid complex functions in the consolidation of associations between neutral stimuli and aversive stimuli. Correll (1957) conducted one of the first studies to use EBS to explore the role of the hippocampus in learning. He trained cats to traverse a runway and to press a bar at the end for food reinforcement. Bilateral, subseizure electrical stimulation of the dentate fascia in the ventral hippocampus was applied during learning. The stimulation did not appear to affect initial response acquisition, but it delayed subsequent extinction. These findings are consistent with reports by Nyakas and Endroczi (1970) that subseizure stimulation of the dorsal hippocampus does not affect retention of a conditioned fear response in rats and with the findings of Flynn and Wasman (1960) that shock avoidance conditioning can occur even in the presence of hippocampal afterdischarges. These results indicate that disruption of hippocampal activity during learning does not severely impede initial response acquisition.

Low-intensity electrical stimulation of other brain structures during learning, including the medial frontal cortex, medial or basolateral amygdala, caudate nucleus, or substantia nigra (Bresnahan & Routtenberg, 1972; LePiane & Phillips, 1978; Routtenberg & Holzman, 1973; Santos–Anderson & Routtenberg, 1976) can also influence memory. Santos–Anderson and Routtenberg (1976) delivered low-level (5 or 15 μA) unilateral EBS to the medial–prefrontal cortex of adult rats during passive avoidance training. Training consisted of placing rats on a platform and delivering footshock upon descent from the platform on to the

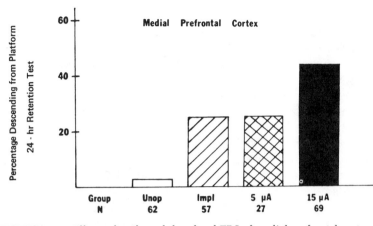

FIGURE 10.1 Effects of unilateral, low-level EBS of medial prefrontal cortex during step-down shock-avoidance learning on retention tested 24 hr later. A greater percentage of implanted controls (Impl) descended from the platform at the 24 hr retention test compared to unoperated controls (Unop) indicating that electrode implantation impaired retention. Stimulation at 15 µA, but not at 5 µA, produced retention impairment over and above that observed in Group Impl. There were no differences among groups in initial acquisition during EBS. (From Santos-Anderson & Routtenberg, 1976).

grid floor. EBS was given whenever the animal was on the platform. Training was continued until animals remained on the platform without descent for 2 min. Retention was tested 24 hr later by observing whether animals descended from the platform within 3 min on each of 5 consecutive test days. The results shown in Figure 10.1 show that at the 24 hr retention test, stimulated animals (15 µA) showed poorer retention than the implanted controls and unoperated controls.

STIMULATION APPLIED AFTER LEARNING

Amygdala Stimulation

In one of the first posttrial electrical brain stimulation studies, Kesner and Doty (1968) reported amnesia 24 hr after an aversive mouth shock in cats if seizure-eliciting electrical stimulation was applied to the dorsal hippocampus or amygdala 4 s after the shock. No amnesia was reported for similar levels of stimulation of the septum, fornix, or ventral hippocampus. Thus, seizures per se were not responsible for the amnesia. They concluded that an intact amygdala is necessary for efficient mnemonic processing of aversive experiences. McDonough and Kesner (1971) later demonstrated that brief, bilateral, subseizure stimulation of the amygdala of cats was sufficient to produce amnesia for an aversive mouth-shock when EBS was delivered 4 s after shock and memory was tested 24 hr later. These effects were time-dependent in that the most consistent amnesia was produced when EBS was applied immediately after training. The timecourse over which EBS given after training becomes ineffective in disrupting memory is often referred to as the *temporal gradient*. The temporal gradient for the effects of EBS on memory is typically, although not always, within minutes after training. However, the precise timecourse depends to a great extent on the nature of the memory task and on the intensity and duration of stimulation. Unilateral, low-intensity, posttrial amygdaloid stimulation has also been reported to produce amnesia for shock avoidance learning in rats (Gold, Edwards, & McGaugh, 1975). Gold et al. (1975) trained water-deprived rats to enter a goal box and to lick water from a metal water spout. After 5 days of training, animals were given a 2 mA, 1-s footshock during the 10th s of licking on the spout. Electrical stimulation of the amygdala (10-s or 30-s trains) was administerd to electrode-implanted animals 5 s after footshock, and memory was tested 24 hr later by measuring individual animals latency to enter the goal box and begin licking. Unimplanted and implanted, but not stimulated, control groups were used. The results of their study are shown in Figure 10.2 below. As shown in the figure, both unimplanted and im-

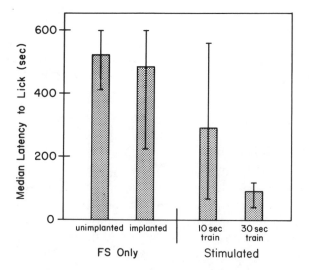

FIGURE 10.2   Median latency to lick (and interquartile ranges) for animals in each group. The stimulated animals had retention latencies significantly lower than those of either control group (From Gold et. al., 1975).

planted control groups (footshock only) showed good retention of the footshock experience as evidenced by median lick latencies greater than 400 s. In constrast, rats receiving 10- or 30-s trains of posttrial EBS to the amygdala showed significantly shorter lick latencies compared to controls. Afterdischarges were not found in these animals and thus were not prerequisite to the memory disruption. It was also found that the basomedial nucleus of the amygdaloid complex appeared to be the most effective site for producing disruption, although the reasons for this apparent site specificity are unknown.

In an attempt to determine whether the amnesia observed following posttrial amygdaloid EBS affected short-term or long-term memory, Kesner and Conner (1974) examined retention of an aversive footshock experience in rats 64 s after shock (short-term memory test) or 24 hr after shock (long-term memory test). Rats with electrodes stereotaxically implanted, bilaterally, into either the amygdala, dorsal hippocampus or mesencephalic reticular formation (MRF), were trained to bar press in a Skinner box for sugar water reinforcement. After reaching stable performance, they were given a 5 mA, 1 s footshock following a bar press. Four seconds later, 5 s of bilateral EBS was delivered through the implanted electrodes, and memory of the footshock was tested 55 s later or 24 hr later. Memory was indexed by supression of bar-pressing during the retention test. Unimplanted and implanted nonstimulated control groups were trained and tested in the same fashion. The results of this experiment are shown in Figure 10.3. Suppression of bar pressing, indicated by suppression ratios below 0.5, was used as an index of retention of training. A 0.5 ratio indicates no change from preshock level of bar-pressing or amnesia. As shown in the figure, control groups showed low-suppression ratios indicating good retention of the footshock at both the 64 s (short-term) and 24 hr (long-term) retention test. This was interpreted as evidence for good short-term (STM) and long-term memory (LTM) of the training experience. Amygdala stimulation disrupted both STM and LTM of training. Hippocampal stimulation disrupted LTM only, while MRF stimulation selectively disrupted performance at the STM test. Since STM and LTM could be disrupted independently, Kesner and Conner interpreted these data as evidence for parallel activation of both short-term and long-term memory processes during learning. This is in contrast to the more traditional sequential model (Hebb, 1949; McGaugh, 1966).

Both lesion and electrical stimulation studies indicate that the amygdala plays a critical role in the processing of emotional behavior, such as anger, fear, and rage. The data previously presented are consistent with this point of view. In order to examine this hypothesis in more

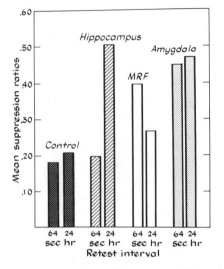

FIGURE 10.3   Mean supression ratios of bar-pressing 64 s and 24 hr after the foot-shock. Electrical stimulation was given for 5 s to the hippocampus, midbrain reticular formation, or amygdala 4 s after the footshock; controls received no brain stimulation. Supression of bar-pressing was used as the main indicator of retention for the FS experience. This suppression was indexed by the ratio $B/(A+B)$, where A represents the total number of bar-presses during the first 5 min of the session before treatment and B represents the total number of bar-presses during the first 5 min of the session at the retest. Thus, a ratio of .50 indicates no relative change in bar-press rate after the treatment. A ratio of .00 indicates complete cessation of responding on a retest. (After Kesner & Conner, 1974).

detail, Kesner, Berman, Burton, and Hankins (1975) studied the effects of posttrial EBS of the amygdala on memory of two unique learning experiences: recovery from neophobia and learned taste aversions. Neophobia refers to the observation that rats show an initial shyness toward novel-flavored foods or liquids and initially consume less of them than they would of a familiar substance (Barnett, 1958; Rozin & Kalat, 1971). If no consequences such as illness follow ingestion, animals will consume normal amounts when the food is presented again. This phenomena has been called recovery from neophobia. Conditioned taste aversion refers to the fact that animals will readily learn to avoid ingestion of substances that have been associated with illness. Taste aversions can be learned by rats in a single trial, even with delays of up to 12 hr between food ingestion and illness. In the neophobia experiments rats were allowed to drink a novel-flavored apple juice solution for 15 min to which they showed a strong initial neophobia. Sixty seconds after removal of the apple juice, 2 min of bilateral amygdala EBS was delivered through implanted electrodes. Three days later animals were again presented with apple juice, and the amount consumed was recorded. Both controls and stimulated animals showed complete recovery from neophobia. When the solution was changed to grape juice and consumption was followed by illness produced by injection of LiCl, then control animals avoided the solution when tested 3 days later indicating acquisition of a strong conditioned aversion. In contrast animals given amygdaloid stimulation as long as 3 hr after illness onset, showed little acquisition of the taste aversion. EBS applied after the initial flavor presentation or during the taste–illness interval failed to affect taste-aversion conditioning. These data indicate that the amygdala may be important for taste aversion conditioning, possibly by mediating the association of negative affective experiences such as nausea or pain with taste. The observation that amygdaloid stimulation did not affect recovery from neophobia, but did disrupt the association of taste with illness is consistent with this hypothesis.

While the data suggest a role for the amygdala in memory of aversive experiences, few studies explored the effects of amygdaloid lesions or posttrial stimulation on memory of appetitive experiences. This is due, in part, to the difficulty in constructing one-trial appetitive learning experiences that result in sufficient learning to provide measurable baseline retention performance. Berman and Kesner (1976) employed a one-trial appetitively motivated task in rats to explore the role of the amygdala, lateral hypothalamus and dorsal hippocampus in STM and LTM. In this task, thirsty rats were allowed to find and lick a drinking spout filled with sugar water. Following this the tube was withdrawn and 4 s later, 30 s of low intensity EBS was delivered through chronically implanted electrodes in the amygdala, dorsal hippocampus, or lateral hypothalamus. Memory of the sugar water experience was measured 90 s or 24 hr later by measuring the number of licks taken by the animals on an identical empty tube. Amygdaloid stimulation did not disrupt memory for this appetitive experience. Dorsal hippocampal stimulation disrupted retention 24 hr following training only, and lateral hypothalamic (LH) stimulation facilitated retention performance at the short-term 90-s test, but not at the 24-hr LTM test. The implications of these results with LH and hippocampal stimulation are discussed later.

Although this study would appear to support the idea that the amygdala functions primarily in the processing-aversive experiences, a more recent study suggests that the amygdala may be involved in mnemonic processing of both positive and negative emotional experiences provided that the experiences are sufficiently salient. Kesner (1981) found

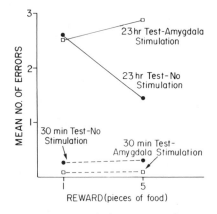

FIGURE 10.4   Mean number of errors before entering the correct arm as a function of expectation of 1 or 5 pieces of food, time of retention test (20 min or 23 hr), and presence or absence of amygdala stimulation.

that posttrial amygdaloid stimulation impaired retention of an appetitive learning experience in a task which varied the level of reinforcement magnitude. Specifically, Kesner reported that rats make fewer errors in returning to a previously reinforced arm of a maze when they have been trained to expect five, rather then one reinforcement upon returning to the arm. This is an example of the *magnitude of reinforcement effect*. In this situation animals receive an initial reinforcement in one arm of an 8-arm maze. Highly discriminable and appetitive flavors were used as reinforcers and also as cues signalling the magnitude of reinforcement on the next trial. Thus, one flavor cued the presence of five reinforcements on the next trial, whereas a different flavor signaled only one reinforcement. As shown in Figure 10.4, this magnitude of reinforcement effect is observed at the 23-hr test. The number of errors made by the *No-Stimulation* control group dropped on trials in which five rather than one reinforcer had been signaled. Stimulation of the amygdala had little or no effect on performance when animals expected a single reinforcement upon reentering the reinforced arm. Stimulation after the cue signalling the large reinforcement disrupted retention. Kesner (1981) suggests that the amygdala may be involved in the encoding of both positive and negative emotional attributes associated with reinforcement contingencies, providing that the situation involves intense reinforcers. These findings are consistent with a large body of evidence that the amygdala is involved in the mediation of emotional responses, such as fear, anxiety, pleasure, and anger, and suggest a general role for the amygdala in the hedonic evaluation of reinforcing stimuli (Ben-Ari, 1981).

Caudate Nucleus Stimulation

Most studies on the function of the caudate nucleus have focused on its relationship with other basal ganglia structures, such as the globus pallidus and putamen, in its role in the control of movement. Early work studied such elicited behaviors as arrest of movement, head turning, phasic limb and facial movements that occur following stimulation of the caudate. However, retention deficits have also been reported at stimulation intensities below those producing gross motor movements.

Wyers, et al. (1968) trained rats to traverse a runway and press a lever for liquid food reward. After stable runway performance was achieved, rats were given an intense footshock while licking and were tested for memory of the footshock experience 24 hr later by measuring the time it took for trained animals to run the maze and begin licking. Unstimulated control animals showed long latencies to approach and drink from the tube, while animals given a single pulse of bilateral caudate EBS 0.1–30 s after the footshock approached and drank far more quickly. Wyers and Deadwyler (1971) later showed that the amnesia was time-dependent because when caudate stimulation was delayed by 30 s to 15 min after training, the least disruption occurred with the longest footshock-brain stimulation intervals. Wyers, Deadwyler, Hirasuna, and Montgomery (1973) further demonstrated that memory was disrupted when measured as early as 100 s after training and EBS and that stimulation of brain regions near the effective caudate sites, including accumbens, cortex, pallidum, lateral geniculate, internal capsule, was ineffective indicating that the amnesia was due to local disruption of caudate activity. Since caudate EBS was effective immediately after training, while EBS delayed by more than a few minutes was not, Wyers et al. (1973) concluded that memory consolidation, rather than initial acquisition or retrieval of memory was disrupted. Gold and King (1972) also report a temporal gradient of retrograde amnesia in rats using a 1-trial shock-avoidance task. One second of 1.5 mA bilateral caudate stimulation 15 min after footshock impaired retention tested 24 hr later. EBS delayed 60 min after training was ineffective as was a lower EBS intensity (i.e., 1.0 mA). Posttraining EBS of some projections to the caudate may also be effective since stimulation of the substantia nigra pars compacta, a major projection to the caudate, also disrupts retention in rats (Routtenberg & Holtzman, 1973). Similar stimulation of the reticular zone of the substantia nigra was without effect, as was stimulation of the media lemniscus and red nucleus. Peeke and Herz (1971) found that caudate nucleus stimulation interfered with food-reinforced maze learning in rats, suggesting some generality of these findings across different learning tasks.

Not all studies employing posttrial caudate stimulation reported amnesia following posttrial stimulation. For example, Wilburn and Kesner (1974) fail to find passive avoidance deficits following low-intensity caudate stimulation in cats. The reason for this discrepancy is unclear, but could be related to differences in stimulation parameters of species.

From the studies described above it is clear that caudate stimulation can interfere with memory for training in a variety of tasks, including shock avoidance and appetitive maze learning. The role of the caudate in memory, however, remains unclear. Kesner (1982) has suggested that different neural regions may mediate specific attributes of memory and that the caudate nucleus may participate in memory of some motoric or kinesthetic aspect of an experience. More research will be required before the merit of this suggestion can be judged.

Hippocampal Stimulation

Several studies using posttrial hippocampal stimulation indicate a role for the hippocampus in memory processes. Both disruption and facilitation of memory have been reported. Kesner and Doty (1968) were amont the first to report that posttrial dorsal hippocampal seizures interfered with the retention of 1-trial shock avoidance in cats. They reported complete amnesia in 8 out of 13 cats when animals were tested for retention 24 hr after training and EBS. Brunner, Rossi, Stutz, and Roth (1970) later reported that rats given footshock after stepping off a platform onto a grid in a step-down passive avoidance task showed amnesia 24 hr later, if bilateral stimulation of the dorsal hippocampus immediately followed footshock. Similar stimulation of the cortex or septal region had no effect. Interestingly, large bilateral electrolytic lesions of the hippocampus failed to disrupt retention of the footshock suggesting that electrical stimulation may be capable of producing more complete interference than lesions of large complex structures such as the hippocampus. Such lesions nearly always leave some connections intact. McDonough and Kesner (1971) then reported that bilateral subseizure electrical stimulation of the dorsal hippocampus 4 s or 5 min after mouth shock impaired retention of shock when cats were tested 24 hr later. Others have also produced amnesia in rats and mice by using subseizure, bilateral, posttrial stimulation of the dorsal hippocampus (Kapp, Gallagher, Holmquist, & Theall, 1978; Kesner &

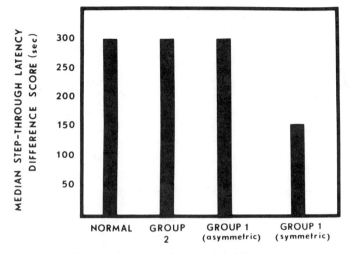

FIGURE 10.5   Median group step-through latency difference scores. Group 2 mice were implanted controls. Mice in Group 1 (asymmetric) received subseizure EBS to asymmetrical electrode placements. Mice in Group 1 (symmetric) received bilateral electrical stimulation to electrodes bilaterally located in the area dentata. (From Zornetzer et al., 1973).

Connor, 1974; Vadaris & Schwartz, 1971; Zornetzer, Chronister, & Ross, 1973). Bilateral stimulation of the dorsal hippocampus appears to be necessary to disrupt memory, and Zornetzer et al. (1973) produced amnesia only when bilateral electrodes were located symmetrically in the area dentata of the hippocampal complex. Asymmetric placements failed to influence behavior as shown in Figure 10.5. This finding is consistent with data from humans indicating that bilateral destruction of temporal lobe structures is an important precondition for severe memory deficits (Milner, 1966). Berman and Kesner (1976) reported that hippocampal stimulation also impairs memory for appetitive experiences. In their study, rats trained in a single trail to find a source of sugarwater showed amnesia 24 hr later if posttrial dorsal-hippocampal stimulation was given. Memory tested immediately (90 s) after training was intact. These results are consistent with the suggestion that the hippocampus may be critically involved in long-term, but not short-term memory.

The role of the hippocampus in memory has been reinterpreted by recent studies indicating that memory for a specific event must in fact be composed of many parallel memories representing attributes of the experience. Examples may be temporal, spatial, affective, and motoric attributes of a memory event. This idea was considered in detail by

Bower (1967) and by Underwood (1969) more than 25 years ago. In one recent version of this hypothesis (Kesner, 1982), memory for a typical 1-trial shock-avoidance task requires an animal to gain information about the relationship between several stimulus variables, such as foot-shock, illumination, noise level, odors, and spatial aspects of the environment and such behaviors as lever-pressing, freezing, and escape. Specific attributes, then, may be abstracted and processed in parallel by different neural regions. According to this view, the hippocampus may be centrally involved in processing spatial–temporal information about the environment, while the amygdala may participate in memory for affective attributes of the experience. In a unique test of this hypothesis, Kesner and Hardy (1983) trained rats in the dark to enter a compartment and lick water from a metal spout. After initial training, a pattern of phosphorescent stripes was inserted into the compartment around the spout to accentuate the environmental aspects of the training environment. Animals were given a 2 s, 1.5 mA footshock after 60 s of licking, followed 50 s later by 5 s of low-intensity bilateral EBS of either the dorsal hippocampus or medial amygdala. Retention of the footshock experience was then tested under two conditions (Test 1 and Test 2 in Figure 10.6). Retention Test 1 was given 24 hr after training with only a single phosphorescent stripe centered around the spout. At Retention Test 2 given 48 hrs after training the total set of phosphorescent lines was present. As can be seen, both unoperated and implanted controls showed good retention of the footshock experience under the partial cue condition (Test 1), and better retention when the complete cue was present (Test 2). Animals that received posttrial amygdala stimulation showed poor retention under the partial cue conditions, but good retention with the complete cue. In contract, hippocampal stimulated animals showed poor retention under both conditions. If one accepts the suggestion by Kesner & Hardy that the complete set of phosphorescent stripes represents an environmental–spatial cue, then the following interpretation is possible. Amygdala stimulaed animals showed improved memory under Test 2 because memory for the environmental context (e.g., stripes) was intact, and the presence of the complete cue acted as a reminder. In constrast, hippocampal stimulation disrupted memory for the environment so that recreation of the training environment was unable to act as a reminder and failed to facilitate retention. This hypothesis is supported by evidence from lesion studies that show that damage to the hippocampus or its afferents and efferents (fornix or entorhinal cortex) appears to selectively impair spatial memory (O'Keefe & Nadel, 1978). However, other interpreta-

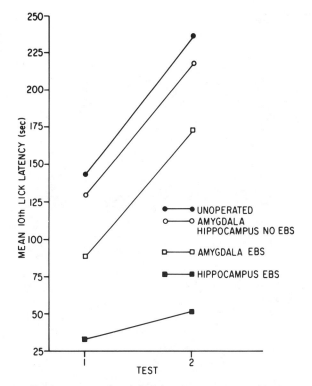

FIGURE 10.6   Groups means of 10th lick latency scores (in s) on Test 1 (partial cue) and Test 2 (complete cue) for unoperated, amygdala, and hippocampus implanted but nonstimulated, amygdala stimulated and hippocampus stimulated animals. EBS, electrical brain stimulation. (From Kesner & Hardy, 1983).

tions of such experiments are possible, and again more research will be required to test this hypothesis.

Hippocampal lesions have also been reported to impair working memory (Olton, Becker, & Handelmann, 1979). Working memories are defined as memories that are useful within one test but are not useful from test to test. For example, rats can learn to enter each arm of an 8-arm maze once in order to obtain food and can retain memory for arms entered within a trial. However, rats do not retain such information from day to day as evidenced by the observation that different patterns of maze running are used from test to test. A possible analogy might be drawn to memory for items in a list, where specific items change from day to day. In order to explore the effects of electrical stimulation of the hippocampus on working memory, Collier, Miller, Travis, and Routten-

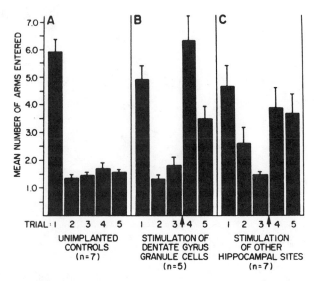

FIGURE 10.7   Effects of hippocampal stimulation on performance on a 5-trial, delayed matching-to-sample task that required rats to return to a baited arm of an 8 arm
maze for food reinforcement. (A) Mean (±SEM) number of arms entered by unimplanted
control animals over 5 trials. (B) Number of arms entered over 5 trials by animals receiving 30 s of 10 uA EBS of dentate granule cells immediately after trial 3. (C) Effects of
stimulation of other hippocampal sites on performance. (From Collier et. al., 1982).

berg (1982) trained rats to find food reinforcement at the end of one arm
of an 8-arm maze. Rats were then trained to return to that same arm
over the next 5 trials, with the specific arm changed from day to day.
Thirty seconds of hippocampal EBS was given during the delay between Trials 3 and 4 of maze running. The results are shown in Figure
10.7. As shown in the figure, unimplanted controls are able to reliably
return to the baited arm over the 5 trials indicating good memory for the
task. In contrast, stimulated animals were unable to return to the reinforced arm on Trials 4 and 5. The effect was not specific for the dentate
gyrus as stimulation of other hippocampal sites was also effective.
These results were interpreted as evidence that working memory can be
disrupted by hippocampal stimulation, that the effects of EBS parallel
those obtained with lesions of the hippocampus, and that the hippocampus is central the processing of working memory.

    In summary, the weight of the evidence indicates that posttrial stim-
ulation of the hippocampal formation is capable of disrupting memory
in a variety of tasks. The nature of the disruption is the subject of
current debate. Earlier work considered the role of the hippocampus in
consolidation of long-term memory, while more recent work focused

on its involvement in memory of spatial–temporal aspects of an experience or in working memory.

Stimulation of the Midbrain Recticular Formation (MRF)

Both disruption and facilitation of memory have been reported to follow stimulation of the MRF. Glickman (1958) reported that posttrial high-intensity stimulation disrupted memory for shock-avoidance training in rats. However, others reported that lower levels of MRF stimulation can facilitate acquisition in cats and monkeys (Fuster & Uyeda, 1962; Sterman & Fairchild, 1966). More recently, Sara, Deweer, & Hars (1980) tested the effects of MRF stimulation on retrieval of maze learning in rats using a procedure that measured spontaneous forgetting in trained subjects over a period of 25 days. Rats that received 90 s of MRF stimulation immediately prior to retention testing 25 days after training showed fewer errors than nonstimulated controls. Sara et al. concluded that since MRF stimulation can alter memory days after initial learning, continued integration of experiential input must continue long after initial learning. No inferences were made concerning the possible role of the MRF in memory formation or retrieval.

In contrast to the studies just described, Kesner and Conner (1974) reported that MRF stimulation disrupted short-term memory. In the experiment described in Figure 10.3, rats shocked while bar-pressing and then given immediate posttrial MRF stimulation showed amnesia when tested 64 s later. No amnesia was observed 24 hr later. Again, Kesner and Connor (1974) concluded that STM and LTM are activated in parallel and that MRF stimulation selectively impairs STM producing amnesia immediately after training, but parallel activation of LTM results in a viable trace measurable 24 hr later. In a further test of this hypothesis, Bierley and Kesner (1980) trained rats in a discrete delayed-alternation task. Briefly, rats were trained in a Skinner box equipped with two symetrically placed retractable levers. Levers were positioned on either side of a reinforcement dipper that delivered sugarwater. On any one trial either the right or left lever was extended into the box. After being pressed, the lever was retracted. After a variable delay of either 0, 5, 15, 30, or 40 s, both levers were extended into the box, and reinforcement was delivered for a barpress on the lever opposite to the one originally pressed. This is a delayed-alternation procedure. Under these conditions control animals can perform above chance with delays of approximately 40 s (Figure 10.8). Stimulation of

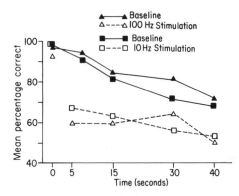

FIGURE 10.8   Effects of midbrain reticular formation (MRF) stimulation (10 or 100 Hz) upon percentage correct performance in delayed alteration task as a function of time delay. (Fifty percent correct responding reflects chance performance.)

the MRF disrupted retention at every delay suggesting that stimulation interfered with the persistence of STM.

Stimulation of Cerebral Cortex

Seizure level stimulation of the inferotemporal cortex has been reported to impair learning of visual pattern discrimination in monkeys (Goldrich & Stamm, 1971). In such studies direct stimulation of the visual cortex did not interfere with learning indicating that the effect was due to a level of information processing beyond initial sensory registration. However, such seizures could spread to other sites, such as the amygdala or hippocampus, where disruption is already known to produce memory impairment. The following year, Kovner and Stamm (1972) used subseizure stimulation of the inferotemporal cortex in a delayed matching-to-sample task in monkeys. They reported that such stimulation disrupted retention only when given during the delay between stimulus presentation or when given with the matching stimulus. They suggest that the inferotemporal cortex may be involved in processing of visual information, such as pattern recognition, into short-term memory.

Posttrial stimulation of the cerebral cortex of rats has also been reported to disrupt memory. Gold, Farrell, and King (1971) found that stimulation of the anterior or posterior cortex 5 s after shock-avoidance training produced amnesia when animals were tested 24 hr later. However, high current levels above 5 mA were required. Zornetzer and McGaugh (1972) also showed that stimulation of the frontal cortex produces amnesia for shock-avoidance training in rats, but only at intensities that result in primary afterdischarges recorded from the cortex. These results suggest that seizures are generally required in order for frontal–cortical stimulation to produce amnesia, and several studies have failed to find memory impairments using subseizure stimulation levels (Brunner et al., 1970; Erickson & Patel, 1969; Lidsky & Slotnick, 1971).

MEMORY FACILITATION BY ELECTRICAL BRAIN STIMULATION

Memory and learning can also be facilitated by localized intracranial brain stimulation. These studies are of particular interest as they indicate that the mnemonic processes of storage and retrieval can be enhanced by experimental manipulations such as EBS, and support the possibility that memory disorders may eventually be amenable to pharmacological treatment. There are difficulties, however, in the interpretation of such studies. For example, memory in experimental animals is always inferred by observing performance on operationally defined memory tasks such as shock-avoidance or complex-maze learning. Performance on these tasks could be improved by a number of mechanisms, including enhanced attentive processes, altered motivation state, and even direct motor effects of EBS, that do not directly, but only indirectly influence memory. However, these same criticisms are also valid for studies reporting memory disruption.

In an early study, Stein and Chrover (1968) found that electrical stimulation of the dorsal hippocampus facilitated acquisition of a Hebb–Williams maze, but only when maze training was conducted under spaced conditions. They trained rats in a series of 15 Hebb–Williams maze problems either with 6 hr between the first and 5 subsequent trials (spaced training), or under conditions of 6 massed trials. EBS was delivered to the hippocampus or caudate after the first trial for the spaced training conditions, or after each trial under massed conditions. The results demonstrated significant savings in acquisition under the spaced trial conditions following hippocampal stimulation, but impaired acquisition under the massed training conditions. Caudate stimulation was without effect in both tasks.

Erickson and Patel (1969) also reported that electrical stimulation of the dorsal hippocampus facilitated learning in rats. Rats were trained to press a lever in response to a tone in order to avoid a footshock. Three seconds of EBS was delivered to the dorsal hippocampus 10 s after each avoidance or escape response. Rats were trained to a criterion of 85%

successful avoidance responses. Rats receiving low-intensity hippocampal EBS (30 μA) reached the criterion faster than unstimulated controls and faster than animals receiving high-intensity (200 μA) hippocampal or frontal cortex stimulation. The effect was blocked by administration of atropine sulfate. The authors concluded that the septohippocampal cholinergic system plays a central role in memory processing by the hippocampus. Destrade and his colleagues have carried out a series of studies examining the nature of memory facilitation produced by posttrial electrical stimulation of the hippocampus. In their experiments, mice are partially trained to lever-press for food and are then tested for retention of training by examining the rate of lever-pressing 24 hr later. Electrical brain stimulation is given sometime after training. In an early study, Destrade, Soumireau–Mourat, and Cardo (1973) found that EBS of region CA-1 of the dorsal hippocampus facilitated lever-pressing acquisition. The effect was time-dependent in that stimulation delivered immediately after initial training enhanced retention, but was ineffective when given 10 min later. Galey, Jeantet, Destrade, and Jaffard (1983) later found that stimulation of the medial-septal input to the hippocampus also facilitated retention of lever-pressing in a time-dependent fashion. They speculate that activation of the septo-hippocampal cholinergic pathway was responsible for the memory facilitation. EBS of the entorhinal cortex (EC), the major direct cortical input to the hippocampus via the perforant pathway, also facilitated retention, but with an unusual temporal gradient (Gauthier, Destrade, & Soumireu-Mourat, 1982). Stimulation of EC delayed by 30 s or 3 hr was ineffective, while that delayed by 30 min facilitated retention. Lesions of the perforant pathway did not abolish this effect indicating that it was not due to direct hippocampal activation, but may be cortical in nature (Gauthier & Destrade, 1984). They speculate that the hippocampus is involved in immediate initial processing of memory, while the entorhinal cortex became active in later memory processing, possibly via interaction with cortical stored memories.

Other investigators have also reported that EBS of the medial-septal nucleus can facilitate memory, but have attempted to relate facilitation to induction of hippocampal theta activity (Landfield, 1976; Landfield, Tusa & McGaugh, 1973; Wetzel, Ott, & Matthies, 1977). Theta is a rhythmic, synchronized EEG activity of 4–7 Hz characteristic of hippocampal neurons that can be driven by low-frequency EBS of the medial septum. Landfield (1977) reported that in rats, when theta was driven by 7.7 Hz stimulation of the medial septum immediately after active avoidance training, memory was facilitated when tested 24 hr later. EBS at 77 Hz blocked theta and did not facilitate memory.

In support of these observations, Wetzel, Ott, and Matthies (1977) found that posttrial stimulation of the medial septal area facilitated learning of a brightness discrimination in rats. They gave rats 40 training trials in a brightness discrimination task and then delivered low-frequency (7 Hz) medial-septal stimulation for 10 min, either 5 min or 4 hr after initial training. Another group received high-frequency (100 Hz) septal stimulation. Retention was measured 24 hr later as percentage savings during retraining of the animals in the original task. They found that 7 Hz stimulation delivered 5 min posttraining facilitated retention tested 24 hr later and produced a 65–79% increase in hippocampal theta. High-frequency stimulation (100 Hz) resulted in only 8–27% hippocampal theta and slightly impaired retention. They concluded that synchronization of hippocampal EEG at some critical point in memory formation can facilitate memory consolidation.

Facilitation of memory by posttrial stimulation of the dorsal hippocampus would appear to be inconsistent with the studies described previously indicating amnesia following such stimulation. Unfortunately, no human studies have yet reported facilitation of memory formation following hippocampal stimulation, so no information is available on the qualitative nature of the facilitation in laboratory animals. However, one possible explanation for the apparent discrepancy may be that dorsal hippocampal stimulation disrupts normal memory processes and that both apparent amnesia and memory facilitation represent different forms of, but nevertheless abnormal, altered memories. The temptation to assume that facilitated performance during tests of retention in laboratory animals actually represents a qualitatively improved memory always exists. However, at present there is no evidence upon which to base this assumption.

Enhancement of memory has also been reported following electrical stimulation of the lateral hypothalamus (Berman & Kesner, 1976; Huston, Mueller, & Mondadori, 1977). Berman and Kesner (1976) allowed water-deprived rats to find a spout containing sugar water. Retention was tested immediately (90 s) or 24 hr later by measuring the number of licks taken on an empty tube in the same setting. Unstimulated controls demonstrated good retention of the appetitive experience, and rats that received LH stimulation immediately after training showed enhanced retention by an increase in the number of licks taken on the empty tube. However, the effect was only significant at the 90 s but not at the 24 hr retention test. Similarly, Houston and Muller (1978) demonstrated similar facilitation of learning following EBS of the lateral hypothalamus in a number of memory tasks. The mechanisms underlying the facilitation may be due to the reinforcing nature of the stimulation, and it has been suggested that this effect may be due to activation of catechol-amine-containing and possibly Substance P-containing neurons in the hypothalamus (Houston & Staubli, 1981). However, Berman and Kesner (1976) did not find direct reinforcing effects with LH stimulation that also appeared to facilitate retention.

Finally, in a fascinating series of studies, Velley and Cardo (1979) report that 4 hr of reinforcing lateral hypothalamic or locus coeruleus stimulation delivered on 2 consecutive days in 15-day-old rats facilitated acquisition of operant conditioning on a CRF schedule when training was conducted 4 weeks later. The effect could also be observed when stimulation was delivered between 10 and 90 days of age. The nature of this effect, although suggested to be due to activation of dorsal noradrenergic system plasticity, remains unknown. However, it does indicate that under certain circumstances, the effects of localized EBS can be long lasting, and facilitation of performance can be observed many weeks after stimulation.

Facilitation of memory following stimulation of the mesencephalic reticular formation has also been reported, and it has been suggested that such stimulation may enhance memory via activation of target structures, such as the hippocampus, more directly involved in memory (Ammassari–Teule, Fombon, & Bloch, 1984).

ELECTRICAL BRAIN STIMULATION IN HUMANS

Wilder Penfield, founder of the Montreal Neurological Institute, pioneered the use of localized electrical stimulation to explore the functional organization of the brain. After completing his medical training Penfield went to Breslau in 1928 to work with the neurologist, Otfried Foester. Foester operated under local anesthesia on epileptic patients and applied *gentle* electrical stimulation to the surface of the cerebral cortex in an effort to imitate the effects of focal epileptogenic lesions. It is this setting that made it possible for Penfield to study the anatomy and physiology of the conscious human brain in an operation using EBS. Penfield was thus able to map the now classical sensory, motor, and speech areas of the cortex. He also made the astonishing discovery that electrical stimulation of certain regions of the brain produced *psychical states*.

These states were classified as follows (Mullan & Penfield, 1959): (1) psychical hallucinations, (2) psychical illusions, and (3) psychomotor automatisms. Patients experiencing psychical illusions during cortical

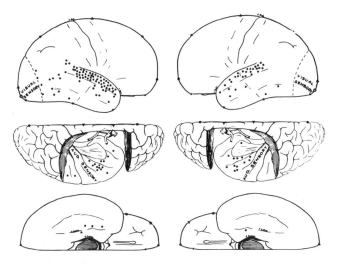

FIGURE 10.9   Maps indicating experiential responses produced by electrical stimulation. (From Penfield and Perot, 1963.)

stimulation appeared to misinterpret present experiences so that friends voices sounded remote, well-known rooms appeared unfamiliar, and feelings of sorrow, fear, disgust, or loneliness were sometimes experienced. These illusions were only produced by EBS of the temporal lobe and surface of the adjoining insula. According to Penfield, the patients were always aware that the altered perceptions were illusions. Psychomotor automatisms were periods of confused behavior, again evoked by cortical EBS, and invariably followed by amnesia for events that occurred during the period. By far the most interesting effects of EBS, however, were the psychical or *experiential* hallucinations reported by Penfield in approximately 8% of the patients he studied. These experiential hallucinations appeared to represent a "recall of past experiences in detail with all that fell within the patients attention at that time. They are better called experiential seizures or experiential responses to stimulation" (Mullan & Penfield, 1959, p. 269). The areas of the temporal lobe from which these hallucinations could be evoked is indicated in Figure 10.9 (Penfield & Perot, 1963).

The experiences recalled were chiefly auditory, visual, or combined auditory–visual. These hallucinations were produced by stimulation of the temporal lobe, and none were elicited by stimulation of other lobes or from dominant speech areas. An example of one of these hallucinations is described as follows:

> This is born out by the results of stimulation in the case of M. M. She heard "a mother calling her little boy" when point 11 on the first temporal convolution

was stimulated. When it was repeated at once, without warning she heard the same thing. When repeated again twice at the same point, she heard it each time, and she recognized that she was near her childhood home.

At point 12 nearby, on the same convolution, stimulation caused her to hear a man's voice and a women's voice "down along the river somewhere." And she saw the river. It was a place "I was visiting" she said, "when I was a child."

Three minutes later, while the electrode was held in place at 13, she exclaimed that she heard voices late at night and that she saw the "big wagons they used to haul the animals [of a circus] in." (Penfield, 1958, p. 59)

The content of these illusions were rarely of experiences that the patient said were of importance. Usually they were described as forgotten events, but the patients expressed little doubt that the experiences were their own. Penfield came to call the area of the cortex from which EBS produced experiential *flash backs* the *interpretative cortex*. Penfield concluded that memories of past experiences were probably not stored in the interpretative cortex. Rather, that this cortical area was a passage way through which electrical current could activate portions of "a record of the stream of consciousness" (Penfield, 1958, p. 58).

The nature of these experiential hallucinations are as difficult to interpret today as they were when Penfield first described them (Penfield, 1938). They have recently been systematically observed by Halgren, Walter, Cherlow, and Crandall (1978). They found that the vivid hallucinations and deja vu described by Penfield following lateral-temporal lobe (LTL) stimulation occur in approximately the same proportion of patients after subcortical medial temporal lobe (MTL) stimulation and concluded that MTL structures (hippocampus, para-hippocampal gyrus, amygdaloid complex, and subicular complex) are more important than the lateral portions of the temporal lobe, areas stimulated by Penfield and his co-workers in evoking experiential phenomena. However, Halgren (1982) argues that experiential phenomena evoked by MTL stimulation are really due to activation of some yet-to-be-discovered site more central than the MTL to the storage of memory. This conclusion is based on the observation that there did not appear to be a relationship between the location of the stimulating electrode and the category of experience evoked. Second, mental phenomena were more likely to be evoked if afterdischarges were also produced and spread to interrelated structures (Halgren, 1982). Third, surgical removal of the MTL does not destroy the memories that were evoked by EBS. Finally, the major effect of EBS is to disrupt activity of large masses of neurons around the electrode tip. The fact that MTL stimulation often evokes specific, complex, and coherent experiences suggests to Halgren that they represent responses of another structure to altered MTL output.

According to Halgren (1982), MTL activity allows us to interpret current awareness, such as sensory information about emotional state and content of recent episodic memory, against a model of the external world (which is semantic memory) elaborated in the association cortex. Halgren (1982) argues that the hippocampal formation may be the critical area activated when MTL stimulation evokes memory images. Evoked memories, then, are due to activation of semantic memory in association cortex due to disruption, or otherwise loss of control, of normal MTL system input. In many ways this view is similar to Penfield's original description of the function of the superior lateral–temporal lobes (LTL) as interpretative cortex, the difference being in the focus by Halgren on MTL rather than on LTL sites.

As discussed previously (see Berman & Kesner, 1981) the major effect of localized EBS is to disrupt normal neural activity at the focus of stimulation. It is not surprizing then that, as in the infrahuman studies described earlier, most clinical investigations report memory impairment following EBS of specific brain regions. In an early study, Chapman, Walter, Markman, Rand, & Crandall (1967) used electrical stimulation to map the cortex of patients being surgically treated for temporal lobe epilepsy, dyskinesias, or intractable pain. Bilateral hippocampal stimulation produced retrograde amnesia extending back approximately 2 weeks in time. Immediate and remote memory were intact. Memory returned within several hours, with complete anterograde amnesia for the period of EBS and the episode of memory loss. Unilateral stimulation of the hippocampus was ineffective. However, unilateral stimulation of the hippocampus in 7 of 15 epilepsy patients resulted in reports of visual images, sounds, or memory fragments. For example, in one subject stimulation evoked fragments of a television commercial, a visual scene of rabbits playing together, rules of a childhood game, and the feeling associated with falling into a deep hole when he was a child. They were not associated with the sensation of reexperiencing an episode, but rather seemed to be intrusions into consciousness. Unilateral stimulation of the amygdaloid complex did not disrupt memory, although 7 of 15 patients reported deja vu following amygdaloid stimulation. These data are consistent with other human data linking amygdaloid function to mental components of emotion (Halgren, 1981).

In line with the research implicating the hippocampus to memory storage and retrieval, evidence links interference with hippocampal activity to the clinical syndrome known as transient global amnesia (TGA). Transient global amnesia is characterized by a retrograde amnesia for events preceeding TGA by weeks or years and simultaneously an anterograde amnesia for events that occurred during the attack. Primary memory (digit span) and remote memory (memory of distant events) are intact. The cause of TGA is unknown, but it has been thought to be due to transient ischemia within the hippocampal formation.

In a test of the role of the MTL in memory, Halgren (1982) studied two patients who were undergoing electrical stimulation of the temporal lobe as a supplementary diagnostic aid in the treatment of epilepsy. A paired-associates task was used in which two words were sequentially presented (cue and response words) for 1.5 s followed by a 3-s presentation of an example uniting the two words. Recall was then tested 30 s later by presenting the cue slides and recording correct recall of response words. In two patients tested, impairment of memory was only noted when afterdischarges were elicited by MTL stimulation. In a subsequent study with eight patients, simultaneous subseizure stimulation of amygdala, hippocampus, and parahippocampal gyrus during either stimulus presentation or recall disrupted memory. Disruption was maximal when EBS was delivered during both stimulus presentation and during recall. No disruption was observed when stimulation was applied between stimulus presentations. Halgren speculates that the MTL structures are involved in both initial experience of an event and in its subsequent recall or recognition.

Ojemann (1982) tested the effects of the EBS of a variety of brain structures on several cognitive functions, including object-naming, reading, short-term verbal memory, facial mimicry, facial memory, matching, and recognition memory. Ojemann, Blick, and Ward (1971) investigated the effects of stimulation of the left ventrolateral thalamus on verbal memory. Lesions of the left ventrolateral thalamus have been associated with impaired performance on standard tests of verbal memory. Twenty-five patients undergoing stereotaxic thalamotomy for treatment of dyskinesias (all but one was a Parkinson's patient) were studied. Subjects were shown a stimulus object, such as a picture of a star, for 4 s and asked to say "this is a star." Subjects then counted backwards for 6 s as a distractor. A 4 s recall test was followed by a 4 s recognition test in which the object had to be picked out from a list. Stimulation was given during presentation of the stimulus object, during the distractor task, or during recall. With left thalamic stimulation given during recall, there was a significant increase in recall errors (35% increase), whereas right lateral thalamic stimulation only produced an 8% increase in recall errors. Ommaya and Fedio (1972) also reported a severe short-term verbal memory disruption following stimulation of the left, but not right cingulum. Nonverbal short-term memory was disrupted by right cingulum stimulation as well as by EBS of frontal white matter. Hippocampal stimulation produced a slight impairment on both verbal and nonverbal memory tasks, but the effect was considerably less than that seen with cingulum stimulation.

Ojemann (1974) later reported that electrical stimulation of left thalamus during acquisition accelerates high mental processes, especially memory. In a study of 26 patients undergoing therapeutic stereotaxic thalamotomy under local anesthesia (24 for dyskinesias, 2 for intractable pain), he reported that left thalamic stimulation during stimulus presentation decreased subsequent recall errors by approximately 15%, but had no effect on initial object naming or latency to name object. Stimulation during the distractor period when the subject was counting backwards accelerated counting rates. Stimulation during recall increased errors by approximately 33.6% but shortened latency to recall. Interestingly, no effect on verbal memory was found when stimulation was given both during presentation and during recall. The conclusion was that left thalamic stimulation produced a specific alerting response for verbal processes and directs attention of the nervous system to active, onging processing of verbal information in the environment.

In an exploration of the human language cortex, Ojemann and Mateer (1979) examined effects of stimulation of language cortex on orofacial movements, phonemic recognition, and short-term verbal memory. Subjects were patients undergoing left anterior temporal lobectomy. Cerebral dominance for language was tested by intracarotid amobarbital testing. Subseizure stimulation levels were used. In the short-term memory test a stimulus object was presented and named. Subjects then read a distractor phase for 8 s followed by a 4-s test of recall. Stimulation effects were studied at each phase of testing. Based on the results, Ojemann and Mateer described three general systems associated with language areas of the human cortex. The first system, found in the left motor and premotor inferior frontal cortex appears to represent a motor output pathway for speech since stimulation impaired all facial movement and generally arrested speech. A second system in the inferior frontal, superior temporal, and parietal peri-Sylvian cortex may represent a sequential motor-phoneme identification system for language, since stimulation of these sites alters both sequential motor movements and phoneme recognition. A third system, largely separate from the others appears to represent a short-term verbal memory system. Memory impairment sites were found in the parietal and temporal, but not the frontal lobe. The memory errors appear to follow stimulation during input, but not during output, indicating that these sites may be involved in active verbal memory storage. The pattern of sites described is shown in Figure 10.10.

Studies on the effects of electrical stimulation of the brain on mem-

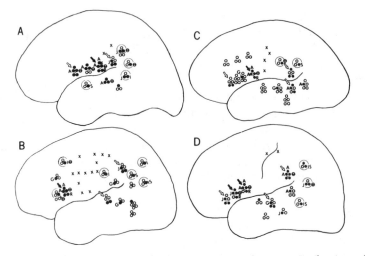

FIGURE 10.10   Sites where stimulation alters language functions in dominant hemispheres of four patients. Large circles indicate major subdivision where EBS interfered
with short-term verbal memory. Filled arrows indicate a major subdivision representing
final motor pathway for speech. Open arrows represent sequential motor-phoneme identification system. (From "Human Language Cortex: Localization of Memory, Syntax, and
Sequential Motor-Phoneme Identification Systems" by G. Ojemann and C. Mateer, 1979,
Science, *205*, pp. 1401–1403. Copyright 1979 by the AAAS.

ory are by necessity rare and difficult to carry out. In general the results
of these studies appear to compliment the experimental findings with
laboratory research animals. That is, electrical brain stimulation of the
hippocampus can impair memory. Both recent (short-term) and remote
(long-term) memories are affected. Halgren's studies indicate that the
amygdala, another medial temporal lobe structure, also participates in
information processing, and stimulation of this structure can contribute to amnesia, or to experiential or affective changes in consciousness.
The human studies also point to the importance of thalamic regions in
memory processing, particularly the research of Ojemann (1982). This
is consistent with the view that damage to diencephalic structures such
as the dorsomedial nucleus of the thalamus (Squire, 1982) can also
impair memory. Indeed, Squire (1982) suggests two types of amnesia,
diencephalic and temporal lobe amnesia, to reflect the fact that damage
to either region appears to produce amnesia. Unfortunately, few, if any,
studies with laboratory animals have systematically investigated the
effects of thalamic stimulation on memory. However, dorsomedial nucleus lesions have been reported to affect memory in cats and monkeys.

The human data further point to the complexity of behavioral effects following EBS, ranging from memory facilitation, arrest of behavior, affective responses, as well as amnesia.

SUMMARY

The past 25 years of research on the neurobiology of memory and learning have made it clear that (1) no single brain structure or region is solely responsible for memory storage and retrieval, (2) some neural regions must be directly involved in storage and retrieval processes, while others primarily serve to modulate memory, (3) many brain regions are capable of being modified by experience, and (4) more than one type of memory exists. Thus, it is not surprising that EBS of many brain regions can alter memory, with results ranging from amnesia to memory enhancement. Furthermore, the results one obtains from such studies are dependent upon the nature of the memory requirements of the learning task and probably even the animal species being studied. The task of the investigator, then, is to draw together the complex and often seemingly divergent findings concerning the neurobiology of memory into a coherent and consistent theory of memory.

The findings with EBS indicate that disruption of ongoing activity in the amygdala, caudate nucleus, mesencephalic reticular formation, hippocampus, and specific regions of the cerebral cortex can alter memory if applied during or shortly after learning. The nature of the altered memory may be either disruption or enhancement. If memories are composed of multiple components or attributes, then each neural region may be differentially involved in the processing of a specific aspect of experiential input. Disruption of amygdala activity is particularly effective in producing memory impairment when the experience to be remembered involves either negative reinforcement such as footshock, or possibly any intense affective response. In turn, the hippocampus may play a role in memory for the spatial–temporal aspects of an experience. A possible role for the caudate nucleus could involve processing of memory for motoric responses, while the MRF may still perform its traditionally assigned role of modulating CNS arousal and thereby the rate of memory storage and retrieval. Finally, specific cortical areas may process event-related sensory input, including visual, auditory, and somatosensory, while other regions may carry out later processing of memory by elaboration of higher order associations between new input and previously stored memories.

REFERENCES

Ammassari–Teule, M., Fombon, A., & Bloch, V. (1984). Facilitation of generalization in spatial learning problems by posttrial stimulation of the mesencephalic reticular formation. Physiology and Behavior, 32, 1027–1031.

Barnett, S. A. (1958). Experiments on "neophobia" in wild and laboratory rats. British Journal of Psychology, 49, 195–201.

Ben–Ari, Y. (1981). The Amygdaloid Complex. Elsevier-North Holland: New York.

Berman, R. F., & Kesner, R. P. (1976). Posttrial hippocampal, amygdaloid, and lateral hypothalamic electrical stimulation: Effects on short- and long-term memory of an appetitive experience. Journal of Comparative and Physiological Psychology, 90, 260–267.

Berman, R. F., & Kesner, R. P. (1981). Electrical stimulation as a tool in memory research. In M. M. Patterson & R. P. Kesner (Eds.), Electrical stimulation research techniques (pp. 173–203). Academic Press: New York.

Bierley, R. A., & Kesner, R. P. (1980). Short-term memory: The role of the midbrain reticular formation. Journal of Comparative and Physiological Psychology, 24, 561–575.

Boast, C. A., Reid, S. A., Johnson, P., & Zornetzer, S. F. (1976). A caution to brain scientists: Unsuspected hemorrhagic vascular damage resulting from mere electrode implantation. Brain Research, 103, 527–534.

Bower, G. H. (1967). A multicomponent theory of the memory trace. In K. W. Spence & J. T. Spence (Eds.), The psychology of learning and motivation (Vol. 1). New York: Academic Press.

Bresnahan, E., & Routtenberg, A. (1972). Memory disruption by unilateral low-level, sub-seizure stimulation of the medial amygdaloid nucleus. Physiology and Behavior, 9, 513–525.

Brunner, R. L., Rossi, R. R., Stutz, R. M., & Roth, T. G. (1970). Memory loss following posttrial electrical stimulation of the hippocampus. Psychonomic Science, 18, 159–160.

Chapman, L. R., Walter, R. D., Markham, C. H., Rand, R. W., & Crandall, P. (1967). Memory changes induced by stimulation of hippocampus or amygdala in epilepsy patients with implanted electrodes. Transactions of the American Neurological Association, 92, 50–56.

Collier, T. J., Miller, J. S., Travis, J., & Routtenberg, A. (1982). Dentate gyrus granule cells and memory: Electrical stimulation disrupts memory for places rewarded. Behavioral and Neural Biology, 34, 227–239.

Correll, R. E. (1957). The effect of bilateral hippocampal stimulation on the acquisition and extinction of an instrumental response. Journal of Comparative and Physiological Psychology, 50, 624–629.

Destrade, C., Soumireu–Morat, B. & Cardo, B. (1973). Effects of posttrial hippocampal stimulation on acquisition of operant behavior in the mouse. Behavioral Biology, 8, 713–724.

DeVietti, T. L., & Kirkpatrick, B. R. (1976). The amnesia gradient: Inadequate as evidence for a memory consolidation process. Science, 194, 438–440.

Doty, R. W. (1969). Electrical stimulation of the brain in behavioral context. Annual Review of Psychology, 20, 289–320.

Ellis, M. E., Berman, R. F., & Kesner, R. P. (1983). Amnesia attenuation specificity: Propranolol reverses norepinephrine but not cycloheximide-induced amnesia. Pharmacology Biochemistry and Behavior, 19, 733–736.

Erickson, C. K., & Patel, J. B. (1969). Facilitation of avoidance learning by posttrial hippocampal electrical stimulation. *Journal of Comparative and Physiological Psychology, 68,* 400–406.

Flynn, J. P., & Wasman, M. (1960). Learning and cortically evoked movement during propagated hippocampal afterdischarges. *Science, 131,* 1607–1608.

Fuster, J. M., & Uyeda, A. A. (1962). Facilitation of tachistoscopie performance by stimulation of midbrain tegmental points in the monkey. *Experimental Neurology, 6,* 384–406.

Galey, D., Jeantet, Y., Destrade, C., & Jaffard, R. (1983). Facilitation of memory consolidation by post-training electrical stimulation of the medial septal nucleus: Is it mediated by changes in rhythmic slow activity. *Behavioral and Neural Biology, 38,* 240–250.

Gauthier, M., & Destrade, C. (1984). Late post-learning effect of entorhinal cortex electrical stimulation persists despite destruction of the perforant path. *Brain Research, 310,* 174–179.

Gauthier, M., Destrade, C., & Soumireu–Mourat, B. (1982). Late post-learning participation of entorhinal cortex in memory processes. *Brain Research, 233,* 255–264.

Glickman, S. (1958). Deficits in avoidance learning produced by stimulation of the ascending reticular formation. *Canadian Journal of Psychology, 12,* 97–102.

Goddard, G. V. (1964). Amygdaloid stimulation and learning in the rat. *Journal of Comparative and Physiological Psychology, 58,* 23–30.

Goddard, G. V., McIntyre, D. C., & Leech, C. K. (1969). A permanent change in brain function resulting from daily electrical stimulation. *Experimental Neurology, 25,* 295–330.

Gold, P. E., Edwards, R. M., & McGaugh, J. L. (1975). Amnesia produced by unilateral subseizure, electrical stimulation of the amygdala in rats. *Behavioral Biology, 15,* 95–105.

Gold, P. E., Farrell, W., & King, R. A. (1971). Retrograde amnesia after localized brain shock in passive avoidance learning. *Physiology and Behavior, 7,* 709–712.

Gold, P. E., & King, R. A. (1972). Caudate stimulation and retrograde amnesia: Amnesia threshold and gradient. *Behavioral Biology, 7,* 709–715.

Gold, P. E., & McGaugh, J. L. (1975). A single-trace, two-process view of memory storage processes. In D. Deutsch & J. A. Deutsch (Eds.), *Short-term memory* (pp. 355–378). New York: Academic Press.

Gold, P. E., & Sternberg, D. B. (1978). Retrograde amnesia produced by several treatments: Evidence for a common neurobiological mechanism. *Science, 201,* 367–369.

Goldrich, S. G., & Stamm, J. S. (1971). Electrical stimulation of inferotemporal and occipital cortex in monkeys: Effects on visual discrimination and spatial reversal performance. *Journal of Comparative and Physiological Psychology, 74,* 448–458.

Halgren, E. (1981). The amygdala contribution to emotion and memory: Current studies in humans. In Y. Ben-Ari (Ed.), *The amygdaloid complex* (pp. 395–408). Amsterdam: Elsevier.

Halgren, E. (1982). Mental phenomena induced by stimulation in the limbic system. *Human Neurobiology, 1,* 251–260.

Halgren, E., Walter, R. D., Cherlow, D. G., & Crandall, P. H. (1978). Mental phenomena evoked by electrical stimulation of the human hippocampal formation and amygdala. *Brain, 101,* 83–117.

Hebb, D. O. (1949). *The Organization of Behavior.* New York: Wiley.

Huston, J. P., & Mueller, C. C. (1978). Enhanced passive avoidance learning and appetitive T-maze learning with posttrial rewarding hypothalamic stimulation. *Brain Research Bulletin, 3,* 265–270.

Huston, J. P., & Staubli, U. (1981). Substance P and its effects on learning and memory. In J. L. Martinez, R. A. Jensen, R. B. Messing, H. Rigter, & J. L. McGaugh (Eds.), *Endogenous peptides and learning and memory processes.* New York: Academic Press.

Huston, J. P., Mueller, C. C., & Mondadori, C. (1977). Memory facilitation by posttrial hypothalamic stimulation and other reinforcers: A central theory of reinforcement. *Biobehavioral Reviews, 1,* 143–150.

Kapp, B. S., Gallagher, M., Holmquist, B. K., & Theall, C. L. (1978). Retrograde amnesia and hippocampal stimulation: Dependence upon the nature of associations formed during conditioning. *Behavioral Biology, 24,* 1–23.

Kesner, R. P. (1973). A neural system analysis of memory storage and retrieval. *Psychological Bulletin, 80,* 177–203.

Kesner, R. P. (1981). The role of the amygdala within an attribute analysis of memory. In Y. Ben-Ari (Ed.), *The Amygdaloid Complex* (pp. 331–342). Elsevier-North Holland: Amsterdam.

Kesner, R. P. (1982). Brain Stimulation: Effects on Memory. *Behavioral and neural biology, 36,* 315–367.

Kesner, R. P., Berman, R. F., Burton, B., & Hankins, W. G. (1975). Effects of electrical stimulation of amygdala upon neophobia and taste aversion. *Behavioral Biology, 13,* 349–358.

Kesner, R. P., & Connor, H. S. (1974). Effects of electrical stimulation of rat limbic system and midbrain reticular formation on short- and long-term memory. *Physiology and Behavior, 12,* 5–12.

Kesner, R. P., & Doty, R. W. (1968). Amnesia produced in cats by local seizure activity initiated from the amygdala. *Experimental Neurology, 21,* 58–68.

Kesner, R. P., & Hardy, J. D. (1983). Long-term memory for contextual attributes: Dissociation of amygdala and hippocampus. *Behavioral Brain Research, 8,* 139–149.

Kovner, R., & Stamm, J. S. (1972). Disruption of short-term visual memory by electrical stimulation of inferotemporal cortex in the monkey. *Journal of Comparative and Physiological Psychology, 81,* 163–172.

Landfield, P. W. (1976). Synchronous EEG rhythms: Their nature and their possible functions in memory, information transmission and behavior. In W. G. Gispen (Ed.), *Molecular and functional neurobiology* (pp. 390–424). Elsevier: Amsterdam.

Landfield, P. W. (1977). Different effects of posttrial driving or blocking of the theta rhythm on avoidance learning in rats. *Physiology and Behavior, 18,* 439–445.

Landfield, P. W., Tusa, R. J., & McGaugh, J. L. (1973). Effects of posttrial hippocampal stimulation on memory storage and EEG activity. *Behavioral Biology, 8,* 485–505.

LePiane, F. G. & Phillips, A. G. (1978). Differential effects of electrical stimulation of amygdala, caudate-putamen or substantia nigra pars compacta on taste aversion and passive avoidance in rats. *Physiology and Behavior, 21,* 979–985.

McDonough, J. H., & Kesner, R. P. (1971). Amnesia produced by brief electrical stimulation of amygdala or dorsal hippocampus in cats. *Journal of Comparative and Physiological Psychology, 77,* 171–178.

Lewis, D. J. (1976). A cognitive approach to experimental amnesia. *American Journal of Psychology, 89,* 51–80.

Lidsky, A., & Slotnick, B. M. (1971). Effects of posttrial limbic stimulation on retention of a one-trial passive avoidance response. *Journal of Comparative and Physiological Psychology, 76,* 337–348.

McGaugh, J. L. (1966). Time-dependent processes in memory storage. *Science, 153,* 1351–1358.

McIntyre, D. C., & Gunter, J. L. (1979). State-dependent learning induced by low intensity electrical stimulation of the caudate or amygdala nuclei in rats. *Physiology and Behavior, 23,* 449–454.

Milner, B. (1966). Amnesia following operation on the temporal lobes. In C. W. M. Whitty & O. L. Zangwill (Eds.), *Amnesia.* London: Butterworth.

Mullan, S., & Penfield, W. (1959). Illusions of comparative interpretation and emotion. *Archives of Neurology and Psychiatry, 81,* 269–284.

Nyakas, C., & Endroczi, E. (1970). Effects of hippocampal stimulation on the establishment of conditioned fear response in the rat. *Acta Physica Scientiarum Hungericae, 37,* 281–289.

Ojemann, G. A. (1974). Mental arithmetic during human thalamic stimulation. *Neuropsychologia, 12,* 1–10.

Ojemann, G. A. (1982). Models of brain organization for higher integrative functions derived with electrical stimulation techniques. *Human Neurobiology, 1,* 243–249.

Ojemann, G. A., Blick, K. I., & Ward, A. A. (1971). Improvement and disturbance of short-term verbal memory with human ventrolateral thalamic stimulation. *Brain, 94,* 225–240.

Ojemann, G., & Mateer, C. (1979). Human language cortex: Localization of memory, syntax, and sequential motor-phoneme identification systems. *Science, 205,* 1401–1403.

O'Keefe, J., & Nadel, L. (1978). *The hippocampus as a cognitive map.* Clarendon Press: Oxford.

Olton, D. E., Becker, J. T., & Handelmann, G. E. (1979). Hippocampus, space and memory. *Behavioral Brain Sciences, 2,* 313–365.

Ommaya, A. K., & Fedio, P. (1972). The contribution of cingulum and hippocampal structures to memory mechanisms in man. *Confin. Neurology, 34,* 398–411.

Overton, D. A. (1977). Major theories of state-dependent learning. In B. Ho, D. Chute, & D. Richards (Eds.), *Drug discrimination and state-dependent learning.* Academic Press: New York.

Peeke, H. V. S., & Herz, M. J. (1971). Caudate nucleus stimulation retroactively impairs complex maze learning in the rat. *Brain Research, 33,* 519–522.

Penfield, W. (1938). The cerebral cortex in man. I. The cerebral cortex and consciousness. *Archives of Neurology and Psychiatry, 40,* 417.

Penfield, W. (1958). Some mechanisms of consciousness discovered during electrical stimulation of the brain. *Proceedings of the National Academy of Sciences, 44,* 51–66.

Penfield, W., & Perot, P. (1963). The brain's record of auditory and visual experience: A final summary and discussion. *Brain, 86,* 595–696.

Ranck, J. B., Jr. (1981). Extracellular stimulation. In M. M. Patterson & R. P. Kesner (Eds.), *Electrical stimulation techniques.* New York: Academic Press.

Routtenberg, A., & Holzman, N. (1973). Memory disruption by electrical stimulation of substantia nigra, pars compacta. *Science, 181,* 83–86.

Rozin, P., & Kalat, J. A. (1971). Specific hungers and poison avoidance as adaptive specializations of learning. *Psychology Review, 78,* 459–486.

Santos-Anderson, R. M., & Routtenberg, A. (1976). Stimulation of rat medial or sulcal prefrontal cortex during passive avoidance learning selectively influences retention performance. *Brain Research, 103,* 243–259.

Sara, S. J., Deweer, B., & Hars, B. (1980). Reticular stimulation facilitates retrieval of a "forgotten" maze habit. *Neuroscience Letters, 18,* 211–217.

Squire, L. R. (1982). The neuropsychology of human memory. *Annual Review of Neuroscience, 5,* 241–273.

Stein, D. G., & Chrover, S. L. (1968). Effects of posttrial electrical stimulation of hippocampus and caudate nucleus on maze learning in the rat. *Physiology and Behavior, 3,* 787–791.

Sterman, M. B., & Fairchild, M. D. (1966). Modification of locomotor performance by reticular formation and basal forebrain stimulation in the cat: Evidence for reciprocal systems. *Brain Research, 2,* 205–217.

Underwood, B. J. (1969). Attributes of memory. *Psychological Review, 76,* 559–573.

Vadaris, R. M., & Schwartz, K. E. (1971). Retrograde amnesia for passive avoidance produced by stimulation of dorsal hippocampus. *Physiology and Behavior, 6,* 131–135.

Velley, L., & Cardo, B. (1979). Long-term improvement of learning after early electrical stimulation of some central nervous system structures: Is the effect structure and age-dependent? *Brain Research Bulletin, 4,* 459–466.

Wetzel, W., Ott, T., & Matthies, H. (1977). Post-training hippocampal rhythmic slow activity ("theta") elicited by septal stimulation improves memory consolidation in rats. *Behavioral Biology, 21,* 32–40.

Wilburn, M. W., & Kesner, R. P. (1974). Effects of caudate nucleus stimulation upon initiation and performance of a complex motor task. *Experimental Neurology, 34,* 45–50.

Wyers, E. J., & Deadwyler, S. A. (1971). Duration and nature of retrograde amnesia produced by stimulation of caudate nucleus. *Physiology and Behavior, 6,* 97–103.

Wyers, E. J., Deadwyler, S. A., Hirasuna, N., & Montgomery, D. (1973). Passive avoidance retention and caudate stimulation. *Physiology and Behavior, 11,* 809–819.

Wyers, E. J., Peeke, H. V. S., Williston, J. S., & Herz, M. J. (1968). Retroactive impairment of passive avoidance learning by stimulation of the caudate nucleus. *Experimental Neurology, 22,* 350–366.

Zornetzer, S. F., & Chronister, R. F. (1973). Neuroanatomical localization of memory disruption: Relationship between brain structure and learning task. *Physiology and Behavior, 10,* 747–750.

Zornetzer, S. F., Chronister, R. B., & Ross, B. (1973). The hippocampus and retrograde amnesia: Localization of some positive and negative memory disruptive sites. *Behavioral Biology, 8,* 507–528.

Zornetzer, S. F. & McGaugh, J. L. (1972). Electrophysiological correlates of frontal cortex-induced retrograde amnesia in rats. *Physiology and Behavior, 8,* 233–238.

V

LESIONS

INTERVENTIONAL
APPROACHES TO MEMORY:
LESIONS

David S. Olton

INTRODUCTION

A lesion analysis examines the behavioral changes that follow damage to the brain in order to draw conclusions about the functional organization of the nervous system. This type of experimental strategy has had a profound effect on the ways in which we think about the brain, behavior, psychology, and the interrelationships among them. Historically, the lesion analysis produced all of our initial ideas about brain function (Thompson & Robinson, 1979). Everyday events like accidents, war, and disease, and experimental techniques such as ablation, provided direct ways of interfering with the activity of brain structures before equivalent techniques were available to enhance or measure brain activity. Currently, a lesion analysis is one of the three experimental strategies (stimulation and recording are the other two) that we can use to examine the functional organization of the brain, and it provides critical information that cannot be obtained from either of the other two strategies.[1]

---

[1] As discussed later (page 391), the lesion, stimulation, and recording analyses can be applied to any neural component: cells, neurotransmitters, ions, etc. Thus, this discussion of the lesion analysis is relevant to any intervention that disrupts normal neural activity.

As is the case with every approach that attempts to elucidate the interrelationships between structures and functions, the interpretation of the results from a lesion analysis requires careful attention to the assumptions and the logic of the analysis. When appropriate steps are taken, a lesion analysis provides a powerful strategy to understand the functional organization of the central nervous system. The present chapter focuses on the rationale for and the logic of a lesion analysis in order to examine the interrelationships between neural structures and memory. It reviews the rationale for lesions, the ways in which the analysis can be misapplied to yield very curious conclusions, the more productive approaches with carefully controlled dissociations in appropriate theoretical contexts, and the application of this logic to examine the brain mechanisms involved in memory.

Many kinds of structures and functions exist, and a lesion analysis can be applied to all of them. An appreciation of these other applications helps to illustrate the advantages and limitations of the lesion analysis. Consequently, this chapter begins with a brief discussion of some of the general issues involved in a functional analysis of any system.

STRUCTURES, FUNCTIONS, AND LESIONS

A *function* is a transformation of an incoming signal to an outgoing signal. A *structure* is the component that carries out this function. An experiment can start with a given function and seek the structures that mediate it, or can start with a given structure and seek the functions that are mediated by it.

Here are a few examples of structures and functions, with the structure first and the function second. Tyrosine hydroxylase is an enzyme that helps transform tyrosine into dopamine. The lateral geniculate is a nucleus in the visual system in mammals that transforms the pattern of action potentials in the afferent optic tract to the pattern of action potentials in the efferent optic radiations. A transformer is an electrical device that transforms one type of voltage to another. The roof of a house is a structure that transforms the vertical movement of rain originally destined to fall on the chair in the bedroom to horizontal movement so that it goes to the gutter to fall on the driveway instead. A turbine in a dam transforms the vertical movement of water into the rotary movement of a shaft to generate electricity. A fan in a ventilation system transforms slowly moving air into rapidly moving air. This list could be extended indefinitely, but these few examples should make the point that structures and functions can be found in many different systems.

A lesion analysis tests hypotheses about the functions of a structure. If a structure carries out a function, then decreasing the activity of that structure ought to decrease the activity of that function. Decreasing the amount of tyrosine hydroxylase should reduce the amount of tyrosine that is turned into dopamine. Removing the roof of my house should increase the amount of rain that falls on my chair. Slowing the movement of the turbine should decrease the amount of electricity.

Hypotheses about the functions of a structure can also be tested by experiments using stimulation and recording strategies. Stimulation enhances the activity of a structure. If a structure is involved in a function, then stimulation of that structure ought to increase the activity of the function. Recording measures the activity of a structure. If a structure is involved in a function, then the activity of that structure ought to vary with the activity of the function.[2]

A lesion analysis makes two contributions. First, it is one of the three strategies that can be used to determine the functions of a structure. Each one of these has disadvantages that severely limit the conclusions that can be drawn from it. Consequently, no one of them can be used alone to draw final conclusions about the functions of a structure. Thus, a lesion analysis provides an important converging operation (Garner, Hake, & Eriksen, 1956) in any functional analysis.

Second, a lesion analysis provides a unique piece of information, one not obtainable by any other experimental strategy. Recording experiments can determine the extent to which activity in the structure occurs during the function, and stimulation experiments can determine the extent to which activity in the structure can produce the function. However, only a lesion analysis can determine the extent to which the activity of a structure is necessary for a function.

The remainder of this chapter focuses on experimental designs that place lesions in brain structures, observe the effects on behavior, and draw inferences about the psychological functions of these structures. This approach is common in behavioral neuroscience; illustrations and

---

[2] *Lesion* and *stimulation* have very specific meanings in this discussion. A lesion directly interferes with the activity and the function of the brain structure in which it is placed. Stimulation directly enhances (improves) the activity and the function of the brain structure in which it is placed. The ultimate behavioral effects of these manipulations may vary widely. For example, a lesion may reduce or increase the probability of a given behavior depending on the excitatory and inhibitory influences of the structure in which the lesion is placed. Thus, these two analyses reflect complementary alterations of the activity of the structure in which they are placed.

applications are readily available, and focusing on a single type of design helps to organize the discussion. Still, the reader is encouraged to consider the broader framework discussed above because it provides a perspective that helps to illustrate the issues raised here in a more limited context.

MISUSE OF LESION ANALYSES

Numerous stories, both apocryphal and true, illustrate some simple ways of misusing a lesion analysis. Two of my favorites, abbreviated from their shaggy-dog versions, are recounted below.

One scientist was studying auditory memory in the grasshopper. An appropriately elaborate behavioral testing procedure was established so that when a tone was sounded, the grasshopper jumped across the table. The scientist thought that the grasshopper might use the ganglia containing the motor neurons going to the legs to remember to jump when the tone came on. Knowing the importance of parametric manipulations, the scientist tested the grasshopper's reaction to the tone after destroying each ganglion, one-by-one, until all had been removed. The grasshopper's response got progressively weaker as each ganglion was removed, and disappeared entirely after the final one was destroyed. "Eureka," the scientist exclaimed. "Grasshoppers store auditory memories in these ganglia, and I can propose a whole new theory of insect memory."

In the second example, the object of study is the radio. The scientist removes a component from the radio and finds that a piercing squeal emerges instead of the music. Knowing about the importance of ABA experimental designs with repeated measures on individual subjects, the scientist replaces and removes this component several times, always to find the same result: music with it in, squeal with it out. "Eureka! I have found the center for remembering music" (see Gregory, 1961).

These, and many other stories, illustrate the fact that lesion analyses can be misused to produce exquisitely confused conclusions. However, stimulation and recording fare no better; equivalently bizarre conclusions can be drawn from them when they are misused. The generality of these problems in no way alleviates the difficulties associated with the lesion analysis (see Lashley, 1964, p. 23; Webster, 1973; Weiskrantz, 1968b), but it does suggest that similar problems may be solved by similar solutions. As will be seen in the discussion that follows, many of the principles that help make structure-function analyses productive apply equally to designs using stimulation, lesions, and recording.

DISSOCIATIONS

The effect of a lesion in a single location on a single behavior is virtually uninterpretable in terms of structure-function relations. That same lesion may affect many other types of behavior, and that same behavior may be influenced by many types of lesions. Consequently, no conclusions can be drawn about the extent to which this given structure and function have a special relationship. Only by comparing the effects of lesions in different locations on the same behavior, and the effects of a given lesion on different behaviors can more specific conclusions be drawn (Lezak, 1983, p. 100; Teuber, 1956; Weiskrantz, 1968a). These comparisons, especially when arranged in a systematic manner along both neural and behavioral dimensions (see the section entitled "Systematic Lesion Analysis") are the basic elements of a lesion analysis.

A brain with a lesion is a malfunctioning, defective system. As might be expected, the strategies used to develop and interpret a lesion analysis are identical to those used to diagnose any malfunctioning system. The examiner carries out a series of tests, each of which is particularly sensitive to and selective for a different type of fault. The results of the tests are compared to identify the functions that proceed normally, the ones that are altered, and the ways in which the malfunctions are exhibited. This pattern of symptoms is used to eliminate alternative explanations of the abnormality. In essence, any function that is shown to be intact by the diagnostic test is subtracted from the list of possible explanations. This subtractive logic is carried out until the correct conclusion is obtained.

This conclusion is often given the ultimate empirical test by an attempt to fix the structure thought to be responsible for the malfunction. A return to the normal state of affairs indicates that the initial logic was correct. A failure to re-establish normal function is harder to interpret. Either the original hypothesis was wrong, the repair was not carried out correctly, or the original damage caused changes in other parts of the system that persisted even after the element that initially failed was replaced.

This general strategy can be seen in diagnostic tests of almost every system. Information about the results of a single test can rarely pinpoint the location of the problem. The results of several carefully chosen tests usually can (Ettlinger, 1968). Mechanics with cars that don't start, programmers who get the result 15.75 instead of the correct answer of 236.2, neurologists with a patient who is losing motor coordination, electricians with a power plant that stopped producing current—all these use the same general strategy (Gauss, 1982; Goodglass & Kaplan, 1979; Jonson, 1984; Laski & Korel, 1983; Lezak, 1983, p. 100). Compared to the brain, many of these other systems are relatively simple, completely known, and come with a handbook explicitly designed to help diagnose and fix the system when it becomes defective. But I am not aware of any reason why these same approaches should not work with neural structures and psychological functions, and the results of many experiments show that they do work in practice (Lashley, 1964, p. 29).

Different types of dissociations can follow a brain lesion, and each of these provides information about the functional organization of different components in the system. For this analysis, a 2-dimensional table is required. One dimension contains the structures in which lesions are made, the other dimension contains the behavioral tests that are conducted. The object is to obtain data for each point in the matrix. The logic of this approach can be illustrated best by examples of lesions in sensory systems and relatively large units of psychological functions. Consider a simple lesion analysis with neural and behavioral dissociations to determine the psychological functions of some of the structures in the visual system of monkeys. The data are summarized in Table 1 (Manning & Mishkin, 1976; Pasik, Pasik, & Bender, 1969a,b).

No Dissociations

Lesions of the lateral geniculate impair choice accuracy in a visual pattern discrimination and in a visual learning set with different pairs of visual stimuli. Thus, no dissociations of choice accuracy are found in these tasks following the lesion. This pattern of results is interpreted as follows: (1) Both behaviors share at least one function in common; (2) This function is required for correct performance in both tasks; and (3) the lesion of this structure disrupts this function. More specifically: (1) Visual pattern discriminations have at least one function in common with visual learning sets; (2) This function is required for correct

TABLE 11.1

A SUMMARY OF THE BEHAVIORAL EFFECTS OF LESIONS IN SOME NEUROANATOMICAL
STRUCTURES RECEIVING PROJECTIONS FROM THE EYE

	Structures destroyed by the lesion		
Behavioral tasks	Lateral geniculate nucleus	Pretectal nucleus	Inferotemporal neocortex
Occular reflexes	O[a]	I[b]	O
Simple visual pattern discrimination	I	O	O
Learning set for simple visual stimuli	I	O	I

  [a] O = No impairment in the behavior following the lesion.
  [b] I = An impairment in the behavior following the lesion. See text for explanation.

choices in both tasks; and (3) Lesions of the lateral geniculate disrupt this function.[3]

SINGLE DISSOCIATIONS

A lesion of the lateral geniculate impairs choice accuracy in the visual discrimination and in the learning set; a lesion of the inferotemporal cortex does not impair choice accuracy in the visual discrimination, but does do so in the learning set. This pattern of results exemplifies a single dissociation; the two lesions differentially affect performance in one task, but not in the other. It is interpreted as follows: (1) The behavior in which the impairment is found after both lesions has a function in common with the behavior in which the impairment is found after only one of them; (2) This function requires the integrity of the structure in which a lesion produces an impairment in both tasks; (3) The behavior in which the impairment is found after only one lesion has a function that is not present in the other behavior;

---

[3] No dissociations may be found with two different lesions and one task (rather than with a single lesion and two tasks as described in this section.) These results are very difficult to interpret. Performance in every task involves many different psychological functions, and disruption of any one of these can impair choice accuracy. Thus, the absence of a dissociation in this type of analysis does not imply that the two structures are involved in a common function.

and (4) This function requires the integrity of the structure in which a lesion produces an impairment in only this task. More specifically: (1) Visual discriminations and learning sets involves a common function that (2) requires normal activity in the lateral geniculate, (3) learning sets involve a function not required by visual discriminations, and (4) this function requires normal activity in the inferotemporal cortex. In short, single dissociations demonstrate that structures and functions are arranged hierarchically. The more basic function can proceed normally without the more advanced one; the structure that mediates it must have both an input and output that are independent of the more advanced structure so that it can be influenced by and influence the rest of the system normally. In contrast, the more advanced function cannot proceed normally without the basic one; the structure mediating the more advanced function must have an input or an output that is dependent on the functioning of the more basic function.

DOUBLE DISSOCIATIONS

A lesion in the lateral geniculate impairs choice accuracy in visual discriminations, but does not affect occular reflexes; a lesion in the pretectal nucleus impairs occular reflexes, but does not affect choice accuracy in visual discriminations. This pattern of results is interpreted as follows: (1) The first behavior has at least one function not shared by the second; (2) The first structure is required for this function but not the second; (3) The second behavior has at least one function not shared by the first; and (4) The second structure is required for this function but not the first. More specifically: (1) Occular reflexes have a function that is not required for visual discriminations; (2) This function requires normal activity in the pretectal nucleus but not the lateral geniculate; (3) Visual discriminations have a function that is not required for the light reflex; and (4) This function requires normal activity in the lateral geniculate but not in the pretectal nucleus. Because each function can proceed independently of the other, each must be mediated by a structure that has both an input from and an output to the rest of the system, and these must be independent of the inputs and outputs of the other structure.

These two dimensions can be extended indefinitely, yet the logic is always the same. These three types of dissociations are the only results that can be obtained from a lesion analysis. In a lesion analysis, every conclusion about brain structures and psychological functions must be made on the basis of these three types of dissociations.

SYSTEMATIC LESION ANALYSES

The art in structure-function analyses comes in choosing the appropriate set of structures and functions, a creative task that can be assisted by a systematic approach to both structures and functions. The object is to localize functions, not symptoms, and attainment of this goal requires close attention to the organization of the functions and structures into working systems (Critchley, 1966, p. 406; Geschwind, 1965; Mishkin, 1982).

Given a structure in the brain, what psychological functions is it most likely to influence? Given a psychological function, what neural structures are more likely to influence it? With the vast number of structures and functions, the probability of choosing an interrelated pair is very small. Furthermore, some dissociations are much more informative than others. Correct intuitions about the right functional questions to ask about a structure, and the right structural questions to ask about a function, are absolutely critical for efficient progress. A systematic approach to both structure and function, with some bootstraps between them, has helped to work through this dilemma. Brain structures do not come as isolated units; each is a component in a system and has distinct afferents and efferents. Thus, if we have some idea about the function of one structure in a system, we can make some rough guesses about the function of the closely related structures. This strategy works particularly well when dealing with structures that have relatively direct connections to either receptors or effectors, but the logic can be applied anywhere in the system.

Psychological analyses are hampered by not being able to gain direct access to structures and functions, but considerable consensus has evolved about the general outlines of the system. The same logic holds here as in the previous examples. If, for a given function, you have some idea of an involved structure, then closely related structures in the same system are likely to have closely related functions.

Two points about this approach are obvious, but should be emphasized. First, a complete description of the brain mechanisms involved in memory is not yet available. Even with computer models, which have few restrictions on the types of mechanisms, describing just the initial perception of patterns has proved to be very difficult (Hinton, Sejnowski, & Ackley, 1984). Clearly, we don't yet have a working computational model of the neural bases of memory. Second, we have learned a good deal about the interrelationship of particular psychological functions and neural structures. Given the enormous numbers of functions that do not require any given structure, and the enormous number of structures that are not necessary for any particular function, this progress is strong evidence for the effectiveness of a systematic approach to both structures and functions when carrying out a lesion analysis.

This systematic use of dissociations along neural and behavioral dimensions has made important contributions to our understanding of the neural and psychological organization of memory. These dissociations clearly demonstrate that amnesia does not have to be a global phenomenon, affecting all aspects of memory equally (Cohen, 1984; Squire, 1981). Consequently, the different psychological processes involved in remembering must be mediated by different neuroanatomical structures. Furthermore, single dissociations are often found after lesions, demonstrating that the involved memory processes must be hierarchical rather than independent. The relatively more complicated aspects of memory processing appear to be developed from the relatively simpler ones in the same way that the relatively more abstract representations of sensory stimuli are generated from the relatively simpler ones.

QUANTITATIVE MANIPULATIONS OF STRUCTURES AND FUNCTIONS

When conducting an initial screen for the possible interrelationship of structure and function, having the maximal possible involvement of both is often optimal. When testing the validity of a relationship that has received some support from the results of the initial screening, quantitative manipulations of the size of the lesion and the importance of a particular function can assist interpretation of the results.

Intentional variation of the size of the lesion can help document the involvement of a structure in a function. Every lesion may cause unintended damage to other structures, raising the possibility that the functional changes following the lesion are due to this ancillary damage rather than to destruction of the target area. Parametric manipulations of the size of the lesion in the target area can minimize this possibility. If the magnitude of the change in the psychological function is related to the magnitude of the lesion in the target area and not related to the magnitude of the lesion in other areas, then strong evidence is provided for the involvement of this structure in this function.

A second benefit of this quantitative approach is information about the parameters of the mathematical function relating the activity of this structure to the effectiveness of the psychological function; parameters are necessary to obtain a working computational model. In many cases, these parameters are positively accelerated. Few, if any, behavioral effects are seen after small lesions, and major behavioral impairments develop only as the lesion involves the final 20% of the structure. Examples include: (1) maze learning of rats following lesions of the neocortex, (2) visual discrimination in monkeys following lesions of the visual system, and (3) eating and drinking following 6-hydroxy-dopamine lesions of the ascending noradrenergic bundle. Parameters for most systems remain to be determined.

As mentioned previously, every behavioral task involves many functions. Consequently, the behavioral effects of a lesion may be due to disruption of functions other than the one of interest. For example, consider an experimental design in which the importance of one function is steadily increased while the importance of all other functions is held constant.

Quantitative manipulations of the extent to which the psychological function is required for accurate performance may help demonstrate that a brain structure is involved in a particular psychological function. If an interaction effect shows that the magnitude of the behavioral change in the group with the lesion increases relative to that of control subjects, then the lesion most likely affects the function that was manipulated, rather than the other functions that were held constant. This approach likewise has the advantage of permitting the estimation of parameters relating the structure and function. An interaction effect shows that these are not linear, but positively accelerated.

This approach is particularly useful when investigating the neural mechanisms of memory. Consider experiments using a delayed conditional discrimination (DCD), for example. At the beginning of each trial, a sample stimulus is presented; it is removed for a delay. At the end of the delay, the animal is given two or more alternative responses. The response that is correct is conditional upon the stimulus presented at the beginning of the trial. Initially, animals are tested with only a single sample stimulus, a delay of only a few seconds, and an intertrial interval of several minutes. Subsequently, these parameters are manipulated to increase the difficulty of remembering the sample stimulus; the number of stimuli to be remembered is increased, the length of the delay between the sample and the choice is increased, and the intertrial interval is decreased.

The results of this type of experiment often show the interaction effect previously described. Normal animals have decreased choice accuracy as these parameters are manipulated to make remembering more difficult. Animals with lesions have also decreased choice accuracy as

the task becomes more difficult, but the rate of this decrease is significantly greater than that seen for the normal animals. Because all aspects
of the task except the memory requirement remain the same, this relatively greater impairment of the animals with the lesions is most appropriately attributed to a failure of memory (Jarrard, 1975; Mishkin, 1982;
Zornetzer, Thompson, & Rogers, 1982). Similar logic has been applied
in the analysis of rates of forgetting (Squire, 1981).

SENSITIVITY AND SELECTIVITY

Sensitivity is the function relating the magnitude of change in a
dependent variable with the magnitude of change in an independent
variable. *Selectivity* is the function relating the magnitude of change in
one dependent variable with the magnitude of change in other dependent variables affected by the independent variable. Lesion analyses
proceed best when the lesion is selective for a particular structure, that
structure is sensitive to the technique used to produce the lesion, the
behavioral test is selective for a particular function, and performance in
this test is sensitive to that function.

The selectivity of the lesion is particularly important, and the sensitivity of the structure to the lesion technique can help obtain selectivity. The more sensitive the structure, the less force necessary to make a
lesion, ahd the lower the probability of producing unintended lesions
elsewhere. The development of relatively selective neurotoxins, chemicals that have a special affinity for particular structures, exemplifies
this approach (Johnson, McKinney, & Coyle, 1981; McGeer, Olney, &
McGeer, 1978). When applied correctly, neurotoxins can produce very
discrete lesions. Their applicability is limited, of course; selective affinity means that they are not suited for other structures because they will
almost always produce unintended damage to the structure that is most
sensitive to them.

The lesion analysis seeks to describe the functional changes following damage to a particular structure as precisely as possible. This
search for precision is severely handicapped when lesions are not selective. The involvement of more structures may alter more functions,
complicating any attempt to relate a specific function with a specific
structure.

Some compensation for nonselective lesions can be made by varying
intentionally the structures that receive the unintended damage. A core
syndrome of behavioral changes probably reflects damage to the struc-

ture that is consistently involved. But the general goal is still clear: The more selective the lesion, the easier the interpretation.

Behavioral tests that are both selective and sensitive are also highly desirable. Unlike neurological manipulations that can go directly to a structure, psychological manipulations can influence and measure a function only indirectly. Performance in every behavioral task involves many psychological functions, and changes in performance can reflect changes in any of these. The empirical measurement of a behavioral change is relatively easy; the inferential judgment about the underlying psychological functions responsible for the behavioral change can be very difficult.

This process is aided by sensitive and selective behavioral tests. The sensitivity means that even a small change in the desired function will produce a large change in behavior. The selectivity means that even a large change in other functions will produce few, if any, changes in behavior. Highly sensitive and selective tests tell us a great deal about the functions being assessed; they are good diagnostic tests. Insensitive and nonselective tests may give us some information about the behavioral effects of lesions, but they can do little to tell us about the psychological functions that are altered.

UNITS OF ANALYSIS

The brain can be analyzed along many different dimensions, and a lesion can, in principle, be placed in any of these. Structures may be cellular components (axons, spines), neurochemicals (enzymes, transmitters), molecules (Na^+, Ca^{++}), or neuroanatomical structures (caudate nucleus, parietal lobe).

Psychological functions can also be analyzed along different dimensions. These include the type of information (visual, verbal), the stages of processing (perception, storage), the types of associations formed (phonemic, semantic), and the behavioral actions required (approach, avoidance).

Choosing the units of structure and function that are most likely to be interrelated is a difficult job in itself. For a particular type of memory process, is the most productive neural analysis at the molecular, neurochemical, cellular, or neuroanatomical level? Alternatively, for a given structure, what theory of memory is most likely to yield the correct functional analysis? These are difficult issues that have yet to be resolved. They complicate the search for the links between structure and function. A concerted analysis of the ways in which different levels of analysis can be interrelated will most effectively help us progress through the myriad possibilities.

TEMPORAL VARIABLES

The brain is a living, changing organ, constantly reacting to the stimuli that influence it. Not surprisingly, it also reacts to a lesion. The changes are numerous and varied. They can begin immediately, continue for a significant portion of the individual's remaining life, and when completed, remain until death. Thus, every lesion has a temporal as well as a structural dimension to it, and the functional consequences following the lesion may change with time (see Chapter 3, this volume, by Crutcher; Finger & Stein, 1982; Schoenfeld & Hamilton, 1977; Webster, 1973).

The age of the individual at the time of the lesion may also influence the functional consequences of it. The younger nervous system can often react more adaptively to damage than the older nervous system so that the earlier lesion may have fewer functional consequences than the later one.

Plasticity and adaptation are hallmarks of the nervous system and of behavior. The principles and processes underlying plasticity in both the brain and behavior have significant theoretical and practical implications. However, they are not directly relevant to the discussion here, and consequently will not be pursued further.

VALIDITY

A systematic approach to brain structures, psychological functions, and the logical analysis of dissociations is the most effective means of gathering information through lesions, and probably through every other approach as well. But, how does one determine if even this most coherent use of lesions is accurate?

A definitive answer to this question is difficult, because no single standard is available to assess the truth of a proposed hypothesis about the psychological functions of the brain. Consequently, we must compare the conclusions obtained from lesion analyses with those obtained from other experimental strategies.

The logic involved in a lesion analysis has been applied effectively in many settings other than behavioral neuroscience. It can localize symptoms in a known system, and these symptoms can lead to conclusions about the functions of the components involved in that system. Thus, the approach is in general valid. The only question is whether it can be applied to neural structures and psychological functions.

Two lines of evidence suggest that it can. First, scientists continue to use lesions and find them helpful in the functional analysis of brain systems. Although this persistence may simply reflect the inertia of a bad habit, it may also reflect the considered judgment of the appropriate expert witnesses.

Second, the conclusions drawn about the psychological functions of neural systems from lesion analyses are consistent with those obtained from stimulation and recording. No one of these three strategies has an a priori claim to be the single method to obtain truth in this area. Indeed, each of them has a fatal flaw that prohibits such status. Still, they can be treated as three independent, converging methods. The fact that the conclusions drawn from experiments using stimulation and recording support those drawn from lesion experiments, which often precede them, suggests that lesion analyses can be correct. Given the incredible number of structures and functions that might be interrelated, this agreement is strong evidence for accurate interpretations.

Thus, a lesion analysis does have value if applied in a reasonable fashion. Further discussion of ways to evaluate the usefulness of lesions in general, and each type of analysis in particular, would help to assess the contributions and limitations of this scientific strategy.

MEMORY

This chapter, for several reasons, has emphasized the logic and rationale of a lesion analysis, rather than its application to a particular structure or function. First, although the usefulness of a lesion analysis has often been questioned, most arguments have not been very thoughtful. Rather, they are based on caricatures like those presented at the beginning of this chapter. I hope that the description of the lesion analysis offered here will lead to a more sophisticated and productive debate concerning the advantages and disadvantages of this analytical strategy (see, for example, Weiskrantz, 1968a,b).

Second, so many different theories have been offered to describe the biological bases of learning and memory that a single chapter could not begin to discuss them all. Furthermore, to choose arbitrarily one particular theory to illustrate the application of a lesion analysis might confound the more important explication of its fundamental nature.

Nonetheless, a lesion analysis has been used to support many different hypotheses about the neural bases of learning and memory. Table

TABLE 11.2

A Brief Summary of Some Applications of a Lesion Analysis to Identify the
Neural Mechanisms Underlying Learning and Memory

Reference	Neural structures	Mnemonic function
Thompson et al., 1982	Cerebellum	Classical conditioning
Cohen, 1984	Temporal lobe	Declarative memory
Olton, 1983	Hippocampus	Working memory
Rawlins, 1985	Hippocampus	Temporal memory
O'Keefe & Nadel, 1978	Hippocampus	Cognitive mapping
Thomas & Spafford, 1984	Septum	Representational memory
Hepler, Olton, Wenk, & Coyle, 1985	Basal Forebrain Cholinergic system	Working memory
Meck & Church, in press	Cholinergic system	Temporal memory
Bartus, Dean, Beer, & Lippa, 1982	Cholinergic system	Geriatric memory
Mishkin, Spiegler, Saunders, & Malamut, 1982	Hippocampus and amygdala	Global memory

11.2 presents a short list of some of these, with a representative publi-
cation and a brief orientation to the neural structures and mnemonic
functions that are discussed. Many of them focus on the hippocampus,
temporal lobe, and cholinergic system, reflecting the growing consensus that these brain areas are importantly involved in memory function.
Each analysis has provided some information about the biological bases of learning and memory. None has achieved the goal of a complete
systematic, working computational model of both the neural and psychological systems. All have relied on the results of a lesion analysis to
support their arguments. I encourage the reader to take one or more of
these approaches, evaluate the extent to which the lesion analysis has
been applied appropriately, and suggest new ways of extending this
analysis within the given framework.

CONCLUSIONS

Lesions provide a powerful analytic tool for examining the interrelationship of brain structures and psychological functions. Systematic
patterns of dissociations obtained from a lesion analysis are necessary
to understand the ways in which the brain mediates behavior and to
determine whether psychological explanations of behavior can be reduced to neural ones. Lesions are not the only tool in this enterprise,
and the scientist who uses only one approach to study a phenomenon

is at a serious disadvantage compared to a scientist who uses many approaches (Platt, 1964). Consequently, this discussion is not meant to champion the use of lesions to the exclusion of all other approaches. Quite the contrary. No one technique has an a priori mandate as the road to truth, and the goal of science is to bring many converging operations to bear on the same question so that the conclusions are not likely to be an artifact of the liabilities inherent in any one (Weiskrantz, 1974). Still, experiments using a lesion analysis vary widely in the elegance with which they are applied, which in turn determines the validity of the conclusions that are obtained. Consideration of the points raised here should help design a lesion analysis that is productive, giving us information about the ways in which brain structures mediate psychological functions such as memory.

ACKNOWLEDGMENTS

I thank R. Kesner and J. Martinez for the opportunity to prepare this chapter, M. Gazzaniga for providing a beautiful setting in which to write it, R. Kesner, J. Martinez, M. Shapiro, G. Wenk, and C. Wible for comments on it, and E. Picken for typing.

REFERENCES

Bartus, R. T., Dean, R. L., III, Beer, B., & Lippa, A. S. (1982). The cholinergic hypothesis of geriatric memory dysfunction. *Science, 217,* 408–417.

Cohen, N. J. (1984). Preserved learning capacity in amnesia: Evidence for multiple memory systems. In L. Squire & N. Butters (Eds.), *Neuropsychology of memory* (pp. 83–103). New York: The Guilford Press.

Critchley, M. (1966). *The parietal lobes.* New York: Hafner Publishing Company.

Ettlinger, G. (1968). The neurological examination of animals. In L. Weiskrantz (Ed.), *Analysis of behavioral change* (pp. 376–388). New York: Harper & Row.

Finger, S., & Stein, D. G. (1982). *Brain damage and recovery, research and clinical perspectives.* New York: Academic Press.

Garner, W. R., Hake, H. W., & Eriksen, C. W. (1956). Operationism and the concept of perception. *The Psychological Review, 63*(3), 149–159.

Gauss, E. J. (1982). The "wolf fence" algorithm for debugging. *Communications of the ACM, 25,* 780.

Geschwind, N. (1965). Disconnection syndromes in animals and man. *Brain, 88,* 237–294.

Goodglass, H., & Kaplan, E. (1979). Assessment of cognitive deficit in the brain-injured patient. In Michael S. Gazzaniga (Ed.), *Handbook of Behavioral Neurobiology* (pp. 3–22). New York: Plenum Press.

Gregory, R. L. (1961). The brain as an engineering problem. In W. H. Thorpe & O. L. Zangwill (Eds.), *Current problems in animal behavior* (pp. 307–330). Cambridge, England: Cambridge University Press.

Hepler, D. J., Olton, D. S., Wenk, G. L., & Coyle, J. T. (1985). Lesions in nucleus basalis magnocellularis and medial septal area of rats produce qualitatively similar memory impairments. *Journal of Neuroscience, 5,* 866–873.

Hinton, G. E., Sejnowski, T. J., & Ackley, D. H. (1984, May). Boltzmann machines: Constraint satisfaction networks that learn. *Technical Report, Carnegie Mellon University* (CMU-CS-84-119).

Jarrard, L. E. (1975). Role of interference in retention by rats with hippocampal lesions. *Journal of Comparative and Physiological Psychology, 89,* 400–408.

Johnson, M. V., McKinney, M., & Coyle, J. T. (1981). Neocortical cholinergic innervation in the rat. *Experimental Brain Research, 43,* 159–172.

Jonson, N. E. G. (1984). An everyday philosophy of diagnosis. *Surgical Department, Central Hospital, S-291 Kristianstad, Sweden* (Unpublished Manuscript).

Lashley, K. S. (1964). *Brain mechanisms and intelligence.* New York: Hafner Publishing Company.

Laski, J. W., & Korel, B. (1983). A data flow oriented program testing strategy. *IEEE Transactions on Software Engineering, SE-9*(3), 347–354.

Lezak, M. D. (1983). *Neuropsychological assessment.* (2nd ed.) New York: Oxford University Press.

McGeer, E. G., Olney, J. W., & McGeer, P. L. (Eds.). (1978). *Kainic acid as a tool in neurobiology.* New York: Raven Press.

Manning, F. J., & Mishkin, M. (1976). Further evidence on dissociation of visual deficits following partial inferior temporal lesions in monkeys. *Society for Neuroscience Abstracts, 2,* 1126.

Meck, W. H., & Church, R. M. (in press). Cholinergic modulation of the content of temporal memory. *Behavioral Neuroscience.*

Mishkin, M. (1982). A memory system in the monkey. *Philosophical Transcripts of the Royal Society of London, B 298,* 85–95.

Mishkin, M., Spiegler, B. J., Saunders, R. C., & Malamut, B. L. (1983). An animal model of global amnesia. In S. Corkin, K. L. Davis, J. H. Growdon, E. Usdin, & R. J. Wurtman (Eds.), *Alzheimer's disease: A report of progress in research.* New York: Raven Press.

O'Keefe, J., & Nadel, L. (1978). *The hippocampus as a cognitive map.* Oxford: Oxford University Press.

Olton, D. S. (1983). Memory functions and the hippocampus. In W. Seifert (Ed.), *Neurobiology of the hippocampus* (pp. 335–373). London: Academic Press.

Pasik, P., Pasik, T., & Bender, M. B. (1969a). The pretectal syndrome in monkeys. I. Disturbances of gaze and body posture. *Brain, 92,* 521–534.

Pasik, P., Pasik, T., & Bender, M. B. (1969b). The pretectal syndrome in monkeys. II. Spontaneous and induced nystagmus and "lightening" eye movement. *Brain, 72,* 871–884.

Platt, J. R. (1964). Strong inference. *Science, 146*(3642), 347–353.

Rawlins, J. N. P. (1985). Associations across time: The hippocampus as a temporal memory store. *Behavioral and Brain Sciences, 8,* 479–497.

Schoenfeld, T. A., & Hamilton, L. W. (1977). Secondary brain changes following lesions: A new paradigm for lesion experimentation. *Physiology and Behavior, 18,* 951–967.

Squire, L. R. (1981). Two forms of human amnesia: An analysis of forgetting. *The Journal of Neuroscience, 1*(6), 635–640.

Teuber, H. L. (1956). Physiological psychology. *Annual Reviews in Psychology, 6,* 267–296.

Thomas, G. J., & Spafford, P. S. (1984). Deficits for representational memory induced by septal and cortical lesions (singly and combined) in rats. *Behavioral Neuroscience, 98*(3), 394.

Thompson, R. F., & Robinson, D. N. (1979). Physiological psychology. In E. Hearst (Ed.), *The first century of experimental psychology* (pp. 207–257).

Thompson, R. F., Berger, T. W., Berry, S. D., Clark, G. A., Kettner, R. N., Lavond, D. G., Mauk, M. D., McCormick, D. A., Solomon, P. R., & Weisz, D. J. (1982). Neuronal substrates of learning and memory: Hippocampus and other structures. In C. D. Woody (Ed.), *Conditioning* (pp. 115–129). New York: Plenum Press.

Webster, W. G. (1973). Assumptions, conceptualizations, and the search for the functions of the brain. *Physiological Psychology, 1*(4), 346–350.

Weiskrantz, L. (1968a). Treatments, inferences, and brain function. In L. Weiskrantz (Ed.), *Analysis of behavioral change* (pp. 400–414).

Weiskrantz, L. (1968b). Some traps and pontifications. In L. Weiskrantz (Ed.), *Analysis of behavioral change* (pp. 414–429).

Weiskrantz, L. (1974). Brain research and parallel processing. *Physiological Psychology, 2*(1), 53–54.

Zornetzer, S. F., Thompson, R., & Rogers, J. (1982). Rapid forgetting in aged rats. *Behavioral and Neural Biology, 36,* 49–60.

NEUROBIOLOGICAL VIEWS OF MEMORY

Raymond P. Kesner

INTRODUCTION

NEUROBIOLOGICAL VIEWS OF MEMORY

The structure and utilization of memory is central to one's knowledge of the past, interpretation of the present and prediction of the future. Therefore, the understanding of the structural organization of memory at both psychological and neurobiological levels is of paramount importance.

Even though scientists have been studying the neurobiological basis of memory for many years, theoretical views concerning the organization of memory are surprisingly diverse. It is the purpose of this chapter to present some of these views.

On a psychological level the overall memory structure can be represented by a set of elements, such as stimuli and responses, and their interrelations. Furthermore, there is a set of rules that organize the interrelationships between elements. On a neurobiological level the overall memory structure is also represented by a set of elements, such as synapses, neural regions, and their interrelationships (neural interconnections). Each theoretician with a psychological and neural view on the structure of memory must determine which psychological units (e.g., set of elements or higher-order levels of organization of these elements) to select and which critical neural units (e.g., synapses, neural regions) to integrate with the psychological theoretical constructs. In order to illustrate more specifically the kinds of decisions that differ-

LEARNING AND MEMORY
A BIOLOGICAL VIEW

ent theoreticians have made, I will use a specific learning situation, in this case an inhibitory avoidance task, as an examplar. In this learning task the apparatus might consist of a two compartment box, with one compartment black and the other one white. During training the animal is placed in the white box; and when the animal crosses into the black box, it received a painful footshock. The animal will most likely jump, try to escape and then freeze. The animal is removed from the apparatus. In order to test for memory for this aversive experience, the animal is returned to the white compartment some time later (usually 24 hours) and the latency to return to the black box is measured. This latency measure is used as an index of the strength of the memory. Presumably the longer the latency the stronger the memory. One can then analyze the neural systems that code, store and organize this specific inhibitory avoidance memory at a number of levels.

First, one can attempt to discover the neural networks that mediate stimulus–response (shock and freezing behavior), stimulus–stimulus (shock in black box), or stimulus–reward (a negative emotional experience in black box) associative units. This approach ignores higher levels of organization, but it lends itself well to a potential cellular level of analysis. Thus, specific associative structures represent the psychological unit of analysis, while a set of synapses might represent the neural unit of analysis.

Second, there are a number of ways one can analyze the contribution of neural elements to a higher level of organization of these associative structural units. For example, specific associative units may be organized in the form of attributes such as spatial–temporal, sensory–perceptual, response, and affective attributes. The spatial–temporal attributes would define the context of the situation, such as the black box in which a specific painful event occurred at a particular time. The sensory–perceptual attributes would include visual cues from the apparatus and pain from shock. The affective attributes could be represented by the emotional consequences of the painful shock, while the response attributes are represented by the organization of jumping and freezing responses. It would then also be necessary to determine the interaction between attributes in forming the inhibitory avoidance memory. This approach encourages the use of multiple indices of inhibitory avoidance memory, such as changes in heart rate or efficacy of a reminder cue, to assess the contribution of each attribute. This latter approach utilizes a multidimensional analysis of memory. The psychological unit of analysis is represented by an attribute and interaction between attributes, while neural regions represent the neural level of analysis.

One could also organize these associative or attribute structural units into a dual memory system. For instance, one could differentiate the new informational aspects of a memory (*data base/working* memory), such as receiving a painful shock in a black box, from the existing aspects of a memory (*expectancy/reference* memory), such as it is always safe to enter dark places or, after the shock, do not enter dark places, because one might get a painful experience. In this case the psychological unit of analysis is represented by the dual system of *working* and *reference* memory, while the neural unit of analysis might be represented by large interconnected neural systems.

A third and very popular approach is to analyze the neural regions that subserve an inhibitory avoidance memory and not be concerned with its possible subcomponents, such as attributes or a working/reference memory dichotomy. A memory is then totally defined by the task, for example inhibitory avoidance memory, while the neural basis might vary from specific brain regions to the brain as a whole.

Finally, since a memory, such as an inhibitory avoidance memory, does not exist in isolation of other memories and might well be different from other memories, one might consider possible differential contributions of specific neural networks to different types of memories usually defined by task exemplars. Thus, one might concentrate on a comparison between memories for aversively and appetitively motivated experiences, between *recognition* and *habit* memory, or between *declarative* and *procedural* memory as the critical psychological units.

It is the purpose of this chapter to present a number of different theoretical views of the neural structural organization of memory at different levels of analysis. The dynamic aspects associated with the development of new memories will be presented in other chapters in this book.

LASHLEY

Karl Lashley was the pioneer in attempting to identify which brain structures might code and store mnemonic information. He trained animals to make visual discriminations, to run through mazes for food reward and to open up boxes fastened by latches. He defined memory by the tasks to be learned and assumed that in the case of visual discrimination, the task reflected memory for a single S–R association, but in the case of maze learning, the task reflected memory for a large set of critical associations. Even though Lashley did not specify the nature of any higher level organization, he clearly attacked the notion that S–R

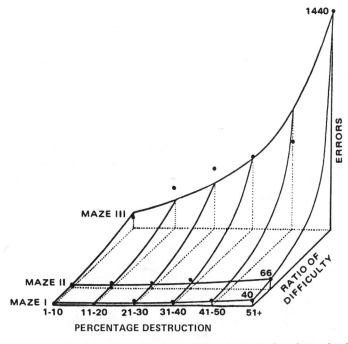

FIGURE 12.1   A demonstration of the Law of Mass Action in the relationship between the percentage of cortical destruction and the errors in running a maze. (From Lashley, K. S. *Brain mechanisms and intelligence.* Chicago: University of Chicago Press, 1929. Copyright 1929 by the University of Chicago Press. Reprinted with permission).

associations are organized in linear chains and assumed that S–R associations were organized within some type of hierarchical system.

His strategy was to systematically destroy specific cortical regions either before training or after the task had been mastered. Lashley found that in the visual discrimination task a large lesion of the visual cortex would abolish memory for the task. However, if even a small part of the visual cortex remained animals could relearn the test. He suggested that there is a great deal of redundant storage of information within the visual cortex and suggested the principle of equipotentiality. Every part of the visual cortex is equally essential for maintaining stored memory representations (Lashley, 1950).

Lashley (1929) also found that in maze learning tasks of increasing difficulty the more the cortex that was removed, the greater was the deficit, as can be seen in Figure 12.1. No specific cortical area was of greater importance than any other area. He concluded that for every complex memory, the cerebral cortex functions as a whole and acts according to a mass action principle, that is, memory traces do not have a specific localization within the central nervous system (CNS). Thus, the neural unit of a memory within a complex task is represented by the cerebral cortex as a whole. It should be noted, however, that the deficit was in part a function of the complexity and difficulty of the maze. Very little deficit was seen when only the simplest maze was used (see Figure 2.1). In addition to the lesion data, there is some support for Lashley's mass action view from the electrophysiological recording work of John (1982). He showed that when a conditioned stimulus is presented to an organism, single and multiple neural activity from single or multiple cells and gross evoked potentials can be recorded from widespread areas of the brain. Based on this data John added an organizational model to the mass action principle. He suggested that coherent patterns of interactions in the transmission between population of neurons throughout the brain represented the key to memory representation.

Even though Lashley was criticized (1) for interpreting all deficits as memory-related rather than perhaps sensory–perceptual, attentional or motivational, (2) for a nearly exclusive use of a maze-learning task to develop a general model of the nature of memory organization, (3) for the exclusive use of cortical lesions ignoring possible involvements of subcortical areas, and (4) for ignoring possible qualitative changes in response output, he nevertheless had a powerful influence on the scientific community. Based on Lashley's notion of equipotentiality within specific neural regions using simple tasks, a number of researchers have looked for the neural locus of critical S–R connections often using cellular analyses in invertebrate (see Chapter 8, this volume) and vertebrate (see Chapter 9, this volume) model systems. I will present Richard Thompson's views as representative of this type of analysis. Others were influenced in attempting to support or refute the notion of mass action representation of memories which characterized complex tasks. Because of the development of new cognitive memory tasks, new technological developments and new theoretical formulations emphasizing higher-order organizational schemas, much greater localization of function has been found in recent years. As representative of this approach I will present Larry Squire's and Neil Cohen's neurobiological views on memory because their ideas are novel and interesting. Also Mortimer Mishkin's theoretical views will be presented because he has developed the most comprehensive neurobiological model of memory organization. Other influential neurobiological views on the structural organization of memory include John O'Keefe and Lynn Nadel's cognitive map theory and David Olton's working-reference memory theory. As a final example, I will present Raymond Kesner's attribute theory concerning the neurobiological organization of memory.

As will become clear, different theoreticians use different terminology, different levels of organizational schemas and different species. Nevertheless, an attempt will be made in the last section to integrate all the different theoretical positions into a single framework. In part this approach is based on the need to have an integrative neurobiological theory of memory, and in part it is based on the assumption that across species there exists both a mental (e.g., mnemonic function) and neural evolutionary continuity.

THOMPSON

Richard Thompson (Thompson, 1980) proposes that multiple brain systems contribute to the organization of memory. Each system might be organized in a somewhat different fashion, varying from a hierarchical to a partly temporal type of organization. Furthermore, Thompson suggests that many of the known neural systems may or may not subserve any psychological units of memory used by various theoreticians. As an example, he points to the cerebral cortex, where one can find a number of general systems including sensory projection, motor, nonspecific cortical fields, cortical projections of the ascending reticular formation, limbic cortical areas and dorso-medial thalamic nucleus-prefrontal cortex system. Thompson does not attempt to specify the exact mnemonic role of each of these neural circuits. Instead he searches for specific neural regions that code primarily critical S–R connections.

In order to achieve this goal Thompson selected as a model system classical conditioning of the rabbit nictitating membrane response with a tone as the conditioned stimulus (CS) and a corneal airpuff as the unconditioned stimulus (UCS) (see Chapters 1 & 9, this volume). Even though many neural regions have been investigated, the early studies focused on the hippocampus, with a more recent emphasis on the importance of the subcortical nuclei of the cerebellum. Thompson has demonstrated that under conditions of paired CS–UCS presentations, hippocampal cellular activity increases by the second trial of training, signifying that a critical CS–UCS pairing has occurred. With continued training hippocampal unit activity forms a temporal model of the behavioral response and precedes it in time. No learning or changes in hippocampal unit activity occurred in animals that received unpaired CS–UCS presentations. However, removal of the hippocampus does not disrupt the acquisition of the nictitating membrane response. This means that even though the hippocampus codes the presence of a significant S–R event, other neural regions must be involved in storing and organization of S–R associations. Such a system was recently found in the dentate and interpositus nuclei of the cerebellum (McCormick & Thompson, 1984). Lesions in this area abolished the acquisition and retention of the nictitating membrane response. Conversely, recordings from these nuclei resulted in the development of unit activity related to learning. Electrical stimulation of the critical recording sites leads to the production of the nictitating membrane response. Based on these data Thompson suggests that the critical S–R associative connections occur either within the dentate-interpositus nuclei or nuclei afferent to this system, implying that memories associated with classical conditioning of the nictitating membrane response are stored in the dentate-interpositus nuclei. Other systems can then contribute significantly to the memory via their interconnections with the dentate-interpositus nuclei.

Thus, it appears that one specific neural circuit is of paramount importance in mediating the storage of the S–R structural component of the conditioned nictitating membrane response. Clearly other neural regions might be of importance in mediating the internal and external context of the situation. Also, there are undoubtedly other neural sites which will be of importance in other classical conditioning tasks.

SQUIRE AND COHEN

Larry Squire and Neil Cohen have suggested that there are two types of memory, which they named *declarative* and *procedural*, with each characterized by a specific set of operations within or between tasks (Squire, 1983; Cohen, 1984). *Declarative* memory is based on explicit information that is easily accessible and is concerned with specific facts or data. On the other hand, *procedural* memory is based on implicit information that is not easily accessible and is concerned with procedures and skills. Squire and Cohen also assume that the two types of memory systems are independent of each other. Furthermore, they propose that the medial-temporal cortex, which includes the hippocampus, and diencephalic human brain areas mediate declarative but not procedural memory.

Support for this distinction comes from studies with human amnesic patients (Cohen & Squire, 1981). Korsakoff patients, with presumably diencephalic damage, and patients receiving electroconvulsive shock

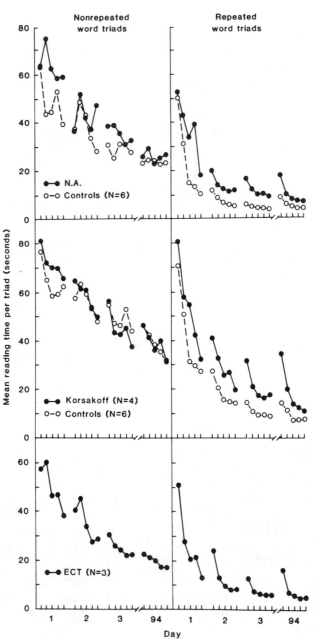

treatments, which presumably produce major disruptive effects in the temporal lobe, could acquire and retain (for at least three months) a mirror reading skill as easily as normal subjects. However, when asked to remember the words they had read, they were severely impaired. The results are shown in Figure 12.2. In another experiment, patient H. M. with bilateral medial-temporal lobe damage, including hippocampus and amygdala, could learn and remember a set of complicated skills associated with solving the Tower of Hanoi problem, yet this patient could not recall any contextual aspect of the task or the strategies involved in solving the task (Cohen, 1984). Thus, it appears that amnesic patients can acquire skills necessary for correct mirror-reading performance or finding the appropriate solutions for the Tower of Hanoi problem, but they cannot remember the spcific facts or data-based experiences of the experiment. Similar dissociation experiments have not yet been carried out in animals. Other support for Squire and Cohen's neurobiological view of memory comes from Mishkin's (see Section on Mishkin) findings that lesions of limbic–thalamic regions in monkeys selectively disrupt performance within a visual delay non-matching-to-sample task. This task is assumed to depend greatly on normal operation of the *declarative* system, because the task requires the animal to utilize factual, trial-unique information.

There are a few problems with the suggestion that the medial–temporal cortex and diencephalic areas exclusively mediate declarative, but not procedural memory. First, there is a possibility that damage to the medial–temporal cortex or diencephalic areas in amnesic patients is not complete, which provides a possible substrate for skill learning. Furthermore, one could assume that the substrate of nondamaged medial-temporal cortex and diencephalic tissue subserves spared short-term memory capacity often seen in these amnesic patients. The possibility exists that new skills can be learned with the remaining short-term memory capacity. An alternative would be to assume that short-term memory capacity is mediated by some other neural system, which could be part of or different from the procedural memory system. This latter hypothesis is difficult to evaluate because Squire and

FIGURE 12.2 Acquisition of a mirror-reading skill during three daily sessions, and retention three months later. The ability to mirror-read unique (nonrepeated) words was acquired at a normal rate by amnesic patients. The ability of amnesic patients to mirror-read repeated words was inferior to the control rate because amnesic patients, unlike control subjects, could not remember the specific words that had been read.

Cohen have not put forth any ideas concerning the neural substrate for procedural memory.

MISHKIN

Mortimer Mishkin has at the present time elaborated the most extensive neural model of memory organization (Mishkin, 1982; Mishkin, Malamut, & Bachevalier, 1984). He proposes that the brain organizes memories into two classes. The first is called *recognition* memory and is assumed to require higher-order level organization of many associative elements. It should be noted that recognition memory is only one form of associative or representational memory. The second is called *habit* memory and is based on stimulus–response association links. Notice the similarity to Lashley's view. Furthermore, he assumes that the two memory systems are independent.

Based on extensive empirical work with monkeys, Mishkin proposes that recognition memory is stored and represented in higher-order sensory areas of the cortex and involves active interaction with limbic-thalamic and cortical-neural circuits. More specifically he proposes that for visual recognition memory, information is processed initially in the primary visual cortex and then, in a sequential fashion, transferred into the secondary visual cortex, posterior temporal cortex (TEO), and then anterior temporal cortex (TE). The TE area is assumed to be the neural site representing storage of visual information. Furthermore, there is parallel activation of the amygdala and hippocampus. This parallel activation is then maintained with an amygdala projection to the medial dorsal thalamus and an hippocampus projection to the anterior thalamic nuclei. Finally, Mishkin assumes that there is a feedback system from the limbic-thalamic structures to the anterior temporal cortex. Mishkin has provided a great deal of empirial support for the proposed pattern of neural organization, with the exception of proposed feedback circuits.

The task examplar representing visual *recognition* memory is delayed nonmatching to sample. First, a monkey is shown a distinctive object over a central foodwell. When the animal removes the object, it receives a reinforcement. Ten seconds later the animal is given the same object and a novel object covering lateral foodwells. In order to receive reinforcement a second time, the animal must remove the novel object and ignore the familiar one. Monkeys can learn this task very quickly, and many trials can be given per day. One can easily vary the difficulty of the task by increasing the length of the delay period and by increasing the number of objects to be remembered.

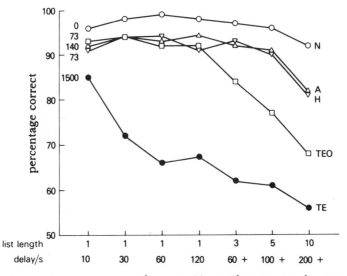

FIGURE 12.3 Average scores on the recognition performance test by groups with bilateral lesions of the amygdala (A), hippocampus and underlying fusiform–hippocampal gyrus (H), posterior temporal cortex (TEO), or anterior temporal cortex (TE), as well as a group of unoperated controls (N). Numerals to the left of the curves indicate average trials to relearn the basic task, which entailed remembering a single object for 10 s, with the first point on the curve being the average final score achieved on this condition. Animals were tested on the six remaining conditions, involving gradually increasing delays and list lengths, for one week each.

In support of his model Mishkin trained his monkeys as just described, and then removed either the anterior temporal area, posterior temporal area, the amygdaloid complex, or the hippocampal formation and then retested the animals for memory of 1, 3, 5, or 10 items at delays that ranged between 10 and 200 s. The results are shown in Figure 12.3 and indicate that there was a mild impairment for amygdala- or hippocampus-lesioned monkeys, but only at the longest delays. There was a more marked deficit at long delays for TEO- lesioned monkeys, and a significant impairment at long delays and list lengths, with only a mild impairment at the shortest delay, for TE-lesioned monkeys. Based on these results Mishkin proposed that TE is the critical area for storage of at least visual recognition memory. In a subsequent experiment he demonstrated that combined amygdala–hippocampus lesions produced as great a deficit as can be seen in TE-lesioned monkeys (Mishkin, 1978). Based on this latter result Mishkin proposed parallel processing of information within amygdala and hippocampal circuits at least for recognition memory. However, differential contributions of the amygdala and hippocampus neural regions might emerge when one searches for specific associative processes or attributes that underlie recognition memory.

Combined hippocampus and amygdala lesions in monkeys do not produce memory deficits in all tasks. For example, monkeys with limbic lesions can learn a multiple discrimination task in which successive trials are separated by intervals of 24 hr (Malamut, Saunders, & Mishkin, 1984). Based on this study Mishkin argues that the multiple discrimination task is mediated by a different memory system, one which requires primarily fixed S–R associations. This system is called habit memory and is assumed to be mediated by the cortico-striate system. More research is needed to support this latter hypothesis.

Even though the model is quite comprehensive there are a few important issues that need to be discussed. First, monkeys with only lesions of the hippocampus have deficits primarily in spatial tasks. For example, deficits are found in a place reversal task, but not in an object reversal task (Jones & Mishkin, 1972). Similarly there are deficits in a spatial delayed alternation task, but not in a go-no-go, nonspatial version of a delayed alternation task (Mahut, 1971). Finally, there is a deficit in a task requiring memory for the location of objects (Parkinson & Mishkin, 1982). In this latter study amygdala lesions have no deleterious effects. Thus, the possibility exists that hippocampus lesions alone produce a severe deficit only in spatial recognition tasks.

Second, performance of hippocampus or hippocampus plus amygdala-lesioned animals in the visual recognition nonmatching-to-sample task is a direct function of the delay between the presentation of the sample and the test. This ability to remember information only for short delays is similar to the pattern of deficits seen in human amnesic patients with presumably hippocampus or amygdala plus hippocampus damage and rats with hippocampus lesions (Kesner & Novak, 1982; Milner, 1978). Mishkin does not elaborate on neural systems that could mediate memory at short temporal intervals (often called short-term memory). There are at least two possibilities. First a different neural system could mediate information within short-term memory. Often the prefrontal cortex has been assigned such a function. Another possibility is that the hippocampus codes the whole temporal domain, so that the greater the damage to the hippocampus the less time the animal or patient has to maintain critical information. As a matter of fact Squire and Zola-Morgan (1983) have suggested that there is more hippocampus damaged in a combined amygdala–hippocampus lesion compared to the hippocampus alone. Thus, there are other plausible explanations of the greater deficit in the combined amygdala–hippocampus lesioned monkeys.

O'KEEFE AND NADEL

The theory of John O'Keefe and Lynn Nadel (1978) concentrates on space as the critical attribute of specific memories. They further divide the spatial attribute into a *locale* system, which codes places in the environment into cognitive maps, and a *taxon* system, which codes motor responses in terms of specific orientations within a spatial environment. They suggest that the hippocampus mediates the locale system and stores a cognitive map. The cognitive map can be used for place recognition, navigation, and coding of context. They do not specify which neural regions code the taxon system. The best evidence for hippocampus mediation of space comes from the identification of specific place cells in the hippocampus (O'Keefe, 1979), the observation that hippocampal theta activity is related to movement in space (Vanderwolf, Bland, & Whishaw, 1973), and the finding that animals with hippocampus lesions perform very poorly in tasks in which memory for spatial location is important (Olton, 1983).

An experiment that strongly supports hippocampus mediation of a cognitive map was carried out by Morris (1983). Rats were trained in a large circular tub filled with water, made opaque by the addition of milk. Their task was to find a platform that was hidden just below the surface of the cloudy water. Even though the starting place was varied from trial to trial, animals could learn this task rather quickly and thus appear to use the locale system. Animals with large lesions of the hippocampus were impaired in learning the task, as indicated by long latencies, to find the hidden platform. However, when the platform was visible, hippocampus-lesioned animals could learn the task very quickly. This latter version of the task requires cue rather than place navigation (see Figure 12.4). More recent observations using the Morris task have not supported O'Keefe and Nadel's prediction. First, when one trains animals prior to removal of the hippocampus, only small deficits are found on further retests. Second, rats with removal of the parietal cortex perform even more poorly in the Morris task than hippocampus-lesioned animals. Finally, there is a large deficit even when parietal-lesioned animals are trained prior to the lesion (DiMattia & Kesner, 1984, 1985). These latter observations suggest that the parietal cortex might be of greater importance than the hippocampus in mediating the locale system.

There are other experiments that are not totally consistent with the exclusive involvement of the hippocampus in storing a spatial map. Walker and Olton (1984) trained animals to enter a specific goal box from each of three different starting positions. After fimbria-fornix le-

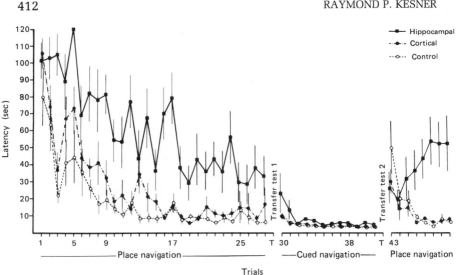

FIGURE 12.4   Mean latency of escape (s +/− 1 S.E.) over the 50 trials of the experiment. The trial number for the first of each series of daily trials is shown on the horizontal
axis, as are the two transfer tests. Note the reemergence of the hippocampal deficit during
trials 43–50.

sions the animals were given transfer tests on a new starting position
and asked to go to the same goal box. Successful selection of the goal
box on the transfer tests requires the utilization of a cognitive map. The
task is conceptually similar to the Morris task. Controls as well as
animals with fimbria-fornix lesions performed the transfer tests without any difficulty.

Thus, there exists a body of experimental data that cannot easily be
interpreted within the model of O'Keefe and Nadel. Most learning tasks
involve temporal as well as spatial attributes. O'Keefe and Nadel's failure to consider the mediating role of the hippocampus for temporal
attributes may explain the limitations of their theory.

OLTON

Olton has suggested that within every learning task there are two
types of memories that organize the critical information (Olton, 1983;
Olton, Becker, & Handlemann, 1979). Based on a distinction made by
Honig (1978), Olton suggested that the specific, personal, and temporal
context of a situation is coded in *working* memory. This would translate into memory for events that occur on a specific trial in a task,
biasing mnemonic coding toward the processing of incoming data. In

contrast, general information concerning rules and procedures (general knowledge) of specific situations is coded in *reference memory*. This would translate into memory for events that happen on all trials in a task, biasing mnemonic coding toward the processing of expectancies based on the organization of the extant memory. One would expect that in any new task to be learned there would be a somewhat greater emphasis on working memory, but that after learning, the emphasis would shift toward reference memory, unless the task requires the processing of new information on every trial. In this latter case both working and reference memory systems would be activated. This distinction between working and reference memory is closely akin to the distinction between episodic and semantic memory as proposed by Tulving (1972).

Olton further suggests that both working and reference memory can operate independently of each other. Based on a large number of experiments Olton proposed that the hippocampus and its interconnections mediate working memory, while some other system, such as the neocortex mediates reference memory. For instance, consider one critical experiment in which food-deprived rats are placed in the center of an 8-arm maze. The ends of each arm contain food reinforcement. The animals are allowed to choose any arm freely. Normal rats learn very quickly to use an optimal strategy, which is to enter each arm once and not to choose a previously visited arm. In addition to reference memory, which includes the knowledge that food can be obtained at the end of each arm and that the maze has 8 arms, this task has an important working memory component, which includes the knowledge of which arms had been previously visited for that trial. Bilateral lesions placed in the medial septum, postcommisural fornix, fimbria-fornix, dorsal hippocampus or entorhinal cortex resulted in impaired performance, with many repetitions of arms previously entered. Lesions of other neural regions, such as caudate nucleus or amygdala complex, did not produce any deficit, suggesting some specificity of hippocampus function for working memory.

As was noted above the radial arm maze also has a reference memory component, so the possibility exists that hippocampus lesions also disrupt reference memory. In order to test for this possibility, Olton and Papas (1979) ran animals in a 17-arm maze with food available in 8 arms and no food available in 9 arms. In order to solve this maze an animal should not enter unbaited arms activating reference memory, but they should enter baited arms only once utilizing working memory. After learning the task to criterion performance, animals were given fimbria-fornix lesions. Results are shown in Figure 12.5 and clearly

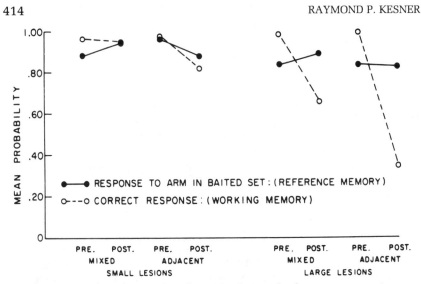

FIGURE 12.5 A summary of performance during the last 10 preoperative tests ("Pre"), and the last 10 postoperative tests ("Post") for rats with the Mixed ("Mixed") or Adjacent ("Adjacent") Pattern after small ("Small") or large ("Large") lesions. The mean probability was taken from the first 8 choices on all 10 tests. Reprinted with permission from "Spatial memory and hippocampal system function" by D. S. Olton and B. C. Papas, 1979, *Neuropsychologia*, 17, pp. 669–681. Copyright 1979, Pergamon Press, Ltd.

demonstrate that lesioned animals have a deficit only for the working, but not for the reference component of the task. It should be noted, however, that during acquisition of an 8-arm maze fimbria-fornix lesioned animals often make many reference memory errors (entries into arms that do not contain food) in addition to working memory errors (entries into arms that have been visited before).

Given that working and reference memory can be dissociated, neural regions other than the hippocampus should mediate reference memory. One possible neural region might be the parietal cortex. Support for this possibility comes from a study by Kesner and DiMattia (1985), who have shown that in an 8-arm maze parietal cortex lesions placed in rats after training on 4 unbaited and 4 baited arms resulted in a deficit in reference but not in working memory. This suggests that parietal cortex might subserve reference memory, at least for spatial information. Together the parietal cortex and hippocampus lesion data support the possibility that, at least after training in a spatial task, reference and working memory might operate independently. Experiments to test whether, during the learning of the task just described, both reference and working memory can operate independently have not been carried out satisfactorily.

KESNER

Based on earlier suggestions by Underwood (1969) and Spear (1976), Raymond Kesner has proposed that any specific memory is composed of a set of features or attributes that are specific and unique for each learning experience (Kesner, 1980). Embedded within this multidimensional attribute framework are some of the explicit associations (S–S, S–R, S–Reward) mentioned earlier.

Kesner has suggested that in most animal experiments there are a set of at least five salient attributes that characterize mnemonic information. These are labeled *space, time, affect, sensory-perception,* and *response.* A *spatial attribute* within this framework involves the coding and storage of specific stimuli representing places or relationships between places, which are usually independent of the subject's own body schema. It is exemplified by the ability to encode and remember maps and to localize stimuli in external space.

A *temporal attribute* involves the encoding and storage of specific stimuli or sets of spatially or temporally separated stimuli as part of an episode marking or tagging its occurrence in time, that is, separating one specific episode from previous or succeeding episodes.

An *affect attribute* involves the encoding and storage of reinforcement contingencies that result in positive or negative emotional experiences.

A *sensory-perceptual attribute* involves the encoding and storage of a set of sensory stimuli that are organized in the form of cues as part of a specific experience.

A *response* attribute involves the encoding and storage of information based on feedback from responses that occur in specific situations as well as the selection of appropriate responses.

The organization of these attributes can take many forms and are probably organized heterarchically. There are interactions between attributes that are very useful and can aid in identifying specific neural regions that might subserve a critical interaction. For example, the interaction between spatial and temporal attributes can provide for external context of a situation, which is important in determining when and where critical events occurred.

Another important interaction involves the temporal and affective attributes. In this case the interaction can provide important information concerning the internal context (internal state of the organism), which is important in evaluating emotional experiences.

Finally, there is an interaction between spatial and response attributes that might result in the encoding and storage of responses that depend upon accurate assessment of one's body orientation in space. This interaction is influenced by vestibular and kinesthetic input that aids navigation in space relative to the organism. It is exemplified, for instance, by the ability to encode and remember right–left responses.

The attribute theoretical framework emphasizes the importance of multiple measures of memory for any specific task, with the aim of assessing the contribution of a single attribute or interaction between specific attributes, and scaling of the difficulty of a task along a single dimension. For example, one can vary the temporal attribute by increasing the time interval between study and test, the spatial attribute by increasing the number of locations to be remembered, and the affect attribute by varying the magnitude of reinforcement. These manipulations are very important because one often finds a reciprocal relationship between task difficulty and lesion size of specific neural regions.

Kesner suggested that specific neural regions might subserve a single or subset of critical attributes. For example, the hippocampus might be critically involved in the coding of spatial–temporal attributes, although it should be noted that the hippocampus is probably also influenced by sensory–perceptual attribute information and can influence selective operation of the somatic component of the response attribute.

Support for this idea comes from the observation that a lesion of the hippocampus causes severe impairments in tasks that accentuate the importance of temporal and spatial attributes, such as Olton's 8-arm radial maze, spatial delayed alternation tasks, inhibitory avoidance tasks with long retention delays, spatial matching-to-sample tasks using long retention delays, and spatial reversal learning tasks (Glick & Greenstein, 1973; Kesner & DiMattia, 1984; Mahut, 1971; Olton, 1983).

As an example, animals were first trained in an 8-arm maze to enter a randomly selected arm in order to obtain a reinforcement (study phase). Ten seconds after finding the food the animal was removed from the maze for either a 1 min or 2-hr delay period. Following the delay period the animal was returned to the maze and given a retention test (test phase). Correct performance during the test phase required the animal to return to the previously reinforced arm. The animal had to use a "win-stay" rule in order to receive an additional reinforcement. After extensive training rats could remember (made few errors) the correct arm after a 1 min or 2-hr delay period and only occasionally made errors. These animals then received dorsal hippocampus lesions and were retested at each delay period. Results are shown in Figure 12.6 and indicate that the lesioned animals made no errors at 1-min delay but made many errors at the 2-hr delay interval (Kesner & DiMattia, 1984). The pattern of results is identical with previous findings

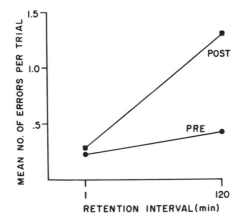

FIGURE 12.6   Mean number of errors per trial at short (1 min) and long (120 min) retention delays before (Pre) and after (Post) dorsal hippocampus lesions.

using electrical brain stimulation of the hippocampus in the same task (Bierley, Kesner, & Novak, 1983).

Thus, with hippocampus lesion, one can observe in spatial tasks selective impairments at long delays with sparing at short temporal delays.

In tasks where the spatial attribute is salient with little contribution of the temporal attribute, such as the Morris water tank test or Olton's multiple location task, one finds either no deficit or a less severe deficit following hippocampus lesions (DiMattia & Kesner, 1984; Morris, 1983; Walker & Olton, 1984). In tasks where the temporal attribute is salient with little contribution of the spatial attribute, such as visual nonmatching-to-sample or taste aversion learning tasks, again one finds no deficit or a less severe effect of hippocampus lesions (Best & Orr, 1973; Mishkin, 1982). In tasks where neither the temporal nor the spatial attribute are of critical importance, such as visual discrimination or classical conditioning of the nictitating membrane, there are no deficits following hippocampus lesions (Squire & Zola-Morgan, 1983; Thompson, 1980).

A further suggestion of Kesner's Attribute Theory is that the amygdala is critically involved in the encoding of temporal and emotional attributes, both positive and negative. The amygdala is probably also influenced by sensory–perceptual attribute information and can influence selective operation of the autonomic component of the response attribute.

Support for this idea comes from the observation that pre- or post-training electrical stimulation, chemical stimulation, or lesions of the

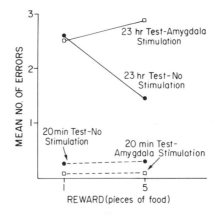

FIGURE 12.7   Mean number of errors per trial before entering the correct arm as a function of expectation of 1 or 5 pieces of food, time of retention test (20 min or 23 hr), and presence or absence of amygdala stimulation. Reprinted with permission from "Preserved learning and retention of pattern-analyzing skill in amnesia: Dissociation of knowing how and knowing that" by J. Cohen and L. R. Squire, 1981, Science, 210, pp. 207–210. Copyright 1981 by the AAAS.

amygdala produce profound memory deficits in a variety of tasks in which reinforcement contingencies of sufficiently high magnitude were used. Some of the tasks used include passive and active avoidance, shock-motivated visual discrimination, taste aversion and delayed matching-to-sample learning (Baker, Kesner, & Michael, 1981; Gold, Hankins, Edwards, Chester, & McGaugh, 1975; Gold, Rose, Hankins, & Spanis, 1976; Kesner & Andrus, 1982; Kesner, Berman, Burton, & Hankins, 1975; Liang, McGaugh, Martinez, Jensen, & Vasquez, 1982; McDonough & Kesner, 1971; Todd & Kesner, 1978). As an example, Kesner and Andrus (1982) trained rats in a symbolic delayed spatial matching-to-sample task using an 8-arm radial maze. When the animals were provided with differential cues predicting a small or large reward, retention at a 23-hour delay was better for the large reward. It is assumed that a large reward results in greater affect. Electrical stimulation of the amygdala, a treatment that is presumed to disrupt normal function of the amygdala, during 10 s exposure to the appropriate food cue, which predicted a large reward, impaired performance. Results are shown in Figure 12.7. No disruptive effects were seen at a 20 min. retention test. These data support the idea that the amygdala is involved in processing of affect and temporal attributes of specific memories.

Based on the attribute theory, one ought to be able to demonstrate that the hippocampus and amygdala contribution to a memory can be dissociated in that it is assumed that the hippocampus codes a spatial, but not an affect attribute, while amygdala codes an affect, but not the spatial attribute. Support for differential contribution of amygdala and hippocampus to a specific memory comes from studies using 8-arm maze learning with its emphasis on temporal–spatial attributes and from studies of taste aversion learning with its emphasis on temporal–affect attributes. It has been shown that lesions or electrical stimulation of the hippocampus impair performance on the 8-arm maze but have no effect on taste aversion learning, while lesions or electrical stimulation of the amygdala impair taste aversion learning without altering 8-arm maze performance (Best & Orr, 1973; Kesner & Berman, 1977; Kesner, Berman, Burton, & Hankins, 1975; McGowan, Hankins, & Garcia, 1972; Nachman & Ashe, 1974; Olton, 1983; Olton & Wolf, 1981).

In a different set of experiments using inhibitory avoidance learning, Baker, Kesner and Michal (1981) have shown that posttrial electrical stimulation of the amygdala or hippocampus can produce amnesia for an aversive footshock experience. However, after the amnesic animals were given a reminder footshock in a different situation, on a second test, only the hippocampus-stimulated animals showed recovery of memory, while amygdala-stimulated animals did not. The data suggest that amygdala stimulation might have disrupted the memory of attributes associated with emotional consequences of the footshock, rendering a subsequent reminder footshock ineffective. Since in the above situation there was an emphasis on processing of affective attributes with the use of reminder footshock, a second experiment was designed (Kesner & Hardy, 1983), which emphasized the importance of the environmental context. In this experiment, animals in the same inhibitory avoidance task were presented with a footshock in a unique environment (light-activated phosphorescent paint). Following training animals received electrical stimulation of the amygdala or hippocampus at the same parameters as the previously-mentioned experiment. Retention tests 24 or 48 hr later indicated an amnesic effect only for the hippocampus- and not for the amygdala-stimulated animals. These data suggest that the hippocampus, but not the amygdala, is involved in the processing of the environmental context utilizing spatio–temporal attributes. These two studies, together with the other studies cited, support the idea that there is a double dissociation between amygdala and hippocampus function, which is dependent upon the relative importance of reinforcement contingencies (affect attributes) and environmental–contextual components (spatial attributes) of a task.

The data are also consistent with the observations of Mishkin (1978) and Mahut, Moss, and Zola-Morgan (1981), who found that combined amygdala plus hippocampus lesions were more effective in producing memory deficits than damage to each neural structure alone. If one assumes that the relative contribution of each neural region depends upon specific attributes associated with a task, (such as the saliency of the environment (spatial attributes) and reinforcement contingencies (affect attributes), then one would expect disruption of the normal operation of two different sets of attributes to be more effective than functional disruption of either one independently.

Kesner proposed that the caudate nucleus is critically involved in the encoding and retrieval of spatial and response attributes. Support for this notion comes from a number of studies showing that neuronal activity within the caudate nucleus of monkeys is often related to performance of a task or to movements instrumental to picking up food (Kitsikis, Angyan, & Buser, 1971; Rolls, Thorpe, & Maddison, 1983). Electrical stimulation of the caudate nucleus can disrupt performance of a complex motor task that requires skilled motor movements (Wilburn & Kesner, 1974). In a different study Potegal (1971) studied Huntington's disease patients, who presumably have caudate nucleus lesions. He presented these patients with a task in which a subject first sees a target and must remember its location. The person's position relative to the target is then shifted without the subject seeing the target. The person is then asked to point to the location of the target from his or her new position. Huntington's disease patients are markedly impaired in performance of this task. In another study, it was shown that Huntington's disease patients were impaired in their ability to learn a mirror-reading skill, but showed normal verbal recognition for the words cued in the mirror-reading task (Martone, Butters, Payne, Becker, & Sax, 1984). In studies with rats, Potegal (1982) has shown that caudate–putamen lesioned rats were impaired on a radial arm maze task where they were required to find a goal box, the position of which was determined relative to the rat's starting position. Caudate-lesioned rats were also impaired on a return from the passive transport task, in which rats were tested in a visually homogeneous octagonal enclosure with a water spout at each corner. The animal was allowed to drink from one spout while confined in an enclosed wagon. Then, the back was closed off and the rat was transported away from and at a right angle to the goal spout. The animal was then released and allowed to find the same spout. Since the animal must navigate on the basis of vestibular feedback, return within the passive transport task can be considered to be a test of caudate nucleus involvement with the interaction of space and response attributes, (i.e., egocentric localization). It should be noted that hippocampus lesions did not disrupt performance on this task (Abraham, Potegal, & Miller, 1983).

Rats and monkeys with caudate lesions also have deficits in tasks like delayed response and delayed alternation (Divac, Rosvold, & Szwarcbart, 1967; Sanberg, Lehmann, & Fibiger, 1978). These deficits can also be explained on the basis of the important contribution of spatial and response attributes in egocentric localization.

In a recent lesion study, Cook and Kesner (1984a) demonstrated that caudate nucleus lesions in rats impair performance on previously learned tasks that (1) involve right–left discriminations between randomly paired adjacent arms in a 12-arm radial maze or (2) require an animal to select adjacent arms when placed at the end of a randomly selected arm in an 8-arm radial maze. Both tasks require the utilization of spatial and response attributes for egocentric localization. These same animals, however, showed no deficits in the standard 8-arm radial maze task or in a place learning task in which rats were placed at the end of a randomly selected arm in an 8-arm radial maze and were reinforced for running to a single arm, the position of which remained constant in space. These latter tasks require the utilization of spatial attributes with minimal importance of the interaction of spatial and response attributes.

There is also some evidence in support of the independent operation of the hippocampus and the caudate nucleus. As examples of a double dissociation between hippocampus and caudate nucleus, hippocampus-lesioned animals perform poorly on the standard 8-arm maze task, while caudate-lesioned animals display no deficit (Cook & Kesner, 1984a; Olton, 1983). Also caudate nucleus-lesioned animals cannot perform a previously learned right–left discrimination, but hippocampus-lesioned animals are not impaired in this task (Cook & Kesner, 1984b). Huntington's disease patients with presumed caudate nucleus damage are deficient in acquiring a mirror-reading task with normal verbal recognition, while Korsakoff's patients with presumed hippocampus and diencephalon damage are normal in acquiring a mirror-reading task with deficient verbal recognition (Martone et al., 1984).

In summary, Kesner proposed a multidimensional view of memory organization with many possible interactions of critical attributes. However, he has not addressed the relationship of attributes to working and reference memory. Furthermore, the complexity of the theory requires a large number of assumptions.

INTEGRATION

A STRUCTURAL VIEW OF MEMORY

At this point any serious student interested in understanding the neural systems that mediate the structure of memory should be totally confused with the multiple distinctions and levels of organization that are made by different theoreticians. Is it possible to integrate all the previously-mentioned neurobiological views of memory into a single theoretical framework? In this section an attempt will be made to present a comprehensive model of memory organization, which incorporates as much as possible the previously presented views.

In this comprehensive model it is assumed that any specific memory is organized into a *data-based* memory and an *expectancy-based* memory system (see Figures 12.8 and 12.9). *Data-based* memory is a system biased toward the coding of incoming data concerning the present, with an emphasis on facts, data, and events that are usually personal or egocentric and that occur within specific external and internal environmental contexts. The emphasis is on "bottom-up" processing. During initial learning there is a great emphasis on the data-based memory system, which will continue to be of importance even after initial learning in situations where trial unique or novel information needs to be remembered. The data-based memory system is akin to Olton's working memory, Tulving's episodic memory, Mishkin's recognition memory, Squire and Cohen's declarative memory, and part of O'Keefe and Nadel's taxon memory.

Memories within the data-based memory system are organized as a set of attributes and their interactions that are unique for each memory. Even though there are many attributes, I will concentrate on only five. They are labeled *space, time, affect, sensory-perception,* and *response.* Of the many interactions between attributes a few appear to be of critical importance. They are labeled *external context,* representing the interaction between time and space attributes, *internal context,* representing the interaction between time and affect attributes, *egocentric localization,* representing interaction between space and response attributes, and *S–R association,* representing the interaction between sensory-perception and response attributes.

Expectancy–based memory is a system biased toward previously stored information and can be thought of as one's general knowledge of the world. It can operate in the abstract in the absence of critical incoming data. The emphasis is on "top-down" processing. The expectancy-based memory system would tend to be of greater importance after a task has been learned, given that the situation is invariant and familiar. In most situations, however, one would expect a contribution of both

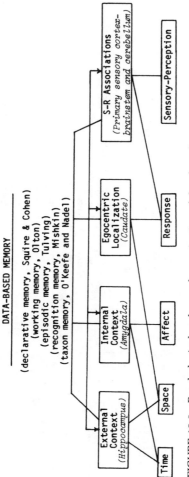

DATA-BASED MEMORY

(declarative memory, Squire & Cohen)
(working memory, Olton)
(episodic memory, Tulving)
(recognition memory, Mishkin)
(taxon memory, O'Keefe and Nadel)

| External Context (*Hippocampus*) | Internal Context (*Amygdala*) | Egocentric Localization (*Caudate*) | S-R Associations (*Primary sensory cortex-brainstem and cerebellum*) |

HIGHER-ORDER ATTRIBUTES

Time | Space | Affect | Response | Sensory-Perception

ATTRIBUTES

FIGURE 12.8   Psychological and neural organization of data-based memory.

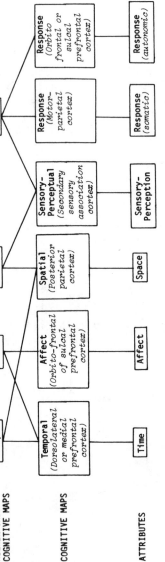
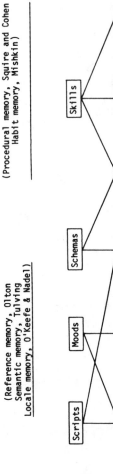

FIGURE 12.9   Psychological and neural organization of expectancy-based memory.

systems with varying proportions of involvement of one relative to the other.

Memories within the expectancy-based memory systems are organized as a set of cognitive maps and their interactions that are unique for each memory. The cognitive maps are labeled *spatial, temporal, affect, sensory-perceptual* and *response* and are composed of a corresponding set of attributes such as *space, time, affect, sensory-perception* and *response*, respectively. Note that the same attributes are also associated with the data-based memory system. Of the many interactions between cognitive maps a few appear to be of critical importance. They are labeled *scripts* representing the interaction between temporal and spatial cognitive maps, *schemas* representing the interaction between spatial and sensory-perception cognitive maps, *moods* representing the interaction between temporal and affect cognitive maps, and *skills* representing the interaction between sensory-perceptual and response cognitive maps. Within the expectancy-based memory system, the combination of moods, scripts, and schemas can be thought of as similar to Olton's reference memory and Tulving's semantic memory, whereas skills can be thought of as akin to Lashley's association memory, Mishkin's habit memory and Squire and Cohen's procedural memory.

The structural organization of these attributes, resulting in increasing higher-order levels of organization (e.g., internal and external contexts, egocentric localization, S–R associations, as well as cognitive maps, scripts, schemas, moods, and skills), needs to be determined. As an initial attempt it is assumed that interactive patterns of independently operating attributes provide the organizational framework for the existence of each unique memory. At the neurobiological level it is assumed that specific brain regions code or store the previously-mentioned attributes and cognitive maps as well as their specific interactions. Furthermore, relative amounts of neural activity within each critical brain region that codes a critical attribute, a cognitive map, or a set of attributes and cognitive maps provides for the total neuronal substrate associated with each unique memory.

Which neural regions can be considered as candidates for the mediation of the attribute-based structure of memory? Within the model presented in Figures 12.8 and 12.9, it is proposed that for the data-based memory system the hippocampus mediates the *external context*, the amygdala mediates the *internal context*, the caudate nucleus influences *egocentric localization*, the primary-sensory cortex and the brainstem–cerebellum circuit mediate the *S–R association* system. Within the expectancy-based memory system it is proposed that the posterior parietal cortex mediates the *spatial cognitive map*, the dorsolateral or medial-prefrontal cortex mediates the *temporal cognitive map*, the orbito-frontal or sulcal-prefrontal cortex mediates the *affect cognitive map*, the secondary sensory association cortex mediates the *sensory perceptual cognitive maps*, and the parietal-motor cortex influences the *response cognitive map*. The interaction between the dorsolateral or medial-prefrontal cortex and posterior parietal cortex serves as the neural substrate for scripts, the posterior parietal cortex and secondary sensory association cortex for schemas, the dorsolateral or medial and orbito-frontal or sulcal-prefrontal cortex for moods and the secondary sensory-association cortex and parietal-motor cortex for skills.

Finally, it is assumed that neural regions subserving higher-order attributes and neural regions subserving cognitive maps can operate independent of each other, even though many interactions exist.

DATA-BASED MEMORY SYSTEM

Hippocampus

According to the model the hippocampus encodes and retrieves information concerning primarily the *external context*, which is composed of temporal and spatial attributes with some modulatory influence from sensory-perceptual and response (somatic) attributes. Furthermore, the hippocampus operates exclusively within the data-based memory system. Data in support of this proposal have been presented in the previous sections, but it is important to point out that place cells in the hippocampus are activated when an animal is in a place coding a real event rather than an expected event (Hill, 1978). Also hippocampal unit activity can be altered significantly after one or two trials of CS–UCS pairing in classical conditioning of nictitating membrane response (Thompson, 1980). Finally, there are a number of studies in the literature demonstrating a greater deficit in hippocampus-lesioned animals in the learning of new spatial tasks than in performance of tasks learned prior to surgery (DiMattia & Kesner, 1984; Jarrard, 1978).

This approach to hippocampus function is consistent with Olton, Squire, Cohen, Mishkin, and Thompson's theoretical views, but it is at variance with Nadel and O'Keefe's theoretical views, who assume that the hippocampus codes only spatial attributes and stores cognitive maps of the environment. It should be noted that this model predicts that hippocampus-lesioned subjects can learn or remember tasks that require the expectancy-based memory system or that do not require extensive operation of spatio–temporal attributes within the data-based memory system. Thus, within the data-based memory sytem there ought not be deficits in tasks emphasizing affect, sensory-perceptual, or response attributes, and within the expectancy-based memory system no deficits in tasks that emphasize the use of cognitive maps. Data in support of these predictions have been presented in previous sections (see Kesner, 1980; Squire, 1983; Olton, 1983; Mishkin, 1982).

Amygdala

According to the model, the amygdala encodes and retrieves information concerning primarily the *internal context*, which is composed of temporal and affect attributes with some modulatory influence from sensory-perceptual and response (autonomic) attributes. The amygdala also operates exclusively within the data-based memory system. Support for this idea was presented in the section on Kesner's attribute theory.

This view is consistent with Mishkin and Squire, who include amygdala within their recognition and declarative memory systems, although it should be stated that for certain tasks in which recognition memory is important Mishkin views the amygdala and hippocampus as equipotential. Olton and O'Keefe and Nadel make no statements concerning amygdala function.

Caudate

According to the model the caudate nucleus encodes and retrieves information concerning egocentric localization, which is primarily composed of spatial and response attributes within the data-based memory system. Data in support of caudate function were presented in the section on Kesner's attribute theory. This system is similar to O'Keefe and Nadel's taxon system. Other theoreticians have not discussed the role of the caudate nucleus.

Primary Sensory Cortex—Brainstem-Cerebellum

According to the model the primary sensory cortical areas in conjunction with their thalamic projections, and the brainstem—cerebellum circuit, encode and retrieve information concerning S–R associations, which are composed of sensory–perceptual and response (somatic and autonomic) attributes. It is assumed that this neural circuit operates primarily within the data-based memory sytem. Mishkin has been concerned with the contribution of sensory systems to recognition memory. Supportive data can be found in Mishkin's research (Mishkin, 1982). Others have suggested that the brainstem–cerebellum neural circuit can mediate the response component of S–R associations (Buchwald & Brown, 1973; McCormick & Thompson, 1984; Moore, 1979).

EXPECTANCY-BASED MEMORY SYSTEM

Posterior Parietal Cortex.

According to the model the posterior parietal cortex (PPC), in conjunction with its thalamic projection, stores and retrieves information in reference to a spatial cognitive map within the expectancy-based memory system. It receives critical inputs from sensory–perceptual cognitive maps as mediated by the secondary sensory association cortex, and it influences the response cognitive map systems as mediated by the motor and parietal cortex. Support for this hypothesis can be found in an analysis of human patients with PPC damage. In addition to problems with attention, sensation, and motor control, there is often a deficit associated with spatial aspects of the patients' environment. These include an inability to draw maps or diagrams of familiar spatial locations, to use information to guide them in novel or familiar routes, to discriminate near from far objects, and to solve complex mazes. There is a general loss of "topographic sense," which may involve loss of long-term geographical knowledge as well as an inability to form cognitive maps of new environments. Thus, memory for spatial events appears to be impaired (Benton, 1969; De Renzi, 1982).

Additional support comes from studies with PPC-lesioned monkeys. These animals demonstrate deficits in place reversal, landmark reversal, distance discrimination, bent wire route-finding, pattern string-finding, and maze-learning tasks (Milner, Ockleford, & Dewar, 1977; Petrides & Iversen, 1979; Pohl, 1973). Similarly, rats with PPC lesions cannot perform in mazes (Thomas & Weir, 1975). In recent research, DiMattia and Kesner (1983, 1984, 1985) and Kesner and DiMattia (1985) have demonstrated that (1) PPC lesions disrupt reference or expectancy-based memory, but not working or data-based memory within an 8-arm maze, (2) disrupt the acquisition and retention of a cognitive map within Morris' water tank task, and (3) disrupt acquisition and retention of spatial recognition memory for a list of one or five spatial locations. In all the previously-mentioned tasks a cognitive map is required for excellent performance. The idea that the PPC might mediate a spatial cognitive map contradicts O'Keefe and Nadel's suggestion that the hippocampus serves a cognitive map function.

Dorsolateral or Medial Prefrontal Cortex

The model suggests that the dorsolateral-prefrontal cortex in humans and monkeys, and the medial-prefrontal cortex in rats, in conjunction with its thalamic projection, store and retrieve information in reference to a temporal cognitive map within the expectancy-based memory system. It receives critical inputs from sensory-perceptual cognitive maps as mediated by the secondary sensory association cortex, and it influences the response cognitive map system as mediated by the parietal-motor cortex. Support for this hypothesis can be found in the clinical literature dealing with human patients with frontal cortex lesions. In addition to problems with lack of initiative or spontaneity, poor movement programming and reduced corollary discharge, there is often a deficit for information concerning temporal aspects of their environment. They cannot remember the order in which information was experienced, nor can they plan and create a complex set of motor movements, nor program a temporally ordered set of activities. Frontal cortex-damaged patients can remember that certain words or pictures have been presented, but cannot discriminate the more from the less recent. Thus, memory for item information is intact, but memory for order information is impaired (Milner, 1971).

In addition, frontal cortex-damaged patients were impaired in a short-term memory task in which two stimuli had to be remembered for a 60-s time interval (paired-comparison task, Milner, 1964). This task requires short-term temporal memory for two events, implying that frontal cortex-damaged patients cannot remember the order of stimulus presentation. In another experiment, frontal cortex-damaged patients were impaired in their ability to self-order a sequence of stimuli presented one at a time (Petrides & Milner, 1982).

In monkeys, dorsolateral prefrontal cortex lesions result in deficits in the temporal ordering of events, a finding that is comparable to what has been described in humans. This temporal ordering deficit is evidenced by impairments in delayed response, delayed alternation, and delayed matching-to-sample tasks, as well as self-ordering of a sequence of responses (Petrides & Milner, 1982; Rosenkilde, 1979). Based upon the previously-mentioned findings, it has been suggested that the prefrontal cortex is primarily involved in temporal structuring of information in short-term memory (Fuster, 1980).

In rats, lesions of the medial prefrontal cortex produce in most studies a deficit in DRL performance, as well as deficits in a temporal go-no-go alternation task (Johnston, Hart, & Howell, 1974; Rosenkilde & Divac, 1975). Deficits have also been observed in tasks in which rats emit a specific sequence of behavioral responses requiring temporal organization (Barker, 1967).

In a recent study Kesner (1985) trained rats in an 8-arm maze to remember the item (spatial location) or order of four spatial locations. After training, animals received medial prefrontal cortex lesions. The results are shown in Figure 12.10 and indicate that medial-prefrontal cortex-lesioned animals had an order memory deficit for all items, but had excellent item-memory for the first item of the list, with impaired item-memory for the remaining items of the list. The possibility exists that poor performance for item information was due to the variable temporal–spatial sequences presented during the study phase. To test this possibility the lesioned animals were trained with a constant sequence, the same four arms were always selected, followed by tests of item- and order-memory. The results are shown in Figure 12.11 and indicate that prefrontal cortex-lesioned animals had excellent item

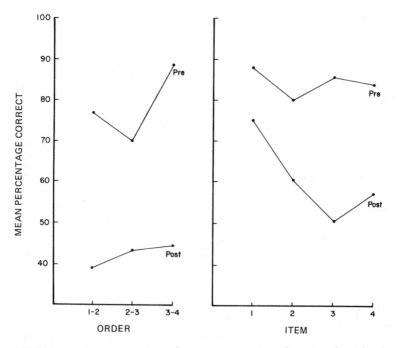

FIGURE 12.10   Mean percentage of correct responses as a function of serial order and serial position (item) before (Pre) and after (Post) medial-prefrontal cortex lesions.

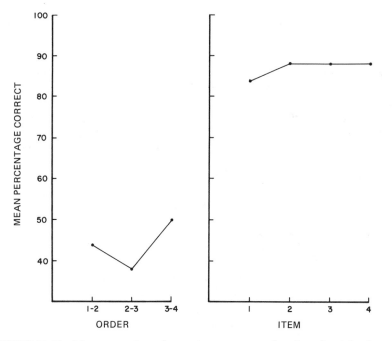

FIGURE 12.11 Mean percentage of correct responses as a function of serial order and serial position (item) using an invariant order for the study phase in medial-prefrontal cortex-lesioned animals.

memory for all items of the list but had no memory for the order of presentation of the items. In additional tests it was shown that this order deficit appeared even when the animals were allowed to self-order the items during the study phase or when the list length was only two items. Thus, both rats and humans can remember the occurrence, but not the temporal ordering of events following prefrontal cortex lesions.

The idea that the frontal cortex might mediate a temporal cognitive map has been proposed by others (Fuster, 1980), but it has not been incorporated within the theoretical schemas of Olton, Mishkin, Squire and Cohen, Thompson, or O'Keefe and Nadel.

Orbito-Frontal or Sulcul-Prefrontal Cortex

It is proposed that the orbito-frontal cortex in humans and monkeys and the sulcal cortex in rats, in conjunction with its thalamic projection, stores and retrieves information in reference to an affect-mediated cognitive map within the expectancy-based memory system. The affect map is influenced by specific sensory input, especially rewarding and aversive stimuli, and in turn, influences the selection of appropriate autonomic responses.

Support for this view comes from clinical data dealing with human patients with frontal cortex damage, including the orbito-frontal cortex. These patients show a variety of personality changes characterized by facetiousness, euphoria, irritability, sudden depression, and impaired social judgment. Most patients so affected are unable to enjoy pleasurable experiences, especially when the rewards are social or intellectual. They seem to have a lack of appreciation of social rules, altered affect, and limited response to and experience of pain. In monkeys, orbito-frontal lesions often cause reduction in aggressive behavior including altered emotional responses to aversive visual stimuli (Butter, Snyder, & McDonald, 1970; Butler, Mishkin, & Mirsky, 1968).

In a recent study with rats, Kesner (1985) found that sulcal-prefrontal cortex lesions disrupted performance on a 5-item list spatial recognition task when reward presented during the study phase consisted of only one piece of food. However, when four pieces of food were presented the deficit was totally reversed, suggesting that the appreciation of affect is of critical importance to sulcal-lesioned animals.

Secondary Sensory Associative Cortex

The secondary sensory association cortex codes high-level organization of sensory information and provides a background for the interaction between stored memories and sensory inputs that result in sensory-perceptual cognitive maps. This system influences all other cognitive maps within the expectancy-based memory system. It should be noted that it is assumed that the sensory-perceptual cognitive map system is important for the operation of skills, but that other cognitive maps can operate independent of this system.

This pivotal role for the secondary sensory association system is in agreement with Mishkin, who has suggested that this system represents the memory store.

Parietal and Motor Cortex

The parietal and motor cortex codes and stores information associated with cognitive response maps. This system is triggered by the secondary sensory association cortex for the organization of skills and by the posterior parietal and dorsolateral prefrontal cortex for the organization of actions that derive from the use of temporal–spatial cognitive maps. This neural system is important for the operation of critical S–R associative processes. It also appears to be one of the systems that is spared in amnesic patients. There are undoubtedly different circuits within this system that mediate skills versus other response outputs.

A Dynamic View of Memory

From a dynamic viewpoint, it is assumed that each attribute activates in parallel neural regions mediating data-based and expectancy-based information followed by subsequent interactions. In the case of spatial attributes, the posterior parietal cortex would be more active than the hippocampus when critical spatial information can be retrieved from a cognitive spatial map within the expectancy-based memory system. On the other hand, the hippocampus would be more active than the posterior parietal cortex when critical spatial information cannot be retrieved from a cognitive map because of novel or varied spatial inputs or expectation of a memory test at long temporal delays. The organism must then attend more to spatial data input within the data-based memory system. The same dynamic model applies to the prefrontal cortex and hippocampus for temporal attributes, orbito-frontal cortex and amygdala for affect attributes, secondary sensory associative cortex and primary sensory cortex for sensory-perceptual attributes, and motor–parietal cortex and brainstem–cerebellum for response attributes.

The operation of the expectancy-based memory system appears to have limited capacity and is short-lived and thus can only be based on short-term neural activation of critical cortical neural systems. Similar limitations exist for most neural systems involved in the data-based memory system with the exception of neural regions (such as the hippocampus and the amygdala), that are capable of coding temporal attributes. These systems are capable of long-term or intermediate term activation, which in turn, could lead to consolidation and a possible restructuring of the expectancy-based memory system. It is predicted that there is short-term memory capacity remaining even in total hippocampus- or total amygdala-lesioned animals, but that this short-term memory capacity would be manifested only in invariant or expected memory tasks.

The above model can be viewed as an elaborate and comprehensive model of the structural organization of memory. The model not only integrates all the neurobiological views of memory organization presented earlier, but it also reveals some degree of agreement among different researchers in terms of the conceptual organization of the data-based and expectancy-based memory systems, as well as the selection of neural regions that subserve these systems.

For example, there is good agreement that the hippocampus subserves the data-based memory system. Other terms for this system include declarative, working, episodic or recognition memory. The suggestion that other neural substrates can also mediate data-based memory promotes the idea that there are a number of different components (attributes) associated with the data-based memory system. Thus, the hippocampus should not be seen as the exclusive mediator of data-based memory. Even though a great deal of research has been done with the hippocampus and the data-based system, in comparison, little neurobiological research has been carried out in differentiating possible neural substrates of the expectancy-based memory system. Thus, it is not surprising that the major differences among theoreticians occur in their conceptual organization of the expectancy-based memory system. For example, Olton and Tulving concentrate on the organization of schemas and scripts, whereas Squire and Mishkin concentrate on the organization of skills. These differential emphases may actually reflect the contribution of different neuronal substrates.

The model can only serve as a heuristic to search for possible dissociations or critical interactions, to aid in design of new experiments, and to provide for a path toward the better understanding of the neurobiological basis of memory.

Summary

As is readily apparent in this chapter, memory is a complex phenomenon due to a large number of potential interactions that are associated with the organization of memory at the psychological and neural system level. As a result, the study of the neurobiological basis of the structure of memory lends itself readily to multiple theoretical views. The views of Lashley, Thompson, Squire and Cohen, Mishkin, O'Keefe and Nadel, Olton, and Kesner have been presented in some detail with a special emphasis on critical experiments. In the last section an attempt has been made to integrate all the different theoretical views into a single model.

REFERENCES

Abraham, L., Potegal, M., & Miller, S. (1983). Evidence for caudate nucleus involvement in an egocentric spatial task: Return from passive transport. *Physiological Psychology, 11,* 11–17.

Baker, L. J., Kesner, R. P., & Michael, R. E. (1981). Differential effects of a reminder cue on amnesia induced by stimulation of amygdala and hippocampus. *Journal of Comparative and Physiological Psychology, 95,* 312–321.

Barker, D. J. (1967). Alterations in sequential behavior of rats following ablation of midline limbic cortex. *Journal of Comparative and Physiological Psychology, 3,* 453–604.

Benton, A. L. (1969). Disorders of spatial orientation. In P. J. Vinken & G. W. Bruyn (Eds.), *Handbook of clinical neurology* (Vol. 3). Amsterdam: North Holland.

Best, P. J., & Orr, J., Jr. (1973). Effects of hippocampal lesions on passive avoidance and taste aversion conditioning. *Physiology and Behavior, 10,* 193–196.

Bierley, R. A., Kesner, R. P., & Novak, J. M. (1983). Episodic long-term memory in the rat: Effects of hippocampal stimulation. *Behavioral Neuroscience, 97,* 42–48.

Buchwald, J. S. & Brown, K. A. (1973). Subcortical mechanisms of behavioral plasticity. In J. D. Maser (Ed.), *Efferent organization and the integration of behavior.* New York: Academic Press.

Butler, C. M., Mishkin, M., & Mirsky, A. F. (1968). Emotional responses toward humans in monkeys with selective frontal lesions. *Physiology and Behavior, 3,* 213–215.

Butter, C. M., Snyder, D. R., & McDonald, J. A. (1970). Effects of orbitofrontal lesions on aversive and aggressive behaviors in rhesus monkeys. *Journal of Comparative and Physiological Psychology, 72,* 132–144.

Cohen, J. J., & Squire, L. R. (1981). Preserved learning and retention of pattern-analyzing skill in amnesia: Dissociation of knowing how and knowing that. *Science, 210,* 207–210.

Cohen, N. (1984). Preserved learning capacity in amnesia: Evidence for multiple memory systems. In L. R. Squire & N. Butters (Eds.), *Neuropsychology of memory,* New York: Guilford Press.

Cook, D. G., & Kesner, R. P. (1984a). Memory for eqocentric spatial localization in an animal model of advanced Huntington's disease. *Neuroscience Abstracts, 10,* 133.

Cook, D. G., & Kesner, R. P. (1984b). Dissociation of hippocampus and caudate contribution to egocentric and allocentric localization.

De Renzi, E. (Ed.). (1982). *Disorders of space exploration and cognition.* New York: John Wiley & Sons.

DiMattia, B. V., & Kesner, R. P. (1983). The role of the posterior parietal association cortex in the processing of spatial event information. *Neuroscience Abstracts, 9,* 133.

DiMattia, B. V., & Kesner, R. P. (1984). Posterior parietal cortex: A part of the cognitive map? *Neuroscience Abstracts, 10,* 136.

DiMattia, B. V., & Kesner, R. P. (1985). Differential contribution of parietal cortex and hippocampal formation in the retention of a cognitive mapping task. *Neuroscience Abstracts, 11,* 833.

Divac, I., Rosvold, H. E., & Szwarcbart, M. K. (1967). Behavioral effects of selective ablation of the caudate nucleus. *Journal of Comparative and Physiological Psychology, 63,* 184–190.

Fuster, J. M. (Ed.). (1980). *The prefrontal cortex: Anatomy, physiology, and neuropsychology of the frontal lobe.* New York: Raven Press.

Glick, S. D. & Greenstein, S. (1973). Comparative learning and memory deficits following hippocampal and caudate lesions in mice. *Journal of Comparative and Physiological Psychology, 82,* 188–194.

Gold, P. E., Hankins, L. L., Edwards, R., Chester, J., & McGaugh, J. L. (1975). Memory interference and facilitation with posttrial amygdala stimulation: Effect on memory varies with footshock level. *Brain Research, 86,* 509–513.

Gold, P. E., Rose, R. P., Hankins, L. L., & Spanis, C. (1976). Impaired retention of visual discriminated escape training produced by subseizure amygdala stimulation. *Brain Research, 118,* 73–85.

Hill, A. J. (1978). First occurrence of hippocampal spatial firing in a new environment. *Experimental Neurology, 62,* 282–297.

Honig, W. K. (1978). Studies of working memory in the pigeon. In S. H. Huke, H. Fowler, & W. K. Honig (Eds.), *Cognitive process in animal behavior.* Hillsdale, NJ: Lawrence Erlbaum.

Jarrard, L. E. (1978). Selective hippocampal lesions: Differential effects on performance by rats of a spatial task with preoperative versus postoperative training. *Journal of Comparative and Physiological Psychology, 92,* 119–127.

John, E. R. (1982). Multipotentiality: A theory of recovery of function after brain injury. In J. Orbach (Ed.), *Neuropsychology after Lashley*. Hillsdale, NJ: Lawrence Erlbaum.

Johnston, V. S., Hart, M., & Howell, W. (1974). The nature of the medial wall deficit in the rat. *Neuropsychologia, 12*, 497–503.

Jones, B., & Mishkin, M. (1972). Limbic lesions and the problem of stimulus-reinforcement associations. *Experimental Neurology, 36*, 362—377.

Kesner, R. P. (1980). An attribute analysis of memory: The role of the hippocampus. *Physiology Psychology, 8*, 189–197.

Kesner, R. P. (1985). Magnitude of reinforcement attenuates item memory deficits in animals with sulcal cortex lesions. In preparation.

Kesner, R. P. (1985). Correspondence between humans and animals in coding of temporal attributes: Role of hippocampus and prefrontal cortex. *New York Academy of Sciences, 444*, 122–136.

Kesner, R. P. (1984). The neurobiology of memory: Implicit and explicit assumptions. In J. L. McGaugh, G. Lynch, & N. M. Weinberger (Eds.), *Neurobiology of learning and memory* (pp. 111–118). New York: Guilford Press.

Kesner, R. P., & Andrus, R. G. (1982). Amygdala stimulation disrupts the magnitude of reinforcement contribution to long-term memory. *Physiological Psychology, 10*, 55–59.

Kesner, R. P., & Berman, R. F. (1977). Effects of midbrain reticular formation, hippocampal and lateral hypothalamic stimulation upon recovery from neophobia and taste aversion learning. *Physiology and Behavior, 18*, 763–768.

Kesner, R. P., Berman, R. F., Burton, B., & Hankins, W. G. (1975). Effects of electrical stimulation of amygdala upon neophobia and taste aversion. *Behavioral Biology, 13*, 349–358.

Kesner, R. P., & DiMattia, B. V. (1984). Posterior parietal association cortex and hippocampus: Equivalency of mnemonic function in animals and humans. In L. P. Squire & N. Butters (Eds.), *Neuropsychology of memory*. New York: Guilford Press.

Kesner, R. P. & DiMattia, B. V. (1985). Parietal cortex lesions disrupt reference but not working memory. In preparation.

Kesner, R. P., & Hardy, J. D. (1983). Long-term memory for contextual attributes: Dissociation of amygdala and hippocampus. *Behavioural Brain Research, 8*, 139–149.

Kesner, R. P., & Novak, J. (1982). Serial position curve in rats: Role of the dorsal hippocampus. *Science, 218*, 173–174.

Kitsikis, A., Angyan, L., & Buser, P. (1971). Basal ganglia unitary activity during a motor performance in monkeys. *Physiology and Behavior, 6*, 609–611.

Lashley, K. S. (Ed.). (1929). *Brain mechanisms and intelligence*. Chicago: University of Chicago Press.

Lashley, K. S. (1950). In search of the engram. In *Symposia of the Society for Experimental Biology*, (No. 4). Cambridge: Cambridge University Press.

Liang, K. C., McGaugh, J. L. Martinez, J. L., Jr., Jensen, R. A., & Vasquez, B. J. (1982). Posttrial amygdaloid lesions impair retention of an inhibitory avoidance response. *Behavioural Brain Research, 4*, 237–249.

Malamut, B. L., Saunders, R. C., & Mishkin, M. (1984). Monkeys with combined amygdala-hippocampal lesions succeed in object discrimination learning despite 24-hour intertrial intervals. *Behavior Neuroscience, 98*, 759–769.

Mahut, H. (1971). Spatial and object reversal learning in monkeys with partial temporal lobe ablations. *Neuropsychologia, 9*, 409–424.

Mahut, H., Moss, M., & Zola—Morgan, S. (1981). Retention deficits after combined amygdala-hippocampal and selective hippocampal resections in the monkey. *Neuropsychologia, 19*, 201–225.

Martone, M. Butters, N., Payne, M., Becker, J. T., & Sax, D. S. (1984). Dissociations between skill learning and verbal recognition in amnesia and dementia. *Archives of Neurology, 41,* 965–970.

McCormick, D. A. & Thompson, R. F. (1984). Cerebellum: Essential involvement in the classically conditioned eyelid response. *Science, 223,* 296–298.

McDonough, J. R., Jr. & Kesner, R. P. (1971). Amnesia produced by brief electrical stimulation of the amygdala or dorsal hippocampus in cats. *Journal of Comparative and Physiological Psychology, 77,* 171–178.

McGowan, B. K., Hankins, W. G., & Garcia, J. (1972). Limbic lesions and control of the internal and external environment. *Behavioral Biology, 7,* 841–852.

Milner, A. D., Ockleford, E. M., & DeWar, W. (1977). Visuo–spatial performance following posterior parietal and lateral frontal lesions in stumptail macaques. *Cortex, 13,* 170–183.

Milner, B. (1964). Some effects of frontal lobectomy in man. In J. M. Warren & K. Akert (Eds.), *The frontal granular cortex and behavior.* New York: McGraw–Hill.

Milner, B. (1971). Interhemispheric differences in the localization of psychological processes in man. *British Medical Bulletin, 27,* 272–277.

Milner, B. (1978). Clues to the cerebral organization of memory. In P. A. Buser & A. Rouguel-Buser (Eds.), *Cerebral correlates of conscious experience.* Amsterdam: Elsevier.

Mishkin, M. (1978). Memory in monkeys severly impaired by combined but not by separate removal of amygdala and hippocampus. *Nature, 273,* 297–298.

Mishkin, M. (1982). A memory system in the monkey. *Philosophical Transactions Royal Society of London B, 298,* 85–95.

Mishkin, M., Malamut, B. L., & Bachevalier, J. (1984). Memories and habits: Two neural systems. In J. L. McGaugh, G. Lynch, & N. M. Weinberger (Eds.), *Neurobiology of learning and memory.* New York: Guilford Press.

Moore, J. W. (1979). Brain processes and conditioning. In A. Dickinson & R. A. Boakes (Eds.), *Mechanisms of learning and motivation: A memorial volume to Jerzy Konorski.* Hillsdale, NJ: Lawrence Erlbaum.

Morris, R. G. M. (1983). An attempt to dissociate "spatial-mapping" and "working-memory" theories of hippocampal function. In W. Seifert (Ed.), *Neurobiology of the hippocampus.* New York: Academic Press.

Nachman, M. & Ashe, J. H. (1974). Effects of basolateral amygdala lesions on neophobia, learned taste aversions, and sodium appetite in rats. *Journal of Comparative and Physiological Psychology, 87,* 622–643.

O'Keefe, J., & Nadel, L. (Eds.). (1978). *The hippocampus as a cognitive map.* Oxford: Oxford University Press.

O'Keefe, J. (1979). A review of the hippocampal place cells. *Progress in Neurobiology, 13,* 419–439.

Olton, D. S., & Papas, B. C. (1979). Spatial memory and hippocampal system function. *Neuropsychologia, 17,* 669–681.

Olton, D. S., & Wolf, W. A. (1981). Hippocampal seizures produce retrograde amnesia without a temporal gradient when they reset working memory. *Behavioral Biology, 33,* 437–452.

Olton, D. S. (1983). Memory functions and the hippocampus. In W. Seifert (Ed.), *Neurobiology of the hippocampus.* New York: Academic Press.

Olton, D. S., Becker, J. T., & Handlemann, G. E. (1979). Hippocampus, space and memory. *Behavior Brain Science, 2,* 313–365.

Parkinson, J. K., & Mishkin, M. (1982). A selective mnemonic role for the hippocampus in monkeys: Memory for the location of objects. *Society for Neuroscience Abstracts, 8,* 23.

Petrides, M., & Iversen, S. D. (1979). Restricted posterior parietal lesions in the rhesus monkey and performance on visuo–spatial tasks. *Brain Research, 161,* 63–77.

Petrides, M., & Milner, B. (1982). Deficits on subject-ordered tasks after frontal- and temporal-lobe lesions in man. *Neuropsychologia, 20,* 249–262.

Pohl, W. (1973). Dissociation of spatial discrimination deficits following frontal and parietal lesions in monkeys. *Journal of Comparative and Physiological Psychology, 82,* 227–239.

Potegal, M. (1971). A note on spatial-motor deficits in patients with Huntington's disease: A test of a hypothesis. *Neuropsychology, 9,* 233–235.

Potegal, M. (1982). Vestibular and neostriatal contributions to spatial orientation. In M. Potegal (Ed.), *Spatial abilities, development and physiological foundation.* New York: Academic Press.

Rolls, E. T., Thorpe, S. J., & Maddison, S. P. (1983). Responses of striatal neurons in the behaving monkey. 1. Head of the caudate nucleus. *Behavior Brain Research, 7,* 179–210.

Rosenkilde, C. E. (1979). Functional heterogeneity of the prefrontal cortex in the monkey: A review. *Behavioral Neural Biology, 25,* 301–345.

Rosenkilde, C. E., & Divac, I. (1975). DRL performance following anteromedial cortical ablations in rats. *Brain Research, 95,* 142–146.

Sandberg, P. R., Lehmann, J., & Fibiger, H. C. (1978). Impaired learning and memory after Kainic acid lesions of the striatum: A behavioral model of Huntington's disease. *Brain Research, 149,* 546–551.

Spear, N. F. (1976). Retrieval of memories: A psychobiological approach. In W. K. Estes (Ed.), *Handbook of learning and cognitive processes* (Vol. 4). *Attention and memory.* Hillsdale, NJ: Lawrence Erlbaum.

Squire, L. R., & Zola-Morgan, S. (1983). The neurology of memory: The case for correspondence between the findings for human and nonhuman primate. In J. A. Deutsch (Ed.), *The physiological basis of memory.* New York: Academic Press.

Squire, L. R. (1983). The hippocampus and the neuropsychology of memory. In W. Seifert (Ed.), *Neurobiology of the hippocampus.* New York: Academic Press.

Thomas, R. K., & Weir, V. K. (1975). The effects of lesions in the frontal or posterior association cortex of rats on Lashley III maze. *Physiological Psychology, 3,* 210–214.

Thompson, R. F. (1980). The search for the engram, II. In D. McFadden (Ed.), *Neural mechanisms in behavior: A Texas Symposium.* New York: Springer–Verlag.

Todd, J. W., & Kesner, R. P. (1978). Effects of posttraining injection of cholinergic agonists and antagonists into the amygdala on retention of passive avoidance training in rats. *Journal of Comparative and Physiological Psychology, 92,* 958–968.

Tulving, E. (1972). Episodic and semantic memory. In E. Tulving & W. D. Donaldson (Eds.), *Organization of memory.* New York: Academic Press.

Underwood, B. J. (1969). Attributes of memory. *Psychology Review, 76,* 559–573.

Vanderwolf, C. H., Bland, B. H., & Whishaw, I. Q. (1973). Diencephalic, hippocampal and neocortical mechanisms in voluntary movement. In J. D. Maser (Ed.), *Efferent organization and the integration of behavior.* New York: Academic Press.

Walker, J. A., & Olton, D. S. (1984). Fimbria-fornix lesions impair spatial working memory but not cognitive mapping. *Behavior Neuroscience, 98,* 226–242.

Wilburn, M. W., & Kesner, R. P. (1974). Effects of caudate nucleus stimulation upon initiation and performance of a complex motor task. *Experimental Neurology, 45,* 61–71.

INDEX

A

1-Acetamine-2-pyrrolidone, brain integrative mechanism enhancement with, 153–154

Acquisition-encoding deficits, in age-related long-term memory dysfunction, 210

Acquisition vs. retrieval, in age-related long-term memory dysfunction, 211–212

Acquisition deficits, in age-related long-term memory dysfunction, 212–214

Adrenocorticotropic hormone
ACTH$_{4-9}$, effect on attention, 154
ACTH$_{4-10}$
central vs. peripheral administration, dose effectiveness comparison, 136
conditioned behaviors affected by, 147
learning modulation and, 147–148
stress-induced release, and brain protein synthesis, 180

Adrenal gland
adrenal medulla removal, effect on action of nicotine and amphetamine, 141
memory consolidation, 24
role in memory modulation, 23

Adrenergic system, peripheral, role in mediating drug effects on conditioning, 141

Aging
Alzheimer's disease, 217–220
basal forebrain cholinergic activity, 217
cholinergic system and, 140
multiple neurotransmitters in, 217–220
naloxone effect, 154
long-term memory deficits, 208–216
animal studies, 212–216
human studies, 208–209
memory loss in, role of locus ceruleus, 220–221
direct electrical activation effects, 221–223
pharmacological activation effects, 223–225
short-term memory deficits
animal studies, 206–208
human studies, 205–206, 208

Alzheimer's disease
cholinergic system and, 140
basal forebrain activity and, 217
multiple neurotransmitters in, 217–220
naloxone effect, 154

Amnesia
antero- and retrograde gradients, 129
electroconvulsive shock-induced, attenuation with magnesium pemoline, 153
induction by
intrahippocampally injected serotonin, 142
protein synthesis inhibitors, 144